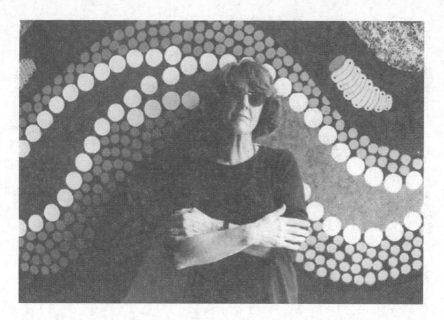

Diane Bell, Tandanya, April 1998
Mural by Heather Shearer.
(Pat Hannagan, *Advertiser*, Adelaide)

Diane Bell is a feminist anthropologist who, over the past two decades, has written with passion and courage of women in Aboriginal society, land rights, law reform, human rights and violence against women. Since moving to the USA in 1989 to take up the Henry R. Luce Chair in Religion, Economic Development and Social Justice at Holy Cross College, Worcester, Massachusetts, she has undertaken comparative research concerning cultural appropriation of Indigenous traditions in Australia and North America. In January 1999 she will take up the position of Professor of Anthropology and Director of Women's Studies, George Washington University, DC. She has published widely in journals of Women's Studies, Anthropology, Law, History, Art and Religion.

OTHER BOOKS BY DIANE BELL

Law: the Old and the New (co-author, 1980/1984)
Daughters of the Dreaming (1983/1993)
Religion in Aboriginal Australia (co-editor, 1984)
Generations: Grandmothers, Mothers and Daughters (1987)
Gendered Fields: Women, Men and Ethnography (co-editor, 1993)
Radically Speaking: Feminism Reclaimed (co-editor, 1996)

NGARRINDJERI WURRUWARRIN

A WORLD THAT IS, WAS, AND WILL BE

by

Diane Bell

Wurruwarrin: Knowing and believing in it is the answer to understanding it.
Tom Trevorrow

𝒮PINIFEX

Spinifex Press Pty Ltd
504 Queensberry Street
North Melbourne, Vic. 3051
Australia
women@spinifexpress.com.au
http://www.spinifexpress.com.au/~women

First published by Spinifex Press, 1998

Edited by Janet Mackenzie
Typeset by Claire Warren
Printed by Griffin Press Pty Ltd

National Library of Australia
Cataloguing-in-Publication data:

Bell, Diane.

Ngarrindjeri Wurruwarrin : a world that is, was, and will be.

Bibliography.
Includes index.
ISBN 1 875559 71 X

1. Aborigines. Australian – South Australia – Hindmarsh Island. 2. Narrinyeri
(Australian people) – Social life and customs. 3. Narrinyeri *Australian people).
4. Sacred sites (Australian aboriginal) – South Australia –. I. Title.

306.089991509423

Australia Council
for the Arts

This publication is assisted by the Australia Council, the
Australian Government's arts funding and advisory body.

Acknowledgements

Completing this project while being here and being there has only been possible because I had much expert assistance; extremely tolerant, thoughtful friends; colleagues with imagination, intelligence and good libraries; students who laboured long and hard and never seemed phased by their somewhat jet-lagged professor; cheerful, talented publishers and editors and; finally, access to technology which when it was good, it was very, very good, but when it wasn't we all knew it!

One of the most trying parts of the research for this book has been locating and accessing sources. A number of colleagues responded to my requests for materials, patiently answered my questions, suggested other sources I might consult and, together we learned a great deal about the attachment functions on our respective email systems. In particular I thank Olwyn Barwick, Jeremy Beckett, Janet Berlo, Rod Foster, Fay Gale, Tom Gara, Jane Goodale, Rod Hagen, Renate Klein, Ian Keen, Rod Lucas, Roger Luebbers, Natascha McNamara, Stephen Muecke, Richard Owen, Adam Shoemaker, Marion Maddox, Jane Simpson, Peter Sutton, Jack Waterford, Irene Watson, Susan Woenne-Green and Karolyn Wrightson. In addition to helping with sources Linda Barwick, Genevieve Bell, Deane Fergie, Steven Hemming, Stephen Kenny, Cheryl Savageau, John von Sturmer, Rod Lucas and Deborah Bird-Rose also read various drafts and provided much appreciated feed-back. I know my demands were an overload on already busy lives and that I variously intruded on vacations, family life and work commitments. Thank you. Without the talent and hard work of Linda Barwick, my most constant email colleague, I could never have completed the section on songs. From existing language files Barry Alpher created an invaluable dictionary of Ngarrindjeri for me and I am grateful for his input on matters linguistic. I thank Vivienne Courto for sharing her translation of Elymann with me in late 1996 and Brendon Reay for his translation of nineteenth century Latin footnotes.

I was fortunate to have the research assistance provided by Jenny Green, Laura Greene, Kaylene Leopold and Marian Thompson who worked on this project at various times and always managed to find the material I requested. I appreciate the hard work of Katie Coyle, Genevieve Bell and Stephen Shaheen on the Chronology and am especially indebted to Stephen for racing against the clock and creating such beautiful maps. At work, Ann Bookman, Bob Henry, Ken Prestwich, Melanie Samsel, Ron Sarja, Kristin Waters and Chick Weiss provided logistic and collegial support which made it possible to be productive even when the network was down, the book hadn't arrived and I had missed a deadline. Through the Heritage application of January–June 1996, I had the opportunity to work again with Pam Ditton and to get to know Annie Keeley, Geoffrey Bagshaw, Neale Draper, Stephen Kenny, Sydney Tilmouth and Jo Wilmot. There were many tense moments but should the non-confidential material generated during the Mathews Report ever become available, it will be apparent that we accomplished an enormous amount under extremely stressful conditions. As the book began to take shape Geoff and Stephen offered all manner of help, by phone, fax and email. Each was dealing with extremely painful personal losses and I am deeply grateful for their friendship and support. Hindmarsh Island has taken a toll on all who have been involved.

I owe a personal debt to a number of friends who made sure I didn't lose touch as my work days got longer and longer and my time to attend to anything other than writing grew less and less. I thank Barbara Drapos, Jean King Fray and Suzanne Patton who let me talk when I needed to and understood when I missed meetings of "The Nine"; Nancy Bentkover, Sally Levinson and others in my aerobics class who kept me fit; Jim Alex, Lois Brynes, Maia Daly, Cynthia Enloe, Rachel Falmange, Serena Hilsinger, Jane Lloyd, Lillian and Geoffrey Lloyd and Joni Seager who offered all manner of care, from food, to retreats, to theatre excursions, to news clippings, to challenging questions; and most especially to Greg Prince and Kristin Waters who have kept pace with the twists and turns of the case and were always ready to help me think through complicated legal and ethical dilemmas. I am proud to acknowledge the input of my daughter, Genevieve Bell, who shared the November to December 1996 fieldwork with me, read drafts, located references, and earned her PhD in anthropology in 1998 at Stanford University.

Many persons who have been involved with Hindmarsh Island matters have found themselves being sued and I do not wish to add to their troubles but thanks for the bacon and eggs that Friday night after a long day's work; thanks for the key to the door and the ready made bed; thanks for access to the phone, computers, copiers and faxes; thanks for the corrections by torchlight in the carport; thanks for the flight from California; thanks for the warm slippers when I was freezing, and the cold beer when I was parched; thanks for the care packages that arrived on my doorstep when I didn't have time to go shopping and thanks for the loans of cars, books, and bits of furniture. I should also thank Mark Smith and his crew who throughout 1998 have been working on my house. They provided endless distractions and we were deadlocked as to who would finish first.

I thank the University of Adelaide for my appointment as an Honorary Visiting Research Fellow in the Department of Adelaide and in particular Jimmy Weiner who made that possible; the staff of the South Australian Museum, Mortlock Library, and Mitchell Library who helped me access their collections; the librarians at Holy Cross who didn't flinch when I repeatedly filed a handful of Inter-library loans; the Center for the Study of World Religions at Harvard University for inviting Ellen, Tom Trevorrow and myself to participate in an international conference on indigenous concerns in November 1997; and the Fulbright Foundation for inviting me to participate in their symposium in Adelaide in April 1998. I thank the Luce Foundation for their generous funding of my Chair and Holy Cross College for the Research Fellowship of 1996–7 which freed me of teaching responsibilities and allowed me to return to this project. Apart from the period when I was under contract (January–June 1996), the travel and research has drawn on personal funds. Fortunately, it is possible to get frequent flyer miles for one's phone bill!

Working with the staff at Spinifex is always a delight and I know that once again I tried their patience as the book grew and deadlines passed. I thank Claire Warren for her inspired design and dedication; Janet Mackenzie for her copyediting; Maralann Damiano, Jo Turner and Libby Fullard for their competent handling of a range of tasks; Renate Klein for her intellectual and moral support and Susan Hawthorne who stayed with me through one week of the last stages of the writing and spent the last weeks of production on phone, fax and email as we sorted through each problem and made it to the printers. Every author should be so lucky as to work with such committed feminist publishers.

In the course of my visits to Australia in January, March, May–June 1996, November–January 1996–97, May–June 1997, February and April 1998, I worked with a number of Ngarrindjeri women and men. I made numerous visits to Hindmarsh Island, Goolwa, Raukkan, Murray Bridge, Tailem Bend, Meningie, Camp Coorong and Point Pearce. Throughout November and December, I lived at Clayton on the banks of Lake Alexandrina overlooking Hindmarsh Island. I thank all those who made those visits such a rewarding experience. I especially appreciated the early morning cups of tea and delicious meals, the warm beds and hot water bottles, the early morning talks in the weak winter sun, the late night talks in the cool of a summer evening and the long days spent pouring over texts, photographs, transcripts and the manuscript. I was delighted when Muriel Van Der Byl agreed to work on the cover and even more delighted when I saw the results. My deepest gratitude goes to Veronica Brodie, Margaret Brusnahan, Vi Deuschle, Sheila Goldsmith, Neville Gollan, Vicki Hartman, Matt Rigney, Dorothy Shaw, Grace Sumner, Maggie Jacobs, Doreen Kartinyeri, Peter Mansfield and his wife Meryl, Sarah Milera, Eileen McHughes, Isabelle Norvill, Shirley Peisley, Valmai Power, Daisy Rankine, Mona Jean and Henry Rankine, Edith Rigney, Sandy Saunders, Elizabeth Tongerie, Ellen and Tom Trevorrow, George Trevorrow, Muriel Van Der Byl, Cherie Watkins, Hazel Wilson, Victor Wilson and Doug Wilson and all relatives, grannies, and friends who were present on various occasions. I cherish your friendship and wisdom and look forward to a time, not too distant, when your stories will be known and appreciated by a wider audience.

Contents

PART TWO: THE POLITICS OF KNOWLEDGE

Contents

List of Maps

Ngarrindjeri Terms

Jekejere, Jekejeri: an ancestral being
kondoli: whale
koyi, koiya, koy: basket
korni, korne: man
krayi: snake
Krowali: Blue Crane, White Faced Heron
kringkari, gringari, gringgari: whitefella, corpse, underlayer of skin
lauwari: Cape Barren Goose
manthari, mantheri, manthuri: native apple
mi:mini, memini, mimini: woman
millin: a deadly sorcery practice
mingka: bird, harbinger of death
miwi: feelings located in stomach, soul substance,
muldarpi, mularpi, mulapi: travelling spirit of sorcerers and strangers
muldawali: Creative hero
mulyewongk, muldjuwangk, moolgewangke, mulgewanki: bunyip,
   monstrous water creature
mutha: grandmother
narambi, narumbi, narumbee: sacred, dangerous, forbidden, taboo
Nepelli: brother-in-law of Ngurunderi
ngatji, ngaitye: totem, friend, countryman, protector
ngia-ngiampe, ngengampi, nhung e umpe, ngyangangyampe: navel
   cord relationship, traders
ngrilkulun: ceremonial dancing
Ngurunderi, Oroodooil: creative hero
nori: pelican
nukkin: look
pakanu: mother's mother
pakari, pekere: prayer song, Dreaming song

pondi, ponde: Murray cod
pulanggi, pulangki: navel
putari: doctor, midwife
ringballin: singing, chanting, corroboree
ritjuruki: Willie wagtail
Rupelli, Rupulle: Leader of *tendi*, landowner
ruwa, ruwar: body
ruwi, ruwe, ruwee: land, country, birthplace
tendi: governing body of the Ngarrindjeri nation
Thukapi, tukabi: turtle
thumpamarldi, thumparmardle: sorcerer
Waiyungare, Waiyungari, Waiungare, Wyunggaree: Creative hero, great hunter
wurruwarrin: knowing and believing
yanun: speak, talk

The Ngarrindjeri (Narrinyeri) Nation

(see Map 3, p. 30)
Portaulan, Potawolin (west of the Murray River)
Ramindjeri (Encounter Bay)
Tangani, Tangane, Tanganarin, Tanganekald (Coorong)
Warkend, Warki (north and west of Lake Alexandrina)
Yaraldi, Jaralde, Jaraldi, Jaraldikald (east side of Lake Alexandrina and Murray River)

Neighbours

Boandik, Bunganditj (southeast of Ngarrindjeri)
Kaurna (Aboriginal people of the Adelaide region)
Narrunga (Yorke Peninsula and Point Pearce)
Potaruwutj (Tatiara)

For my Ngarrindjeri friends and "family",
For your good humour, good sense, and trust.

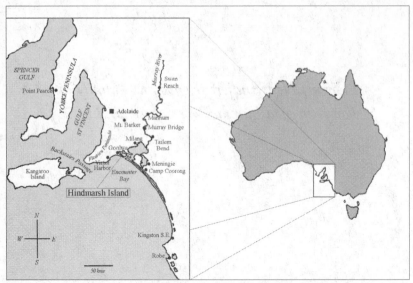

Area of Study (Map: Stephen Shaheen)

Sacred Waters: The car ferry between Goolwa and Hindmarsh Island
(background), proposed site for the bridge. (*Age*, 15 December 1997)

Prologue:
Being Here: Being There

Massachusetts, December 1995. A White Christmas and another blizzard forecast for New Year. I dream of Australia as I shovel the snow which is blowing off the frozen lake on to my driveway, do mental inventories of the contents of the cupboards (candles if the power goes

Leicester, Massachusetts. (Diane Bell)

off, water if the well fails, food that doesn't need elaborate cooking) and check, yet again, on the eighty-year-old beech tree which is leaning towards the house—I should have dealt with it over summer. A telephone message from lawyer Pamela Ditton of Alice Springs, with whom I have not spoken for over a decade, changes all that. "Do you have three weeks to work on a new Ngarrindjeri application? The Royal Commission[1] has found them to be fabricators and Tickner's ban on the building of the bridge has been quashed. The appeal has been denied. I need an anthropologist."

I am working on a book on New Age prophets. I have just on three weeks before teaching resumes. I value these times and the writing is going well. I've been researching this book for several years and am now ready to write. But Hindmarsh Island? At one level it's tempting. Although I have had no contact with the case, I know the issues. A group of Aboriginal women, claiming that a site of special significance to them will be desecrated if a bridge is built and basing their claim on knowledge which is privileged to women, have been

1

accused of making it up to frustrate development. This is an all-too-familiar dilemma in the history of site protection in Australia. With the written record mostly mute on the subject of women's interests in land, and the consultative bodies dominated by authoritative men, women's voices are often not heard until quite late in a development project. Getting the ethnography right in the first place is something I have advocated for the past two decades. Meetings at which decisions might be negotiated are no substitute for field work in the classic participant-observation mode, where one not only has the time to ask, but can also see how statements are played out in everyday lives. However, three weeks is hardly enough time to do this, and there is little chance of getting an extension.

Everything is rush, rush, rush. By the time I come on board, the case has a legal, political, and popular history which constitutes a significant constraint on what an anthropologist might do. On 19 December 1995, the same day the South Australian Royal Commission report is published, thirty-one Ngarrindjeri women and thirteen Ngarrindjeri men lodge an application under Section 10 of the *Aboriginal and Torres Strait Islander Heritage Protection Act* 1984 (Heritage Act). This is Commonwealth legislation, designed to be brought into play when all else fails. And all else has failed for the Ngarrindjeri applicants who are seeking, for the second time, a declaration for protection of an area, including the waters, between Goolwa and Hindmarsh Island. As their lawyer, Pam Ditton has good reason to move speedily in lodging the application. For me the fast pace means I will have no hand in shaping this critically important application, but any reports I write will need to address it. The timing is neither mine, nor the applicants', nor their lawyers'. But, without this new application, there is nothing to stop the developers from beginning work on the bridge. To Pam I say, "Give me a day to check it out."

Since moving to the USA in 1989 in order to take up the Henry R. Luce Chair of Religion, Economic Development and Social Justice at the College of the Holy Cross, in Worcester, Massachusetts, I have maintained my research interests in Australia and initiated new ones, but I have not undertaken any new consultancies in the Aboriginal field. This has been deliberate. I have wanted distance and time to reflect, to write, and to do comparative research. I have been enjoying, nay thriving on, being here and being there. Clifford Geertz's (1983) characterisation of anthropological location and dislocation has been much in my mind (Bell 1993a: 293-6). When I lived in Australia, I was always there. From 1994 onwards, on each visit to "there", I have been asked what I think about the "women's business" claim. What do I think? The media hype and the lack of a contemporary ethnography for the region make it impossible to have a considered opinion on the specifics. (I know of Philip Clarke's (1994) doctoral thesis, but have not yet read it.) So I answer in general terms. Site claims stripped of context are fraught. What is the history of the region? What is the scope of the sources? Whose voices have been recorded by the nineteenth-century missionaries and "learned gentlemen"? With whom did the twentieth-century anthropologists, linguists, historians, and archaeologists work? Have there been trained women in the field who have actively sought out knowledgeable women as "informants"? I reflect on my experience elsewhere in terms of working with women on contested claims. None has been simple. One needs to know the "factors and actors", as my colleague John von Sturmer once said of the Alligator Rivers Region.

Australian anthropology is a small field, so, although I have not worked in this particular region, I know a number of individuals who have been involved in the matter. Also, there are my long-standing research interests in issues related to Aboriginal women's religious beliefs, relations to land, sacred sites, and customary law. These are all matters on which I have published, and my work in that respect is part of the public record. I remember having met several of the applicant women at a conference in Adelaide in 1980 and at various functions at the then Australian Institute of Aboriginal Studies in Canberra. In terms of applied anthropology, I have undertaken a number of consultancies but, for the most part, these have concerned matters in the Northern Territory. Once again my reports, submissions, exhibits and testimony generated in these contexts are part of the record. Hoping that this history of work will be a resource rather than a liability, I agree to undertake the work and, after some creative rescheduling of my professional and personal commitments, I am on a plane to Adelaide and in the dry heat of a South Australian summer four days later.

3

New Year 1996 and a new application. As I fly to Australia, I reread the Commonwealth Heritage Act and a bundle of clippings I put together during a summer visit to the Australian Embassy in Washington, DC, where I can peruse hard copy of the daily papers. I start working on a chronology of events and a "genealogy" of the key actors. The legal and political history of this matter is intricate, and I invite the reader who is interested in following the twists and turns in greater detail to refer to the chronology at the end of the book. All I am doing here is highlighting key moments and tracing the contours of the terrain on which the application I have agreed to work on is being contested. The rules which govern a Section 10 application under the *Aboriginal and Torres Strait Islander Heritage Act* are by no means settled; this application is going to generate deeply troubling questions, some of which will be addressed in a report being prepared by Justice Evatt.[2] The Heritage Act sets out the following steps. After receiving a Section 10 application seeking protection of an area, the federal Minister for Aboriginal and Torres Strait Islander Affairs nominates a "Reporter" who deals with matters of significance and desecration for the Aboriginal applicants, and the nature of the impact a declaration would have on other interested parties. After consideration of the report, any representations attached to the report, and any other matters he thinks relevant, the Minister may make a declaration in relation to the area. This is just what Robert Tickner did in 1994.

As the federal Minister, Tickner had heard from Professor Cheryl Saunders, the Reporter. With the exception of one envelope marked "Confidential Appendices 2 and 3: To be read by women only", he had read all the representations. With respect to these confidential appendices, which had been prepared by Dr Deane Fergie (1994), Minister Tickner had the Saunders Report (1994) and he took advice from a female member of his staff who had been authorised, by the applicant women, to read the contents of the envelopes. Armed with this information, Tickner was satisfied that the area was significant and that it would be desecrated by the building of a bridge. But why had it become necessary to invoke the powers of the federal Minister? Was not the purpose of the South Australian legislation to protect sites? What had satisfied him that a declaration was a proper use of the Commonwealth legislation? Tickner (1994: 51) agreed that indeed the South Australian *Aboriginal Heritage Act* 1988 did afford protection. However, in the matter of the site at Goolwa, the state legislation was not affording protection. The site had already been registered under that legislation but was now at risk. On 3 May 1994, Dr Armitage, the state Minister for Aboriginal Affairs, had exercised his ministerial discretion under the state legislation and authorised such damage to the site as might be necessary for the building of the bridge.[3] The earth-moving equipment was in place. In such circumstances the federal Minister needed to act and act quickly if the site was to be protected. Thus, on 12 May, Tickner issued an emergency declaration under Section 9 of the Heritage Act and then, on 10 July 1994, after hearing from the Reporter, issued a twenty-five-year ban. The Ngarrindjeri applicants celebrated.[4]

The Tickner declaration of 1994 was an affirmation for the Ngarrindjeri applicants of the tenacity of their survival. It was also a statement that the work of the Council for Aboriginal Reconciliation[5] may have significance for the lives of peoples in the "settled south", not just the peoples of the far north and central desert regions of Australia. For the most part, over the past several decades, Aboriginal people in these "remote" regions have been able to protect their sacred places.[6] Although they too have faced difficulties, generally it has been easier for them to demonstrate their on-going responsibilities for and genealogical relationships to their sacred places, than it has been for Aboriginal people in the so-called "settled south". Courts and legislators are much more comfortable in recognising

BRIDGE BUSINESS, 1993–1994
1993
April Bridge approved
October Protection sought unhder *Aboriginal Heritage Act 1988 (SA)*
1994
20 April Protection sought from federal Minister
3 May Destruction of sites authorised by state Minister
4 May Amelia Park protest rally
12 May Temporary emergency declaration by federal Minister
26 May Cheryl Saunders appointed as Reporter
5 June Barbecue, Goolwa wharf
9 July Saunders Report
10 July Tickner issues 25-year ban
8 August Binalong Pty Ltd goes into liquidation

Ngarrindjeri applicants and friends celebrate at the Semaphore Workmen's Club, July 1994
Edie Carter, Val Power, Shirley Peisley, Muriel Van Der Byl, Sandy Saunders, Irene Allen, Joan Varcoe and others
(*Advertiser*, 10 July 1995)

"traditions" amongst peoples who still speak Aboriginal languages and still have an elaborate ceremonial life. From the mid-nineteenth century onwards, the Ngarrindjeri have felt the bite of assimilation policies as administered by missionaries, protectors, police, welfare officers and educators. Their families have been torn apart; their languages and their ceremonies suppressed (Berndt *et al.* 1993: chapter 20; Jenkin 1979; Mattingley and Hampton 1988). Demonstrating that the area was of significance and that the bridge would violate their traditions was a major victory.

For the developers, Wendy and Tom Chapman and their son Andrew, Tickner's ban was an exercise in ministerial discretion that added to their problems. They had already gone into receivership. They took their grievances to the Federal Court where they sought judicial review of Tickner's declaration. By 15 February 1995, the Federal Court had agreed that the advertisement of the original application was flawed and that the Minister should have read all the representations, even those confidential to women. The Tickner declaration of July 1994 was quashed.[7] Even though the court had ruled on procedural, not substantive grounds, the Ngarrindjeri applicants had once again to prove their case. Tickner and two of the applicants appealed the quashing to the Full Federal Court.[8] It was to be another ten months before the results of that action were known, and there were rumblings in the Lower Murray region that not all Ngarrindjeri believed in the "traditions" on which the original application had been made. The most bitter moment for the applicants was March 1995, when Ian McLachlan—then federal

BRIDGE POLITICS, 1995
7 February Federal Court quashes Tickner's ban
15 February Tickner appeals quashing
6 March McLachlan brandishes the "secret envelopes"
10 March McLachlan resigns
26 March Nanna Laura Kartinyeri's letter tabled in parliament
19 May Dorothy Wilson's and Dulcie Wilson's claims of fabrication on TV Channel Ten
6 June Doug Milera's claims of "fabrication" on TV Channel Ten
8 June SA Government announces a Royal Commission
27 July Doug Milera retracts
7 December Tickner's appeal dismissed
19 December Report of Royal Commission

Minister for the Environment, and member for Barker, a district which takes in Goolwa and Hindmarsh Island—revealed in the parliament that his office had copied the so-called "secret envelopes". How many copies were made was contested, as was whether he had actually read the contents, but his general attitude was one of contempt for Aboriginal women's restricted knowledge. "The more documents you send, the more I will copy," he was reported as saying.[9] Within a week he was forced to resign, but the case grew murkier and cries of "hoax", "fabrication" and "conspiracy" grew louder. By April 1995, political reporter Chris Kenny (1996: 139ff.) had begun to investigate the charges and to flesh out the claims that the "women's business" was "fabricated by men". On 8 June, the Premier of South Australia, Dean Brown, announced that a Royal Commission would inquire into the fabrication charges and the then federal Minister, Robert Tickner, announced that an independent inquiry would begin once the outcome of his appeal was known. The rules governing a Heritage application may be specified at law, but the process by which and the conditions under which a declaration is sought have been increasingly politicised (Brunton 1996a, b; Maddock 1988; Merlan 1991; Nile 1996).

The appeal against the quashing of the Tickner declaration was denied on 7 December 1996 when the Federal Court agreed that the Minister should have read the contents of the envelopes. All those working on Heritage claims realised this decision would have dramatic ramifications. How were applicants to provide documentation when gender-restricted information is central to their claims? Aboriginal men may reasonably expect to speak with a male Reporter and have their words read by a male Minister. Even if the matter should go on appeal, there are plenty of male judges on the Federal and High Courts. The courts and parliament are, after all, male-dominated institutions. Thus, when it comes to material that should only be read by women, the decks are stacked against women. The applicants had little time to think through this one. The findings of Commissioner Iris Stevens (1995: 299) that the whole of "women's business" was fabricated for the purpose of obtaining a declaration, were published on 19 December 1995. The "dissident women" celebrated.[10]

The dissident Ngarrindjeri women celebrate, December 1995.
Left to right: Beryl Kropinyeri, Betty Tatt, Dulcie Wilson, Bertha Gollan, Dorothy Wilson, Vena Gollan, Audrey Dix, Jenny Grace
(Leon Mead, *Advertiser*)

During the six months spent investigating Ngarrindjeri women's beliefs regarding the significance of the Hindmarsh Island sites, the Royal Commission divided the Ngarrindjeri community into those who believed in the "women's business" (the "proponent" women) and those who didn't (the "dissident" women). It pitted anthropologists against anthropologists; provided the local media with a tale of intrigue; and left the general public tired, vexed, and disinclined to believe the word of these politicised Aboriginal women applicants. Will the taxpayers be willing to endure another year of Hindmarsh? At that time I had my own reservations concerning the case and how it had evolved, and I knew it would take time to work through the documents, consult with relevant persons, and make up my own mind about the "women's business". Looking back, I would say at that stage it had not really sunk in just how deeply scarred were all those who had worked on matters Hindmarsh. Nor did I fully realise how bitterly matters Hindmarsh had soured the research climate.

January 1996: First field work. As I begin my first field work in the Lower Murray region of South Australia in January 1996, I know that Jane Mathews, a Federal Court judge, will be the Reporter who will hear representations from the applicants and other interested parties. She will report to Senator Rosemary Crowley of the Australian Labor Party who has been appointed by the Prime Minister to act for and on behalf of Robert Tickner, in relation to the application. With a woman judge and a woman Minister, the Ngarrindjeri women should be able to present a full account of their claim. But I am becoming familiar with the context of the claim and sense the frustration of the applicants when asked to focus on the rectangle of land designated for construction of the proposed bridge. They want to explain the significance of the wider area within which the ferry now operates. They want to speak about the damage done to the area of the Murray Mouth in the 1930s by the building by the River Murray Commission of the barrages which hold back the salt waters and keep the lake water fresh for agricultural purposes. They want the judge to understand how the landscape has changed: soakages have dried up; the salt table has risen; and native flora and fauna have been devastated. They have concerns about disturbing the burial places of their ancestors, about violating the integrity of the waters below and the skies above. For them the Murray Mouth, Goolwa and Hindmarsh Island area is a complex of stories, sites and resources. They stress the inter-relatedness of their beliefs about the region and their particular histories of knowing about country.

Late January 1996 and the first field work is done. I am back in the US, to teaching, a dead car buried under a snow drift, frenetic writing, library and archival research, and much trans-Pacific communication. In Australia, a federal election is called for 2 March and I wonder what impact the outcome will have on the process. Am I still writing for a woman Minister? By the time I know it will be too late to rewrite the report. I sign off on "A World That Is, Was and Will Be: Ngarrindjeri Women's Traditions, Observances, Customs and Beliefs", a 114-page confidential report, in which I examine the women's claims regarding their beliefs and practices within the context of the literature I have been able to access and review. The title, which is also the sub-title of this book, plays off *A World That Was* (1993), a book by Ronald M. Berndt and Catherine H. Berndt with John E. Stanton, on which the Royal Commission relied in coming to its finding of fabrication. By now it is apparent to me that Ngarrindjeri applicants are not to be written of in the past tense. Dr Doreen Kartinyeri's verse: "To all the mothers that was; to all the mothers that is; to all the mothers that will be" makes this explicit.[11] Some of my report does, however, become past tense, when the Labor government is defeated in the March polls and the new Minister for Aboriginal Affairs, Dr John Herron, repeatedly refuses to appoint a woman to receive Justice Mathews' report. On the instructions of the applicant women, some thirty pages of my initial report are withheld. If a woman Minister is appointed, they may be submitted. They never are. They remain unread. They never become part of the case. The applicants do not want this gender-restricted knowledge placed in harm's way.

March 1996: The USA and Australia. In the USA it is now spring break. My students head off to do research in their home communities. I fly to Adelaide where the biennial Arts Festival is in full swing in the city and the early autumn air is still warm and thick.

Further south, around Encounter Bay, the days are getting chill and the wind off the dunes stings. I'll have a little more time working with the women and will be there for the first three days of their oral representations, as their testimony ("evidence") is called in one of these proceedings. The women speak of their lives, attachment to the area, knowledge of Ngarrindjeri traditions, commitment to teaching their daughters and grandchildren, respect for their aunties, mothers and grandmothers. I expect to be called to speak to my report, answer questions, and then, at the conclusion of the evidence, after having had a chance to read the representations from other interested parties, to be able to prepare a final report. But this is not how this application is going to proceed. I've worked on some seven land claims in the Northern Territory, given expert testimony in various cases involving customary law, been a consultant to the Australian Law Reform Commission and various Aboriginal Legal Aid Services. In 1984, back in the early days of the legislation, I even acted as a Reporter on a Heritage claim, but I have never worked on a matter quite as complex, chaotic, changeable and conflict-ridden as this one.

April: Back in the USA. Spring break is done. I read the balance of the men's oral representations on transcript, watch the video of the men's and women's testimony, and continue teaching a course on the New Age that is by now taking on a surreal feel, quite over and above the subject matter. "Why is it that the consumers of New Age texts, that purport to be accounts of journeys of Western wisdom-seekers with Indigenous persons, are so vulnerable to these questionable testimonies?" I ask my students. They present their field work reports. They tell me that the public libraries in their home communities, mainly in the northeast, hold multiple copies of the book *Mutant Message: Down Under* by Marlo Morgan (1993), but no ethnographies on Australian Aborigines, and none of the recent writings by Aboriginal authors. They find books about Native Americans in the children's books section, but little about the peoples of the northeast of the USA where they are located. The students find they could spend hundreds of dollars a day attending workshops where they might experience a sweat lodge, make drums, participate in a vision quest, or learn shamanic journeying. They find that local Native American organisations, starved of funds, are highly critical of the practices of these "plastic medicine men". Some communities have turned to running casinos, but most Native Americans live in poverty, pale shadows of the more luminous characters that people the New Age accounts of Native spirituality. The construct of the noble savage, the intuitive native, and a religion that integrates all life forms into one harmonious world, is far more appealing than the historical reality of peoples whose lands have been over-run, whose children have been stolen, whose food sources have been destroyed, and whose beliefs have been under attack since first contact. In the reimagining of the "native" as untouched and willing to share wisdom, the real lives, struggles, histories, and rights of Indigenous peoples can be set aside. These are not the "real people". Instead, the romantic reconstruction has become the standard against which to measure the authenticity of those claiming to be Indigenous.

There are many parallels to be drawn with their research and mine. Like the southeast of Australia, the northeast of the USA was settled early in the history of European colonisation of the continent. These are the peoples who bore the brunt of first contact and they are at a distinct disadvantage when it comes to making claims against the very state which dispossessed them. When the Mashpee of Cape Cod sought restoration of their lands in 1976, they found what was at stake was their identity as a tribe (Clifford 1988). The Ngarrindjeri in 1996 must first prove they are the custodians of the sites and of the knowledge of their forebears. Can people who no longer live a "tribal life", like that of the peoples of central and northern Australia, or the peoples of the Plains and the Pueblos of North America, expect to receive the benefits of legislation that requires evidence of "tradition"? What is "tradition" in this context? These questions have arisen in previous cases concerning heritage issues, land rights, and sacred sites (Maddock 1988; Merlan 1991; Brunton 1996a, b). Each new case brings new speculation and contesting of the concept of "tradition". Can traditions change? Be relearned? Be reasserted? Can there be a tradition of innovation? Are anthropologists part of the "invention of culture"?

The Ngarrindjeri with whom I am working are interested in their culture, in telling the stories of their forebears, in re-learning their language, and in protecting their places. In this sense they are

13

politicised. There is no denying this. But what are the forces shaping their interest and how much do these political forces account for the content of their beliefs? Native American poet Linda Hogan (1987: 126) says of her grandmother's move from an Euro-American life back to "a very traditional one in Oklahoma . . . Maybe any life of resistance to mainstream culture is traditional Indian". That is surely part of it. The peoples of the Lower Murray have had over at least 170 years of accommodation and resistance. They have lived under different political and administrative regimes. Following the 1967 referendum, which gave the federal government concurrent rights with the states to legislate for Aboriginal peoples and required that they be counted in the national census, new spaces and resources have been made available. Federal and state Departments of Aboriginal Affairs have been established. Aboriginal organisations have flourished. New community-based meeting places have been built. Education programs in the schools, a Centre of Aboriginal Studies in Music, exhibits, oral history and family history projects in the South Australian Museum, Heritage Committees, and NAIDOC (National Aboriginal and Islander Day Observance Committee) have all been part of the refocusing of attention on Ngarrindjeri language, music, art, story telling and history. Those Ngarrindjeri who have flourished in this new climate would certainly understand their lives as ones of resistance in Hogan's terms, but the stories which sustained their old people and the stories which are nourishing this generation draw heavily of a distinctive body of knowledge and practice which is more than the product of resistance to oppressive policies. It is grounded in oral traditions passed from generation to generation, albeit traditions which have accommodated change, absorbed new ideas, and thus survived.

But not all Ngarrindjeri have been caught up in this cultural revival, and not all Ngarrindjeri are reflective about their culture, any more than all Australians have an abiding interest in and extensive knowledge of constitutional debates. Not all Christians are familiar with the history of the church and its controversies over the nature of religious authority, yet they may still call themselves Christians. One can be Ngarrindjeri without being engaged by

14

questions of tradition. One can be a believer and not be reflective. There are many ways of being Ngarrindjeri. The applicants have explained theirs to the Reporter Jane Mathews at some length. As their consultant I set about explaining the importance of individual and family histories as a context for understanding their stories. As the Ngarrindjeri with whom I am working are fond of saying, Not everyone needs to know everything for it to be true. Moreover, the Commonwealth legislation does not require that everyone know, nor that everyone endorse the application. Section 9(1)(a) simply speaks of an application from an Aboriginal or group of Aboriginals.

Mid-April: Another report. The snow has almost gone in Massachusetts. I am still in daily contact with the legal team. I sign off on another report: "Ngarrindjeri Oral Submissions Thus Far: An Interim Supplementary Report". In this twenty-three-page analysis I set out the arguments advanced for the significance of the area and the bases of authority from which these Ngarrindjeri applicants speak. The stories they know are primarily from the old people, not books. In a fifty-page attachment of women's evidence in a Northern Territory land claim, I suggest that their evidence is consistent with, and no more detailed than that which has been offered by the applicants. But the judge wants more of the stories than the women have been prepared to disclose. The men are supportive of the women and have taken the judge by boat along the Coorong, the inland waterway which runs parallel to the coast for some one hundred kilometres. They have explained the ways in which particular places in the Ngarrindjeri world are inter-related. They have pointed out where the salt and fresh waters meet; where the wildlife proliferates; where their old people are buried. They have spoken of the damage done to the land and waterways by barrages and the drainage of the southeast. They explain they "know" *of* "women's business", but they do not "know" the details. With a woman as Reporter, they find themselves in the position well known to Aboriginal women required to give evidence about their beliefs to a male judge. The Ngarrindjeri men explain they cannot reveal details of their gendered knowledge to Jane Mathews. The existence of gendered knowledge presents a real problem for a legal system which claims to be gender- and race-neutral. There are women and men with knowledge of the existence of certain sites and accompanying stories, but it is inappropriate to speak of the "business" of the other. It is both dangerous and disrespectful.

May 1996: More reports. How then to explain Ngarrindjeri beliefs, especially those which entail gender-restricted knowledge? By the beginning of May, Geoffrey Bagshaw, who is working with the applicant men, and I have co-authored "Seven Sisters Dreaming: The Ngarrindjeri in Perspective", a twenty-seven-page report. We establish a framework for knowledge of sites and Dreamings and fill in evidence that women and men know of the critically important Seven Sisters story and practices. In the creative era, known as the Dreamtime, ancestral heroes travelled through the land, and established the religious law. The lore and law of *Ngurunderi*, the culture hero who created the mighty Murray River and initiated major rituals, have been recorded by various observers of Ngarrindjeri culture (Meyer 1843; Taplin 1873; Berndt 1940a). *Ngurunderi*, whose canoe can today be seen as the Milky Way, like the Seven Sisters, who are visible in the summer skies as the Pleiades, established a relationship between earth and sky. Through story, ceremony, song, dance, and ritual designs, this knowledge has been passed from generation to generation. The Royal Commission, however, found no trace of the law and lore of the Seven Sisters in Ngarrindjeri lands. Commissioner Stevens (1995: 278) stated that this story was "never part of the Dreaming of the Ngarrindjeri people". However, Geoff Bagshaw and I cite sources for Ngarrindjeri beliefs and namings of the Pleiades constellation in Ngarrindjeri which date back to 1930. Peter Sutton (1996) reports on the mention of the Seven Sisters across Australia and speculates regarding the meanings attached to the Ngarrindjeri Seven Sister stories. I have since found nineteenth-century references (Taplin 1873: 18) to the Pleiades. Can the finding of fabrication by the Royal Commission be sustained in the light of this evidence? Unfortunately, challenging a Royal Commission takes more than facts. What of the scholarship of those "experts" who testified in the Royal Commission that the Dreaming story was an importation? To whom are they accountable?

More questions. It seems we have established to Jane Mathews' satisfaction that the area is significant to the applicants, but this is not enough. The Reporter wants to hear why a bridge would desecrate this significant area. In "Injury and Desecration: An Anthropological Assessment of the Submissions", thirty-two pages long, I set out an argument concerning the nature of the harm that a bridge constitutes for the Ngarrindjeri applicants. I write as an anthropologist, not as a lawyer. I explain the beliefs regarding the consequences of violating Ngarrindjeri law, of the way in which Ngarrindjeri lore keeps the knowledge alive and vivid. In a one-page report "Re: Final Report", I explain what could be addressed in a final report if we had been given time, and what might be gained from oral submissions from the anthropologists working on the matter. There is another snow storm, and four inches of soft white stuff covers my newly sown lawn. It is also getting chill in Adelaide.

I make a third trip to Australia in late May, do more field work, and am still expecting that there will be some need for *viva voce* evidence. The anthropology of this case is so fraught, and we keep finding written documentation in overlooked or newly available sources which supports the oral claims made by the applicants. However, there is no time to do justice to these research findings. The judge wants all representations in writing and to her by 17 May.[12] To further complicate matters, in the last few weeks, before the lawyers close their case, we have seen two significant breaches of confidence, been in and out of the Federal Court, and tried to accommodate the changing rules of the game occasioned

HERITAGE BUSINESS, 1995–1996

1995

8 June Tickner announces intention of a new inquiry

19 December New application lodged

1996

16 January Crowley names Mathews as Reporter

19 February Chapmans seek $12,115,317.36 in damages

2 March Howard wins federal election

16–18, 25–7 March Women's evidence

2–3 April Men's evidence

12 April Mathews: More details

30 April–3 May Women's confidential disclosures

28 May Crocodile Farm (WA) case re confidentiality

29 May Mathews: Confidential material no longer protected

30 May Ngarrindjeri withdraw all confidential material

27 June Mathews Report

22 August Evatt Report

6 September High Court rules Mathews appointment ineffective

17 September Mathews Report tabled; Special legislation proposed

26 September Herron tables Evatt Report

by a decision in a Heritage case in Western Australia.[13] The applicants balance the dangers that will befall them if they disclose gender-restricted knowledge against the harm that will be done if the bridge is built. In order to protect their heritage, it seems, they must violate their religious teachings; there is no guarantee that, if they do allow the confidential material to go to the Minister, he will understand the importance of the stories. What does he know of Aboriginal people? What has he read? Ethnography? New Age? Travelogues? The *Adelaide Review*?

8 June 1996: Adelaide. I deliver a sixty-one-page report, "Myth, Ritual and 'Women's Business'", in which I recapitulate what can be known of women's knowledge from the non-confidential evidence, and argue that the definition of "women's business" relied upon by the Royal Commission was flawed in that it focused on ritual, not myth (i.e., on practice, not on beliefs). Myth and ritual, I argue, implicate each other. Further, we don't need to be apprised of the inside details of women's restricted knowledge to know that there is a sincerely held belief. I point out that we already know a great deal of the structure of women's knowledge, the authority of the elders, the texture of Ngarrindjeri beliefs, and the consequences of violating Ngarrindjeri law. We don't need the three or four pages of transcript and the three paragraphs of one of my confidential appendices that have been withdrawn.[14] There are some several thousand pages of evidence left, and they tell the story of an area of significance to the applicants and beliefs about why a bridge constitutes a desecration. By now I have written myself to a standstill, and the judge and her party have retreated to the Barossa Valley to write the report for the Minister.

Summer: The USA. I return to the USA, to summer, to a million things that have been neglected, but the faxes and phone calls continue. The twists and turns of the legal and political process require constant monitoring if one is to stay current. On 27 June, Justice Mathews completes her report, but the Minister decides to sit on it until the High Court rules on the matter of the Mathews appointment as a Federal Court judge to be the Reporter.[15] By September I have almost caught up on the outstanding jobs that accumulated during the first half of the year. I have filed the reports, the research, the correspondence, the various decisions, and my study is almost back to normal. I am back to my writing. I have a research fellowship for the academic year 1996–7 and I had planned to finish work on a book on social justice issues in Australia and North America. *Just Dreams* concerns the framing of key moves by Indigenous peoples for social justice and the contexts within which such moves are attempted, interpreted, supported and thwarted in Australia, the USA and Canada. I am exploring the dilemma Indigenous peoples represent for our theorising around issues of justice. How do we redistribute resources equitably without encroaching on the rights and liberties of individuals? Indigenous peoples, I suggest, present what is perhaps the most telling test for those who would argue for the minimalist state and those who would argue for the state as the site of redistribution. How can we be fair to people who have been denied access for so many years? Is it possible to speak of justice at local, national and international levels, or are we just dreaming? In what sense can Indigenous peoples self-determine? Is the "self" of "self-determination" gendered? I have been thinking that the Hindmarsh Island affair will be the final chapter to *Just Dreams*. It does, after all, encapsulate the debates I intend to address.

September 1996: Canberra. The High Court rules. In a six-to-one decision they find that Mathews' appointment breached the constitutional separation of powers of the executive and judiciary.[16] "What then is the status of her report?" I ask the lawyers. "Will we have to do it all over again? Surely the report cannot now be used for Ministerial decision-making." On 17 September, the crunch comes. The Mathews Report is tabled in the Senate and the federal government announces that the bridge will go ahead. A one-off amendment to the Commonwealth Heritage Act will be introduced to facilitate this. After all, the reasoning goes, another report would be a waste of money. It would be "vexatious". What all this means at law is moot. What is clear to me, after writing some 300 pages of submissions, reading 800-plus pages of transcripts, filling some seven large filing boxes, is that the Ngarrindjeri applicants are yet to have their day in court. Political expediency in the parliament, poor drafting of the act, states' rights, media sensationalism and partisan reporting, disgruntled developers, an ill-informed public, hurried and harried anthropology, a lack of political resolve, legalism masquerading as fairness, and constantly shifting ground rules have proved to be a potent mix.

There are more things to ponder about the timing of the tabling of the Mathews Report. The Report of Justice Evatt which reviews the Heritage Act (22 August 1996), advocates handing the matter of heritage sites back to the states from the Commonwealth, and spells out strong provisions regarding confidentiality. Has the Minister taken its recommendations into consideration with respect to Hindmarsh Island? He certainly had the Evatt Report before he decided to table the Mathews Report on 17 September. The Honourable Elizabeth Evatt (1996: 303) has cautioned that requiring that confidential information be disclosed as a condition of protection may discourage Aboriginal people from using the Act. Her report is tabled on 26 September and allowed to languish. The Mathews Report does and does not exist. In so far as the Minister can cite the Reporter as saying that, without the withdrawn pages of transcript and several paragraphs of a confidential appendix of mine, there is not enough in evidence to make the case for desecration, it has a political life. But at law, the report does not exist. It has no legal force. If it were alive at law, it could be challenged by the applicants.[17] There is much in the report on which to reflect. There is, Mathews (1996: 3) writes, sufficient material to find that the area is significant to the applicants. This is important in that it contradicts the findings of the Royal Commissioner. For the area to be significant, the "proponent women" must have had some traditional knowledge. But these are not matters which the media finds "newsworthy". They have a compelling narrative of fabrication to tell and, with notable exceptions, are sticking with it.[18] The applicants continue to believe that they have been denied justice by the Minister's refusal to appoint a woman to receive the report and say so in letters to the Prime Minister and the Minister for Aboriginal Affairs (Kartinyeri 1996).

There is, I decide, a pressing need for a public document which provides a context within which to read the Ngarrindjeri claim for protection of the site. There are other narratives of Ngarrindjeri knowledge and they are ones I think the public should know. The anthropology of the two Heritage applications and the Royal Commission has attracted much comment, but most of the commentary is ignorant of Ngarrindjeri ethnography. Further, because all the reports have been confidential, non-participants can only speculate as to what was learned during the Mathews reporting process. Those prone to find succour in conspiracy theory are doing their best to portray all the inquiries, other than the Royal Commission, as a denial of "natural justice" because evidence taken "in confidence" cannot be tested.[19] With one exception, none of the proponent women gave evidence in the Royal Commission. They chose not to recognise the jurisdiction of a commission which was inquiring into their religious beliefs.[20] There are stories they want to tell, but they want to do so in a dignified and respectful manner. I have requests from the applicants to do something with the material I've generated. It will take much negotiation to sort out what can be in the public domain and what must remain private, but at present the material on which the public, the media, the parliament, and even my colleagues can draw is extremely dated and limited. The focus of most commentaries on Hindmarsh Island and Ngarrindjeri culture is the Royal Commission, not the more recent Mathews Report on which I have been working. And, although Mathews was not convinced that a bridge would desecrate the site, she did agree it was a site of significance. This needs to be widely known. What if I were to take the reports and transform them into a book? a number of the applicant men and women ask.

November 1996: Back to Australia. I begin to plan my fourth trip for the year. My daughter, Genevieve, who is finishing her PhD in anthropology at Stanford University, offers to come along as my research assistant. The Committee on Research Fellowships at Holy Cross agrees to my changes in plan for 1996–7. *Just Dreams* will have to wait, or maybe the moment has passed. I submit a proposal to the Ngarrindjeri working group named on my contract for the initial consultancy of January–June 1996, and leave it to Stephen Kenny, the instructing solicitor, who is now acting for both the men and women, to advise his clients. In my contract I had agreed not to comment on the case or use knowledge I had acquired during the consultancy, so I need to be released from this contract if I am to work on a book. It's getting chill again in Massachusetts, but my autumn plantings are thriving and the beech tree has been felled. The hurricane season passes without drama.

The response to my proposal has been enthusiastic, so Genevieve and I plan to spend November and part of December in Australia. I have a position as a Visiting Honorary Research Fellow in the Anthropology Department at the University of Adelaide; thus I have access to libraries and archives, a community of scholars who know quite a bit about Hindmarsh Island but by no means agree, and a rented house at Clayton, on Lake Alexandrina, overlooking Hindmarsh Island. In the interests of fairness and because I consider not having been able to talk to the "dissident" women to be a gap in my research, I approach their solicitor, Nicolas Iles, and request permission to interview his clients. At first he is favourably disposed but, after consulting with his clients, informs me they do not wish to be interviewed and that they are on the public record for all to see. I express my regret that I shall not be able to speak with them directly; state that I consider it necessary to deal with their concerns; and point out that my approach was ethnographic not adversarial.[21]

While the negotiations regarding release from my contract have been in train, it has become apparent that one family has significant reservations about my proposal to write an ethnographically oriented book. They request a full meeting of the working group with whom their lawyer, Stephen Kenny, has been negotiating regarding my book proposal. Their questions are interesting: "Can a non-Indigenous person write an ethnography?" They fear the book I am proposing will become the authority and I may get it wrong; I may be given false information; I may unwittingly transgress. These are all matters which concern me also. I have already suggested that a new working party be formed and I am happy for them to read drafts, as I would have been happy for the "dissidents" to read what I might have written of them had I had the opportunity to speak to them. The issue of the money to be made from the book is raised at the meeting. I offer to enter into a joint venture: to share the profits and losses. I am already significantly out of pocket with the cost of the various trips and research. I have no outside funding for the research for this project.

Had I waited to apply for a grant to cover travel and so on, it would have been another year before I could begin, and I didn't think this project would wait. Journalist Chris Kenny's book, *Women's Business* (1996), appears and I marvel at his cavalier approach. Ignorance has become a knowledge claim. No time-consuming negotiations for him. Has he breached Section 35 of the state *Aboriginal Heritage Act* 1988?[22] Has he libelled individuals? He certainly has exercised journalistic licence in his reconstruction of conversations at which he was not present, and here I am laboriously negotiating every sentence of conversations in which I was a participant.

An Australian Christmas. The negotiations around what can be used and what can't; and around who wants to be included and under what conditions; in addition to driving from community to community, chasing down obscure references, getting access to tapes, photographs, and special collections—these are all time-intensive and at times extremely frustrating. Through this process of consultation I learn a great deal about the politics of knowledge being played out in the South Australian Museum as well as in the Ngarrindjeri community. From Ngarrindjeri I initially hear as much about the deep hurt, anger, and mistrust engendered by the Royal Commission as about Ngarrindjeri ethnography, but as I get to know people better, as they visit my place and I theirs, as we chat on the phone, go shopping, work through photographs and documents together, we move beyond that. The work begins to feel more and more like participant-observation field work and I want to keep going. People want to talk, and they know a great deal that is not in the sources, in Mathews, the Royal Commission, or my previous notes of interviews. I also want to spend more time with anthropologist Norman B. Tindale's papers of the 1930s and 1940s, which are now lodged in the South Australian Museum, and with the journals (1859–79) of missionary George Taplin, which are lodged in the special collection in the Mortlock Library, Adelaide.[23] The notes of these two men are yielding rich results. By mid-December my daughter Genevieve has returned to California and I have decided to stay until New Year. I email those I've invited for a festive meal in Massachusetts. Christmas in Australia with Ngarrindjeri friends will be fun and will complete a cycle of work begun a year ago.

Field Work Area

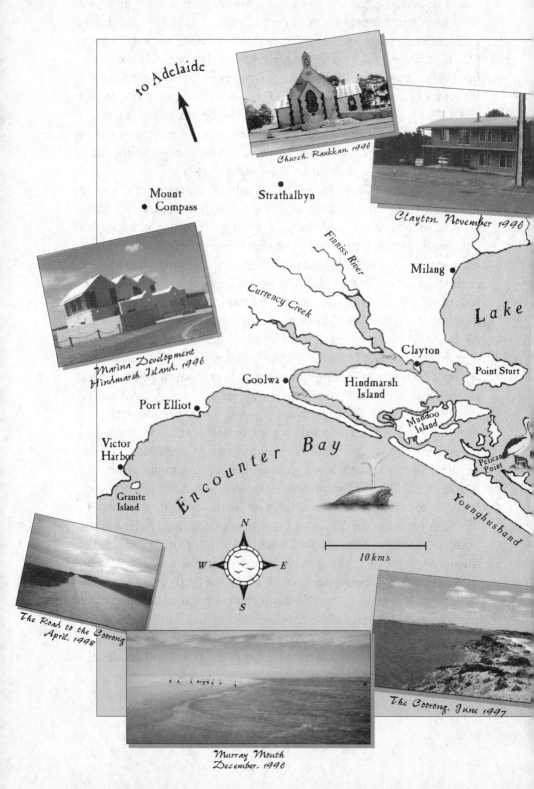

to Adelaide

Church. Raukkan. 1996

Clayton. November 1996

Mount Compass

Strathalbyn

Milang

Finniss River

Currency Creek

Lake

Clayton

Point Sturt

Marina Development
Hindmarsh Island. 1996

Goolwa

Hindmarsh
Island

Mundoo
Island

Port Elliot

Pelican
Point

Victor
Harbor

Encounter Bay

Younghusband

Granite
Island

N
W E
S

10 kms

The Road to the Coorong
April. 1998

The Coorong. June 1997

Murray Mouth
December. 1996

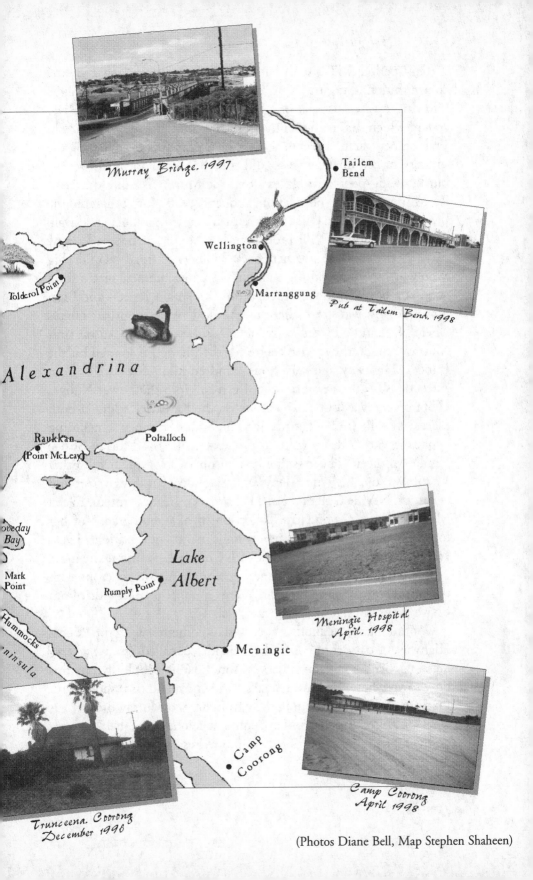

Murray Bridge. 1997

Tailem
Bend

Pub at Tailem Bend. 1998

Wellington

Marranggung

Tolderol Point

Alexandrina

Raukkan
(Point McLeay)

Poltalloch

Loveday
Bay

Mark
Point

Rumply Point

*Lake
Albert*

Meningie Hospital
April. 1998

Hummocks

Peninsula

Meningie

Camp
Coorong

Camp Coorong
April 1998

Trunceena. Coorong
December 1996

(Photos Diane Bell, Map Stephen Shaheen)

This period will also be a time to get a better sense of the communities, along the Murray, on the mission, and in Adelaide. Growing up in Australia one learns of the Murray–Darling River system which drains the southeast of the country. As a ten-year-old I remember tracing the journeys of the explorers and pondering the mystery of the inland rivers—did they flow into an inland sea?—but knowing people in places along the Murray is quite different. At Murray Bridge, population about 12,000, I photograph the bridge built 1879, the first to cross the river. If I park here and walk back up to the hotel I'll probably see a couple of people I know playing the pokies; further back along the road at the big Woolworths others will be shopping. I know the best places for a good cup of tea in town—there is only one main street—and I can now find my way from there to the neat brick suburban houses where Ngarrindjeri families live side by side with other Australians. Murray Bridge, the service centre for the district, is located on the Princes Highway, an easy one-hundred-kilometre drive from Adelaide. On the way into town I can call into the Lower Nungas Club; on the way out I can detour via the Kalparin Farm. At both places I will find Ngarrindjeri men and women, including applicants, at work on cultural projects. I like the Murray Bridge families I meet. The hospitality of Isobelle Norvill, her brother Victor Wilson, his wife Glenys and extended family is warm and generous. Neville Gollan, I quickly learn, is a great raconteur. Eileen McHughes has a wonderful collection of old photographs of her forebears, and her extended family joins in our conversations. I visit Harold "Kim" Kropinyeri. I talk with Connie Love and many more people who are interested in sharing stories. All are generous with their time, but I realise there are many younger people with whom I have had minimal or no contact at all.

Continuing south another twenty-six-kilometres along the Princes Highway, I pass through Tailem Bend, so called from *tagalang* meaning bend in Ngarrindjeri.[24] About 1600 people live in this busy town where the Murray takes a wide turn and runs southward. Liz Tongerie was commuting daily from here to Murray Bridge, but when at home was sure to have some delicious home-baked goods on the table. It's another fifty-two-kilometres on to Meningie, from the Ngarrindjeri *meinangi*, meaning the place of mud flats, on the banks of Lake Albert.[25] I don't know many of the families in this fishing and tourist hamlet of under 1000 people, but I am enjoying dropping into the bakery for fresh bread and pies. Camp Coorong,[26] the race-relations camp, is another ten-kilometres on; it is here that I usually catch up with Ellen Trevorrow, her mother Daisy Rankine, Ellen's husband Tom Trevorrow, and his brother George. The place is always a hive of activity which revolves around groups attending workshops at the camp, the daily business of maintaining the facilities, and their extended families of the Trevorrows. If I'm lucky, there is Coorong mullet for lunch. Coorong, pronounced *Kurang*, is from the Ngarrindjeri word for "neck", *kuri*, a word which also carries the meaning "river" and "voice" (Meyer 1843: 73). A little further south-west along the Coorong I drop in to see Peter Mansfield Cameron and his wife Meryl at the old homestead at Trunceena, which is written *Thrunginyoong* by his aunt Lola Bonney Cameron. A cup of tea, photograph albums and historic letters are soon on the table. On the way back I can take the turn-off from the Princes Highway to Narrung, *Ngarrarrar*, place of she-oaks (Taplin 1873: 130); I cross on the ferry to the old mission at Point McLeay, now called Raukkan, meaning "ancient place"[27] on Lake Alexandrina where some one hundred people live in a range of houses, from modern brick places to the rendered and old stone dwellings of another era. Life here is quieter than in the towns. I visit Jean and Henry Rankine and usually see their daughter Natalie, her girls, and sometimes one of their sons. I sit and chat with Dot Shaw, Grace Sumner, Hazel Wilson and Sheila Goldsmith. With others working at the Council Office I have a nodding acquaintance.

To reach Goolwa, where Sarah and Doug Milera live, I have to go around the lake. I can cross the Murray by ferry at Tailem Bend and from there head towards Strathalbyn, a gracious town of some 2000 founded in 1839 by Scottish migrants led by Dr John Rankine who, with his brother, also took up land on Hindmarsh Island in the 1840s. Genevieve and I enjoy foraging in the secondhand stores of "Strath", as it is called locally. We meet no Ngarrindjeri residents in either Strathalbyn or Clayton, the tiny windblown hamlet where we have a house. It is a short walk to the fish and yabbie restaurant that is featured in all the guidebooks. Looking westwards we can see where Finniss River and Currency Creek flow into the Goolwa Channel and at night we can hear the breakers the other side of the hummocks. We can almost touch Hindmarsh Island across the channel, and later I learn that this was the site of "Rankine's Crossing", where stock were first brought onto the island in the 1840s. From Clayton, there is a back road, or rather a network of back roads, to Goolwa, a town of some 2400, where tourists and fishers far outnumber the Ngarrindjeri who visit and live in town. In the heyday of the paddle-steamers in the middle to late nineteenth century, Goolwa, surveyed in 1840, just after the colony of South Australia was proclaimed, grew into a thriving town with foundry, boat-building facilities, flour mill, courthouse, stately homes, and an Aboriginal fringe camp. Pre-contact, *Kutungald* (Goolwa) was a residential, trade and ceremonial centre for a number of Ngarrindjeri clans.[28] Today, where Ngarrindjeri once tended their fish traps and collected cockles, there is a marina and big houses isolated on small blocks. Without a bridge they will not be more fully developed. From Goolwa, in just over an hour, I can be back in Adelaide. There a number of Ngarrindjeri, including Margaret "Aunty Maggie" Jacobs, sisters Val Power and Muriel Van Der Byl, Vi Deuschle and Shirley Peisley, Edith Rigney, Veronica Brodie and her brothers Doug and Graham Wilson, Margaret Brusnahan, Margy Dodds, and many other Ngarrindjeri family members variously live, work, attend meetings, gather for functions at Tandanya (Australia's first National Aboriginal Cultural Centre opened in 1989) and attend the Community College. Adelaide is where I settle into libraries, although the Strathalbyn library is good and accommodating. To visit Doreen Kartinyeri and her family I usually need to drive for more than two hours around the Gulf of St Vincent to Point Pearce, a former mission on the Yorke Peninsula.

There is no single village, no long-hut, no town well or market at which people might gather. This is not field work in the Malinowski mode, but then Ngarrindjeri are not Trobriand Islanders. They are, at a conservative estimate, some 3000 persons,[29] the majority of whom live in the southeast of Australia, with significant populations in Adelaide, Murray Bridge, Tailem Bend, Meningie, Gerrard, Berri, Glossop, Raukkan (Point McLeay), Point Pearce and Mannum (smallish). Some Ngarrindjeri live in Victoria and others in New South Wales. Although the extent of Ngarrindjeri lands and the divisions within their territory are not beyond dispute, Norman Tindale's map is a helpful starting point.[30] Running from Swanport on the Murray River, down to Kingston in the east, and Cape Jervis in the west, Ngarrindjeri lands take in Lakes Alexandrina and Albert, Encounter Bay, a number of small off-shore islands and rock formations, the Coorong and the hummocks, the scrub back-country to Strathalbyn, salt lakes, claypans, numerous fresh-water wells, valleys where river gums create deep shade, and the mighty Murray as it winds to the mouth where it debouches into the chill waters of Southern Ocean. It is generally agreed that peoples who lived along the Coorong were known as the Tangani (Tangane, Tanganekald); those who lived on the east side of Lake Alexandrina and Murray River, the Yaraldi (Jaralde, Jaraldekald); the Ramindjeri occupied the Encounter Bay region; Warki (Warkend) lands were on the north and west of Lake Alexandrina; and the Portaulan were on the western banks of the Murray River. Across the Mount Lofty Ranges were the Kaurna, with whom the Ngarrindjeri had some links through trade and marriage but whose ceremonial life and language were quite distinct.[31] There were marriages, trade and much visiting up river and to the south east to Mount Gambier. Some would include Mt Gambier within Ngarrindjeri lands to the east, others would go further west than Cape Jervis.

Ngarrindjeri memories take in the experience of living under the infamous *Aborigines Act of South Australia* 1911 which gave the Protector (1911–39) and later the Protection Board (1939–62) enormous power over the daily lives of Aborigines; the shift from policies of assimilation to those of self-determination and self-management in the 1970s; a range of residential arrangements from missions, to fringe camps and the town; the interventions of welfare, police harassment, and more recently the intense scrutiny of the courts and media.[32] Above all, the Ngarrindjeri about whom I am writing are literate and care a great deal about how they are represented to a literate world. They are constantly confronted by

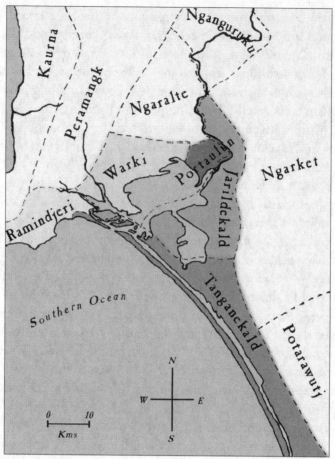

"Tribal" boundaries (after Tindale 1974, Map Stephen Shaheen)

accounts of their beliefs and practices in print. Representing this complex reality will require a departure from the form and style of classic ethnographic monographs written in the timeless land of the ethnographic present. I have chosen to write a historically grounded ethnography, one that is in dialogue with the sources, oral and written. The postmodern turn in anthropology has significantly opened up possibilities in writing about the "other", but I find much of this work to be jargon-ridden, elitist and morally vacuous.[33] It is my hope that this book will reach beyond my colleagues, to a wider audience with an interest in Aboriginal Studies, questions of justice for Indigenous peoples and women, and the exercise of religious

30

freedom. These are not matters that can be settled in one book; nor is this my final word. I have not exhausted the written sources and I most certainly have not exhausted the knowledge of living Ngarrindjeri.[34] However, the political climate is getting more and more hostile towards minorities and this book needs to see the light of day.

In mid-December 1996, the Senate Committee considers the bill to amend the Heritage Act so that the bridge might be built and retires for Christmas. But the High Court has another bombshell. The Wik decision comes down on 23 December 1996. This decision clarifies the relationship between the rights of pastoral leaseholders and native title. It is found in a four–three decision that these rights can co-exist. Once again the media is filled with calls to amend the *Native Title Act* 1993, with criticisms of an activist High Court, and with pronouncements of doom and gloom that will follow their decision. On 10 February 1997, the Senate votes down the Hindmarsh Island Bill. The Commonwealth Heritage Act is still in place. What now? A new application? Will the Minister simply exercise his discretion? Will the conservatives introduce a new bill? The matter bounces back and forth. Tom and Wendy Chapman, the developers, are back in court. I hear that the "dissident women" have been to the South Australian Museum and seen the nineteenth-century photographs in which cicatrices (scarring) on a young woman's body are clearly visible. Will this evidence of women's rituals convince them? In March 1997 Doreen Kartinyeri speaks to the United Nations Special Rapporteur for Religious Intolerance, Abdelfattah Amer, in Alice Springs. Will this case become yet another source of international embarrassment for the Australian government?

May 1997: Australia. At the second attempt, May 1997, the Hindmarsh Island Bridge Bill passes both houses and once again there is nothing to stop the bridge. Neville Gollan and Doreen Kartinyeri seek to challenge the constitutionality of the *Hindmarsh Island Bridge Act* 1997 in High Court. The South Australian Attorney-General agrees that there will be no development while the matter is under appeal (McGarry and Windsor 1997: 5). But the developers are not having any of that. They make application in the Federal Court seeking damages of $69.62 million, plus a further $20,000 per day,

THE *HINDMARSH ISLAND BRIDGE* ACT

17 September 1996 Special legislation proposed

23 December 1996 High Court: Wik decision

February 1997 Hindmarsh Bill voted down

22 May 1997 Hindmarsh Island Bridge Act commences

29 May 1997 Chapmans seek $62.62 million in damages

5–6 February 1998 High Court hears challenge to *Hindmarsh Island* Act

1 April 1998 High Court rules 5 to 1, the Act is constitutional

for losses suffered by Binalong, the company of which they are directors. They name the anthropologist, Dr Deane Fergie, the Reporter, Professor Cheryl Saunders, and Luminis, the consultancy services at Adelaide University, as responsible for their loss of income.[35] There is a resounding silence from other anthropologists. In the months ahead more people who have expressed an opinion or been involved in some way will find themselves being sued. My professional indemnity insurance does a hike.

Through all this I am trying to write and planning a further trip to Australia. I'm hoping to have a draft manuscript to take with me. After more negotiations, the situation with the family who is opposed to the preparation and publication of a book appears to be resolved. I agree not to mention them or their genealogy in this book and not to repeat what I have learned from them while under contract January to June 1996. Everyone else has released me from the contract and given permission to access all representations generated in their names. Nonetheless, I consider I am obliged ethically to negotiate the right to use individual stories and where I draw on the applicants' oral and written representations, I do so with the permission of each individual. Mostly people told me, Use what I said. I meant it then, and I mean it now; but others review their words, add to their stories and retell in more detail. By June 1997 I have, in effect, duplicated all the research, library and field work I did for the Mathews application. It is now legitimately mine and not tainted by any previous agreements. This extra work has been worthwhile, if time-consuming. But, I am still walking on egg shells. I see the Mathews Report reviewed in the *Aboriginal Law Bulletin* (Charlesworth 1997: 19-21) and the evidence of one of the applicants is quoted. This is the family who has said that I am to repeat nothing of theirs.

Had they been asked, would they have consented to having their material in the report, or to having it repeated in a review? Because the Minister chose to table the report, their name and testimony are firmly in the public arena. Should I now repeat those matters? The reviewer can plead ignorance, but I can't. Despite written requests, the Minister has not returned the materials generated during the Mathews Report to the applicants. Is he in violation of Section 35 of the South Australian Heritage Act? There is no funding to pursue any of these matters and the media does not find them fascinating.

From reports to a manuscript. At least I can now enter into a contract with my publishers, Spinifex Press. We begin to discuss what all these negotiations regarding permissions, ethical and legal, mean for publication. A select number of anthropologists continue to thug Hindmarsh out in conferences, journals, and the media. I read the exchanges and hear reports of oral presentations, but I am not part of the disciplinary discourse. This is partly by design, and partly because I am not there. And when I am "there", I'm in South Australia, a satellite state for the Sydney–Canberra axis of anthropological action. I return to Australia in late May to mid-June to work with the publishers and do further checking of sources. I want the people on whom I have relied to read what I have written. Throughout 1996 and 1997 we've stayed in touch by telephone, fax, letters and cards. They are ready for my visit and take the task of reading their words, now in written form, extremely seriously. I take photographs of the storm of 1 April 1997 that buried my house and car, and a group of Ngarrindjeri weavers plan a trip to the USA in June. Being here and being there is becoming less distinct.

The 400-page manuscript I have taken with me to Australia in mid-1997 bears little resemblance to the reports I'd written in 1996. Then I had thought I could simply revise, edit and update, but somewhere during the 1996–7 field trip, I knew I wanted to write quite differently of the Ngarrindjeri than I had during the Mathews application. During the 1997 visit in the southern winter, more stories are forthcoming. Negotiating oral accounts into written texts, I am beginning to think, is something like writing glosses in the margins of a medieval tract. I have comments on the comments on the texts. I am invited into a more intimate world, and see more of the daily pressures on the Ngarrindjeri with whom I am working. I write of many of these exchanges and negotiations in the present tense, in part to capture the immediacy of the moment and in part because the scenes remain vivid for me and the people with whom I am working.

Whereas in 1996, the Royal Commission genealogies were at the forefront of people's minds, by mid-1997 it is the findings of the National Inquiry into the Separation of Aboriginal and Torres Strait Islander Children from Their Families, published as *Bringing them Home* (Wilson 1997) which dominates conversation. Members of the "stolen generations" talk about the healing yet to be done. I stand in awe of the compassion, gritty determination and integrity I hear in their voices. Relations of kin and country, of person and place, are at the core of the Ngarrindjeri world with which I've become familiar, and it is these very relations that have been abused, ruptured and denied in past government policies on land, sacred sites and families. The report on the Stolen Generations honours the stories that have kept alive these core values. The bipartisan Council for Reconciliation is dedicated to improving relationships between the settler and Indigenous population, to "sharing history" and to "valuing cultures" different from those of the mainstream.[36] But neither of these national initiatives, the Reconciliation Council nor the Human Rights Commission, intrudes on the South Australian Royal Commission's understanding of stories of past injustices.

The Royal Commission found fabrication in the oral accounts of the proponent women. In so doing it tapped into modes of contesting Aboriginal oral claims about sacred sites that have been well honed over the past few decades. Firstly, without any independently generated written documentation, a claim is open to the challenge that "it is all made up to frustrate development". "No texts; no sites" was the mantra of the Royal Commission. Secondly, when extra or new information about an important site or Dreaming is disclosed during, or late in, a development project or hearing, it is regarded as suspect. "Why wasn't there information about the Seven Sisters on the original application?" ask the developers. "It must have come from somewhere else." In the now highly politicised southeast of Australia, Ngarrindjeri no longer control the flow of knowledge. Nor is Ngarrindjeri ethnography the sole province of anthropologists. Lawyers, politicians, developers, journalists, religious leaders, environmentalists and "the people", as heard on talkback radio and in letters to the editor, all have something to say.

The questions posed by the Hindmarsh inquiries have not been asked before of this ethnographic record; asking them now has made a number of people extremely nervous. However, my research over the past two years has revealed a number of references supportive of the oral accounts of living Ngarrindjeri people. I have already mentioned the Seven Sisters Dreaming, and in subsequent chapters I will be further examining the stories about the "Meeting of the Waters", the *mulyewongk* (bunyip), the culture hero *Ngurunderi*, and the rites of passage for women in Ngarrindjeri society. There are sources on which I am relying which were either ignored by, or not available to, earlier hearings on the matter of the bridge. And there are sources that have not been not subjected to the sort of scrutiny I have brought to bear. There is no conspiracy here. Research takes time and a willingness to follow all sorts of leads. Perhaps the most disturbing question is: what might the Royal Commission have looked like had the material I have now been able to read and digest been available in 1993? Tickner would have been presented with a very differently documented application for protection of the bridge site in 1994. I'm rapidly coming to the conclusion that there would not have been a Royal Commission in 1995 and the proponent women would not have been placed in a position of having to carry the case. To understand why this could be so, I need to take the reader through the intricate weave of Ngarrindjeri culture, as I came to know it, and through the contexts within which knowledge of Ngarrindjeri culture is generated, contested and consumed.

In writing this book I am shifting from the role of consultant to that of ethnographer, or, as some would have it, from applied (read "advocacy") to fundamental (read "value-free") research and writing. All research has a politics, some is just made explicit (be it by circumstance, or by choice of the writer). Here let me simply state that as a consultant to the Ngarrindjeri, I saw my role as first to provide a sketch of Ngarrindjeri culture as a context within which

I might explore the particulars of individual beliefs and practice; and second, to locate what I had learnt through field work within the written record, specific and comparative. I did not consider it to be my role to specify the content of the women's beliefs. It was their knowledge and it was up to them to decide how much they wanted to disclose. In writing now, this remains my position: the beliefs and practices detailed herein are ones that the holders of the stories have agreed may be published. As I said, I am no longer acting as a consultant, but I am writing and respecting the limits that the applicants have placed on confidential and private material. However, I am not under contract to write a particular sort of book. Making this distinction clear in the hostile environment created by adversarial proceedings is extremely difficult, as my exchange with Nicolas Iles demonstrates. I am not willing to accept that all social relations and all research are to be regulated, monitored, and interpreted by lawyers. But nor do I wish to be sued for a breach of Section 35 of the state Heritage Act.

From manuscript to book. The book is divided into two parts which sit between this prologue and an epilogue. My sketch of Ngarrindjeri culture in the first six chapters (Part One) spells out its salient features as a distinctive weave of ideas, practices and beliefs. I focus on the ways in which the women and men with whom I worked present their knowledge of Ngarrindjeri culture now, and I look back to the sources. The dissident women are part of this weave, and I regret I have not been able to explore their strands in more detail. The Ngarrindjeri voices that carry the argument regarding the dynamic nature of contemporary Ngarrindjeri culture spell out an epistemology in which "feelings" are central and they detail the "respect system" which underwrites the authority of the elders. I introduce the reader to a number of Ngarrindjeri who offer accounts of their experiences and recount stories which have been passed down through the generations. I explore the different contexts and histories within which the stories are told and find meaning. In their own voices women and men explain the importance of telling stories and reading the signs; of weaving, making feather flowers, and singing; of *ngatji* (one's totem), *miwi* (the locus of feeling and wisdom) and genealogies. They speak of a world of intimate relationships to place; where beliefs about healing, sorcery, the living and the dead, structure their daily lives. They tell of a land alive with meaning, *gendered meanings*, of land as body, of restricted and sacred places. Individual women and men recount stories of the beings who live in the waters, on the land, and they speak of the cautions with which they were reared and those they teach their children. Theirs is a rich, vital world within which the living and the dead constantly interact; where there are birds who bring messages and whales with whom one can talk; *and it is a gendered world.*

From the sources we know that there were many ways in which stories might be told. Ngarrindjeri, it seems, have always tolerated, perhaps even delighted in ambiguity and shifting emphases in story-telling. I am not arguing that we can achieve a perfect understanding of Ngarrindjeri culture, or that "cultures" are neat structures. Rather, I am alluding to the texture, colour, pattern, gauge, and design of the Ngarrindjeri weave. And yes, there are rents, rough and frayed edges, broken threads, colours that clash, motifs that elude explanation, worn patches, crudely stitched and shredded pieces. But, in spite of the disruption and dispossession of nigh on two centuries, there is a live, vibrant Ngarrindjeri culture which people consider worth fighting over and fighting for. This is the context within which to explore Ngarrindjeri stories of kin and country. The lengths to which the Ngarrindjeri applicants were prepared to go to prevent injury and desecration to their sacred places is evidence of their attachment to and concern for their places and their old people. The nature of the contesting of cultural knowledge is part and parcel of a society which both honours the rights of individuals to find their own truth and meaning in life, and insists that the knowledge of the old people be respected and not questioned. How this is played out in late-twentieth-century Australian society is a complex and often painful matter.

In Part Two, I address what I am calling the politics of knowledge. I look to the rules of access and transmission in an oral culture, to communities of belief and a culture of dissent, to strategic silences and considered disclosures. Knowledge within Ngarrindjeri society is restricted on the basis of age, gender, and family in ways that mystify a print-oriented society which, nonetheless, has its own rules, albeit not always made explicit. I explain how I negotiated access to the stories which appear in this book and why the record will always be incomplete. There is more to be learned from contemporary Ngarrindjeri and they tell a range of tales. How then to understand the process of finding meaning in a rapidly changing world? The written sources on Ngarrindjeri culture in general, and women's beliefs and practices in particular cry out for a critical, contextual reading. I look to the who, where, when, and why of the written sources and find silences, omissions and assumptions about the nature of women and women's bodies. What might be learned from a feminist reading of the sources? There is ample evidence to support the claim that Ngarrindjeri women had rituals from which men were excluded; that women were considered sacred at these moments; that there were ritual experts whose expertise drew on central Ngarrindjeri values; that these concerned women's beliefs about their bodies and the ways in which body/land and spirit were interwoven. It is possible to know of the existence of these rituals without knowing the content of the rituals themselves. There are also good reasons why certain knowledge is restricted and women are increasingly reluctant to broadcast the intimate details of their lives and embodied beliefs. In the oral and written record there are fragments of the stories of the coming into being of the Ngarrindjeri universe which point to a cosmology every bit as complex and interwoven with survival as that of other Aboriginal groups. Of Hindmarsh Island, the Murray Mouth and Goolwa area, I find there was a complex of clans, Dreamings and resources that made this the focus of much traditional activity. In this area where clans cluster, where salt and fresh waters meet; where *ngatji* (totems) proliferate; where the *mulyewongk* (bunyip) lives; where *Ngurunderi* camped and the Seven Sisters Dreaming visited, there are important sites to be protected.

So what do the flawed findings of the Royal Commission and Mathews Report (1996) mean for our understanding of Ngarrindjeri culture in general, and of legal inquiries in particular? It's a complex matter. What it meant to me as I was completing the research and writing, was that this story had to be told. The story goes to the heart of values held dear by democratic societies. That's how this book happened. There is of course much more and, in the following chapters, I will be introducing you to some of the individuals, their stories, the sources, and the issues. This Prologue is by way of setting the stage, and I urge the reader to follow the ethnographic path I am laying out before engaging with the nitty-gritty of the various legal inquiries. A Royal Commission, two Heritage applications, and appeals in the Federal and High Courts are not particularly good starting-points for one seeking to understand the dynamics of Ngarrindjeri culture.

In the Epilogue I return to the explosive mix with which I began the Prologue and reflect on the significance of the Ngarrindjeri struggle in late twentieth-century Australia. Should Aboriginal rights in land, and respect for Aboriginal religion, be a matter of balancing competing interests? What does the Mabo decision mean now that Native Title has been eroded? What is the role of the courts, the parliament, the media, anthropology? To whom can Indigenous peoples turn when the courts, parliament and the general public weary of their stories? More generally, what does the continued contesting of indigenous claims mean for the promised social justice package? For the Reconciliation movement in Australia? For Human Rights? How will Australia represent itself in the Olympic Year, Sydney 2000?

Genevieve Bell photographing Veronica Brodie, Coorong, December 1996
(Diane Bell)

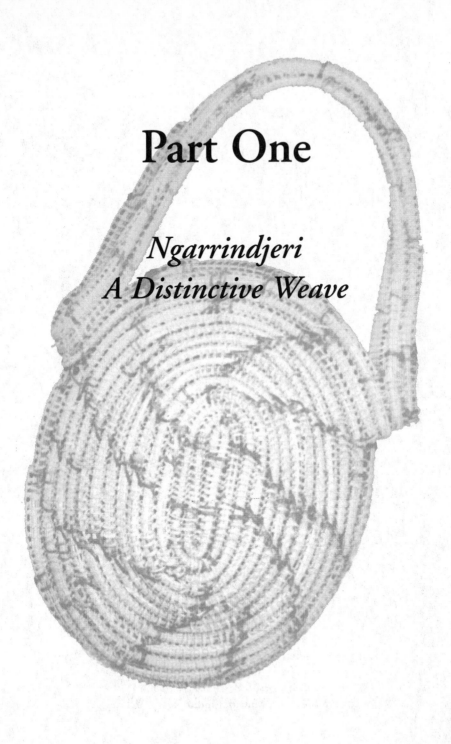

Part One

Ngarrindjeri
A Distinctive Weave

Previous page: A "sister basket" made of sedge by Ethel Watson, 1939
(M. Kluvanek)
Collector: N. B. Tindale A15951
South Australian Museum Anthropology Archives

1

Weaving the World of Ngarrindjeri

Weaving Women

When we weave with the rushes, the memories of our loved ones are there, moulded into each stitch. And, when we're weaving, we tell stories. It's not just weaving, but the stories we tell when we're doing it. Daisy Rankine explains. *Wukkin mi:mini*[1] means the women's business of weaving and all the cultural and sacred life which has been part of the Ngarrindjeri people's ancestry. Ngarrindjeri women are known as weavers of mats and baskets of enduring value and high distinction. They know where the best rushes grow, when, and how to cull and work them. They extol the fineness of the fresh-water rushes; and admire the bundles that other women have prepared. Ellen Trevorrow, the eldest daughter of Daisy Rankine, is rarely seen without a piece of weaving in her hands or close by. When I pick rushes I reminisce and I recall Nanna, yes, Nanna Brown. I lived with her at Marrunggung [Brinkley] and I was named after her. She was a hard worker. Ellen asks that the first time I mention her, I give her full name, Ellen Brown Rankine Trevorrow Wilson, so that her heritage will be known. One does not call names lightly.

Ellen Brown, after whom Ellen Trevorrow is named, was the daughter of Margaret "Pinkie" Mack, a major source of information for researchers in Ngarrindjeri lands. Pinkie Mack's mother, Louisa Karpeny, could recall when the first white explorers came into her lands. The stories told in this family reach back to first contact, and the family speak with enormous respect of their "old people". It is "Queen" Louisa, and Daisy Rankine always identifies Pinkie Mack as "the last initiated Ngarrindjeri child". When Daisy Rankine speaks of the creation of Ngarrindjeri lands she invokes Pinkie

43

Louisa Karpeny
1821–1921

Margaret (Pinkie)
Mack 1858–1954

Laura Kartinyeri
1906–1995

Ellen Brown
1905–1979

Mack: Nanna told stories of the waters and the *mulyewongk* [bunyip] underneath; of the pelicans and the sea turtle come into the deep reaches; and of the *pondi* [Murray cod] come down this way. From Queen Louisa, down through Pinkie Mack, to Ellen Brown (and her sister Laura Kartinyeri who was not as interested in weaving), to Daisy Rankine, and Ellen Trevorrow, this is a distinguished line of weavers and story-tellers. The next two generations are growing up in a world rich in history, oral and written.

There is a whole ritual in weaving, says Ellen, and for me, it's a meditation. At Camp Coorong I watch as Ellen patiently encourages a child to begin the circle, to take the lace and to tighten each knot. Deft fingers work the bundles of rushes. The form of the piece emerges. From where we actually start, the centre part of a piece, you're creating loops to weave into, then you move into the circle. You keep going round and round creating the loops and once the children do those stages they're talking, actually having a conversation, just like our old people. It's sharing time. And that's where a lot of stories were told. Ellen's quiet, confident manner holds the children as they struggle to form the centre by twisting the first knotted bundle back on itself. Then they get into the rhythm of the looping through, tightening, and adding new rushes. There is a busy buzz in the classroom. The technique is deceptively simple, and initially it is the sociality of the activity that draws me in to the weaving and from there to the stories of the weavers. Women smile as they recall memories of a favourite aunt or grandmother weaving late into the night and admit that, when they weave till the wee small hours, their children and husbands understand their tired state at breakfast. There is indeed a ritual, a rhyme and a rhythm to weaving.

As a weaver I have to pick and dry the rushes, and when I go out for rushes, Ellen explains, I go with my children and my sister's children and friends. Through this sharing, teaching and learning, when they get to an age, they'll know. They're learning about the land, about the best places for rushes and how to pick them, about the different species, *kukundo* and pinkie, from the southeast, and *marnggato* from the Coorong.[2] To talk about weaving is to talk about family and country in an intimate way. All my children are weavers, Ellen announces with pride, And now, Corina, my granny [grandchild], she's five, said to me the other day, "Nanna, it's my turn now."

Daisy Rankine
1936–

Stories and memories of loved ones sustain and structure the Ngarrindjeri social world; explain the mysterious; provide a secure haven in an otherwise hostile world; bring order to and confer significance on relationships amongst the living; hold hope for future generations; and open up communication with those who have passed on. The stories of cultural life recall the creation of the land, of the seas, rivers, lakes and lagoons. They tell of the coming into being of fish and fowl, of the birds of the air and beasts of the fields. They spell out the proper uses of flora and fauna. These are stories of human frailty and triumph, of deception and duty, of rights, responsibilities and obligations, of magical beings, creative heroes and destructive forces. Everything has a story, but not everyone knows every story. Nor does everyone have the right to hear every story, or, having heard it, to repeat the words.

Ellen Trevorrow
1955–

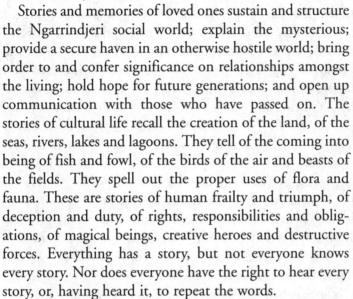

Tanya 1978–

"Get Aunty Maggie to tell you that ghost story," I'm told when I ask about *muldarpi*, the travelling spirits of the sorcerers, strangers, and clever people, who visit after dark, and whose appearances and behaviours are carefully analysed by those present.[3] "Ask Aunty Veronica," I'm told when I inquire about the Seven Sisters Dreaming and the transmission of women's restricted knowledge about that story. I learn that sisters Val and Muriel will tell me about the mysterious water monster, the *mulyewongk* at Marrunggung; and I already know that Dr Doreen Kartinyeri is an expert on family history, and much more. And so it goes. This one knows about being taken away and raised in an institution, that one of growing up on the mission at Raukkan (Point McLeay) or at Point Pearce (Yorke Peninsula), another of surviving in the fringe camps of the towns along the Murray River.

Ellen 1996–

45

Almost everyone to whom I speak knows about the *mingka* bird, the harbinger of death, but people differ regarding the call and how to read its significance. Ron Bonney of Kingston and Mrs Jean Gollan of Point McLeay name Mount Barker as a *mingka* bird site (Hemming 1987: 8), but Eileen McHughes is the only person I hear from who has seen the bird. Her story of the encounter weaves family and familiar places. I remember her telling us, says her younger sister Vicki Hartman, after Eileen has finished telling her story to an enthralled audience. Most everyone knows that the *ritjaruki*, the willie wagtail, is the messenger bird, but once again there are different interpretations of its behaviour. Doreen watches the one in my garden at Clayton to be sure everything is all right. Is he always there? she asks me. I've seen it before, although it is the Murray magpies and the galahs who mass overhead and fill the trees who wake us in the morning. Doreen pursues the question. What was he doing? "Just flying between the house and the fence," I tell her. "I saw a pair." She watches for a while and relaxes. He's happy.

Isobelle Norvill is concerned that variations in detail, pronunciation and interpretation of certain words may be misunderstood. She explained to Judge Mathews: You can go round this area and you talk to different people, and you might hear different words and pronunciations that make it appear that the women you're talking to are wrong, but nobody's wrong. You might get a name different to Kumarangk for Hindmarsh Island; it's still not wrong; it's still the same, the very same place. The same principles stay and changes happen by conditions. I think that's very important because it could confuse you a little bit and I don't want anybody hurt by any statement made like that. Ngarrindjeri "cultural and sacred life", as Daisy Rankine called it, is a weave of many voices, personalities, histories, remembrances, perspectives, beliefs and practices. At the centre there are "principles", as Isobelle called them and these can be specified.

The "ownership" of stories is respected by the Ngarrindjeri with whom I speak. "That ghost story" remains Maggie Jacobs' story. There are many others I am to hear from Aunty Maggie and other women, especially late at night, when we are comfortably settled and all is still. In March 1996, I was present when one *muldarpi* story was told for the first time. Henceforth, I was able to partake in the retelling and note how the significance of the events is determined. Different people emphasise different aspects of stories and, at each telling, the story is made relevant for the listening audience. It changes "by conditions" as Isobelle said. Stories belong to different places. The *mulyewongk* at Marrunggung is but one of a number of the creatures who live in the treacherous waters of the Lower Murray River and lakes. Called "bunyips" by early settlers of southern Australia, these large menacing beings made for fascinating children's and bush yarns, but Ngarrindjeri know theirs is much more terrifying than these whitefella representations and their story has several layers of meanings.

Knowledge is attributed to the elders of this generation and the "old people" who have now passed on, but it takes more than age to be considered an elder. Elders must be wise in the ways of the land and bestow their knowledge on members of their families who are worthy of such wealth. When Leila Rankine was dying, she deemed her younger sister, Veronica Brodie, to be ready to hear the story of the Seven Sisters constellation. But what Veronica Brodie was told of the Pleiades remains Leila's story. The relationships in which knowledge is embedded are honoured, and the elder from whom the knowledge came is owed respect. The use of the term "Aunty" for women older than oneself captures something of this notion of respect. Often people were reluctant to name the particular elder, especially if they had passed away. One lesson which has been learned over the past few years is that sacred knowledge may be mocked in the media and the courts, and this is disrespectful to the elders. I also think that for Ngarrindjeri themselves, there has been no need to nominate a particular elder as a source. The "old people" is a sufficient source and taboos on calling the names of the dead, now somewhat relaxed, would have meant that a personal name would not have been available anyway.[4] A kin reference would have sufficed for those present when stories were being told in family groups.

Here and in the following chapters, through the stories of knowledgeable, reflective Ngarrindjeri women and men, I invite you to become familiar with individuals who, story by story, act by act, strand by strand, are actively engaged in weaving their world. Each

47

has a distinctive story to tell. They track back to the knowledge of their forebears and, where possible, I provide a counterpoint from the written sources. At times one echoes the other, but there are also important differences to be noted and explored. The stories celebrate Ngarrindjeri struggles to protect their heritage and are grounded in the current battle over the bridge and earlier intrusions into their land. Through their stories, some handed down from previous generations, others more contemporary, the texture, shape and scope of Ngarrindjeri knowledge, beliefs and practices are made manifest. The stories are for their children and grannies so that they may read of their lives, lore, beliefs, and commitment to the future, and for those who wish to learn more of Ngarrindjeri *wurruwarrin*, of how these Ngarrindjeri know and believe in their past, present, and future.

Sustaining Stories

I'm Doreen Kartinyeri, a Ngarrindjeri elder. I've been interested in recording kinship, Aboriginal history and traditions since working with Professor Fay Gale and the South Australian Museum. I have been able to publish books of genealogies on the Raukkan and Point Pearce families. The first one was *The Rigney Family Genealogy* in 1983. But my main interest since 1994 has been Kumarangk, Hindmarsh Island. Before the white settlement our families' ancestors lived there and we do have ancestors buried there. I will do everything I can to protect our sacred sites, heritage, culture, tradition and our grandmothers' lore. Doreen Kartinyeri has done extensive research into Ngarrindjeri families and what she knows is an important resource in a community for whom kinship is a major topic of conversation and contention. Doreen's memory for names and dates is something anyone would envy. With her quick mind, inquisitive nature, and respect for knowledge, it is little wonder that her elders invested in her.

Doreen Kartinyeri has been called a "fabricator" by Commissioner Stevens (1995: 287-99), and "theatrical" by Chris Kenny (1996: 136). Philip Jones (1995: 174), of the South Australian Museum, described her as delivering a "standard haranguing" and detailed her treatment of co-workers (*ibid*.: 4247).[5] Before Hindmarsh Island became a household name in Australia, Doreen Kartinyeri's work was well known to researchers in the Aboriginal field. I first met Doreen in 1981 at a conference with Aboriginal women from all over Australia that I'd helped to organise in Adelaide (Gale 1983). There Doreen Kartinyeri (1983a: 136-57) spoke of her pioneering work on family history at the South Australian Museum; of her long-standing interest in tracing her ancestors and those of other related families; of her concern not to pry and offend; of how she ensures confidentiality; and of exercising discretion (*ibid.*: 140, 143, 145). Doreen Kartinyeri relies heavily on memory, but she also utilises archives, and the Register of Births, Deaths and Marriages. "It was always very important to me to find out

An honorary doctorate: Doreen Kartinyeri with her cousin Edith Rigney, University of South Australia, Adelaide, 1995 (Doreen Kartinyeri's personal collection)

what was right. I used to make it my business to find out the truth," she said at that conference (*ibid.*: 140). This was her position in 1981. She stated it again in the book of Rigney genealogies (Kartinyeri 1983b: xvii) and it remained her position in 1996. Working with her throughout that year, I had ample opportunity to listen, question, check and double-check. Her accounts of events at which she was present were consistent, and her accounts of relationships with her elders were confirmed by others who were close to her family. When Doreen was not present, or had heard something from someone else, she always said so. She would correct me if I erred. Once when I said she had told me about the animosity between Albert Karloan, who worked with researcher Ronald Berndt, and Clarence Long (Milerum), who worked with Norman Tindale, she said, No. My father told me.

The shared memories of Ngarrindjeri such as Doreen Kartinyeri, Maggie Jacobs (née Rankine), Daisy Rankine (née Brown), Veronica Brodie (née Wilson), first cousins Eileen McHughes (née Kropinyeri) and Isobelle Norvill (née Wilson), the sisters Val Power (née Karpeny) and Muriel Van Der Byl (née Karpeny), Sarah Milera (née Day), Mona Jean (née Gollan), Henry Rankine, Neville Gollan, George and Tom Trevorrow reach back across the generation of their parents into the nineteenth century, to the first contacts with white explorers, whalers, sealers, settlers, welfare officers, missionaries and to the visits of various anthropologists. Clarence Long (Milerum) from the Coorong, on whom Norman Tindale relied so heavily for information and knowledge, was a neighbour of Maggie Jacobs at Raukkan, and Granny Ethel Watson (1887–1964), a noted weaver, from Kingston, known locally as "Queen Ethel" was Tindale's nursemaid. Daisy Rankine remembers the Berndts interviewing her grandmother at Brinkley in the 1940s, and Doreen Kartinyeri has had exchanges regarding her research with both Ronald and Catherine Berndt and with Norman Tindale. The Ngarrindjeri I have met may not always know what has been written about them, but they remember who was visited and asked questions, and they have opinions about the quality of the interactions.

We didn't have bookshelves, so we put stories onto the land, says Muriel Van Der Byl. The Karpeny sisters, Val Power AM (born

Val Power at Marrunggung 1974 (*News* 19 November 1974)

1936) and Muriel Van Der Byl (born 1943), moved from Wellington when their father died in 1944. They lived briefly at Raukkan, while their mother cared for her dying father, and then relocated to Berri where their father's brothers were settled. They travelled back and forth to Tailem Bend, spent time with their father's sister, Aunty Janet, visited Goolwa and learned about Hindmarsh Island. Just there, just past where the ferry comes in, that was the camping place of Jenny Ponggi on Hindmarsh Island. Val Power points to the sweep of land to the south-east of the ferry extensions to indicate the site.

Muriel Van Der Byl
(Lisa Tomasetti)

Jenny Ponggi (Pu:ndji), who died in 1911 at the age of 100, remembered Charles Sturt's voyage of "discovery" down the Murray River in 1830. In fact, according to long-time resident H. F. Dodd, who had heard her on the subject while she was camped at Lalawa Station of Lake Albert, the old lady often described how she ran away with her folks when frightened by Sturt's approach (Tindale 1938–56: 260). Her knowledge informed what her son, Albert Karloan, told Ronald Berndt in 1939. Jenny Ponggi was a mother's sister to Louisa Karpeny, and Val Power is proud to be a descendant of this powerful woman. Jenny Ponggi's camping place would have taken advantage of the coastal mudflats of the island, a resource-rich ecological zone. Since the building of the barrages, the water level is about a metre higher than it would have been in Jenny Ponggi's time. Many sites are now submerged. Val speaks also of burials and medicinal plants on the island, but declines to give locations. Stories of vandalised grave sites and the lack of respect shown to existing registered sites are significant inhibitors.

51

Jenny Ponggi, *c.*1908
(M. Angas Collection)

Val Power and Muriel Van Der Byl now live in Adelaide and visit daily. Val, recently retired, was in the public service for twenty-eight years, where her staunch defence of Aboriginal rights and her concern for women and children was well known. Muriel has also worked in the bureaucracy, but is now spending more time on her art work, some of which was shown at the Fringe Festival of the Adelaide Arts Festival in 1996. They playfully called the exhibit "Tratuoballa: Silk and Wire". Patrons of the festival asked was this "tratuoballa" a Kaurna word, the language of the Aboriginal people of the Adelaide region, or was it Ngarrindjeri? No. It was "all about art" spelt backwards. As Muriel sees it, the "silk and wire" indicate the contrasting tensions of the hard and the soft, of the negative and positive, working together as a strength.

In 1973 Val was appointed an Inspector under the now defunct *Aboriginal and Historic Relics Preservation Act* 1965. In 1975 she purchased the lease to the land which had been obtained by her grandfather George Karpeny (Pinkie Mack's brother), in 1882 and renewed in 1897. That's right, says Val, as we sit reading the manuscript and sipping hot coffee in her living room. It's a chill winter day. Val has not been well. Her sister quickly moves to wrap a shawl around her shoulders and tuck in a rug around her knees. And now, our grandfather's dream is finally coming to fruition with a new fence around our burial ground and building allotment. That's where I want to go back to live. This is the fulfilment of a promise to Aunty Janet to look after the land, that was why she wanted us to get the lease. Val is at once on her feet. I have a picture. She disappears for a bit and returns with a news clipping from 1974 of Janet Smith with her weaving and herself at Marrunggung. I make a note to get a copy from the *News*.[6]

Out at Raukkan, Henry J. Rankine OAM, JP, and his wife Jean, fresh from a visit to the USA, settle back into the routine of Raukkan life, where Henry is now chairman. His Churchill Fellowship of 1996 took them to many native communities in North America. Henry and Jean share their many observations about the similarities of Indigenous people in both countries with their

Left to right: Natalie, her mother, Jean Rankine and grand-
daughters, Kemisha Moh-gene Hester Lawrie Rankine and
Sarafina Mariah Lawrie Rankine (Genevieve Bell)

53

children and grandchildren. Jean talks about her aunt and her great-grandmother who taught her weaving. Of her own weaving, she says: I just can't stop. It takes over your mind once you start. Jean, a thoughtful hostess, who always has a proper cooked meal waiting if one visits at lunch, worries about her children and grandchildren. The trip to the USA was the first time in thirty-five years that she and Henry, now in their fifties, had been away from their children. Jean guards her privacy and objects vigorously to publication of details of her family life that were acquired through what she considers to be covert research. It's not that she does not want to bring others into her world. Jean is a talented teacher. Rather, it is a matter of being respectful. When Jane Mathews visited Raukkan, Jean Rankine, with the permission and backing of her elders, acted as a guide and spoke with depth and feeling of her connections to the mission.

Aunty Margaret "Maggie" Jacobs (née Rankine) born 1920, in a wurley (traditional shelter)[7] at Raukkan, simply says, I'm a descendant of this area and her lineages reach back through the Rankine and Koolmatrie lines to Yaraldi, Tangani and Ramindjeri country. Her knowledge comes from Granny Koomi (Rebecca Harris, Veronica Brodie's mother), Mummy Lola (Lola Sumner), and her grandmother, Ada Koolmatrie. Aunty Maggie now lives in Adelaide, but she has travelled widely; when she visits Raukkan, as she often does, other women gather to hear what she has to say. When she sits down to sing, be prepared for a treat. Her repertoire is extensive and features old Raukkan hymns. Like many who grew up on the mission, Aunty Maggie is a devout Christian. One morning, as we are about to begin talking about matters Ngarrindjeri, she selects a saying from a little box of cards, her "Promise Box", which contains quotations from the Bible. Daisy Rankine, Maggie Jacobs and Veronica Brodie, and a number of other Ngarrindjeri I have heard on the topic, find no conflict in their fight to protect their sacred sites, their beliefs in the ancestors who shaped Ngarrindjeri land, and the Christian message.[8] "If He didn't want me to do this, I'd know," is a common sentiment. The stories of these women can accommodate both the Christian message of forgiveness and redemption and Ngarrindjeri relations to kin and country. Aunty Maggie: God has been in Aboriginal people before. They knew about God before the mission, before we had to go to church. I believe in God. He is not going to stop me. He doesn't want me to lose sight of my culture. I don't do things I shouldn't do. I don't condemn other people. The Royal Commission made me bad. I began to swear. I didn't before. I can pray for other people, but it's up to Him. Usually every morning I pick a psalm, like Proverbs 3, "Lean not unto thine own understanding, but in all thy ways acknowledge Him and He shall direct thy pathways," and He has done that for me.

Margaret Jacobs (Aunty Maggie) making ashes damper, Raukkan, 1992
(Steven Hemming)

At Camp Coorong, the race-relations cultural education centre, where school groups visit, where conferences and workshops are held, there is a happy business-like hum. Tom and Ellen Trevorrow live on site and, along with Tom's brother George, shoulder the responsibility for running this complex. There is always work to be done and Tom, after having told me of the many groups who had been through in the previous year, comments somewhat ruefully. If I can't get time to take my children out, they won't know the stories. I'm going to organise it next year so I can take the time. His son Bruce adds, We need to know, so we know what to protect. The on-site museum, warm with the smell and colour of weaving, carvings, feather flowers, photographs and books, is a talking-point for visitors and locals alike. From the Northern Territory there are mats from Borroloola and baskets made by the Maningrida women from Arnhem Land. The women from the tropical north and temperate south shared their fibres and weaving techniques with each other at a series of workshops in association with an exhibit "Two Countries: One Weave" at Tandanya in 1991.[9] Each used the coiled-bundle style but, looking at the brilliant colours of the Maningrida women's boiled and dyed pandanus strippings and the natural hues of the Ngarrindjeri rushes, there was no mistaking whose work belonged to whom. Each artist knows her own work. Looking at the pieces by Glenda Rigney, Rosalyn Karpeny, Noreen Kartinyeri, Millie Rigney, Simon Smith and Billy Rankine, along with that of Ellen Trevorrow, her mother Daisy Rankine, and the display case on loan from the South Australian Museum, the difference in the fibres is clear. Ngarrindjeri materials are distinctively theirs. The sedges (rushes) are of this place. A sister basket made by Ellen catches my eye. Irene Watson tells me that Amy Gibson, from Kingston in the

Ellen Trevorrow, holding a sister basket, and her mother, Daisy Rankine, at Camp Coorong, 1996 (Genevieve Bell)

Ellen Trevorrow, "Ngarrindjeri Sister Baskets" 1995
Freshwater rushes. Reproduced from "Below the Surface": A contemporary textiles
exhibition 27 July–31 August 1996, Goulburn Regional Art Gallery
(Lesley Goldacre)

south-east, made one for Tindale in 1924–25 and it too is in the
South Australian Museum. I have seen the one made by Ethel Watson
(1880–1964) of Kingston in 1939. Two identical coil woven pieces
are sewn together, and the pattern made by the redder strands of
pinkie grass that grow in the Kingston area radiates out from the
navel-like core. The sister basket, an important one, says Ellen.[10] The
first one I made is in the South Australian Museum. The one here is the
second. The genealogies of woven pieces are known and, while
people enjoy viewing the pieces that have found their way into the
museum, they are not always as sanguine about how they got there.

Sitting in the shade at Amelia Park in December, Sarah Milera
(née Day) tells me, I was directed to Goolwa through my dreams,
powerful visions. I know it here. It's the closest to God you're ever going
to get. You can't change your relationship to a special place, to where
your learning comes from. It's a powerful thing. The birds talk to you. A
lot of people know that. And I'm very upset that I'll lose my strength. I
remember my first conversations with Sarah some eleven months
earlier and subsequent ones; her quiet, intense voice and wry
humour; her encouragement and support; the time she organised a

57

meeting with her sisters Rachel and Mary so that I might understand more of her family and place within it. Sarah traces back through her mother's father's father to Peter Pulami, known as the last Rupelli (head) of the *tendi*, the governing body of Ngarrindjeri affairs.[11] I'm a descendant of that paramount law and I have knowledge of things that I can't talk about. I have responsibility to get it right for Black and White. In returning to Goolwa in 1992, Sarah, now in her fifties, assumed that burden. She continues to research her family and in June 1997, Sarah happily told me she'd learned, My great-grandmother was Nellie Russell, who was associated with Joe Walker, and a mother's sister to Albert Karloan. This genealogical fragment links her to the area and to knowledgeable individuals. It can be cited should her authority be challenged.

First cousins Eileen McHughes (née Kropinyeri) and Isobelle Norvill (née Wilson), both in their late fifties, live and work in Murray Bridge, but they grew up in different parts of the state. I was a mission girl and she was a camp person, says Isobelle. Eileen: Dad was exempted[12] so we had to get permission to visit Raukkan. In the fringe camps along the Murray River, where Eileen spent her formative years, she was surrounded by her own family and other

Sarah Milera at Amelia Park, Goolwa, 1997 (Genevieve Bell)

Ngarrindjeri families who reminisced in the evening about what the old people had done, said, and knew. They took her out on bush trips where she learned the names of edible plants and medicinal plants. Isobelle was reared at Point Pearce, a mission far from Ngarrindjeri heartlands, by a strict grandmother, Martha Kropinyeri, known as "Mumadie". At the age of ten, Isobelle was taken to Fullarton Girls' Home in Adelaide. By the time she was thirteen her family had moved to Tailem Bend and lived for a while with Eileen's parents, who by then had a house in town. As young

Isobelle Norvill, Goolwa, 1996
(Genevieve Bell)

mothers, their paths again diverged. It was only in the mid-70s that Isobelle moved back to Murray Bridge, worked with her mother, Aileen Wilson, and helped build the Lower Murray Nungas Club[13] on the west side of town. The history of the impact of government policies is inscribed on individual Ngarrindjeri lives.

Doreen Kartinyeri is telling me about time she spent at Point Pearce. Aunty Rosie [Rosetta Rigney, 1894–1981] was a married woman when she went to Point Pearce to live just after 1931. We were in contact from 1954, when I was married, until 1981 when she died. Over that period of time I learned more than I would have anywhere else. We talked on a regular basis—it was really every day. We'd be making feather flowers, or baskets. I'd also help her make toffee apples or wind the wool off the skein, whatever she needed. Aunty Rosie would mend nets too and she used a peg made from a sharpened calf bone from a kangaroo leg. It was tied around her wrist so she wouldn't lose it. She'd swing it and use it.

Gertrude Kropinyeri, Eileen McHughes' mother, at Boundary Bluff, *c.*1930
(Eileeen McHughes' personal collection)

Aunty Rosie taught me about being a young married woman. If I'd been there as a teenager, she would have taught me about that too, but I was in the home at Fullarton and then working for the Dunns. Aunty Rosie was concerned about my welfare and was like a mother figure to me and my brother Oscar—she was very fond of him. Over at Point Pearce, she'd ask me about different ones at Raukkan because she hadn't been there for a while. She'd only go for funerals for members of the family. She came over when my mum died in 1945. I was only ten. But sometimes, if she hadn't heard when someone had passed away, she'd say how sad it was. There were other families who had moved from Raukkan to Point Pearce to live: my grandmother's brother Wilfred Varcoe—I called him Papa Varcoe—his wife, Olive [née Rankine], their children, and my grandmother's sister Ada and her husband, Tony Wilson. The last two children of Wilfred and Olive were born at Point Pearce. My grandmother Sally [Doreen's father's mother, Sarah Varcoe, 1881–1959] stayed at Raukkan. So, the only time I spoke the Raukkan language was with Aunty Rosie and when I met up with Wilf and his family—even his children were beginning to lose the language. Aunty

Olive and Hilda, her oldest daughter, were the only other ones speaking words like me.

The level of detail in Doreen's accounts can easily overwhelm the novice, but it is one of the things that had impressed me when I first met her. In January 1996, fifteen years after this meeting, when Doreen and I met again, she was thinner, and obviously stressed. However, her quick wit had not dimmed. Throughout the Mathews Inquiry, Doreen was always ready to assist, to puzzle over complicated genealogies, and to take time out from her own work, but the stomach ulcers which had developed the year before during the Royal Commission were giving her trouble. Then, in July, 1996, she shocked us all with the news that she had stomach cancer. Repeatedly she had warned of the consequences of women's secrets being read by men. She had said people would get sick and now she had cancer. In November, although weak and having to eat six to eight small meals a day, Doreen readily agreed to work with me at Clayton on this book. She is one of the few people who is completely comfortable with a tape recorder. Although everyone loves to hear "the old people" on tape, most resist being recorded. The tapes we made then, on which I am relying now, summarise many of the topics we had discussed previously and recapitulate on matters we'd raised in conversation. Doreen and I have found we can work together for long stretches of time, from early morning to late into the night. Every now and then Doreen would get up and go out onto the verandah or into the garden for a smoke. She'd come back in, refreshed, and recite from memory the genealogy we'd been puzzling over, identify the people in an old photograph, or sketch out an area I'd been asking about.

The Respect System

Always Doreen Kartinyeri spoke with respect of her "elders" and of the "old people" who had passed on. Indeed the use of a "language of respect" was one of the striking characteristics of all the Ngarrindjeri stories I have heard over the past two years, and it is to be found in the written sources (Ely 1980: 32, 34). Further, the deference due to one's elders is not simply a matter of speech, but rather a central consideration in all social interactions. The "respect system", as I have come to think of it, is something about which people are quite explicit. This is not a set of vague rules that one learns through observation.[14] There are clear instructions given to those who are learning, and that included me. Maggie Jacobs: We weren't allowed to answer back. You treated your elders with respect. Jean Rankine: I listen to my elders. I ask questions when suitable, Muriel Van Der Byl: If they said don't go somewhere, you didn't question it, and they weren't always specific. Val Power: It meant to have patience and wait for answers to come. Veronica Brodie: If we're told something, that's good enough for us. I didn't question my grandmother any more. I wouldn't have dared. I've been around important women and been told to leave the room. Sometimes it is as diffuse as I heard it from the old people, or, I'll have to speak to my elders. Tom Trevorrow was asked to specify to whom he was referring in the Royal Commission: I really didn't want to answer it, you know. I didn't want to bring my old people's name up in a place like that. Henry Rankine: Growing up we were taught to have respect for the people who died and their remains.

The respect system sets out the proper way of behaving; it specifies who may know what, when, and in what detail. The code is strictly followed, constantly reinforced, and it is not possible to engage in conversation of any depth or meaning if one does not abide by the rules. They are simple. *The elders know. Don't ask. Don't answer back or challenge. Wait to be told.* The respect due to elders applies to this, as well as to earlier generations of elders. When one is told by an elder, one doesn't question the authority, or the rationality. Respect, says George Trevorrow, That was one of the most important things the old people taught me throughout my life. Respect for the old people; respect for the dead; respect for the land; respect for our spiritual beliefs. Sarah Milera says, It's the law and I don't break it. I'd be sick if I did. It comes through the Manggurupa [clan] law.[15] Her statement doesn't require a further rationale. The justification is in the authority of the elder—in her case from the Pulami lineage—and the invocation of his clan name. Isobelle Norvill: She said, well, this is our way. Liz Tongerie: We weren't allowed to ask questions, just listen.

Respect for one's old people is marked in the everyday Ngarrindjeri speech. A person who is older than oneself is never called by a first name alone. It is disrespectful and overly familiar to address or refer to an older person thus. Sometimes one hears Mr or Mrs So-and-so, but most frequently the respect due to one's elders is achieved by the use of an honorific or courtesy title: "Aunty" or "Nanna" for women and "Uncle" or "Grandfather" for men. An "aunt" or "uncle" may in fact be only a little older that oneself, and need not necessarily be a blood relation; as they grow up, children have many more persons to whom they can turn and from whom they can learn than their nuclear family. Regardless of how one is related, it is Aunty Dodo (as Doreen Kartinyeri is fondly known), Aunty Daisy, Aunty Janet and Aunty Maggie. I call her Aunty Leila, says George Trevorrow. Now Veronica is her sister and I call her Veronica. It's not because I love one more than the other, it is just that Aunty Leila held a special place in our group, amongst the Ngarrindjeri people. It was something about her, with the knowledge she had.

"Nanna" is most often used, as in Nanna Laura, and Nanna Rosie, for a woman considerably older than oneself, but so is Granny, as in "Granny Unaipon", the mother of author David Unaipon. Jean Rankine uses "Gram", while Ellen Trevorrow calls her mother's mother "Nanna Brown" and her mother's mother's sister "Nanna Laura". However, Laura Kartinyeri died in 1995 and, as a mark of respect, her name will be avoided for several years. Sometimes an older person will use "Mummy", as Maggie Jacobs calls Lola Sumner, or Mummy Laura as Daisy Rankine calls her mother's sister. I have heard "sister" used by close cousins who are about the same age, but usually on its own, without a first name. Isobelle Norvill calls Doreen Kartinyeri "sister" and that is what Doreen calls me. But that is more about marking our common research interests and friendship than it is about age. I have noticed that, since my daughter Genevieve's visit, I am asked by people around my age, "How is my niece?" Through this it is being signalled that I am in a sibling-like relationship with them.

People who in their life-time were highly respected are often just called by a kin term. This is a way of not calling dead names without drawing attention to the practice and thereby becoming a target for mission repression. Daisy Rankine usually calls her grandmother, Pinkie Mack, by the term for mother's mother, *pakanu*, not *muthanu*, which would be father's mother. Those who still know and use these kin terms are communicating information not available in the English term "grandmother". The two little daughters of Natalie, daughter of Henry and Jean Rankine, rarely hear English kin terms. The world of close family in which they are being raised is named in Ngarrindjeri and, without any explicit teaching, they can distinguish maternal from paternal kin. Grandchildren are usually simply called the "grannies", a term which Ngarrindjeri realise might be confusing to whitefellas. There are, no doubt, many reasons for the use of courtesy titles: some are deeply embedded in the specificities of the pre-contact Ngarrindjeri kinship system, and some are accommodations of the changes of the last two centuries.[16]

But young people do not live a closed world, and educators like Isobelle Norvill recognise the conflicts that they face. Isobelle Norvill, who has trained many young people for jobs in the white world, recounts how the discipline they have learned at home makes them "shamed" when they have to interact with officials. They know

Aunty Rosie Kropinyeri at her grand-daughter, Thelma's house, Maitland, *c*.1960. (Eileen McHughes personal collection)

the difference and have to operate within two sets of rules. I send them back in, like going to the Post Office. They come out but I send them back in. I say, "You do it." But there are memories of humiliation of having homes inspected by superintendents and not being able to say, "Leave my children alone." In order to bring about changes, you need to know the rules in both, and that's what I teach them. Operating in this bi-cultural world requires skill and, if done well, it is invisible to the outsider.

Within the homes where stories of the old people are told, the elders are respected. Doreen Kartinyeri's Aunty Rosie is "Aunty Rosie" to Doreen's contemporaries and "Nanna Rosie" to subsequent generations. Her words are revered. When I located a taped interview with Catherine Ellis made in 1966, on which Aunty Rosie speaks, Doreen was close to tears. Her daughters listened attentively and shushed the chattering children. It wasn't just hearing the voice of a loved one. It wasn't just that she spoke with authority. It was also a vindication of what they had been telling me about the "old people". She knew, but she wasn't going to blurt it all at once. She was holding back. Nor did people tell me everything at once. Our conversations are works-in-progress and, rather like the weaving, they keep circling back on themselves and growing larger as the design becomes visible.

Making Baskets: Making Family

One of the things Doreen Kartinyeri talked about with great insight and enthusiasm was basket weaving and making feather flowers. Before Mum died, she taught me how to knit, crotchet and she started to teach me how to weave and to make feather flowers. First she was teaching me how to prepare the rushes. Then, when she died, my Aunty Martha [1906–84], Dad's sister, started to really show me how to make sprays and things like that. Aunty Myra Wilson [1912–89] was good at making baskets and when she went to Point Pearce, she was trying to teach them to make baskets because they didn't go into weaving like the Raukkan women did. Rushes were plentiful and we learned how to pick them as kids. I knew how to prepare them before I got to sitting down to weave them. They were plentiful around Raukkan, at Teringgie, down Big Hill way, and all around the lakes with the jetties. But where Alison and Frank Lovegrove lived on the lake, the rushes were coarse and we didn't use them for weaving. I know Aunty Laura Kartinyeri [née Sumner] and them used to go and pick rushes near Tailem Bend, where she lived and up the river, around Mannum, you could get good ones there too.

"What makes these places good?" I ask. We've been out driving on the Point Sturt Road. Doreen has been pointing out various sites to me, identifying plants, and volunteers that David Unaipon, son of James Ngunaitponi, Taplin's main informant on language, used to preach through here. We find some sedges (rushes), but they are the wrong kind, having two prongs, not three. On other occasions women have indicated camping places, favourite places—some for yabbies, some for rushes—and then bemoaned difficulty of access and scarcity of rushes, the damage done to the environment by sheep and cattle grazing, four-wheel-drive vehicles, pesticides and the like.

Fresh waters. The best rushes are fresh-water ones. We tried to use some of the rushes around Point Pearce, me and Aunty Rosie, but we found that they split. Sometimes Aunty Rosie would send a message over to Raukkan saying, "Send some rushes over to me because I want to make a couple of baskets." When you get the rushes, you're not allowed to pull them up by the roots. You had to pick them one at a time, although sometimes you can't help it if the sand is loose. But you shouldn't pull them up in bunches because you're stopping the growth and, if you're pulling them all the time, you get blisters. When we got home with the rushes we'd cut the heads off, like the three little spikes at the top and the part that went into the root. Then we'd lay them out to dry for two to three weeks. I remember my mum would get sugar bags, hessian ones from Uncle Dan Wilson [Veronica Brodie's father] at the store. They'd take the sugar out of the big bag and put it into little ones. She used these hessian bags to wrap the rushes up, because after you've picked them, you have to keep them damp and pliable. In the bag roll you could just dampen them down and they wouldn't split. You could unroll them and check them. As Doreen explains this to me, she reaches for a bundle of wooden barbecue skewers and a tea towel to demonstrate. I can't find the word for this action, so I'll show you. I'd unwrap them and roll them with the tips of my fingers and the palm of my hand, and I was told not to take them off the hessian, and then I'd wrap them up tight again and sprinkle them with water. In the summertime you had to keep them damp. I remember once Mum used a blanket, but they went mouldy. The hessian let the air in. Mum tried to clean them down and used them as the ones you insert.

I know the rushes she got from Raukkan, from Aunty Phyllis that were sent over with Uncle Jimmy Cross. She used those good ones for lacing. She wouldn't use the Point Pearce ones except for filling. I said, "Let's try them. They look good." But every time we tried to rub them back on the knife, they'd split. She'd be holding the knife in one hand and then she'd pull the rush over the blunt side to make it smooth. We'd get an old knife and just use the back part of the blade near the handle. They would rub it to make the rush smooth and flatten it out. She never wasted things, so the ones that split were used on the inside as fillers. You have to keep inserting different lengths of different rushes so that you can weave around, and then you don't have just one weak spot in one place. You wouldn't just get a bunch and stick it in. You keep adding one or two to keep the same thickness. She'd keep the stitches close together, the closer the better, and the holes, you punch ahead of where you are, and then you can pull the rushes through and tighten each one as you go. The tightness of the stitches is like the closeness of the family. This last observation, almost a throwaway line at the time, I later learn is a key to Ngarrindjeri symbolic representations of their world. As I come to understand more of the ways in which Ngarrindjeri wisdom is transmitted and beliefs confirmed as true knowledge, as I read more of the sources and women begin speaking about matters dear to women, I begin to appreciate more and more the way Daisy Rankine linked weaving to the sacred and cultural life. But for now, Doreen is intent on demonstrating the skills of a weaver and I have not yet asked questions about the possible inner meanings of this activity. I am hoping they will arise spontaneously. They do, but later. There are more things to be introduced, more strands to be woven, before we can understand those aspects of the design.

Doreen produces a packet of dolly wooden clothes pegs to show me how her father would make the hole punch. You put the knife in the split of the peg and hit it with a hammer or stone, and then use a piece of broken glass to sharpen the split end. Then you could tie it around your wrist and use it for making the holes when you were weaving. These are skills that have been passed down, but Doreen, the researcher, also has an interest in the documentary record. If you see the film of Milerum making his baskets, even though I never knew him personally, I can see that nearly everyone had the same way of weaving that Milerum shows. Tindale has a tape of him showing how to work the fibres and make them into string. Milerum would have been the last one who would have been doing that. So that would be something we could have been teaching if we knew the techniques. I never learned that skill myself. As she speaks of this method, Doreen rubs her thigh with the palm of her open hand, a gesture I have seen in central Australia, where it signifies hair string. Here it has to do with the working of fibre which is chewed, rubbed on the thigh, and worked into twine. Doreen is always clear about the limits of her knowledge. She names her source, and does not claim to know things just because she has seen others do it. Where she has a right to know, she says so. While working in the Museum, Doreen has seen old fish nets made of fibres from roots and plants, and there are drawings by George French Angas from the 1840s in which Ngarrindjeri work is visible. Tindale (1934–7: 164) writes of *kandari,* a net made of chewed fibre, steamed, from rushes, characteristic of the peoples of Encounter Bay.[17] On the basis of my reading, I ask about the names of different rushes, reeds and grasses. Doreen says she does not know. But, she hastens to add, she does know where they grow and how to use them. She also knows that introduced items could be put to work.

Mum used a lot of wire. She got that from Dan Wilson at the store too, off boxes. She used the wire to strengthen the handle, and sometimes she would weave it into the pattern and it kept its shape. The only time I ever used wire was when I put the handle on. Aunty Martha showed me how to do it. You'd have your second-last row and weave over it just like it was ordinary rushes, and go around and do the other handle and do the same thing. The last row would finish off the handle. Ellen listens as I read this section. I remember Nanna Brown doing that with wire. Doreen: The most difficult thing for me to learn was the beginning of it. They all start the same way. One of the things Aunty Rosie was saying to me over at Point Pearce, "*Nukkin* [look] the way we still do everything in a circle" and I thought, even though she is a long way from home, she still had thoughts about being there, in a circle that's tying us all together.

It's binding us together. And the more we'd weave, she'd be there laughing and telling us yarns and I'd be sitting down watching her. Sitting down watching Ellen weaving, I could see she had been taught the right way. She does a really good job.

Doreen moved her foot around in a circle as she spoke. People had a pattern the whole year round. They travelled in circles and followed the food. They would camp here and there, depending on where the food was. This is something I have heard from Neville Gollan. The months were marked by what was in season. In June it was swan eggs, and in mid-winter, July, it was mushrooms. Then came the fishing season in mid-August to early September as the waters began to warm. We'd get flogged if we swam too early and told we'd turn yellow. Now [late December], the *muntharies* [native apples] are out. They're early this year because of the rains and now it's warm. Summer is a time of plenty. Maggie Jacobs tells me, We lived by the seasons. In late November I hear, The *lauwari*, Cape Barren geese, they'll be on the saltpan at Poltalloch, just before The Narrows. Neville Gollan adds: They come down when the lucerne is all green and then they leave as quickly as they came. It depends on the warmth. I was explaining to Doug Wilson, Veronica Brodie's brother, where we were staying at Clayton. Had I seen the *lauwari* were yet at Tolderol Point? he asked. I explained we drove south from Milang. Where the road swoops around before heading into Clayton, they'll be there, he assures me. Sure enough, as we drove home the next day I saw they'd arrived. I then remembered when, about the same time last year, I first saw them massing on very similar swampy land on Hindmarsh Island. They know how to make fresh water of salt water, Neville Gollan explains, That's their business. Next visit, I drove straight back to the Hindmarsh Island site and there they were. For a brief moment, the intertwined rhythm of the seasons and sites was mine to know. Doreen Kartinyeri ties it together: It was the same with the rushes. It was a cycle and they travelled around in a circle. And now, with meetings, especially after Hindmarsh Island, we form a circle. It is for solidarity and friendship amongst us. It might not have meant that in the olden days, but it was part of their life. And now the language is being taught, we're weaving, making feather flowers, and learning about the plants.

Ellen Trevorrow is one who knows well where the best rushes

grow. The rushes like fresh water and a lot of considerate farmers are leaving them so we have supplies. I move around and just thin out the good places. I'm finding it very hard down our end close to the Coorong, because there was a lot there, but the salt water table is taking over. We need the fresh water. Sometimes along the roadside, because it's not on farmer's property, but just where the water runs off the road, the rushes are growing very nice, and you'll see someone picking them. But I move around in a circle. I pick and move and let the other lot grow; they grow very quick. I never pick them out completely. Later, I can return when the young ones have come up again. You can see where I've been.

It was sixteen years ago at a workshop that was arranged by the museum with Steve Hemming and Aunty Dorrie [née Gollan]. She was an elder and I enjoyed it, because I reminisced on my life, my childhood and my grandmother, my family, and the basket weaving. From then on I was teaching the basket weaving and my first class was a Year 9 art school class in Meningie. I've been teaching ever since and working towards exhibitions. Out at Raukkan, Dot Shaw (née Rigney) laughs when she hears this and says that Ellen is now teaching her to weave. Ellen learnt from Aunty Dorrie who learnt from my mother, Fanny Rigney [née Sumner]. So now the circle is complete. It's come back to Gracie Sumner [née Gollan], her sister and me. Ellen continues: I feel there have been really different cycles in my life. I was around with my grandma at Marrunggung but it was Aunty Dorrie Kartinyeri [the wife of Doreen's father's younger brother] who taught me. She was the one who first started me on basket weaving.

Nanna Brown made baskets to sell or to make a trade for some clothing or something for us. After the age of eleven, I moved to Bonney Reserve with my mum. I look back now and my stepfather was a shearer, so we ate a large amount of sheep. I did all my schooling at Meningie, and straight from my schooling I went into a family with my husband Tom Trevorrow. He's a fisherman and we eat a lot more fish. My life is based from Marrunggung to Meningie, and that's where I still am today, here with my family, weaving. It's cultural weaving because it was the same rushes that they prepared—it's a three-pronged type—there's a lot of different types of rushes, but this is the one that was used, because it lasts a long time. Weaving is not just something I do to make money. I don't sell a lot. I work towards exhibitions. I love teaching; I love sharing the basket weaving.

Ellen's sister basket, on loan from the South Australian Museum, was on display at the Adelaide launching of the Indigenous Peoples' Basket Conference, held in the week of 18–22 November, at Camp Coorong. There, eighty full-time delegates and hundreds of visitors from other parts of Australia, the USA and New Zealand renewed old friendships, and established new ones. The brochure announced: "Basket weaving is one outward sign of people living in touch with their land. Joining in a basket weaving group is a means of communicating, connecting and solving problems of present society." In the final session the participants shared their concerns as women weavers in a rapidly changing environment. They identified the problems caused by the disappearance of their raw materials as lands have salted up and been polluted by insecticides. They bemoaned the theft of indigenous knowledge through registration of patents,[18] and lack of respect for women's knowledge. They told of their spiritual connections to land. Ngarrindjeri weaving, story-telling and survival continue to go hand in hand.

One hot January day in 1996, over an early-morning cup of tea with Ellen Trevorrow, we discuss the nature walk that her husband Tom has planned for us, and I admire the rushes that are carefully stacked along the side of the bench in the kitchen. Tom takes tours of children through the Bonney Reserve, a piece of land long under Ngarrindjeri control. It shows. Whereas other parts on the land side of the Coorong are eaten out, this section is thick with vegetation and animal life. Here is Old Man's Beard, which Eileen McHughes has already told me about—boiled up it's good for colds and as a compress for rheumatism. The *muntharies* are in season. I realise in rereading my notes and the sources that *muntharies* season was a time which people anticipated and relished. Taplin (11/2/1868) noted that by February all the local people were gone "to get muntarris on the Coorong". Angas (1847: 65) writes of the natives dispersing over the sandhills in search of "monterries" and returning in the evening with their baskets filled.

On our nature walk we see pigface (*Portulacca*), *ngunungi*, numerous edible berries, *puyulangki*, *kalathumi*, and roots, gum from the wattle tree, banksia honey, and a she-oak that moans and murmurs. Tom tells me of the importance of the she-oak (*Casuarina stricta*) in the story of *Ngurunderi*'s creative acts in the Lower Murray. It is something Eileen McHughes has also mentioned. I've read about this tree in Tindale and much of it concerns sacred matters which are not discussed openly. What can be said is that *tungi*, the female she-oak tree, marked with colour and considered sacred, are distinguished from *kula*, the male she-oak tree (Tindale 1931–4: 152, 156). *Tungari*, Tindale (1934–7: 30, 31) records, is a "secret language" "spoken at a distance" between *Ngurunderi* and his brother-in-law *Nepelli* and "practised by old men who have prestige". Through the sacred tree (*tungi*) "imbued with spirits", native doctors could convey messages to each other (*tungari*) and their communications were audible when "branches chafe together" (1931–4: 165). At Katal, meaning "talking tree", at the southernmost named Tangani place, there is just such a sacred tree. The landscape is full of meaning, and these meanings are reinforced and renewed through human interaction with the natural world.

On school trips Tom makes the children use their memory and, at the end of the walk, asks them to recapitulate. Although some may forget some bits, usually the class is able to reconstruct what they have been told. It shows them the strength of working together, says Tom. Risking his displeasure, I take notes and add the plants he has told me about to those I have learned from other Ngarrindjeri. At the end of that first period of field work, I cross-check what I have with Appendix 6 in the Berndts' book (1993); I find that contemporary Ngarrindjeri have named most of the plants mentioned there, but their knowledge is not from books. They know things that are not in the books and are mildly amused, even smug, when white people find a scientific basis to their traditional knowledge.

Pelicans on Lake Albert, Meningie, 1996 (Diane Bell)

Feather Flowers: The Land of Pelicans

I used to watch my mother making feather flowers. She made roses, with swan feathers, the white ones of the black swan, but usually we used pelicans, says Dorothy Shaw (née Rigney). I learnt to weave from Aunty Fofon, and my uncle would go for the pelicans, adds Sheila Goldsmith, who was raised by her adoptive parents James and Alma Kartinyeri. Ellen Trevorrow is reminiscing with her mother: Some twelve to thirteen years ago, Tom had a piece of driftwood and said he would like some feather flowers to go around it. Do you remember, Mum? You did it for him and we've still got it on our windowsill today.

The Lower Murray is the land of pelicans. I've photographed these gregarious birds at the Goolwa barrage, at the ferry crossings at Narrung, at Meningie, and at the Sturt Park Murray Bridge. At these sites I've seen Ngarrindjeri women fan out looking for feathers. Any children in the party are shown how to preen the feathers into a bunch. I now find myself walking and scanning the ground for the pelican feathers, though I am not yet able to identify the fifty to sixty different parts Doreen tells me are on a pelican. At the Goolwa barrage Edith Rigney (née Kartinyeri), Doreen's first cousin, quickly collects a bunch that she says are probably from the

Feather flowers made by Doreen Kartinyeri, Devon Park, 1981
(Doreen Kartinyeri's personal collection)

73

Christabel Wanganeen, Doreen Kartinyeri, Cheryl Travis, Lydia Wanganeen,
Devon Park, 1981 (Doreen Kartinyeri's personal collection)

breast part of the pelican. "Who taught you, Aunty Edie?" I ask.

We called her Mummy Fofon, or Aunty Fofon, and this is what my old
Aunty Fofon and a lot of the old ladies taught me when I was a young
woman. They taught me how to make feather flowers. We used to take
them to the canteen. This was when the Salvation Army used to run the
canteen on the mission at Raukkan, and whatever food we needed or
anything, we exchanged it for the feather flowers. I bought a dinner set,
my first little dinner set, through the canteen with feather flowers.

Doreen was taught by her mother: To prepare the pelican skins, they
used to salt the back part and nail it up, stretched, to dry. When the inside
was dry, we used to cut it up into small portions. They have beautiful
feathers on the neck. Usually the women used those as the centre parts of
the flowers and they were like a spiral thing. Under the breast the feathers
were almost the same. The back of the pelican has another shape feather,
and you'd sort them out for different flowers. Under the wing, you would
have to pull them out because you couldn't cut the wings, like you could
the skin. The feathers under the wing and on top were a different shape
again and most of the women used those for petals. Aunty Myra, Aunty
Fofon, Aunty Martha, a lot of them, they all knew which ones to use to
make it look like certain flowers. Ellen listens to this passage: I saw that
around my grandmother, and Mum does the same today.

Doreen: I was friends with Polly Rankine, Aunty Fofon's eldest daughter,

74

and I was allowed to go to the lake, after school, with Polly and that's when I saw, for the first time, Aunty Fofon making a fan out of pelican feathers. Now she used the wing feathers to make this and not the long pointy ones she used for leaves, but from along the wings, the long-stemmed ones, and she made a beautiful fan. It was Auntie Rosie who said to keep the binding even and really tight and close, when you're working the feathers, just like the weaving, otherwise the feathers could get out.

Sheila Goldsmith was also taught by Aunty Fofon. Feather flower arrangements became wedding bouquets, a dress corsage, a table centrepiece of flowers and driftwood. A while ago, Aunty Sheila's niece made her feather flowers for Mother's Day. "Where did Aunty Fofon learn?" I ask Doreen. Annie I. Rankine, MBE, or Aunty Fofon as she is fondly known, the daughter of Polly (née Beck) Long, is one of the elders whose knowledge is highly respected. It is in the papers of her father, Clarence Long (Milerum), collected by Norman Tindale, that I have found much that echoes the oral accounts of today's elders. Henry Rankine, Milerum's grandson, acts as a custodian for his grandfather's papers, which are held in the South Australian Museum. The ways in which the oral and written records intersect, converge and diverge is always a lively topic for conversation.

The art of making feather flowers may have been taught by missionaries from Victoria, but men and women had numerous ceremonial and pragmatic uses for feathers and were already adept at working them. I ask: "Aunty Daisy, did the old people use feathers?" The tribal people used the feathers for wiping down the bodies of the dead and for ceremonial dances. They wore feathers on their arms and ankles and put them on the end of their spears. They used the bigger feathers, the ones on the wings and they also had the feathers for brooms to clean out their wurlies, or a branch off the trees. Nothing was wasted. I ask Doreen: In some of the old photographs, I saw one of Peter Campbell and his grandson, all dressed up and they had feathers in their dress. They were used traditionally in their corroboree. "*Ringballin?*" I ask. "I don't know the language name," Doreen responds. This is a term I have heard Sarah Milera and Daisy Rankine use for "corroboree". Eileen McHughes has another, *ngrilkulun*. Both terms are in the early literature; Neville Gollan tells me that *ringballin* is "singing" whereas *ngrilkulun* is for ceremonial singing and dancing.

Daisy Rankine: In the 1940s, during the depression time, it was hard to survive then, so we did the weaving and feather flowers and we sold them to visitors coming from Goolwa by steamer to Raukkan. At that time the wages was small, our father's wages was small, and you'd see the women every fortnight on Friday, they'd be up on the Captain Sturt monument up on the hill; they'd be up there with all the feather flowers and weaving to sell to the visitors. In the fifties I sold quite a few at the Coffee Palace in Tailem Bend. My sister was a waitress there. It took me ten minutes to make the flowers for a spray. But since the 1960s, when the new law came in, and you could only get one pelican per year, we have to make those feathers last through the year till we'd get another pelican.

Doreen Kartinyeri: Nowadays, they mostly shoot them. Earlier they would have trapped them and the men would skin them. When making feather flowers, you had to prepare them to get them nice and clean a long time before you were ready to work them. If it had been shot, you had to wash the blood off. Some when washed weren't any good, so you'd have to throw them away. Feather flowers were another income for the family, same as baskets and that. My Aunty Martha used to send them up to her sister, Aunty Connie, who lived at Tailem Bend. She would put them in the chemist and the tourists would buy them from there. In 1983, I got Syd to shoot a pelican for me so I could make feather flowers to pay for the publication of the Rigney Book.

It was Aunty Martha who really taught me how to dye the feathers. To get a variety of colours, we used to break the skin into different parts so that we could dip each piece into a different colour: red, green, blue, yellow, purple, whatever. We used crepe paper, food colourings, Dolly dyes, blossoms, and clays. We did it in jam tins. We'd wash them out, take off the paper labels and then boil them on an open fire. As long as you didn't keep them in the sun after they were made, they wouldn't fade. They were really good. Back in 1981 I made heaps. I had to get a permit from Parks and Wildlife to shoot a pelican. On that occasion I was demonstrating the feather flowers to Steve Hemming, and he took photographs and he has me on tape talking about it.

The difficulty of getting feathers is a common complaint, but there are creative ways around this. If a bird is electrocuted, the rangers will save it for the feathers, and freezers come in handy. Women have diversified and some have even tried the feathers of chickens. Aunty

76

Janet, who died in 1980 at the age of 97, had begun to improvise with string, rough and thick, when she couldn't get rushes. Her niece, Muriel Van Der Byl, tells me, And she made beautiful mats. The doctors told her not to go collecting any more, so she used string. Sometimes Val and I would collect rushes for her. Feather flowers and weaving thrived on the mission; found an outlet in tourist trade; were collected by museums; and provided private spaces where women could work and talk together. The skills are still being taught in the families and in workshops. Down at the Goolwa barrage, Edith Rigney finishes telling Judge Mathews: I was always learning, from when I got married, that's the time I did start learning more about my language, making feather flowers, and a bit of basket weaving. That's when I started getting to really know and wanted to learn more about the culture and our language, because I didn't know anything before, just a few little words here and there which we always heard, you know.

Janet Smith with weaving made from rushes and rough jute, 1974
(*News*, 19 November 1974)

Weaving the Past

Language long suppressed is being revived. Grannies are being addressed in Ngarrindjeri; elders are returning to school to learn language, weaving, and Aboriginal history. People are actively seeking to connect with and care for the land. Women's work is one way of tapping into and appreciating this cultural resurgence. Feather flowers and weaving keep people in touch with their world in tangible ways. Collection of material takes you out into the country, with family. It forces you to look. The activities associated with weaving and feather flowers became the focus of sharing specialist knowledge about the country and its bounty. It was a way in which histories of the land might be constructed. I hear snatches of conversation: Last year we found rushes in this place, but next year? We need new places so we don't pick them out here. My grandmother used rushes from here. We no longer have access. The land is salted up. The land is under water. Pelicans, now restricted game, have become scarce. Stray feathers are picked up and saved. The things are named. The names are savoured. The value placed on women's crafts by Europeans may have helped sustain production and created a niche for new items, but the quality of the interaction with the land, and the pride in the thing made of the land by Ngarrindjeri hands, is distinctly Ngarrindjeri.

Ngarrindjeri women knew how to make baskets, big baskets for carrying fish and little baskets for special items, winnowers, fish scoops, mats to be worn, mats to sit on, mats as back warmers, and mats that are folded over to make coffins. Charles Sturt (1833: 155) describes the round mats on which women sit. Artist George French Angas (1847: 85, 61) wrote in 1844 of the child sheltering in the large circular mat, fastened upon a mother's back and tied in front, "so that they almost resemble the shell of a tortoise", and of women's net bags, laden with mussels. His drawings illustrate the range of Ngarrindjeri women's distinctive basketry work. In his vocabulary of the language of the Encounter Bay area, missionary H. A. E. Meyer (1843: 62) uses the sentence "the woman is making a basket", to illustrate the utility of the particle *il* in *wark-il lakk-in koye* and *warke laggel-in koyel*, and to point to the complex relationship between agent and object.[19] On the mission, women made baskets to sell. They made traditional pieces for the South Australian Museum, pieces which may now be studied by contemporary cultural weavers. They made novelty pieces which found their way into the museum, like the rush mono-plane made in the 1920s by Janet Watson at Kingston: "I made this plane because my brother left in it when he left home to go shearing. It was the first time I saw a plane" (Giles and Kean 1992: 4.7.3). Yvonne Koolmatrie, whose work includes a three-dimensional turtle, was commissioned by Tandanya to reproduce the mono-plane, as a celebration of innovation in Ngarrindjeri culture (*ibid.*). As Ellen Trevorrow reads this she comments, I want to make a wurley out of rushes.

Louisa Karpeny (right) and companion, *c.*1915.
(M. Angas collection, SAM Anthropology Archives.)

79

The making of beautiful baskets and mats by the "first generation" is confirmed in a number of sources. In a much-published photograph of "Queen" Louisa, dated 1915, she and her companion, both probably in their nineties, are bedecked with baskets and mats. In another she carries a bundle of rushes. Louisa Karpeny, "Queen" Louisa, known in Ngarrindjeri as Kontindjeri, believed to be over one hundred years old when she died in 1921, was an adult woman when George Taplin (1831–79) established the mission at Point McLeay on the banks of Lake Alexandrina in 1859. Taplin mentions that the women "make a great many mats and baskets of different kinds" (1873: 43) and in his journal records that on 4 March 1875, he "attended to some women who had mats to sell". Weaving was encouraged on the mission, but while Taplin's diaries are a rich source of information on daily activities and Ngarrindjeri lore, there is little on Louisa, scant mention of weaving, and not a whisper of the stories that might have accompanied such work. We are more likely to be able to retrieve the name of the person who collected the item than the name of the person who collected the materials, made the piece, and told stories about the peoples and places it evoked. Today, alert Ngarrindjeri eyes regard the quantity and scrutinise the quality. Where did she collect the rushes and with whom? Contemporary weavers can usually identify the species and they know the techniques, but the social dimension is missing. We can only speculate.

Louisa Karpeny, like many of her generation, did not live on the mission. When she visited, which she did for periods of time, Louisa camped off the mission, in a wurley by the lake, not in one of the mission-built Christian houses. Mostly she lived at East Wellington, on what became the Brinkley Aboriginal Reserve, where George Ezekiel Mason (1810/11–1875/76),[20] the Sub-Protector of the Aborigines east of the Murray River, had established his camp in the 1840s. Karpeny connections with the area have continued to the present. Other families lived down the Coorong, some at Goolwa, on Encounter Bay, at Milang and Point Sturt, some up the river. And, from Taplin's journals we can see that Ngarrindjeri were highly mobile in the nineteenth century. There was frequent traffic back and forth across the lake, up and down the river, and along the

Coorong. As she reads this section, then in manuscript form, Daisy Rankine tells me of the markings clans left on their camping grounds when they'd go to the mission for rations. Clear as a signpost to those who could read the signs. These marks warned others of the danger of trespass and brought the travellers safely home. In Tindale (1931–4: 71-2) I find reference to the boundary mark *kinari* made with a pole displaying the *ngatji* (totem) of the land-owner or head male person.

Louisa Karpeny, the mother of Pinkie Mack, and her mother's sister, Jenny Ponggi (*c.*1811–1911), mother of Albert Karloan, stayed lucid to the last. The historical memory of these two women was central to twentieth-century researchers seeking to reconstruct the lifeways of the Lower Murray before the colony of South Australia was officially proclaimed in 1836. Louisa provided information to Edward Stirling (1911: 13-20) about the devastating smallpox epidemic of the 1830s, the second such epidemic which had ravaged Ngarrindjeri lands.[21] However, Stirling records nothing about her weaving. Jenny Ponggi also assisted Stirling. And although, according to Ramsay Smith (1924: 201), Jenny Ponggi was blind, when he visited her at Trunceena, she was mat-making. Again, if he sat with her, there is no mention of any stories she might have shared with him, or her companions. He was more taken by the "velvety softness" of her pleadings for tobacco (*ibid.*). His all-male party covered a great deal of territory in a short time: hardly conducive to getting to know an old lady and her stories.

Margaret "Pinkie" Mack (1858–1954), Louisa's daughter by George Mason, was born at the Brinkley homestead. Situated on the east bank of the Murray River, just above where it enters Lake Alexandrina, the community at Marrunggung (Brinkley) could protect a number of nearby sacred places. From this secure home, they could visit, attend gatherings at which conflicts were resolved, trade, hunt, and attend to ceremonial obligations, including burial rites, arranging marriages, and initiation. Yes, but in the late 1950s McFarlane fenced off the main camping place at the lodge, Daisy Rankine interjects. I have also heard this as a complaint from the Karpeny sisters, Val and Muriel. Daisy Rankine remembers Nanna Pinkie rowing across the river to sell her weaving to passengers on the steamers which would

Pinkie Mack at Brinkley. R. M. Berndt Collection.
(SAM Anthropology Archives.)

come down the river and stop at the punt. Pinkie Mack was a valued "informant" of anthropologists Ronald and Catherine Berndt in the early 1940s. Indeed, she was their major source on women. Her grand-daughter directs me to a photograph taken by the Berndts (1993: 16-17) in 1943 at Brinkley. That's me on the step, the bigger girl, says Aunty Daisy of the seven-year-old standing behind Nanna Pinkie.[22] That day they were talking to Nanna, and my sister and me were sent out of earshot to clean up the garden. We were burning the grass. We weren't allowed to be around. Then she called us over for the photograph. "Who was talking to Nanna Pinkie?" I ask. There was Ron and Catherine Berndt and another woman with them. She was older than Catherine. Who was this woman? The Berndts did not drive and relied on others for transport. Was this woman their driver? Someone from the museum? From welfare? Did she make any notes on the meeting? There might be some mention in the field-notes of the Berndts, but these will not be available to researchers until 2024.[23]

In the 1930s Nanna Pinkie had assisted South Australian Museum ethnologist Norman B. Tindale with his extensive research in the southeast of the state. Her skills and remarkable memory are noted, but did anyone sit with her while she was making that coffin basket for Ronald Berndt (Berndt *et al.* 1993: 241, 274)? Daisy Rankine remembers her nanna was at Raukkan, where she made it, and where she waited for Ronald Berndt in 1943. Did the authors of the authoritative texts ever collect and prepare rushes with Pinkie Mack? Did they record the stories that are shared at such times? The Berndts (*ibid.*: 98) are explicit about their field priorities: "time and interest did not permit us to record the various techniques of net, basket and mat work". Of course they may have observed the production process and not recorded it, but it seems safe to say that their knowledge of weaving is not based on participant-observation field work. Tindale's film does provide details on techniques, but not the accompanying sociality. On film in 1937 Milerum makes baskets and mats, some with his own totem feathers, but they were made at the behest of a researcher, not in the company of his peers. These too are in the museum. It appears, from his notes, that Tindale worked one-to-one, not with groups of people engaged in an activity like weaving. My point here is not to disparage the work of these researchers—there is a great deal to be learned from the written records—but rather to set their work in a context. There are certain questions that can usefully be asked of their records and others for which the response will be silence. For their part, the Berndts (1993: 282) do not claim to have produced an exhaustive account of the knowledge of their chief "informants", let alone the entire Ngarrindjeri nation.

The written record may be silent on the sociality of basket making, but Ngarrindjeri conversations begun over baskets will shape the Ngarrindjeri world, and it will be one that weaves in diverse strands. Weaving is something that younger people are doing, especially those who belong to weaving families, and the sociality of the activity (the aspect which first drew me to weaving), is creating intimate contexts for story-telling. I saw Ellen in 1996 just before New Year. She was of course weaving. Her family had gathered at Camp Coorong. Her daughter Tanya was in hospital and soon herself to be the mother of a daughter. Little Ellen Sandra Alice Rose Wilson, born into this distinguished line of weaving women on 29 December 1996, will be surrounded by stories of her forebears, told by her elders. Tracing back through her four grandparents to "Queen" Louisa and "Queen" Ethel, the Ngarrindjeri world this child will come to know will also include accounts of the efforts of her great-grandmother, Daisy Rankine, her grandmother, Ellen Trevorrow, and Louisa's grand-daughter, Laura Kartinyeri, to protect the places, stories, and relationships that give that world meaning.

L–R: Ellen Trevorrow, Daisy Rankine, Ellen Sandra Alice Rose Wilson, Tanya Trevorrow, 1997 (Ellen Trevorrow's personal collection)

Weaving New Worlds

Isobelle Norvill looks to the future and the possibilities of a better world for her grandchildren: Unfortunately, because of the movement by the Protection Board, I didn't grow up in this area, even though my mother was a Ngarrindjeri woman and I learnt a lot of things from my old grandmother and the old lady we call Granny Rosie. I've got a grand-daughter now and I bring her down here, to the Murray Mouth, as many times as I possibly can, and, with the help of all her aunties, I'm teaching her so that she doesn't have to miss out on some of the things that I feel hollow inside about missing out on. So Edie will show her tonight with

L–R Back row: Sisters, Ellen Brown, May Sumner; front row: Laura Isobelle Kartinyeri (née Sumner) with brother Hurtle Sumner, early 1970s, Murray Bridge (Doreen Kartinyeri's personal collection)

the little feathers she collected and she'll make a little flower. I'm going to get some more feathers and Edie will actually make her one to take back home to put in her collection. So like I said, I feel really empty inside about not being around to be rich in the Ngarrindjeri knowledge and I just want to make sure that my grand-daughter doesn't go through the same thing.

Today's weavers are teaching their daughters, and some are also teaching their sons to weave and to make feather flowers. Ellen's five sons are all weavers. It is clear from a number of sources that both women and men could and did weave. However, for the most part, women made those items they used in their daily work (carrying baskets, cradles and baskets for storage) and they also made the coffin baskets. Were there items that were kept separate from the opposite sex? Reaching back into Tindale's (nd, a) notes, in the folder marked "Jobs Needing Further Attention Before Typing", I find: "Both men and women wove coiled basket numbers, men using their products for fish traps; baskets for fighting clubs and for protecting and transporting ceremonial objects which they do not disclose to women." In one of his journals, Tindale (1931–4), cites Mrs Catherine Gibson (5/4/1933) who told him of the *waninga*, a hair string cross not to be seen by women. Tindale and Long (nd: 4) remark on *taiaruk*, the "thread cross", made of "fur, hair string with tufts of feathers on all four arms, held in hand in men's ceremonies and not witnessed by women". If this is so, why was a woman telling Tindale? He explains that the old people, knowing these ceremonies were being curtailed, showed the item to the women of the last generation to witness the dances. Ethel Watson, Catherine Gibson's niece, dated this as about 1876 (*ibid.*).

Did women have items which men did not see? Given that there were few women researchers in the field in the nineteenth century, and that activities such as weaving were not seen as sacred, it is hard to imagine how such information may have made it into the written record and, had it got there, been accorded value as an activity of both sacred and profane significance. We are, as I have pointed out, hampered in reconstructing the significance of women's weaving by the silences in the written record. However, several trends in the study, documentation and analysis of activities such as cultural weaving hold some promise for the future. There are now museums where Indigenous peoples set the agenda for collection and curation; there are Repatriation Acts under which items are returned to their home communities; and there is an ever-growing body of literature on the religious significance of weaving, singing, dancing. The stories are beginning to be told and recorded.

For missionaries, encouraging women to weave may have been part of their notion of what women should do; an antidote to those idle hands becoming the devil's plaything; and a step towards assimilation. However, as far as Veronica Brodie is concerned, the ignorance of what women might be doing when they were with other women, allowed certain important women's activities to remain invisible. Time spent collecting materials was time out, time that the mission didn't question, time that women could spend undisturbed with other women. Some of them, when they left Raukkan, or wherever they were, would bring their weaving. They would carry whatever they were making. And it didn't come to me until my sister Leila said, "You think about it. They'd tell the White Christians they were coming away to pick rushes, and to do more weaving. They'd be gone for a few days. Mum would come with her grandmother. While they were here doing the women's business which the White Christians didn't know about, they would also take in a bit of trading. So, you see, the women's business was always taken care of but no-one knew what was going on. All they knew was that the women had gone away from there to do some weaving, pick more rushes, and the only ones to know about it were the ones that they knew that were trusted. Goolwa was a trading place. They told Taplin they were getting rushes and that they were trading, all of which was true. Speaking of strategies of resistance can be dangerous, as can allowing outsiders to record one's stories. I have included this one and have heard others, just as I have heard people find significance in the words of their ancestors where others hear only silences. Silences and absences cannot be read as proof of ignorance or the non-existence of certain practices, but I am all too aware that those who believe that women had no sex-specific knowledge will do just that.

The comparative literature on the sacred nature of weaving in other Indigenous cultures offers clues regarding Ngarrindjeri practice. Increasingly, anthropologists are recognising how much may be learned of a culture from a study of women's work. Comparative research also can indicate gaps in the ethnographic literature and demonstrate the importance of feminist scholars with their persistent question, "Where are the women?" Malinowski, so-called father of the participant-observation field work method of anthropology, in his study of Trobriand Islanders provided detailed accounts of trade, ritual, kinship, and the famous *kula* ring, but he missed what women were doing. They were there as wives and daughters, but not as actors in their own right. Anthropologist Annette Weiner (1976) found through her study of mortuary ceremonies that the women had their own trade in mats and banana leaves. Janet Berlo (1991: 439), surveying the textile traditions of Mesoamerica and the Andes, writes: "Textiles are eloquent texts, encoding history, change, appropriation, oppression, and endurance, as well as personal and cultural visions. . . . For indigenous Latin Americans, especially women, cloth has always been an alternate discourse. Only recently have we begun to listen."

David Guss (1989: 91) has written eloquently of the Yekuana of the South American rainforest and their weaving. He argues that only when narrative, graphic, textual, and functional elements have been considered can baskets be viewed in their true cultural context. Baskets, he demonstrates, provide yet another expression of the Yekuana conceptualisation of the universe. "For like all things made . . . they are intended as portraits of the society that inspired them." The society that inspired the Ngarrindjeri baskets and feather flowers has changed dramatically. Ngarrindjeri mother and child are no longer wrapped within a round rush mat; men no longer secretively transport objects in special-purpose baskets; but women still make distinctive mats. The coiled design, like the radiating design Guss analysed in South America, is a window onto the world that inspired and continues to inspire weaving.

Australian collectors of material culture have catalogued and categorised fibrework. Baldwin Spencer (1914: 381-9) makes an intriguing mention of a little knitted bag worn by men only amongst the Kakadu, but carried by a young girl in Tiwi initiation ceremonies. W. Lloyd Warner (1937: 329) made mention of woven items, such as women's dilly bags containing sacred objects in the mythology, but until recently with ethnographies such as that of Ian Keen (1994: 200ff.), not much attention was paid to exploring the symbolic meanings embedded in baskets. Louise Hamby (1995) has paid particular attention to the Djanggawul story from Arnhem Land and the significance of the sacred woven objects carried by these ancestral women. For the southeast, no-one appears to have pursued the gendered meanings attached to specific baskets; to have probed the significance of their structure; or to have asked if, like certain ritual paraphernalia, baskets might act as mnemonics for the relationship of person to place. The "sister basket", visible in the early photographs and still being made today, invites just such an analysis. In 1997 Ellen Trevorrow was working on a set of seven sister baskets. We have the story and it came to me to make the set. As the women attest, the very act of weaving binds family together. All the weaving begins the same way, from a centre knot, but, I've been told over and over, you're never sure what shape it will assume until you're finished. But, only when it is complete, can the whole be appreciated. In the recurrent symbolism of the circle in Ngarrindjeri speech and in the cycling of the seasons, Ngarrindjeri anticipate the whole. It is assumed that events will achieve closure. They are constantly seeking to close the circle, to complete the cycle, and it is the assumption about the nature of the whole that provides security in a rapidly changing world. It will come back. It will return.

2

Shared Designs, Different Strands

Ngurunderi: Landscape and Culture, United and Divided

When I go to Victor Harbor I remember *Ngurunderi*. When I walk on the Bluff I think about him. . . . I stand up on the hill and look out on The Pages [small rocky islands] and Kangaroo Island and up along the southeast to Kingston. At night, I look at the Milky Way and think: one day will I be there or not? said George Trevorrow (Department of Education 1990: 50) in 1988. Henry Rankine, whose sombre tones are heard in narrating the story of this creative hero on the video, *Ngurunderi: A Ngarrindjeri Dreaming*, says: In the Dreaming of the Ngarrindjeri people, *Ngurunderi* is the shaper of the land, the laws and creatures. He could travel through time and space, along rivers and hills, across lakes and seas. His mind and spirit sometimes took human shape and he travelled as a man.

In the Dreamtime, in search of his two wives, *Ngurunderi* travelled down the Murray River which at that time was only a small stream. A giant Murray cod, *pondi*, swam ahead and with each swish of its mighty tail widened the stream. *Ngurunderi*, in pursuit, tried to spear the cod from his canoe. *Lenteilin*, Long Island, near Murray Bridge, represents one spear which missed. At Tailem Bend he threw another spear and the *pondi*, wounded, surged ahead, eventually escaping into Lake Alexandrina. With *Ngurunderi*'s help *Nepelli*, his brother-in-law, speared the giant fish and *Ngurunderi* cut *pondi* into pieces. As he flung each piece into the surrounding waters, he named his creation. From one large body, *Ngurunderi* created

the various species of fresh- and salt-water fish for the Ngarrindjeri nation.

Meanwhile his wives had made camp and were cooking bony bream, a fish prohibited to women. *Ngurunderi*, smelling the aroma of the cooking fish, stood on his huts, now the two hills at Mount Misery, and placed his canoe in the sky, where it became the Milky Way. He then pursued his wives. In their effort to escape, the women built a raft of grass-trees and reeds and crossed Lake Albert. At the spot where they landed, their raft turned back into grass-trees and reeds. The women hurried south. *Ngurunderi* followed them south to Kingston where he met, fought, and finally triumphed over *Parampari*, a great sorcerer whose burned body is now visible as granite boulders. *Ngurunderi* then travelled north, and made camp several times on the Coorong, where he dug soakages and fished. Continuing along the coast, he crossed over the Murray Mouth and, amongst other deeds, made a fishing ground at Middleton by throwing a huge tree into the sea to make a seaweed bed. At Victor Harbor, still not having found his wives, he became so angry he threw his spears into the sea where they became off-shore islands. Finally, near King's Beach, he heard his wives laughing and playing in the water. His club, which he hurled into the ground, became the bluff known as *Longkuwar*. His wives, realising that he was catching up with them, fled in terror until they reached Cape Jervis. He strode after them. They began to hurry across the land bridge to what is now Kangaroo Island. Seeing his wives once again escaping, *Ngurunderi* called out in the voice of thunder for the water to rise. Wave after wave rushed in, drowning the women, whose bodies became the rocky islands known as The Pages. *Ngurunderi*, knowing that his time had come, crossed over to the island and travelled to the western extremity. There, after throwing his spears into the sea, he dived into the water. From there he rose to the sky to become a star in the Milky Way.

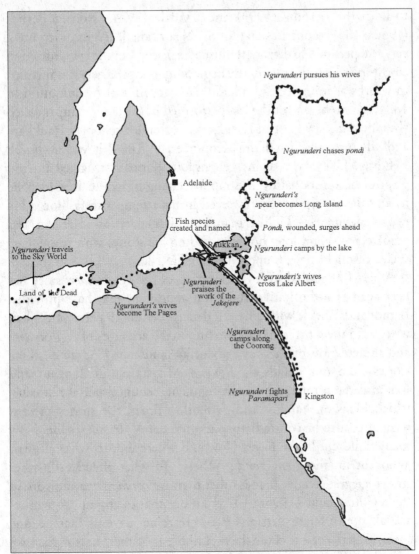

Ngurunderi pursues his wives

Ngurunderi chases *pondi*

Ngurunderi's
spear becomes Long Island

Pondi, wounded, surges ahead

■ Adelaide

Fish species
created and named

Ngurunderi camps by the lake

Raukkan

Ngurunderi travels
to the Sky World

Ngurunderi's wives
cross Lake Albert

Land of the Dead

Ngurunderi
praises the
work of the
Jekejere

Ngurunderi's wives
become The Pages

Ngurunderi
camps along
the Coorong

Ngurunderi fights
Paramapari   ■ Kingston

Pioneers of the Lower Murray   (Map: Stephen Shaheen)

This account draws on the written and oral texts which accompany the multi-media *Ngurunderi* exhibit at the South Australian Museum.[1] For the most part, the exhibit relies on the account Albert Karloan related to Ronald Berndt (1940a) in 1939 at Murray Bridge. A Yaraldi man of the Manangka clan of the west coast of Lake Albert, Karloan (1864–1943) provided a wealth of cultural and linguistic information to both the Berndts (1993) and Tindale (1974). Ronald Berndt (1940a: 185) emphasises that for the Ngarrindjeri, "Ngurunderi was a very real person. No deviation must take place from the laws, rites, and ceremonies he instituted in the beginning. His greatness was revealed to youths at initiation." And Karloan's account of his initiation in 1884, said to be one of the last performed in the area, is unparalleled (Berndt *et al.* 1993).[2] But Karloan also attended school at Raukkan, and when he married Flora Kropinyeri in 1884, it was a church wedding. Like many of his generation, Karloan struggled to find ways of accommodating the rapidly changing world in which he lived, but was repeatedly thwarted in his attempts to fashion a life of independence.[3] Unlike many of his generation, Karloan was prepared to spend long hours recording his stories with researchers such as Ronald Berndt and Norman Tindale.

Albert Karloan's detailed recounting of the *Ngurunderi* story has been read as authoritative, though it appears he may have provided Berndt and Tindale with different details (Berndt 1940a: 172). When we turn to the written record, we find many accounts of *Ngurunderi* and the creation of the Lower Murray landscape.[4] At times, these stories flesh out details of *Ngurunderi*'s travels in Tangani and Ramindjeri territory, and thereby augment accounts, such as Karloan's, which focus on Yaraldi lands. At other times, the stories present what appear to be contradictory accounts of *Ngurunderi*'s life. How many children did he have? How and where did his wives drown? Who cut up the giant *pondi*? Where? To what effect? Still other stories suggest creative heroes other than *Ngurunderi* were at work in the region. Clarke (1995b: 147) cautions that to attempt to synthesise all the different versions is to create an account that no one Ngarrindjeri person could have authored. Rather, he suggests we read the different versions of the *Ngurunderi* story as a reflection of the power of local knowledge to generate distinctive accounts. He explores those stories which have "a coastal bias and those that emphasise the inland aspect of the Murray River" (*ibid.*). I would add that the existence of various accounts should also serve as a caution. Where there is no canonical Indigenous text, but rather myriad perspectives on central mysteries of the relationships between all life forms, the land below and the sky above, it is folly for a researcher to seek the "authentic" or "pristine" version. As Keen (1994: 217) notes for Yolngu ceremonies, if the people themselves offer "multiple interpretations, no anthropological reading of the ideological significance of myth or ritual can be given 'objective' validity". Like oral traditions everywhere, the story-teller speaks face to face to an audience most often comprising closely related people. The stories are presented in ways that are relevant to both person and place. When we read written accounts of stories that belong to an oral tradition, we need to ask about context. Who told the story? To whom? When? Why? In response to what question?

One early and interesting local strand of *Ngurunderi's* travels was recorded by Dr Richard Penney (*c*.1815–1844), "Surgeon to the whale fishery at Encounter Bay" in the early 1840s.[5] In Penney's account the wives follow Ooroondooil (*Ngurunderi*) and drown.

> After he had made all there is in this country, he left it, by swimming, to make other lands. Two of his lubras, who tried to follow him, were drowned and turned into the two islands, called "The Pages" at the entrance to the Backstairs Passage, at the east of Kangaroo Island. He made Kangaroo Island [Kukakun] rise out of the sea, and went on making countries to the westward; where he still lives, though, by this time, a very old man [Penney 1843].

In this account *Ngurunderi* does not become part of the Milky Way but remains earth-bound. The wives are devoted rather than defiant. Should we then say, given that Penney recorded this account a century earlier than Berndt (1940a), that his is more authentic and that Karloan's is a fabrication? I think not. There are different ways of construing the relationship between *Ngurunderi* and his wives, just as relationships between husbands and wives are not constant in everyday life. The *Register* of 4 September 1872 carried an account in which there were three wives who were drowned when, out of curiosity, they followed *Ngurunderi* (cited in Clarke 1995: 148).

Meyer (1846), who like Penney is writing of the Encounter Bay region, introduces Pungngane as the one responsible for cutting up the fish and throwing them into the sea. What of the fresh-water fish? What of *Nepelli*, who is not mentioned? Were all subsequent researchers duped? Again, I think not. Angas (1847: 96-7), a contemporary of Meyer, writes of Oorundoo (*Ngurunderi*), travelling down in his canoe and commanding the water to rise and form the river, and then drowning his wives by making two lakes (Alexandrina and Albert). There are many ways in which we might contextualise the different accounts as products of different times, minds and relationships, as well of different places. The stories were, we need to remember, spoken, not written, and their vitality relied on gifted story-tellers who could bring the narratives alive for their audience.

This is our culture, our beliefs, our newspaper, our environment, says Henry Rankine who learned about the *Ngurunderi* Dreaming from his father when he was ten or twelve. I don't know how many people know about that Dreaming story. These stories are handed down from generation to generation. When I was young I learned that the old people would talk to you about our Aboriginal tradition and culture if you were willing to listen and learn. If you were silly and said that you didn't want to believe it, then they would tell you to go away and they would not talk to you about anything.

Stories might be told in different ways, but they could also be "heard" and recorded in different ways by a researcher who asked different questions and had different interests. Tindale and Pretty (1980: 43), for instance, with an interest in systems of land tenure, note how *Ngurunderi* shaped the river as he passed through different clan territories. Penney also noted Ngarrindjeri territoriality but did not tie it to clans. Rather, he identified larger regional configurations. Penney (1843) writes: "He made the Big Murray, or Eastern tribes first, and then the Lower Murray people; teaching them all the arts of life that they possess, and instructing them in the knowledge of their mysteries, and in those rites which they still continue to observe." In his epic poem of "The Spirit of the Murray", Penney (Foster 1991: 82) credits Ooroondooil (*Ngurunderi*) with instructing his children that "A separate realm I give to each / To rule and fill with life". Beginning in the east, each established his own territories which he then had to guard. In this account, the powerful hunter, *Ngurunderi*, transforms the landscape and sends his offspring to colonise far and wide. And the land being created is distinctively different from what it had been before his arrival. Alf Watson (Tindale 1934–7: 58-9) told of how the Crow, *Wark* "magically cut the country up into separate living spaces", and then offered

Ngurunderi's nephews a choice of a place to live.

In fascinating ways, stories recorded about *Ngurunderi* mirror the archaeology of the area (Flood 1983: 113). They tie changes in the landscape, to the migration of peoples into the Lower Murray; remark upon the drowning of the coastal reaches, the emergence of the river and lakes, and the disappearance of mega-fauna. Taplin (25/6/1860) writes of the great hunter *Wyunggaree* who made the salt lagoons by pegging out the skins of the kangaroos he killed. The animals were so large that one skin covered each lagoon. The account of the drowning of the wives by the rising waters not only addresses the separation of Kangaroo Island from the mainland but also provides an insight into the time depth of certain oral traditions. With the end of the last ice age, and rising waters, the flora and fauna of the region changed gradually, but nonetheless dramatically. By 10,000 BP, Kangaroo Island had separated from the mainland. By 6000 BP sea levels had reached their present level (approximately) and, over the next few thousand years, Aboriginal habitation intensified. Roger Luebbers (1981; 1982) writes of the evolving settlement patterns of the Southern Coorong, which involved increasing levels of economic complexity as food supplies became locally less reliable.[6] By 2350 BP there is evidence of large semi-sedentary and sedentary populations and recurrent occupation by small, clan-like groups. This is the well-regulated society governed by the laws instigated by *Ngurunderi*, and this is the society which many researchers have sought to reconstruct.

It took the skill and vision of a great hunter such as *Ngurunderi* to move successfully into this newly emerging landscape, and it no doubt took many generations for the system of land tenure and the system of governance to achieve the sophistication described by Taplin (1879: 34-6), Tindale (1974) and Berndt *et al.* (1993: 58ff.). Taplin (1873: 2-3) suggests that *Ngurunderi*, who found the country already occupied by a tribe under the Chiefs Waiungare and Nepelli, "united his people with them and gained ascendancy over the whole". Songs tell of a migration southwards (Tindale 1937: 108-9). The Berndts (1993: 223) have *Ngurunderi* coming into Ngarrindjeri lands from the Upper Murray and also link *Ngurunderi* with *Baiami*, a hero of considerable ritual importance in northern Victoria and southwestern New South Wales. Harvey's (1943: 112) story is of a migration from the Wimmera. The Ramindjeri, Tindale (1974: 133) suggests, appear to have been more sedentary and then, with the arrival of the Tangani who had travelled from the east through the Wimmera and the Yaraldi who had come down the Murray from the northeast, were hemmed in and compressed into the toe of the Fleurieu Peninsula.

Taplin certainly understood *Ngurunderi* as a historical figure, but with his interest in saving souls, paid more attention to the moral character of this hero. Taplin (15/10/1859) had dubbed *Ngurunderi* the "devil" but was also comfortable in promoting the idea of him as "God" (25/6/1859, 22/11/1859), the translation often given today. Victor Wilson, Isobelle Norvill's younger brother, in explaining this translation to me, says, *Ngurunderi* was on the beach before Jesus. It's a chronology I have heard from others. While the missionaries may have sought to capitalise on the commonalties of the creative deeds of *Ngurunderi* and God, there were Ngarrindjeri who forged their own dynamic understanding of the relationship between the two systems. It was one which allowed their beliefs in their old people, *muldawali* (creative heroes), and localised spirits to continue to shape their lives. They absorbed certain elements of the Christian story, a process facilitated by their ability to live in ambiguity and not feel threatened by a multiplicity of localised possibilities which were also an amalgam of the beliefs of migrations into the region over a period of time.

One of the difficulties faced by missionaries looking for analogies in Indigenous religions is that important Dreamings frequently have both good and bad characteristics (R. Berndt 1979). They are not divine in the sense a Christian God is imagined. Further, promoting *Ngurunderi* as the creator had significant consequences for Ngarrindjeri world-views. The importance of other creative heroes was marginalised, the singular creator/God was gendered and, once he was identified as a male, those female Dreamings, such as the Seven Sisters, were moved from centre stage. In a single move the world was gendered, sanitised, and a monotheistic regime imposed. The South Australian Museum exhibit has further entrenched Ngurunderi as *the* creation story. The ambiguity which was not only tolerated but was celebrated by different peoples in the Lower Murray is being erased, as literacy and Western notions of what constitutes "tradition" threaten to synthesise and standardise the many stories of this creative hero. It is a sad irony that the museum exhibit which has done so much to focus interest on the Indigenous culture of the area, may also have generated what will become the canonical text against which all other stories will be measured.[7]

Fortunately, active Ngarrindjeri story-tellers continue to subvert this move. Oral transmission of knowledge is still the primary mode of learning about the ancestors, and there are other stories of the creation of the Murray River. At the Museum at Signal Point at Goolwa, there are displays which tell of the lives of the peoples of the Lower Murray. Goolwa, one learns, is the "elbow" of an ancestral giant. On the introductory video, which features sweeping shots of the Murray River and of the abundant wildlife of the region, there is a segment Henry Rankine narrates, "I'll tell you a story of how the river was created long ago . . .". It is about *Krowi Thukapi*, the giant turtle who, having travelled across the country, from the Darling district, began to make the Murray River, with its many billabongs and backwaters. "Going this way and that way, still walking and all the way [*Thukapi*] could smell the sea." Henry Rankine told Philip Clarke (1994: 114) that *Thukapi* was looking for a place to lay her eggs. "As she went, the drag of its tail made the river, its flipper carved out the lagoons and banks. You can see where it went. When it got to the lake, it pushed itself into the sea." In narrating the video, he explains that *Thukapi* then went back into the Dreaming. All this happened before *Ngurunderi* was on the scene. In another version *Matumari* chased a giant fish from the Murray Mouth up through the lake. Near Poltalloch he caught, killed and tore the fish to pieces (Tindale and Long nd: 10). I have also heard stories that recall the role of the Seven Sisters in creating these inland waterways.

Many paths, many stories. In yet another account of the creation of the Murray River, it is a woman who creates the river and opens communication to the sea. Penney (1842b) writes of *Corna*, the progenitor of the region who, when living in the north east, was threatened by the fires his neighbours had lit. The fires had already killed many tribes. *Corna* and his family were overcome and near death when, from the dying form of the old wife, a female form arose. Stamping upon the ground, she brought forth the Murray River from a cleft in the ground, extinguished the fire, and the river flowed on till it came to the sea. In a similar story, Tindale and Long (nd: 10) depict *Ngurunderi* as living in the mallee country with a wife older than he, while he was waiting for his young wives to be old enough to join him. One hot north-wind day when a bushfire threatened to engulf them all, the older wife warned the camp, saved her companions by damping them down, and created the Murray River. "The old woman was engulfed in flames and died but as the people fled, her body leaped up like a great flame and she thrust her digging stick into the ground and the Murray River appeared."

In Tindale's (1986a) "Work in Progress" folder, the following note indicates that even the most basic component of the *Ngurunderi* story—that he widened the river in the pursuit of the Murray cod— is contestable. "According to some, *Ngurunderi* cut the valley of the River Murray by pursuing a gigantic Murray Cod with a spear, according to others the 'spear' was a phallus, and the river channel being carved by its aid and flooded with urine. In yet another variant, the phallic origin of the channel is maintained but the river flow is the urine of his two wives." It is, I think, easy enough to see why recorders with an eye to the sensibilities of say, museums, missionaries, and educational programs may have privileged one version over another and why Ngarrindjeri "informants" may have omitted certain details and favoured certain versions. Explicit sexual references, be they to the male or female body, in accounts of the activities of the ancestral heroes are common in Aboriginal mythology. It has also been common for such references to be read as evidence of the "primitive" nature of Aboriginal beliefs and to be treated with a singular lack of respect.

Clearly men and women participated in the making of their worlds but, for the most part, it is men whose voices have been recorded. If women had been recorded in similar depth, what might they have said? One researcher, Alison Harvey (1939), who spent but a few days with Pinkie Mack, learned that one of *Nepelli*'s wives carried a basket for cockles. This would relate to the wives' activities along the coastal reaches, and most likely there was story attached to both the basket and the cockling. While the single-line entry in Harvey's notebook cannot answer such questions, it provides a link between weaving and the Dreamtime and makes me wonder what further details more intensive field work might have revealed. In all the recorded accounts I have read, neither *Nepelli*'s nor *Ngurunderi*'s two wives are named. When the latter appear, they are fleeing *Ngurunderi* and their bodies remain in the landscape as a cautionary tale for women who defy the rules. But perhaps they also stand as a reminder of the independent ways of women in days of yore. What might we have learned of the flight of *Ngurunderi*'s wives from their angry, vengeful and easily roused husband had a senior woman been asked? Perhaps the wives, who are related as sisters or close cousins, have links to stories of travelling women from other regions, just as *Ngurunderi* has links up the river to other travelling heroes. It is, after all, the wives who precede *Ngurunderi* into the new lands. It is his pursuit of them that is the impulse for explorations of new lands, and it is their transgressions that vivify gendered food taboos.

Without an exegesis from a woman of some standing, we can only guess at their identity and the meanings women may have attached to the exploits of the wives. The Berndts (1993: 227) were told, "The reason for his wives leaving him was not revealed." It would be interesting to know whom the Berndts asked. Unfortunately, women's motives and desires are rarely probed. Although it would appear that the wives were wilful, spirited young women who were capable of surviving in new lands, they are not presented as knowing subjects. Even in Unaipon's (1990: 19-32) story of "Narroondarie's Wives", the focus remains on the man. Despite the lack of agency credited to the women, the *Ngurunderi* story does illuminate the nature of polygynous marriage. A man's first marriage was most likely to an older woman, maybe the wife of a deceased brother. His subsequent wives, "promised" to him at initiation, were considerably younger than he, so *Ngurunderi* was waiting.

In the *Ngurunderi* exhibit, contemporary Ngarrindjeri voices are interwoven with historical accounts, artefacts, photographs, tapes, images and objects. On the video we hear Henry Rankine as narrator and see his children as actors as they present an account of the travels of this ancestor. In the displays we trace the journey and are introduced to various aspects of social, economic and religious life. Ngarrindjeri input was critical to ensuring that these reconstructions were faithful to Ngarrindjeri beliefs and practices and it was a task they took seriously. The Lower Murray Aboriginal Education Consultative Committee worked with the museum curators (Hemming 1994b). On several occasions Doreen Kartinyeri, who was undertaking research at the museum, alerted the curators to details which were inconsistent with her experience and knowledge of Ngarrindjeri culture. In one display the fire was located so that it would have smoked out the camp. In another the women were sitting in a way which was inappropriate for a family camp. This piece of gendered knowledge was not available to the male curators.

The stories are not static. They reveal different information to different people. To my mind, the differences as well as the underlying commonalties of various stories and the various accounts of the "same story" offer clues about the Ngarrindjeri conceptualisation of their world. *Ngurunderi*, who was also responsible for establishing major rituals of Ngarrindjeri society, has left more traces in the written record than the story of *Thukapi*. However, there are elders, like Aunty Daisy, who know this story as one passed down in their families, not from the Goolwa Museum.[8] Both stories provide meaningful accounts of the creation of the mighty river which drains the south-east of the continent. Both concern larger-than-life beings whose exploits are inscribed on the land. Both concern a search: the one for wives, the other for a place to lay eggs. Both entail acts of reproduction: be it in the laying of eggs or the division of *pondi*.[9] And, as Clarke (1994: 114) indicates, both force "the enlargement of a stream into the river". Some force, then, was needed to break through from the river to the Southern Ocean. We know that the mouth has closed over at various times. We know that the course of the Murray has moved over the centuries. The land which was the reference point for the oral traditions was not static, and neither were the stories. They speak to different periods, to a time when the rich coastal lands were being inundated, to different migrations, and to changes in the flora and fauna. They can accommodate more than one location of the Murray Mouth, more than one bend, billabong, and backwater in the river.

In the creation of fish species and in the colonisation of the land by *Ngurunderi*'s sons, the stories recorded by Penney and Berndt offer ways of thinking about the relationship of the part to the whole. At the macro-level, the account of the creative hero *Ngurunderi* stresses "the over-arching importance of *Ngurunderi* as law-giver and as the main shaper of the distinctive landscape in which Ngarrindjeri people still live today" (Hemming *et al.* 1989: 4). This was a framework within which people could continue to find meaning when, post-contact, their lands were colonised and populations decimated. At the micro-level, there are stories concerning specific sites which reflect more localised perspectives, interests, and affiliations. Thus stories from the Encounter Bay area emphasise *Ngurunderi*'s role in creating the coastal landscape, while those from Yaraldi provide a lakes and river perspective, and those of the Coorong concern the uniqueness of that ecological zone. Fragments of these stories have survived in certain families, have been held in trust by respected elders, and have been transmitted to privileged individuals who, like their forebears, tell the stories as ones of relevance, guidance and sustenance to their kin.

Ngarrindjeri weavers and story-tellers express confidence that despite their many differences, there is a world which is distinctively Ngarrindjeri. It has a past, present and future, and contemporary Ngarrindjeri can and will have a hand in determining its shape and design. On the one hand, there are stories that weave a world of unity around shared concerns, histories, beliefs and practices; on the other, there are stories that explain regional differences. There are the writings of literate Ngarrindjeri, and the oral accounts of this generation of elders. This generation of story-tellers has begun reflecting on the complex ways in which their individual lives intersect and diverge; on the relationship between their experiences on missions and in fringe camps; of being taken away to homes; of the way in which the policies of church and state have variously constrained and enriched their lives. They recognise that the materials of which their world has and will be fashioned are not of a uniform texture and quality. Their stories are not ones of passive acceptance of authority but of spirited resistance, of intelligent accommodations and adaptations, of respect for their elders, of cultural resurgence when the climate is conducive, and of dignity in the face of repression, cruelty and abuse of human rights.

Raukkan, 1997. The Church viewed from "Bummers' Corner" (Genevieve Bell)

Life on the Mission: From Taplin's Time On

Today Raukkan is a self-governing community run by the local Point McLeay Council to whom the land was handed back in 1974 as part of the government's policy of self-determination. My first glimpse of Raukkan was one fine summer day in 1996. I was shown around and quickly learned of the importance of Taplin's time. From his arrival in 1859 to his death in 1879, George Taplin worked hard to address the moral, spiritual and physical well-being of his charges. There had already been a mission at Encounter Bay where, from 1840 to 1846, H. A. E. Meyer of the Lutheran Mission Society of Dresden ministered to Ramindjeri who had been in contact with whalers and sealers for several decades.[10] And, since 1840 there had been a fairly stable population at Wellington. However, it was the mission run by the Aborigines' Friends' Association (AFA) at Point McLeay on the banks of Lake Alexandrina which became one of the enduring residential foci for Ngarrindjeri life. In the view of historian Graham Jenkin (1979: 171): "In times of hardship, ill-health or persecution, Raukkan was a safe, reliable, and friendly place of refuge." In oral traditions, Taplin is recalled as a strict disciplinarian who was both loved and feared. Through his journals covering his period at the mission, one can trace the unrelenting campaign Taplin (1873, 1879) waged against those who wanted to initiate young men and women, arrange marriages, practise sorcery, and dispose of the dead in traditional ways. He sought to break the hold of the old people over the young, and in many ways he succeeded. Girls sought refuge in the school-house so that they could avoid promised husbands; young men cut their hair and thus avoided painful rites of initiation; old men and women agreed to be buried in the ground and not smoked on the traditional platforms. Taplin also kept Ngarrindjeri Christians on a short leash. James Ngunaitponi, who was to be one of Taplin's chief sources of linguistic information, took up residence at Point McLeay after he was converted by missionary James Reid who was at Wellington 1861–63. When Ngunaitponi went off preaching on his own, Taplin made him do penance on his return (Howie-Willis 1994: 117).

The tenor of Taplin's time is represented differently in written and oral accounts. David Unaipon (1953: 6) observed that Taplin would promote his regime with youth in school and would consult with the old men, win their co-operation, and thus have things done his way. Jenkin (1979: 124-5) attributes the arresting of the "slide into oblivion" to Taplin's work. Judy Inglis (1964: 115) paints a bleak picture of a people on Point McLeay and Point Pearce a century later as no longer having a distinct culture. Today, some Ngarrindjeri hold Taplin responsible for destroying the language: We were forced to give up our language and had to pray to God in English because Taplin said God did not understand Ngarrindjeri. However, it is also evident that Taplin was dedicated to learning and recording the language. He translated sections of the Bible. He offered up prayers and preached in Ngarrindjeri.[11]

Taplin was genuinely fond of many Ngarrindjeri, grieved for them as true friends when they died, and would grow incensed were any of his charges cheated by the locals (Jenkin 1979: 98). It is one of the contradictions of the man that he could dedicate himself to learning the language, could write about it with respect and admiration, and could translate scripture, yet be so committed to breaking the old ways. Taplin reasoned that he could better bring the people to Christianity if he could talk with them in language. He was a pragmatic when it came to conversion. "We cannot stoop too low to save souls," wrote Taplin (1873: 77). His choice of translations was strategic and his interventions focused. Taplin would withhold resources that were destined to become part of traditional ceremonies and shut the doors to latecomers to worship to teach punctuality. How one writes and speaks about Taplin's time depends to a great extent on the value one places on assimilation as a goal.

Taplin established dormitories where the boys and girls lived in separate quarters during the school week, a practice which some people today credit with hastening the loss of language. Jenkin (1979: 88) argues that Taplin did not force parents to relinquish their children, but once again oral traditions suggest that notions of parental "consent" in such situations are problematic. The parents were frightened and it was hard to say "no" to Taplin when you were living on the mission and wanted your children to be educated. Taplin himself was conflicted about how to best cope with educating youth. He proudly recorded incidents when youth preferred his rules to those of their elders, but then complained about the lack of discipline amongst his newly enfranchised coverts. Taplin (1873: 103) wrote of "young fellows intoxicated with vanity, conceit and self-assertion." Today Taplin's published works are read with interest by some Ngarrindjeri, who find in them accounts of family members and stories they have heard from their old people.

Taplin and those who followed him faced the same problem: the land set aside for the mission was too small and too poor to be self-sustaining, and local residents ensured that the mission did not encroach further into their lands.[12] By 1913, and some eight superintendents later, the days of the AFA mission were numbered. The Royal Commission of 1913 recommended that the South Australian government take control and it did in 1916. David Unaipon (1913: 33), the son of James Ngunaitponi, was only seven when Taplin died, but he detailed the decline in morale and work opportunities at Point McLeay and urged a government take over. To a man, the Ngarrindjeri witnesses agreed (Royal Commission 1913: 32-45). No doubt they were hand-picked, but their testimony does offer a rare glimpse of their aspirations in their own words. Successive witnesses repeated the position of John Wilson senior

106

(1913: 36): I think that children should be brought up on the mission station. They could leave the mission when they reach manhood. . . . I think the government should provide blocks of land for the natives who are capable of working the land successfully. Three of his sons worked off the mission, whereas two remained because, Wilson testified, "they did not want to leave their wives behind". The witnesses wanted their children to become skilled tradespersons. Jacob Harris (1913: 37) wanted to know that his children would be treated properly, but agreed: "If it were for his good, I would let him go." Those who recalled Taplin's time spoke of a happier period. John Wilson senior (1913: 36) observed: The mission has helped me a great deal for the forty-four years I have been here. . . . Conditions are not the same here to-day as they were thirty years ago; fish and game are not so easily obtained now. The commission heard stories of people in dire need. Mathew Kropinyeri (1913: 45) complained that the rations being dispensed at Wellington were insufficient, but allowed that, "Much praise is due to the Association for what they have done in the past." However, the AFA, he points out, was starved of funds.

The witnesses saw their future as independent farmers where they could support their families. Alfred Cameron and Henry Lampard were both already farming on land for which they held leases. Henry Lampard senior (1913: 37-8) who had been away from the mission for eighteen or nineteen years, stated: "I tried my level best because I wanted to get away from here with my boys . . . I have a little piece of land—120 acres—on the Coorong . . . I am pleading for my sons. I would like them to get a piece of land." Dan Wilson (1913: 36-7), born 1860, suggested blocks of 300–500 acres would be appropriate. He had worked in the vineyards. Pompey Jackson (1913: 34-5), born in 1849, grew to manhood during Taplin's regime. He had worked for thirty-three years on Narrung and, in his view, farmers preferred native labour, but white shearers didn't want them in the shearing sheds where they could earn equal wages.

No Ngarrindjeri women testified to this commission but that did not stop the committee inquiring into their welfare and formulating policies "for their benefit". It appears weaving was viewed favourably. David Unaipon (1913: 33) spoke of Susan Campbell, crippled but still capable of making mats. F. G. Ayres (1913: 598), a local farmer, in making the argument that the government should take over the mission at Point McLeay, stated, "let those old people go in for basket-making and other things that they are capable of doing". Patrick Wilfred Francis, a teacher at Point McLeay since 1904, had observed that the natives knew how to weave and thought that this could be taught to the children. "I think we can teach a lot through the fingers" (1913: 43). The matron, Elizabeth Jane Hunter (1913: 44-5), noted that the girls could be taught domestic skills but, because they no longer went straight from school to the dormitories, as they had in Taplin's times, she had little control.

Families who stayed beyond the reach of the mission on farms like that of Alfred Cameron on the Coorong were able to educate their children, but it was a struggle. Cameron had first approached the Land Board for land but was refused, so he bought it himself. He told the Royal Commission (1913: 38): "I earned the money to pay for it. I worked for 14 years with Mr Hackett, of Narrung." Now he was looking to expand his land base, as what he had was insufficient to support his large family. "I would be satisfied with the Needles property," he told them. However, he was not optimistic because he had spent the past twelve years applying to the Protector as well as to the Land Board, and the leases on the Coorong held by the AFA were being sub-leased to local farmers (*ibid.*). The very people who should have been assisting these independent-minded Ngarrindjeri were instead working closely with local landowners. The Royal Commission provides little or no information on cultural life, but it does offer insights about the values of hard-working people determined to carve out a living in a hostile environment. These were not passive victims being shuffled around the landscape, but active participants, albeit operating under significantly restricted conditions.

Once the mission became a government reserve, the population of Point McLeay found that, instead of the threat of Christian retribution, they were subject to the control of the *Aborigines Act* 1911 and their lives monitored by Protectors. Residents of Raukkan have set down their memories of the period of the Protectorate in their own words. In 1986 Leila Rankine (Department of Education 1990:

170) recalled the 1930s and 1940s: In my own time at Point McLeay I have seen young Aboriginal men chained up to a fence in the middle of the summer. Not even given a drink of water. Handcuffed to the superintendent's fence in the middle of the summer. One of the most painful aspects of this period was the power of the Chief Protector to commit children of Aboriginal descent to an institution for their "care, control and training". Aboriginal people are on record as protesting against this practice. Matthew Kropinyeri (1913: 37) distinguished between taking children away so that they might be educated, and "complete alienation from our children" which he characterised as "an unequalled act of injustice". The concentrated population on the mission made people vulnerable to police and welfare raids on their children. In the fringe camps there was some hope of hiding, but this was not always successful, as George Trevorrow illustrated; he described how his brother, at age three months, was taken by welfare and didn't return until he was sixteen, at which point he was confused and angry (Department of Education 1990: 170-1).

Religion: On and Off the Mission

Dot Shaw is thinking on the old days. She regrets that so much knowledge of the old people was treated disrespectfully, but says, I didn't hear the old people growling about Christianity. And our walk [the Long Walk of November 1996] was blessed, because He makes everything clear if you just trust Him. I was already Ngarrindjeri. I asked Him to bless it, and everything was found. We couldn't have been doing anything wrong. You have a choice about how you want to live: sharing, caring, loving, and always putting Him first. Veronica Brodie draws a distinction between her mother's relationship to Christianity, which she terms "religion", and her "culture", which is all embracing. Mum lived *with* her religion as well as *in* her culture. She believed in both. She had her culture to begin with. She was raised in that. It no longer exists in a traditional sense, but who says it's finished. Even within a single family there could be very different attitudes towards religion and culture. Grace Sumner: We weren't allowed to swear. Going to church was like going to school. We had to go. We went three times on Sunday: church, Sunday school, church. My grandmother tried to tell me more traditional yarns, I remember her trying to tell us about people getting *millined* [a form of sorcery]. However, my father didn't like that and tried to stop us hearing those stories. He did stop us. The old people were strict. Within families and within marriages there were divisions in terms of religiosity. As Aunty Maggie explains, Marj Koolmatrie, Lindsay Wilson and herself were age mates. They had been in school together and enjoyed their work sessions with the museum researchers. Dulcie Wilson, a staunch member of the Salvation Army and thirteen years younger than her husband, stayed more in the background. You can hear her reminiscing about life at Raukkan in interviews with Steven Hemming (1994a: 15–17).

The missions at Point McLeay and Point Pearce were home to a number of Ngarrindjeri, and people found various ways to accommodate their "culture" with their Christian beliefs. For Maggie Jacobs, there is no conflict. I can't do anything without God. He must have a reason. God has been in Aboriginal people before. They knew about God before. Then it was only when we . . . when Taplin founded the mission, there was Christian Endeavor, and we had to go to church. I do believe in God—He is not going to stop me. I was Congregational. There's been so much religion through Raukkan they don't know who or what to believe. Now I go to the Baptist Church. He doesn't want me to lose sight of my culture. I don't do things I shouldn't do. I don't condemn other people. The Royal Commission made me bad. I began to swear. I didn't before. I can pray for other people, but it's up to Him.

Doreen Kartinyeri lived on the mission, went to Sunday school and listened to her nanna and her nanna's sister, Mumadie, read the Bible. Old Mumadie would never tell you anything except if it was about Christianity. I didn't go along with that, so I stopped asking after a while. "Do you consider yourself a Christian?" I ask Doreen. Yes, but I didn't get converted by the Salvation Army. I believe in God but not in the style of preaching of the Salvation Army. I liked the way the Rev. Henry Reed conducted the service. Doreen is proud of her Aunty Rosie, who stayed beyond the reach of the missionaries; revels in talking about Mulparini, the "Black Heathen", the woman who stayed defiantly beyond the reach of the mission. Others, whose families have always lived off the mission and who view missionaries with disdain, remark on the freedom they enjoyed and the time

110

they were able to spend with their extended families. Alf Cameron's great-grand-daughter, Liz Tongerie, recalls: Every night I'd lie and look at the stars, that was our roof. I was never on the mission. My mum and father would tell stories about the stars. That is our connection. Other people have other beliefs. They spent a lot of time talking about the old days. That may be why those people that lived on the mission don't know things.

Isobelle Norvill knew the strict discipline of life on the Point Pearce mission: Mum came over from Raukkan to Point Pearce as a young woman. My father was born on Point Pearce. His people came from Encounter Bay, Cape Jervis way. Point Pearce to me, when I look back now and I can see it from an adult perspective, was a place—it's a horrible word to use—but it was basically like a dumping ground. It was sort of stuck in the middle of Yorke Peninsula and it was in a very dry, barren place. We had to get water carted to us. People used to have big drums and water used to get carted, because there was no water. We had the beach, not far, because as children we used to walk to the beach and swim, but there was a variety of people at Point Pearce. I would say there was about maybe eight Ngarrindjeri families at Point Pearce. There was people from the west coast, because that's where I was quite fascinated by these riding boots and their horsemanship skills and things like that. As children we used to watch them ride and thought, you know, how good they were, because they were stock people.

Mumadie was feared by everybody on Point Pearce; nobody ever crossed her path. She had a tongue, oh, she was shocking. I was brought up very, very strict by Mumadie. She would read the Bible to us all day long, and wouldn't let us go swimming with boys and a whole host of other things. She was the organist in the church and my grandfather was a lay preacher, and I used to help her prepare for the church services because everybody had to attend church on the mission. You weren't allowed to miss, unless you were sick, and actually that's where I learnt to play the organ in church when I was only about eight, propped up, because I used to watch her fingers and do it. But Mumadie lived to a very ripe old age; she was in her eighties when she died, but it's really interesting, and Dodo [Doreen Kartinyeri] and I were discussing it one day, Mumadie had three generations of us. She more or less just took us, and brought us all up really strict. "Didn't she, Dodo?" She took my

111

proper grandmother, Connie Varcoe; she took my mother Aileen Varcoe, and then she took me. Doreen agrees and adds, I gave up asking her questions. It was always about the Bible.

Isobelle continues: Granny Rosie [Kropinyeri] and my grandfather were brother and sister and, like I said, all the Ngarrindjeri people stayed together and Granny Rose, you know, I saw her on a daily basis, and that's when Dodo used to be up there with her all the time, and her brother Oscar. There was another old Ngarrindjeri lady whose daughter, my aunty, still lives today, and we look on her as a mother figure now, Hilda Wilson, she's eighty-six. She was Varcoe and her mother was the midwife at Point Pearce. She delivered me. We used to call her Granny Ollie. There was eight children in our family; two were born in hospital and the others were born in the house, and me being the elder daughter, every time mum would go into labour, my father would say, you know, run down and get Aunty Ollie to deliver the child because the baby's coming. But the Ngarrindjeri women all stuck pretty well close to themselves.

Mumadie, who raised me, had a brother Wilfred. We used to call him "Pop Wilfie", and if we were good, we were allowed to go down there and he'd tell us stories. He was a story-teller. He used to talk about the *mulyewongk*—the white people call it the "bunyip". He used to tell us stories about the *mulyewongk,* and different other stories about the things that he as a child used to do and he was—and he was also a very good dancer, and a tap dancer. I don't know where he got that from, but he used to be always dancing for us kids, so he was a lovely old man to be around.

Doreen Kartinyeri summarises the restrictions and impact on the transmission of knowledge: We lived under three laws: the government laws, the mission laws and the Protector's law. You can see why we lost so much. The laws were strict. People wanted to practise their traditions, but they were not allowed to. Taplin stopped them after he set up dormitories. At night time he took the children from school home to the dormitories so they wouldn't practise their traditions and he didn't want the children to speak their language while they were in school and the dormitories. They had very little time to communicate with their parents, to be speaking Ngarrindjeri, and by then they weren't practising their culture like they were on the Coorong, around Tolderol and Wellington, where they didn't have the mission.

112

Dulcie Wilson (1996a: 40), one of the leading "dissident women", has a different view on the assimilation era and the role of the church.

> I personally believe that the greatest injustice to Aborigines in this country was labelling them as different. By making Aborigines a separate people, this label has created the problems and the divisions we face today . . . For Aborigines to achieve a high standard of living and a greater measure of liberty, they themselves must face up to what has happened and repudiate the sham excuse that their problems are the result of colonisation. . . . Many Aboriginal people who were victimised and oppressed, not only by the system of this country but by their own leaders, are now rejecting the claptrap with which they were brought up. They are now more aware than they once were of the deception and the manipulation by some of their own leaders.

Dulcie Wilson is a speaker in demand at various functions where she delivers her message. It is very similar in tone to that expounded by critics of policies of self-determination who are fond of saying that Aboriginal rights create a special category of rights not enjoyed by other Australians.[13]

Dulcie Wilson, the daughter of Spencer Rigney and Lorna Sumner, now in her mid-sixties, was born and educated at Point McLeay. When she was eighteen she married Lindsay Wilson, Bertha Gollan's brother, and by the time she was twenty-six, the couple with their three children had moved to Millicent, where their fourth child was born. All her adult life Dulcie Wilson has been a committed member of the Salvation Army and in 1957 was a delegate to their conference in England. In 1985 she was awarded the "Citizen of the Year" in Millicent (Stevens 1995: 265). Various political leaders and business people call her friend (Maddox 1997) and newspaper reports of her talks, such as the one she delivered to the Rotary Intercity meeting at Murray Bridge (Anon. 1994) and to the Millicent Men's Probus Club (*South Eastern Times* 29/4/1996), indicate her local standing. During the Royal Commission, Wilson rejected the proposition that her mission upbringing had alienated her from Ngarrindjeri culture and pointed out that Christianity had not prevented her husband from being consulted by anthropologists (Stevens 1995: 266). Further, she argued, she was friends with Leila Wilson and had mixed with older knowledgeable women. The life of which she spoke had much in common with the so-called "proponent women", and this is a point that many commentators have made, including Judge Mathews (1996: 90) who notes the close genealogical relationship and similarities in life histories of both groups. Like other Raukkan women, Dulcie Wilson had partaken of bush tucker, camped on the Coorong, and learnt to make feather pillows from her mother who was a skilled weaver (Stevens 1995: 265). Mathews (1996: 90) concludes that "the only thing that appears to distinguish them as separate groups is the position they take with respect to the existence or otherwise of restricted women's knowledge". I am suggesting it is a little more complex.

Dulcie Wilson (1996b) wrote to the *Adelaide Review* and expressed her bewilderment and hurt at the way in which some churches had "come out in support of so-called Aboriginal spirituality" and stated that "scripture clearly tells us that we cannot serve God and Mammon". Wilson (1996a: 38) has consistently said she has no interest in whether or not the bridge is built, but is simply trying "to restore dignity and credibility to the Ngarrindjeri people of whom [she] is a descendant". Church support for those who hold that Ngarrindjeri tradition and Christian beliefs can co-exist has caused great pain to Dulcie Wilson (*ibid.*: 43) who cites a letter written by the Moderator of the Uniting Church in South Australia to a friend of hers. It illustrates one aspect of the dilemma created by the dissidents' modelling of culture:

> We must confess that it is the missionary movement of our Church which created the dilemma Dulcie Wilson expresses in her articles— for missionaries, particularly in Southern areas of Australia, did teach that conversion demanded relinquishing of Aboriginal spirituality. But we, or the missionary societies involved, were wrong. Over the past 75 years the missionary churches have discovered that there is an important distinction between gospel and culture . . . we have learnt that God was not without witness in the cultures we call pagan.

With respect to Dulcie Wilson's religious beliefs and involvement in the church, it is well to remember that the church is not mono-lithic; there were many different missionaries who passed through Point McLeay; and there are many ways in which Christianity has been incorporated in individual lives. Veronica Brodie draws a distinction between the Christianity of Dulcie Wilson in the Salvation Army and that of her mother who was brought up in her culture and when the Christians came, it didn't sway her. It didn't deter her from believing. She had that base to begin with. The "dissidents" speak of "tribal life" as finished and cannot envisage the possibilities of a culture that is neither "tribal" nor Western—that is, Christian —but respects the knowledge and authority of the old people. There are, Anne Pattel-Gray and Garry Trompf (1993) argue, a range of possible Aboriginal theological styles from the traditional (or non-Western) to the "Aboriginal" (or post-western). Within this framework, Marion Maddox (1997) explores the "conservative and liberal forms of 'missionized Christianity' imposed by non-Aboriginal evangelists, and 'story-telling theology' in which Dreaming stories and images are interwoven with Christian theology so as to offer a 'non-conservative, non-evangelical' hermeneutics grounded in Aboriginal tradition". Maddox locates Dulcie Wilson, whose Christian faith emphasises personal salvation and rejects syncretism, at the conservative end. Dulcie Wilson, Maddox (*ibid.*) points out, looks to a future where Aboriginal and non-Aboriginal will live together and where one God, rather than competing beliefs, will provide guidance and support. Dulcie Wilson (1996b): "As one of the dissident women I am not ashamed to bear witness to Christ's teachings, nor have I anything to gain by speaking the truth, other than a clear conscience which was guided by God in the face of strong opposition." At the "liberal" end, Maddox (1997) discusses Victor Wilson's position as an example of Pattel-Gray and Trompf's "post-denominational, post-Western 'Aboriginal theology'". Victor Wilson's ability to find in Dreamtime stories a "timeless guide for active engagement" and to lean "heavily towards biblical justice" has much in common with the view expressed by Aunty Maggie, Veronica Brodie and Dot Shaw. Reflecting on the way in which some Ngarrindjeri meld Christian beliefs with their traditional beliefs and those who feel the need to choose, Doug Milera, whose taped interview on Channel Ten (6/6/1995) sparked the Royal Commission (Stevens 1995: 186ff.), distinguished between "authentic tradition and personal beliefs" (Maddox 1997). Unfortunately, in the quest for the sensational sound-bite, Maddox's (*ibid.*) fleshing out of "the

115

links between political and historical experience and theological orientation which Pattel-Gray and Trompf suggest" is too subtle, too nuanced, for the evening news. Yet it is only with such an approach that we can make sense of the various competing positions on Ngarrindjeri "traditions".

Life on Farms and in Fringe Camps: Learning by Word of Mouth
Cousins, Shirley Peisley and Vi Deuschle grew up in the south-east. Vi Deuschle: My grandfather lived on 160 acres of land, thirteen miles out from Kingston at "Blackford" and we lived there as an Aboriginal family group. Although our fathers and uncles went out to work in the White world, we lived there in a little community ourselves and we didn't have any missionary influence because we were left to survive. Grandfather brought up his family there—he had thirteen children—and there were a school down the road and we used to go out into the bush on picnics. A social gathering wasn't just a social gathering. There was economics about how to pick the materials for weaving, the mothers and aunties did a lot of that. It was women's work down our way. Shirley Peisley adds: Even as a little girl, I knew how to make sure that we covered over the area where the spring waters were, so people who came along always knew where it was. We made sure it was cared for properly. And Gram told us women's stories about women and really emphasised what my role and responsibility and purpose in life would be when I grew up. All the Dreaming stories ended with our spirits going up into the stars. I realise now the story of *Ngurunderi* is very much part of what Gram knew. She was saying "Well there's the Milky Way. That's where he is."

There were those independent families like the Camerons and Vi's grandfather who raised their children away from missionary and welfare influence, and there were other families who lived in fringe camps and were able to stay reasonably mobile. Eileen McHughes: I was born in 1941 at Murray Bridge and grew up at the Three Mile out of Tailem Bend with elders around me: Nanna Laura, the Kartinyeris, Rigneys, Loves, Lampards. We'd be up and down to Tailem Bend and the One Mile at Meningie. We lived in humpies with dirt floors, no running water. There were camps around the towns along the Murray River and around the lakes, like the One Mile Camp out of Meningie and the Three Mile Camp out of Tailem Bend.

116

There, families lived in makeshift homes built of tin, hessian, canvas and some traditional materials. There were also camps along the Coorong. Although people engaged in seasonal work, hunting and gathering continued to provide important supplements to their diet. On the one hand, they had a measure of independence; on the other, because they had refused to live on reserves, their housing situation did not improve until the late 1950s when, in keeping with the government policy of assimilation, houses were made available in towns such as Meningie and Tailem Bend.

Unlike those families on the mission where literacy was possible and those independent-minded individuals who saw their future through a white man's education, the Ngarrindjeri in fringe camps looked to their elders for their education. Neville Gollan: I missed out on an education, but I'm one of the few elders around my age group that was lucky enough to be living in these areas, starting off from Meningie and other parts of the Coorong. And I've lived all my young days through the whole of the Coorong. They might take you past a place and then further down the track say, "Don't go there," and that was good enough. We weren't allowed to go there. And, maybe three months down the track, they say, "You know why we told you not to go near that island?" And it would be added to. It wouldn't be given all in one, and as you matured, you'd be given more information. The restrictions on movement that kept mission residents isolated did not apply to those who lived in the fringe camps. George Trevorrow: I was brought up in this part of the country and we had a chance, more of a chance than some people, to be in particular places at particular times, to hear our old people talking and to get an understanding of the layout of our country. Others look to those who had those experiences as the repositories of Ngarrindjeri stories. Matt Rigney tells me: Neville Gollan told us the story of the blue crane years ago. He'd say "*Nukkin the krowali,*" and then he'd tell the story. And, it's not just a story, it's our history. It's the substance of life.

Access to one's elders, of which Liz Tongerie also speaks, is critical in terms of who knows what. In the fringe camps of the nineteenth century through to the late 1970s, extended families lived near other extended families. There was seasonal movement, travel, and plenty of time for children to learn from their grandparents. They learned of the stars, the land, medicinal plants, hunting and gathering techniques, and family history. They heard language being spoken. Occasionally they saw their elders dancing in the traditional style and heard them singing in language. Isobelle Norvill: Grandmother Connie, Mum's biological mother, she used to dance every now and then in front of Eileen and myself and Eileen's other two sisters. She'd just tell us about how people used to dance and she used—she said the word "*ngrilkulun*". Is that right, *ngrilkulun*? And she used to do the dancing for us. We used to all sit lined up while she used to do it and then we'd get down and try and do it.

Tom Trevorrow: I grew up here in Bonney Reserve as a child. Right down the end. It was a ration station in the early days, but not any more. That history has been passed on to me by my elders who were around here at that time. Not all Ngarrindjeri people from along the Coorong went off to live on the mission. Just out of Meningie, we have the old One Mile Camp and the Three Mile Camp and down at Bonney Reserve, the Seven Mile Camp. We set up camps in these areas because there was a lot of fresh water around here then, and there was still a lot of scrub land around here, with all our animals, plenty of kangaroos and emus and echidnas and pigeons. All these big lagoons used to fill up with water. There used to be swans and ducks used to nest in here and that is why it was such a good place. There was still plenty of our traditional tucker, food, that we lived off of.

Our old camp site used to be in this area just here and it was made up of the old tar drums. When the Highways Department was building the roads through here, the old fellas would go and pick up the tar drums and cut the bottoms out and the tops out, split them in halves and make a sheet of tin, and that is what we would put up on the windward side and the rest of the rooms and that were made up of wheat bags. So we would sew the wheat bags together and that was our rooms. Even wheat bags were our bedspreads that we slept with. We were happy still living out on the land like this. The hard part, though, was we went through the welfare days, when the welfare would come in and do raids on the camp and the children were taken away from here.

George Trevorrow: The final threat of the government of the day was that if you do not move into town and away from the fringe camps, we are going to take all your kids away from you. So the women sort of took on a bit role in them days and they moved off with the children. It really put the squeeze on people and I know, with our mother, she used to have to go to the police station with a little ticket and get it signed so she could go to the store for some goods if the police was there. If they was not in a good mood, they'd tell them to go away and come back another day but, you know, we packed up our swag from here at one stage and we moved down to Victor Harbor where we lived for a long time down there. You know, we moved to Kingston. It was all our territory. We could roam right through and our camps went right from Kingston to Victor Harbor, right through the whole country and, you know, we moved around a bit. We were lucky in some senses I suppose we never got picked up by the welfare people.

A lot of our people did, our cousins, brothers, a lot of people got picked up by welfare. When the big black car used to roll in with the police behind it all the old people used to tell us kids to all go, and it was always the responsibility of the older kid to grab the younger kid, and we would run for the bushes and we would hide out on a big hill over the back there for however long it took. Then when the old people used to come out the back and stand on the little hill here, and it was a sign to come back into camp when them people had gone. It was horrible having to run around like that all the time but we survived it, I guess. I think it made us stronger people.

Some people, like Isobelle Norvill, went from the mission, to a girls' home, to a fringe camp and finally to a real home. When we left Point Pearce, we came across to Tailem Bend, because Point Pearce was becoming an open place then, and people were drinking and Mum said that she didn't want us to stay on the mission where there was drink. So we came and we stayed with Eileen McHughes's family, in a railway cottage at Tailem Bend, because Eileen's dad was my mother's brother, so we stayed with them until we got our house. And we all came down to Hindmarsh Island on a family picnic and that's the first time that my mother ever said to me that this was a special place, but I would be told one day about it. But then I put my age up and went to work because it was very hard for my father to get work—he was a shearer and a wheat lumper—so I went to work on the farms as a domestic, and used to help Mum and Dad, with my wages. That was a familiar thing with a lot of girls at those times—we went out and put our ages up and got jobs, grape picking, domestic mainly, and working in the old pub at Tailem Bend, peeling potatoes and all that stuff.

As a young girl I worked around Victor Harbor and Goolwa in the guest houses, when I was nineteen, twenty, twenty-one. A lot of Aboriginal girls came down here and done seasonal work in the guest-houses, so—and we'd all gather together and yarn and sing, because music is a very important part of our life, we like music. So I spent quite a bit of time down here at Goolwa and Victor Harbor mainly, and come down here as much as I can. With the publication of *Bringing them Home* (Wilson 1997), the report of the Human Rights Commission Inquiry into the Stolen Generations, many more of these stories are being told, lives are being pieced together, and the fact that they survived is being celebrated.

Life in the Home: Being Taken Away

Edith Rigney was born at Point McLeay in 1935, where she and Doreen, only two months apart, were reared like sisters by Doreen's parents. Then, at the age of ten, Edith was taken to a home: I was put into Fullarton Girls' Home, Salvation Army Girls' Home because Aunty Thelma [Doreen's mother] died. I was in and out of Fullarton until I was about sixteen. Doreen was there for a while, Isobelle Norvill, and a few other girls from Raukkan. We went home to Raukkan during the school holidays, but there was a couple of Christmases that we missed and I don't know what it was—whether it was because of a sickness that was going around, whether it was polio, or something—but we couldn't go home a couple of years for Christmas because the place was under quarantine. We had to stay there. Then at sixteen I went to work for a family in Rose Park, Adelaide as a housemaid. When I was about eighteen, I met a girl, Miriam Sumner that lived in Port Elliot and was going down there where her grandmother lived. But her grandmother died, and she had to go home to Point McLeay where her mother was living. She worked at Cliff House down at Port Elliot, so they were looking for girls to work, so she got me to go down with her. Aunty Marj and Uncle Hector Sumner, and Uncle Herbert and Aunty Agnes Rigney lived at Goolwa and I visited them on weekends.

In 1954 I married Clyde Rigney, that's Dorothy Shaw and Hazel Wilson's brother. We lived on Point McLeay and in '65 we moved to Lameroo. After she got married, I only saw Doreen on some occasions, mainly funerals I'd see her. She was living at Point Pearce and I remember Aunty Rosie, she used to be always growling at us. I suppose she'd say we was lazy. She said, "I used to go out and get in the boat, go and run the nets, bringing the fish in, clean them, gut them, take them to the fish buyers and some of them I'd keep and I'd smoke them." So little things like that, that's all she ever said to me. She just sort of made, like, with her hand, you know, she'd say, "Oh, we used to have that stick standing up like that, the bar standing up like that, and we'd have the fish all hanging inside and make a little fire." But I didn't question her what kind of wood she used, you know. Never ever asked her. I would have been in my thirties then, when Aunty Rose was talking about that. I could remember people mentioning Hindmarsh Island, Mundoo Island, and all that, but I never ever questioned about it, you know. I also feel sad that I never had the chance, even though my grandparents were still alive, I never had a chance to meet or mix with them, you know. Because when you're taken away, you lose everything. Doreen has also told me of Aunty Rosie smoking fish. The techniques are those described in Tindale and the Berndts (1993: 110-11).

Like Aunty Edie, Isobelle Norvill spent her teenage years in a home. Both had begun their education within the extended family networks of missions, were removed, married young, and in their middle age have been able to build on that early knowledge. So I lived on Point Pearce till I was thirteen, then they come and took me, the Protection Board, they come and done a swoop and they put me in Fullarton Girls' Home, and they just said. "Yes, well, she's a brainy little one. She might be able to get educated, this one." So they took about four or five of us, because Fullarton was another sort of a pot-pourri of people—like you had the ones that were in there because their parents had died and I was in there for education. I hated it. Hated it. I was there about two years and I got sent back to the Briar Bush, because I was really naughty. I used to run away as much as I could. Mum used to come and take me out for weekends and stuff like that. They sent me home on the bus if I was good, for school holidays, but like I didn't even know when Victor— that's my youngest brother, Victor Wilson—was born. Mum come one day with a baby and I said, "Whose baby is that?" She said, "This is your little brother." Because they wouldn't give us any messages.

I used to help one of the girls that had polio, but I'd get caught out, so they'd lock me in the cellar or in the coke room where the boiler was and all the coke would be in there. It was a very small room, with a great big burner in it. Just this great big red glow and just this noise. It was terrifying and sometimes they'd forget—they left you in there. I could squeeze through the grate and I'd go to my Aunty Amy and she'd keep me for a while, but then she'd have to take me back because the police would come. So as part of my punishment, I wouldn't be given any mail, because my mother used to write to me, and Mumadie, they used to write and send me lots of little packets of goodies. I thought I was lucky because I'd get a little box from my parents. I'd get toothpaste and they'd call me "Cuzzy Colgate". Yes, I was one of the lucky girls in Fullarton in as much as getting parcels. Wasn't I, Edie? You were in Fullarton with me. Every time it was mail call, I always got parcels from home and my mother kept contact as much as she was able, but she had to get permission.

Isobelle and I have worked through her sections of the manuscript and we've settled into her comfortable chairs, in front of the fire, in her new house, which is rapidly becoming a home. The garden is being planned; the plants brought from the last place and friends' gardens are being repotted; the boxes sorted; and the decor is developing, as Isobelle, a canny shopper, finds bargains. She's cooked up a storm in the crock-pot, just right for a cold winter night. Isobelle is pensive. She has been reflecting on the launch of the report on the Stolen Generations in Melbourne and the Ngarrindjeri who gathered for the occasion. It was profoundly moving and discussion of this report dominates conversations during my May–June 1997 visit, just as those about the Royal Commission did in January 1996. This night I'm bone tired. "Go to bed," says Isobelle, the caretaker. "We'll talk more in the morning." She's made up a bed. It's her daughter's bed, splendid with ruffles and deep eiderdown, and comfortingly warm: Isobelle has put two hot-water bottles there. Her daughter won't be sleeping in this bed for a while. She is in gaol. Isobelle called in all her resources to get the best legal assistance, but her daughter is a casualty of the system. She fought, but she got tired of running. I go to sleep thinking of Isobelle being torn from her mother and how important is it for her now to be able to mother.

Huddled over the radiator the next morning, we continue our conversation of the night before. Isobelle, who is working on a new project on grief and trauma in the local community, says: I've been thinking about when I was taken away and my grand-daughter without her mother. It's still happening. It's in a different way but we're still being separated. I'd never really stopped to think about it, but being with the other women and talking about being taken away, it really hit me. I was the total mother and Pat was the total father. I wouldn't let anyone hurt my kids. But under the Act, that's the way it was and I'm really sad that Mum and Dad didn't have total control over their kids and that someone else could decide what was best for us. It's going to take time. I need to reflect and to heal.

Veronica Brodie was born at Raukkan and at the age of fourteen went from Grade 7 there to Tanderra, a breakaway from the Colebrook Home.[14] There were Aboriginal girls there from everywhere and the ones who'd been there before had more privileges. When we first went there we weren't accepted by the other girls. We had to fight to be recognised. We were strangers and made to feel like it. When I went back the second year, I said, "They're not going to tell me what to do." In the first year I saw the discipline and I fretted. So did the other girls. When we came back in, they'd search our bags. My brothers sent me money and Mum would come down and buy me things. The board provided all our clothes and daggy old underwear. Matron read the Bible at breakfast and tea and we had church four times on Sunday. At the end of three years, no wonder we didn't want to go to church. There was lots of taboos. Anything that was fun, like going to the movies. Now I see Matron was getting us ready for living after the Protection Board. Years later I learned that the board was keeping the money I had earned and was holding it "in trust". I had walked out on my job and then my father had a heart attack; asked to go home and they said no. I went to the Ombudsman and he intervened with Mrs Angus and put me on the train. I had a pass for the train and a permit to be on the mission. The train went to Tailem Bend and then I went by rail bus to the reserve. I got back five months before he died.

I worked at Narrung on the switchboard for a little while. Then I got married. I was nineteen. Because my husband was classified as a "white person" who was totally exempt, I was issued with my "little dog ticket".

Then, when my daughter was about two or three, I got a letter telling me that I was an Aboriginal. So I went and demanded my entitlements as an Aborigine for my daughter and husband. I tore up the paper in front of Mrs Angas. The three born before the referendum were "white" and after 1967 they gave us back our Aboriginality and I've got a letter informing us we could get benefits due to us as Aborigines.

People were separated from their parents and isolated from family in a number of ways, but they still found ways to visit their places. It is important to contextualise the gaps in knowledge. This can be done by reference to life history material which explains, for example, why "sisters" Edith Rigney and Doreen Kartinyeri have such different degrees of knowledge regarding Ngarrindjeri culture. Further, reference to government policies and missionary practices illuminates different levels of knowledge, plus the onslaught on language and ceremony. Not all experiences of Christianity were the same. Not all experiences of being in a home were the same. It depended where, when and with whom, and there were even differences of opinion and acceptances within families.

One evening Cherie Watkins and Veronica Brodie are discussing other ways families were fractured. Cherie is one whose father, working for the Highway Department, moved his family around as the roads were being built. We lived in a tent. Now recently I've been told that people remember my family at the Three Mile, when we were camped there for a short time. Dad [Fred Turner] was born at Ravensthorpe in Western Australia. His family went there for the gold rushes. That was before there were any records being kept. So it's possible he was Ngarrindjeri, but had never been documented. Veronica Brodie is thinking out loud: People were just sent away and you were not told who your relatives were, then forty-five years later you find family. His family never told him. When my great-grandfather Dan Wilson went transcendental travelling, he'd return and say he'd been up north to see his relatives. My brother Graham was told to keep away from one of the Turner girls, and I assume this was because they were too closely related. "That's your own," meant don't marry within the blood lines. My mother used to say we were related to the Turners, and we never questioned her. George Turner would come down to Tanderra, and he'd say hello to Aunty Koomi, my mother. Then she'd ask about his people, and I was

124

always his cousin, and Cherie's dad was always over at his Aunty Koomi's [Veronica's mother], and then I'd visit. I met George Turner before he died, and he sang out "Veronica", and he came running, "my cousin". Fragments. What do they mean? Do they fit together? These sorts of reconstructions are the stuff of arguments fuelled by the ways in which families were fractured; records kept on some families and not others; and the old people talking in riddles. This generation is trying to find its place in a literate world which is increasingly requiring that Aboriginal people specify the one group to which they belong. Like many other people of the southeast, she is still searching for stories of her forebears, and the search takes in a number of regions and languages.

Cherie Watkins: We lived at Victor Harbor when I was about nine or ten years old for about three years, and Dad would take us down to Tauwitcheri, and he loved fishing around there and in Encounter Bay, and we'd go out at night with the Tilley lamp and spear the fish. They'd be attracted by the light. Some old lady we used to visit there who used to teach us weaving. Veronica interjects: "It might have been Marjorie Sumner". Cherie continues, "We didn't realise that was what he was doing. He was using Ngarrindjeri words. When I hear it I remember. I know."

Ngarrindjeri of High Literary Degree[15]

Ngarrindjeri with an interest in their language and culture and a desire to reweave surviving strands back into Ngarrindjeri designs look to their elders for guidance. There are the stories being told today and there are the stories that have been set down in writing. The long and honourable tradition of literacy amongst the Ngarrindjeri, both on and off the mission, is proving to be a boon for those who wish to know more of their forebears. Indeed, the first Aboriginal author to be published in Australia was Ngarrindjeri. David Unaipon (1924–25) wrote: "As a full-blooded member of my race, I think I may claim to be the first, but I hope not the last—to produce an enduring record of our customs, beliefs, and imaginings." Many have followed. Reuben Walker's (1934) manuscript tells of the life of the Ramindjeri at Encounter Bay and his plight as a mixed-race child. Lola Cameron Bonney's (1990) stories and poems tell of life at Teeluk, in the southeast. In the 1980s Leila Rankine's poems, interviews and speeches are eloquent testimony to her attachment to and knowledge of the Coorong. Doreen Kartinyeri's books of genealogies (1983, 1985, 1989, 1990), *Ngarrindjeri Anzacs* (1996), and her work in the Family History Project at the South Australian Museum, establish her as a researcher of some standing. Vi Deuschle (1988) is a speaker who has also published. She wrote the foreword to *Survival in Our Own Land* and was a contributor to *We Are Bosses Ourselves*. Margaret Brusnahan's poems address the dislocation and loss experienced by many Ngarrindjeri.

However, literate Ngarrindjeri who have written of their own culture have found themselves in a double bind. Their writing provides invaluable insights, but the authors are accused of being less than authentic "natives" because they read and write. The Berndts (1993: 9), for instance, say of David Unaipon's two published legends (1926, 1930) that they were "far removed from typical Narrinyeri accounts". This may be so. The language is not that of everyday Ngarrindjeri, but then neither is that of song, and Unaipon (1925, 1926, 1929, 1930, 1951, 1953, 1959a, b, c, 1990) wrote more than two legends. Unaipon was a scholar of the classics. He read Milton and Bunyan. To be sure it was unusual to find an Indigenous person writing of religion, using a theological vocabulary, and struggling to explicate the metaphysical bases of Aboriginal religion. Not what one would expect of the "native" at all. Yet I do not think Unaipon's work can be dismissed out of hand as "inauthentic". In his "Story of the Mungingee", Unaipon (1925) outlines the rites of initiation for women as instigated by the Seven Sisters. Beston (1979: 346) argues that Unaipon treated his material "pretty freely". The ordeal of pain which the Seven Sisters must endure is the ritual of tooth avulsion (i.e. knocking out the front tooth), which is not practised by Ngarrindjeri. Therefore, the reasoning goes, Unaipon must have borrowed the idea from male initiation. Beston (*ibid.*) also suggests that the cicatrices on the girl's breast may be adapted from male initiation practices. Had Beston checked the sketches of Angas from the 1840s he would have seen the cicatrices on Ngarrindjeri women's bodies. But tooth avulsion? It is a not unusual to find the creative heroes engaged in behaviour that is not replicated by those who follow the law established by the particular Dreamings. The ordeals which Unaipon specifies follow a general framework of submitting to the authority of the elders and demonstrating discipline. Within the Mungingee story there are references to *yartooka*, young girls, as in the *yatuka* of Berndt *et al.* (1993: 164), to bunyips, and *muldarpi*. Unaipon has the Seven Sisters looking down from the sky, along with *Ngurunderi*, *Nepelli* and *Waiyungari* (1990). I shall be returning to this story in Chapter 10. And, I should add that, for that to be possible I have talked with Harold "Kim" Kropinyeri in Murray Bridge who is the custodian of his great-uncle's papers.

So who was this man, David Unaipon? Something of an enigma, it seems: an inventor: a preacher, a writer, defender of his people, the face on the $50 note. David Unaipon, 1872–1967, the fourth of nine children of Nymbulda and James Ngunaitponi, was self-taught.[16] It is clear from various other sources that Unaipon was familiar with Ngarrindjeri customs and would go to some lengths to protect his lands. On 27 July 1918, Unaipon wrote "In defence of the Aborigines" in the *Register* to explain that there was no truth to the assertion that Ngarrindjeri were robbing swans' nests and thus preventing their hatching. "I never take eggs in the way indicated, because I strictly observe the old aboriginal law, which still holds good, that only the first eggs shall be taken for food." Unaipon was the model citizen at the height of the assimilation era. He espoused the merit of adopting Christian values: "Look at me and you will see what the Bible can do" (Jones 1993: 304). Unaipon was proud of the trades a man could learn; his inventions, like the modified handpiece for shearing, his lifelong fascination with discovering the secret of perpetual motion and various patent applications earned him the title of Australia's Leonardo (*ibid.*). In 1926, in one of the many bitter ironies of his life, David Unaipon spent time in gaol for idleness after being picked up on Point McLeay where he was collecting stories from his people.[17] Cath Ellis recorded criticisms of Unaipon in the 1960s when he worked with her and with Strehlow in Adelaide, and Tindale recorded "the gossip" about Unaipon in 1940, when Unaipon was working for Ramsay Smith and was being paid to collect stories.[18]

Philip Jones (1989) deconstructs the myths that have become the Unaipon legend and points to inconsistencies in Unaipon's biography. The story we most commonly read is of David Unaipon who, having travelled and read widely and having thereby developed a comparative perspective, was no longer in touch with his Ngarrindjeri roots. But his roots were deep. His mother, a Tatiari woman, commonly known as Granny Unaipon, was born around 1834, but at 100 years old when interviewed by Tindale, she was still lucid. On the basis of work with her, which he had overlooked in formulating his 1974 opinion on clan boundaries, Tindale (1934–7: 77) said he needed to revise his position on Ngarrindjeri territoriality. David's father, James Ngunaitponi (1834–1908), a Portaulun man, was Taplin's main informant and one of the reasons Yaraldi speakers don't always recognise vocabulary items.[19] Beston (1979: 335) ponders the lack of biographical information about David Unaipon: was he protecting his family from prying eyes? The Ngarrindjeri of Raukkan and Murray Bridge know his genealogy well. On a large poster display in the Lower Nungas Club in Murray Bridge one can track down through the generations.[20]

I had read the secondary material on Unaipon and his published legends before I had the opportunity to consult his thirty-chapter manuscript in the Mitchell Library (Unaipon 1924–5). It has been there for decades, yet it appears from their published work that neither the Berndts, nor Clarke nor Jones has paid detailed attention to its contents. The manuscript includes descriptions of Ngarrindjeri marriage, the navel cord relation, witchcraft, and a "fishing competition" that are amongst the best sources we have for these Ngarrindjeri activities. Certainly they are the most detailed from a member of the culture. There is no confusion regarding to whom his stories relate. When the stories are from New South Wales, he says so, but when they are Ngarrindjeri they are intricately interwoven with his intimate knowledge of the kinship system and local geography. His familiarity with several languages and his wide reading permit generalisations. To be sure, his writing is not what one would expect from a person with no formal qualifications, but the work is in his hand. In my view, the ethnographic value of his manuscript is enormous. Yet his writing has been overlooked.

Perhaps, as I have noted, this is because of the florid language, his assimilationist politics, his willingness to find common ground between the stories of his forebears and Christian values, or perhaps because Ramsay Smith published the work under his name (Jones 1993: 304). The circumstances of that piece of plagiarism are not well known.

The entry for Ramsay William Smith (1859–1937) in the *Australian Dictionary of Biography* (Elmslie and Nance 1988: 674-5) states that he was a "physician, naturalist, anthropologist and civil servant". He certainly worked with Aborigines (David Unaipon in particular), published two major works, *Myths and Legends of the Australian Aborigines* (1930) and *In Southern Seas* (1924), and contributed to the section of Aborigines in *The Australian Encyclopaedia* (1925–6), but his professional training was in medicine. His medical career was punctuated by unfortunate incidents and unpopular opinions, and worsened when he discovered bubonic plague in Adelaide in 1900. His anthropological record is also a mixed bag. His glass negative slides of Aborigines at the Murray Mouth are an invaluable record, but his role as a "recorder" of myths and legends is less than transparent. In Smith's (1930: 7) introduction he states: "It is a collection of narratives as told by pure blooded aboriginals of various tribes who have been conversant with the subject from childhood." When the book appeared, Smith was criticised in the *Times Literary Supplement* (1931: 233) for his "pretty pretty" language and importation of a "whole Olympus of deities". In his "Informants File" Tindale (nd, b) writes that Ramsay Smith wrote "romantic rubbish"; harsh words, he admits, but in his view, Smith used "highly improbable concepts entirely foreign to the real stories of an Australian prelithic [*sic*] people". Tindale was aware that Unaipon contributed some of the stories, but held Smith responsible for rewriting them in a "florid style more characteristic of collections of European myths" (*ibid.*). However, it would appear that the flourishes are Unaipon's, not Smith's. Indeed Smith (1930: 8) states that the changes he has made in the indigenous narratives are "few and slight" and the Unaipon (1924–5) handwritten version predates Smith's interest in the material.

There are various reports of the way in which Unaipon collected the stories that appear in Ramsay Smith's book. In the *Register* (Anon. 1925) I read an account of a suggestion by Sir Joseph Verco that Mr Unaipon collect materials, which was taken up by the Director of the Museum, Edgar R. Waite and the Professor of Anatomy at Adelaide University, Wood Jones; they, together with fellow member of the oversight committee Dr R. H. Pulleine, hoped to raise money to finance the travel. In early 1996 I had read Smith's (1930: 345-50) account of the Seven Sisters story. Later that year I read the Unaipon handwritten manuscript and the version of the story he published as "The Mungingee" in *Home* (1925: 42-3); and in 1979 in *Southerly* I found that, save for a few minor changes in phrasing, the handwritten version of 1924 was the same story word for word, paragraph for paragraph, as appeared under Smith's name in 1930. What was the chronology? Happily, the Mitchell Library not only holds David Unaipon's manuscript, it also has the correspondence between Ramsay Smith and George Robertson of the publishing house Angus and Robertson (1932). It appears that for £150, in March 1927, Smith bought the copyright to Unaipon's stories. Unaipon had been paid "two guineas per 1,000 words" towards two 50,000-word volumes which Angus and Robertson planned to publish. Unaipon had delivered the manuscript by October 1926 but told Smith, whom he had known for some twenty years and whom he had previously approached for assistance in funding his story-collecting travels, that he had heard nothing from the publishers in twelve months (*ibid.*: 100). Smith was not prepared to do anything about the material until he clarified how things stood between Unaipon and the publishers. This he did in late 1926 (*ibid.*: 103). The typescript manuscript was sent to him and by September 1927 Smith wrote to Robertson (16/9/1927) of his "enormous amount of pains-taking work" on the manuscript: "I think the literary result will prove that it was worth writing". I am not sure what this could have entailed but in 1930 *Myths and Legends of the Australian Aboriginals* appeared under Smith's name. It contains Unaipon's (1924–5) stories almost word for word. All Smith owned was the copyright. He could reproduce the material but why was he able to pass it off as his? Jones (1989: 11) suggests perhaps Unaipon was unaware of the fraud. Wherever the truth lies, it is plain that

Smith appropriated Unaipon's material. There is still the question of moral rights in the material and that needs further attention.

David Unaipon might have been the first to be published, but in 1934, Reuben Walker (*c.*1859–1935) wrote a wonderful account of growing up amongst the Ramindjeri of Encounter Bay and Yaraldi at Raukkan.[21] Reuben's spelling and expression in this forty-page manuscript require some concentration, but I know of no comparable document for the Ngarrindjeri. The typed manuscript is in Tindale's *Journal of Researches of South East of South Australia* (1934–7: 185-217). Although it is obvious that he has drawn on it in developing his understanding of the navel cord relationship, trade, seasonal camping sites, apart from an acknowledgement in Tindale and Pretty (1980), he has not written of Walker as one of his prime informants. What might Tindale have learned had he had the opportunity to work further with Reuben Walker or asked old Mark Wilson (1868–1940) to write for him also. Mark Wilson was literate and could type; his grandson, Victor Wilson, tells me "the scholar", as Mark Wilson was known, could also take shorthand. One wonders if there is not a manuscript of Mark Wilson's hidden away in some collection of papers.

Reuben Walker's life story encapsulates the early history of contact for those Ngarrindjeri living on the coast. He was the son of a Ramindjeri woman, of the Rapid Bay side, and an unknown early whaler or sealer at Encounter Bay. His mother, Elizabeth, was the daughter of Martha (Suke), a Parnkala woman of Port Lincoln and one of the "lawless whites" of Kangaroo Island. Initially Reuben Walker lived amongst the Ramindjeri at Encounter Bay, but he was scorned by both whites and his mother's people, as his name Pulpulumi, "outcast" or "friendless one", indicates. His mother died when he was still young and he was reared by Old Harry of Rumply Point and his wife. He considered them grandparents and writes fondly of his relationship with Old Harry. By 1872 his grandfather had taken Reuben to Raukkan to be taught by Taplin. However, Reuben stayed less than a year. The children there called him names that disparaged his racial heritage (Walker 1934: 191). By his own account he learned to read and write not at Raukkan, but from a young woman when he was working at a station in the Ninety Mile

131

Desert. He was eighteen and there must have been other distractions, but he paid her half his wages for eight months for the privilege of learning. Reuben Walker considered Point McLeay to be a hostile environment, but when he visited Poonindie Mission at Port Lincoln in 1884 he described it as a "horror mission station". Eventually he settled in Goolwa in 1887 and remained there for the rest of his life. Through his travels and family connections he was familiar with Ramindjeri, Yaraldi and Kaurna culture. He mourns the passing of the old people: only Clarence Long and Karloan are left, he says. Walker (1934: 199) claims the last Ramindjeri, Tommy Holmes, was buried in 1912.

At times in Walker's accounts, it is clear that mission attitudes have had an impact. With respect to mourning, Walker records that women shave their heads, and daub the body with charcoal and ashes. This he witnessed as a boy. Writing at the age of seventy-five, he considers it "the most filthy thing" women do (1934: 210). We also need to read over his references to older women as "hags". It is a designation found in other ethnographies, until quite recently (Hart and Pilling 1960). What is important is that Walker is offering eyewitness accounts of the daily lives of the Ramindjeri at Goolwa and in these accounts women are engaged in rituals that require discipline and skill.

The family of Alfred Cameron were literate but, as for Walker, literacy came at a price. Also like Walker, the Camerons have left many important written documents. Lola Cameron Bonney (1923–93), his grand-daughter, published a number of Ngarrindjeri stories, and there is a great deal yet to be published. Peter Mansfield has much of it carefully catalogued at his place at Trunceena on the Coorong. Nancy Taylor explained in her letter to Peter about Lola's family. Grandfather Alfred Cameron was the son of Jack Cameron, a Scot, and Princess Nellie (daughter of the "Chiefteness of the Temprominjeri Tribe"). For a period, Alf and his wife Jessie Cameron (née Forrest, adopted by George Mason), lived at Point McLeay, so that their children, including Lola's mother, Lily, could be educated, but it was an unhappy time. In 1903 Alf Cameron sought permission for his children to attend the all-white school, eleven kilometres to the north-west of "The Needles". Before they could be admitted, all families attending the school had to agree. All but one family signed. It seems in this family literacy was worth enduring a number of indignities. Cameron (1913: 747) told the 1913 Royal Commission that he bought a vehicle so he could get his children ten kilometres to school.

Lola Cameron Bonney lived with her grandparents from the age of five. Her book *Out of the Dreaming* (1990) is a collection of poems, photographs and stories passed down through her family. Her short vocabulary of Ngarrindjeri words indicates a knowledge of plants, fish, and the many spirits that occupy Ngarrindjeri lands. In Cath Ellis' notes (1962–6 (1): 52-4) there are several of Lola Cameron Bonney's poems. As well as writing, Lola Cameron Bonney was willing to be recorded and her descendants spend many happy hours listening to Aunty Lola and Uncle Ron. It is apparent that the telling of stories about family, special places, signs and sorcery was common place in her family. It is also apparent that there is an accommodation of other religions: "I went to Sunday school as a kid and was taught different things about religion. I just remember that someone is up there who sees the whole thing and is looking after you. Here we call him *Ngurunderi*, along the Coorong, he taught us" (Bonney 1982).

Leila Rankine (1932–92) worked for the Centre for Aboriginal Studies in Music (CASM) and her interviews (Breen 1989) tell us a great deal about Ngarrindjeri musical practice. In putting together *The Ngarrindjeri People* (1990) for use in schools, the South Australian Education Department drew on her stories. Annie Koolmatrie (Ely 1980: 53) remembers Leila Rankine telling stories she'd learned from her parents and grandfather on holidays on the Coorong. Her poetry celebrates the beauty of the Coorong, her affection for and connection to Ngarlung. I have also located a typescript of a lecture she gave at the Goolwa Seminar, University of Adelaide, 10 January 1974 during their Summer School of Environmental Studies. There she describes Raukkan, where she lived until 1963; the plenty of the waters; the vineyards, orchard and vegetable gardens; and the repressive permit system. Everyone needed a permit to live on the reserve and one even needed to get permission to have deceased relatives buried at Raukkan. When her fourth child was born in 1959, Leila was asked if she had a permit for the child and was informed that, as she did not, the two-week-old baby could be removed from her care. "Over my dead body," Leila replied. In 1986 (Department of Education 1990: 172) Leila dubbed "assimilation" a "dirty word". It was their policy to take the children away, grow them up in the city, educate them and so dies out the Aboriginal race after three generations . . . That was their policy of assimilation. Maybe it was their own way to create a genocide. At Goolwa Leila Rankine (1974a: 3) had said: There was nothing done to encourage the preservation of the age-old traditions and culture of the Coorong and Lower Murray tribes. In her opinion, Aboriginal people were encouraged to leave the reserve, but no training was available to help them become self-sufficient. In light of her portrait of life on the mission, the accomplishments of David Unaipon and the record he has left in his writing are even more remarkable. Veronica listens as I read this section: In 1962 my husband Jim and I had to get permission from the Protection Board to go home for my grandmother's funeral and I had to get permission for Margaret, my daughter, too. She was about ten months old. We were given twenty-four hours or the welfare or the police would come and take Margaret from us. Like other literate Ngarrindjeri, Leila Rankine has not escaped the nay-sayers who mutter that she didn't really write those poems.[22]

There are no doubt other records of Leila Rankine's speeches to be found. However, when she is remembered, it is for what she was able to pass on by word of mouth, to the next generation. Veronica Brodie: I believe today and from what my sister has told me that what's there is very precious to us, in those waters. It's a part of the women's business and being one, I guess, who's been entrusted with this story, I feel that I have to respect what's there, and I don't know just how much of it I can tell . . . it's a very big strain on me, in particular, because I know what Leila has passed on to me, what Mum gave her, that I want to tell it; I want to clear this air and I know that there's women like Ellen, Debbie, my daughters, and other young women out there that we need to tell it to now because, like I say, we always say we'll tell it one day, but I may never be here tomorrow; I only live for one day at a time. George Trevorrow: Aunty Leila was one of the, you know, special ladies within our group which I think everybody had a lot of respect for. She

134

was lucky in one way that when it came time for her to go, you know, she had time. During that time she had time to express to her family or her immediate family her orders on when she was going to pass away.

Aunty Daisy Rankine also writes. She has decided it is time to tell some of the stories and for the past ten years has been working on a book: I'm putting all the knowledge in it and by the time I'm finished Ellen will be fifty years old. Ellen typed up the story of my lifestyle. I lived a corrupt life after my late husband passed away and I then became a Christian and got baptised in Lake Albert at Meningie, and it hit me then it was time for me to do my duty and put it down on paper. I'm a great-grandmother of six and there's many more to come, and I think it's time for me now as a great-grandmother to put my family history down on paper. Ellen hasn't seen the traditional part. She will get the sign. She will be touched. The spirits will be with her. Ellen smiles quietly, I'm listening to the stories now. Several of Daisy Rankine's stories concerning the sacred nature of the waters of the Lower Murray have been in typescript form since at least 1995. They are stories I have heard her tell on a number of occasions, of the *mulyewongk*, *thukapi* (turtle), *nori* (pelican), of *ngatji* and the creation of the land, river, lakes and sea. The authenticity of her stories has also been doubted because she is the only person who has set down certain versions (Mathews 1996: 165ff.).

With the work of literate Ngarrindjeri discounted, oral traditions held to be the products of fallible memories, and many Ngarrindjeri themselves hostile to any recording of their culture, the experts remain the outside observers: the museums, libraries and archives. The gatekeepers to the field and the repositories of wisdom are the curators, archivists, and anthropologists. Doreen Kartinyeri's books establish her as a serious research scholar. In Tindale's papers he has a clipping from the Adelaide *Advertiser* (11/6/1981) about her work on genealogies. He saw her as a researcher. But the Royal Commission did not consider her one of the museum "experts". The Berndts (1993) did not take account of her published material on genealogies. Her view of her culture was not that of the guardians of the written word. The hallmark of "authenticity" in an oral culture is transmission of knowledge from one generation to the next, not literacy. Because she is literate, Doreen has been dismissed as an "expert" on her own culture, rather than understood as heir to a long-standing Ngarrindjeri tradition: literacy and an interest in recording aspects of Ngarrindjeri culture. She is also heir to a long-standing tradition of mistrusting literate Aborigines on matters of tradition by "expert" outsiders. If, for a number of reasons, "objective outsiders" did not happen to write of things mentioned by the literate insiders, the latter is found to be at fault. When they theorise, it is "nonsense".

But let a Ngarrindjeri poet have the last word. Margaret Brusnahan (1992) has published several volumes of poetry and her work contains searing critiques of mission life. For her the publication of the report on the Stolen Generations was belated recognition of the harm done to her as a young child taken from her home and reared in a foreign religion.

Threads of Dreamtime

Accept my Life Style as I accept yours,
Your ways your system governed by Laws.
Or should I agree that you're right and I'm wrong.
Believe as you do that my culture is gone.

You want me to believe your Christian views.
Well as a black person I'd like to ask you
When somebody's dead should I then deny.
That I already knew from the minca bird's cry?

So don't question my culture, let my spirit fly free.
For my ties to this Land are important to me.
My land, my people are spirits entwined
In a Life that is woven with threads of Dreamtime.

© Margaret Brusnahan

Wururi: Many Dialects, One Body

The threads are woven in stories such as those about *Ngurunderi* where the strands and design, the part and the whole are made manifest. Another Ngarrindjeri story, that of *Wururi*, the spider from whose body language is generated, also concerns the relation of the part to the whole. It tells of the coming into being of language in the Lower Murray, and provides a way of understanding both the underlying unity of the language and the differentiation into dialects (Meyer 1846: 204-5; Berndt *et al.* 1993: 237-8). Today people speak of the Ngarrindjeri language but from the early vocabularies it is apparent that a number of "dialects" were spoken in this region.[23] These languages or dialects—Yaraldi, Tangani, Ramindjeri, Warki and Portaulan—belong to the Pama-Nyungan language family. They are closer to the languages of the southeast and Victoria than they are to Kaurna, the language of the peoples on the other side of the Mount Lofty Ranges.[24] Most frequently, one hears "Ngarrindjeri" for land and language, but I have heard lively and passionate debates around these terms. Val Power is insistent that I use "Yaraldi" as the language name. The Berndts use "Kukabrak". Daisy Rankine is the only person I know who has spontaneously used that term.

Taplin (1873:1) observed that the "Narrinyeri" might fight amongst themselves but they presented a united front to outsiders. On the other hand, Clarke (1994: 81) writes that a high level of political cohesion has never been a characteristic of the region. Obviously, context is important. The Ngarrindjeri lived in small family groups within which there were conflicts but there was also an overarching structure. Should we consider the Ngarrindjeri a loose confederacy? A nation? A constellation of closely related languages? One manifestation of the underlying unity was the institution of the *tendi*, a unified system of governance which operated at clan and interclan levels, with formal "leaders" known as *Rupelli*.[25] Disputes could be resolved at the local family or clan level and at the level of the Ngarrindjeri nation. The spider body as the origin of language is another way of thinking about the relationship between different entities. But what is the nature of this unity symbolically represented in the body of the spider?

Wururi is said to have roamed about at night, scattering fires while people slept—a dangerous practice—and she further exercised her bad temper by "growling", that is, condemning others (Tindale 1937: 117). When she died, there was much happiness and the people gathered to feast and celebrate. The Ramindjeri ate of her flesh first and, as other groups arrived from the north and the east, they too ate, each devouring different parts of the body and each

137

then speaking a distinct language. The sequence of the arrivals mirrors that recorded in stories and songs of migration into the area. No one, we should note, arrives from the west. The Ramindjeri, in this account, are the most westerly of those sharing the language and body of the spider, and indeed the languages further west are very different from those of the Lower Murray. According to the *Wururi* story, the differentiation of languages happened before *Ngurunderi* made his journey down the Murray River. It was through his various interactions with existing life and land that he created the landscape as we see it today and laid down the law for Ngarrindjeri to follow, but the language groups were already in place.

The Berndts identified the spider as a "tarantula", a species not native to Australia. However, a corruption of that name, "Triantelope", is commonly used for the huntsman spider, one of the few spiders not averse to contact with humans (McKeown 1936: 85) and almost certainly the spider in the story of *Wururi*. Huntsman spiders are harmless, remain hidden during the day and, rather like *Wururi*, hunt at night. The female huntsman spins a complex, layered, cushioned egg sac, which she protects by holding it wrapped within her legs. When her spiderlings first venture forth from this protective sac spun from her body, they stay connected and supported by silken threads. To feed they crowd around their mother and from her mouth eat pre-digested food. Finally they scatter far and wide. These are powerful images which can enrich our understanding of the *Wururi* story. We can imagine the spiderlings feeding around the mouth as "eating language". When they scatter, these newly nourished spiderlings flourish as independent but related dialects, just as *Ngurunderi's* sons went forth to settle new lands. All this must remain speculation, but whatever it is that caught the attention of early Ngarrindjeri story-tellers in the behaviour of the huntsman spider, it is unlikely that the identification of that spider species with the origins of language was random.

Neither the Berndts nor Meyer comment on the significance of associating language with a spider, a female one at that. However, it is, I think, noteworthy that language originates from a woman's body who, as a spider, is a spinner of webs, in particular a protective egg sac in which to nurture her young. The symbolism of the female spider runs through the stories of many Indigenous peoples. Spiderwoman is a well known and revered character in Native American stories. In her poem "Grandmother", Paula Gunn Allen (1984: 14) writes of Spiderwoman who spins the world into existence out of pure thought, from her own body. This is no pragmatic, profane activity, but a sacred moment of creation. Having created she disappears, but for those who follow:

> After her,
> the women and the men weave blankets into tales of life,
> memories of light and ladders,
> infinity-eyes, and rain.
> After her I sit on my laddered rain-bearing rug
> and mend the tear with string.

Mending the tear is a task that Ngarrindjeri have begun, but the work to be done is vast. The generation who spoke language fluently has passed. There were explicit acts of repression and rather more subtle messages to the old people that the language was "primitive", and ultimately an embarrassing hindrance to their children. Scottie (Alan) Cameron stated his father spoke twelve languages, but would not teach his children at all, a practice Scottie considered to be silly. He told Cath Ellis (1962–5 (3): 9): The race is dying, and these things are very interesting. Jean Rankine remembers when the language was repressed; she has been part of the revival; and today addresses her children and grandchildren in Ngarrindjeri: I was born here at Raukkan, then went to live at Point Pearce when I was six till I was eleven or twelve and since then I've lived here. I did work in the school, prior to working in the Council Chambers, and I got very much involved in heritage and history with teaching the language to children. That was from 1976 onwards. This is one of the oldest educational buildings in South Australia and we're very proud of that fact. But in those days they weren't allowed to practise their culture or their language. And if they did, they were punished severely. So way back from when Taplin first came here at Raukkan, it was stopped right up until my husband's days, it wasn't allowed to be spoken in school, the language. But when I started up there, I was given the choice of being able to teach the children in their own language, about their culture and to be able to give them their identity back, which gave me a lot of pleasure. Right to this very day, I have young adults coming up to me and saying, "Do you remember those days, Aunty Jean, when we used to sit around and talk?" I call it *yanun* time. That was just sitting around like the old people used to, like Nanna. They'd sit in a circle and it gave me a lot of pleasure that the kids wanted so much to learn about their culture. We were making the circle bigger. And in fact, we practise it at home as well with our grandchildren. We talk to them in language as well.

The Circle of Language

In her lifetime Leila Rankine contributed to the documentary record of Ngarrindjeri language, song, poetry and history, but it is memories of her spoken words that are cherished by her descendants. Veronica Brodie will cite her sister as a source, just as Doreen Kartinyeri will cite her Aunty Rosie, but both these women are also prepared to engage with the literate world. It is an unusual situation to work with people who place greater value on what their elders have told them (when their elders would talk) than on what is written about them in scholarly texts, but who are prepared to go back to school to learn their language; to work through the early vocabularies of missionaries such as Taplin and Meyer; and to struggle with Tindale's genealogies. Edith Rigney and Veronica Brodie, for instance, attend classes at the Tauondi Community College at Port Adelaide where their General Studies classes include language and weaving taught by a Ngarrindjeri woman. Teaching materials in the schools draw on Ngarrindjeri speakers and nineteenth-century vocabularies. The circle of language is being woven from the knowledge of the elders who still know a significant amount of language and who can "read" the different orthographies of Taplin, Tindale and the Berndts, as only a native speaker can. The circle of language learning is expanding. It radiates outwards like a beautifully coiled Ngarrindjeri mat.

One of the things my father always impressed on me was that his pronunciation of the words was correct, Leila Rankine (1974b: vi) observed, while complaining that whites miss the beauty of the language in their interpretations. The early vocabularies can only hint at the richness of the language—it takes a speaker to bring it to life—

140

and, apart from the Berndts (1993), and Taplin's bible translations, there are few texts in Ngarrindjeri. Penney (1842b) castigated those colonists whose prejudice led them to overlook the poetry "which evinces a greater amount of original and imaginative genius than our imperfect knowledge of their tongue will allow us to demonstrate by a translation". Taplin (1873: 123) recognised Ngarrindjeri pride in their beautiful, distinctive language "possessing inflections ours does not". On the other hand, Wyatt (1879: 160) complained of their "slovenly habit of clipping, or contracting words in ordinary use" (an aspect of the language that Taplin finds worthy), but recognised their creativity in compounding words to form new ones. "Hat", for instance, was *kurl-inyeri*, literally, "what appertains to the head" (Meyer 1843: 74). The language was dynamic. It could encompass introduced items. A loaf of bread was known as *laialdurar*, from the word for "a large piece of gum composed of a number of drops stuck together" (*ibid.*).[26] The language also encoded gender distinctions: *mayoo kombo* for the outer or man rainbow and *ummaiche kombo* for the inner or female rainbow (Wyatt 1879: 170).

Ngarrindjeri called whitefellas *kringkari* because of the similarity of their skin colour to that of a corpse after the scarf-skin had been removed in the smoking process of mortuary rituals. The first white men at Encounter Bay were considered to be returning ancestral spirits, and some Ramindjeri thought they "recognised certain of the strange white individuals as their forebears" (Tindale nd, c; Meyer 1843: 60). Explaining the appearance of strangers in this way brought them within the Ngarrindjeri world; by categorising them as "dead", their bad behaviour could be explained and maybe even made amenable to Ngarrindjeri law. The word *kringkari* is still in use—I heard myself being referred to as the *kringkari mi:mini*—but there is now a more historically grounded explanation of the arrival of whites in the southeast.

There is a care and comfort in speaking to another who understands *nukkin*, "look"; *noppin*, "walk"; *porli*, "child"; *mi:mini*, "woman"; *korni*, "man"; and the difference between a *krink* (short for *kringkari*) and a *Nunga* (Aboriginal person).[27] Such speech is also a way of signalling to outsiders that they are in the presence of difference. Certain topics, especially those that concern the body and sexuality, are more easily broached in language. As Doreen Kartinyeri explained: They don't sound dirty when I say them like Aunty Rosie did. Neither clinical nor vernacular language affords the respect and privacy that is possible in Ngarrindjeri. Important plants, animals and fish are rarely called in English by the older generation. Isobelle tells me she is warned if she uses Point Pearce words at Murray Bridge. I'll quickly get corrected. People say, you know, you're a Ngarrindjeri person, don't talk that language. I have heard people use Pitjantjatjara words and words from other Aboriginal languages, but when challenged they always know when it is not Ngarrindjeri.

The people of this region take an interest in their language and are great folk etymologists. From the earliest records onwards we find examples of people finding meaning, albeit different ones, in their language. As we have seen, the place-name Goolwa has many different meanings attributed to it. People play with words, appropriate phrasings they like, imitate the Raukkan accent, the Point Pearce accent, and Scottish accents as well. The speech of Ngarrindjeri today carries information about early and more recent contacts. Peter Sutton (1989) has pointed out that in the Adelaide region of South Australia a number of people of Aboriginal descent speak a distinctive dialect. One feature he identifies is the post-vocalic 'r', as in the standard North American pronunciation of Victor Harbor (and spelling). There is a pride in names that carry certain European ancestry and an interest in their Scottish forebears, those mad Scots on whom certain behaviours can be blamed.

The Ngarrindjeri I know have a sense of humour which is robust and relies on inside references to shared experiences that are interpreted in a distinctively Ngarrindjeri fashion. Victor Wilson puns until it is painful. What is a pun? he asks. "I'll tell you the next time you do it, Victor." A little later he comments that what I am saying, Doesn't ring a "bell" and laughs. On one occasions we're singing hymns, What about "hers"? comes the mischievous question from a senior man to a senior woman. There is also an intellectual curiosity about language and people ask about words they don't know. Veronica asks what is a "think-tank". I explain. They're running on empty, she retorts. What is a prurient interest? I am asked of a submission I was writing. I explain. Oh, kinky white men, comes the quip in reply. What mean "pike"? Tom Trevorrow asked me as we were driving due west from Boston. I delivered a brief historical account of turnpikes and customary payment of tolls for use of such roads. It probably didn't make much sense. You need to live here to appreciate the reliance on cars, absence of public transport, and resistance to tax-funded highways. Similarly you need to be around Ngarrindjeri families to know of their concerns, their respect for their elders, their love of language and song.

As I got to know people better, I realised there was a formal, polite English, heavily mission-inflected at times, which older people use when speaking to outsiders and then there is the language they speak with each other. On such occasions their conversation is peppered with references to the names of relatives, places, and resources in the Ngarrindjeri language. To follow, one needs some knowledge of genealogies, institutional histories, personal achievements, local geography and history. Story-tellers like Maggie Jacobs punctuate their presentations with *ána* (isn't it), the interrogative particle. It is part of a story-teller style wherein the listener is engaged in the story by being asked to confirm certain details.

"Many of us", write Joy Harjo and Gloria Bird (1997: 21-2), editors of *Reinventing the Enemy's Language: Contemporary Native Women's Writings of North America*,

> are using the "enemy language" with which to tell our truths, to sing, to remember ourselves in troubled times . . . In our tribal cultures the power of language to heal, to regenerate, and to create is understood. These colonizers' languages, which often usurped our own languages or diminished them, now hand back emblems of our cultures, our own designs: our beadwork, quills if you will. We've transformed these enemy languages.

By becoming attentive to the power of language to "capture" native peoples and reduce them to unidimensional stereotypes, these writers are part of a decolonisation process. These Indigenous writers have reinvented and redirected the language imposed on them into a powerful tool of resistance and resilience (Murphy 1997: 10-11). "There is a native tenacity to persist through . . . Our physical presence denies the American myth of the vanishing red man. The stories and songs are subversive" (*ibid.*: 30). Ngarrindjeri story-tellers, songsters and weavers may have incorporated non-Indigenous items and they may no longer have fluency in the languages of their grandparents, but, like the women of whom Harjo and Bird write, they have transformed the enemy language. These Ngarrindjeri have made the English they speak and the songs they sing theirs. The songs and stories resonate with Ngarrindjeri imagery and the rhythm of the land. This may, ultimately, be one of their greatest triumphs.

3

Singing: *"Pakari Nganawi Ruwi"*
(Prayer song for my country)

Pinkie Mack leads the Big River Corroboree, Goolwa
(*Advertiser*, 12 February 1951)

Pinkie Mack: Singing of Welcome and War

"Pata winema ngama leiwuninang ania akaka . . ." sang Pinkie Mack
at the Sturt Re-enactment in 1951. Ten-year-old Veronica Brodie
saw the party who had retraced the 1600-kilometre journey of
Charles Sturt down the Murray River come ashore at Raukkan.
I was there when the whaleboat pulled in. The fellows started to dance,
Les Gollan, Havelock Carter, and Big Bert [Wilson], my brother, was

dancing. Grant Taylor, who was playing Sturt, backed down, it was so realistic. Then they came back and walked up to the Sturt monument. Henry Rankine was eleven and remembers Big Bert, also called "Big Eagle", who rushed down and frightened those disembarking from the army duck. Doreen Kartinyeri, sixteen at the time, remembers that army duck coming out of the water. Everyone was in shock. We were in a big group, waving to the whale boats and motor boats, but the big one was coming in and we thought it would get stuck in the sand in the shallow water. There was Rodney Taylor playing George McLeay and Grant Taylor played Charles Sturt.

From Raukkan, the party moved onto Hindmarsh Island, where they spent the night, and the next day pushed onto Goolwa. Vietch (1951) wrote in the Adelaide *Advertiser* of Pinkie Mack at Raukkan sitting on a hillock near the men as she thumped a pillow, rocked from side to side, chanted the native war song and urged the young men, who were liberally daubed with black and white shoe cleaner, to "drive the white men back to the sea". On Hindmarsh Island he states they danced the "Big River" corroboree:

> the native traditional story of the Murray River. Most of the natives had not taken part in this corroboree before, but they were taught the legend and steps of the dance by 81-year-old Mrs. Pinkie Mac, a full-blood native of Point McLeay. While the painted young natives danced, whooping, shouting, and brandishing weapons, Mrs. Mac stood beside them chanting, singing, and crying to urge them on.

There is a certain romance in declaring that only one old lady knew the story and song for this ritual, and certainly a lack of appreciation for what was being transacted to depict her as the enthusiastic teacher thumping and rocking while her students, the men, whoop wildly and attempt to repel the invaders. There are also factual errors. Pinkie Mack was closer to ninety-three than eighty-one and her name "Pinkie" supposedly came from the "spoiling of her colour" from her white father, George Mason, the Sub-Protector of Aborigines.[1]

Fortunately we have other accounts of the 1951 event. Daisy Rankine, aged fifteen, was there when her grandmother sang. Looking back she recalls the mixed emotions. *Pakanu* [mother's mother] was a traditional woman and when she sang her welcoming song, that was the last corroboree. She was dancing with a pillow, like

146

the traditional rolled skins the women used to beat the rhythm. The pillow stopped her from hurting herself, so she would not get too excited with the men dancing and doing what she could, telling them how to dance and sing. At Goolwa, they waited till nearly dark and it was a great strain, but by doing this Nanna Pinkie saved the family title. At Tailem Bend Janet Smith was helping Nanna by welcoming them there, through her father's title, that's George Karpeny [Pinkie Mack's brother]. And yes, Nanna was angry, like she was mourning the loss of ceremonies. We weren't allowed to speak language or *ringballin* [corroboree] and we weren't allowed to complain. But that day in 1951, the descendants of Louisa Karpeny had affirmed it was their land. That day Louisa's daughter, Pinkie Mack, and Louisa's son's daughter, Janet Smith, were giving ceremonial permission for the "strangers" to come ashore, and also asserting the position of their family vis-à-vis other Ngarrindjeri lineages. That day in February 1951 the law of "Queen" Louisa Karpeny ran through the land as Ngarrindjeri "performers", not for the first time, were officially permitted to sing and dance. There is, of course, a bitter irony that this celebration was to mark an event on the colonists' calendar which had heralded the beginning of the dispossession of the Ngarrindjeri. Charles Sturt had traced the Murray River to where it emptied into the Southern Ocean in 1830; by 1836 South Australia had been proclaimed as a British Province and by the 1850s Goolwa was a thriving port. The tensions inherent in that "welcoming moment" of 1830 and the re-enactment of 1951 were not lost on the participants. Daisy Rankine: A couple of weeks after the Sturt Re-enactment, Nanna Pinkie's nerves went on her. The stress was too much. She was admitted into Glenside just after that and she died in 1954.

Neville Gollan was thirteen in 1951. He had taken care to position himself where he could see what was happening, but not be caught. We were in the woolshed, up in the top of the pulley, watching and keeping quiet, but someone coughed or sneezed and they said, "Come down here", and we got a good hiding and then they painted us up. There was Uncle George and Havelock. They were much older than us. As we talk about the re-enactment, Victor Wilson and Neville Gollan dispel any notion that this was the first time this ceremony had been performed. The men were really getting into it, jumping through the fires.

Every marking they had on their bodies had a meaning. Doug Wilson explains that the men had rehearsed, by themselves, out of the sight of women, up on Big Hill behind the she-oak. We had to do it properly. The dancing had to be fast and brief. The leg movements needed to be perfect. Pinkie Mack was in charge of the performance on the day, but she did not "teach" the men everything they knew.

Victor indicates the spears in the photograph. All the spears were made by Proctor Wilson. I call him grandfather, on my father's side, really his uncle. Afterwards Mrs Angus, Mr Bartlett and Mr Swalling took the spears. When Doreen reads this, she adds, Ross Swalling was a superintendent at Raukkan and so was Clarrie Bartlett until the mid-1940s, after that he was a Protector. Doris, my sister, was named after Clarrie Bartlett's sister. I'll ask Mrs Angus if she knows where those spears are now. The Camp Coorong Museum would be an appropriate place for these ceremonial objects where, set amongst other Ngarrindjeri work, they would pay tribute to those women and men who kept the knowledge of ceremony alive into the 1950s and beyond.

What Pinkie Mack brought out in 1951 was neither new nor unknown to the Ngarrindjeri participants. There had been an earlier re-enactment in 1930, on the centenary of Sturt's voyage down the Murray, and some Ngarrindjeri attended both events. Maggie Jacobs, Marj Koolmatrie and Lindsay Wilson were still at school in 1930 and, along with the other children on the mission, contributed to the cost of the Sturt Memorial built to mark that occasion. Uncle Lindsay Wilson spoke with pride, albeit tinged with irony, of being the first to save up for a stone for the monument (Hemming 1997: pers. comm.). In the 1930s, there were still people alive who had participated in traditional ceremonies and, according to Uncle Lindsay, it was Milerum (Clarence Long) and "Muthani" (Stanton White, a relative of Pinkie Mack), who told the people how to paint up and to dance. By 1951, Uncle Lindsay said, there were not many who knew (*ibid.*). That may be so, but enough was known for there to be three performances in two days: the first one mid-day at Raukkan, the second that evening on Hindmarsh Island, and the last the next day at Goolwa. After a century of repressive policies and depopulation, Pinkie Mack could still marshall sufficient dancers who could put on the paint, have feather-bedecked spears to brandish, and be prepared sing and dance through that weekend in February. In the photograph of Pinkie Mack "urging the men on", we can see thirteen hand-held spears and the painted bodies of the men.[2] In the photographs from Grandmother Lola Sumner,[3] taken of the performance at Raukkan, when the men danced on the sandy shore of the lake down by the jetty, some thirty people are visible, including women standing on the rise above the men. In the other photograph of the group of seated men, some sixteen spears are

Ngarrindjeri men painted and dancing at Raukkan, 1951
(Lola Sumner, personal collection. SAM Archives.)

Ngarrindjeri men seated: Back Row (left to right): Geoff Carter, unknown,
Clyde Rigney, unknown, Les Gollan, Fred Sumner,
Havelock Carter, Bert Wilson, Sonny Rankine.
Front Row: Howard "Jack" Sumner, George Harris, Clark Rankine, unknown,
Oscar Kartinyeri, unknown, Adrian Rigney. (Also present: Andrew Sumner,
Lance Walker, Fred Long, Clarrie Long, Vernon Carter)
(Lola Sumner, personal collection. SAM Archives.)

visible and the men's bodies are painted with several different designs, indicating perhaps their membership of different clans (Woods 1879: xxvii). This occasion required preparation and co-operation. Just as women reminisce while they gather rushes and weave, so would the men have told stories as their bodies were painted and the spears decorated. Perhaps other songs were sung over the ritual paraphernalia as the paint was applied. The photographs are helpful in that they fill in some gaps, but they pose as many questions as they answer.

I had signed off on this section of the manuscript when, quite by chance, I located a tape fragment of Pinkie Mack singing. I had heard from a colleague that the ABC (then the Australian Broadcasting Commission) had recorded the entire Sturt Re-enactment. Each night interested Australians had tuned in to hear of the progress of the whaleboat down the Murray. I even have some dim childhood memory of sitting by our wireless at home. (The lot of the "explorers" was a favourite topic of my grandmother.) Perhaps, I thought, there is some mention of the singing and ceremonies on these tapes. Perhaps some Ngarrindjeri were interviewed. A couple of international phone calls and a research fee settled the matter. Radio Archives in Sydney dispatched copies of the "Sturt Report" as broadcast 8–11 February 1951.[4] There were excerpts from the speeches made by local dignitaries, marching bands, schoolchildren, property owners and a descendant of Charles Sturt, but not one Ngarrindjeri was interviewed. The noon-time visit to the mission, which Vietch (1951) depicts as "more than 300 natives" crowded onto the jetty to "goggle" the Sturt party, and which is remembered so vividly today as having an element of surprise, may indeed have been impromptu. Reporter Talbot Duckmanton (ABC 1951) recounts that the whaleboat and army ducks, having made good time crossing the lake on their way to Point Sturt, decided to call into the mission for "a bite of lunch". Doreen Kartinyeri, who was working as a "maid" for the superintendent at the time, says she had been busy running around and preparing food for days. So why was I doing that if they hadn't planned on calling in? she asks me. Duckmanton (*ibid.*), reports that some twenty young men donned their "warpaint" and performed a welcome dance. They were instructed by an old Aboriginal woman who he doubts knows how old she is but is said to know more about corroboree in this section of the river and lakes than anyone else.

The report follows the party as they rowed on to the overnight camp on Hindmarsh Island. Dancing took place as planned that evening but unfortunately there is no sound recording of that event. The focus of the "Sturt Report" is on the arrival of the Sturt party at Goolwa on Sunday, 11 February. These are the events that are scripted. The Army is thanked and the crew of the whaleboat join in a rousing singing of "*Viva la compagnie*". Anthony Sturt is presented with a medallion and reads from the journals of his great-grandfather. I check the entries of this part of Charles Sturt's (1833: 168-76) journey and find that as the party struggled through the muddy shoals and quicksands of the Goolwa Channel to the Murray Mouth, they were under constant surveillance from local people, who kept abreast of them and lit fires. Of the latter, Sturt (*ibid.*: 172) says, "the size of the fires at the extremity of the channel, seemed to indicate the alarm our appearance had occasioned". Sturt did not linger, as his men and supplies were close to exhausted. We do not know what might have happened had he explored the hummocks and Murray Mouth in any detail, but it is clear that the Ngarrindjeri, who already had some experience of whitefellas at the whaling stations at Encounter Bay, were not about to extend a warm welcome. Watchful Ngarrindjeri men were poised, ready to intervene should Sturt's party violate their law by desecrating sacred sites or interfering with their womenfolk. Several years later, Ngarrindjeri would kill Captain Barker at the Murray Mouth. This was not a place where one wandered about at will.

But what of the Ngarrindjeri descendants of the fierce land-holders of the Murray Mouth and their planned corroboree at Goolwa in 1951? It is only a snatch of sound and the tape quality is not good, but the voice of Pinkie Mack is clear, strong and vibrant. It pulsates. The men's cries punctuate the singing and their feet pound out the rhythm being marked by Pinkie Mack on her pillow. Tal Duckmanton (ABC 1951) describes the men in "full warpaint", accompanying Pinkie Mack's singing of the "Nuriya" corroboree which told of the first white man coming down the

151

river. Could this be a reference to *Ngurunderi*? No one appears to have interviewed Pinkie Mack, who could have given her age and perhaps clarified "Nuriya". Who, I wonder, told the ABC team that "Nuriya" was the name of the dance and provided details of the story? I make a working copy of this precious tape, cue it on my machine, phone Pinkie Mack's great-grand-daughter Ellen Trevorrow, and play the tape over the phone. I try to imagine how the sound is being received across the Pacific at Camp Coorong by the descendants of Pinkie Mack. Hitherto I knew this renowned songster only through the stories I have been told and the written records. Now I am riveted by her voice. This is not the solo performance for a research archive. This was not sung into a tape recorder. This was made in the context of an outdoor performance. The voice is strongly projected and, musicologist, Linda Barwick (1997: pers. comm.) tells me, with the use of vibrato and nasal overtones providing the amplification of sound needed to cut through the other noises being made by the dancers. And the song I am hearing is not the "*Pata winema*" song. When Daisy Rankine hears the tape, she tells me it is the "Big River" corroboree. *Pakanu* Pinkie sang that one too. She used to sing to us, all us grannies. Her daughter Ellen adds, You heard them when you were young and I had to wait until I was forty-two to hear them on tape! For those over sixty who were present, the 1951 celebrations are part of their lived reality. For the up-and-coming generations, it is near history about which they can now ask their elders.

It would appear that there were at least two songs sung during the Sturt Re-enactment. The group was "welcomed" at Raukkan and the "Big River" was celebrated at Goolwa, a pre-contact site for ceremonial gatherings. "Big River?" I ask Tom Trevorrow. "Is that about *Ngurunderi*?" "No. Big River was when all the groups gathered." Penney (Clarke 1991: 94) distinguishes between Milmenyra as the "Big Murray tribe" of the Coorong and the "Picannini tribe" of the Murray River.[5] Goolwa was a meeting place for the Ramindjeri of Encounter Bay, the Tangani of the Coorong and the Yaraldi of the lakes, so it would seem a particularly appropriate place for the "Big River" song to be sung. Doreen Kartinyeri adds that when Pinkie Mack sang "*Pata winema*" she was always seated, with the cushion on her lap, and she would pat on her right thigh. So the photograph of Pinkie Mack "urging the men" on is in all likelihood at Goolwa where she sang the "Big River" corroboree.

Until I played the tape and heard the snatch of that song, I had no idea I could ever hear a Ngarrindjeri ceremony. I had fallen into thinking that this was part of the "world that was". I had no way of asking about other songs that might have been sung in 1951. I now imagine there were more songs sung than these two, and I mutter away to myself about how notions of "authenticity" impede our understanding of what it is that people are actually doing when they sing on such occasions. Neither the Berndts nor Tindale was able to record songs as part of a performance in the 1930s and 1940s, yet in 1951 there was such an opportunity—not in the context of an initiation, but a performance nonetheless—in which men and women participated, with dancing, painting, ritual objects and a story. Unfortunately, there is a certain snobbery when it comes to according the status of "authentic" to ceremonies performed at the behest of non-Indigenous outsiders. Ceremonies performed far from the gaze of the "civilisation" are more likely to be deemed "real" than those performed on occasions such as the Sturt Re-enactment. However, drawing on my experience in other parts of Australia, I would say there is much to be learnt of local "traditions" from such "command performances". In areas where ceremonial life still flourishes, where people are still fluent in their languages, and where they still live on their own land, "command performances" are often a way of getting the necessary resources to stage a big ceremony. In some instances, it is the very request for a ceremony that makes the performance possible. Every time a ceremony is staged, it is a statement of the power and authority of the landowners to do so. Thus, asking for a performance legitimates the activity and constitutes a recognition of the authority of those involved. It also implicates the persons making the request in the performers' lives.

The organisers of the 1951 celebration provided logistic support (often crucial in staging big ceremonies) by allowing the party to use the barrages to cross over to Hindmarsh Island in time for the evening performance. Further, the Ngarrindjeri were being invited to perform at a time when things traditional were being actively undermined by the policy of assimilation and the practices of the Protection Board which separated families and rewarded those who pursued a western lifestyle. It is doubtful that the underlying reciprocity of the exchange was grasped by the organisers of the Sturt Re-enactment, for whom the Ngarrindjeri appear more as props than as persons with a stake in the "celebration". But the nature of the exchange did register on Ngarrindjeri lives. Pinkie Mack cracked under the strain. She had one opportunity to make a public statement about her authority and that of her lineage over the land. Moreover, the invitation came from the descendants of the colonisers, who thereby were acknowledging her authority. Could it be that the first performance is remembered fondly because it was the impromptu one where the Ngarrindjeri, as far as was possible within mission constraints, were in control of the agenda? And, much to their delight, they surprised the actors.

What sort of a report might an anthropologist have made of the performances in 1951? With the help of Ngarrindjeri who were present, especially Doreen Kartinyeri, some thirteen of the eighteen visible in the group photograph have been identified and another five known to have participated named. With further genealogical research I could map how the participants were related; time with Tindale's data might reveal something of their clan affiliations and marriage lines. I'd like to know the sequencing of the dancing and songs and whether the "audience" participated. How does Ngarrindjeri ceremonial life compare with other practices across Australia? Are there more tapes, photographs, and artefacts from the 1951 performance in existence? Perhaps, tucked away in personal or public archives, there may be documents which could add to our understanding of the 1951 re-enactment.[6] There may even be some film footage of the dancing. A film crew is mentioned on the "Sturt Report" of 10 February. With the assistance of Linda Barwick, a start has been made on the analysis of the various recordings of the "*Pata winema*" song. How well does this song fit within what we know of the music of the southeast of Australia? What might be learned of the meanings of the symbols and songs? What can this song tell us about the continuity of oral traditions in this area? How does this performance compare with other recorded instances of Ngarrindjeri ceremonial life? There are several accounts of nineteenth-century ceremonies, Ngarrindjeri testimonies regarding their singing, and the documentation of various observers through which I can explore some of these questions, but much will remain speculation.

Many Meanings: Few Recordings

Sung in a mixture of languages, including Pidgin, "*Pata winema*" was probably composed in the context of nineteenth-century fringe camps where there was a mixture of languages and intermarriage between groups from different regions. It is quite common for people to borrow words from elsewhere and even to sing songs with meanings which are obscure or unknown to them. Taplin observed of certain songs: "They will learn it with great appreciation if it seems to express some feelings which theirs does not" (1873: 143-4). Restricting access to the meaning of songs was also a way in which authority was maintained by the elders whose interpretations were accepted and trusted. Mike Gollan (Ellis 1962–6 (1): 31), having listened to Milerum singing, told Catherine Ellis in July 1963 that he couldn't get the words for the songs and the language but he supposes it must be so if Clarence (Milerum) says it. Only the sages of the society could interpret the songs that held the keys to mysteries of their world and their interpretations were believed.[7] Thus, it is not unusual for people to sing words they don't understand; but it may also be, when they say they don't know, that they are not the proper person to ask, that it is the wrong context in which to ask, or that the person asking does not have the right to be told.[8]

Albert Karloan told the Berndts (1993: 172) that the "*Pata winema*" song was sung during his 1882 initiation, but offered no further explanation. Daisy Rankine identifies "*Pata winema*" as a "welcoming song", whereas Flora Smith (née Kropinyeri) told Steven Hemming (1984; 1997: pers. comm.) it was a "cursing the white-fellas" song. It is quite possible that each saw the nature of the "welcome" to be given to the new arrivals in a different light. On the one hand a "welcome" can be hospitable, but on the other a "welcome"

155

might be quite war-like. It may be that the meaning attached to "welcome" has changed over the years to accommodate changing circumstances, and understandings of frontier relations. Annie Koolmatrie, recorded by Will Lobban (1969), offered no interpretation but in 1988 told Steven Hemming that the "*Pata winema*" song was about the coming of the white man, the taking of land, and had been composed by "King John", a relative of Jenny Christmas, from the mid-Murray Hills region.[9] In 1984 Flora Smith explained to her son, Paul, and Steven Hemming (1997a: 7-9) that the song was about the "*Whitepellie* (whitefellas)" coming from "*mileaway* (miles away)" and that when the old people did this corroboree they were "*piein, piein,* that's cursing, cursing". Hemming's tentative translation is: "Let's corroboree about the whitefellas from miles away who came and sat down on our country."

There is no recording of Pinkie Mack singing "*Pata winema*" at the 1951 re-enactment that I have been able to locate. I have, however, been able to hear, and play for their descendants, the 1965 recording that Catherine Ellis (LA 124) made of Pinkie's daughter, Ellen Brown, who sings "*Pata winema*" three times. When Ellen Trevorrow heard it, she recalled that she was with Nanna Brown that year, just before she moved to the Bonney Reserve, but she knew nothing of the recording. You see they didn't tell us what they were doing. I was living with her and didn't even know about it. Rosie Kropinyeri sang "*Pata winema*" for Ellis in 1965 (LA 106) and Doreen Kartinyeri recognised the song as soon as she heard it. Others also recognise the song and it is commonly referred to as "Nanna Pinkie's corroboree". However, neither Ellen Brown nor Rosie Kropinyeri gave Cath Ellis (*ibid.*) a translation of "*Pata winema*". Rosie Kropinyeri, having sung the song, comments, I forget the words. I don't really know what it is about, but I know they always used to sing that when I was with the ones that used to corroboree, and it stuck in my memory ever since. I used to sing it for my grandchildren. They laughed and laughed about it. They thought it was funny. She may not have recalled the details, but even in this brief account, it is apparent the song was learned in a ceremonial context.

But then there is James Brooks Kartinyeri who, in 1964, singing snatches of "*Pata winema*" several times for Cath and Max Ellis (LA

120a), was quite explicit that the song was about the gathering of cockles at Goolwa. It is an association which, according to Taplin (1873: 130), is encoded in the meaning of *Gutungald* (Goolwa), which he translates as "place of cockles". It is a place, I would note, that women today say had excellent cockling beds before the barrages raised the water levels and drowned them. James Brooks Kartinyeri learned the song from George Pantoni, who had spent quite a bit of time in the Goolwa–Victor Harbor area and "used to make a corroboree or two". When Kartinyeri demonstrates the action by which the sand is being stirred up by the cocklers, Max Ellis mistakenly thinks it is a dance step, but Kartinyeri corrects him: dancing would be *ngrilkulun*, this is getting cockles. The way one stirs the sand is distinctive and James knows the difference. The story James Brooks Kartinyeri tells of the song is localised and particularised in ways that other explanations of "*Pata winema*" are not. James shifts back and forth between story-telling mode and songs as he engages his audience with questions. "Sing it straight through", requests Max Ellis, but James has a picture to paint of the art of cockling, of the greeting of strangers, of the discovery that they are "our people" who then join in and all sing together. In this sense his version could be seen as a welcoming song in that the newcomers are accepted and included in the activity of cockling. Unfortunately James is so intent of telling the story of the song to Max and Cath Ellis, that he never actually sings the song straight through. However, from the text and rhythm it is definitely the same song.

James explains that now he lives on his own, it is hard to remember, but he says: When I am sitting by the fire, lying on my bed and my mind is just floating, I think about the old days and sometimes they come into my mind . . . and then I start singing. I'll get the sticks and then I'll just do as they were doing. For Max and Cath Ellis, James improvises with two wooden spoons. He recalls: *Koyi* means a basket, about that long, with a neck from one side to side of it, to put over the shoulder. They get the cockles. They put it in the sand and when the waves come up, it washes through. They get the cockles without dirt. . . . It's about this man and his wife. They were down there getting cockles. And then some others came over the hill and they looked and said, "Uh *ngangga*."

157

They were looking to see. . . . It was [at the] Nine Mile they was getting cockles. "*Ngangga*. Who there? Who are they? They look something like someone I know. Who are they? Oh, *nga:tjagha*. Oh, they are ours. *Ku, li:wenl*. Oh, they are poking for cockles. *Ku, ku,* come on down. Let's get them cockles. James then sings a line, "*Parta winema, Nine Mile, li:wenena: nga; many many, tjatupulanda alpuli o malowo*", and continues his explanation of the questioning of the newcomers and establishes that they are *nga:tjagha* (us). They are our people. Then they all are into it. "*Partay winemay Nine Mile, li:w/ngn(h)ena, many many tya:rtepelanda:l peliy an ngerruwuw, rrrrrrr.*" "What is the "rrrr"?" asks Max Ellis. They're getting cockles, James continues, they are down to fish and to bake in the ovens . . . and save some for fishing and . . . with the backwash of the waters, they take the dirt and leave the holes in the sand . . . That's what it means. That is it. That happened down the Coorong.[10]

While minor word changes may be explicable as individual variations, and at a stretch we could see all the versions as different kinds of welcome, the meaning James Brooks Kartinyeri gives to the "*Pata winema*" song is radically different from those Hemming was given. It has story content and place-names, and is about a traditional activity of the Goolwa area, at a named place, the Nine Mile. Further, James says he learnt the song down on the Coorong. *Koyi*, the basket which James mentions, is also the basket named by Pinkie Mack as one which *Nepelli*'s wives carried (Harvey 1939). The Berndts (1993: 211) mention a ceremonial basket called *koiyi* made out of human hair, two of which represented the full expanse of the turkey's tail feathers.[11] What might James have known of these items had he been asked? He certainly is one of the most forthcoming persons interviewed by Cath Ellis. At a minimum, we know that the cockling basket is celebrated in song and associated with one of the major Dreamings of the region. There may be a men's and a women's basket, of the same name but with a different structure.

James' exegetical style is very similar to that of Milerum working with Tindale on song texts. There are a few words to be translated, but there is a whole story to be told. It could be that George Pantoni brought it from up-river and localised it. Taplin (1873:

112; see also Berndt *et al.* 1993: 523) mentioned "Pantuni" as a young man in 1867, so he would have been initiated before Karloan (born 1864). Karloan and Pinkie Mack probably both learned it in similar contexts and their versions are close. It could be that Pantoni's version pre-dates the Pinkie Mack version which has now become a generic welcome song, no longer tied to a place and a particular encounter. It could be that Pantoni's and Karloan's teachers both learned versions from up-river people and each then made the song their own in different contexts: one at Yaraldi initiation and another on the Coorong with Tangani. Linda Barwick (1997: pers. comm.) adds, "The co-existence of seemingly contradictory explanations is evidence that meaning-making is an ongoing process."

Linda Barwick has compared the song text of Pinkie Mack (Berndt *et al.* 1993: 172) with other versions: the recordings of Albert Karloan (1989), by Tindale in the late 1930s, the three versions sung by Pinkie Mack's daughter Ellen Brown for Ellis in 1965, the one sung by Rosie Kropinyeri for Ellis in 1966, by Annie Koolmatrie for Lobban in 1969 (A1729), Flora Smith (née Kropinyeri) for Hemming in 1984 (5: 3/1/1984), James Brooks Kartinyeri for Ellis in 1964, and Hilda Wilson in 1998 for her family. She concluded that, while there are differences in the actual words, this is the same song.

Karloan's rendition of "*Pata winema*" is close to the Berndts' transcription from field notes (not a recording) of Pinkie Mack's version. Despite the intervening years of suppression of Ngarrindjeri language and culture, the renditions of the 1960s and 1980s are closely related, and sufficiently similar to those of the Karloan and Pinkie Mack from the 1940s to all be considered the same song. In the opinion of Linda Barwick (1997: pers. comm.), the similarity in tempo among the various versions is primary evidence of oral transmission—there's certainly none of written transmission —and also the type of variability that shows up in the morphology and melody fits with Ong's (1988: 31–77) characteristics "the psycho-dynamics of orality". Barwick elaborates:

> The Karloan version suggests significant virtuosic improvisation, while
> the later versions, although much less complex, maintain to varying

159

Part	Line	Phrase	Albert Karloan	Pinkie Mack	Ellen Brown	Rosie Kropinyeri
I	1	A	Pata winema	Pata winema	Pata winema	Pata winema
		B	namaliwunina	ngama leiwuninang	lanma leiwuninang	nanma leiwuninang
		C	iniya akaka	ania akaka	iniya akaka	alinya akaka
I	2	D	Mariya papataya	Maria pailpata	miniwa papataya	—
		E	manimani	manimani	manimani	wuliwuli
		F	tjatupulanda	tjatupulanda	tjatupulanda	tjatumalanba
		G	alpili ayi	waipali ai	opuli owan	walpuli yana
		H	malowa	malo-a	balawan	malal
II	1	A	Pata winema	Pata winema	Pata winema	Pata winema
		B'	nama liwuninanya	ngama leiwuningang a	nanma leiwuninanya	nanma liwuninaya
II	2	J	A ya	Ai	aya	a ya
		E	minimini	manimani	miniwa	manganmi
		F	tjatupulanda	tjatupulanda	patupulanda	tjatumalanba
		G	alpili ayi	waipali ai	wopuli owan	opuli yana
		H	malowa	malo angk	balaban	malal
			(repeats I, II)			
III	1	A	Pata winema	Pata winema		
		B'	nama liwuninanya	ngama leiwuningang a		
III	2	J	—	Ai		
		E	Manimani	manimani		
		F	tjatupulanda	tjatupulanda		
		G	alpili ayi	waipali ai		
		H	malowa	malo angk		
			(repeats I, II)	(repeats I, II)		
			coda: AB'J [I.1] EFGHAB'' [I.2] JFG [cfr I.2] HAB'FG [II.2]	coda ABH + tr tr tr		

Comparison of eight versions of "*Pata winema*" song sung by Ngarrindjeri performers 1930s–1998. The division of the texts into "parts" and "lines" follows the numbering given for Pinkie Mack's version reproduced in Berndt *et al.* (1993: 172). These correspond to subdivisions of the melody. The "phrases" (A–J) have been labelled by Linda Barwick on the basis of textual and rhythmic correspondences.

160

Singing: "Pakari Nganawi Ruwi"

Annie Koolmatrie	Flora Smith	Hilda Wilson	James Brooks Kartinyeri
Pata winema	Pata		Pata winema
namana	winiwini [E]		nanmali
namana	tjatupulanda [F]		wunina …
	waipeli o [G]		
iniya akaka	winiwini akaka		[manolowa]
—	Pata		
—	winiwini		minimini
—	tjatupulanda		tjatupulanda
—	waipeli o		alpuli o
—	—		malowo
Pata winema	—	Patai wanma	Pata winema
namana	—	leiwuninana	nanmali
namamana			wuninanya …
Pata	Tjata	a yu	—
winema	minimini	minimini	minimini
namananama	tjatupulanda	tjatupulanda	tjatupulanda
waipeli o	waipeli o	watpili aran	alpuli al
wini	wina		
malowei	malowa	bolow	manolo
(repeats x3)		(repeats x3 or x4)	[fragments]
	coda: wh wh wh wh		coda: trrrr

degrees important structural elements. It's significant that, as the tradition is becoming more attenuated, with text elements dropping out and consequent distortion of the melodic skeleton, different singers maintain different elements that allow us to make sense of the Berndts' written record. Flora Kropinyeri continues the "tr tr tr" dance cue. Ellen Brown maintains the full text and melody in skeletal form (all the elements from which I hypothesise that earlier singers, Pinkie Mack and Albert Karloan, created more elaborate versions and repeats and melodic improvisation). Annie Koolmatrie applies and elaborates melodic variability and repetition, even though her text is somewhat abridged. Rosie Kropinyeri gave information on performance practice in conjunction with performance, and James Brooks Kartinyeri maintained and elaborated meanings for the words. In other words, the song has been looked after through dispersal within a network of knowledgeable Ngarrindjeri people, each with his or her own take on it. When we bring all these versions together, we see how antithetical it all is to a centralised dogmatic form of maintenance and transmission through writing. Utterance of the characteristic text/rhythm/tempo signature is the thread that links them all, but the shape and weave of each version is contingent, dependent on the materials and knowledge available, the purpose of the performance, the context of the performance, the relationship with the recordist and so on.

Cath Ellis (1984: 164) writes of what she calls "perfect time", which rather like perfect pitch can be identified by objective measures. In a series of recordings of small songs from the far north of South Australia, Ellis (*ibid.*: 165) notes that the performers were not always the same people, but key performers were present in all recordings which were made in Adelaide and Indulkana over a period of some eight years. "The duration of the rhythmic pattern and text for the identical small songs varied remarkably little over this total span of nine years." Small songs, Ellis (*ibid.*: 184) concludes were not learned by rote and thus indelibly imprinted on one's memory. Rather, the singers learn "the musical logic" which allows them to manipulate elements within a unified frame. It would appear that the singers of "*Pata winema*" have also internalised a logic such that, when Ellen Brown and Rosie Kropinyeri sang "*Pata winema*" for Cath Ellis, their tempo was identical to that of Albert Karloan. This is very strong evidence that these songs are part of an oral traditional of some standing.

Right from the outset we need to distinguish several different levels at which variations can occur. Firstly the words of the song can vary with the singer, and even the same person may sing a song differently on different occasions. For example, Milerum's *pekeri* (Dream) song (Tindale 1937: 109) and the later version, also by Milerum (Tindale 1941: 233), exhibit minor differences, similar to the variation between the different renderings of "*Pata winema*" by Ellen Brown and that of Rosie Kropinyeri. Secondly, there may be different translations given for the same words within a song. This is something the Berndts (1993: 578, 584, 590, 592, 593) note in their translations of songs of Albert Karloan and others. The words may be obscure or archaic, but the song can still be full of meaning (Tindale 1941: 236; 1937: 109). Thirdly, as Strehlow (1971: 127) argues, the way in which words are constituted for the purposes of a song text may deliberately obscure sacred meanings. For central Australia, Strehlow (*ibid.*: 64) demonstrates how the difficulty of identifying individual words and obtaining translations led many to assume that Aranda songs had no meaning. Similarly, Ellis (1985: 62-3) points out that the syllables of a song text may be grouped differently to form words that offer the possibilities of different readings, and this is certainly so with *ngama*/Nine Mile. James Brooks Kartinyeri, by singing "Nine Mile" clearly as a place-name has made the *ngama* of the other versions transparent. Without giving any context, I ask Neville Gollan, "Do you know of a place called the Nine Mile?" He tells me "The Nine Mile" is on the beach side of the Sir Richard Peninsula, just past the barrage and just before the Murray Mouth. This is in the area where Sturt's men collected cockles in 1830 (Sturt 1833: 170). Cockles and baskets, songs and stories, historical texts and creative heroes are all part of the weave of this region.

Fourthly, at the level of the meanings wrought from a song, there can also be wide variations. Even when the words can be isolated and translated, there is still need for a context. The words in themselves are usually cryptic, repetitive, and function as a mnemonic. There are songs that recite place-names and it would require an expert to provide the stories for each place, but the singing of the song will keep the names and the order straight in the memory. We cannot, for example, get directly from a literal translation of the words of song to the meaning without engaging with the Ngarrindjeri world. Milerum, for example, provides Tindale (1937: 108-9) with a richly textured account of when the Tangani first arrived from the scrub country and heard the ceaseless roar of the Southern Ocean. "*Tango'walo'ngan!* (What will we do now?)" asked one man and the name of the Tangani tribe was thus established. This rhetorical strategy of asking one's location and then naming it, is a familiar story-telling style and one James Brooks Kartinyeri also employs in his account of cockling.

Lastly the meaning attributed to songs can change over time, as one moves from the immediacy of the moment to more generalised feelings and lessons that come to be associated with a song. For example, a song sung about a particular widow who had not waited the prescribed year of mourning before considering remarriage, after a few generations becomes a song that sets out the rules of remarriage and is a mechanism of social control (Tindale 1937: 116). James' account could be generalised to one of general meeting and welcome. Changing circumstances may be reflected in the metaphors on which the interpreter draws in explaining a song. Thus when Milerum spoke of the sound of waves crashing on the hummocks as a "noise which brings you to a sudden stop", he likened it to "white men in city streets" who rush around without any order (*ibid.*: 109). The urban-based metaphor is evidence of the way in which new experiences are incorporated within a pre-existing world depicted in song. In earlier times Milerum may have likened the sound to an inter-tribal gathering.

When confronted with various interpretations, translations and exegeses, it is tempting to shrug and say, the Ngarrindjeri no longer know anything; but I don't think that sits particularly well with what we know of the language of songs and their interpretation within Ngarrindjeri country, nor does it sit well with what we know of the individuals offering the explanations. Each is respected for his or her knowledge. From elsewhere in Australia, we know it is not unusual to find variations in the texts of songs, even from the same person. Marett *et al.* (1997: 9) note that multiple meanings in song texts are well attested in the literature on Aboriginal music; they provide a detailed analysis of a song of Bobby Lane (1941–93), a Wadjiginy songman of the Cox Peninsula (Northern Territory), for which there are a number of different meanings, "all of which people at Belyuen now agree are correct" (*ibid.*: 29-31). Ray Keogh (1996: 255-64) reviews the literature on song text interpretation and explores the divergent interpretations of a *nurlu* song text[12] in the Kimberleys. The variability of interpretation he suggests should be understood in the light of three factors: "the state of the tradition, the transmission procedure, and the nature of the song language" (*ibid.*: 261). Each is relevant to Ngarrindjeri songs. The ceremonies have not been performed on a regular basis and thus there may be difficulty remembering the "original meaning". But what does it mean to posit the existence of such? Songs are transmitted through singing by actual songsters who may have different understandings of the meanings. And, as we have seen, song language is a complex matter. Can we then say one is right and another wrong? What may have been an explanation that relied on an historical event can in several generations become mythologised and thus decontextualised (*ibid.*: 263). In the process, the song can achieve a greater reach and meaning. It will also require an expert to interpret it.

In exploring the song language of two Aboriginal totemic song texts of the western Roper River area of the Northern Territory, Francesca Merlan (1987: 146) proposes that textual opacity "forces the learner (whether outside analyst or local person) to rely largely, even entirely, upon knowledgeable interpreters (and usually, ones who are recognized for some reason as being legitimately so, for others refuse to comment)." This variability of interpretation is manifest in a number of Aboriginal expressive media. Merlan (*ibid.*) cites Nancy Munn (1973) on the productive and multivocal nature of Warlpiri symbols; Howard Morphy on the difficult-to-interpret geometric Yolngu clan designs which productively encode a multiplicity of meanings; and Ian Keen's (1978) explication of an "economy of religious knowledge" wherein knowledge is controlled "in terms of notions concerning its legitimate release, receipt and use." As far as legitimacy or "correctness" is concerned, it is "often inferred directly from the legitimacy of its source (not vice versa)". As Keogh (1996: 257) concludes, "the more legitimate the source of

165

knowledge, the more legitimate the knowledge". Or, as Peter Sutton (1987: 88) writes: "Mystery is in the hands of the few. Those who control mystery control change, as well as the status quo."

Strehlow (1971: 197) in his analysis of Aranda songs suggests there may be three levels of meaning in any one song text. A song may be interpreted as a story that is told to outsiders (the uninitiated, foreigners and so on) which masks a deeper meaning, sometimes erotic, told to young adults, which in turn masks a deeper spiritual meaning only available to those schooled in the law. No wonder at different points in their careers different researchers are told different things. From the song texts of the Berndts (1993) it appears they were being offered level one, as would be appropriate to their age and status in the early 1940s. This tolerance of many meanings and willingness to participate even when the song texts are not understood has, as we have seen, a counterpart in Ngarrindjeri story-telling. However, songs offer a perspective on change that is quite unlike what we might say for myth. They have stable melodic, rhythmic and textual structures. These may be varied, but only within certain confined parameters (Ellis 1994: 5). And, more importantly for my argument, they can be charted in ways that allow us to track a form of expression, such as a song like "*Pata winema*", through time. Thus I can say that, because of certain factors, this song is an example of oral transmission of some stability over a period of time and that it is completely independent of written texts.

Songs of the Southeast

In all analyses of Ngarrindjeri songs, we are dealing with a slim database. In fact most of what we know of "traditional" Ngarrindjeri music comes from one man, Milerum (Clarence Long).[13] Tindale (1986b: 498) considered Milerum, who became a close friend and colleague, to be the "final repository" of details of his culture. Milerum, born around 1869, grew up in the southeast of Ngarrindjeri land and spent his early years learning from the old people, including his traditionally conservative grandparents. Drawing on knowledge from his Tangani father, his Potaruwutj mother, and time as a young boy in Bunganditj country, Milerum was able to provide Tindale with a wealth of material from the southeast. The nineteen songs, two Yaraldi and seventeen Tangani, that he sang for Tindale (1937, 1941) constitute a small fraction of what Milerum knew and of what would have been known a century earlier, when they would have been sung in ceremonial contexts. Milerum was known as one of the last initiated men of the Coorong and thus, as with Pinkie Mack, we can expect to find stories and songs related within the framework of an oral culture.

While Ellis is at pains to stress that her research has not been comprehensive and that there is more work to be done reclaiming what she terms "remnants of tribal affiliations alongside information on cultural and social transition", nonetheless Ellis (1963–5: 54; Ellis *et al.* 1988: 156-7) provides a description of what she calls the "Southeastern" style of songs which is quite different from others in South Australia. The song characteristics are: (i) highly ornamented upper note which never occurs at the start of the song, but as a central or final climax; no clear tonic; (ii) free rhythm, with some changes of tempo; (iii) many ornaments, particularly on upper notes; (iv) clear tenor voice (Ellis 1967: 15). A question that cannot yet be answered, but which Ellis raises in an intriguing way, is whence came the Southeastern song types? Ellis (1967) traces the diffusion of song styles as a means of illuminating the migrations of peoples to and within Australia. Perhaps this exercise could also illuminate the diffusions of ceremonial culture, in particular, those rituals which concern women. According to Ellis, the picture of song styles for the Southeast is complicated. It would appear that an older, relatively simple, Central Australian style was supplanted by a more recent musical style that had moved around the eastern and southern coastlines and then moved northwards and westwards. The Western Desert style which Ellis *et al.* (1988: 157-8) say derives from a second Central Australian style, is thus more recent than the Southeastern style. Thus, to argue, as did Commissioner Stevens (1995: 278), that Ngarrindjeri have borrowed from the Pitjantjatjara (Western Desert style) is to reverse the possible lines of diffusion. It is more likely, by this reckoning, that there will be compatibilities with Western Peripheral style which was formed by a westwards move from southeast. By way of support, Ellis (1967: 15) notes that, in both these areas, unlike other parts of Australia where women use shallow wooden carriers, women carry their babies in baskets. In the Ellis schema, the Southeastern would be prior to the Western Desert and Peripheral styles. Perhaps the latter borrowed from the Ngarrindjeri. All this, of course, is speculation. Styles, Ellis *et al.* (1988: 158) allow, can be syncretised and obliterated.

From the various accounts of the "*Pata winema*" song, Linda Barwick (1997: pers. comm.) concludes that the melodic structure shows more similarity to the songs of eastern Australia than to Central Australian styles:

> The use of ascending as well as descending movement in the contour, the pitch range of more than an octave, and the use of discrete pitches rather than microtonal subdivisions and portamenti are also found in other southeastern song styles (e.g. the songs analysed by Gummow 1995 and Donaldson 1995). This song was not used by Ellis in arriving at her characterisation of southeastern song styles.

Thus we can say that the "*Pata winema*" song, sung in 1998 by a senior woman, is consistent with that of the 1882 initiation song of Karloan, and is consistent with the Southeastern style based, to a large extent, on Milerum's singing.

While it is true that our understanding of so-called traditional Ngarrindjeri music is considerably hampered by the lack of recordings and transcriptions, it is not accurate to say that traditional songs were not being sung. The fragment of the performance at Goolwa in 1951 indicates not only that there was traditional music, but that more than one song was known and that people today recognise those songs. Aunty Dot Kartinyeri, Grace Sumner's sister, could sing in the fish when she was fishing, Kenny Sumner, her nephew, told Steven Hemming (1998: pers. comm.). The more I ask about songs, the more is recalled. I have been able to reconstruct a genealogy of sorts for "*Pata winema*". The song has left traces in the written record. As this goes to press, the account of Mrs Hilda Wilson's knowledge of the song is still unfolding. How many other songs are there which have not left traces?

We can be sure some songs have gone unrecorded. Taplin (1873: 37-8) reports he was "too ashamed" to look upon the "disgusting displays of obscene gesture" as "he stood alone in the dark". There was "nothing of worship contained within it". When it was the women who danced, Taplin found them "very immodest and lewd" (*ibid.*). We have no translations of any of these songs. Despite his antagonism towards Ngarrindjeri ceremonial life and his lack of interest and at times embarrassment regarding their songs, Taplin (1879: 35; 1873: 144) does note the range of occasions on which people sang, from marriages, through initiation to burials. And, while he is inclined to view these activities as dramatic spectacles, Taplin (1879: 107) did recognise the powerful emotions aroused by singing, even when the song had been learned from another tribe and the words were not understood.

Unfortunately we have the sketchiest of accounts of songs sung as part of ritual performances. Taplin (1879: 106) provides a transcription and translation of one song he had heard some eighteen years earlier. "The Narrinyeri are coming; soon they will appear, carrying kangaroos; quickly they are walking." Here is a song that could be read at a number of levels; it probably began as a description of an actual hunt and in time became one that extolls the plenty of the land and the skill of the hunters. Barwick (1998: pers. comm.) notes that "this style of rendering 'native music' is typical of nineteenth-century tropes of 'primitive music' from whatever country, Africa, the Americas or Oceania."

Despite the lack of recordings, there is much to be learned from what we have, especially the detailed explanations Milerum proffered. What I found particularly interesting in these texts (Tindale 1937; 1941) is that many of the songs record events that have occurred within the memory of the last few generations. Here is evidence that the corpus of song is alive and adaptive, that songsters have the capacity to absorb, explain, and manage change. I do not think this phenomenon is a colonial artefact. The most "traditional" of all songs, *pekeri tungar*, those that tell of the creation of Ngarrindjeri lands like the journey of *Ngurunderi* down the Murray River, were at some point in the history of the region "new songs", which told of the migration into and colonisation of the lands by a strong hunter and his clan. In time this historic event has become mythologised in that it no longer has the specificity that would attach to the song about a known person (see Wild 1987:

109). The song about a dispute between the Tatiara and Tangani in Milerum's day (Tindale 1937: 119) had that specificity, but, in time, such a song would lose the references to particular times, places and persons. It would become an instructive account of more general abstract matters such as relationships to others, the land, and the nature of intrusion.

Pinkie Mack was recognised as a wonderful singer, who could sing up the river to Swan Hill and down to the Coorong.[14] Like Milerum, her songs reflected her world. In Tonkinson's (1993: xxi) words they "encompassed both timeless and traditional concerns and the impact of alien influences, such as money, paddle-steamers, alcohol, shepherding, and dresses with bustles, as perceived by Aborigines in the last quarter of the nineteenth-century". Songsters like Pinkie Mack were the repositories of the stories of the people and their songs addressed matters of importance to the society, food, birth, death, marriage, initiation, relations with neighbours, disputes and resolution of conflict. Unfortunately we are missing much detail in her repertoire. By the time Cath Ellis began recording in the 1960s, Pinkie Mack had passed away. In her report on field work within a 320-kilometre radius of Adelaide, Ellis (1963–5) finds little by way of knowledge of traditional songs or language. It was her surmise in the mid-1960s that "the culture was forced out very rapidly between the time of David Unaipon (now 91) and Banks Long (now about 70)" (Ellis 1962–6 (1)). However, there are several individuals noted by Ellis (1963–5) as knowledgeable, and they are persons cited today as sources of traditional knowledge. Ellen Brown knows a "great deal more than most people in this area", including "a great deal of history", notes Ellis (*ibid.*: 14). When Ellis (1962–6 (4): 4; 1996a: LA 106) interviewed Rosie Kropinyeri on 8 January 1966, and recorded a few words, the *Pata winema* song, one about Indian traders, and information about genealogies and midwives, she noted: "Very friendly. Did know legends, but couldn't remember them. Used to sing and dance with Banks Long." "Reputedly knows a lot", Ellis wrote in her notebook (1963–5: 8). Aunty Rosie did know a great deal, but she did not tell Ellis all she knew during that brief visit. On the tape you can hear her beginning to talk about more intimate matters and then letting it slide as Ellis moves onto another topic. It was these women who were keeping the songs alive.

Ellis also found other sources of "traditional" knowledge. Olive Varcoe "can speak and sing" (Ellis 1963–5: 12); Rita Mason did know songs (*ibid.*: 37). These summaries are filled out in four note-books (Ellis 1962–6 (1-4)), where we learn something of the song repertoires of various individuals. Mrs Varcoe and Mrs Mason are each remembered as singing (*ibid.*: (2): 34-6). Ellis (*ibid.*: (3): 9) reports that Scottie (Alan) Cameron, who was living on the Bonney Reserve in 1963, "made it a hobby to learn songs from different areas, and he knows four or more—one Coorong, one Lakes, one River. Ellis did not succeed in getting him to sing them and there are some clues in her notes that help explain the silences. Bob Wanganeen said he had heard the old people sing and would rush home from school in the hope of hearing them sing, but they did not let him listen and would not teach anything (*ibid.*: 2 : 52). Others told Ellis how the songs had become a matter of fun for children.

Tindale's recordings of Milerum's knowledge of songs and language have come down to us in loving detail. We have no comparable record from women, yet I suspect that much survived through the descendants of Pinkie Mack. Ellen Brown observed that Clarence Long (Milerum) and her mother, Pinkie Mack, would have a jolly good laugh together. This, she reasoned, was because they knew what they were singing about (1965: LA 124b). If this knowledge had been tapped we would have a vastly different understanding of Ngarrindjeri music and ceremony today. From what people have been able to recognise today from the fragments of recordings I have been able to locate and play back, it seems the songs are still part of cultural memory. What has been gone for a century or so is the large-scale ceremonies which provided the context for learning and performing the songs.

Songs and Ceremonies of Yore

The 1840s' eyewitness accounts of ceremonies by Meyer (1846) at which 200–300 gathered and celebrated in song and dance the creative acts of the pioneering ancestors are the earliest I have

171

located. Meyer describes male initiation in the warmth of summer evenings when several tribes meet for fighting and afterwards "amuse themselves with dancing and singing". He writes of the times all join in and of the women's distinctive high screaming that accompanies the men's dancing.

> The women sit apart, with skins rolled up and held between the knees, upon which they beat time. The young men are ornamented after their fashion with a tuft of emu feathers in the hair; and those who are not painted red, ornament themselves with chalk, by making circles around the eyes, a stroke along the nose, and dots upon the forehead and cheeks, while the rest of the body is covered with fanciful figures.

Taplin's account (1879: 107) of a ceremony at which some 200 were present is strikingly similar to that of Meyer (1846) and also to the Sturt Re-enactment of 1951. In each the women beat time on rolled-up skins; the men are decorated with white circle and line designs; the firelight is used to dramatic effect.[15] In most of the reports it is the men who are dancing and the women who are singing and keeping time. But in Taplin (1873: 38) we also get a sense of the reciprocal roles of men and women. Sometimes men dance while women sing; sometimes the roles are reversed. Campbell (1934: 30-1), citing George Wallace, a long-time local resident of Millicent, states: "The womenfolk did the singing and beat their sticks on rolled-up opossum skin rugs, while the dancing consisted chiefly of a simple leg-shaking sort of dance." This is a style I have seen women today demonstrate as what they saw their female kin doing in the 1950s and 1960s and is a style well known in other parts of Australia. In 1984 Flora Smith (née Kropinyeri) told Steven Hemming (1997a: 8) that they'll do a dance together, men's, all mens dance first, when they've done their dance the womens on their own. No men allowed there . . . [the women] used to tuck their dresses between their legs and shake their legs . . . they used to dance around. They'd beat and they all stamp, stamp, as soon as they'd [dance?] they go sit down, have a drink of tea. They'd turn their backs and the men get up then and they had their dance. It would appear that, like other Aboriginal people, the Ngarrindjeri have activities that are gender-specific and others that require co-operation of both sexes.

172

It is my impression from reading the sources and talking to people, that large gatherings occurred off the mission. Taplin (24/11/1859) reports one some 100 kilometres away which included people ranging from Encounter Bay to the Darling River, but there were also gatherings at Raukkan. In early May 1876, Taplin recorded that a smaller group from the Coorong had gathered for *ringballin*. Campbell (1939: 29), citing a report of W. Warren, a native officer of the Aborigines Department at Guichen Bay in the southeast, states that over the "last four years Robe Town, has been regularly visited during the winter by the natives of the 'Coorong', of 'Salt Creek', and 'Mount Gambier'". The visits of these "intelligent, industrious, workmen", capable of making their own contracts regarding fencing, colt breaking and so on, never extended "beyond two or three months and are regarded as tokens of friendship by our natives, no disturbances ever having taken place between them rendering interference of the police necessary". Campbell (1934: 30-1), in his quest to draw together the fragmentary and scant record for the southeast, notes gatherings at Mount Burr, for which messengers were sent to groups as far away as Kingston and the Coorong. From this it would appear that Ngarrindjeri were in contact with other groups and travelled outside their territory for ceremonial and economic purposes.

Another large gathering for which we have an eyewitness report occurred in November 1867, when the Duke of Edinburgh visited Loveday Bay, some eight kilometres from the mission. This was another occasion on which Ngarrindjeri ceremonies marked important moments in the colonial calendar and on which, contrary to Taplin's regime, they were able to perform *ringballin*. Five hundred had gathered for the festivities which Taplin had prepared, but *ringballin* was not part of his agenda. Taplin (10/11/1867) notes that on the Sabbath, "The blacks behaved very decorously all day. There was hardly any singing or dancing." But on the next evening, "I could not be present", writes Taplin (12/11/1867). It is not clear whether he deliberately absented himself, but it is clear that the Ngarrindjeri seized the moment, as they did when the whaleboat came ashore at Raukkan in 1951. Fortunately for the record, J. D. Woods (1879: xxxii-xxxiv) was present. His account notes yet again the particular designs on painted faces, the white dots and bands; and the seated women chanting and keeping time by beating on folded possum-skin rugs. He traces the way in which the singing and dancing builds to a crescendo as the voices of the men "swelled the song of the women, and their action was carried on in most admirable time".

Woods (1879: xxxii) is mystified as to what it all means: "Some think it a war-dance—others a representation of their hunting expeditions—others, again, that it is a religious, or pagan, observance; but on this the blacks themselves give no information." One wonders what sort of exegesis might have been deemed satisfactory; what questions he asked and of whom. Like Taplin, he found their ideas to be less than coherent. "The idea of religion possessed by the blacks are very indistinct, besides being ridiculous and contradictory" (*ibid.*: xxx). Angas (1847: 69) glimpses the totemic nature of these gatherings when he observes several dances that celebrate the frog and emu ancestors at Bonney's waterholes, but is more impressed by the "demon-like shouts and wild chanting" than the potential for religious expression. These "first contact" witnesses are reluctant to acknowledge that what is being transacted is religious and that the rituals go to the core of Ngarrindjeri beliefs about their relationship to the natural world. On the one hand there is a reluctance to see the activities as religious, and on the other no great enthusiasm by Ngarrindjeri to provide anything other than the most rudimentary sketch of what is happening. Such knowledge could only be gained through the lengthy process of training.

Missionaries had a vested interest in not acknowledging the deeply spiritual nature of ceremonies and in undermining the authority of the elders who, as far as Taplin was concerned, took his promising charges and corrupted them. "Some have fancied that they saw in it a religious significance. It may have in some tribes, but I do not believe it has amongst the Narrinyeri," wrote Taplin (1879: 107). There was little to challenge such a view. Through the writing of men such as Radcliffe-Brown (1918), Howitt (1904: 672-5), Brough Smyth (1878), and R. H. Mathews (1900), the Ngarrindjeri became one of the prime examples of "Aboriginal culture" and thus known to the world. However, it was not the religious importance of their songs and ceremonies that was featured. The interest was in social structure and evolutionary models. Aboriginal religion remained a problematic category well into the twentieth century, and still is for some. W. E. H. Stanner (1979: 143) writes of the shift in consciousness necessary to see that "religion was not the mirage of the society, and the society was not the consequence of the religion. Each pervaded the other within a larger process".

The Berndts (1964; 1988) are anthropologists who have written with passion of Aboriginal religion, of the authority of ritual experts, of taboos and restrictions on certain knowledge. Yet a constant refrain throughout their writing about the Ngarrindjeri is that they are different and this includes their rituals not being deemed religious. The evidence they adduce is not particularly satisfactory. For example, they report Albert Karloan "did not speak of his initiation as a religious experience", as religion for him was something that concerned adults (Berndt *et al.* 1993: 185). Now the distinction between a religious experience and religion is worth pondering. Does the baby at baptism have a "religious experience"? The child is certainly part of a religious ceremony that is a central rite of Christian religions, just as the young man in an initiation ceremony in a participant in a central rite of passage in his society. Religious experience remains subjective, and the presence or absence of same in no way can be considered evidence of the existence of a religion. I ask my colleagues at Holy Cross College about this and members of the Religious Studies Department join in: "A sacrament, no matter how badly done, accomplishes its ends," I learn.

The Berndts (1993: 210) state: "Performances that did approximate a religious orientation were held publicly and were more in the nature of a ceremony rather than a re-enactment for the major commemoration of particular mythic personages and the events they had experienced." What they mean by this turns on their understanding of the nature of ceremonial performances, on whether they were religious, or had some other purpose. The Berndts (*ibid.*: 368) allow that *pekeri* (dream) songs "in a general way could be deemed to be religious—or at least a tendency in that direction". In an earlier analysis, Berndt (1974: 26) made reference to his unpublished material concerning "sacred rituals attended by men and women" that "dramatized the behaviour of various natural species, the clan totems". Certain songs were learnt with stories, suggesting "they were clan or Dreaming songs, concerning natural species noted in myth", the Berndts (1993: 368) allow. On the other hand, they state that "in this particular context there is no reference to their being religious and it is unlikely they were considered as such" (*ibid.*: 368). What does this qualification mean? For whom were the songs not considered religious? What would it take for the songs to considered religious? The Berndts' description of the occasion for which the songs were sung, male initiation, has all the hallmarks of a religious ritual in terms of what is being taught; the ritual taboos being observed; the authority of old men over young men; the gatherings of witnesses to the ceremony; and the totemic nomination by the boy.

The songs about the Dreamtime which Tindale calls *pekere tungar* capture key episodes in Ngarrindjeri history. One tells of *Ngurunderi*, another of *Jekejere* at Goolwa. Tindale and the Berndts are in basic agreement about this category of songs (and it is one that has some currency today) but from there on they differ in detail, emphasis and naming.[16] Both Tindale (1937; 1941; 1974: 34) and the Berndts (Berndt 1940a; Berndt *et al.* 1993: ch. 14) struggle to organise the fragmentary material into categories, but they end up with lists that conflate subject with purpose and the context in which they were sung. Tindale (1937: 103) identifies magical songs, songs associated with sickness and death, totemic songs, hunting songs, dramatic songs, and epics and fighting songs. The Berndts (1993: 215-18, 222) identify five categories of songs and write of those with accompanying actions, of sorcery songs, healing songs, *ngatji* songs, "gossip" songs, death songs, growling songs, hunting songs, social control songs. Providing a satisfactory way of categorising Aboriginal songs has proved elusive. Ellis *et al.* (1988: 152-3) argue that Aboriginal songs are normally magical and commemorative and may be based on everyday events. They divide the social functions of songs into three categories: ecological (increase songs, control over rain and so on); social control (education and safety of children); and dealing with human life events (birth, love, emotions, death, healing songs, which maybe too powerful to be sung). All the above researchers admit that their typologies of Ngarrindjeri songs are less than satisfactory, that there are variations within areas, and that they are frequently contradicted by their informants.[17]

In the nineteenth century, even before official white settlement, songs rendered the inexplicable consistent with the Ngarrindjeri worldview. The smallpox epidemic of 1830 is "explained" in songs about a *maldawuli* (a creative being of the long ago) who came out of the Southern Cross, like a bright flash and, as he travelled westwards, beckoned in a smoke signal, for others to follow (Tindale 1931–4: 251-2; 1937: 112; 1941: 233-4).[18] Veronica Brodie said it was like a wind coming through the rushes from her grandmother's country. Jenny Ponggi (Stirling 1911: 40) says it came from the east and with a loud noise, whereas Louisa Karpeny said it was from the west. What remains constant in the accounts is the association with a natural phenomenon as explanation of a disaster. By the 1930s, a century after the epidemic, the songs of that smallpox-related *maldawuli* were associated with the McGraths Flat area and were sung when people were worried, ill-at-ease, or when someone was sick (Tindale 1941: 234). This is a good example of the way in which a specific event is woven into the fabric of Ngarrindjeri life. What began as a story to deal with the horror of an unprecedented epidemic became a song for troubled times in general. For the women with whom Hemming was working, "*Pata winema*" had become a song to curse whitefellas.

One theme that recurs in Ngarrindjeri songs is that of longing for country, both in a specific and more generalised sense. In an early journal entry, Taplin (30/6/1859; see also 1873: 117) mentions two songs of which the words were known: one about *Ngurunderi* and the other a lament for land: "Shall I ever see my country again". This song was slower, very "plaintive and wild . . . One of the men asked if I could write what they sang in a letter." It began as a low chant:

> all through the piece they say the same words over and over again, then the chant rose higher and higher with the beat of the *tartengk*, a native drum, then it sank again and the men's voices broke in shouting in time

to the chant and brandishing their weapons in the wildest excitement. Then the shrill treble of the women broke in like an imploring vociferation in answer to the shouts of the men.

The Berndts (1993: 582) also recorded songs lamenting the emptying out of clan territories and the passing of clansfolk. Catherine Berndt (1994a: 639–40) writes nostalgically of "tears of grief" running down Pinkie Mack's cheeks for "the long-gone past, or for scenes evoked by specific songs. . . . Where are all these Piltindjeri now?"[19] In later years this Piltindjeri lament was sung when there was a disturbance. This is another song that began with a specific focus and over time became more generalised. When sung by Pinkie Mack it expressed grief at not just the move off the clan territory but the death of so many Piltindjeri.

Meyer (1843: 52) had already noted the repetitious nature of their songs: "All their songs appear to be of the same description, consisting of a few words which are continually repeated. This specimen, it will be observed, consists of two regular verses:"

$$— \cup | —— | \cup — | \cup — \cup$$
$$— \cup | —— | \cup — | \cup — \cup$$

This is a form that resembles the cyclically repeating text typical of the Central Australian, Western Desert and Lakes styles more than a Southeastern style. But as Barwick (1997: pers. comm.) is quick to point out: "There is not enough information to be categorical." Repetition is a feature of songs recorded by the Berndts (1993: 586), as in the song about calling the name of places, including Goolwa (*Kutungald*) of which the songster is proud.

New technologies, especially those which aided travel, were noted in song and were sufficiently interesting to be recorded by researchers. Meyer (1843: 52) recorded the song: "What a fine road is this for me winding between the hills!" of the road between Encounter Bay and Willunga, that goes high between the hills.

> *Miny-el-ity yarluke an-ambe*
> what is it   road   me for
>
> *Aly- el- arr   yerk-in yangaiak-ar!*
> here are they standing up   hills.

In his translation of "The Railway Train", Taplin (1873: 39) captures the Ngarrindjeri imagery of this new technology. The smoke "looks like frost,/ It runs like running water,/ It blows like a spouting whale." Tindale (1941: 234) recorded George Spender's rendition of his "Song of the Murray Bridge" in which the native crossing is contrasted with the white man's bridge. This song was created between 1876, when the first bridge was built over the Murray, and 1886, when the railway line arrived; it was, writes Tindale (*ibid.*), one of the last songs made by the Tanganekald. In a handwritten note that did not make it into his publications about this song, Tindale says: "Bridge at Murray Bridge where pylon of bridge stands in swamp was *Muldjuwangk* [bunyip] place and was sacred. Only very old people could fish there. Mud was supposed to be very deep. Wonder why white can make a pylon there" (Tindale and Long, nd: 11). He does not say who was doing the wondering, but it appears that the bridge desecrated a sacred site, certainly a site associated with a powerful being, the *mulyewongk*, and it was a site with restricted access. Why was there no outcry? Why sing of something that desecrates a site? We know nothing of the context of the song or how it was received. We do know that, at the time the song was composed, there was no forum for complaint, no heritage legislation, and no protection of sacred sites. Celebrating technology in song was one way of making it intelligible and was obviously of interest to the whitefellas who dutifully recorded these songs. Were Ngarrindjeri singing the songs that this audience wanted to hear? Were they awed by technology, as have been generations of people world-wide, only to find that a bridge, a dam, a hydro-scheme—in other words, a development beyond the reach of their own experience and religious code—brings disaster to their lands and families? Meaning is sought in the wisdom of the sages of the society, those who can find the stories and songs to explain the new and bring it within the ambit of the known world.

Captain Jack sang "O the turkey at Goolwa" which Taplin (1873: 36) explains referred to a gilt figurehead representing an eagle from a shipwreck. The "turkey" had found a home on the door of a house in Goolwa. Here is a song that may be interpreted in a number of ways. At the most literal level it is about a piece of flotsam, a striking piece to be sure, that was part of the history of the coming of whitefellas into Ngarrindjeri lands. It is worth noting that the song, like James Brooks Kartinyeri's account of "*Pata winema*", and songs recorded by the Berndts (1993: 586), expresses an attachment to Goolwa. But why a turkey? The Berndts (*ibid.*: 211–12) describe the "turkey dance" with the basket-weave tail feather as one involving surprise and mystery.

The Sturt Re-enactment was not the final chapter in the story of Ngarrindjeri ceremony, nor was Pinkie Mack the last songster. In the privacy of their homes, their camps, and down by the lake, singing continued. Vi Deuschle recalls Granny Ethel, who died in 1964, dancing, but the songs she sang were never translated and, she adds, There were no men around when she danced. Tom Trevorrow remembers his Uncle Bigalong singing in camp. "Wilfred Wassa knows the dance to that song . . . they used to dance to it and clap thighs together", reports Cath Ellis (1962–6 (3): 8-9). According to a number of Ngarrindjeri, in their fifties and older, there were occasions on which older people sang at Raukkan, down by the lake and up on the hill with the older people. Also Pinkie Mack was not the only knowledgeable person. Connie Love, for instance says, that at about seven years of age, her big brother Oscar Kartinyeri was "in it"; and that the men knew what to do. She remembers the 1951 re-enactment as happening several years later.

Music, Cath Ellis (1985) contends is the main intellectual medium through which Aboriginal people conceptualise their world. She writes:

> Through song the unwritten history of the people and laws of the community are taught and maintained; the entire physical and spiritual development of the individual is nurtured; the well being of the group is protected; supplies of food and water ensured through musical communication with the spiritual powers; love of homeland is poured out for all to share; illnesses are cured; news is passed from one group to another. [Ellis 1985: 17]

Elaborating on Ellis's ideas, Barwick and Marett (1995: 4-5) write of the "essence of singing" of the "very ephemerality of sound that draws attention to the evanescence of existence itself", that takes one back to the creative era, and "the substance of song", and the role of indigene and analyst in understanding this form of communication. So what world were Ngarrindjeri communicating in their songs? From what we know, it was a world of heroic deeds, fearful encounters, new items and forces, feelings of nostalgia, connection and power, warfare, maintenance of social order—indeed a catalogue that reflects the times in which the songsters lived.

Ngarrindjeri voices have been much in demand on "official occasions", from the visit of the Duke of Edinburgh in 1867 to performance at Camp Coorong at the conclusion of the Weavers' Conference in 1996. In church, at social gatherings, in glee clubs, and school choirs, Ngarrindjeri continued to sing. Today songmen and songwomen are "given" songs in much the same way as their ancestors were. Ngarrindjeri continue to sing about their lives and their land, albeit lives very different from those who greeted Sturt in 1830 and those who were at the 1951 re-enactment. Their songs include Ngarrindjeri words and the idiom is decidedly Ngarrindjeri.[20] Teasing out the various strands of Ngarrindjeri singing is no simple task, but once we set aside the idea that western music replaced the "traditional music", now "lost" or "forgotten", some interesting questions about the nature of social change, resistance and cultural persistence emerge, as does appreciation of the creative process. By focusing on a song such as "*Pata winema*" we can see the continuity of an oral culture at work.

George Spender's song was not the last one in Ngarrindjeri. Ngarrindjeri continued to sing of their changing world and to catalogue the new. In 1966 Rosie Kropinyeri sang of Afghan traders (Ellis 1966a: LA 106; see also Berndt *et al.* 1993: 584). Bessie Rigney (née Gollan) sang lullabies, and Ellis (1963–5: 11) commented that she knows "much of tribal lore". The assault on language and the assault on Ngarrindjeri ceremonial life is linked in the minds of those interviewed by Catherine Ellis. Bessie Rigney expresses sorrow at losing the language, but was still singing to babies (Ellis 1965: LA 125ab; see Reay 1949: 96).[21] Harry Carter, speaking at Berri on 26 January 1965, says to Cath Ellis (1965: LA 124b): Don't ask for songs. We don't know any songs. He says that the worst of it is, when we meet somebody, we can't even form a sentence. He had gone away for work, and when he came back all his mates were gone, and the people who could speak language were gone. He added, They had a song for everything, for every corroboree, a song for their sacred corroborees, to wind them up they asked God to help wind them up. Ellen Brown and Hughie McHughes talk about songs and language and Edgar Lampard recalls they used to sing and chant with Ellen's mother, Pinkie Mack (Ellis 1965: LA 124b). The attacks on language and the attack on ceremonial life struck at the core of certain sorts of knowledge in an oral culture. While the songs were sung, the places and their stories were secure. But it was a long process by which one learnt the songs, and gained sufficient status to be able to sing them. It required time spent with the old people, time on site at sacred places, time in the country learning while doing. There was little of this time during the era of the Protector. The church became one safe place in which to sing. Anthropologists work with the "last" of the singers. Her descendants mourn, but undeterred, Ngarrindjeri continued to sing.

Gospel, Glee Clubs and Guitars

Maggie Jacobs: I like all those hymns, but my really favourite one is "I Stand Amazed In Thy Presence". It's an old Raukkan favourite. I learned to sing at school, under W. T. Lawrie, the headmaster at the school. He was the one who would stick a ruler in your mouth to make you sing and he'd put his fingers in your back to make you sit up straight and numb your head with a flick of his fingers. Lindsay Wilson was made to sing in front of us, and we were all laughing. Marj Koolmatrie, Lindsay Wilson and me, we were all in the same class. Mr Lawrie made him sing "There is a Land Where Summer Skies." The mission school choir would serenade visitors and the passengers on paddle steamers that regularly pulled into the Raukkan jetty.[22] The children would dive for pennies, I've been told. Maggie Jacobs: Every Friday, one boy and one girl would go down to escort the passengers around Raukkan. They would visit the school and that's where they would sing for them. And the same boy and girl would take them to where the women were making mats and to where the men, like Clarence Long [Milerum], Jack Stanley and my grandfather Rowley, were carving.

Veronica Brodie's older sister, Leila Rankine[23] (1974b), was a talented musician. She sang, played the trombone and was chair of

CASM, the Centre for Aboriginal Studies in Music, at the University of Adelaide 1976–86: The church was packed every Sunday night. Everyone came to church. We all grew up with the church influence. Whether you regarded yourself as a Christian or not, you came along to church and you enjoyed the singing. You'd hardly find a spare seat. There'd be say 200 people sitting there enjoying the hymns, at least four or five hymns a service . . . After the Methodists, we had Church of Christ, Congregationalists and then the Salvation Army was resident there (quoted in Breen 1989: 35).

Ngarrindjeri were well known for the "beautiful and disciplined sound of their choral singing," writes Breen (1989: 31; Jenkin 1979: 18). Albert Karloan was a member of the Raukkan Glee Club who sang at Government House in 1895 to welcome the governor, just thirteen years after his initiation where "*Pata winema*" was sung. In 1910, twelve Ngarrindjeri travelled to Tasmania where they sang at the re-enactment of colonisation. Old Dan Wilson (1860–1921) was one of the party, as was David Unaipon (1872–1967). Veronica Brodie remembers her mother talking and laughing about the Glee Club. The church played an important part in providing a forum in which people could sing, and sing about matters of belief, but the democratic nature of this forum—one did not need to be an elder to sing—must have undermined the authority of the older generation, as I imagine Taplin's translations of hymns into Ngarrindjeri must have also. In Taplin's church, one did not need to dedicate a lifetime to learning the songs and their significance. One could attend the service and sing. And Ngarrindjeri were called upon to sing on occasions where their presence as Indigenous persons could be used to legitimate the genocide of other Indigenous people, such as the Tasmanian Aborigines and their own dislocation in the lands of the Lower Murray.

By Leila Rankine's generation, Ngarrindjeri had taken over from the wife of the missionary or superintendent as the church pianist. [O]ne of the older players for the church was Auntie Janet Smith. She also played the concertina. . . . She's one of the very few people that can relate a lot of stories and history about the earlier days. (Breen 1989: 35) Dot Shaw recalls: My father played the organ, and that made him feel good in order to be able to give it all to the Lord. The only Sunday he would ever miss was if he was sick. It couldn't have done him any harm to serve the Lord. That's how I feel now. I feel hurt that our language and culture have been taken away. I'm sad about that. But I wasn't living back then. I feel sad I missed out and I'm envious and in awe of people in the North and what they have.

Leila Rankine spoke of the people who played the piano in the hall; the people who played by ear; the dances that ranged from waltzes though barn dances, to the military two-step and the concerts at the Ashville Hall on the Main Road which were attended by people from the surrounding districts. I can remember Bessie Karpany [deceased] who played the piano with a real swing. She never learned music, but she could play very well and was in great demand for dances when the hall was built (Breen 1989: 33). "She was a beautiful player," says Maggie Jacobs as she reads this section of this manuscript. Leila Rankine (*ibid.*: 34-5): There was no lack of musicians and you didn't have to have a big group in order to have a singalong, or a concert, or a dance. People were really enthusiastic to show their skills. They would have learned by listening to the radio, watching travelling shows, or in the shearing sheds. Some learned by correspondence; Mark Wilson, my grandfather, learned this way and taught his skills to two or three girls on the pedal organ. My mother also learned music and elocution by correspondence . . . My brother and I (he played the guitar and I played banjo mandolin) would sit in the house and play for the sheer joy of it. At CASM too, we encourage Aboriginal students to pass on their skills to younger ones coming in.

Singalongs are remembered fondly. Catherine Berndt (1989: 12) recalls Pinkie Mack would initiate the singing on social occasions in other people's homes. In the 1950s Leila Rankine remembers there were singalongs, usually on the weekends, in people's houses. They sang Stephen Foster songs and other popular songs of the day. People got to talking, thinking back over the years and someone would mention somebody and they'd sing a song that was his or her favourite and then other people's favourites as well. . . . After tea, at nightfall, it was popular to build a fire by the beach or lake, or sit outside the cottage and have a chat and a singalong. You'd find people with guitars, and harmonicas were popular too. Or maybe someone would come along who could play an old concertina or gum leaf. I can remember my uncles and others playing with just the gumleaf and guitars, items for concerts or dances. There were people who played the bones and some autoharps, but nobody played banjos (Breen 1989: 32). Not all Ngarrindjeri agree about the absence of banjo players. Neville Gollan played one. Also the ukulele, he informs me. Don't ask him to teach you to play, Doreen tells me, He's left handed.

Songs, like stories, recalled people and places; but the songster, like the story-teller, always brought the message home. A song that Leila's grandmother taught her (and which she sang to her grandson) was about mice in a barn. "Three Little Mice," says her sister Veronica, "And it's been translated." Leila Rankine: We'd always get the moral of the story told to us after we'd sung the song. It was about being careful not to stay out after dark, but also helped us to be more responsible for our actions and realize what would happen if we did something foolish without thinking it through. There were lots of stories that they told too, that had morals for us—even some of the Aboriginal legends (Breen 1989: 32-3).

There was and continues to be a range of musical styles. Ngarrindjeri have sung hymns, ballads, hillbilly, country and western, and more recently rock or reggae. It seems to me that at various times they have taken a popular music form and made it theirs. Olga Fudge's well-trained voice sang the "Pelican Love Song" at Raukkan (Ellis 1962-6: 2: 41). She sang in Ngarrindjeri. Was there a connection between the healing song of the pelican clan (Berndt *et al.* 1993: 579) and a love song to the pelican *ngatji*? Cornish carols were sung on the Reserve and down at Narrung at Christmas. At times the humour was slapstick. In earlier days there was Cecil Gollan who played the button accordion. At any concert or social function, he was very much in demand to sing "The Parrot Song" . . . you'd find yourself laughing your head off because of the antics. . . . Cecil passed on, but his son Neville sings it and so does my sister Veronica Brodie. (Breen 1989: 33). Leila Rankine (*ibid.*: 32): We also knew "Little Black Coon", but I changed the words as I grew up, to "Mummy's Little Aborigine". I did not hear any "coon songs" and am inclined to think that moment has passed. Even when they were current, as Leila demonstrates, the Ngarrindjeri were not passively singing songs that contained derogatory images of black people. They took the tunes and harmonies they liked and changed the words. During the Royal Commission several of the women applicants began working on a Gilbert and Sullivan opera with patter songs that put the "model of a modern major-general" in a new context.

Before contact with Europeans, Ngarrindjeri music had been primarily vocal, with a percussive accompaniment on the "native drum" with clubs, boomerangs, or lap clap. By the twentieth century Ngarrindjeri were playing a number of instruments which had the effect of stabilising intervals and metre (Ellis *et al.* 1988: 61) and the "non-narrative patterned repetitions of corroboree song texts could not be successfully combined with the stanzaic constructions of introduced songs" (Donaldson 1995: 144). The increased song repertoire may have delighted many, but the songs being sung had a near universal quality that Ellis *et al.* (1988: 151-2) claim obliterated the significant regional variations. I think this may be true for a musicologist, but this anthropologist saw people taking songs and making them local and personal. A song became "owned" through repeated singing. Like Pinkie Mack's "*Pata winema*" song, Annie Koolmatrie took a melody and made the song about the Coorong hers; Leila made a lullaby of a racist song.

In the *Song Book of Narrunga, Kaurna and Ngarrindjeri Songs* (Amery *et al.* 1990), produced at a two-week song-writing workshop funded by the National Aboriginal Language Project at Tandanya in March 1990, a number of the best-loved songs were recorded and new ones composed. There is a range of styles: some are in English, some a mixture of English and language, others all in language. There is one based on a story in Taplin (1879: 39) of *nori*, the pelican, and his fight with the greedy magpies at *Tipangk* (Point Sturt). There is another, "*Ngarrindjeri Ringbalin*" by Smokey Varcoe, Cathy McGrath and Chester Schultz, sung in language with the accompanying dance movement and part singing indicated so that children may partake of a "performance". Amery (1995: 76) writes of revival and reclamation of Nunga languages: "The content of most songs seeks to affirm Aboriginality, dealing with aspects of Nunga life, Nunga history and Aboriginal values."

At Daisy Rankine's sixtieth birthday, celebrated at Camp Coorong in early November 1996, for the first time I hear Ngarrindjeri singing. After the speeches, the cutting of the cake, the saying of grace, and thank-yous to all present, Syd Graham sets up his sound equipment and Auntie Maggie settles in. With some coaxing, Veronica Brodie joins her, and arm in arm they sing "The Old Rugged Cross", "Just a Closer Walk with Thee", "I'll Never Love Blue Eyes Again", while the little children dance their own swirly-twirly dances and those of us who can remember the words join in, harmonise, and tap the rhythm. Favourite songs written out by hand are tucked away in a handbag and they laugh when they miss a cue. On other occasions I have seen song folders in which carefully arranged typescripts are protected by plastic sleeves. Aunty Maggie and Aunty Veronica adjust their glasses so they can read the words.

Mostly people play by ear. One weekend several of the women had come to stay with us at Clayton. We'd agreed that running up and the down the stairs was not an option, and made up beds downstairs. Veronica Brodie spies the electric organ under the stairs. "Do you have the key?" I'd never thought about it. I don't play, but I love singing. The key of course was in the seat and Veronica quickly was making music. "Where did you learn?" I ask. "In the home at Tanderra from sitting next to Dora Hunter. She was two years older than me." We sing a range of songs. By now I'm becoming familiar with the repertoire. My daughter recalls the singing we did on long trips when she was younger and that I still do. I remember my grandmother who sang and what that meant to me then and now.

Aunty Maggie is known as a great singer, and indeed I have seen her sing people half her age hoarse. When she arrived at the Christmas carols gathering, Graham Wilson broke into a sweet rendition of "Maggie". Aunty Maggie and Veronica settled in, sang their favourites, the teenagers were doing their thing in the living-room, and the grannies [grandchildren] were cuddled up with their aunties. The last songs to be sung were children's mission songs, in language, with Aunty Maggie teaching the children the actions to show "love", and "generosity" for "Thank God for the Flowers". All was well with the world. Around 11 p.m., with the remaining food shared, the laundry retrieved and loaded in a big plastic hamper in my car, Veronica decides that I should see the Christmas lights in the homes of residents in the Largs Bay area. Bonney, her grand-daughter, is delighted. We're still humming. I recall Aunty Rosie talking about going down to the lake to watch the old people corroboree: In the night time we thought it was like going to a picture show now. That's all we had (Ellis 1965: LA 106). Veronica is telling me, I wish there were more times we could gather like this, where there is community and fellowship, not trouble, where we can forget the stress and enjoy the fellowship, but the young ones are not really interested. A great number of young ones aren't interested, but there are a few and they have important role models, albeit sometimes reluctant ones.

Pakari Songs: Twentieth-Century Dreaming

"I can hear the people singing, singing songs of long ago," Annie Koolmatrie sang. She always included her "Coorong Song" in her repertoire, Leila Rankine observed. The "Coorong Song", sung by Annie Koolmatrie, in old slow ballad style to a variation on the tune of "Lay My Head Beneath a Rose", recalls her husband Jack's country on the Coorong. Annie, born at Swan Reach in the 1890s, was the daughter of Rita Mason, who lived into her nineties and whose song talents were noted by Ellis (1963–5: 37). Accompanying herself on the button accordion, Annie Koolmatrie was in demand at social gatherings. She too sang "The Old Rugged Cross", popular music, and her own compositions. It is Annie Koolmatrie who is one source for the meaning of the words to "*Pata winema*".

Ocean Bay, The Coorong, 1996 (Diane Bell)

188

Singing: "Pakari Nganawi Ruwi"

In an extended interview conducted in the late 1970s, Annie and Jack Koolmatrie (Ely 1980) talk with Leigh Hobba about the old times; about why people are reluctant to divulge details; and the traditional knowledge that is still accessible. Annie Koolmatrie travelled up and down the river and remembers her father speaking his and other people's language. I'm only the last one around by the end who can do the corroboree. I can dance. My grandfather was a great dancer. He invented quite a lot of corroborees and that was one of the corroborees I dance . . . you've got to do them right. I'm a bit disappointed in all the younger ones . . . There were songs . . . [for] when they were troubled and sad . . . This is all gone. I can remember the rejoicing part of that corroboree what I sang (Ely 1980: 17, 21). This sentiment that the younger ones know little and that no one was as knowledgeable as one's own grandparent echoes down the generations, but in the late 1990s the refrain has become more poignant. There have been generations of Ngarrindjeri raised with little knowledge or regard for the music and stories of their forebears. In a later interview with William Lobban, Annie Koolmatrie (1969: 1729A) said, We know a lot of places but we don't say nothing. However, her songs are an important moment in the history of Ngarrindjeri singing and, although they are unlike the traditional songs of Milerum recorded by Tindale, they nonetheless tell of Ngarrindjeri lands.

Annie Koolmatrie's "Coorong Song" evokes the singing of the old people of the Coorong. It establishes a link with their feelings and the land. Her reference to change, as inevitable as the changing of the seasons, and the longing for people and place are not dissimilar to that Taplin (1873: 117) noted in the song, "Shall I ever see my country again?" and the Berndts (1951: 89) in the Piltindjeri lament. The sentiments expressed in songs and the sentiments about songs endure. The language is English and the musical form non-Indigenous, but the people and places are Ngarrindjeri.

"The Coorong Song"[24]

Let me sing about the Coorong,
where the mighty seas roar,
sounds like music in the spring time,
singing sounds of long ago.

189

First chorus:
Birds of every kind are whistling
as when the evening shadows fall.
I can hear the people singing
singing songs of long ago.

When the stormy winds are blowing
and the rolling waves are free
and game grows full and plenty
and on their tribal grounds they lived.

Second chorus:
Round the camp fires they are singing
all their songs of long ago.
Oh I hear the people singing
all their songs of long ago.

As I travel through the Coorong,
thinking of the long ago,
proud and happy were the people
and all their songs of long ago.

Repeat second chorus:
Now today the times are changing
summer comes and winter goes
strangers coming to their country
and living on their tribal grounds.

Repeat second chorus.

Leila Rankine's poem "The Coorong" celebrates similar relationships.

Land of my father's people
Place of my ancestors' past
Never will I forget you
For you are dear to my heart.

For Dorothy Shaw, now in her early fifties, Raukkan is home, but her feelings for Ngarrindjeri places she visits are strong and reflected in her music. We sit on her porch at Raukkan and talk. She plays "Call of the Coorong",[25] then talks about "The Dreaming of a Ngarrindjeri *Memini*" and its composition in 1994. Auntie Dodo had shared with us some of the stories of Kumarangk, just enough for us

190

to understand. I said to the Lord, "Lord, if what Auntie Dodo said has meaning for us, to know about our history, can He please show us?" And all that week I was down there, I just kept humming the tune, and I didn't know what it was, because I hadn't heard it before, and when I came home, I kept talking to the Lord, and the words started to come for the chorus. I knew it wasn't a verse, and then the rest of it started to come, and talk about the land, and it fell into place. It is a miracle that He gave it to me. God is the creator of everything, and to know the story that Aunty Dodo shared. The chorus was just there, and it came out in the tune. People say to me that I should get copyright, but the money doesn't mean anything to me. Someone else might sing it, and that's OK by me if others sing it and praise the Lord.

> The Dreaming of a Ngarrindjeri *Memini*
>
> This island is not just any island
> It belongs to the Ngarrindjeri *Memini*.
> It shelters her from the stormy weather
> Kumarangk is all of life to the Ngarrindjeri *Memini*.
>
> *Chorus:*
> Follow your heart, your dreams will come true,
> Every day, every breath you take,
> God will bless the way.
> Never give up, but keep your faith,
> Believe in His Holy grace,
> Ngarrindjeri *Memini*, Kumarangk is our home.
>
> This island is not just any island,
> From the River Murray to the Coorong Hummocks.
> It's welcomed everyone who lived in these homelands,
> Kumarangk is all of life to the Ngarrindjeri *Memini*.

Doreen Kartinyeri recalls when Dot Shaw "started to get" the song: Down at the Murray Mouth, at the mound, between the Mouth House and the Murray Mouth, some of the women walked out when the tide was out, but that place was so peaceful, just to be there, just to sit there. When I first took the girls down there, the young ones in their late twenties and early thirties, they couldn't believe the feeling they had. The first meeting after Graham's Castle and we all went over to the island and just sat there. Some started to cry and felt overwhelmed. A couple of the girls had lost their mothers recently and that's the closest they'd felt to their mothers for a long time. They were at peace, content, strong in themselves and I told them I've always felt that there. I could reach out and touch her. We used to camp not far from there. This day Dot was playing the guitar, that's when she started to get the song. It was just amazing to see Dot do that. She was putting together something that would be with us for a long time, the Kumarangk song.

On occasions when the Ngarrindjeri applicants gather, they may sing the "Kumarangk Song". It was sung at the Murray Mouth, during the Mathews Inquiry and at the Weavers' Conference. It was sung in Pitjantjatjara lands, and no doubt in the USA on the weavers' trip also. Listening to the Raukkan schoolchildren, singing "Kingston Town" and "Somewhere" at the close of the Weavers' Conference, I wonder how long before they will be singing the songs of their own composers? There are bands, tapes and CDs in circulation. Jimmy Rankine, son of Jean and Henry, is there one morning when I call in to see his parents. He tells me, Music taught me about strengthening myself. It comes from where I feel. I'm singing the truth. On his CD *Rough Image* (1994) Jimmy sings, You can modernise us but we don't want to be westernised. And then there are Victor Wilson's songs which take a strong stand on Ngarrindjeri struggles to survive in the face of intrusion into their lands. His 1995 composition "Clan Woman Sister" has by now been sung many times. Dot Shaw: When we went to Melbourne in March 1997, we sang Vic's song then. He gave us permission. He said, "It's your song as well as mine." Maggie Jacobs and Veronica Brodie sang it too and we changed it a bit when they sang it. He laughed when we told him.

My clan woman sister, We owe so much to you, Victor Wilson sang to a gathering of Ngarrindjeri and their friends at Goolwa. I'd heard the words the week before when Genevieve and I were visiting Victor's older sister Isobelle in Murray Bridge. Vic, via the speaker phone, gave us a preview of the words he had been "given".

> My clan woman sister,
> We owe so much to you,
> You're our mother, our aunty, our grandmother too.
> You're a stateswoman, freedom fighter, defender of our land.
> My clan woman sister, we stand in awe of you.

Maybe a tune will come to me, he said, at the moment it is a poem. By the end of the week it had a tune. Vic's band is popular; there is a brisk trade in tapes of his songs; and he has much experience to record in song.

It is an earlier song I've heard Victor singing at his place in Murray Bridge, his *Pakari* song that I ask about in June 1997. In this song Victor shifts from English to Ngarrindjeri as the litany of the things for which he is giving thanks grows. The form is not unlike that noted by Meyer (1843: 52) and expresses sentiments similar to those recorded by Taplin. "*Pakari?*" I comment. "That's in Tindale and Berndt, except they render it *pekeri*." The Berndts (1993: 222) say the songs concerned *ngatji* (totem) traditional themes and were sung to clan tunes. Pinkie Mack knew one about the pelican, *nori*, that could cure sickness and "it was not to be played with lightly" (*ibid.*: 215). "*Pakari Nganawi Ruwi*", it's a prayer song of my country, says Victor. We don't spend enough time listening to the spirit. The power of the spirits to speak is not something experienced by this generation alone. The Berndts (*ibid.*: 213) write of a famous composer of songs, especially *pekeri*, who drew inspiration from his dreams. In addition, people would come to him with unusual dreams. "Once he had the details, he would lie full length on his back, close his eyes and rhythmically tap out the words on his chest, putting them together to fit the chant or tune." By lying on his back on the land he could make contact with the power of his country. Tindale (1931–4: 230) records Milerum as saying: "Sometimes when you are dreaming half asleep, half awake, a song comes to you. When it comes like this you must sing it straight away, that is how we find new songs." James Brooks Kartinyeri told of how he also needed to lie down and tap out the rhythm. In other parts of Australia songmen and songwomen struggle to find the words to explain the mysteries of the communication of the spirit. Bobby Lane (Marret *et al.* 1997: 15) explained that his "cousin brother" had appeared to him in a dream. I was fast asleep . . . but I can hear this . . . spirit come and sing to me. Next day I wake up and I keep on practising wherever I go, then I get that song."

Vic and I have finished reading his part of the manuscript and he has volunteered phrases from "*Pakari Nganawi Ruwi*" that are appropriate to the text. I ask him what he thinks of my idea that there is something enduring in the way songs tell of feelings and the way they are composed. I use the word "found". Victor quickly corrects me. *Given*, songs are given. And yes, it's the same spirit.[26] I read back through my notes and of course this has been the verb that Dot Shaw and Doreen Kartinyeri used and Jimmy Rankine spoke of, that special black way togetherness so gifted to us from young and old.

Pakari Nganawi Ruwi
(Prayer Song of My Country)

Take us back
To our country
To the place
Where we call home
Ngarrindjeri Ruwi
Nganawi Ruwi
To the place
Where we belong
Nangi Winamaldti
Made it for us
In the Dreamtime
Long ago.

He taught our *Pakanus*
To take good care of it
He made all good things there for us
Like *Kungari Ngartjara*
Kanmeri Pilakar
Ke-Ah Nukun Malawi
Wrukkun Kurangkgai
Trokkari Ngantin
Ratharathi Kykulun
Ritjarooki Ringbalin
Unngarrindjeri Ruwi
Ngarrindjar Ruwa
Nganawi Ruwi
Unguni Ngninta
Nganawi Ruwi
Nganawi Ruwi

© Victor Wilson 1996

Celebrating the Long Walk, Goolwa, November 1996
Belinda Stillisano, Cathy Carter, Glenys Wilson, Victor Wilson,
Marshall Carter (Genevieve Bell)

Vic Wilson's songs, like those recorded by Tindale, were composed for a particular moment but will in time come to represent a more diffuse cluster of issues and more generalised feelings. "Clan Woman Sister" was sung for the first time at Amelia Park, the site of the bridge protests at Goolwa, a traditional camping site and place of ceremonies, a site already damaged by road works and threatened by future development. Goolwa, a place celebrated in older Ngarrindjeri songs, was a significant location for the first public performance of Vic Wilson's song, but so was the occasion, the conclusion of the Long Walk, a five-day trek from Adelaide to Goolwa.[27] After the Weavers' Conference in November 1996, many Indigenous and non-Indigenous persons who supported the Ngarrindjeri in their stand against the bridge joined the weavers in the Long Walk. The walk brought together black and white, young and old, male and female, environmentalists, unionists, feminists, politicians, lawyers, citizens for reconciliation, and supporters of religious freedoms. Each evening the numbers swelled as others who were working during the day joined the camps to eat, sing, and converse with the walkers who later slept under the stars. Those who were not up to the physical rigours of the walk travelled by bus, visited with friends, shopped, and cheered on those who were

195

walking for them. Spirits were buoyed. People felt good. After so many body blows from the courts, the parliament, the media and "the experts", the walkers were making a clear statement that they could still walk tall. A thousand people lent their support. The young Ngarrindjeri present were attentive to the needs of their elders and saw the walk as one way they could "testify" to their beliefs. Veronica Brodie is correct when she says they need more occasions in which young people join in. It is true there are many who know little. The lament about the passing of the Piltindjeri is as relevant today as it was when composed in the 1880s. However, one of the unintended consequences of the applicants' struggle to protect their sacred places has been a new fellowship, a generation of occasions for new forms of fellowship, and a sharing of stories and songs across the generations.

Ngarrindjeri have continued to sing in church, in their homes, at social gatherings and political rallies. They have adopted some styles and rejected others, but I think we can tease out threads that tie their songs and the songsters of today to enduring values of Ngarrindjeri culture. Tamsin Donaldson (1995: 157), exploring the range of motivations that underlie the various mixes of Indigenous and introduced song styles, emphasises the inventiveness with which the heritages that people are currently concerned to "learn back" have been "continuously reworked, redirected and enjoyed in new ways whatever the larger circumstances of each successive generation of inheritors". I was struck and charmed by the obvious enjoyment of singing and the seriousness with which songmen and songwomen are held within Ngarrindjeri society, and the evocations of person and place in their songs. Where there has been considerable disruption and intrusion on Indigenous lands, Donaldson (*ibid.*) argues, Aboriginal musical life serves "as a site for creative and sustaining cultural responses to the facts of that history itself." This is true, and for Ngarrindjeri the creativity is associated with feelings and songs are still said to be "given". They are not composed by the songster. Their genesis is beyond the world of mundane reality. The lives being celebrated in contemporary songs may be vastly different from that of a century ago, but the "principles", as Isobelle Norvill called them, remain.

To be a singer in the days before the mission, one needed to know more than the words and melody. Songs, like genealogies, brought people back to the land, to its sacred places and stories. Songs, like *ngatji* (totem), were embedded in cryptic codes. A deceptively simple image, phrase, or even a single word could evoke the complexities of Ngarrindjeri religious symbolism. To sing such songs one needed authority and power. Singers were revered. Songs were sacred texts. In reaching back into the historical record, there is much to be learned regarding Ngarrindjeri beliefs and practices regarding totems, kinship and marriage, land tenure, governance and sorcery, but little on the songs that were sung. Singing together offered a sense of fellowship, but was also a way of fixing certain facts, and sequences. The songs were mnemonic devices which fixed in memory place-names and clan names in particular. Songs belong in complex webs of meanings, in sequences and hierarchies; when these are interrupted as dramatically as they have been during the past 170 years, there is an impact on all knowledge, not just that of the songs themselves. But the land is still there. The stories are being reclaimed. The weavers are out there marking the rhythm of the land and the seasons. Songsters are being given the texts that link them to the power of the land and the ancestors.

Tamsin Donaldson (1995: 143) poses two key questions: What has become of the inherited Aboriginal forms of music and their performance contexts; and what Aboriginal responses have there been to the introduced music? She traces the "selective persistence of the modified old and selective appropriation of the modified new" as inter-related processes that have thus far generated a range of macaronic texts (mixtures of Aboriginal and English languages), but not any "truly syncretic forms or performance contexts". Ngarrindjeri certainly have a strong musical tradition today and it is one that acknowledges and draws on a range of musical influences. What is distinctively Ngarrindjeri about the songs is the evocation of particular places (not just a generalised sentimentality about country as expressed in some popular songs and ballads); the ways in which the songs memorialise key moments and individuals. The songs look back to pre-contact days with the call and pull of the old people, remembered or singing in language; they provide rallying points in contemporary struggles; and they anticipate a future for the grannies, who cuddled in the lap of a favourite aunt or nanna are listening and absorbing the atmosphere. It will be interesting to see what meanings will be ascribed to the "*Pata winema*" song as language revival plays itself out in the Ngarrindjeri community.

Diana Eades (1981) asks can people who no longer speak language and do ceremony be "traditional? It would be convenient to say they cannot be "traditional" and that is what many commentators have done. Eades offers ways in which we might understand "traditions" as continuing forces in the lives of people living in southeast Queensland, but intends her argument about the importance of relationships and the different registers of English to hold for all of settled Australia. Jerry Schwab (1988: 78) focuses on identity among Aborigines in Adelaide and asserts it is "fundamentally a matter of kinship". In both southeast Queensland and Adelaide "lingo", or "the language", made up of a limited number of local words interwoven with English, is a powerful tool, to be used when, and where, and how it is needed. It resonates with histories of lost lands and peoples, of discrimination and oppressive policies, but it also defiantly marks out a distinctive social domain. Rather than see Ngarrindjeri songs as having been obliterated by contact, I think we can track a dynamic between the wider society—especially the church which created safe places for singing, and more particularly spaces where singing remained spiritually important—and Ngarrindjeri love of singing today, their cherishing of songmen and songwomen, and the vitality of their composers. The musician, Ellis *et al.* (1988: 154) write, is a powerful person who in knowing the music knows about life. The life of the late twentieth century is significantly different from that of the early nineteenth, but songs and songsters provide intricate and loving links between these worlds and hope for the future. At the conclusion of the Weavers' Conference in 1996, the participants made a "world mat" into which everyone wove their pattern of shells, beads, feathers and fibres. It will travel to future conferences and it was said to carry "a song waiting to be sung".

4

Family, Friends and Other Relations

Ngatji: "Friend, Countryman, Protector"

Ngatji, mainly he's your friend. He'll guard you. Doug Wilson volunteers in one of our first conversations. We are sitting at the kitchen table enjoying a cup of tea with his younger sister Veronica Brodie. A formal portrait of their father, Dan Wilson, from the Tindale collection, and more recent family snapshots are carefully arranged on the shelves in the living room. On the kitchen bench are still more prints waiting to be framed. I am slowly getting to know the Wilson clan. I've met brothers Doug and Graham, but I only know their sister Leila, who died in 1992, through their stories, her poems and photographs. Veronica's daughters and the grannies bustle in and out of the house and chat on the phone. Today Doug is talking about his mother's mother: Our grandmother, Laura Harris, would see different birds in the lake and in the river and suddenly up would come a musk duck. It would dive, not fly, and my grandmother would be talking to him, just like another human being, and down he'd go and swim. She'd talk to him in language and ask him questions, just like chatting to a person.

In a small box of treasured items, kept on the bureau in her bedroom, Veronica Brodie has a photograph of herself with what she calls a "rogue pelican" at Meningie. She writes on note paper with a pelican motif. In Hahndorf, I find her a pelican fridge magnet for her collection. My *ngatji*, she says fondly: When I was about four, we'd go down to Pelican Point and there's a landing there, a strip, where all the pelicans come in at sundown. I always used to look at it when I was little and think that was the end of the world. I called it Land's End. And I would run up there and get in amongst the pelicans

199

Rogue pelican and Veronica Brodie
at Meningie, late 1980s
(Veronica Brodie's personal collection)

and run around amongst them. Veronica holds her arms outstretched and is at once a child wheeling, swooping and banking amongst these birds. They were beautiful and they'd wouldn't bite me or anything. And I'd just run there and play with those pelicans. They used to just sit there and I'd run round and pat them, and then I'd run back to the camp. The old people watched to make sure I didn't run the wrong way into the channel. And I grew up with that, the pelican as my *ngatji*. Every year I'd look forward to *nukkin* the pelicans. There in the sources is *nori*, the pelican, one of the *ngatji* of the Wilson clan (Radcliffe-Brown 1918: 22-39; Berndt *et al.* 1993: 309). There also is the story of *Nori*, *Thukeri* (bony bream), and the magpie at Point Sturt (Taplin 1879: 39), a story which was memorialised in a song composed at the 1990 workshop at Tandanya (Amery *et al.* 1990: 32).

Leila Rankine, Veronica's older sister, wrote with longing of the Coorong and her favourite places. Her poems "The Journey" and "Journey's End" conjure up a land of plenty, and one she excitedly anticipates visiting. Year after year different families would return to their camping sites along the Coorong. The Wilson clan returned to Pelican Point. Maggie Jacobs, Leila Rankine's sister-in-law, tells the story of the way in which the pelican, *nori*, provided the necessary sign the day that Leila Rankine's ashes were scattered down the Coorong. It is a story she has told on other occasions (see Hemming 1996: 30) but each telling brings tears to the eyes of

200

those who hear it. Aunty Maggie, tall and straight at seventy-eight years of age, has a particularly majestic way of recounting the story.

Sisters-in-law Maggie Jacobs and Leila Rankine, 1989
(Margaret Jacobs' personal collection)

I'll tell you about *ngatjis*, that totem. You know it was Leila's wish to come down and have a last look at all the countryside before she died. Well, the pelican is her *ngatji*. We brought Leila from Camp Coorong to Raukkan, and we had a bit of a service for Leila there. And when we went to go off, to leave Raukkan, and we came down to the ferry and, you know that little jetty at the Raukkan, there's always hundreds of pelicans, you know, they're always sitting there. *Ánu?* We started to come across but there was no pelicans. You see them in the water swimming, see them sitting, four of them sitting there. But that day there wasn't a pelican to be seen. We come along to the ferry and just before we pulled into the ferry, one pelican was sitting there and he just looked in and we had the window open, and he, only one pelican, he just looked in to Leila and he just went like this with his wings [Aunty Maggie folds her arms in and out across her chest], you know, three or four times, and Veronica said to her sister, "Leila, look, he's saying good-bye to you." And this is exactly what he was doing, you know, he was saying good-bye. And Leila said, "Yeah."

201

Then, after she died, and we was having a service at Pelican Point, one pelican flew over, flew right over us, the group that was on the bank there. And Lizzie Rigney said, she said, "Oh look," she said, you know, "There's Aunty Leila, the pelican," because when we see a pelican we'll say, "Oh, there's Aunty Leila, or old Granny Koomi [Leila's mother] or somebody like that," because that's their *ngatji*. Anyway after we finished the service and we got in the ranger boat to come down to Ngarlung and then all of a sudden there was another pelican and the pelican, you know, usually you see them in the dozens, you know, but this time there was only one pelican, and this one pelican, other than the one that flew over then when we started off, there was one pelican, and when we got in the boat, the ranger boat, and the pelican flew low on the water, like this, right in front of us. [Aunty Maggie swoops with her arms.] It skimmed.

One pelican flew right in front of us; took us right over to where we were, but when we got off at Ngarlung and the women were singing the hymn "God be with you". I carried Leila's ashes. Veronica and I went to walk up and we found it a bit hard, you know, because the sand was a bit heavy. And Tom said, "No, it's not this place; it's down further." There was only just a few of us, those that were pretty close to Leila, and we started off again. And this one pelican, just the one pelican again, he was just almost touching the water and he flew right up, right to where we buried Leila, to where we put Leila's ashes, then he disappeared, see. All right, then, that was all right. You know, Roslyn Milera, Leila's care person, she couldn't get over it, but we know this is what happens, *ánu*, Veronica? That's the *ngatji*, you see. Our animals tell us everything.

Like many other people of southeastern Australia, Leila Rankine, Veronica Brodie, Doug and Graham Wilson have a multi-cultural heritage on which they can draw. They have impeccable Ngarrindjeri credentials through their father, Daniel Wilson (1890–1959), the man from whom Aunty Rosie got wire for her weaving and hessian sacks to wrap the rushes; and his father Old Dan Wilson (1860–1921), a young man on Taplin's mission, a member of the Glee Club and an important source of information for visiting researchers. On their mother's side, they can trace back to her maternal grandfather, to yet another Ngarrindjeri ancestor, George Spender of the Coorong. His wife, Latarlare, generally acknowledged as a Kaurna woman, spent much of her life in Ngarrindjeri lands. Latarlare and George Spender travelled around, as people did in those days, Veronica explains. It was only when her daughter Laura got a house at Raukkan, that Latarlare settled down and went to live there. Laura Spender, who had married a Ngarrindjeri man, Jacob Harris, in 1892, also lived with her husband's people. By marrying into the Ngarrindjeri side she learned the language and ways of the people and was accepted, Veronica adds. It was common for women to settle on their husband's territory and to raise their children to be wise in the ways of that land. And it is knowledge of the rivers and lakes and her kinship with the rich bird life of the region that Doug's story of grandmother Laura recalls. It was knowledge she needed to survive, but she also was very much of that country and she chose to be buried on Ngarrindjeri lands. Leila Rankine had chosen to return to Ngarrindjeri lands also, but she did not neglect her Kaurna heritage. She asked to be buried with all her old love letters and her wedding bouquet made of ibis feathers, a Kaurna bird, from her grandmother Laura Glanville. Veronica, who was responsible for seeing that this was done, added: It was a privilege in those days to have it made of a tribal totem.

Veronica Brodie begins to talk of her mother, Koomi (Rebecca Harris 1897–1974). It was her voice on a tape from the 1960s that brought Veronica into the Royal Commission, and it was there she was called upon to reconcile her Kaurna genealogy with her Ngarrindjeri knowledge.[1] How could she claim that her sister, Leila, and mother, Koomi, knew of Ngarrindjeri women's stories when their matriline back through Laura Glanville and Latarlare was Kaurna? At each generation level these women married Ngarrindjeri men and spent significant periods of time in Ngarrindjeri lands; there they heard stories of the land and, based on their interactions with local people and places, began to generate their own stories. Veronica's grand-mother and mother, her aunties and great-aunties, all grew to woman-hood in multi-cultural families with Ngarrindjeri fathers and with mothers who had ties to both Kaurna and Ngarrindjeri lands. Similarly, on her father's side, aunties, cousins and grandmothers were part of the family within which the children were raised. It is easy to fall into the trap of thinking of families as limited to primary kin, but Ngarrindjeri stories, as we have seen with those of Doreen Kartinyeri, reach out to include vast networks of extended kin. Women learned through these networks, but they also learned through direct interaction with the land and from their *ngatji*.

"What did Latarlare know of Ngarrindjeri rituals?" I ask Veronica. Well her husband was "smoked" on Mundoo Island, so she must have participated in that ceremony. I check the dates: George Spender died in 1897 and Latarlare in 1916. So in this family there was still active knowledge of traditional mortuary practices available into the twentieth century. Veronica Brodie spends a great deal of time puzzling over her complicated family history, one she is researching, more through talking to the old people than in archives, but she is happy when she finds written records and particularly photographs. There are gaps in her genealogy—she is still trying to learn more of the parents of Latarlare and speculates that her father may have been Ngarrindjeri. I don't do a lot of reading, but my interest came with my grandmother's side, her side of her history. In the Berndt book on the Spender side, because my great-grandmother Latarlare, Rebecca Spender, is in that book with Pinkie Mack and Queen Louisa Karpeny. They're all, they're sitting together with a group of women at Point McLeay [Berndt *et al.* 1993: 32] and I have been trying to find my connections with her side in regards to Hindmarsh Island, because my grandmother's brother, Alf Spender, was born on Hindmarsh Island and I know my grandfather, George Spender, was smoked on Mundoo Island. And so Latarlare had a lot to do with Hindmarsh Island. As a little girl, Koomi visited Hindmarsh Island with her grandmother, Latarlare, and Pinkie Mack. By then Pinkie Mack would have been in her fifties, certainly old enough to know of the importance of the place.

I find a reference in Taplin (7/8/1878)) to a Caroline Latarlare being beaten by her "half-caste husband Gollan". Was "Latarlare" functioning as a surname? Was Caroline a sister of Rebecca Latarlare, Veronica's great-grandmother? I find another reference to a Latarlare in Taplin's (1879: 56) chart of measurements. Standing five foot six and a quarter inches at age twenty-five, Latarlare was taller than her contemporaries. Taplin identifies her as of the "Coorong clan". If this is the same Latarlare as married George Spender, she was already known as being part of Ngarrindjeri lands.

If it is Caroline, it appears that the Latarlare family has a connection to the Coorong. Others find the puzzle interesting, and Veronica has spent happy hours at Trunceena with Peter and Meryl Mansfield looking at photographs of "The Needles" where George Spender was born.

Doreen Kartinyeri has also puzzled over *ngatji* and family affiliations: I remember talking to Uncle Nat [Aunty Rosie's husband] about where he fitted into the Kropinyeri family. He had a little bit of a number of clans in him. He filled me in about totems and that's how I found out the pelican was our *ngatji*. My great-grandmother was born at Pelican Point. Her name was Mulparini. I thought I was Kartinyeri by blood line, but Aunty Rosie told me that wasn't so and I checked it out later and found that Archie Kartinyeri, my father's father, was fathered by a white man, Archibald George Clarke. Archie wasn't Albert Kartinyeri's son, but he took the name of his stepfather and married my grandmother, Sally Varcoe, under that name. He wasn't a Kartinyeri by blood and their totem was "wild dog". I thought that suited me. I have heard others say their *ngatji* must be a certain creature because they resemble it, or it is all about in their life, or was present at a significant moment. When I first moved into the house at Clayton, a little swallow that was nested under the carport flew into the house, upstairs, and settled against the window overlooking Hindmarsh Island. It allowed me to pick it up and take it back outside where it then sat on the "For Sale" sign and watched Genevieve and me unpacking. When I told Victor Wilson, about this episode, he said, Must be your *ngatji*. It knows you have work to do. He's come to help you.

George Trevorrow, always sensitive to the questions raised by cross-cultural communications, explains to Justice Mathews: *Ngatji* to non-Aboriginal people is like a totem which each one of us has and each group belongs to. It could be the pelican. It could be the swan. It could be the mullet. There are different species of—you know, animal, fish, plant, but each group belongs to that *ngatji*. A *ngatji* is something that is more than a close friend. It's more than your best friend. It's something that is more closely to you.

It's even closer, Tom Trevorrow told my class the day he and his wife Ellen spent at Holy Cross College, than a husband and wife. Like Laura Harris and her grand-daughter Leila Rankine, George

Trevorrow is also close enough to his *ngatji* to communicate. It's something that can speak to you, can give you information, can let you know of safety and danger. It's a very, very close affiliation with something that can relate to you as a whole, you know. According to the Berndts (1993: 237-8), a long time ago people conversed with their *ngatji*, *Wururi*, the spider who brought languages to the Ngarrindjeri, by climbing up "with their legs till they reached a *ngatji* person's head". Albert Karloan added that there were only two men of Tatjarapa, Efram Tripp and Manson Tripp, who could still talk to the *ngatji* in this way.[2]

Whether or not one may eat one's "totem" and under what conditions, is a matter of some speculation in the anthropological literature. Milerum, in the 1930s, told Tindale and Long (nd: 1): "A totem is one's 'friend' just as an elder brother, a father, and a father's father are one's best friends. Its flesh is like your own flesh." Doreen Kartinyeri remembered asking if the pelican could be eaten, but she had never heard anyone say it was permissible, or heard of anyone eating it. Veronica Brodie, with reference to the swan, her *ngatji* from Latarlare, alluded to the general belief that one should not eat one's *ngatji*. In some parts of Australia, such a practice would be akin to eating one's own flesh. Taplin (1873: 63) records taboos on eating one's *ngatji*. Berndt *et al.* (1993: 123) note the difficulty of obtaining "a complete coverage of *ngatji* taboos" in the 1940s, but state that when a particular *ngatji* was not killed or eaten it was said to be *narambi* (sacred, separated, taboo). That *ngatji* derives from the kin term for the maternal grandfather, *ngaityanowe* adds further depth to the "same flesh" aspect of the taboo.[3] Tindale (1974: 18, 24) writes of the people gathered for feasting on beached whales sung to shore by their "clever men", and notes that this was one of the few occasions when people entered the territory of others and ate their *ngatji*. As with all rules, there are exceptions. Taplin (1873: 63) said one's *ngatji* was taboo "except if it was good for food". In such a case, where one might eat one's *ngatji*, "great care was exercised in destroying the remains, lest an enemy get hold of them, and by his sorcery cause the *ngaitye* to grow inside of the eater, and cause his death" (Radcliffe-Brown 1918: 241; Taplin 1873: 63). Daisy Rankine added another dimension to the issue of what taboos apply to one's totem. I made feather flowers out of pelican feathers till I found out the pelican, as well as black swan, was also my *ngatji*, so it sort of stopped me from continuing to make feather flowers.

William Kropinyeri, whose *ngatji* was Willie wagtail, composed a love song in which he calls the object of his affection after his *ngatji*. The Berndts (1993: 586) translate the song text as concerning the bird with a small heart and two trees grown for shade. "The man and woman in the song had earlier planted two trees especially for themselves to sit under in the shade. She was sitting under one of these when William comes by. She did not want him to sit with her. He said, calling the name of the bird, that she has a small heart, and that the shade of those two trees was made for more than one person" (*ibid.*: 218). The song is interesting in several ways. Here is William Kropinyeri, a devout Christian who was obliged to relinquish one wife on becoming a Christian, composing a love song.[4] Here is a man composing a love song to woman with the same *ngatji* as himself, a person he would call "same flesh". The love is unrequited, as it must be, but this has not stopped the song being composed or sung. In looking to stories and songs to explicate Ngarrindjeri lore and law, we need to bear in mind that Ngarrindjeri lived complex lives which were not without contradiction and ambiguity.

The people with whom I am working pay attention to closeness of *ngatji* relationships, and *ngatji* affiliation is central to their identity as Ngarrindjeri. Exegeses of this complex term appear to have remained remarkably consistent over time. In Meyer's (1843: 86) vocabulary we find *ngayte* as "friend, countryman, protector" and this is perhaps the first recognition in the Australian literature of Aboriginal totemic ideas, and while it also captures the sense of current usage, Tindale (nd, e) points out it does not acknowledge the component of emblem. However, Ngarrindjeri are aware of this component. Albert Karloan (Berndt *et al.* 1993: 241) spoke of men who carried part of the *ngatji* animal into battle as an emblem of the clan and the young men who wore a necklace of claws of their *ngatji* which was passed onto a young brother (*ibid.*: 359). Taplin (29/11/1859) recorded *ngaitye* as meaning countryman, a father, a protector, and noted that his friend Captain Jack was named

207

"Tooreetparne" after his *ngatji*, wild dog, and "Paate" after frost which he also claimed as a countryman. A century later, the Berndts (1993: 25) gloss *ngatji* as "friend, mate", and referring to "a natural species or phenomenon". In 1966 Richard Kropinyeri volunteered to Elaine Treagus (1966: LA 3461A) that *ngatji* meant friendship.

Neither Veronica Brodie nor Doug Wilson has read any of these sources nor listened to the tapes, but they do use similar language to that in the written sources and they do allude to the special affinity that existed between a person and their *ngatji*. Their understanding comes from the old people who watched them at play, took them fishing, and told stories around the camps in the evening. Milerum was a contemporary of Old Dan Wilson, Doug and Veronica's grandfather, the man of whom Radcliffe-Brown (1918: 239) wrote as his "best informant". Milerum would have been a respected "uncle" for their father Dan Wilson at Raukkan. It is reasonable, I think, to claim some continuity for the term *ngatji*. However, what it has come to mean in practice for people who, for the most part, no longer live on their clan territories is another matter.

Ngatji: Accommodating Change

Working with Taplin's figures, Radcliffe-Brown (1918: 229-30) estimated that in 1840 there were approximately 4000-4500 Ngarrindjeri. Given the ravages of the earlier smallpox epidemics, it is reasonable to suggest an even higher figure for the 1700s. By 1877 Taplin could name only 613 Ngarrindjeri. One the critical consequences of this dramatic and rapid depopulation was that there were not sufficient surviving Ngarrindjeri to maintain the indigenous systems of land tenure and marriage. Clans amalgamated, some boundaries blurred, Ngarrindjeri married outsiders. Throughout the nineteenth century people moved (or were moved) into the towns and fringe camps and onto the missions. It is little wonder that, by the time systematic observations were made, there were competing versions of who belonged to which tract of land and what the territory should be properly be called. Taplin (1873: 2) identified eighteen *lakalinyeri*, which he translated as "tribe" or "clan"; Radcliffe-Brown (1918) named thirty-five clan/hordes, of which twenty-two were Yaraldi and ten Tangani; Tindale (1974: 23) mapped twenty-two Tangani clans and the Berndts (1993: 307-10) list seventy-eight Kukabrak clans of which thirty-eight are Yaraldi and nineteen Tangani (plus eight from other sources). It is an interesting exercise to attempt to tabulate the various findings of these researchers and in some cases the fortunes of certain clans as they amalgamate with others, split, and adjust their *ngatji* affiliations.[5] Most clans had several *ngatji*, and by tracking these one can sometimes figure out which clans, or subsets of clans, have moved where. Today fewer species are identified as *ngatji* than was the case in the 1940s, but given that *ngatji* connects one intimately to certain places and that Ngarrindjeri have not been able to visit certain places for decades—especially since the 1950s when properties began to be fenced, and in some cases for over a century—we might expect to see some accommodation of this in contemporary practice and belief.

The fact that all of Taplin's *lakalinyeri* were not located by twentieth-century researchers may say just as much about the way each did his field work and how each understood the nature of local and social organisation, as it says about the dramatic changes in Ngarrindjeri lands and lives. Even the Berndts and Tindale, who were working around the same time and often with the same "informants", mapped different clan and *ngatji* affiliations. Different questions will elicit different answers from different people. The Berndts' key "informant", Albert Karloan, knew well the Yaraldi country around Lake Albert and east of the Murray River. He was less sure when it came to Tangani land down the Coorong. Clarence Long (Milerum), on the other hand, knew the Coorong, and Tindale's mapping of this area is one of the most detailed we have in the pre-land rights literature for Australia. Taplin had worked with James Ngunaitponi, a Portaulan man, whose land was west of the Murray on Lake Alexandrina and, unlike Tindale, neither Taplin nor the Berndts did much on-the-ground mapping. Rather, they recorded details where they lived, be it Raukkan, Murray Bridge or Wellington. As any researcher knows, there is no substitute for visiting the country with Aboriginal people, camping near important sites and hearing the stories *in situ*.

To me the differences in the sources are evidence of an indigenous land tenure system of considerable complexity which was under enormous stress; it was mapped by researchers who at different historical moments asked various "informants" questions informed by particular models of social organisation. The idea that Ngarrindjeri lands could be divided amongst a specified number of patrilineal, patrilocal clans, each named (often after important sites), each with its own unique *ngatji*, and each having members marrying geographically and genealogically distant members of other clans was just that, an idea. Nonetheless it was a powerful idea and one that has shaped how Ngarrindjeri have been depicted both in the mid-nineteenth and late twentieth centuries. The nature of so-called totems, their relationship to clans and the most accurate ways in which to characterise local groups is the stuff of Australian anthropology (Peterson 1976; Tindale 1974; Sutton 1998) and Ngarrindjeri ethnography figures prominently in the literature.[6] We read of Ngarrindjeri lands, lands of abundance, lands of plentiful food and reliable water, where clans were relatively small and boundaries were jealously guarded, and where inter-relations with other clans and with the neighbours of the Ngarrindjeri, such as the Kaurna, Bungandidj (Boandik), Narungga, and Tatiara, were established through trade, marriage and various ritual relations.

It appears that Ngarrindjeri had ways of accommodating change and, although the velocity of change has intensified over the past two centuries, the patrilineal, patrilocal clan was more flexible than it might first appear. Two clans with the same *ngatji* were considered like siblings, or, as I have heard people say, "same blood".[7] This was one way of dealing with demographic imbalances pre- and post-contact. Another was that *ngatji* affiliation could be traced through both parents (Berndt *et al.* 1993: 33). This became increasingly important for those whose fathers were non-indigenous or not Ngarrindjeri. In 1966, Rosie Kropinyeri told Cath Ellis (1966: LA 106) that her mother's *ngatji* was black duck, but that she didn't know her father's as his family was from Western Australia. Reuben Walker (1934), whose father was a white man, took his country from his mother's side. It is his *ruwee* (country) at Goolwa of which he writes longingly. Veronica Brodie and her siblings have pelican, from their father, as their *ngatji*, but from the story of Leila's burial it appears that Koomi was also able to communicate with the

210

pelican, the *ngatji* of her husband. *Ngatji* affiliation could also be reckoned from place of birth, *ngatjurtul*, (Tindale and Long nd: 1) and this became important for those born on missions away from their own country. In pre-contact times, when Ngarrindjeri wives came to live on their husband's clan territory and children were born on their father's country, they could be said to inherit his *ngatji* by descent. But they were also growing up in a place where the behaviour of his *ngatji* would be noted by other clan members who would reinforce the child's attachment to the place and its species. Thus place of birth and father's *ngatji* may come to mean the same thing. Some of the confusion regarding *ngatji* affiliation for those families who have not lived on the clan territories for several generations, I think, arises from this conflation of place of residence and place of birth. Those who were reared on the river may assert *pondi* as their *ngatji*, even though, if we could go back through their genealogy, it may not be the clan *ngatji* of one of their parents. Of course, not all children were born on their father's land. People travelled into other territories; and there are accounts of wives staying on their father's country. Tindale (1941: 242) recorded a song of a man who had lived so long on his wife's country near Yankalilla that all who knew him thought he spoke only their language, Merildakald. Only when he was an old man did he sing in Tangani the song he had kept secret all those long years, which told of his frightening experiences in a strange land.

Despite the difficulties, dislocations and dispossession in Ngarrindjeri lands, people continued to strive to be in close contact with their country and kin; key individuals kept alive the stories that connected them to people and places. Certain families continued to holiday down the Coorong; and to pay careful attention to the genealogical closeness of young persons contemplating marriage. There were well-established mixed populations in a number of centres where key families, rather than clans, organised large gatherings, and were identified with specific areas. Clan names are still known, especially by those who live on or near their clan territories, and some of these families function as *ad hoc* clans with respect to their land, but clan names are not the primary identifier which is most commonly evoked in discussions and disputes about who may properly speak for what land, story, or genealogy. Today people commonly speak of the "families", a unit held together by blood lines, but lines that may be traced through all four grand-parents and even by reference to one's great-grandparents and their siblings. Thus the "family" is larger than what might have been a clan group and smaller that a dialect/language grouping such as Yaraldi or Tangani.

It is my impression that, in addition to the shift from clan to family as a unit of identification for Ngarrindjeri, there are now what might be called "regional *ngatji*". Point Pearce people are known as "butterfish". Others say, "We come from the river so we must be *pondi*, the Murray cod"; or "We were born at Raukkan so we must be black swan." At Point Pearce Isobelle Norvill recalls the term "*pondi* breed" for the river people and it's one I've heard used in Murray Bridge. Ellen Trevorrow had assumed that her *ngatji* was *pondi* because she came from the river, but her mother Daisy Rankine explained it was black swan because Ellen was born at Raukkan. These are ongoing discussions, I learned in June 1997, as Daisy Rankine and her daughter considered the comparative importance of blood lines, residence, place of birth and personal attachments. It is a conversation I have heard also with reference to living at Point Pearce but being Ngarrindjeri by birth. Victor Wilson posed this question to his sister Isobelle, who was raised at Point Pearce and sometimes uses Narrunga words: Your parents who are German born and bred are travelling in a train across Europe. You are born as the train passes through France. Are you French? Through these family discussions what it means to be Ngarrindjeri and the way *ngatji* affiliation informs that identity, contemporary Ngarrindjeri identity is negotiated and made known.

Ngatji Stories: *Krowali, Krayi* and Others

Neville Gollan, son of Cecil Gollan and Jean (née Walker from the New South Wales coast), grandson of Adeline Sumner and Michael Gollan (Eileen McHughes' mother's father), has extensive and intimate knowledge of the Coorong. Now in his late fifties, Neville Gollan grew up between Point McLeay and the Coorong, and lived for seven years on Rabbit Island. His father had a dairy farm at

212

Boundary Bluff. At around the age of nine or ten, he began to learn from his grandfather. As he explains the places where he and others have lived and travelled, he draws in the sand. The story of the *krowali*, the white-faced heron, commonly called "blue crane", is one he told to Jane Mathews at Stoney Well, on 25 April 1996. The location was important.[8] Stories told on or near the site or sites to which they refer often provide details not deemed appropriate to disclose when the story-teller is in foreign territory. It doesn't "feel right" to speak of matters of spiritual importance under those circumstances. Nonetheless, Neville Gollan adds to the story as we read the manuscript together in Murray Bridge over a year later. The story concerns the ills that befall one when the rules regarding *ngatji* are not followed. It does not matter that there was no ill intent. There are no innocent mistakes in this system of summary justice. One has to heed the signs and the instructions of one's elders.

George Trevorrow's grandma Rosie asked my uncle, George Koolmatrie (her husband) and myself, if we could go down and get a duck or a swan because that's our natural resource food. So we took the rifle with us and we went down between Stoney Well, a mid-way camp for road maintenance, and Wood's Well which is the next little station

L–R. George Trevorrow, Neville Gollan, Tom Trevorrow
at Camp Coorong, 1996 (Genevieve Bell)

213

on. We came along the shore looking for a duck, or a swan. Now normally if you get a bit of breeze there will be ducks and swans flying, or sometimes just feeding. Anyhow we came along all the way, roughly two mile, walked along the shore, and we couldn't see none. I happened to look out in the water and sitting out there on a stick in the water was a blue crane and we call him, *krowali*, the blue crane, he's a *ngatji*, to the Kingston people.

Anyhow, I said, "Uncle, look out there." He said, "We can't get a duck, that will do." So anyhow, bang, he fired and got the bird with the first shot and he drifted in. He came in with the wind and I said, "Right, I'll carry him." So we carried him. It wasn't far down from where we shot the bird and I came along. Anyhow, we got back to the camp, and as we were getting there I could see Tom and George's grandmother watching for us to come back with the bird. She was behind the fire and I could see her outline as we were coming in and I knew it was her. There was no other lady there of her age. Uncle said, "Mum, we couldn't get anything else." He said, "We couldn't get a duck or a swan. All we could get was this," and he pulled out this blue crane and when she saw this crane she went off, really went off at us. "You two knew that you should have more sense than to shoot that bird. That's our *ngatji*," she said, "from Kingston. I don't want that bird. You take it back to where you got it and you burn it." So anyhow we went back a bit. We said, "No need to take this any further, we'll throw it away." We threw it away. "The foxes will get it." She was a lady of good calibre, good living, in very good health. So anyhow we went back to the camp.

No more was said about it. I went to bed that night and for some reason or another in the early hours of the morning I could hear, because each tent had a wooden floor in it, I could hear movement and I thought, that's very unusual. There was another lad with me and I tried to dig him with my toe, foot to foot, and he wouldn't move. Anyhow, eventually he did wake and I said, "They're around early this morning." Anyhow, we were about to get out of bed because we used to go out on the tractors with them. We were about to get out of bed and the next thing, my father came in, him and another gentleman, Andrew Sumner, my uncle, and he said, "You two stay there, don't you dare move." So no more was said, but those days one word was enough, or just a look from the old people. You weren't to question or anything. You did as you were told, otherwise

214

you would get flattened with whatever they could put their hands onto, that's the way we were brought up, to respect.

So anyhow, away they went and everything went quiet and I thought, strange, no vehicle going out, no truck or tractor moving. So eventually they came back about seven o'clock in the morning and they said, "Now you two can get out of bed." I did not ask why we were made to stay in bed, but they said, "Now you know why we made you stay in bed? You know that old lady—I called her Granny or Aunty Rose—you went to get the duck for yesterday?" "Yes." "She died." That's my strong belief in the *ngatji* and that's why I am telling this story. I honestly believe that had a lot to do with it, because we destroyed her *ngatji*. We have different *ngatjis* that come and gives us signs. Tom Trevorrow who had been told about *ngatji* by the old people, and respected *ngatji*, said that hearing Uncle Neville's story deepened his understanding and quickened his fears about the devastation of the bridge site. I'm afraid for the *ngatji* and what could happen. This story is not a hypothetical account of what might happen. It concerns Granny Rosie, the mother of Tom and George Trevorrow's mother, Thora (née Lampard). I ask Neville why his uncle didn't know about the danger of damaging her *ngatji*. George Koolmatrie was a Coorong man. He may not have known about the southeast, Neville suggests.

That *krayi*, we call the snake "*krayi*"—is carved around it and put into the walking stick, Tom Trevorrow is explaining to Jane Mathews. You see, and the *krayi* was the *ngatji* of one of the clan groups of the Ngarrindjeri. And they were put onto the sticks like that. When Ngarrindjeri people look at the trees or at the bush, you can already see the shape that's there. And we just take it down, trim it down, and then we've got our snake, our *krayi*. It's the same with the carved birds and other pieces—we see it in the tree. In the museum at Camp Coorong, along with the women's weaving, there is a range of wooden items, traditional items made a long time ago, and ones made more recently. Like the women's weaving, the carvings can be read as sacred texts; men know their own carving, take pride in its distinctiveness, and point out what is Ngarrindjeri and what is not. Like the women, they also have no interest in claiming ownership of that which is not theirs. The Ngarrindjeri carvings carry stories of their lands, their practices, and those of their forebears.

215

Tom Trevorrow explains that traditional objects are once again being made. We've got items that we've started making again such as what we call *plongges*. A lot of people call them "waddies" or "clubs". But, I remember when I was growing up, we was hunting with these, rabbits in particular. Because a lot of rabbits were around then and we supplemented rabbits as traditional food because a lot of our other foods had disappeared. But these clubs are made out of local wood and put on display here for people to look at. So the wood carving is still around in the Ngarrindjeri people. When I grew up in the camps, we were making boomerangs still. We were going out, still hunting ducks in the One Mile and Three Mile swamps because there was still a lot of ducks and swans around. The items that were made a long time ago, by the old people, they haven't changed. *Plongges* are still *plongges*, *kunarkis* are men's fighting clubs and we were still using them in the 1930s and 40s. The *taralyes*, that's our spear thrower. Our *kayikes*, the reed spear, is special. It has a high profile. It's fast. So, it's still there. All this stuff that has been made locally by Ngarrindjeri people and it's still there. They're different from the ones made in other places in Australia. We can pick them out straight away. We know what's from any other area. We have our own style and the most particular thing that makes it stand out is when you know your own timber, your own trees, and what wood it's made out of.

Taplin's (1879: 106) record of "weapons of the Narrinyeri" includes spears, clubs and shields, but inter-tribal warring was on the wane; by the turn of the century, when Elymann (Courto 1996) saw Old Dan Wilson making weapons, they were primarily for tourists. These weapons, decorated with their secondary *ngatji*, and "imbued with magical properties by secret rites of their own", had been carried by men to court cases at the *tendi* (Tindale and Long nd: 9). The *ngatji* was an identifier and protective of its bearer. Steven Hemming (1991: 125) argues that a rich tradition of carving existed in the Lower Murray but, unlike the women's weaving tradition, which is more or less continuous with the past, carving had to be revived. Paul Kropinyeri's bark shields, featured in the Nyoongah Nunga Yura Koorie exhibit at Tandanya during the 1992 Adelaide Festival (Giles and Kean 1992) are an important part of this revival. Growing up in the fringe camps along the Murray River, Paul was able to spend time with the old people. He was able to draw on the knowledge of his mother Flora Kropinyeri and her contemporaries, who had included Albert Karloan (*ibid.*: 4.4.0). From Dick Kropinyeri (Old Mutti) he learned "the different layers of the river gum bark that you need to be aware of to successfully take a shield from a tree" (*ibid.*: 4.4.2). Paul had also seen the shields of Clarence Long in the Museum. In the early 1980s, when he was looking for suitable trees, Paul Kropinyeri would come across "old scars from shields and canoes, along the Murray River in the area from Overland Corner to Berri. The scars left on the trees will serve as a symbol of Ngarrindjeri culture in the future (*ibid.*: 4.4.4) and become a site for future story-telling.

While the shields of this generation of carvers are made of the same materials and employ the same skills as the generation who passed away in the 1930s, there are gaps in knowledge. Hemming (1991) points out that the symbolic designs which had been part of the traditional shield-making had been set aside quite deliberately. Lindsay Wilson, who as a child helped Clarence Long, remembered him burning an owl design, his *ngatji*, into the shields that were sold to tourists. Annie Koolmatrie (Ely 1980: 39) remembered burning "tribal marks" on spears for her father. But in 1930 Clarence Long (Milerum) made the decision to no longer use the carved design that had been part of this tradition. As weapons of war the shields had little meaning and at that time the only persons interested in their manufacture were museums and tourists. The sacred designs were not for them. The Ngarrindjeri men who are carving once more, out of respect for the old people, are not using the *ngatji* designs. The meaning of the symbols would have been taught at initiation when *ngatji* designs were displayed and cut into one's flesh (see Chapter 9). Without this experience and attendant knowledge, it would be sacrilege to use the designs. It is dangerous to use sacred symbols to which one has no right, and in certain parts of Australia there are restrictions regarding use of your own design.

That *ngatji* have continued as an expression of one's distinctive way of being Ngarrindjeri is an excellent example of ways in which critical information concerning one's personal relationship to the world of the ancestors is maintained. Whichever way *ngatji* is being reckoned, the aspects of *ngatji* affiliation that have the greatest potency and meaning for people today are personal ties to place, and the role of *ngatji* as a messenger, guide, protector, friend.

Miwi: Feeling and Knowing

That's in us. We have that feeling, Aunty Maggie Jacobs explains. I really felt the hurt from our old people, Ellen Trevorrow notes. Now, we went there that day and we didn't feel right, George Trevorrow observes. As soon as they put their foot on the ground, they knew that this was the right place, Tom Trevorrow confides.

Early in my research, after visiting particular places, I'd be asked how I felt. The question took a while to register. Having lived in the USA for nine years where psychobabble often passes for serious introspection, I parried the questions. It sounded too much like getting in touch with my inner child and the intuitive self that New Age workshops promise to deliver. Nonetheless, I faithfully recorded occasions on which I heard people talk about their feelings, and eventually I began to see the patterns in the stories. Visiting sites with Ngarrindjeri dramatised the connection between feeling and knowing. Some places are peaceful—a visit is restorative, a chance to communicate with one's relatives, and to rehear the stories. At some places one feels ill at ease, there are restless spirits around, or perhaps one is on alien territory and thus in danger of being ensorcelled. I began to ask: How do you know? How do you feel? Where do you feel it?

At the same time I was beginning to recognise Ngarrindjeri words in conversation. When I heard *miwi*, it was said rarely and with reverence. It is not a word that is bandied about in casual conversation. From reading the Berndts, I was familiar with the translation "soul substance" (Berndt *et al.* 1993: 287). They locate *miwi* in or behind the stomach and regard it "as the source of emotions, as an eternal part of men and women through which all important feelings, experiences and thoughts were expressed" (*ibid.*: 133-4). David Unaipon told Elaine Treagus in 1966 (LA 3462a) it was where "impulses" of the body comes from, where all feelings come from. For Daisy Rankine it permeates every aspect of her life: *Miwi* is my wisdom that I grew up with. *Miwi* is part of life and it's also a part of the women's business, but the feeling of *miwi* within oneself is

218

in the diaphragm. It's there down reaching our soul. Everything that we do throughout the day, throughout each day, whatever we do, is all wrapped up in weaving and each stitch in weaving meant the part of our lives through the *miwi* wisdom.

Ellen said she felt it "in her tummy", and when she tells this story she is visibly moved. I didn't know anything about the island, but when I first came across onto the island and I came down to the mouth, and we stood there, all of us in a circle, and when I went home to my husband, I was saying, I felt it. I really felt it, in my tummy. I felt it—it, you know, it really touched me that the island means a lot and I don't know all the stories as yet and I just said to Tom, there's definitely something here, there's definitely something. Because I feel it, and I felt it so much that day that I cried and I cried. The gathering at the Murray Mouth with Professor Cheryl Saunders in 1994 was the first time a number of the women had the opportunity to visit the site, feel its power, and hear the stories. This occasion is remembered by all as one of heightened emotion, albeit mixed— joy, peace, comfort, sorrow, renewal. Sheila Goldsmith agrees: A strong place, I could feel it. We held hands and sang at the Murray Mouth. Dot Shaw sang of the feelings in "*Kumarangk mi:mini*".

Tom Trevorrow, in commenting to Geoffrey Bagshaw on the significance of the strength of his wife's feelings said, It's where we get our understanding of things and our feelings and our instincts from. And *miwi* we're told comes from your *pulanggi*, we call it. Navel. . . . through your *pulanggi*. Not through your ears, or your eyes, or your nose, or your mouth, or anywhere else. It's through your *pulanggi*. And I was told by my elders that everybody's got it . . . Everybody. Blackfella, whitefella. But he said, "They gotta know what it's all about and they gotta know how to use it and they gotta know what it means." But everybody's got it. But knowing and believing in it is, you know, the secret [i.e. the key] . . . It's a really powerful thing and when you really feel it, you'll know what it's all about, you know. Had Ellen said she knew for any reason other than her *miwi*, Tom says he would have questioned further, but when she said where she felt it, he knew it was true. When you want to find something out and if it's true or correct—that's here you feel it . . . I've felt it. . . . And it's when I go to places and feel that in my stomach, my *putra*, my *pulanggi*, you know, and it's telling me about something of this area. I can go to other places along the Coorong and feel nothing, you know what I mean? And that's how it works.

The power of one's *miwi* may be apparent in group situations, such as that gathering at the Murray Mouth, but it remains an intensely personal experience. Eileen McHughes also felt the power of the place when at the Murray Mouth. I'm not Christian but spiritually I feel things. I feel very comfortable when I'm on the island. This sense of knowing one's relationship to a site can be acknowledged and communicated to others, but others cannot know it vicariously. Eileen continued: It wasn't up to me to tell Dorothy Wilson about it. I'm comfortable, not disturbed. The ability to understand the knowledge that one's *miwi* makes available is one that is cultivated: everyone has the capacity, but not all develop this aspect of their sentient selves. In Eileen's view she could not force her *miwi* wisdom on another. She was, however, certain of hers and reminded me of how she was drawn to the other side of the island and later learned that had been Tangani clan territory.

Veronica Brodie said, When I go to Point Pearce, I know, I feel this is not my country. It hasn't got the feeling that Raukkan or the Coorong has. The feeling tells you where you are and where you belong. If you didn't have those feelings, you'd be nothing. The first time we drove to Goolwa Edith Rigney told me: I always feel better once we get past Mount Compass [the northern boundary of Ngarrindjeri territory]. *Miwi* not only tells one what is important, it may also alert one to places where one should not be, and do so at a very precise level. The Berndts (1993: 594-5) recorded songs of strange feelings; "I'm frightened, I haven't been here before." The instance of "feeling as knowing" that is indelibly imprinted on my memory concerns one March day in 1996 when we had taken Jane Mathews to see a fish trap near the Goolwa barrage. Although the day had been bright sun when we set off, it clouded over as we drove onto the island and then the skies opened. Those of us who were not directly involved in the videoing of the women's evidence got out of our vehicle and sheltered under one umbrella. Daisy Rankine also got out. She was cold and wanted to put on her jumper (sweater) but, in the scramble to keep equipment and judge dry, Aunty Daisy was shut out of the van. When we got back in she was ashen. "What's wrong?" I asked. I could see she was cold, but there was something else—she was in pain or frightened. I was standing on a clan boundary. I shouldn't have been there and it's about the burial ground, she said. I could feel it. And she was terrified. Unfortunately this moment was not captured on video. Would it have been appreciated had it been? She told the story later but, without a context, the significance was lost.

Aunty Maggie tells of a place called Elliston, outside Port Lincoln, where a number of Aborigines were driven off the cliff by white settlers. Because of the violence and evil of that time, if you camp there now, in the night, you can feel it. It's horrible and you can hear the wailing. My grandmother, Ada Koolmatrie, told me, and about the strychnine that they gave to them on Hindmarsh Island. I was very relieved when the place I was renting at Clayton was said to have "a good feeling". As people became aware that I too was interested in these feelings, I heard more. Doreen Kartinyeri had already told me of her visits with her Aunty Rosie at Point Pearce but now I began to hear more about her moods, about the places at which she was relaxed and those where she felt stressed.

One story that is told over and over concerns finding the right place to scatter Aunty Leila's ashes. Maggie Jacobs: One of Leila's wishes were that before she died, she said, "I want to go back to the Kurangk [Coorong]." Leila Rankine had always felt at home on the Coorong. When she was dying in 1992, she set about putting her affairs in order. Knowing that it was not possible to have her remains interred on public land on the Coorong, but that it was possible to have her ashes scattered, she arranged that Tom and George Trevorrow each sprinkle half of her ashes on the Coorong. It was a wonderful opportunity for her. She did everything that she wanted to do with her Ngarrindjeri culture and then we brought her back to Adelaide to die. But this is very dear to me, this country down here and I feel the spirits when I'm here—I feel like I'm home. I could live in Adelaide for months on end, but I go to Raukkan or I come here, and I'm at home, and that's what's born within you, those feelings, that's what makes you the Ngarrindjeri that you are.

Tom Trevorrow: At the end of the day it was *miwi* that told us where we had to come to, *miwi*, which is inside. Aunty Leila said. "You'll know the spot." She never named a location. She left it on us to find a place. She

The Scattering of Leila Rankine's ashes, Coorong 1992
L–R Kenny Sumner (great nephew), William and Kier Rankine (grandsons),
George and Tom Trevorrow. (Margaret Jacobs' personal collection)

knew we'd have to know it. She put us to the test with our *miwi*. When we were down the track, a few hundred yards we knew that it wasn't right because our *miwi* was talking and then when we came up here, everybody knew, as soon as they put their foot on the ground that this was the right place with the Coorong, the river and where she could hear the ocean. So that's how we understand that. This is an area of which Aunty Leila (Rankine 1974b: vi) had often spoken in fond terms.

Victor Wilson tells a similar story of how his *miwi* helped him to locate Tom, George, and Uncle Neville. We was all together in the cars, until Salt Creek, and as we were getting ready to go, Nev's son, Derek, wanted to go to the toilet, and in the rush to go, he got left behind by the bus. So we thought we might teach him a lesson. "It's your turn to learn now," we told him. "If you're travelling together, you need to get back in time if you don't know where you're going." There were two roads and we didn't know which one they took. He said, "The bitumen." So we drove a long way down and we keep asking, "Where are they?" Finally he admitted he didn't know. We swung off the road looking for

222

tracks. There were lots. We asked a white family if they'd seen a bus go by but they said they'd seen nothing and they'd been there all the time. I stopped and asked for spiritual guidance. Then I jumped out and said, "There they are, down there." We had to backtrack to get to them. I was talking to the *miwi* and the *miwi* guided me in. It's not a voice. I believe it goes up and comes down and you have to let go. We were trying to track, but you need to let go and trust the feeling. When you're on your own land, you get a strong indication, but not all the time. Neville Gollan nods as I read this story: *Miwi* is inside you, he affirms.

On the third day of the Long Walk in November 1996, Genevieve and I had joined the walkers at Cole's Crossing on the Finniss River. It was not an easy site to find and we were not the only ones who did a circuit of Mount Magnificent on the forest roads before catching sight of the support vehicles. The camp was deep in a hollow, dark, damp and quite wooded. Aunty Maggie, Doreen Kartinyeri, Edie Rigney, Grace Sumner, Hazel Wilson and Dot Shaw were nowhere to be found. They had relocated, half-way up the hill, and by the time we found them, they were comfortably settled down in an almost completed house overlooking the valley. The siting was spectacular. Aunty Maggie and Doreen were discussing the camping site at the crossing. Doreen, curled up on a two-seater couch, was adamant that the site at the crossing was dangerous. Maggie Jacobs, reclining on a cane *chaise-longue*, agreed. It was, she said, "a good place for *thumparmaldi* (sorcerers)" but this place, further up the hill, would be OK. I'm on Ramindjeri land and know I will be safe. "How?" I asked. I can feel it, Aunty Maggie replied. Doreen was in agreement, and added more pragmatic concerns. The old people would not have camped at the bottom of the gully. The site was hemmed in with bushes and there was no escape in the case of fire. It was a dangerous place. *Miwi* wisdom is not disconnected from the physical world. It would be wrong to categorise *miwi* as a mystic power of esoteric value alone. *Miwi* wisdom is at once disarmingly pragmatic and profoundly spiritual.

Miwi fuses the emotional and intellectual into true knowledge. It is, as Tom Trevorrow said, a matter of *wurruwarrin*, of "knowing and believing". It can be cultivated and trained, but it is always there. This makes sense of the pride with which stories are told about how non-indigenous people have felt the power of Ngarrindjeri places and their desire to have me feel it also; to know that the trees murmur; to note how the water laps the sandy beach; to recognise the unease at certain burial places. In a sense the belief that everyone has a *miwi*—something one is born with, that can't be bred out, or married out—is a defiant way of dealing with whiteness. The *miwi* can bring a Ngarrindjeri home and over-ride all other aspects of one's background and personal identity. Feelings and sentiment are acted upon; they carry important messages, are reported, analysed, nurtured, and remembered. With pride Jean Rankine says of her children, they have the same "feelings" as she does; they know when she's sick, worried, or in trouble. Songs about the strength of feelings for people and places continue to be composed.[9] For Ngarrindjeri, paying attention to feelings is critical to staying in touch with the land, and the feelings are grounded in the particularities of kin and country. Thus when a person speaks of their feelings about a place being hurt, they are providing a reason why certain practices are injurious.

Berndt *et al.* (1993: 245) locate *miwi* as part of the "psychic life". However, I am more inclined to see *miwi* as the basis of a way of knowing, as a central component of an epistemology that relies on numerous oral traditions of elders as the authoritative texts within which to interpret signs and feelings. The stories provide the framework for understanding the signs, and the orator provides a concluding section to his or her story that brings the story home and grounds it in the experience of those listening. The stories thus become about what is happening now, not just about past events. They speak to the wisdom of knowing the past as a way of living in the present and as a way of ensuring a future. They contain cautions as to what will occur if the signs are not heeded. People communicate with their *ngatji*. So that ancestors can communicate with the living, the recently dead may appear and, depending on their demeanour, bring good or unsettling news.

The notion that one could know by feeling goes against the rationalist grain. If it can't be proved or disproved, can it considered knowledge? As heirs of the scientific method, westerners tend to be afraid of feelings and sentiment. It is disconcerting to be told that only by letting go will one know truth; or find a particular place. That feelings can confirm a place as good, or dangerous, as one's own or as that of another, is greeted with skepticism. How can the body be a site of knowledge? How can such a proposition be tested? The body is subjective, unknowable, unreliable, and unshared. Of course those Ngarrindjeri who trust their *miwi* have no need of tests. *Miwi* is manifest in their daily lives. Their bodies are real. The power of the *miwi* pervades Ngarrindjeri stories and songs and I will be relating more in subsequent chapters. The examples offered here of how this "feeling as knowing", and of how knowing and believing, *wurruwarrin*, works in practice, should clarify and reassure the rationalist that this is a system of knowing that has its own checks and balances.

Ngia-ngiampe: Birth Relations

It's all to do with where you're born, and it's to do with your "umbiblical" cord and when you're born and your life comes through your "umbiblical" cord to your body. And that's why the "umbiblical" cord is removed from you when you are a baby and it's handed over to other members of the family, Tom Trevorrow told Geoff Bagshaw. Some time later Tom and George also talked with me about this. They always say "umbiblical" for umbilical and it is a rendering I've come to appreciate. With its evocation of "biblical" it seems an appropriate gloss for this sacred relationship. Daisy Rankine says with reverence: It's a feeling you're born with. It starts with the cord and when it's cut and the child is initiated and the rest should be kept to ourselves. It's sacred.

A radical separation of body and soul, the physical and spiritual, the rational and the intuitive, has limited value for an understanding of the dimensions of Ngarrindjeri identity and culture. Both men and women have *miwi*, and because it has a cognitive as well as affective texture, it can be strengthened through training and hence is likely to be stronger in older people, where it indicates the acquisition of wisdom. I think there is particular significance in the importance placed on feelings, the location of *miwi* in the stomach behind the navel, and the *ngia–ngiampe* relationship that permits communication, trade, and a sibling-like relation to exist between

225

the partners to the exchange of umbilical cords. The rituals associated with birth make explicit this symbolic complex (Chapter 9).

As Aunty Daisy said, "It's sacred," and much of what one might say about the importance of the navel cord is restricted. Figuring out what can be written about here has not been easy. Just because there is published material on a topic does not make it open for Ngarrindjeri, and my purpose in writing has not been to further expose deeply held religious beliefs to ridicule by a voyeuristic media. I have often heard women talk about the importance of the *putari*, Ngarrindjeri midwives, and rather less often of the actual practices and problems caused by western obstetric practices. These are private matters and conversations about actual births were always conducted in women-only groups. One evening after spending a day in archives, I was telling Veronica Brodie about some notes on the navel cord I'd located from the 1940s. I thought she would find them interesting. Instead, she looked at me askance: "What? Who wrote this? She was game," Veronica said in a tone I had not heard from her before but which, in central Australia, I associate with particularly egregious violations of knowledge boundaries. I was upset that I had unwittingly caused hurt and I knew that saying sorry would not undo the harm. The anthropological literature is replete with references to the navel cord relation and it is easy to be lulled into a false sense of security. From Taplin (1873: 33-4) onwards we read of how the cord was saved and sent to a distant "tribe" with whom one then established a lifelong relationship.

In quiet moments I had been told of the rituals associated with the cutting of the cord and of the trading of the cord. However, until December 1996, I had never heard the word *ngiampe* said out loud, although, in various forms, it is a term with which the literature on Ngarrindjeri is saturated. This day Tom and Ellen Trevorrow had taken their son Bruce, Margaret and Matt Rigney, Genevieve and me on a trip down the Coorong. We had visited the Murray Mouth, the place where Aunty Leila's ashes had been scattered, passed through the Goolwa barrage, walked on the hummocks, observed the change in water colour from the blue of the Coorong to the muddy murkiness of the river and lakes, and much more. At the end of the day, George

Trevorrow and Daisy Rankine had joined us at Camp Coorong where, in the late-afternoon sun, we were sitting talking about the day. I was plotting our trip on my map and asking Tom and George for clarification of a story I had heard them tell. The men were sitting at one end of the patio and the women near the door. When either George or Tom wanted to check a genealogical detail they would call across to the "old lady", a term of respect for Aunty Daisy. Ellen was reading a transcription of her story to check which bits I could use in this book. I was half listening to several conversations and watching the interplay between family members. Then I heard George mention *ngiampe* to Tom. Probably too quickly, I reeled and began asking questions about the word.

The story that they then told took my understanding of this relationship way beyond the sources and grounded it in the practice of midwives and their continuing relationship to the child they have helped bring into the world. It also introduced some new questions. George explained that he had always wondered why it was that Aunty Beatty (Beatrice Karpeny, née Gollan) would straighten his shirt, comb his hair, and so on, whenever he saw her. She gave you life, his mother told him. She found you. And, says this serious, strongly built man, Violet, her sister, used to call me her "Little Coorong rabbit". "What about the trade relationships established with the exchange of the cord?" I ask George. Traders are different. Every one can't be a trader. But the *putari* is like a second mother. She gives you another set of parents. It gives a child more family and more protection.

Others tell me the same thing. Val Powers and Muriel Van Der Byl explain how Ngarrindjeri mothers would come into town to have their babies. Muriel Williams (née Rankine), sister of Olive, Ivy and Beryl, all of whom were practising midwives, delivered Muriel Van Der Byl who is named after her. My mother came to her place at Hampstead Place off Carrington—it's not there now—to have me. Muriel Williams—she'd married into Point Pearce—was like a cousin to my mother and like a godmother to me. If I was in Adelaide I knew I could get a feed and warm clothes and she'd make sure I didn't roam around. She protected me when I was in town. I remember her and the comfort, the security and lots of love. Val continues: Our mother was a midwife and they sought out midwives they trusted when it was their time. I was delivered by Girly Kestle, a cousin of my mother, in Waymouth Street. She was Ngarrindjeri and Narrunga. Our mother was a midwife and Sarah Milera's mother was still delivering babies in the 1950s. Muriel and Val agree that Muriel Williams and Girly died in the late 1960s, but had given up their practice before that. It was when the Queen Elizabeth Hospital was set up that the midwife practice declined. The last was probably still practising into the late 1950s. Midwives continued to practise at Raukkan, and the hospital at Meningie is used to having people around and allows kin to be present. Men are conspicuously absent on such occasions, although they willingly enumerate the midwives in various communities.

Veronica Brodie, when I ask, tells me: Aunty Beatty delivered me at Raukkan. I was a special baby, only two pounds, two ounces, and she nursed me through all the heat. They had a fire going in the kitchen to keep me at an even temperature. She says that she suffered for me and she always watched out for me. Beatrice's brother was married to Koomi's sister and Muriel reminds me that Aunty Beatty was their father's first wife. James Brooks Kartinyeri (Ellis 1962–6: (3) 42) spoke of the midwife who attended his mother as the lady that "found" him. I'm still working on the kin networks and social fields implicated in these relationships and the outstanding questions about how the relationships established through the midwife relate to what is written about *ngia–ngiampe*. I think about my sketchy knowledge of such matters in my own life. I know the names of the doctors who delivered my children, but not those of the nurses who were present. I have no idea of the identity of the doctor who delivered me and no expectation of a close relationship with any of these individuals. The Ngarrindjeri world I glimpse through stories of midwives, *ngatji* and *miwi* is a weave of unfamiliar relationships that need to be understood as part of family and community histories.

The Power of Naming

During a stay at my place at Clayton, Isobelle Norvill, Eileen McHughes, and her sister Vicki Hartman, had been going through the books and papers I had with me and were pointing out family members. I had asked about names. With pride Isobelle tells me that her name goes back to Mutyuli Isabella Sumner. Eileen's niece is Sally Anne, from Sally Kartinyeri: "She had a nice personality like Sally. No one took on the name Martha ["Mumadee" from Point Pearce] except Isobelle's mother was Aileen Martha Varcoe". Isobelle: "We look out for people with the same name". Eileen: "Aileen was Isobelle's mother, and is my daughter's name. I avoided using Gertrude, my mother's name." Isobelle: "Aileen, out of all of Eileen's kids, is the one I give help and my last granny is Bianca Brooke Eileen." "How do you keep them all straight?" I ask. Isobelle: "Names skip a generation, and that is coming back with real force. But we use nicknames. Sometimes we don't even know people's names. Now kids are getting flash names. Like Eileen's daughter is called Georgina, after her father, George."

While it would be neat if names did indeed skip a generation, like that of "Ellen" in Daisy Rankine's matriline, and thus form a bond between grandparent and grandchild, there are many counter examples. The name Connie from Isobelle's mother's mother and Eileen's father's mother has been passed down to Isobelle's sister Connie, but then a brother Bill has a daughter, Connie, also. I think there are at least two considerations at work here: the structural principle of alternating generations and the force of sentiment which sometimes coincides and sometimes doesn't, but is phrased as having to do with individual personalities and choices. Doreen tells me it was Taplin who encouraged the practice of repeating names at each generation level and that sometimes there are more than one with the same name in the same sibling set. No wonder people get misplaced on genealogies.

Many different "rules" and considerations are enunciated in the historical record. Meyer (1846) says names come from the totem, circumstances of birth, and that adults exchange names as a mark of friendship. Angas (1847: 92, 59) also says names are associated with place of birth and gives an example of an exchange of names. An elderly man told Angas (*ibid.*: 59) that he was now called "Mr Mason" and that George Mason at Wellington was henceforth "Mooloo". Taplin (1873: 51) says children are named as soon as they can walk and that names carry information about birth and *ngatji*. Radcliffe-Brown (1918: 229) notes how names, clan and totems are related. Reuben Walker (1934: 205-6) says that children were not given personal names until around twelve to fourteen; that spouses address each other as "husband of mine" or "wife of mine"; and after the birth of the first child did not use personal names at all but rather say "father of a boy", "mother of a boy", and so on. The Berndts (1993: 359, 506) state that names have the power to influence a child's adult life and that after death one is known by the name of the country. They divide names into three categories: first, a personal and private name; second, a patrilineal name bestowed by men on their sons or a matrilineal name bestowed by women on their daughters; and thirdly, a secret name, given around the age of five, that was known only to themselves, father and male members of the family (*ibid.*: 148). It was known as a "*kalalwonmitji* (long ago, from the Dreaming) name and was *narambi* [sacred, forbidden]". It is not clear how this third name worked for girls, but it is clear that the name linked young people to the stories of the past and was part of the religious identity of the bearer.

Traditional Ngarrindjeri names, ending with *yeri*, meaning "belonging to", derive from clan names, which in turn are often called after a place within the clan territory, or a *ngatji* of that clan. Such names, in a very literal sense, take one back to the land, clan and its spiritual identity. Other names, such as say "Rankine", while coming from the brothers William and John Rankine who migrated to South Australia from Scotland in 1839, still evoke a relationship to place. Old Yami Rankine, of the first generation to take a European surname, was born on Hindmarsh Island, near the site now called Rankine's Landing. Yami was nicknamed "Doc Rankine" because he was a sorcerer and maybe also because the white Rankine was a doctor. Thus even the name Rankine takes Ngarrindjeri family members back to that place. There were many ways that personal names, clan names, and European names became surnames for Ngarrindjeri families. Doreen offers two examples. Koolmatrie as a surname comes from the wife of Pulami, who was given the English name Peter. Their children then took her name Koolmatrie as their surname. He had three wives. His daughter Nymbulindjeri married James Ngunaipon. They are the parents of our famous David Unaipon.

"*My name is Tsoai-talee. I am, therefore, Tsoai-talee, therefore I am,*" writes Scott Momaday as the opening line in his book *The Names*

(1976). For his story-teller this was the first thing to be known because he believed that a "man's life proceeds from his name, in the way that a river proceeds from its source". Momaday is writing of the Kiowa of the Plains in the USA, but his emphasis on the power and primacy of naming resonates with Ngarrindjeri storytelling. "You *pilaki*, you callop, said *Ngurunderi* as he cut up the giant *pondi* and threw the pieces into the fresh and salt waters." Momaday (*ibid.*: 1) writes: "The names at first are those of animals and birds, of objects that have one definition in the eye, another in the hand and features on the rim of the world, or of the sounds that carry on the bright wind and in the void." In the "*Pata winema*" song James Brooks Kartinyeri tells us the people out cockling want to know the identity of the newcomers: "Are you one of us?" Having eaten of the *Wururi*, the languages are named and the new speakers scatter.

To conjure with a name is to unpick this intricately named world and to imperil all who live within its weave. The names of the dead are not called for fear of calling forth the spirit. The names of the old people are uttered with respect. Powerful forces are named with care. *Miwi* is not a word to be bandied about. Speak of sorcerers and they will hear you and appear.

Personal names, it seems, link one to place and one's identity remains rooted in that place, even after death. Names are not called lightly. They invoke a presence and although missionaries and welfare officers significantly undermined the practice of not mentioning the personal names of the dead, there is still a reluctance on the part of close relatives to call them.[10] Throughout the Royal Commission, in a rare acknowledgment of Aboriginal sensibilities regarding not calling the names of the recently deceased, Laura Kartinyeri was referred to as "the daughter of Pinkie Mack", but the larger issue of the rights of families in genealogies was ignored.

Genealogies: Families First

Liz Tongerie unfolds a letter in which her family history is recounted: It takes you back to your land and it helps you know who you can marry. Genealogies are very important because it's your own identity, where you belong. Doreen Kartinyeri says of the documents on which she

231

is working: Well, the important thing for our people is that they get their right identity and then it takes them back, because I've got tribal names and tribal areas where they come from, and Tindale recorded most of this, it takes them back to the land where their ancestors came from. Muriel Van Der Byl's anguish at the publication of genealogies as part of the Royal Commission (Stevens 1995) is palpable. The Report is now a public document. Our genealogy is public knowledge. This is extremely private information.

Genealogies are undeniably one of the "sacred texts" of Ngarrindjeri culture: they are held dear; they carry information regarding the cycling of names; they are powerful tools against an adversary; they are hotly contested; and they are not for trafficking. Misuse or mis-citation causes grievous harm to individuals and their families. It is not a matter of finding the proverbial skeleton in the cupboard, but rather a violation of rights in culturally sensitive knowledge. The passion and pain in Ngarrindjeri responses to the publication of genealogies as an annexure to the Stevens Report (1995) indicates the centrality these representations of relations in Ngarrindjeri life. Through genealogies one can trace back to land, to the upper generation, and from there to an important ancestor. The "first generation" of names, i.e. those recorded at the time of contact, includes personal names like Mulparini, Minkuluti, and Mutyuli, and family names like Karpeni (Karpenyeri) Koolmatrie (Kulmatyeri), and Kropinyeri; they are said with reverence. To be able to trace back to one of these individuals, or establish a blood line to one of the original families, is a mark of status and belonging. To be able to trace back through one's parents and grandparents to several important lineages augments one's authority.

Eileen McHughes can trace through the Kropinyeris, her father's line, to Old Kropinyeri who died in 1875; through the Gollans, her mother's father's line to Old Gollan (1817–77); and through her mother's mother's father's line to Adeline Sumner (1890–1932), born on the Coorong. These are impeccable Ngarrindjeri credentials which, in the days of the *tendi*, the governing body, would have given one a key role in decision-making. In Doreen's opinion: It is the lineage that takes us back to our land, and Eileen's is very strong and through powerful families because all these families are the ancestors of

Ngarrindjeri people living in this nation today. I learnt a lot about kinship from my Aunty Rosie (1894–1981) when I went to Point Pearce to get married in 1954. She was living on the beach, about five to six kilometres away, because she and her husband, Nat Kropinyeri, were exempted and not allowed to live on the mission. Aunty Rosie and her husband had a shack there with other families who were exempted. My husband and I would visit them on the weekend, bring down the mail, and take notes back to the store for things they needed. On Friday afternoon we'd take her grandchildren down, she had five of them, and bring them back on Sunday to Point Pearce, if it was wintertime, so they didn't have to walk to school on Monday morning.

One of the first genealogies I remember asking about was Aunty Isobelle Rigney's husband, Lionel Campbell, because his brothers and sisters are Karpenys. I couldn't get the relationship and I didn't know their mother. So Aunty Rosie filled me in about how he was born before his mother and father was actually married. I asked about our family and she told me about the Challengers in a lot of detail. I heard my grandfather Ben was fathered by a white man and his brother Ted too. But she gave me the story of how Isabella Mutyuli was taken away as a young girl and went to Melrose to work and was attracted to a much older man. He was sixty-one and she was eighteen.

Then Isabella came back to Point McLeay and married Philip Rigney, who had come over from Western Australia to Poonindie with Archbishop Hale. He played up there and the Reverend Craig took him to Point McLeay where he was put into a little cottage to look after Charlie Peake who had been injured on the Warburton expedition. And, it was funny, because Isabella was found living in a hollow tree with her two illegitimate children. She was also returned to the mission and put in charge of being cook and washerwoman for Charlie. It was only a few weeks after Charlie died that they [Isabella and Philip] got married. Aunty Rosie gave me all the details. She didn't talk to others like this. My family was close but I asked a lot of questions and she'd say well this was from my mother's side or father's side.

All that Aunty Rosie told me about my mum's family and her dad's family, I followed up when I began to work for Fay Gale. I tried to stop a couple of times but Fay encouraged me to stay on. Because I never had any education, they said that they couldn't give me the pay that I really

233

should be getting. I only went to Grade 3 in school. Fay tried to tell them that it didn't really matter; I had the knowledge so therefore I should get paid, so they eventually started to pay me a small salary to compile these genealogies together.

On the basis of extensive field and archival research Doreen has published four books of genealogies and in mid-1997 had another five ready to go. It is not only intellectual curiosity that drives her research. Genealogies takes us back to the people who owned the land, and we could say, "Oh, this is home; this is where we belong." And then when you know something like this, you'll go out and you'll try and learn more about your culture, especially for the ones that's been taken away and we have thousands of them that's been removed by Welfare and the Protector. I've had it in my family. I was taken at ten when my mother died, and my sister was only a month old, so I do know the experience of being taken away.

But I was fortunate. I came back. I got kicked out of school at thirteen and I didn't have a European education. I knew then that I'd lost my chances but I wasn't going to let my life slip away, not when I had so much that was more to me than white man's teaching. So I did stick it out and I learnt as much as I could. I wasn't told everything by everybody; some of the older ladies didn't even want to talk about it, but my Aunty Rosie she wanted me to learn. She felt that she could trust me; she knew I'd listen well, and I always asked her sensible questions that she wouldn't really get mad at me, so I really know I had a very good teacher with her. Harold "Kim" Kropinyeri, son of Clyde Kropinyeri and Melva Carter, remembers this teacher–student pair. Doreen, he said, was always around her Aunty Rosie who was "just like a mother". She was a terrific woman, and smart, and really respected in the community. She was everyone's granny. There was no talk back. Over and over I was told about the likeness between aunt and niece. "Who do I take after?" Doreen would ask. "Nanna Rosie", her daughters would say. Then, when I heard Aunty Rosie on a tape made by Cath Ellis in 1966, I knew, too, whom Doreen took after. Connie Love remembers her sister Doreen Kartinyeri and her Aunt Rosie as "two of a kind", a description confirmed by many others. And, Nanna Laura, she's our aunty too. She spent a lot of time with Dodo as well. Kim Kropinyeri says of his father's sister: Margaret Lindsay [born 1926] was raised by Aunty Rosie too and her daughter Jenny Grace said in the Royal Commission, so "Why didn't Aunty Rosie tell her mother [Margaret Lindsay] too?" But her mother was away and not interested in the traditional culture the way Doreen was. Margaret Lindsay did know a lot about social history, as is evident in her daughter's account of life on the Murray (Grace 1990).

Audio cassettes, especially those of the generation born around the turn of the century, are becoming treasured texts. Some are from the South Australian Museum; some from the Australian Institute of Aboriginal and Torres Strait Islanders Studies (AIATSIS) in Canberra; some are home-made. Segments concerning family, language and stories of days gone by receive rapt attention. People love listening to the tapes, but producing my tape recorder usually killed conversations. So I took notes, verbatim notes, read them back, checked, and double checked. People watched and knew what I was doing. As I got to know people better, began to follow some of the genealogical puzzles that were the stuff of daily conversations, and ventured to ask the odd question, the documents came out. From a back room, safely stowed on top of a wardrobe, carefully folded in tissue paper, rolled with care and tied with soft ribbon, in plastic protective sleeves, in albums, framed, but always handled with respect, came a steady stream of letters, clippings, certificates of births, deaths, marriages, and exemption.

Liz Tongerie, born in 1950 at Point McLeay, is the great-grand-daughter of Alfred Cameron. Born a century earlier, the child of a Scottish father and Ngarrindjeri mother, Alfred Cameron, while making the conscious decision to succeed in the white world, did not turn his back on his mother's people. By 1914 he had acquired the lease to "The Needles" on her clan territory. Through her father, Stephen George Lampard, Liz traces back to Old Lampard, and to her father's grandmother, known as "Queen" Ethel. Both Cameron and Lampard were good farmers, were independent of the mission, and wanted to be self-sufficient. Through her mother, Mary Lampard, who died when Liz was only ten, she is related to the Rankines. Clarence Long (Milerum), was first cousin to her great-grandfather Alfred Cameron. Living in various camps, including on the Bonney Reserve, always surrounded by her family, and in close contact with others families, Liz heard many stories concerning her famous forebears. Aunty Lola Cameron Bonney was a favourite and Liz spent a good deal of time with the Cameron sisters Lillian (Lil), Nell and Pearl and their niece Lola.

Pearl Cameron at The Needles, *c.*1960
(Eileen McHughes' personal collection)

Genealogies have to be straight. That is why we fight over them. They are our ties to the land. They are where we come from. These genealogies that I have, I keep them as very important. In 1988 Liz Tongerie (Department of Education 1990) expressed the same sentiment about the importance of passing on stories; "It helps us know where you are, where you come from and who you belong to . . . you have your full identity." On 11 February 1993, her aunt, Lola Cameron Bonney, wrote a five-page letter with information of Liz's ancestry.

The details that her aunt considered important are instructive. The letter begins with a precise account of clan boundaries, the alliances between families that were established through marriage, the role of "ngart-chees" [*ngatjis*] in organising marriages, and the problematic status of the term "Narranjiries" as a gloss for groups who were often in violent conflict with each other. The bulk of the letter deals with her clan territory at "The Needles" and rights of succession.

This document was written for Liz. It is her title deed and her genealogy. Her permission is required before it may be cited, and in her view, just because it has been shared with one person, the document is still confidential. She knows with whom she has shared it and thus can control the spread of the knowledge. Written records, like the letters from her elders, are highly prized, but they create a problem which did not exist when everything was by word of mouth. They can get into the wrong hands. They can be abused. Doreen was very aware of the problems, ethical and factual, she faced when she began her research on Raukkan and Point Pearce families. Everybody was really scared when I made an announcement to them that I was going to do their genealogies. I think they were really scared that I was going to write things in there that they felt shouldn't be written, because it's a personal thing and I knew this. When I'd finished and they saw the book, people were starting to give me information then. They'd ring me up and say to me, "Can we send this information?" and they'd send it down, and they started to lend me photographs, old photographs. This level of participation and respect is quite different from several critical experiences for Ngarrindjeri of genealogical material making it into the public domain in recent years.

Whose Genealogy?

That the genealogies contained in *A World That Was* (Berndt *et al.* 1993) and the genealogies appended to the Report of Commissioner Iris Stevens (1995) became public documents caused considerable pain for many Ngarrindjeri. These were personal matters. Genealogies belong to the families, not to anthropologists, lawyers or governments. The document headed "Genealogies of Aboriginal People Involved in Hindmarsh Island Bridge Royal Commission", a single chart 56 by 92 centimetres, was simply folded and included as an insert to her report: in January 1996, discussion of this document was the leitmotif of field work. No meeting was complete without a reference to the deep hurt, insult and outrage it had caused. With a price of $50, the report was certainly beyond the reach of most of Ngarrindjeri, but word of this document spread like wildfire through the families. The questions were fast and furious. How dare she publish our names without permission? Why are some people there when others are not? Would you publish a genealogy of whites and say that this one was "unwed", "born outside marriage", or "mentally impaired", show another as the issue of an incestuous union, and define yet another as a "half-caste" or "full-blood"? This is private information. Is there no protection to be afforded at law? How come she had access to and can publish records in the museum that are supposed to be restricted?

Muriel Van Der Byl, as a representative of the Karpeny family, pursued such questions in a complaint she lodged against the State of South Australia and the Commissioner, Iris Stevens, under the *Racial Discrimination Act* 1975 at the Equal Opportunity Commission in January 1996. The chart in Stevens itself offers little by way of illumination. It is not cited in the body of the report, so one wonders why it is there at all. It is a hodge-podge of information with the worst format I have seen in twenty years of reviewing and preparing genealogies to be submitted as evidence in land claims. As if to excuse the presentation, across the bottom of the chart is written: "This chart has been typeset from the exhibit which was approximately twice as deep and half as wide again, and different generations which had been clear, reading vertically, are now less so, through necessity." I am not sure what this means and, as there is no exhibit number, I can't refer back to the original. Another caveat appears in a side box: "This genealogy is not intended to be complete but shows relationships between many of the Aboriginal people mentioned in the report." But many shown there were not involved and many, including one of the dissident families which was involved, do not appear. So, who is to be held responsible for this chart? The only clue to authorship is in another box: "Compiled from: Dr. Norman Tindale – research notes; Professor Ronald and Catherine Berndt – *A World That Was*; Dr. Doreen Kartinyeri – museum publications; Dr. Philip Clarke – research notes". What is the passive voice masking here? Compiled by whom? Does it violate Section 35 of the South Australian Heritage Act? Were the custodians of personal data consulted? In land claim hearings one of the first items to be negotiated is the confidentiality to be afforded to genealogies. Even in a closed session with Justice Mathews on the genealogies, Doreen declined to name people or discuss genealogies unless she had permission.

Doreen Kartinyeri was still smarting from how her material had been used a few months earlier: I felt very angry when I saw the Royal Commission genealogies and I had to explain to some of my relatives, very close relatives. There was an indication of incest, and the name of an illegitimate child, and the father was on it. The person was very angry because it has never been publicly known before that was her father. I got into deep water over it and I didn't have anything to do with it. I felt a little bit responsible because my name was on it, although I didn't put it there. Here was a group of people who were being called fabricators, and whose private family details, without their consent, were now common knowledge. To them the way in which Aboriginal family information was being thrown about was reminiscent of living under the Act. Why are not the white people subjected to the same scrutiny? asked Muriel Van Der Byl. There are some interesting relationships to be mapped and they overlap in significant ways with the Aboriginal people in the area. For instance Diana Laidlaw, a Legislative Council member since 1982 made the announcement as Minister for Transport in 1994 that the bridge would go ahead while her brother-in-law, Dr Michael Armitage, authorised the destruction of the Aboriginal Heritage sites (Symons and Maddox 1997). However, I doubt that a chart showing how local pastoralists, police, missionaries, schoolteachers and protectors were inter-related would be considered relevant and proper without some justification.

In her statement of 12 January 1996, Muriel Van Der Byl set out the strength of her family's ties to Hindmarsh Island; the farcical and discriminatory nature of an inquiry into Ngarrindjeri religious beliefs; and the nature of the insult and injury caused by the inclusion of her family on the genealogy. First and foremost, her family were not a party to the Royal Commission, nor did they give evidence to it. She had been present in the court and had, on one memorable occasion, been challenged regarding her identity as Ngarrindjeri. Now Muriel is a brilliant mimic (her Scottish brogue is delicious), a natural story-teller, and her stories are faithful to the details of the day. I have heard a number of her stories told over and over, and the account of who said what to whom, when, and in what voice remains constant. I have also been present when an event, that later became the basis of a story, occurred, and I know that Muriel captures both the facts and the feel.

The first time I met Muriel in Adelaide she was in the process of lodging the papers. She breezed in, her mass of long, wild, curly hair loose; her elegant caftan flowing. Her mood was anything but free. The story she told concerned the Royal Commission and how she had been required to prove she was Ngarrindjeri before being able to sit in on a closed session. It was about a quarter to twelve so I said, well if you adjourn for lunch and by the time you come back this afternoon, I will have my credentials. So then we had to go and get our genealogy out of the Wilson book [Kartinyeri 1990], the family book, and I was thinking to myself, where is it, where is it? And we're rushing against time. So I had the mobile with me and I got to my sister who's like from here to the next street corner away and so I yelled out—on the phone—what page is it, she said, where are you? And she said, look, come and get me. So, I went around the corner to get her and she brought her little trolley with her—she carries it 24 hours a day. She marches in there, and the place is open, and she comes up and she says, "Right-oh, my name is Valmai Blanche Power AM. I am the Women's Advisor to the Premier [and, Val adds for my benefit, the Aboriginal Women's Family and Youth Officer for the State Department of Aboriginal Affairs who advises the Minister on Aboriginal Affairs involving Aboriginal families]. Now I believe there is some problem here. I have come to verify that these women are Ngarrindjeri. I vouch for them being of Ngarrindjeri descent" and stuff like that. "Thank you very much Mrs Power." But it makes me angry that no-one, none of the other women or men had to prove that they were Ngarrindjeri.

The subsequent publication of flawed genealogies in the Stevens Report added insult to injury. However, because of the thinness of resources and the push to get the representations done for Judge Mathews in January 1996, the breach of faith and confidence that

240

the publication of genealogies constituted was not registered as strongly as it might have been in the courts by the "proponent women", who now as the "applicants" are intent on explaining their beliefs to Judge Mathews. Further, by the time sufficient people had read the document, considered their opinion, consulted with the appropriate persons and reached consensus on what should be done, the Stevens Report had been in circulation for a month or so and the damage was done. Unlike a hurt or a harm concerning damage to property, the damage to goodwill caused by actions such as the publication of private information cannot be easily undone. There is no compensation. The line is just drawn closer the next time information is required and the level of trust placed in the written word and official documents is further tarnished.

The genealogies that both fascinate and upset many Ngarrindjeri are those published by Ronald and Catherine Berndt in *A World That Was* (1993).[11] Doreen Kartinyeri: The first time I met Ron and Catherine Berndt was when they came over from Western Australia to meet with Chris Anderson and Peter Sutton and the anthropology staff at the museum. We sat around the staff tea-room table and we were looking at the manuscript. It was not yet published. Ron had heard about my work and I about his. I hadn't seen anything he had done, so he gave Steve Hemming a copy of his genealogies and Steve was to make copies for me. Every time I talk about this my head gets crazy. I pointed out a few things to him where I saw the names of families, and mistakes and things they seemed to have overlooked. But they were not taking any notice of me. I looked at the Rigney section, my mum's family.

The Rigney book was already out, but I didn't have the part about Isabella and James in it because I thought it irrelevant to what I wanted to achieve. So in the Berndt book I saw where Isabella was married to James Rankine. Well I had heard they'd had an affair while they were working together at Wellington in the Lodge. So I queried why he had it down as a marriage instead of a liaison, or something. But I never got much from them that day. Catherine was quiet that day and Ron did most of the talking.

I never met Tindale, though I spoke to him on the phone and had written a letter to him and he'd written to me. In the Tindale material, if there is a reference to another page, you can be sure that same information will appear there, whereas with Ron Berndt's genealogies, he's got numbers for people—we look like criminals—and you've got to track back to find the name and if they're married. Sometimes it has the name but usually it is a number and then you have to look for that. I checked some of his early marriages in the Register's Office and I can't find them. I've checked Tindale's marriages and would get copies when they existed. I'd go with the name and the year and I'd look at the age of the oldest child and go with that year. When Barry Craig and Vincent Buckskin [in the anthropology division of the South Australian Museum] and I would go to look something up from Tindale's genealogies, we usually find the marriage certificate, but not with the Berndts. Say you were looking for John Wilson who was married in a certain year—if you found the one married to Martha and you knew her maiden name was Reed and her mother was Annie Angie, then I would know I had the one I was looking for.

I took the copy of the genealogies back to Cummins, where I was living at the time, and stapled them together. I didn't even know the name of their book then. It was just genealogies. Then when I was in Sydney for a conference, I met up with John Stanton and I said, "I don't like the genealogies." I'd seen every possible mistake I could find. I'd seen where an uncle was put down as marrying a niece. Maybe it was a typing error, but I couldn't believe there were so many. I asked him why he had to put the genealogies in the book. Why not just have the older people and the family names and say they are Ngarrindjeri families. You wouldn't put in the Rigneys because they don't come from this way, just by marriage. But no, he didn't want to do it that way. You could have your families like Isabella from the Coorong and then Rigney as a name that marries in. That would be one way of showing identity. But John Stanton just sat there saying, "Yes. Yes. Yes. But Prof. doesn't want it that way. He wants it this way." Ron Berndt had died by then and I thought maybe I could get through to Catherine. This is when I said we should not have the Museum name linked to it, because once people started looking at those numbers, a lot of people would think there was incest in their families. The Berndts did not do what Tindale did. He wrote up the incest about how they wanted the old man killed because he went with the daughter and if that wasn't bad enough, he went with the grand-daughter too. He was only one man and he was an outsider and came in and you can see how he acted.

Ron Berndt has people married to aunties and uncles and he's got cousins married and it's not as consistent as Tindale. If you're going to do it, you should do it properly. I know I have a problem looking at the Berndt stuff, even though I want to continue to look at it, even though it blows my mind sometimes, I still feel there may be something I can see there that is true, so I'll try to follow along. After Ron Berndt died, Catherine wanted so much to come over to Adelaide. So John Stanton brought her back and we went to have dinner across the road from the Museum and we talked about the book. It was already in press. I became very fond of Catherine and talking to her about things. That time she was very frail and I didn't want to tackle her. She sent me a signed copy. You can just read her signature. I really thought we'd get through to Ron when I was going through the loose pages and going back and forth to find the names. Ron didn't want me to be the one to tell him there were mistakes. I saw the expression in his face a couple of times when I said something, and I didn't like it. I've had that feeling before when I try to correct a whitefella: "What's this little black-fella doing telling him his job?" But if I don't know I ask. With Fay Gale I'd say, "What do you mean?" and she'd explain it. But if I know for a fact something is definitely wrong, I will say it.

So I took them and I studied them and I nearly had a heart attack. They had my great-grandmother married to a man she wasn't married to [Berndt *et al.* 1993: 516-17], and Edna Lovegrove married to her aunt's husband [*ibid.*: 536]. Now, there were two Victor Rigneys and we would say, well anybody could make that mistake, but there were too many. This Victor, who married Edna, had a second name. He was Victor Reid Rigney. Victor Rigney, the son of Isabella Sumner and Phillip Rigney, was married to Edith Mack and she was the sister of Rose Mack, Edna's mother. Edith and Rose were the daughters of John and Pinkie Mack. Then I couldn't work out about Aunty Elva, she was née Rigney but she had married a Milera—she didn't have eight children like Ron has down for a Elba Rigney [*ibid.*: 514]. I thought it might have been Elsa Rigney who at the time of this material being collected would have been a Sumner, because she married Lesley Sumner. But Berndt has this woman recorded as Elba Rigney, mother of eight children. I don't know who that is—not that I claim to know everybody—but I don't know her.

Genealogies are not disinterested accounts of relationships, and those who prepare them need to pay attention to what is being negotiated in their preparation and publication. This may leave some gaps. Although Doreen is passionate in her concern to get it right, she acknowledges: In cases of incest, I'd leave out the actual father's name and just put in the family name. And, if people don't want to be recorded, I'd most probably say well that's entirely up to you. But I tell them the importance of it. It may not be for them now because they're older, but what about the younger ones? I do try and encourage them to change their mind, but some of them are that very strong that they don't really want to do it. I've explained this in nearly every workshop, every place I've been to talking about Aboriginal genealogies that it's important that we record it and we record it properly so that the children of the future can trace their identity and themselves back to their land and their tribe and their culture and their clans and whatever it is. Not everyone is going to be able to do that in the future, because I don't think I'll live long enough to finish my books anyway. But, I have to respect people's wishes.

There are no genealogies to accompany this book. I realise it is difficult to follow the accounts of family relationships at times but that is how the knowledge is transmitted amongst and within families. I have given maiden names where possible, as that is information which is available to most Ngarrindjeri and it is taken for granted in many conversations. I admit I have found it extremely frustrating that I have not been able to sit down and generate page after page of incredibly detailed genealogies as I have been accustomed to do in central Australia. I feel handicapped and constantly at the edge of my competence in working with the material. However, the experience has taught me new respect for what genealogies represent to people who have been missionised, had their names changed, had families broken up, been denied access to records, and been reared with great deal of mistrust of the written record and white experts.

Family Connections: Something Old, Something New

In the ethnographic literature and in the rhetorical assertions of people today, residence was patrilocal and rights in land and *ngatji* inheritance passed through the male line. I have heard this termed the "paramount law". Today there is uneven knowledge of *ngatji* affiliation, but for those who are interested, there are ways of figuring out what one "should be". For those who still have contact with knowledgeable elders, this may be as precise as a clan *ngatji*, reckoned through one's parents' affiliations. In the absence of this knowledge, it appears it is possible to take what I have called the "regional *ngatji*" of the place where one was born or grew up. For those who wish to ground their identity by being able to specify a *ngatji* affiliation, making a connection is what matters. Connection may be made at the macro-level by the assertion of being Ngarrindjeri. Connection may be made at the local level through membership of one of the Ngarrindjeri families. It seems to me that continuity of a grounded identity relies most heavily on these two levels of identification. This is not to deny that there are still people who know their clan names, or that there are still people who distinguish between being Tangani, Yaraldi or Ramindjeri, though this is most likely to be by reference to the Coorong, the river and lakes, or Encounter Bay, than by reference to one of the dialects of Ngarrindjeri. And I have heard long, detailed debates regarding who is and who isn't Ngarrindjeri. Passionate debates such as those concerning Ngarrindjeri identity and family affiliation indicate the importance of knowing who may make legitimate claims and according to what principles. Indeed many of the most rigorous genealogical discussions I have heard focus on the definitions of "family". It's in the blood, to be sure; but it's also in the reckoning.

I think of these "families" as large cognatic local descent groups,[12] who are known by names which connect them to particular places, such as Campbell, Carter, Gollan, Harris, Karpeny, Koolmatrie, Kropinyeri, Lampard, Rankine, Spender, Sumner, Tripp, Walker, and Wilson. The Berndts (1993: 57) state: "In nearly all cases, except for incoming names, they [family names] were correlated with a specific clan—at least up to the early 1940s. Some European patryonyms were not (e.g. Rigney), but in the first generation of Rankines, the mother's clan designation was adopted." For each of these "families" there are nodal ancestors, such as Queen Charlotte, Queen Louisa. Queen Ethel, Mulparini, Mutyuli, and King Peter Pulami; their wisdom is transmitted several generations down by elders such as Nanna Pinkie, Aunty Laura, Aunty Koomi, Aunty Rosie, and Aunty Janet, who have intimate knowledge of the practices, beliefs and traditions of their families. Of course, not all possible descendants of a nodal ancestor will claim family membership (the groups would become large and unwieldy), and individuals make choices. Some choose to identify with several families. In defining the limits I think the Berndts' notion of "kindreds", that is the group of people recruited through cognatic ties to five other clans, with whom a clan member interacted most frequently and intensively, and from whose ranks spouses could not normally be selected, is helpful.

Today names still go through the patriline, but the residential pattern is more likely to be matrifocal, wherein there is an extended family with much activity revolving around a strong, knowledgeable woman. All those within her sphere of influence defer to her authority and knowledge of family. On the one hand, the tendency to matrifocality is a consequence of work histories—men pursued seasonal work while women maintained homes, kept the children in school, and became the centre of residential structures. On the other hand, matrifocality could be understood as the activation of an inchoate principle wherein people had affiliations with the five clan groups the Berndts call "kindreds". Thus today we find people emphasising "blood lines", but not necessarily reckoned solely through the father. Geographer Fay Gale, working with Aboriginal people in Adelaide documented a tendency to matrifocality (Gale 1972; Gale and Wundersitz 1982). Raukkan people, she tells us, were the largest Aboriginal constituency married into the Adelaide population, and, in 1960, marriages were still being arranged between families. It would be interesting to know what family alliances and country affiliations were being played out in these marriages. Gale forecast that these family arrangements would diminish over the next decade and that there would be more mixed marriages (Gale 1972: 168-9). Her findings, she points out, are similar to those of Diane Barwick (1963) for Melbourne, where kin and country continue to structure behaviour, where one goes for holidays, whom one marries, and where one is buried. If it were possible to do a census of Ngarrindjeri families in Adelaide, Raukkan and Murray Bridge, Tailem Bend, Meningie, up the Murray and down the southeast, one could possibly plot these changes more accurately and in greater detail. Historically there are many reasons

246

people resist being "written down" or counted in a census, but in the shadow of the Royal Commission, such research is almost impossible to suggest, let alone conduct.

Kin and country, people and place, these are the ties that bind. Keeping up with kin, visiting, celebrating birthdays, and attending funerals occupies a great deal of time. There are aspects of the kinship system on which people remark and others which may be observed. Kin terms are still known and used. Although the old law about mother-in-law avoidance is no longer followed strictly, I did see instances of "avoidance behaviour" in older women which had all the hallmarks of this institution. Of course, if avoidance behaviour is being rigorously observed, the casual visitor would never know that certain persons did not sit in each other's company or speak the other's name. Such things would be invisible. By observing who cares for the grannies; who cooks when several generations of women are present; who shops for whom and with whom; who answers whose phone; who takes the kids, disciplines them, teaches them, and buys the treats; and who attends funerals; one can gain an understanding of the content of key relationships. In these extended family networks, it seemed to me that aunties, nannas and grandmothers were more likely to be the teachers than parents. Thus, with whom one spent time as a child, where, and at which point in one's life, place in family, plus the quality of the relationship, and how interested the child was in learning, are all critical factors in assessing who knows what.

What mean "family"? I wonder. The question echoes Tom Trevorrow's: "What mean Pike?" I liked the formulation of the question, so: "What mean family?" The complex inter-relations of various aspects of Ngarrindjeri beliefs about what constitutes personal and group identity and the relationships through which they are made known implicates close and distant kin and makes family out of others. There are still things to be learned of Ngarrindjeri culture and there are still many knowledgeable Ngarrindjeri with whom one can work. But you need to be there to learn. By telling the stories of how I learned the stories, I am hoping to demystify and clarify what it is that an anthropologist does and how it is different from say a journalist, lawyer, literary critic and certain archive-oriented historians.

247

A Land Alive:
Embodying and Knowing the Country

A Living, Changing Land

Doreen Kartinyeri: Looking at the Ngarrindjeri nation, the sites, the burial grounds, the middens and the people, it's all one, it's connected together. It goes in a circle and that circle should not be broken, not with sites, not with people, not with land, skies and waters. Veronica Brodie agrees: We've got our hummocks on that side, but we've also got this side where our old people lived, where certain things took place, where we grew up, living and loving, and learning from the land, from the waters, living and learning our old people's ways. George Trevorrow adds: Through the peninsula system, there's huge midden mounds which tells us a lot about our history of the people, our people who lived on there. For ten years or more, Tom and I have been bringing groups over here, showing them the peninsula, walking it, and looking at the midden mounds. We tell non-Aboriginal people who visit us that's just not an Aboriginal problem to look after these sort of things. Those things hold a lot of history for us, us as Australians, not us as just Ngarrindjeri people alone. The land that these Ngarrindjeri love, look to for spiritual and physical nourishment, and are willing to fight to protect, has changed dramatically over the past two centuries, but people still know their special places, continue to visit and care for the country, and to tell the stories that keep it alive.

Explorers, missionaries, occasional visitors and professional researchers alike have remarked on the beauty and breadth of Ngarrindjeri lands; have recorded stories about the creation and integrity of the lands; some have even lamented the damage done through European settlement. Naturalist George French Angas (1847), who wrote vividly of his extensive travels in the southeast and whose fine drawings depict a lifestyle well adapted to the local conditions, paused atop Mount Lofty, and surveyed Ngarrindjeri lands. A "stupendous and magnificent scene" was before his eyes (*ibid.*: 42). Tindale (1974) mapped the lookouts and boundary markers at which Ngarrindjeri also stood and saw their lands. "Among the Lower Murray tribes every clan had one or more such watching place," (Tindale nd, c); maybe a lookout hill, especially in the sandhills where men might make camp and keep watch (Tindale 1941: 242); and Tindale and Long (nd: 12) mention that Milerum's *ngatji*, the *Krowali*, would be cut into a pole to mark his rights within the clan territory of his wife. They too told stories of the pioneers, of the creative ancestors who gave form and meaning to the land. Our country is like a book, George Trevorrow explained as he "read" the landscape. Writing of the "noble" Murray River, some ten kilometres above its junction with Lake Alexandrina, Angas (1847: 51-2) delights in its "blue waters meandering through a vast extent of reeds, the vivid green of which was truly refreshing to the eye. Its course was so gentle as to be barely perceptible; deep and broad, and smooth as a glassy mirror, it flowed tranquilly and majestically onwards in silent grandeur to the ocean." He has entered Ngarrindjeri lands and is beginning to appreciate the complex waterways. "Mount Barker, deeply purple in the shades of evening, shuts out the view to the westward", but from the high ground on its opposite bank, Angas (*ibid.*: 57) has a "fine view" of the river, "winding in the most graceful sweeps, between 'fields of living green'". This path is one the Ngarrindjeri have mapped in their stories and ceremonies, but the changes in the flow and colour of the waters occasioned by irrigation systems upstream and the barrages down stream have tarnished the land and the stories. "Floating islands, covered with reeds, are frequently to be seen on this river," notes Angas (*ibid.*: 54). These also are part of Ngarrindjeri lore.

Over a century apart with their observations, both Tindale (1974) and Angas (1847) were awed by the Coorong. "[R]unning parallel to the coast for 90 miles; being divided from the ocean only by a ridge of stupendous sand-hills", the Coorong, says Angas (*ibid.*: 64-5), is "a truly wild and desolate place". Tindale (1974: 61-2) remarks the dense scrub covering the hummocks; the wide lagoon teeming with birdlife, fish and on the landward shore, the *tengi* shore with its numerous freshwater "sucks" where birdlife congregated, behind that Mallee scrub, yucca and honeysuckle. The rivers, lakes and ocean, hummocks, saltpans and scrub country are home to a wide variety of life. Plentiful freshwater and salt-water fish, yabbies, cockles, mussels, swan eggs, various marsupials, birds, berries, roots and seeds sustained a population of a density higher than for most other regions of the continent. Even so, people moved with the seasons. There were-well established summer and winter camps. The *talamandi* camps were used throughout a season, the *ngawandi* was designed as a one-night camp (Tindale 1934–7: 155) and *milangawand* was a temporary camp for fighting (Tindale nd, e).

Angas (1847: 64) appreciates the seasonal round, the plenty of spring and the measures taken to survive the winters, the ingenuity of Ngarrindjeri semi-permanent camps. A rhythm of life marked by a seasonal round is detailed by Reuben Walker (1934) nearly a century later. The winter thaw in the mountains brings the cold fresh water to the sea; as the days lengthen into summer, people gather, trade, and conduct ceremonies; as the days shorten and nights grow chill, people move to their wurlies, weather the cold wet winters and await spring, the return of life; and so it goes. These were not a nomadic people, but ones with deep ties to particular places and their own clearly defined clan territories. Tindale and Long (nd: 12) write of the permission needed from traditional owners when crossing places of economic and ritual importance: "At times when mullet were crossing the shallows in shoals, their permission would be eagerly sought after." Doug Wilson: Within a fifty-mile radius of Goolwa there was a number of tribes. You never cross into another territory and you wait for contact or a messenger, wait a day, however long it takes. You never deliberately enter, unless you have permission, even if it meant going around and taking days. There were markers for a boundary, hill, a stone, and that would let you know. On Lake Albert, where Campbell House was, my father would say, "Never be afraid here. This is your land here." They'd be watching out and they'd say there is five of them coming across the open country and they'd go down a bit of a dip and lose sight for a bit and then it was only my Dad and his mate. "Where are the other three?" So he said, "Must be your ancestors accompanying you." And there in Berndt *et al.* (1993: 309) is Doug's father, Dan Wilson, with Liwurindjeri on Lake Albert as his clan territory.

George Trevorrow, literate in the ways of the land, reads a story of survival: During the wet season the peninsula actually acts like a big giant sponge, because it's got the sea on one side which is salt water, the Coorong on the other side. And that soaks up all the rain throughout the year. Now when it comes to a dry time like this, when the waters are down, you can poke holes in the side of the hill over there in certain places and out'll come bubbling fresh water. With the assistance of archaeologists and other experts, more information about the middens is being extracted (Smith 1924: 189; Noye 1974: 111; Luebbers 1981): It's incredible how much it can help all of us. It can tell us seasonally how things operated: how high the seas were before, so many years ago; how high they may come up again; what sort of fish was in abundance; what sort of animals were there; what may be extinct, you know; and what may be becoming extinct. There's a wealth of information in this country if we'd be prepared to look after it.

Tom Trevorrow has deep concerns about how the Coorong has been looked after: The fresh water used to come from the southeast, from the next town down at Kingston, right through from Mount Gambier. And that water kept the Coorong alive. Now, when we look at the Southern Lagoon of the Coorong today, it's dying. It's going stagnant because of what happened in the southeast, a part of the Coorong has been damaged very severely. And to us, as Ngarrindjeri people, it's like, it's damaging us. It's like cutting one of your arms off, or one of your legs off. In the end you start losing the full capacity of your body. We look upon the land in the same way. And what has happened down the southeast is slowly affecting the land here today. Because all through this lagoon down here, the water would flow through and it would freshen up the Coorong, make it a combination of fresh and salty water which kept the fish here and all the bird life. And that was all a part of survival of the waterways and the land. That is a part of the survival of the people.

In 1935 Tindale and Long (nd: 10) wrote of the "sacred place Ngerakerang on the hill where Marangane left his spears which became mallee trees which had so much meaning to people, now half a dozen pits in the limestone on the south side have been quarried for road making. This is a place where in olden times the Salt Creek waters came out through several lakes." In the short-term memory of older Aborigines, Tindale (1938: 20) notes, islands in the lakes have been eroded, dune sand rivers have poured over the outer barrier and entered Coorong lagoon to change its configuration, and changes in salt-water level have altered vegetation, with "the clearing of sandy ground, the stocking of the Coorong with sheep and cattle, and its invasion by rabbits, leading to rapid drifting and alteration of old fixed sandhills, lookouts and other landmarks". In his notes Tindale (1934–7: 57) elaborates on how the dark green line of vegetation has been replaced "by mile after mile of drifting sand. Most of the coastal sucks were buried and the camping places overwhelmed. The very hills of the totemic legends have blown away." A number of animals vanished, native herbs were eaten out. Lake Albert became salty, and the weed-covered shallows of Lake Alexandrina where fish bred have disappeared. Each new place I am taken, my guides make sure I understand how the land has been damaged, and they care very much about this continuing onslaught on places they would like to be able to protect. Alf Watson observed: Our *maldawuli* told us, long, long ago, to "beware of the ants". White men must be ants. (Tindale 1938: 20).

Sarah Milera spends much of her time working with local people on environmental concerns, but the perspective and knowledge which drives her interest is from her Ngarrindjeri heritage. She indicates a bush growing near the Goolwa barrage: That's *karlo*, and I had that presented in America on ecology, but I only know it by my Ngarrindjeri word for that bush. We used to get the seeds off that, and we used to get the gum off the trees, it's very important in health, and there's no evidence of that around here now. All the plants are dying and the plants that was under the ground, that's all dying. Some plants I have to keep secret because they belong to women and only women know about them. I can't disclose them to anyone. One day the teaching will be for women to use those plants. There's a lot of my friends who's learning that story with me, is going to go and replant all those kind of plants for the health reasons.

Older Ngarrindjeri women and men have quite extensive knowledge of bush foods and medicines: they know the taboos, where to go, with whom they should go, what is in season, and they are open to creative adaptations. *Muntharies* (native apple) were in season in January and Liz Tongerie had made the best chutney I've tasted for a while. Eileen McHughes, who also knows a great deal about "bush tucker" and herbal remedies, remembers the collecting: We'd go, Mum and the kids, and get *kulithumies* [native currant], *ngunungies* [pigface] and *muntharies*. They'd do the fishing and the sort of gathering of the small stuff, like eggs and yabbies and those sort of things, and the men used to get the bigger game. Sometimes we'd get the swans and the ducks and the emus, kangaroos, so I've tried just about everything. And then my grandfather—he didn't make it to the war—so he stayed home, and he used to do rabbit trapping, and Mum and—I'll call her mother, that's my grandmother, but we was always brought up to call her mother, and my real mum, I called "Mum". They used to go out and set the lines for Murray cod. And they said when you caught it and cut it open, you could hold it up to the light and see *Ngurunderi's* tree. Much later I find this story in Tindale (1934–7: 39) and it has an interesting age and gender twist to it. "The Murray cod is Ngurunderi's fish and only old people are allowed to eat it. When young men spear *pondi*, they open it up and hold its apron up to the sky. If it shows a *wurie*, a network of blood vessels like a red gum tree, then it must be eaten only by old people as it is Ngurunderi's fish. If no red tree, then it is all right for young men and women."

Doreen Kartinyeri: *Ngunungies* they call them and they'd squeeze the juice out onto the palm of the hand and put some on the eyes. They suffered at Raukkan from bung eyes and conjunctivitis from the fine sand and ringworms from cats. A range of folk remedies are in use. On a visit to Goolwa, Isobelle's grand-daughter had sore eyes which were treated with tea bags. The next day when Chantel was feeling better, her "aunties" were proud of how effective their remedies had been. Both of these treatments have been learned from the older generation, and there is a pride in being able to cure loved ones, but the women can and do distinguish tea bags from the Ngarrindjeri pigface. It is the spirit of the healing that persists. Veronica Brodie reminds me about the *watji* bush which looks like a leek, has an

254

acid taste and cleans out the mouth. She then relates the curative value of blue mud. They were putting the stands to hang the nets on and I dived in. I was bleeding badly from the gashes from the coral. The blue mud stopped the bleeding. Later I was treated with iodine.

Sarah Milera has native plants in her garden. She is keen to see the land regenerate and for the balance to be restored. Her well-being is at stake: We need trees so that everybody is replanting around Goolwa in the Land Care area and out on the island where there's salt, because salt is important to us. Salt was in aid of burials. When they burnt bodies it controlled the smell of burning bodies and when the trees go, it loses its impact, and you need the trees around to keep that salt pure. My mother was a powerful woman and she always taught me that, to have respect. Those areas still exist and things have been there for all of my life and I remember my mum talking about salt and when I go to the island, it feels like a spiritual wounding; it's like—it is a spiritual wounding for me. It's heavy going for me to go out on the island and see the salt coming in, because the salt is going to envelop all over. You see it when you go out there. It's a sadness because the trees and the vegetation is not around the way it was, but there's still echidnas on there, on the island. There's still some—there's birds. *Lauwari* [Cape Barren goose], they're there now.

This is a spiritual place, and I am at peace here. I know it at Goolwa. It's the closest to God you are ever going to get. They're breaking our religion, if they build a bridge there. No, you can't change your relationship to a special place, to where your learning comes from. It's a very powerful thing. The birds talk to you—a lot of people know that. And I'm very upset that I'll lose my strength. I'm carrying a big weight for my nation. When we talk about spiritual things—Ngarrindjeri have visions—we see what we were, and what we are able to be. The spirits take its place, and releasing them, and it takes one person to do that, and I've done it. And that's taking up our responsibility. It binds you to that place. To sell a place and leave, it is desecration of the soul. I've been teaching this to white people. How can we be so wrong? The Coastal Protection people said, "Oh, well, we'll clean up, we'll spend a million dollars cleaning up this area." And you can't, because you need the power of the river and the power of the sea and those in combination and the mixing, and you've got to have salt water to have fresh water, because you can go in the middle of the island and get fresh water, but then those barrages are the altering things and we had no control over it. But the land is regenerating.

While on the Goolwa side of the ferry, Isobelle Norvill stood and looked out across the channel, back at the midden exposed by road construction, and down at the ground. Clicking her tongue in disgust, she pointed at the murky water and the dog faeces on the bank. This site would have been clean. Having it like this is disrespectful. It was quite horrifying to see this, the condition of the water, you know, because when I first came down here, we used to be able to, you know, play in the water and stuff like that. But all the pollution and the slime that's happened now because of the boats being there and obviously all the extra tourists and stuff like that. You couldn't even get in there today because you'd just come out riddled with diseases and ear problems. You couldn't let the children go in there." This had been an area where women went cockling, where the limestone cups held fresh water, where at low tide one could walk out to the island.

Maggie Jacobs: See, now we got nothing since white man has stepped on here. The water used to be low. We could get cockles. Now there is nothing. This is all wiped out. At Ngarlung we got sugar-bag, about a tent bag full. There's still some there, but up at Ti-Tree Crossing and other places, they're being fished out. Look at them over there at the Murray Mouth, it was only so wide, only narrow, but with the campers and four-wheel-drives, it's wide. See, there's a sand bank up there. You can see a sand bank there. The channel is only so wide. All along here, blackfellas lived all along here. They made their camps and they fished and we—now—our culture—this is what I've been taught is that the earth, the land, the water, we all got to live by water and the plants and the animals. And it makes me so angry. All they want is to get rich themselves.

The rising water has also covered the fish traps. One trap, right at the marina on Hindmarsh Island, was exposed one January day in 1996 when the wind blew the water away from the shoreline. Tim Goldsmith, a local resident, photographed the stone arrangement which was quickly recognised by Ngarrindjeri as a fish trap. I had heard from both Maggie Jacobs and Val Power that there were fish traps all along the coast. Their information came from the old people. Tom had also told me, You'll see them standing out when you get the right winds and low tide. Lola Cameron Bonney (1982) told Roger Luebbers that between Salt Creek and Woods Well, you can see the stones, but only when the weather is good or the water clear. It's not a big thing. It's not wider than a table but it looks as if the stones were put there. Her husband Ron Bonney added: There is another one that Joe Bonney knows about. Fish traps, such as these, stabilised clan territories along the coast. They were markers of industry and plenty. In her poem "Fish Traps" Leila Rankine (c.1980) imagines

> families working
> in groups, carrying to and
> fro, building stone, upon stone
> and row upon row upon row.

Ask about fishing and hunting stories, and one learns not only about the behaviour of animals, but about territoriality, *ngatji* affiliations and Ngarrindjeri humour. Doug Wilson was out hunting *lauwari* with his father. They would be just out of reach, and my father would put on a red hat (any bright colour) and put his head just above the reeds, and move it back and forth to attract the attention of the birds. They would come to see it, and then he would shoot it. I said, "Why, Dad?' And he said, "Because they're inquisitive." And I said, "What's that?" And he said, "Don't tell everyone." Another time Doug was out getting duck eggs with his father, and had not seen the snake that was coiled up in the nest. It was there sucking out the eggs. His father shot it, and all the eggs. Doug credits his father with saving his life. On another occasion: I was under ten and was fishing down at The Narrows. I threw my line in and my grandmother and father called "*Marmar*". They were calling out to the fish to bite and then I'd feel the bait, "*Ngolkin* [bite] Dougie's line" to the fish they say. I was only little and it worked fine. I have spent many hours listening to tapes of the 1960s, where a Ngarrindjeri person is asked to recall names for body parts, the elements, and legends and, having failed to recall many, is categorised as having little "traditional knowledge". "Ask about fishing," I say under my breath, "It's still there."

Of her research at Point McLeay in the early 1940s, Catherine Berndt (1989: 13) stated the culture of the people "no longer survived as a living force", but that those who grew up around the mission or along the river "were able to get acquainted with basic information about topography, resources and events that adults already knew". Knowledge of their places included where the whales might come in, during which season, the location of residential and burial sites. I also saw this attentiveness to a constantly changing landscape. At each ferry crossing the women would lean near the edge to see what was happening with the reeds and rushes; as we drove along they'd point out where the geese are to be found and where to catch yabbies, and bemoan the fact that some sites were now fenced off. Noting and reporting what is growing where is an important demonstration of care of country. It is an ethic of respect that is grounded in precise knowledge of micro-environments, but is framed within an understanding of the interconnectedness of bird to water, plants to salt, birds to plants, and so on in different localities. Improper use of resources, taking too much, eating too much, swimming in the wrong places, gathering eggs in restricted places, eating prohibited foods, being in the wrong country, will wreak havoc on the living and not necessarily on the perpetrator, and this knowledge is a powerful inhibitor for believers. Non-believers make the country uninhabitable, and hence the interest in educating others. These Ngarrindjeri know the consequences of not having been able to protect their land in the past and now, when they have the possibility of protecting a site from damage under legislation, the responsibility is awesome. They must act, but they must do so within their cultural code of respect. Catherine Berndt's (*ibid.*) observation that Ngarrindjeri culture "no longer survived as a living force" may have characterised attitudes in the 1940s, but it is no longer accurate. Knowledge did survive and, in the late 1990s, there are those for whom it is a living force. The knowledge is acted upon.

It may well be that there is a hidden history of resistance and protest, one that is just beginning to be told (Reynolds 1981). Eileen McHughes remembers the old people telling her to keep away from the barrages. Others referred back to the problems caused by the building of the barrages and resistance of old people. Maggie Jacobs recalls that the men would go out in the evening, sneak down, and break the barrages, knowing that they would have to continue work on them the next day. Veronica Brodie and Aunty Maggie agree: There was Wilf Wassa, we called him "Wolfado", and Uncle Mervyn Carter, we called him "Skidder", Alan Campbell (Amelia's father), and "Big Bert (Bert Wilson). There are others who contest these accounts and claim no knowledge of such acts of sabotage. The changes in the landscape are not contested. Doreen Kartinyeri: The barrages stopped the flow of the water with the tides. It destroyed the rushes that people used for weaving. The foods and medicine plants have gone and the fish is not as plentiful. The birds don't come here as often now because of the people here. When I asked Doug Wilson about what the old people said about the barrages, his answer was a complex interplay of knowledge of the flora and fauna that had disappeared and realisation that the significance of those changes only became evident with time. The old people could see what the barrages were doing to their fishing. I remember Lake Alexandrina before the barrages: the water was salt and fresh. I remember where the last block was built where there had been Mulloway—you'd get two to three ton at a time and only spend a half hour on fishing. The nature of the desecration occasioned by the barrages was the change that ensued, as much as the thing itself. It was the disruption of relations central to the balance of the Ngarrindjeri world that was the harm. There was no "rule" about barrages in Ngarrindjeri traditions. They were not part of the world created by *Ngurunderi* but they certainly restricted realisation of the rhythms of that world. In April 1998, the Murray Mouth was almost closed over. It had closed completely in 1981. The colour photograph in the Adelaide *Advertiser* (11 April 1998: 3) was passed around the people with whom I was staying at Camp Coorong over Easter 1998. In the silty blockage they saw a sad confirmation of what their old people had taught them and what had been mocked in the Royal Commission: We know. We said it would happen. They don't believe us, but there is the proof.

Concern for the land moves back and forth between stories about particular places and stories about the interconnections of places, peoples and histories. Writing of the 1940s Catherine Berndt (1989: 13) stressed the attachment to the region, to the land as a collection of sites rather than a focus on individual places. I agree that the Point McLeay people, of whom she is writing, do have a sense of themselves as sharing a history. However, in my experience, the level of detail about country and sites depends on where one is, with whom, and what is being discussed. On my first visit to the Coorong, I wanted to see McGraths Flat, site of the 1842 killing and the place where Taplin notes his charges are forever visiting. Ngarrindjeri recalled it as the site of the meteorite crash, memorialised in the story of the *prupi*, the cannibalistic old woman (Tindale 1938). Today they speak of nearby Rabbit Island, the birthplace of Milerum and other of their old people. Rabbit Island once sustained farms, but now it is overgrown with weeds and the salt is taking over. Neville Gollan, who as a boy had lived on Rabbit Island, had told me of how he had swam to shore, hessian bag on back, to get supplies for his mother and family. As I walked across the channel of the Coorong to the island, I sank deep in the mud and made an indelible print on the land. I now heard stories of others who had been bogged at this site and of times when the channel had flowed. These stories were alive and belonged to the place.

As I noted with reference to *ngatji*, place of birth has always been important, but residential sites, I think, have become increasingly important as people moved to live on missions, reserves, and the fringes of towns. Living in these new communities, they began to interact with the new places, and local resources, and to imprint their histories on the land; to develop sites of historic importance to their families; and to interact with the spirits of that place. As one woman said: I lived at Raukkan all my life: it's all I know. Some sites were connected to particular resources, the best place to get rushes, bark for canoes, wood for spears, red ochre for ceremonies, yabbies and swans' eggs. Some sites have to do with where international gatherings occurred. At Goolwa, Sarah Milera indicates where different peoples camped when they came there for trade, ceremonies, and to arrange marriages. Other sites have to do with where people holiday, picnic, and visit. At each place one can hear what information is being transmitted to the next generation and observe how attachment to place is made manifest. On our trip down the Coorong, Tom points out the camping sites of various Ngarrindjeri families. Leila Rankine (1974b: iv) notes that the Dodds, Sumners, and Rigneys went to Mark's Point, while the

Wilsons, Macks, Lovegroves and some Rankine families went to Ngarlung and Pelican Point. This remains active knowledge.

Val Power did not want to speak of her land and family at Marrunggung in a faraway place. I'm not talking in an office in Adelaide, on Kaurna land, about what it means to us and how it feels, with the river flowing by, in the distance Poltalloch Hill, and with our place where the Murray flows into the Lake Alexandrina only a kilometre away and where my family travelled to Hindmarsh Island. On our land I can give some information about our cultural, sacred heritage. There are a number of aspects to the affiliations to local places Val then specifies. Her father, Louisa Karpeny's grandson, lived and died at Marrunggung. His sister, Janet Smith, Val's aunty, who was very important in her upbringing, lived there. Jenny Ponggi, who was Val's "great-grandmother" (father's mother's mother's sister) and Albert Karloan's mother, camped on Hindmarsh Island. The Karpeny family met with other neighbouring groups, which Val calls "clans", such as the Campbells and the McHughes, during summertime down the Coorong. They visited Raukkan, and the Wilsons, in her mother's line, but her family did not want to be Christianised. They wanted to keep to their rituals and to be able to fish and hunt and be free.

Today, as people comment on the disappearance of fresh-water soakages on the Coorong; the salting up of the land; the polluted cockle beds; the stripping of vegetation and overstocking; and changes in the landscape; the rising of the waters at Goolwa where one used to be able to walk across; the exposure of burial sites on Hindmarsh Island, at Goolwa and along the Coorong; and the holiday houses clustered along the Coorong shore, there is a bitter sense of resentment. They have protested in the past but had little control. A seemingly pragmatic comment regarding the rubbish at a site is a clue to this aspect of lack of control. Ngarrindjeri stewardship of these ecologically diverse lands was and continues to be a complex interplay of religious, economic and social relationships. In the nineteenth century, clan territories were relatively small and thus it was important to establish a variety of relationships through which one might gain access to resources not available in one's home territory. There were stories and rituals that made this possible, all within the over-arching law made known through the activities of the pioneering heroes. In the late twentieth century, Ngarrindjeri continue to care and worry for their land. The means of expressing these sentiments may have changed radically, but so have the land and the lives of its peoples. Ngarrindjeri culture is neither a museum artefact, an anthropological invention, nor snippets of memories of a passing generation, although it exists in concert with and contradistinction to these elements. Rather, when it comes to land, it is a dynamic, vibrant, resurging, adapting and tenacious mix of peoples, places, beliefs, and practices.

In the cool of an evening after a 41-degree January day in 1996, Tom and Ellen Trevorrow, their children, Ellen's mother Daisy Rankine, Aunty Maggie (Daisy Rankine's sister-in-law), and a number of the grannies were feasting on cockles gathered that day from the Coorong. They were sitting at the back of the house; the power had been off, and their camp was lit by the glowing coals of the fire over which they'd been roasting cockles. Delicious. The tone was happy, peaceful and respectful, and the younger generation listened to the stories of their elders. They spoke of the best places for cockles. They talked about the cockle beds drowned by the raised water levels. They remembered the bounty of other cockling expeditions. I didn't know all the people and places mentioned in their stories, but the tenderness of the tone transcended such specifics. In such intimate settings, the value and dearness of Ngarrindjeri culture is clear. If I had turned my back on the buildings of Camp Coorong, this family group could have been one encountered by Angas 150-odd years earlier.

Ruwi and *Ruwar*: Land and Body

Calling me back, home to my *reuwee*, wrote Reuben Walker (1934: 195). Ngarrinjar *ruwar*, one body, all the people, sings Victor Wilson (1996). Tom Trevorrow used the metaphor of the body both to explain the integral nature of the Lower Murray region and to illustrate how he felt about damage done to that balance. Sarah Milera spoke of a spiritual wounding that was inscribed on her body. People speak of "breaking" the land as one would break bones; of the land sickening and dying; and, in the case of the

262

whales, of the land coming back. In Ngarrindjeri the word *ruwe* captures something of this complex of meanings, feelings, and associations. Today *ruwe* is most commonly translated as "country" or "land" (in the sense of one's territory).[1] In their translations of Albert Karloan's texts, the Berndts (1993: 358) gloss *ruwa* as "body", and I wondered about the "*ruw*" of *ruwa* and the "*ruw*" of *ruwi*. Was the body/land metaphor encoded in the language itself? In one text the Berndts (*ibid.*: 190) translate *ruwa* as ground and say "*ruwi*" also meant "body" so it would seem their informants made a connection. The *ruwi/ruwar* in this text is spoken of as getting hot (*ibid.*) and thus we have the sense of both land and body as excitable. In another text *ruwalan* is translated as the nerves of the body *ruwa* (*ibid.*: 422). From the Berndts' translations it appears the land has feelings and the land is alive.[2] From his preliminary analysis of the available material, linguist Barry Alpher concludes that the "Ngarrindjeri terms *ruwi* 'land, country, ground' and *ruwa(r)* 'body' probably contain the same root *ruw*."[3] In a number of ways, the oral and written sources support this position.

The first chapter of *A World That Was*, "The Land and its People" (Berndt *et al.* 1993: 13) opens with a passage that clearly identifies

The Murray Mouth, June 1983 (Nick Harvey)

the texture of intricate and enduring Ngarrindjeri beliefs about their *ruwe*, with their *ruwa*.

The great River Murray . . . was like a lifeline, an immense artery of a living "body" consisting of the Lakes and the bush hinterland that stretched across the Adelaide Hills and over the southern plains and undulating land. This "body" also included country to the east, most of which was only partially relevant to the Narrinyeri. Its "legs" spread south east-eastwards along the Coorong and south-westwards along Encounter Bay and beyond. The "body", symbolic of *Ngurunderi* himself, embraced five different environments which merged into one another: salt water country, riverine, lakes, bush (scrub) and desert plains (on the east)—a combination that had particular relevance to the socio-economic life of the people.

Along this artery flowed knowledge and resources. Marriages such as that of Pinkie Mack were contracted up-river; migrations such as that led by *Ngurunderi* came down-river.

In this metaphor of land as body, we have another way of thinking about the relationship of individual sites to the larger area of land in the region. Catherine Berndt (1989: 13) contends that, when men and women "voiced their discontent with the restrictions and disadvantages they were experiencing", they spoke of "their prior ownership of the land: not so much in terms of specific sites, but in terms of the larger, overall expanse of country". In so doing they could hold in their minds an image of the whole, of the integrated body. Within this body, individual sites, like specific limbs and organs, were vulnerable. Individual sites have been destroyed and with them the stories, but the land, albeit much changed, is still there and the health of the individual parts still has relevance for the survival of the whole body. Daisy Rankine has another explanation of the unity of Ngarrindjeri lands and it is one that employs a body metaphor also. The black swan, she says, can be seen in the land: Lake Alexandrina represents the body, the Coorong the neck, with the beak at the end of the Coorong past Salt Creek. And the wings spread out over Lake Albert, right up to Swan Reach with the beak going into the sea. What of the Murray Mouth?" I ask. The Murray Mouth would have been the whale, it needed to be big to open it, she tells me. The Berndts (1993: 14) write that the "debouching of the River waters into the sea was referred to as urination". The land is a living, functioning body.[4]

Ngarrindjeri place-names offer another window onto *ruwi/ruwa*.[5] Ngiakkung (armpit) is a name for Loveday Bay and Tipping (the lips) for the end of Point Sturt (Taplin 1873: 130). The most common etymology for the Coorong, or *Kurangk*, as it is pronounced by Ngarrindjeri speakers, comes from *kuri* for "neck", and *angk*, the preposition "at" when used with a proper name (Meyer 1843: 41). However, *Kurangk* could also be from *kuri* for "leg", or *kur* for "river".[6] *Ku:lwa* (Goolwa) may well be from *kuke* for "elbow" (Meyer 1843) but it may also mean the "place of cockles" (Taplin 1873: 130). Then again Gurawa/Gulawa (Goolwa) was said to mean the place where fresh and salt water meet (Morison 1978: 39). It may mean all three, depending on context, who is speaking and so on. Linguists may well find that the etymologies native speakers offer defy the rules with which they work, but when Ngarrindjeri offer their own folk etymologies they are exhibiting an interest in their language and continuing a tradition evident in the early records: Ngarrindjeri delight in their many meanings.[7] In this Ngarrindjeri is not unlike many other Aboriginal languages.

Where we can go back to the stories of the pioneering heroes, we find that it is their bodies that give form to the land. *Ngurunderi* is variously said to have left an imprint of his forehead in the rock where he knelt to drink on the Coorong (Berndt 1940a: 176). By stamping his feet, he created Kungkengguwar, Rosetta Head, (Meyer 1846). Before the bodies of the drowned wives became the rocky Pages Islands (Berndt 1940a: 181), the two women had been swimming in circles and had "stirred up the water so much that they formed a semi-circular sandbar (at King's Point) which later turned to stone" (Berndt *et al.* 1993: 226). In these accounts both men and women are interacting with land; both men and women imprint on the land in their own distinctive ways. The linking of specific physical features of the landscape with the deeds of the ancestors is a common feature of Aboriginal beliefs, nicely captured in Strehlow's (1970) phrase "geography and totemic landscape". The land is indeed the text from which one can read the history of one's forebears, the southward migration of *Ngurunderi* down the Murray–Darling river system, the formation of the land, and the rising of the water that cut off Kangaroo Island from the mainland. The *Ngurunderi* narrative also provides an explanation for anomalous features, such as the clump of grass trees at Rumply Point, as a transmogrification of *Ngurunderi*'s wives' raft (Hemming *et al.* 1989).

When the land is damaged, the response is visceral. The land, *ruwi*, has feelings and nerve endings as does the body, *ruwa*. For Eileen McHughes, breaking the surface of sacred ground registered on her body: We were all standing there, all the women, all my cousins; we're all related, all blood related somehow, and Isobelle and I were standing fairly close together. On the truck there were two toilets and the first one they put down was a women's toilet and it sort of moved, put a dent in the earth, you know, and sort of pushed it up to one side. It was just like we'd been stabbed in the heart. We had this terrible feeling and it's hard to describe unless you've got those kind of feelings as well. It's like as if someone had dug up my mother's bones or something, you know? It was a terrible. It was a real hurt. It was real, like a real grieving sort of feeling, sad and hurtful. It was like we were physically hurt ourselves. And I didn't know how Isobelle felt, and she didn't know how I felt, until afterwards, when we was talking that night. The site at Amelia Park where this happened in 1994 was registered under the South Australian Heritage Act. But the South Australian Minister had given his permission to allow such damage as might be necessary to be done in order for the work to begin on the bridge. This exercise of his discretionary powers was one of the factors leading to the first application for protection under the federal Act. That day in May 1994 Eileen's *miwi* was confirming what the registrar of sacred sites had already recorded. The site needed protection.

Isobelle Norvill: They had the police, and they had us barricaded and we weren't allowed to go in there. They were trying to keep people off so they could get the stuff in and Chantel, my granny, was with me. She was five. And when that first thing off the back of the truck hit the ground and cracked the earth open, it was very powerful. And after it was all over Channie said to me, "Nanna why are you crying?" and I said, "Well, there's a lot of nannas and papas buried here and we shouldn't do digging up where people are buried." Chantel knows all about death, about cemeteries, what happens to people when they die. I think it's important for her to learn very early. We went back to the Bunkhouse where we were staying. Everybody was very quiet and it was almost like we'd come back from a funeral. It was very sad and very quiet. We just went through the motions of getting meals and even the kids were very quiet. And Channie went missing. When we found her in the Bunkhouse, she was crying and she said, "I don't want them to dig up nannas and papas." We told her, "That's why we're here. We're going to try and stop that." So even as a five-year-old she was very sensitive to what goes on about things.

But, as Sarah Milera emphasised, it is not only a feeling. The injury can put you in hospital: Up behind Signal Point is where babies were born. When they drove the pegs into the ground I felt a spiritual wounding; I carry a wound. It's like—they rushed me to hospital. They didn't know what to do with me, because I was wounded by pegs going into the ground in where children were born. I was really hurt. They didn't know what to do with me in the hospital. When you get a spiritual wounding there's no medicine that can help you; it's beyond help and the only confidence was that people were standing by and protecting it. The council has shown no respect and they're still doing it. That site is why I come back because I couldn't face it. I can't face it spiritually if a bridge is built and into that spiritual waters that wounding can actually kill you; it is that serious, and I've been sick enough.

To drive pylons into sacred land constitutes an act of violence against the ancestors whose bodies reside in the area. George Trevorrow: With this part of the country, I can't get away from our belief. The Coorong is a body, is a whole, is one thing, a part of a body. That's what's been taught to us from our old people. The body needs sustenance to make that body survive and go through the seasons. If you start taking away from that body, that body starts dying, along with it our belief, a lot of our spirituality and things that link us in with that start dying as well, and as a people, inside, you start dying as well. This, George explained, may look like environmentalism, but he could

267

not separate out an issue as "the environment". It was part of an integrated world view. I must make that very, very straight. We can't do that. It is one. One block. You know when we talk about the Coorong, the southern part is dying, but there is still some hope for the northern part. The body may be hurting, parts may be seriously diseased or disabled, but the body is still there. One of the arguments I have heard is that the area around Goolwa is already damaged, so why worry with the sites that will be further damaged by the bridge? Do we license amputation of a leg by arguing that the patient has a broken arm?

The complex identification of land as a sentient body and as kin, of damage to land as constituting a desecration of skeletal remains and an injury to the living, is apparent in the way in which women speak about intrusions and changes to the land. It includes the relationship of the land to the water. Eileen McHughes, in explaining why the river should flow unimpeded to the sea, argued: The salt water used to come up as far as Tailem Bend and then the river would be coming all the way down which kept all the environment balanced. It flushes everything out. It's like our bodies. If we don't drink enough water to flush out the poisons, hey, we get sick. Sarah Milera pointed to where the cutting was made for the road to the ferry at Goolwa: That land has all been broken to make that roadway there, but they don't know the power of the water. It's nearly killed people here, and I tried to advise them that when the two powers are coming together, well you've got to be very careful. They don't know the mystery of the waters. The land has dropped a bit. When they took the trees out, the land got weak, and it fell into the water and that's what's hurting all of us Ngarrindjeri people. Deborah Bird Rose (1992: 108-9) captures this nicely when she writes of the relationship between Aboriginal people and their country as reflexive "damage to country, and to Dreamings in particular, causes death or injury to the people who are responsible for the site, and vice versa". This moral relationship of people to land is one with which I am familiar in other parts of Australia. What is distinctive in Ngarrindjeri lands is the power of individuals through their *miwi* to know of a relationship which is at once visceral and intellectual.

268

A Gendered, Embodied Land

Damage to the land, as damaging women's bodies and their health, has a history that Doreen Kartinyeri knows: I can't go into details because of the sacredness of it, but I can tell you about what my Aunty Rosie told me about when they were building the jetty at Raukkan. Her old Aunty was alive then and told her the story. Right from when they started to construct the jetty, the women were in a lot of pain, young babies were dying and women were having miscarriages. There were things that the other women were trying to do for the women, but I won't go into that. They felt the pain. There was an agony. There was crying. There was moaning. And the older women were rolling around just like they'd had a stake driven into their side. It continued right till the jetty was built. In Taplin's journal (16–17/7/1879) I find a reference to the building of the jetty. There is no mention of the women's agony, but could we expect him to have recorded it had he noticed? More important, does faith in the power of a belief that certain practices are dangerous require empirical verification for it to be a recognised as a belief? Do we ask for evidence of the hell to which sinners go in order to acknowledge that following the Ten Commandments is a central Christian belief? Stories such as those of Doreen Kartinyeri, Sarah Milera, Eileen McHughes and George Trevorrow about land as body are the context within which women give meaning to their various experiences. Everyone does not need to have the same experience for these to be powerful beliefs. It is the consistency of the accounts, fragmentary as they may be, the power of the *miwi* in identifying particular places, and the visceral nature of the damage that is so telling.

Doreen has tried over and over to find the most appropriate way of explaining this: It's very much like having something done to our whole body, a scar, a cut, a gash, and these are things that the Ngarrindjeri people, even today, are scared of happening. In the olden days the women would have really felt the effect of it, the damage happening to their own bodies. Now those women looked on Lake Alexandrina as their womb and Philip Clarke has it in his thesis that as being the body of a man—this might be—but my teaching is the body, is the woman's body and when you put a stake in it you're going to destroy it. You're going to feel it. You're going to destroy what's in that woman's stomach.[8] In anthropological texts, especially those seeking to generalise across the continent, the association of the land with the male body may make certain comparative analyses more elegant. Thus the Berndts (1988: 17) and Maddock (1972: 107-10) can compare a dominant male creative figure in the southeast with a female figure in the northeast. However, once the stories are examined in detail, these generalisations are revealed as far too sweeping to accommodate all the regional and personalised versions of the meaning of Ngarrindjeri lands. In the *Ngurunderi* story women were imprinting on the landscape before *Ngurunderi* made his creative sweep through the Lower Murray, and they continued to leave traces of their deeds during his travels.

Doreen Kartinyeri's understanding of the landscape as a gendered body comes from the teaching of her Aunty Rosie: When my first son Terri was born on the fourth of December, 1954, we went up to the school at Point Pearce. I put him in the pram, and I had taken the plate for lunch. As I closed the door, I saw the map on the back of it. It was one of those cloth maps with a sealed surface, and a board at the top and bottom to hold it straight.[9] Joyce O'Laughlin was with me, but she is now dead. The other person with me was Elva Wanganeen, Hilda Wilson's daughter. I looked at the map, and I knew where it was. I was looking at Mundoo and between Hindmarsh Island, and I could see the inside of a woman, like it represented the shape of the womb and the ovaries. On that map I saw Hindmarsh Island, and I went back to my Aunty Rosie. It was a shock to see it. I was at the school lunch for the end-of-school break-up party, and my baby was being passed around and admired, but I wanted to ask Aunty Rose about the map. It was from Port Augusta down, and it looked really . . . it took my breath away. When I went down to see Aunty Rosie, with her mail on Saturday (the mail had to be taken to Hollywood on a Saturday), I was with the baby and my husband. I had already heard about the story from her, and I said to her, "How did you fellows know?" She said, "You've got to believe them. No lies." It was of the Goolwa area. I think of Angas overlooking Ngarrindjeri lands, and wonder what he might have written had he known that land was body. I think of the lookouts of which Tindale writes, and wonder what he might have been told had he been a woman travelling in the company of senior women. I think of the women who rowed through these waters, the midwives on their way to deliver babies, and the expert fisherwomen. They knew the shape of the land. They told stories as they travelled. Unfortunately few researchers pondered how women might understand the features of the landscape that are a result of female agency and that represent women's bodies.

Doreen Kartinyeri continues: When she was about eight years old, Aunty Rosie was playing at Raukkan and fell over. One of the big girls fell on her and dislocated her hip. She was in pain for a few days and then they took her down to Adelaide hospital. This was in the early 1900s and they didn't know enough to treat her, so she grew up and spent the rest of her life on crutches. I remember her using the crutch when she was writing things in the sand for me at Point Pearce. She would draw it, with her stick, then rub it out with her crutch. Much later, when she was at Hollywood on the beach, she had a fall and they took her to Adelaide again and tried to find out why she had been a cripple all these years. The doctor said it was only a dislocated hip and if they'd found out earlier she wouldn't have been a cripple, but it was too late by then.

Drawing genealogies in the sand is an instructional style I know from central Australia, but the way in which younger people are told over and over, that they will "know" when the time comes, is not. It is not an empty gesture. I have heard older women say, That's what she meant. The meaning becomes apparent as one learns how to read the signs and strengthens one's *miwi*, but the experience is flagged as significant when it occurs. This is a story that Doreen knows is significant and she remembers her aunt saying, When Aunty Rosie walked down on the Coorong, the crutches would sink into the softer ground and she was always told to walk in the middle of the road. Keeping to the paths is something that children learn. There are many dangers if one strays: restricted, sacred areas, malignant forces that lurk ready to snatch a stray child. David Unaipon (1924–5) mentions the paths that had to be avoided while men of several clans were demonstrating their fishing prowess. Angas (1847: 67-8) mentions the many narrow native paths leading towards the river. I began looking at stories about paths after I heard this story from Doreen.

Aunty Rosie said not to dig into the ground, unless it was for good. This is an exception phrased in a similar way to that about eating whale (Taplin 1873: 63). With respect to staying on the paths, other children didn't need this instruction. They respected their elders. They would keep to the paths and not hurt the land with their light touch. But Rosie Kropinyeri could drive her sharp unyielding crutch into the soft soil of the Coorong. She could break the surface of the land, the soft body of the land, the *ruwi*, and the nerve ends of that body would feel the jab, a land that in certain place is identified as female. It was like a pain in the stomach when it hit the ground, Isobelle recalled of the day at Amelia Park. Doreen recalled as a young woman being prodded with the crutch when she sat in the wrong way; being taught kinship by the drawings made in the sand; and also being alerted to ways in which one should respect the land. Doreen Kartinyeri, now an elder, reflecting on the meaning of the story of the crutch digging into the ground, prodding her body, a story imprinted on her memory as indelibly as the crutch into the soft sand of the Coorong, knows this is a trespass of gender, a breach of respect for the land.

In Marj Tripp's family there are also stories from Aunty Rosie. In 1997 she told Steven Hemming (pers. comm. 11/8/1997): My son Jeffrey Kropinyeri was living in Mannum with Clyde and Beryl Kropinyeri in the late 1970s and 1980s. They often collected turtle eggs for sale and were planning a trip to Hindmarsh Island. Granny Rosie Kropinyeri was visiting and she told them they shouldn't do this. She said Hindmarsh Island was a sacred women's place, and she was particularly disturbed by the idea that they would be poking long pieces of wire into the ground to find eggs. She said they should not do this. Jeffrey has told this story on other occasions, including in the presence of Chris Kenny (1996) who, unfortunately does not include it in his book. It is a story, like others told of the island, which suggests that Rosie Kropinyeri was a custodian of certain women's knowledge for the place.

The living body on which pain registers is a gendered body. Parts of the landscape are the result of female agency, others that of male agency. Some places are for women, some for men. We know rather more about men's perspective on this gendered world than the women's. According to Meyer (1846), the Kaminjerar clan distinguish rocks and several large stones along the beach by sex and name. "One rock is an old man named Lime upon which women and children are not allowed to tread; but old people venture to do so from their long acquaintance with him. They point out his head, feet, hands and also his hut and fire." Roger Luebbers (1981: 68) working with maps annotated by Tindale between 1932 and the 1940s, states that Tindale wrote of an island in the Salt Creek area: "island sacred to people, go there to place rocks in trees". On another map, but of the same site, he had written: "island sacred to people, go there to place dead in trees". In a 1980 discussion with Luebbers (1996), referring to the same island as viewed from aerial photographs and maps set out before them on the desk, Tindale said: "Aboriginal elders were said to have visited the island to place sacred stones in trees and to sing male songs. Women were prohibited from viewing the island whenever ceremonies were taking place." Luebbers (*ibid.*) points out that Salt Creek, as the only known discharge point for fresh water in the Southern Coorong, was an area of enormous significance to Ngarrindjeri.[10] Not unlike the Murray Mouth area for the Northern Coorong, Salt Creek, for the Southern Coorong, this was where fresh and salt waters mingled; where the Coorong was flushed; where access and information was restricted. It also appears that both were important burial sites. On another notation on a Landseer Map, Tindale has an arrow pointing to a fence line near a waterhole north of the road, some kilometres north of Kingston: "Carved tree hereabouts on hill top (burned now), women do not see it." This was remembered by Mr W. Tapfield, a close relative of Tindale, who visited their farm regularly when travelling with Milerum in the southeast (Luebbers *ibid.*). It would appear that there were sites where men could restrict women's access. There were also names that were restricted: "Tanganekald place names tend to be of several strata of culture," write Tindale and Long (nd: 6) and include descriptive, functional, totemic-linked names and some which were kept "secret by the older men."

So, were there sites that were exclusive to women? I ask Sarah Milera: There's areas where women just sat, because they were tenders of this land while the men were out at their law business, and they were doing law, so I'd be happy if I couldn't talk about this area too long, because there's some things that's gone on here that I'm not happy with and it relates to all this area. Veronica Brodie: I knew there was a place up there but not exactly where. Aunty Nell told me about a women's place up there on the Coorong. Liz Tongerie: I have to get that land. That's why she [Lola Cameron Bonney] wrote that letter. Our people were born there and buried there. There's a special place there at "The Needles", for women. It's where I go when I'm not feeling well. I have to look after it and keep it safe. Are there places men don't go? I ask. The delivery room, I was told over and over. We do not follow that new law about men being in the delivery room. Even women who were extremely close to their husbands expressed real discomfort at the idea that men should be present while they were giving birth. This does not mean men ignore birth. When Tom and Ellen's daughter was in labour, Tom fielded the phone calls while Ellen rested. As Tom said, She'll be up tonight.

The degree of exclusion of the opposite sex depends on the nature of the activity being conducted at a site. Some things should not be seen. Others should not be heard. The constant theme running through the stories of gendered places is the respect each has for the places of the other. Neville Gollan, standing at Parnka Point, explains about two different sites: If you look down there, directly south, that black patch down there, it's an island. That was an island of women's business. I know that by word of mouth from the old people. I can't elaborate on more on that, but just to say that was a women's island. And, directly across that hill, there was another little place that was men's place, for their business to attend to. And I can't elaborate on that no more because that's sacred stuff to us. We knew that at all times it was women's business. It wasn't anything to do with the men. And vice versa with the men's business, the women knew nothing. Neville Gollan learnt about these places when he was around nine. As a young man, when he travelled in the Goolwa area, he asked of Hindmarsh Island, What's that place over there? He was told, Not allowed to go there, it's a women's place. So we weren't allowed to go there. When we read this section of the manuscript, Neville asked how precise I wanted to be with the locations from Tindale's maps. There is more to be said of these places and it is said amongst the

274

men. There is no need to write it down when it is living knowledge. Why invite desecration?

"Are there any places here where women can't go?" I asked several women on my first visit to Raukkan. Yes, Bummers' Corner. It was just for men. We would get into trouble as kids if we went anywhere near and there were never any women there. I can't say any more. However, when I asked what was being transacted there, in a space that was clearly visible from the church and school, a place where women and children could and did come and go freely, I heard two different answers. There were those who said it was serious and we had to avoid it, and there were those who said the men were just gambling, playing draughts, and telling stories. It is not unusual for certain restricted activities to be conducted within view of others, but to remain restricted in terms of participation or knowledge of content—Keen (1994) gives examples of this for Yolngu. Nor is it unusual for white people to be told that it's just "gossip"; that way they don't probe any further.

"At men's places were you told things that were just for men?" I ask. Neville Gollan: Bummers' Corner was where the men met, normally towards sunset. Sometimes they would talk about the running of the place, general discussions and then the nitty-gritty part was to get back to men's business. Just to do with men. I can't say it. It would depend on what they had to talk about, and whether they would tell you anything there, but this was where I started, as I said, from nine years of age at Meningie at One Mile Camp and at Bummers' Corner, Point McLeay was where certain stuff would be handed to you. If they told you not to say nothing, you were not allowed to tell anything. Stories were told in there about certain things that I cannot divulge on camera [to Judge Mathews] or to anyone, that I carry with me now to my grave. I ask to be shown Bummers' Corner (see Chapter 2, p. 104). It's now a vacant lot but in the 1950s it was in an area where women and children were coming and going. Obviously they could see the men. "How did the exclusion work?" I ask Neville Gollan. Women and children were totally excluded from that and there was a Primary School within ten yards of them passing, but they were not allowed to go anywhere near those men and they never did. They would not go and interrupt those meetings. Doreen Kartinyeri: The women would walk past, but never sit down. The men were still sitting there in the

1950s, a little after that photograph was taken. It could have been taken by Leila Rankine or Dan Wilson. She had a little camera and then Dan Wilson got a developing kit and they'd develop their photos and then he got a tinting set. The exclusion was, in a sense, dramatised by the proximity; the possibility of breaching the boundary of the restricted area was ever present and the discipline of keeping away was learned through direct experience. One could see but not participate.

Bummers' Corner, *c.*1940s L–R: Ern Rigney, Big Bert Wilson, Theo Kartinyeri (at back), Percy Rigney (white hat shielding face), Jerry Varcoe, Lindsay Wilson, Manuel Wilson, young Frank Lovegrove
(Neville Gollan's personal collection)

Grace Sumner had been told by her grandmother, who lived near Goolwa, that she should keep away from Granite Island and Hindmarsh Island. She told me and another cousin who is passed away now. We were the oldest amongst the grandchildren and that is why I assume she told us two. She said these places were special, sacred, but she did not give any details. Another place she told me we shouldn't go was Chiton Rocks. My cousin and I sneaked away when we were about thirteen or fourteen. We went to Chiton Rocks where we weren't supposed to go. We walked from the shores across the rocks. The water was about up to our knees. We played around on the rocks, pulling things off and then when we was walking back, the tide just came in fast, and I was nearly drowned. My cousin helped me. More recently I have learned from Tom Trevorrow there is men's business at Chiton Rocks. Of course he didn't tell me any details. But that brought back my memory of the day I nearly drowned when I went to the place my grandmother told me I shouldn't have gone to. This grounding of beliefs in the assertions of one's elders means that, if we are to assess the merits of certain beliefs, then we need to examine the basis of the authority, as much as the content of the belief.

Doreen Kartinyeri, speaking of her childhood, notes that when her father took her camping at Mark's Point on the Coorong, her grandfather would warn the older boys not to go to different places. Of course I never questioned my grandfather then. When he said it like that, we just did what he said. Now I've been wondering if they were sacred places from the old days that he didn't want us to go near, but I didn't know why. It was the boys who dug for water on the Coorong when they were camping there as kids. Frequently it is only later that the significance of the teaching is apparent.

It would seem that there were men's places and women's places, and appropriate behaviours associated with each. There is unevenness in the knowledge of the elders. It depends where you grew up; where you visited; who was around to ask; and how seriously your quest for knowledge was taken. There is symmetry in the landscape but not in the sources. Nonetheless there are clues. Angas' observations of women's use of space are instructive. "In the open forest country," Angas (1847: 87) writes, "the women frequently make little retreats of bark and decayed wood; building them amongst the roots of fallen trees, and in retired places, where they remain unobserved during the absence of the men." Women sometimes fled at the approach of his all-male party, "the sounds of their low jabbering voices becoming less distinct as they sought their hiding-places" (*ibid.*: 58). On one occasion the women swim to an island in the centre of the lagoon while their menfolk make signs of peace (*ibid.*: 68). On another, at Ross's Creek, on surprising a group of women in their camp amongst the she-oaks, his party amuse themselves "by examining their utensils and domestic arrangements" and leave a slice of "damper" in each of the baskets, which were of "beautiful workmanship" (*ibid.*: 149). Angas

277

obviously did not see this as a violation of the women's privacy, nor did he appreciate the breach of etiquette constituted by his opening and sampling of the sweet fresh water in the native wells on the shores of Lake Albert (*ibid.*: 63). What Angas did see was a gendered landscape.

Certain issues of access to knowledge did not arise when Ngarrindjeri controlled passage through their lands. Boundaries were clearly marked and one always asked. However, today, people travel in mixed groups: men and women, young and old, Ngarrindjeri and non-Ngarrindjeri. Still, there is a grace to the ways in which their law is maintained. When Tom and Ellen Trevorrow and their son Bruce, Matt and Margaret Rigney, my daughter and I were on a trip down the Coorong, we visited a site opposite Mundoo Island. Tom wished to explain something to Matt. He called Matt's name softly and motioned him down the beach a little. Ellen thought Tom had called her and walked to join the two men. Her son, who had heard and seen his father's directions, moved quickly and deferentially into her path. He said "Matt", not "Mum". It's men's talk. She immediately returned to where the rest of us stood. It was all over in a second and would not be an episode that would be recalled as an example of how knowledge is managed, though that was most certainly what was happening.

A Restricted Body: *Narambi*—Dangerous and Forbidden

> We were approached by a droll-looking fellow: a tall muscular native, perfectly naked, armed with a *wirri* and a spear, and having his beard, whiskers, and other parts of his body most carefully plucked out. From crown to head he was copiously plastered with red ochre and grease, which dripped from his long matted ringlets; and his hair was ornamented with kangaroo teeth, fastened into it with clay, which hung down over his forehead. [Angas 1847: 58]

Angas had encountered a man who was *narambi*, dangerous, forbidden, sacred.[11] His body, aglow with a mixture of fat and red ochre evokes *Waiyungari*, Mars, the red planet, made from the red excrement of his mother. In his human form, *Waiyungari* was responsible for spring, with its regeneration of life and fertility. As a red-man, he is the quintessential *narambi* youth, but, when he

278

elopes with the wives of his older brother, *Nepelli*, he breaks the taboo on contact with women while in this sacred state. The water exuding from stretched drying skin in the *Waiyungari* story becomes the lagoons which impede the progress of the fleeing lovers. Angas learns that this fellow had just been through the ceremonies which "consist of initiatory rites into the state of manhood" of his "tribe" (*ibid.*). In his hands the initiate holds a green eucalyptus, "being symbolic of his situation according to the 'rainmakers' or wise old men". Angas does not explore the symbolism of the fertility and renewal fused in the fresh new green growth of spring and the activities of red *Waiyungari*/Mars. For this wealth of detail, we need to turn the Berndts' (1993: 75, 112-13, 223-40) recordings of Albert Karloan. While earlier accounts pay little attention to symbolic meanings, they do emphasise the strict nature of the taboos and their relationship to learning in Ngarrindjeri society. Meyer's description captures key elements of male initiation, ones that Taplin sought to eradicate, and the gendered significance which the Berndts sought to minimise.

Meyer (1846), on the basis of direct observation, fleshes out male initiation. Once weaned, around the age of five or six, boys begin to accompany their fathers, who teach them of hunting and the country; between ages ten and twelve they may be scarred on the upper body; by age fourteen or fifteen the boys begin to join the men in inter-tribal wars; and by eighteen or nineteen are ready to join the ranks of men, to become *rambe* (*narambi*). Older men have prepared the grease and ochre, nominated the boys to be initiated and the timing of their "capture", which both Taplin (1873: 41) and Walker (1934: 193) say was kept secret. While the boys are still in the general camp, and while the women are singing, the old men seize the boys and carry them off. Henceforth they may not speak to women, and certain foods become taboo to women, others to the young men. Walker (*ibid.*: 206) explained that children and women were warned that if they ate taboo fish they would become old and grey in a few days.

During the two years following their initiation, the novices are isolated from the social life of the camp; they must pluck their body hair and remain red-ochred. Karloan, speaking of his own initiation, describes the wiping off of the red ochre as signalling the end of the *narambi* period, after which all their possessions are replaced and as new men, "*mokari kon*", they wipe clean their body "*ruwar*" (Berndt *et al.* 1993: 381-2). Only then may the men seek wives. Tindale (1930–52: 263), under the heading "Separation of the Sexes", documents just how serious this period was for the *narambi* youths. Mark Wilson told him of a time when some older men were informed that some youths had been talking to some girls at a place near Point McLeay. "When the young men returned to camp, they had clubs thrust into their hands by their fathers and father's brothers and were then attacked. One youth fought his father and gave him heavy punishment, whereupon the father 'cursed him'. Within three days the youth was dead" (*ibid.*). Similarly, Taplin (1873: 18) sets out the prohibitions on *narambi* youth "any violation is punished by the old men with death". Here, then, is the reason one does not challenge authority. It does not require a rationale external to the caution. The rules were to be followed and, as with Neville Gollan's story about the *Krowali*, the consequences of violation, albeit unwitting, are known and the stories are being passed on.

The structure of male initiation described by Meyer, Taplin and the Berndts will be familiar to anyone with knowledge of initiation practices in other parts of Australia, from the "surprise capture", through seclusion and its associated taboos, re-emergence and reintegration into the community. One interesting aspect of Ngarrindjeri notion of sacred states is that the same word, *narambi*, applies to women when they are secluded (Berndt *et al.* 1993: 153, 156). They too were dangerous and forbidden. Meyer (1846: 4) juxtaposes male initiation with the education of females, which in his view is "simple" and culminates in marriage. Of course, like Angas (1847: 58), from whom women ran and hid at the approach of his all-male party, Meyer is at a disadvantage in making direct observations of what women do in their secluded spaces. There was no need for the *narambi* man to run and hide. Angas, like Meyer, could make detailed observations. Not surprisingly, we have rather better accounts of male *narambi* states than for women. I will be returning to the rites of womanhood in Chapter 9; here I merely point out that, even though his access was restricted, Meyer

understood there were strict rules applying to the separation of the
sexes during male initiation, and also during birth and
menstruation (*ibid.*). These are echoed in Taplin (1879: 40-2),
Albert Karloan's account of his initiation in 1882 (Berndt *et al.*
1993: 364ff.) and Tindale's (1930–52: 263) entry on "Separation of
the Sexes". Each notes the physical separation at key moments and
the intricate web of food taboos. These variously apply to men and
women, to young and old, to initiated and uninitiated, and to
persons who are considered *narambi*.

The education of boys regarding what foods are to be avoided, by
whom and when, begins when they are still young (Meyer 1846).
They learn that the roes of fishes are forbidden to women, young
men and children: only old men may eat them. This boys learn
from their fathers and girls from their mothers. This learning occurs
on the country to which it relates, and food and place taboos are
clearly interwoven. Taplin (28/5/1859): "It is also thought that if
any of the natives eat mountain ducks they will become grey, or if
they step on a certain island in the river, or even spit on it, the same
result will follow." Taplin's journal entry for 13/11/1861
enumerates the foods forbidden to young men and boys. Young
men may not eat *Nakkare* (black duck), *Ngerake* (teal duck),[12]
Kinkindele (small tortoise), *Wheri* (big tortoise), *Ponde* (cod),
Pankelde (Murray goose), *Tyeri* (golden perch), *Punkeri* (widgeon),
Kalperi (shoveller duck), *Parge* (wallaby), *Tilmuri* (female musk
duck), *Pomeri* (cat fish), *Kupulli* (Blue Mountain parrot), *Rekalde*
(water rat), *Puldyokkuri* (water hen), *Talkinyeri* (native turkey),
prolge (native companion), *Wanye* (mountain duck), *Tarki* (lake
perch), *Korneok* (pink-eyed duck). Of this list boys were only
permitted to eat black duck, teal, cod, goose, water rat and water
hen. Neville Gollan was familiar with all the taboo species, but few
are part of the diet today. When I ask Tom Trevorrow, he
immediately mentions cat fish.

Generally, when I've asked about what foods were eaten, the
answers have concerned the fat content and need to eat a healthy diet.
The way in which western scientific knowledge echoes Ngarrindjeri
knowledge encoded in their stories is a matter of pride: fats were
rationed, fish was good for the brain, and so on. Milerum told

281

Tindale (1934–7: 146-7) the sea mullet or *poronti*, a large fish which is full of fat, is only to be eaten by old men and women. Young men were utterly prohibited from either eating or touching it. This is not some vague rule. Tindale is able to support it with Milerum's behaviour. He recalls that "once a great big incursion of the sea water brought these fish into the Coorong and only old men were allowed to have them. He as a young man did without" (Tindale 1934: 119). Tindale records that Mulloway, having swum right up the Coorong, would spawn in shallow water, in the holes in limestone rocks. "Young men were prohibited from catching these spawning fish; only old men were allowed to touch them" (*ibid.*: 119). In contrast, today they're caught before they can spawn by fishermen who string their nets across.

Narambi taboos also applied to store-bought guns, nets and lines for getting food for the initiates, all of which were to be kept away from women: even the smell of the cooking that is "brought secretly from the camp to where the novices are in seclusion" must be avoided by women (Berndt *et al.* 1993: 354-6). The food they eat is *narambi* and no female may accept any food from them, not even from her brothers. She is not even allowed to smell the meat cooking, for such will arouse desire in her (*ibid.*). Meyer (1846: 3) reports that the *narambi* status also applies to the fires on which the foods are cooked. Mission buildings also became *narambi*. Taplin (1879: 69) finds that the place where the flour for cooking for the initiates is stored is *narambi*, and that allowing girls to sleep in the kitchen provokes a vicious fight. Literate Ngarrindjeri have also recorded their views. Reuben Walker's (1934: 206) note on "*nar.um.bee*, sacred or forbidden", focuses exclusively on food and the consequences of violating the taboos which include premature ageing. In other words, there is ample evidence that the *narambi* state for men sets them apart from women in concrete and heavily circumscribed ways.

Relationships established during initiation, especially those concerning marriage, were also hedged in with strict rules. Several songs recorded by Tindale (1937: 116-20; 1941: 240) concern marriage rules and the behaviour of widows. Despite the stress on Tangani marriage regulations that occurred with the reduction of population after white occupation, when some men broke the rules and married anywhere, Tindale (nd, f) tells us, violators got killed. "The women were sent back. The old people used to tell us not to be seen talking (even two or three times) to women who were not of our *ronggi*" (i.e. stood in the relationship of potential spouse). There were also sex-specific rules when it came to the treatment of a surviving spouse (Berndt *et al.* 1993: 357). A widow would be fed because to do otherwise would be disrespectful of her deceased husband and might cause her to come into contact with other men before the period of mourning was over. Widowers, on the other hand, are expected to feed themselves. A woman seeking her own food constitutes a danger that is qualitatively different from that of a man.

Throughout Tindale's material there are references to places to which access is restricted on certain bases. In the "Tangane Data Folder" we read of Karingigal, a place where the dead were exposed over water, and as such forbidden; and of a place on the eastern shore of Lake Albert where, for fear of becoming ill, people may not spit or urinate. This place name, Tungurunganggal, was a place for totemic dances and songs (*tunguri*). Milerum (Tindale and Long nd: 1) knew of a Potaruwutj place where stone for axes was obtained which was "kept as secret by the Kulakulak clan people"; and of the Taldemadeorn ancestor who brought people to the McGraths Flat area, and who created the lagoons, springs and fresh water and swampy places where ducks feed. "He held certain places as sacred and not to be visited, for fear of driving the food animals away." One swamp near his home was where "people were forbidden to go" (*ibid.*: 2). "There were restricted areas to which only duck hunters were privileged to go, others giving them a wide berth." As Milerum expressed it, "ordinary people must keep away" (*ibid.*: 4). Ju:untung, at the south end of Loveday Bay and Creek, was "a magically charmed place to prevent trespass by Jaralde people where a leg bone taken from a magic marker is concealed" (Tindale 1934–7: 4). Duck "flyways" were so important as to be forbidden places to all except the men engaged in the netting of the birds (*ibid.*: 25). Taplin (5/12/1862) mentions an island in Lake Albert where, if one spits, one turns grey. David Unaipon (1924–5: ch. 5) says that the paths leading to the fishing place are also taboo. These restrictions have different bases—protecting food; a sacred ground; excluding other clans; excluding certain categories of persons, be they women, youths, the uninitiated; not getting ill—but all have to do with knowing the land and following the law of the ancestors.

The Berndts (1993: 122ff.) bring some order into this complex of restricted relationships. They identify three major categories of *narambi* taboos. The first concerns the eating of *ngatji*; the second is a general taboo on particular foods designated *narambi*; the third includes four kinds of taboo generally linked to mythology, which, if broken, brought supernatural punishment. In this category we find those taboos that relate to the whole group; specifically to women; to boys only; and to the initiation of youths. As far as initiates were concerned, everything associated with the novices was taboo, and the boys themselves were *narambi*. And, as always, there are exceptions that serve to dramatise the taboo. Sex was prohibited to youth, but there was a period of sexual licence (Taplin 6/3/1861, 19/7/1861; Berndt *et al.* 1993: 180). One's *ngatji* was not to be eaten, except in certain cases. Milerum (Tindale and Long nd: 4) told Tindale that: "The men of the Potaruwutj tribe held ceremonies from which women were excluded." However, there were times when women were present during men's ceremonies. "As soon as a novice was red-ochred, he was *narambi* and until released from this ritual condition, he was taboo and forbidden to have any interaction with females (except one) and certain categories of males" (Berndt *et al.* 1993: 126). The exception was an old woman, but not even she was allowed to prepare his food. Milerum also noted the exceptions: "At the ceremonies which were *narambi* or secret, only a few old women were allowed to be present, others being excluded" (Tindale 1934–7: 223). Reuben Walker (1934: 193), writing as a mature man in the 1930s, is comfortable in recounting the prerogatives of age and gender: I think that it is one of the finest sights that a Person can see the old Men and Women starts the corroboree with a rush out of the darkness the Dancer alivance into the fire Light I Have seen as many as a Hundred and fiftey. In those days of Corroobooree go on till they would get their young men eccited. some of the young ladies would be let into the know they would Call out to the young men. Here Reuben Walker offers multiple clues regarding the dynamics of age, gender and ceremonial knowledge. It is the elders, men and women, who have the responsibility of opening the ceremony in a dramatic gesture. The emotions run high and, with the knowing co-operation of young women, the young men are brought to an emotional high pitch.

In the rich, bountiful and diverse lands of the Lower Murray, how could power be exercised over another? How could leaders compel their clansfolk to abide by the rules? If one wished to leave and establish a new homeland, it would be possible. If youth wanted to rebel what was to stop them? One way to create scarcity was to place restrictions on access to certain choice resources, to special places, to certain persons, to certain knowledge, and to certain ritual occasions. Thus we have food taboos on some of the choicest of foods. Women and youths were not to eat the tastiest of certain fish and game. Places were restricted so that only old people could visit certain places. Young men were controlled by not being allowed to comb or cut their hair after the age of ten. Through these taboos the elders could assert their authority. Always there were exceptions, which, rather than lessening the taboo, threw it into sharp relief. A consistent facet of Aboriginal ceremonies is the way in which restricted information, objects, songs and designs are brought into the open, only to be removed, or held just beyond the line of vision, or on the edge of hearing, rather like the men's conversations at Bummers' Corner. With reference to the Yolngu, Nancy Williams (1986: 45) notes that "at certain times during the performance of a ritual men may carry ritual objects in open procession, objects otherwise kept wrapped and hidden, and available only to men". In male initiation ceremonies I have attended in central Australia, one sits with one's kin and country group and, depending on one's relationship to the initiate, may see the boards in the flare of the fires, but the fact that the women with whom I was sitting had seen these sacred objects was never discussed out loud, nor would a woman claim to "know" about the boards. But, beware, exceptions were not the basis for special pleadings if one violated a taboo: the sanctions were well known and known to work. One area of social life where taboos continue to have a strong force in people's lives concerns death and burials.

Burials: Ensuring a Safe Place, Coming Home

I want to be buried where I can rest, said Jean Rankine. Raukkan is where I live and I want to be buried here. It's like the umbilical cord, bringing me home. George Trevorrow set out the law: Where the people must go, they must remain. They can't be dug up and moved elsewhere. We cannot tamper with the place of the dead, the tools of the dead, the things sacred that are left with the dead, or the dead themselves. It is a spiritual thing, a belief that you go through when you put someone away. There is a whole episode of events that lead up to putting somebody away, and then, when they're away, there's certain things, that are located in certain places, and there's things that are put with them. I suppose you could almost say that they become sacred, that they are very spiritual places. So you can't upset them, you know, because the spirits are the people which are moving, you know, and you can't upset that. They're put away specifically for that reason so they can have peace and go away, but if you interfere with them, you know, it brings something back on you. So that's why you can't interfere with them and we would like that other people don't interfere with them as well. That's our spiritual belief. With the middens, and the burials, you know, it's something we don't feel very good about. We don't like it when people interfere with them, because we know what effects it has on us as a people. George Trevorrow's quiet frustration and deep hurt are echoed in the stories of many Ngarrindjeri. Further, is not only Ngarrindjeri who will be harmed. Sarah Milera speaks of the "spiritual illness" that will befall all those who disturb burial places, whether intentionally or unintentionally. Leila Rankine (c.1980) wrote in "Ration Day" of years ago

> When the land was safe
> And free, burial grounds are
> Now bulldozed and sacred sites are being seized.

Tom Trevorrow told Jane Mathews: I just want to share with you, while we're here, near Aunty Leila's place, one of the stories that has been passed down to me by one of my elders who is Eddie Wilson. Eddie Wilson is still with us today and he still tells me the story that when they came from Raukkan and they were all camping, out the back here, where there is one of our big burial grounds. Now, the old fellows always told them when they go over to the beach to get cockles, always go

286

around the burial ground and never go near it and don't touch anything that's in it. Now, what happened, one time when they was young, they went over to the beach and as they were coming back one of the young fellows went near the burial ground and removed an item from it and brought it home to the camp. That night, everything felt strange in the camp. They could hear strange noises. They knew something was wrong. The old fellows looked at the young fellows and said to them, "Which one of you went near that burial ground?" And they looked at all of them and they picked out the one who was guilty and they said: "What did you take from that burial ground?" He showed them that he took a stone from there. Well, they winged him under the ear hole and they said: "You take that stone right back to where you got it from and you put it back in the exact spot." He took it back and when he came back everything was back to normal again. The Ngarrindjeri instinct was right again, what we call *miwi*, everything was settled again. That's a story that is still getting told to us today of why we should not touch our burial grounds, why we should not go near our old people. When they're put there to rest, that's where they stay. That story is still being told to us today and we still feel very strongly about that.

George Trevorrow adds: I could tell a story myself where a young girl brought some stuff back from a burial one night, and the camp went wild, similar to the story that Tom was saying, and the winds howled and everybody was crazy, and the old fellas looked at the young ones. There was a young girl there who had picked up what she thought was a pretty stone and it was a tooth, and she got flogged right back to the burial mound that night, in the middle of the night, in storms, to put it back in the ground again, because the spirits were very unhappy. Upon putting it back in the ground again, everything went quiet. The camp went back to normal.

Sarah Milera spoke of finding a spear in the reeds. I put it in Signal Point because women are not allowed to have spears. She spoke of her son's anguish on finding a stone axe which, in accordance with her law, had to be reburied. Things from another time are things that shouldn't be touched, she stressed. Liz Tongerie recalls a time when she was with her friends, just "mucking about in the sandhills", when they came across a burial ground. We picked up this skull and some bones and we ran. We were so excited. We ran all the way home and by the time we got there they made us run them all the way back, and we were really petrified because we had to take them back, and bury them in the exact spot where we got them from. And I was always frightened about touching things because you don't know whether the spirits would enter you, so from that day onwards, I was petrified that now someone had entered my body, but I didn't know if they did or not. In the 1940s Albert Karloan explained to the Berndts (1993: 510) that one had to bury the belongings of the dead or the spirit came back "tormented", looking for them. In his story, the leaders with "strong *miwi*" ask that the spirit not revisit them and frighten the children. Once the belongings are located and buried, Karloan said, "He doesn't return" (*ibid.*). This belief still informs Ngarrindjeri behaviour and the stories are being passed on to the grannies.

The fear of unwittingly disturbing burial grounds is compounded by the history (much of it unwritten) of massacre, poisonings and epidemics, and the dramatic ecological changes in Ngarrindjeri lands outlined above. The rising of the waters after the barrages were built has submerged a number of burials. Erosion has exposed others. There are, as Sarah Milera knows, places where Ngarrindjeri are buried that are not burial grounds. On Hindmarsh Island, Sarah Milera indicated two areas: I can feel the difference, she said. I don't say this one is a burial ground; I say people died there, because there's artefacts embedded in the ground. My son buried them really deep, because there's artefacts found through this area that are still there and they remain there. I asked the young fellows that are here to respect it and leave them because they don't belong to our times, so they've reburied stuff there and we need money to protect that area and put trees back there so the sand won't drift down and bring out skeletal remains there, because I'm still actually worried about that area because it isn't a burial ground. I know that for a fact.

Sarah then indicated a nearby site. Now, over there where those trees are, that is a burial ground; that's where trees are protecting it. There is a burial ground over there, that's a certainty. Many older people know that skeletal remains have been unearthed at various places. For example, Smith (1924: 178-9) mentions bones on the hummocks enwrapped in hair with a tinge of red ochre, some found in a sitting position, some lying. People know that various "scientific expeditions" have removed bones from burial sites, such as at Swanport in 1911 (see Stirling 1911: 9). They know there are remains in museums in Australia and in Europe. Val Power tells me the reason many are afraid of hospitals and insist on having the coffin open to the last is that coffins weighed down with rocks have been sent to communities. People know that non-Ngarrindjeri landowners are reluctant to notify the authorities should they find remains on their properties. They hear stories of bones being trucked off Hindmarsh Island,[13] of bones being used as skittles, and they want the bones to be at rest, so they too can rest. It is not that there was a total taboo on handling skeletal remains. The skulls of certain individuals were used as drinking vessels and this, I was told, was an honour and was done with the appropriate rituals.[14] But, for the most part, a Ngarrindjeri person who had pieces of bone was more likely intent on sorcery.

Where burial grounds have been under Ngarrindjeri control, there is a sense of peace. Val Powers is comfortable speaking about her family and her land at Marrunggung. Glenda Rigney, the great-granddaughter of Pinkie Mack, grew up hearing stories from Ellen Brown, her grandmother. Of Marrunggung, she says: That's where my grandmother and my mother and brother and all my aunts are buried and my heart is there with them and with the Raukkan people. Jean Rankine speaks with a calm pride about the site at Raukkan where her family is buried: We don't call this a cemetery. This is a burial ground. A cemetery is something where you've got to pay to be put away and our burial ground, it's free. And notice, all the graves, the heads are facing west. The reason for this is because our people's spirits will travel to those she-oaks up there. They travel backwards and forwards and their souls are connected to Kangaroo Island, all the spirits go that way. And that's their final resting place. But the reason for the burial grounds to be up here is so that they can see Raukkan. . . . And this is something that we are handing down to our children, that the spirits are there, spirits that are connected with Mundoo Island, Hindmarsh Island, Kangaroo Island. It's all a part of us. At the place of burial one may commune with the dead and the dead may speak with each other.

Hindmarsh Island is, in Maggie Jacobs' view, like a cemetery. Our ancestors are buried there. Veronica Brodie added: Aunty Maggie is

289

right and that is what you'd love to be able to say to your daughters and sons: "This is where your ancestors are buried." Doreen Kartinyeri knows that her great-great-grandmother Mulparini (née Sumner) is buried on Hindmarsh Island, but not the exact location. She was known as the "Black Heathen" because she was never Christianised. Edith Rigney: I feel so sad and I think about our old great-great-grandmother and our ancestors, you know, their bones being scattered about, dug up, and it just makes you feel sad, emotional. We don't know where they are, where they're lying, where their bones are. At times sand drifts have exposed bones in such numbers that the old people said they were the victims of smallpox.[15] Can you imagine what this little island is going to be like? Veronica Brodie asks. A desecration. We wouldn't desecrate cemeteries, as Aunty Maggie said. Our old people, would break our bones, our hands, if we desecrated a cemetery. So many old people are at rest here, so many babies. So many other things are buried here that it's mass desecration. Should the bridge get built and development take place, there will be nothing left of that Ngarrindjeri culture. They'll go from Hindmarsh Island, to Pelican Point, to the hummocks. There are burials there. Look at what has been done at the Murray Mouth. Maggie Jacobs: There will be no more cockles. It will dry out. Veronica Brodie: We're not going to have nothing to hand down to our younger ones except to tell them.

Ngarrindjeri recognise that they are not the only people whose burials grounds have been desecrated, and they feel the hurt when it happens to others. Jean Rankine: Up river there was a road that was made with skeletal remains. That affected us very, very deeply, and yet that's the Riverland people and we're the Ngarrindjeri people, but it still affected us. It affected our feelings. It affected our culture. Because we know that there are middens, so we know that there's burial sites there. You can dig anywhere and you'll dig up a bone. And it will affect us and just knowing that if that bridge gets built. I feel like nobody cares, you know, about my children, and my children's children, my grandchildren and so on. And then there's going to be more bridges, but who cares? Nobody cares.

Ngarrindjeri have protested against the traffic in bones and disrespectful attitudes towards burial grounds for generations. In the 1940s the Berndts (1993: 16) reported that "Albert Karloan and

Pinkie Mack were outspoken about those who excavated burial mounds and camp sites and sharply criticised Aborigines who helped Europeans in such activities, condemning them for desecrating their land." A particularly poignant plea for respect is contained in an eight-page postscript to "The Memories of Mrs. N. Taylor", a document dated 20 September 1983, and held in trust by her nephew Peter Mansfield Cameron at Trunceena (Thrunkinyung). In her clear longhand, "Aunty Ellen" records "the wishes of our grandfather, who could not now speak for himself". Alfred Cameron, her mother's father and Peter's mother's mother's father, was eighty-three years old when he died in 1949. Nancy Taylor terms him "a Chieftain in his own right", a man of "impeccable character, and unswerving loyalty. . . . 'The Needles' was part of Alfred Cameron's tribal seat of the Milmendjerie tribe", but his authority was not recognised by the local government at Meningie.

Aunty Ellen's letter addresses the matter of a by-law of the Meningie District Council that provided for a public road through her grandfather's land, and permitted not only the "passage of all and sundry through this tribal land, but also committed the direst and most unforgivable desecration of passing over a tribal burial ground". The last of Alfred and Jessie Cameron's thirteen children is buried there. Knowledge of the burial of their youngest, a daughter who only lived a few hours, was "imprinted indelibly into the memory of these parents for the rest of their lives. A body—or *being*—is a sacred thing. . . . Surely we, of later generations of this lineage, can do something in righting a very unnecessary injustice— that is a public road of no real consequence, to passing over the "Millarouan" ("The Needles") burial ground." You find that interesting? Peter Mansfield asks as I take notes from the letter. "Well, to me it says that burial grounds were sites of religious significance. It also says that there have been incidents which pre-date the bridge proposal where people have objected. Their protests fell of deaf ears because there was no Heritage legislation at that time to require the Meningie Council to protect sacred places. We know about Alfred Cameron's protest because Aunty Ellen could read and write. How many others have spoken and been ignored? How many have suffered in silence?"

Sarah Milera tells people who find bones to leave them *in situ*, but she believes many have been disturbed and not reported. George Trevorrow asked how the locals would feel if Ngarrindjeri brought bulldozers into their cemeteries and started to do earthworks. They said that I was stupid and I shouldn't talk silly. I said, "Well, you're saying the same thing to me." No, it's very important in our culture that the bodies remain where they've been placed. It has a real big effect on the Aboriginal people, on Ngarrindjeri people. It's hurtful. The non-Aboriginal people are hurting our people from way back whenever they were put in there, it's hurting us today. It is the same effect as if they were digging up someone we buried there yesterday. The same effect.

People would rather protect such places by keeping them private. Erecting signposts puts the matter into the hands of whitefellas and Ngarrindjeri lose control but, without mutual respect for burial places, which whites refuse to offer, there is no remedy other than to exclude. When the development of a caravan site at Meningie threatened a burial ground, it took some creative thinking and good humour to find a solution (Hemming 1987: 4; Luebbers 1996). Tom Trevorrow: At Meningie, where they were developing the new caravan park and they wanted to dig out our burial ground and we said, "No, do not do that please. Leave it there and revegetate it." They agreed to and when you go there and look now today, trees all grown up nice and it is a nice sheltered area. We, as Ngarrindjeri people, are happy because our old people are there. They are a part of the earth, they are a part of nature and they are happy with the sheltered caravan park. So in that situation both parties were very happy with what happened.

The same thing will go on today. If we come across one of our burial grounds in an area that has been uncovered and been exposed, we will be asking those people—say, if it is a farmer, we will be asking the farmer, can we revegetate that area and look after it, because that is our old people there and that is our belief that they must not be just left open like that. We must cover them, we must protect them and must look after them. So we would be doing that if we found any. We would be carrying out the same practices that our old people have done and that they have passed on to us and showed us. You go and you break the boughs off—the ones with the seeds just right—and you bring them back and you spread them out over top of the burial ground and you let them

292

revegetate themselves. From the place of the dead, new life springs forth. Burial grounds become where one can come to communicate with the dead amidst trees, symbols of the living, but also species intimately connected with *Ngurunderi*. The revegetation of these places creates sacred groves where Ngarrindjeri can also be in contact with the living, with other animal species who pass on messages, or act as signs for the living. Here one finds the peace of a sanctuary of "natural woods" (Frazer 1959: 72).

Burial grounds and mortuary rituals hold a central place in the Ngarrindjeri world, but why have burial grounds become the focus of much protest in Ngarrindjeri lands? At one level, it is a matter of legislation. Under the Heritage Act, these sites have been ones that could be documented and could be registered. George Trevorrow recalls that the "consultative process" left something to be desired, but that ultimately all parties were satisfied: When this first came about, back in the '80s, the local council here at Meningie wanted to bring the bulldozers in and bulldoze down this burial mound. It took a lot of negotiation and a lot of consulting with local council. There was elders brought in from Point McLeay and Murray Bridge to sit down with the local council and explain the importance of burial grounds and why we should leave them alone. Now, there's a lot of stories that evolved out of this place that was told to us by the elders. A lot of those people are nearly all gone now. As time went on, after we saved this place, more and more stories came out. Our people were so glad that it was able to protect this place. They wouldn't tell us the stories prior to because they were too important, but after the fact, and they knew they were saving this place, they started to tell us more about this particular spot, and it's very important to us culturally and we're able to tell our children or our people, at some stage in time, when we think that time is right.

You know, it's always been known to us that was one of our last in this part, and that is why we didn't say anything about it until they were going to put the bulldozers in and asked me to pick up the bones. It was very hard for a time here. The council said to me, "Well, George, if you're concerned about your burial, get a few of your boys together with some wheat bags and walk alongside the bulldozers and you can pick up your bones and relocate them elsewhere." You know, that's not good enough. When we put our bones in one spot, they must remain always in that spot. There's been too much damage and desecration around this area. The whole town would be just about situated over our main sites. This was the last existing site within the township area and after a long time of consulting with people, appropriate people, we managed to get them to see the importance of saving this place here. Not only for the benefit of Aboriginal people but for the benefit of the community as a whole. We believe that it is important. Sheila Goldsmith added: I was on the Point McLeay Council at the time and it was important to me that we find a solution. A lot of our places were being destroyed and I wanted to be able to see it and show it, not just as a white caravan park. Not much is said about our places.

George Trevorrow: Everybody refers it back to "Aboriginal" all the time and say: "Oh, it's important for the Aboriginal." You know, we're sick to death of that business. This is important for all of us as a people in this area and people in Australia. Our sites are meaningful. There's a lot of information around them and that can come out of them, but people are too hell-bent on destroying them because they believe there's not worth, there's nothing in them, and they always put the issue back on Aboriginal people. You know, there is time stop that. That's enough of that. These places affect all of us and we can learn from them and learn how to live together properly in this country, if we want to give them proper protection and learn from them things. Here we have one of our burial grounds fenced off. It's protected and as well the people can have enjoyment of their caravan park on the shores of the lake.

The other thing, is that once we did save it, they asked us did we want to put a monument or sign or something on it and we told them, no, we didn't, because if we put something on it we find that it is worse for us because people will get interested, people will go in and start destroying it anyway. So we leave it unmarked. It just looks like a lovely little park and a shelter for caravan park, so we leave it like that. It's probably only a few acres of land-wise but it's mounded up fairly extensively and there are quite a number of bodies in there. It is an important big burial ground, that's why it is mounded over as such, you know, and the whole area around it is very important. In actual fact, they took a few out to study at the museum at one stage but we filled in the gap at the top, put them back and covered it all up again. Because they're the people— that's our belief.

294

There are other areas around the countryside, through Ngarrindjeri lands, where you hope that the thing will never ever come about. You leave it to the last moment in that hope because you see a lot of things that can come up over the years. They come up with a big splash and you're worried, but a lot of them disappear too, they don't happen. I don't want to give examples because some of those sites have never been touched because of developments and things not happening through other reasons, and I think it is up to the Ngarrindjeri people to leave them be, and leave them be unknown until such time when they're under threat. It is a community decision to tell about a location of a site and I haven't got permission to talk from the community in relation to other sites, only these, in relating to helping this here. I've heard others tell stories of successful negotiations. Jean Rankine tells of how Dr Neale Draper, archaeologist for the Department of State Aboriginal Affairs, helped negotiate the fencing of a burial ground near Poltalloch. Victor Wilson shows me "Sunnyside Rescue: A Report of the retrieval and reburial of Aboriginal remains discovered at Sunnyside Shack Subdivision, S.A." by Allen Hutchins, Archaeology Student, University of Adelaide, Underdale. We're not hostile to the practice of archaeology, Vic tells me. You can oppose things or submit but we prefer to negotiate. He emphasises that such negotiation would need to honour Ngarrindjeri beliefs, including relations to place, authority structures and restricted knowledges. Roger Luebbers (1996) describes the way in which he was given permission, albeit reluctantly, in 1986–7 to conduct an archaeological survey from Pelican Point to Poltalloch Bluff. Throughout, despite their obvious distress, Ngarrindjeri remained willing to co-operate. Luebbers reports that, in the fifteen years he has known Ngarrindjeri people, "protection of burial remains and sites of cultural significance has been a constant aspiration in all negotiations".

Where there has been damage to sites, people have sought to protect them in a number of ways, not all immediately obvious to the untrained eye. George Trevorrow at the Old Seven Mile: In the distance there you will see that vegetated area. That is one great big burial ground of old people. Now, this area was cleared through here in the early years and that area became wind-blown down there and with soil erosion all our old peoples remains started showing, so what the old people done is they went up in the bush here and they broke down boughs off the trees and they brought them back and they spread them all over that sand drift area and that was done in about 1930. Tom Trevorrow: Now you look at it today, you see the trees all growing there? They are all over our old people. They are there under the ground but we do not mind that because that is a part of us. We are nature. We are the trees and that is the method that old people done when our burial grounds were uncovered. There is several examples of that along the Coorong here where our old people revegetated the burial grounds when they were uncovered.

Those Ngarrindjeri, like the Trevorrows, Victor Wilson, Sarah Milera, Doreen Kartinyeri, Jean Rankine and Val Powers, who can read the land do not need signposts. As we were travelled down the Coorong in December 1996, Tom pointed out the ti-tree clusters on Mundoo Island, but left it at that. George had already explained about the significance of these trees. Ngarrindjeri people used to contain the body, in burial form, within the ti-tree branches sometimes, and the platform. So, the ti-tree used to be one of the main trees for burial. Some of them we refer to as like the burial circles, the ti-tree circles, and most of the circles that you see of ti-trees have been vegetated at some stage by the Ngarrindjeri people, and they are all important burial sites. They are here. They do exist. They've been recorded, and we have major concerns for the safety of those burials, as we do for the ones that exist all over Hindmarsh Island as well. You know what you're looking at if you know the country. During times of importance in the mortuary rituals, Mundoo Island was exclusive to men. George: It's been a place where a lot of ceremony has taken place for man in the past, and it is particularly a man's area.

Eileen McHughes learned from Michael Gollan about traditional burials and burial grounds: Yes, my grandfather told me about Mundoo Island. He said that was where they used to prepare people for burial. Now, I know they "smoked" them. However, I didn't know the process, because Grandfather Mike told me that they didn't bury the people in the ground. They used to put them up on platforms, and he said once when they were going home from Raukkan, they could hear a baby crying and they'd always hear it at a certain spot. When they went there in the daytime, they found apparently the body had fallen out of the tree, so they put it back up in the tree and they never heard the sounds any more.

Men carried the major responsibility for the actual burials while the women were the primary mourners. There were times when women were excluded from certain places, and Mundoo Island is one such place. Sarah Milera: Mundoo Island, that was man's business and they left the women here and the women had their laws and—not that the women were left isolated and left alone. The men come back at times, but they had all business at Mundoo. It first started at the Murray Mouth, but they thought this is not going to work because the women were there, so they changed to Mundoo and that's where serious stuff is. Women are not supposed to go to Mundoo or even mention the name, and if we have our photo taken it's wrong, very wrong, you can get in trouble. You had to have watch places for the law purposes. You had to come in on an invitation, so they were very spiritual grounds. It held very powerful things and they're still evident and particularly strong in this area; very strong in this area because you never know what you find under the ground or the water. There's a lot been taken and bulldozed off here and those people don't have no respect for it.

The practice of performing burials at Murray Mouth is recorded in the ethnographic literature from Meyer onwards.[16] Moriarty (1879: 51) described rituals of mourning, including the "smoking", the keening, the wrapping, and the keeping of the decaying body in the wurley of the nearest relative. "This rite being both offensive and injurious to the public, I do not allow it to be performed in any settled part of this district. It is always done at the Murray mouth." There are frequent references in Taplin to the movement of people to and from the Murray Mouth and their intention of drying a body out of his sight. For example, on 22 July 1867 Taplin writes, "The blacks are on the move to the Murray Mouth. A daughter of old Charley's is dead and they mean to dry her." A day later he records: "A large number of blacks went off to the Murray Mouth and Islands."

Just where the Murray Mouth may have been in 1867 we cannot know with any certainty, although it would appear that it was further east, almost opposite the Mundoo Channel, closer to where it was in 1981. Nor can we be sure exactly where the gatherings at

297

the Murray Mouth occurred. But we do know that the rituals required access to ti-trees. Reuben Walker (1934: 101) told Tindale that the best place to see burials would be on Lucerne Island. In the dense ti-tree thickets, here many bones should still be present. There is every possibility that many skeletons will be unearthed. There is the note from Tindale (1938–56: 261) regarding Matilda Long, mother of Clarence Long, who was buried on an island area covered with ti-tree at the bottom of Lake Albert. "It was there amongst the ti-trees that the aborigines smoked their dead. They named the place Kurandi because of the black ti-trees which were called Kura:di". We do know that these ti-trees grew in abundance on Mundoo Island (Berndt 1940a: 184) and also down Salt Creek way (Smith 1924: 193). Doreen Kartinyeri also pointed out a site on the northeast of Hindmarsh Island, now cleared, from where trees could have been cut and floated around to Mundoo. Our ancestors were buried on Kumarangk and our ancestors were smoked and buried on Mundoo Island. Taplin's policies regarding burials may have considerably disrupted Ngarrindjeri practice, but there are still relatively undisturbed, safe places, where people can conduct their mortuary rites.

Taplin actively campaigned against the practice of smoking bodies and tried various strategies, including withholding resources. "The blacks have been teasing me very much for the twine but I will not be moved. I always make their drying of dead bodies as inconvenient to them as possible. All sensible men of the tribe are against it" (18–19/7/1872). His views were well known and formed very early in his stay. In November 1859, only five months into his mission, his writes in his journal that the sight of a platform burial is a "disgusting spectacle" and that "surely the funeral rites of these people are the most revolting ever known". Complaining of the stench of decaying bodies in the wurlies, Taplin (9–10/6/1870) writes, "I wish this practice could be stopped". He tries to dissuade people from participating in these funerary rites while promoting the idea of Christian burials and succeeds with his converts. While devastated by the death of his friend Teenminnie (21/8/1869), "a truly excellent woman", Taplin is happy she is buried on the hillside at Raukkan. On the other hand, on 28/1/1871 he writes that "the old blacks mean to dry Pelican's body at Teringie" but notes with a certain satisfaction that the "young people ridicule the idea very much".

Burial practices were not, as Taplin imagined, a loathsome custom that could be eradicated. They were a part of *Ngurunderi's* way, part of his legacy. Berndt (1940a: 182) provides the story of the burial rites instigated by *Ngurunderi* for his son Matamai (see also Tindale 1934–7: 51). After waiting three days for his son to recover, *Ngurunderi* placed his son's body in a sitting position on a platform, under which he lit a fire, and smoke-dried the body. He then called the people together and for a certain period they mourned the death. Milerum told Tindale of the Ramindjeri who, looking across the Backstairs Passage from the high land of Cape Jervis, saw the low thick scrub of Kangaroo Island away to the southwest, and called the area Karta, after this vegetation, which they considered useless. It is to this land that the spirits of the dead, following the ancestral hero *Ngurunderi*, cross over. They travelled to the west, over the waters, on the symbolic rafts of their burial platforms, into the setting sun, as—John von Sturmer tells me—the spirits of the dead in Western Cape York Peninsula also do. The Ngarrindjeri were "believed to chatter and talk as they followed along the western cliffs and crossed over the water to their spirit land". Karloan's father, who died in 1894, was an expert in mortuary rites and the making of symbolic canoes for the journey to the land of the dead. Interestingly, he was buried Christian style although he had opposed Taplin all his life (Berndt 1994b: 537), a defeat which made a deep impression on his son Albert.

It is obvious that there was a struggle throughout Taplin's mission for the minds and souls of Ngarrindjeri. It does seem, though, that even those whom Taplin considered converts would at times simply disappear when it became necessary for them to participate in ceremonial practices that he was known to oppose. Thus James Ngunaitponi, a convert of the Rev. James Reid and one of Taplin's key informants, would disappear for long periods. There were times when Ngarrindjeri elders simply voted with their feet. To Taplin's disappointment, there were cases where an old person who had indicated that he or she wished to be buried Christian style was in fact dried according to Ngarrindjeri customs. No doubt some younger people were charmed by the possibilities of being supported in their rebellions against the authority of the elders. By following Taplin they found they could avoid initiation practices, traditional marriages, and the implications of the navel cord exchange. Taplin's push for Christian burial certainly eroded the power and authority of the elders, and there is a rich irony in Taplin's (1873: 103) complaint that the young men need discipline.

Taplin saw these burials as disrupting his mission and bringing ill-health to his people but, despite the best efforts of church and state, the custom of "drying" bodies survived and continued into the twentieth century (Luebbers 1996). This refusal to yield has required that Ngarrindjeri engage in certain deceptions. In Taplin's time much activity was beyond his reach. On 28/1/1870, he mentions that Annie Lawson has been taken to the lower lake on the pretence of meeting her father, but he believes it is so she can be dried not buried. We should not be surprised that there are no written records of such occurrences. I know from my own field work in central Australia in the 1970s that people found ways of eluding state authorities when it came to death, especially in remote areas, and that ceremonial life continued in settled urban areas of Alice Springs long after it had been declared "gone" by the experts (Strehlow 1971). Further, what was happening at Raukkan cannot be seen as the norm for Ngarrindjeri in the nineteenth century. As I have pointed out, there were other centres of population and much to-ing and fro-ing. By the 1870s, Ngarrindjeri mortuary practices could take a number of different forms, depending on where one lived, contact with missionaries and proximity to an agent of the state like Police Trooper Moriarty.

Taplin (20/11/1864) complains that Raukkan is being seen as a sickness place because people are coming there to die and thus the mortality figures for the mission are distorted. In his entry for 19–20/7/1867, Taplin notes that a lot of Murray blacks have come down with the body of a woman from Morrundee and "the foolish people have brought her body all down here to dry here. I am sorry for this as it unsettles our natives much." It also appears to be true that many of his converts died young (Taplin 22/10/1864), and no doubt this was seen as a victory for those who still believed in the old

300

way. Taplin (1873: 78) writes of Waukeri, who died of pulmonary consumption after the old men threatened to kill him because he had washed the *narambi* ochre off his body. Those who had put themselves outside the time-honoured system had been shown to be vulnerable. I think there was another force at work here. By burying one's old people at the mission, albeit Christian style, Ngarrindjeri, living under a repressive regime, could ensure that their old people were there, that they could talk to them still, and that Raukkan was indeed an ancient place as its name suggests: *rawu*, "ancient"; *kung*, "at". Being buried at Raukkan can be seen as an articulation of attachment to country. We do, of course, need to distinguish between the importance placed by Ngarrindjeri and by the Christian missionaries, on where the body was buried and where the spirit was thought to reside. For Taplin, the body was unimportant, indeed it was repugnant; to be disposed of as quickly as possible, it could be put in the ground. The focus was on ensuring the soul went to heaven, and that was divinely ordained. In the Christian schema, the land cannot be bodyscape. For the Ngarrindjeri, the proximity of the body is central to the maintenance of an orderly world which entails a complex set of separations. The fats from the smoking body drip down, the odours go up, the flesh is lost, the bones are kept. The spirit travels, the bones must remain. Indeed, Luebbers (1996) documents middens where there is evidence of multiple burials, and concludes that "camping resumed at the site and activities normalised following burial rites".

Jean Rankine: When my mother died—she had been living in Victoria—I brought her back here. Her husband understood, I wanted her back home at Raukkan. I didn't attend my mother's funeral. It was just too traumatic. A fortnight later, my two sons—they were living in Adelaide—and they came home for a weekend visit. Somehow it came up about Mum. . . . They are always talking about dreams. Seems that my mother had come in a dream to both of my sons and told them that everything was OK, and she pointed with her nose, she always did that, that she was OK, and she was with her two sons, my sons' two uncles, and my mother were standing there. When my mother died she had grey hair, and in the dream her hair was jet black, and I was happy because I knew where she was, and it's things like that keep me going. Reuben

Walker (1934: 197) wrote of burying "the only friend he ever had", his grandfather, in "his own country where I knew it was he longed to rest".

I have observed this phenomenon in other parts of Australia where reservations have been set aside for Aboriginal peoples and groups have been forced to share territory, and to live in daily interaction with peoples who would have resided at a distance. One way of legitimating one's presence is that over several generations children and grandchildren who are born on a mission, a reserve, a town, a station, become of that place, sometimes by being named after a feature of the place, sometimes by being initiated at the place, sometimes by being "found" as "spirits" (i.e. conceived) at the place, and finally the connection is confirmed by being buried at the place. After several generations, they begin to have rights in the place and to be known to others as having rights in the place. It helps if the site already had hosted inter-clan gatherings and if a number of the ancestral heroes had visited the general vicinity. This provides a number of ways in which people may trace legitimate links to a site. John von Sturmer (1987: 70-1) writes of the power of songs to bring the spirits into the camp, the need to send away the new spirits who are considered dangerous, and of the power of old, more benign spirits to control the environment. It is thus that land and body fuse.

With the passage of heritage and sacred sites legislation, Heritage Committees, like that for the Lower Murray, have sought to protect burial grounds. These are truly matters of life and death. More particularly, the two modes of protecting sites—under state law by notification, signposts, and fines for violation, and the Aboriginal method of keeping knowledge restricted—have been on a collision course. It was one that was averted at Meningie. By scattering the ashes of Aunty Leila, another accommodation between two legal systems was found. Where burial grounds are under the control of the appropriate Aboriginal custodians, such conflicts do not arise. Val Power at Marrunggung and Jean Rankine at Raukkan find peace when they visit their respective burial grounds. Too often the legislation to protect sites has let them down, and mistakes cannot be shrugged off as clerical errors or political expediency.

Changing Practice: Persistent Values

Meyer (1846), in his note on burials, stated that the mode of disposal of the body depended on the age and sex of the deceased. Children who died a natural death were carried by mother or grandmother. Angas (1847: 75) observed a mother wandering in search of roots, with her digging stick on hand, almost naked, her dark limbs "thin and poor", carrying a heavy load, the "loathsome and decaying corpse" of her dead ten-year-old son. She had carried it for three weeks. Similarly, Wyatt (1879: 165) repeats that women are so strongly attached to their relatives that they hesitate to part with a dead body. One report of one instance, repeated several times in various sources, becomes a cultural trait, widely known to be true. Hence, it is a "fact" that "women carried corpses". In actuality, we have one report of such a custom. More interesting is the way in which the importance of an individual had an impact on the mode of disposal of the body. For instance, Taplin (2/12/1861) wrote that Louisa's body was put on a platform like that of a man.

At a death both men and women observed speech taboos, and cut their hair (Taplin 15/11/1859; Berndt *et al.* 1993: 505). The wearing of plaited cords made from such hair was said "to give them quick sight", make their "eyes large" and "enable them to see spears thrown at them in battle, and thus be able to avoid them" (Taplin: 15/11/1861). However, for the most part men and women had specific ritual responsibilities during a burial and the period of mourning (Taplin 14/11/1859). Widows covered their bodies with a mixture of fat, mud and excreta, camped separately for six months, and wailed a high-pitched keening at dawn and dusk (Meyer 1843; Berndt *et al.* 1993: 273ff.). They were not supposed to remarry for a year, and then the brother of the deceased was the preferred spouse. Veronica Brodie knew about this period of mourning as one that showed respect for the dead. In the comments on burial practice we glimpse something of the life of women, their role as mourners for the dead, speech taboos, widow remarriage, the trouble that unattached women constituted for this society. We also see how similar the practices of Ngarrindjeri are to those of their neighbours, and indeed to those of other Aboriginal groups across the continent. Of the neighbouring Boandik, Mrs Smith (1880: 9) stated: "After burial the women keep on lamenting and mourning for the departed, chanting all his or her good deeds, and burn their hair and scratch their faces with their fingernails." Remarriage to the brother of the deceased spouse is also reported by Brough Smyth (1878).

More than a century later, how relevant are these details regarding burial practices and beliefs in sorcery? There are no longer platform burials at the Murray Mouth and mothers do not carry their dead children around for months, but places where children are buried are revered as stories of "The Needles" and Signal Point attest. Funerals are where people gather and where disputes are resolved. In that sense they are like the large multi-purpose ceremonial gatherings of several generations ago. It continues to be important to be buried at one's place and for many that is Raukkan, or Marrunggung, or, as Doreen disclosed, at Point Pearce where her children are. The need to have the old people nearby persists. And, for this place to be a safe place, it needs to be somewhere that is under Aboriginal control.

What sense then are we to make of cremations? Isobelle Norvill said she had never heard of that practice at Point Pearce and was horrified by the idea. Doreen said she could not remember any cremation either. I have found no hint of it, except for stillborn babies, in the ethnographic literature. Doreen Kartinyeri appreciates the horror of cremations: I asked Aunty Rosie about cremations and she said when they smoked the dead, they don't burn them to ash. They don't finish up as ashes where you could just put them in a bottle or an urn, or something. But with the smoking of the dead, they do go back into the land, to the ground. Where if it's a cremation the whitefellas, they would have been finishing up on somebody's shelf I suppose. When Leila Rankine, one of the most revered Ngarrindjeri elders, was cremated, she was not put on a shelf. The only way she could be "buried" on the Coorong was to have her ashes scattered. Today she is spoken of and addressed as being at that place. That site was chosen for several reasons. It was a favourite Wilson lookout, one from where Leila now has oversight of the spiritual breeding grounds. In scattering the ashes, George and Tom took care to make Leila's place far enough back from the water's edge that any erosion would not disturb her. By coming home to be buried, Leila Rankine made an immensely important statement about whose land it is and who should care for the place. Future generations are being taught how to read those facts. Being cremated was a necessary accommodation to achieve that goal.

George Trevorrow: On the day we buried Aunty Leila, we had about sixty Ngarrindjeri people in boats all come across here into the bay while we carried out that ceremony and while we put Aunty Leila to rest here. She said this place. She wanted to come to here because it's a special place. She was able to relay a lot from sitting on the point just behind us there and looking down over Hindmarsh Island and over Pelican Point there and you can see where *Ngurunderi* cut up the big Murray cod, the *pondi,* when it came down and created the River Murray, and then he was able to throw the pieces into the different waters to create the fishes that exist in our waters today. So it is a very important place which is linking all along to other places. She said this is where the meeting of the fresh and salt water began. So that's why we brought Aunty Leila here. That was her wish and we carried it out. Aunty Leila is here.

Isobelle Norvill: When Mumadie's husband died, he was the first dead person, I'd ever seen in my life and that's when I started to take notice of the traditions about the funerals. We were children, you know, we were to be seen and not heard—and they used to have the body in the front room, and then mourning period came and people would come to the house and us kids, we used to sneak in and have a look around, you know, to see grandfather lying in the bedroom like that. And then after about three days, and the old horse and cart would come with a box on it and they'd take him down to the burial ground over there.

All the time I worked for a government department—I was a public servant for twenty years—and one of the hardest things that we had to battle was to get away for funerals. People often come up and they say, "What is your religion? What do you believe in?" We'd say we believe in life; we believe in death; we believe in the before; we believe in the hereafter. But when it comes to the reality of ringing up and saying, "Oh look my aunty's died and I won't be in today," you know, well, you're told, you're going to get docked. That happened all the time for the twenty years I was with the department and it is a real priority with Aboriginal people. We come from miles away and even when my mother died I held her funeral up for an extra day to allow people that were interstate who wanted to be there, because that's a token of respect after you've gone. So you've got to allow all the people that want to come. So I guess that's just another part of us, that we all very much hang on to and we will not let go.

Doreen Kartinyeri: I've had to do the same thing. Within a period of about six weeks, at Yalata, Point McLeay, and Adelaide and Point Pearce, I had four funerals, so I was—I thought well, I'll take two weeks off, without pay, to get to these funerals, because it's important that the people come back. We always look to come back with one another, even if it's a close relative, or a very close friend, or a very dear friend, you still make that effort to come back, because you feel you need to be there with them, to pay your respects and you feel you need to be there with their family. We always feel terrible when we can't make it, but we'll do everything in our power to ring through a message on the phones, and someone will pass that message to the minister. I had to do this on several occasions in the last couple of years because I haven't been in the best of health and I haven't been able to attend many, so I usually send a fax through or ring up. Even the Superintendent would wait. It was only in summertime he insisted on burying in two or three days. Sheila Goldsmith is listening: When my mother died I was pregnant with one of my children and I said, even if I can't get there. I'll be there is spirit.

Doreen Kartinyeri: Deaths and funerals are very, very important to us. In fact, death is very much like saying good-bye to a person, because they're going home now. Today, well, usually if you die somewhere apart from where you're born, they will do everything they can to bring you back to your birthplace, because you need to go back home. My funeral arrangements is entirely different because my children are living at Point Pearce and I have requested that I get buried at Point Pearce when I do go. But under any other circumstances I would be taken back home.

Philip Clarke's (1994: 298-311) description and analysis of a Ngarrindjeri burial at Raukkan resonates with those of Doreen Kartinyeri and Isobelle Norvill. He details the importance of getting the word out, which is greatly facilitated by Aboriginal people working in the public service who have access to phones and vehicles, and the importance of attending the funeral. Although the service may appear to be organised along European lines, Clarke (*ibid.*: 302) argues that funerals are a moment when the "Aboriginal people of the Lower Murray present themselves as an ethnic population" and the participation of people from far-flung communities "reinforces local Aboriginal identity". During funerals people put aside their differences and "actively socialise as a community" (*ibid.*: 303). It is a time for catching up with family and "enforced good humour". Clarke (*ibid.*: 302) estimates that people will "attend in excess of a hundred funerals during their lifetime". After the burial people are alert to sightings of the spirits of the dead and take note of their behaviour, which Clarke (*ibid.*: 305) notes does not seem to be dampened by their Christian beliefs.

By keeping the dead close by, one could talk to the ancestors, but this relied upon the proper rituals having been observed. In a spiritual and physical sense the land contains the power of the ancestors. To disturb burial sites causes a rupture in the Ngarrindjeri world and it has consequences for the living. Doreen Kartinyeri: Even though we don't have gravestones, we do have burial sites and even though we don't have houses, we do have camp sites, and that's where our middens are. George Trevorrow: You know, when we're driving through it, when we're riding through it with our children and grandchildren, we're able to point out the places, the meaning of those places to them, where their grandmothers died, where they were born. Where their grandfather was born, where they died, and where their *ngatjis* are, where they're not. And it's just like a big book to us. This whole land. Now, over the years, people been taking—like tearing pages out of our book so there's bits and pieces getting lost. Sometimes it's like whole chapters torn out of that book and then that leaves us, you know, with a big blank. You know, if we take out the centre part of our country, you know we've taken out a whole guts of our book, we're tearing it right out. From that part it would be hard for teaching to carry on after that point.

So our country is a big book. Every mile is a page in our history. We keep taking them out, there's nothing left for us as a people. You know, it's a wonder that the Ngarrindjeri people have survived this long because of the damages that have been done to important things in our life, in our way, our culture, you know. It's a wonder we're here. It's a wonder we're talking to you today. But we know if there is continuous damage, especially to the most important site in our part of the country, there's not much hope for us as a people any more. You're taking too much away then. There won't be enough to go on with for our kids. A book to be read by those literate in the ways of the land, a body to be nurtured by those still attached to their *ruwe*, a world worth fighting for.

6

Signs and Sorcery:
Finding Meaning in a Changing World

Reading the Signs

My *ngatji* is *lauwari* from my mother and none of my brothers or sisters would eat *lauwari*. I'm not sure about my *ngatji* on the Rankine side, but I say the swan is mine because of this thing that happened. Well, my nieces, Margaret and her husband, Daryl Long, they had a birthday party for one of her little ones. He'd gone to bed and it was one a.m. and I said to Daryl, "You do the dishes and I'll vacuum." We go out for a smoko, and we were sitting in the cool. And he said, "Listen, listen to that noise." I couldn't recognise it. It sounded like *mingka*, but it wasn't. Then the black swan came, right under the verandah, and almost smacked both of us with its wing. Daryl said, "I'm going to bed." I said, "That's a sign." We could hear the swan crying from where he came, straight to the cemetery. You don't hear birds at one in the morning, and the way he swooped us, and he cried all along, from the corner, as he passed us, and as he went. Then I found out a few days later. They were trying to ring me in Adelaide, but I was in Raukkan. Young Tony had been shot in the head, and died.

Maggie Jacobs told this story to me in late 1996 and she had told it many times before. Annie Rankine (1969), Henry Rankine's mother, Aunty Fofon to the elders of today, told another story of the night David Unaipon died. That night in 1967 David had been taken ill and was in hospital. In the early hours of the morning his *ngatji*, his "pet bird", began to sing out. Unaipon used to talk with this bird, which Aunty Fofon calls "his tribal bird". Her daughter thought the bird was hungry, but Annie Rankine knew it was the "sign" because the "bird flapped his wings and looked straight toward Tailem Bend, and that was where Uncle David was in hospital. He died that morning."

One aspect of Ngarrindjeri stories that I find striking is the high level of interaction between the world of the spirits and that of the living. In introducing *ngatji*, a number of Ngarrindjeri spoke of their importance as messengers. She-oaks carry communication between native doctors; the Willie wagtail brings news; and the *mingka* bird foretells death. Key to understanding one's place within this portentous world is being able to read what people call the "signs". This is not a subject about which I have heard Ngarrindjeri wistfully reminisce. The stories of times gone are not regarded as being of a mythic past. They are true. They are fact. Signs, when read by those who know the stories, confirm the power of the past to shape the present and future. The level at which they might be read depends on the trust one is prepared to place in the power of one's *miwi* and one's knowledge of stories of people and place.

Across the Australian continent, Aboriginal peoples have stories and songs in which the behaviour of the busy, ubiquitous, black and white Willie wagtail is significant.[1] And its darting, flitting, tail swinging movements are certainly distinctive. In Ngarrindjeri country, some say *ritjaruki*, the Willie wagtail, always brings bad news (Clarke 1994: 138); some say you need to watch how it behaves (Unaipon 1990: 28), or note the colour of the beak before making such a determination. Berndt *et al.* (1993: 124, 253) associate capture of the bird with certain illnesses and sorcery. On the other hand, there was William Kropinyeri's song where he called his lover after his *ngatji*, the Willie wagtail (Chapter 3). Again, a number of interpretations are available in the literature and in contemporary story telling, but all agree one should pay attention to *ritjaruki*. When Sheila Goldsmith was engaged, the Willie wagtail would let her know when a letter was coming from her fiancé who was at Point Pearce but, she added somewhat wistfully, "I don't see them as often any more." Victor Wilson sings *"Ritjukur ringbalin, unNgarrindjeri ruwe"* of the Willie wagtail dancing on Ngarrindjeri country and tells me, "If it dances at the door, someone is coming." For Neville Gollan, the Willie wagtail is one of the "main blokes". If there's something wrong, he'll be there. It's the way he flies. He may peck on your window. That's not natural for a bird. Then you might go over to the window and try to shoo it away, but it'll go away and keep coming back and that's the *ngatji* relationship, that's the type of relationship.

The behaviour of birds, all manner of birds, is carefully noted. This humid December afternoon in 1996, Maggie Jacobs and I have been enjoying the cool of her living room while going through photographs and drinking tea. She is telling me about "signs". Last year, it was November 1995, Margaret Finlayson, Veronica Brodie and I went to Melbourne. We called in at the Grampians, and on our way we went into the art gallery restaurant there—it's shaped like a cockatoo— they call it "the land of cockatoos" there—and there were two cockies that flew over us. They told me when the cockie sees a person for the first time, they circle and bring others. Usually they fly on, but they came back to us. I felt strange, and I thought something was wrong. A bit further on, on the way home, we called in to feed the kangaroos, and Veronica and I started to have a chat, and I started to sing and I cried all the way to the main road. I said, "I'm telling you, my tears will follow." Then we were coming up West Terrace in Adelaide. It was about 1.30 to 2 o'clock in the morning, and I said, "Something bad has happened." They dropped me home. I heard something fall and then I saw a shadow. Then my niece from Riverland called me. "Aunty Maggie, are you all right? Is Hazel there?" "No," I said, "she is not." "Sure no one is there with you?" "Yes, I'm sure." I said, "Is your mother all right? Is Aunty Daisy all right?" Then she said, "Don't tell me I have to tell you that Jimmy passed away, Jimmy Jackson, my sister's son? I said you must be away." In the morning my other niece rang. I told her that I know when there is a death in my family. A sign tells me it's my family. When the cockies flew over it was 3 p.m. and that's when he died.

Christmas Day 1996, after a splendid lunch with the Wilson clan, and a tour of the Kalparin Farm, Neville Gollan and I relax in late afternoon sun outside his office. His grandchildren play with their new bikes. Do you have time to sit? he asks. "Of course I do." I am aware that Neville is a respected and knowledgeable man, fondly called "The Professor", but I have not had the opportunity to spend all that much time with him, though what time I have spent has always been pleasant. This is to be an unexpected and most appreciated Christmas present. We talk about genealogies, his boyhood on Rabbit Island, life in the fringe camps, and his work at

Kalparin. Then, saying, This is how strong my culture is to me, Neville introduces a story of the events of September 1992. It is one he has told others, including Judge Mathews. It was late one night, between ten and eleven o'clock at night and I was nearly asleep and I heard this bird flying from the east. I knew all the tunes of every bird in the bush, every whistle and call and every bird on the lake and the rivers. There are those that call at night and those by day. There's only certain birds fly at night, but I'd never heard this one before. It was whistling, coming towards me, and it came and sat on my window, just a small awkward window, up high, and it whistled. It stayed about ten to fifteen minutes. I thought, "I wonder at you, I don't know what you are." My son was away in Adelaide at the time and I thought, "Something's wrong." It was dark and I didn't want to go out and have a look, but I knew what it was. It was something coming to tell me something.

The next morning, the more I thought of it, I was wondering because my son was away in Adelaide. Another man, who was going with my daughter, asked me what the noise was about. The bird had gone to his window before it came to me, but I said, "I don't know. I haven't heard that bird before. We'll find out." Then, later that same night, the police came and I knew they were coming. They pulled up and asked where I was. Before he knocked, I had the door open. I knew. My son had got killed on the railway line, near Elizabeth. He was twenty-nine. I knew he wasn't coming back when he left, but I thought he was going to run away, not going to be killed. I said to that fellow, "See, that's what made the noise." So that bird was a message of that.

The *Mingka* Bird

The *mingka* bird, unlike the highly visible *ritjaruki*, is rarely seen and its call uniformly announces death. Every bird comes to my place. They know my care. I'm like a mother hen with the birds following me, says Sarah Milera. At a death it is a *mingka* bird that cries, but only privileged people can see a *mingka* bird. Doreen has also told me this. Then, while we're sitting around chatting at Clayton, Eileen McHughes agrees to tape her story of her encounters with the *mingka* bird. Her words still all chatter: Down at the One Mile at Meningie, I guess I was about eleven or twelve, I remember Aunty Marj Koolmatrie and Bill, Tingie and Nulla, Granny Rosie from Kingston way, Nola Johnson and Aunty

Thora Lampard [Tom's and George's mother] were all there. It was getting on towards evening and all us kids, we were playing outside, running through the bushes and scaring each other, when we heard this noise. We knew it was a bird, but we didn't know what kind of bird it was. The old people just gathered us up and popped us inside. They even covered the windows up. It was a *mingka* bird. The next day, we knew something had happened because they had begun crying, and it wasn't crying like we cry. It was wailing, and it went on all day and half the next day.

I reckon I'd seen it, although people dispute it. When we lived at the Three Mile at Tailem Bend, I also heard one up there. We were all out spotlighting in the horse and cart. I can't remember how old I was. I heard a baby crying and I thought it was a little baby. Previously I thought the *mingka* bird was a mopoke, but it's not. It's different. It's a grey bird. The one I saw was about the size of the Murray Magpie, like the ones we hear here at Clayton. It was when we'd moved up to Tailem Bend, and I was going for a swim at the river. I was about twelve. I walked past the trees going down and something caught my eye. I went back and parted the leaves and there was this little bird. The face looked almost human. It had actual, real eyelashes. People really think I'm weird by now [in telling the story]. Dad came looking for me. When we walked back up the cliff, I told Dad about the bird and showed him. I could almost touch it with my hand. He said that was a *mingka* bird. I know not many people have seen it, but I'm sure about what I saw. They told me when it cries like a baby, a baby dies. When it cries like a woman, a woman dies, and when it is a deeper sort of cry is when a man dies.

Isobelle Norvill: It was the same at Point Pearce. The *mingka* bird was there too, except we weren't told about the different cries. It was just when the *mingka* bird was crying, it was a death. We always had to be in the yard before the sun went down and everyone adhered to that rule. You'd hear someone at the end of the mission start singing out to come home now and then it set off the call from all the houses. I was a lagger. I liked to get the most out of every day. So I didn't always hit the curfew. I'd miss by just that much and consequently I got into a lot of trouble. I remember someone saying, "Now there it is over there, sitting on the post." But I was scared and took off. It was crying like a baby. **Eileen adds:** I remember actually catching a mopoke and bringing it home, but it was different. I didn't scare easily, but I was frightened that day.

313

Eileen's account of the *mingka* is remarkable in several ways. She not only saw the bird and had it identified as a *mingka* by her father, but it was sighted during the daytime. In most stories, the *mingka* bird makes its appearance at night. Tom Trevorrow: One night when we was here, at the Three Mile camp, and we was sitting down, and just over the road in the tea-trees, over the other side, the *mingka* bird was there. I remember Dad said to me and George, "Shoosh, you listen." We listened to it, to the horrible noises that it was making. So he said, "Come outside here with me boys," and he took us just over on the point just there and he said, "You stand here now and you listen." We were listening to the noise and it was crying and it was screaming. It was moaning, crying like a child, hungry. It was like a woman being strangled. It was making all these strange noises and that is when he said to us, "You know that bird," he said, "That is the *mingka* bird," and he said that somebody is going to die. "He is telling us now." We come back and a day or so later and we heard about a family member who had passed away. I was about seven years old then, so that was my first experience of the *mingka* bird. I was introduced to it by my father and that just happened over the road here. George Trevorrow smiles as I read this: We didn't finish our homework that night.

The *mingka*, as Isobelle noted, may be heard outside Ngarrindjeri country. Her brother, Victor Wilson, tells of such an experience: I heard the *mingka* at Yardi Station, up north, out from Iron Knob, off the Ceduna—Port Augusta Highway. We were fencing, sitting around the camp fire and we could hear him, crying like a baby. There was a big tree with a caravan under it and it was like he was in it. Rodney Raynor said, "*Mingka*". I said, "We're going to hear bad news." Our last night, we packed up and headed back into Iron Knob and his wife came out and said, "George Wilson was looking for you. His grandmother died in Tailem Bend". In all the stories of ways in which death is announced, there is a sense in which the death disappears as the event is possessed, claimed and made known in the accounts of the appearance of the sign. There is also a metaphorical clinging to the dead, just as there is a literal clinging to the dead in the woman who carried her dead child, and the extended mortuary rituals of platform burials.

The elusive *mingka* bird makes an appearance in most twentieth-century sources on the Ngarrindjeri. Tindale (1931–4: 86, 151, 163,

171, 228) variously records it as a "sinister being" who may assume the form of a totemic animal; as a large species of owl with ears, which lives in the hills and walks about at night; a story told to frighten children; as probably a boobook owl (previously known as mopoke); called *merambi* in Tangane; a man in eagle disguise; and a small man, three feet high with a black face and shining eyes seen in the dark. Lola Cameron Bonney (1990: 21) translates *mingka* as "Body changes to that of a [blank] but it retains the head of a man." Peter Mansfield remembers his mother Dot Walker, Lola's cousin (her mother's sister's daughter), also saying that it could change its shape. Berndt (1940b: 461) makes mention of the *mingka* in connection with the *mulyewongk* as haunting caves and dark places along the banks of the Murray, but does not attempt an identification any more specific than they "may have been owls". Clarke (1994: 135-7) also provides a number of accounts of the bird in which he identifies it as "essentially a night time spirit"; a cautionary tale for children; as having the power to rise phoenix-like from a single feather; as having the ability to shape change; as strongly associated with death; and as consistent with beliefs about omens and death in the southeast of Australia. He notes that there is a northern and a southern *mingka*. Maggie Jacobs says, He's the tiniest little bird, like a finch, and I've heard it is like a curlew. Sheila Goldsmith says, It's the frogmouth owl. At Raukkan, the *mingka* bird is heard calling from the trees near the burial grounds. In the 1980s Leila Rankine wrote of as a child hearing "the lonely curlew call" in her poem "Spirits".

It appears that there are many interpretations of, and experiences with, the *mingka* bird and they reach back across the generations. The *mingka* bird is a Ngarrindjeri traditional story which I have never heard anyone query. However, when I go back to the nineteenth-century sources, I can find no mention of the *mingka* bird by name. (Nor, for that matter, can I find a mention of *ritjaruki*.)[2] It may be that *mingka* was simply missed by those who passed through quickly. However, Taplin, who is quite forthcoming in recording data on the matter of beliefs about death, says nothing specifically of the *mingka*. Of course, people may have withheld the name and only told him of the general belief in a messenger of death. While the early sources may make no mention of a bird called *mingka*, the phenomenon of birds being ill omens is well documented. Early observers identified several birds *muldarpi* (*mooldtharp*, *muldaubie*)[3] which may be the Willie wagtail. Angas (1847: 96) mentions a "flycatcher, of a black colour" that performs "all manner of graceful manoeuvres in air" that is called "*mooldtharp* or devil". Penney's epic poem (Foster 1991: 52) mentions "foul friend", *Muldaubie*, as a screech owl: "Children of superstition ill omen cry./ He knows that death is nigh." David Unaipon (1990: 24) mentions only "the screeching of the night owl, which was a sign something was wrong".

One possible explanation concerning the absence in the nineteenth-century sources and presence in the twentieth-century ones is to be found in Tindale's (nd, l) Potaruwutj Vocabulary Cards, where he records *mingka* as a *muldarpi*, "the name really of the wedge-tailed eagle which is believed to take on the guise of men on the ground". His information is from Mrs G. F. Gaile, who states the *mingka* was an evil being which warned about death or trouble. Ron Bonney told Steven Hemming (pers. comm. 1997) that the bird was from the southeast, as did Doug Wilson. Could the word *mingka* have travelled from Potaruwutj country (i.e. to the east of the Tangani) into Ngarrindjeri country, where there was already a belief in birds as *muldarpi* which could foretell death? If the bird that had been the death bird in Ngarrindjeri country was the southern stone curlew, as Berndt (1940b: 458 n 17, 460) suggests, and if, as Clarke (1994: 135) states, this bird has not been heard by his informants since the 1950s, it may be that the *mingka* has filled the gap of a now extinct bird. It may be that, in time, the *mingka* will come to be associated with a particular species and that Eileen's account may be prophetic.

There are, however, some problems with this line of reasoning. The southern stone curlew is the bird whose cry is routinely described as wailing and mournful, and usually heard at night. The birds' camouflage is excellent and when they squat unmoving amongst shadows on the ground they are barely discernible. These characteristics fit the behaviour of the *mingka*. Also, Eileen McHughes' mention of eyelashes appears to be consistent with the *mingka* being the stone curlew. The bird has a particularly distinctive eye marking, with white bands above and below the brow, which a child may have taken to be eyelashes. The expressive eyes that stare out of the pictures I have seen of this bird remind me that Ngarrindjeri stories encode information about certain species —the pelican is a gregarious bird, the Willy wagtail likes human company—and then draw inferences from that behaviour. The solitary pelican of Maggie Jacobs' account of burial of her sister-in-law Leila is significant, as is the lone black swan at night. It means something. The striking, human-like eye of the stone curlew which brings messages of the dead to the living mediates between the human world and that of the dead. Here is the bird assuming human form at certain times. On the basis of all these factors, it would not be unreasonable to identify the *mingka* bird as the southern stone curlew.

But, in the 1970s the southern stone curlew, *Burhinus magnirostris*, was said to be extinct or disappearing fast from its former haunts, especially in settled areas.[4] It is not reported in the list of *Flora and Fauna of the Coorong National Park* (Kluske 1991: 121-3). Dr David Paton (pers. comm. 1996) of the Department of Zoology, University of Adelaide, on the basis of work in 1987, tells me it is believed that the bird has been wiped out by foxes. So, can the *mingka* be a bird which is now extinct, or are there still some stone curlews living in grassy woodlands, said to be their favourite habitat? I should add that this sort of forensic exercise regarding the basis of people's beliefs is one in which I would not normally engage. There is no question that there is a widespread belief in the *mingka* bird which has been handed down from generation to generation. This knowledge was imparted by the generation born in the early twentieth century and it is being taught as a Ngarrindjeri tradition to the next generation. Contemporary beliefs about the call of the *mingka* bird as heralding death are part of Ngarrindjeri culture. Had I not gone back to the nineteenth-century sources, the question of the provenance of the name would never have arisen. Why not leave it at that? I have pursued the matter as a way of illustrating how problematic it is to require that beliefs be consistent with a western scientific logic. Suppose that traditional beliefs in the *mingka* bird were the basis on which Ngarrindjeri were seeking protection of a sacred site. Would it be ruled a fabrication for want of a nineteenth-century written record?

George and Tom Trevorrow listen respectfully to my hypothesising about the identity of the bird and its Ngarrindjeri name. They have another explanation that is consistent with their experience of the sources on which I am relying. It is also consistent with what they say about disclosing sacred information. In 1988 George Trevorrow is on record as saying: "We'll always hold back some, that way we've got something, otherwise you drain it all out and it's all gone" (Department of Education 1990: 25). Thus, when there are gaps in the records they are not surprised. Further, they are inclined to read these silences as significant. The word *mingka*, they tell me, is not a word that is said lightly. To call it evokes the presence of the bird. I don't like talking about it, said George, and I've heard Sarah Milera express similar feelings. Just because Taplin did not record the word and Tindale has it as a Potaruwutj word, we cannot rule it out as a nineteenth-century Ngarrindjeri belief, or word. The silence in the sources may point to the danger of uttering the word; its currency in contemporary society may demonstrate an opening up of certain restricted knowledge.

The Return of the Whales

If the mysterious *mingka* bird and *ritjaruki*, the busy Willie wagtail, provide ways of reflecting on the nature of cultural continuity and discontinuity in the sources, stories and physical environment, stories of the return of the whales provide a powerful metaphor of cultural resurgence. Hunted to near extinction in the nineteenth century, the whale population has taken over a century to regenerate. Maggie Jacobs, at our first meeting, impressed upon me the importance of these huge mammals to Ngarrindjeri, and especially to women. Veronica Brodie told me when women's ceremonies began to fade, the whales began to leave. Janet Smith, Muriel Van Der Byl's father's sister always used to say, Don't worry my girl, they'll come back one day. You watch, they'll come back. That this prophecy of the return of the whales is now being realised is confirmation of the wisdom of the elders. And, says Veronica Brodie, It's time for that story to come out. We have to start telling it again because certain things are coming back.

Certain things have made their way back to us, I believe. I mean, I was up on the cliff at Port Elliot, just before Christmas, and the most beautifullest sight I ever saw in my eyes, and I was so excited. There were three beautiful whales out in the water and I couldn't believe it.

Maggie Jacobs tells of a spiritual encounter that, by involving the old people painted for ceremony, provides a channel of communication to the time when the whales were more plentiful. This is another way in which continuity is achieved. This story was told at the Murray Mouth, a place for which the whale is *ngatji* (Tindale 1937: 107). There was a woman in there, staying, and our fashion and custom and our beliefs is that the spirits is going to come out at some time or other, you know, even the Bible says, talks about spirits. Well, what happened here, just before Christmas, a lady was in there and there was no wind. And the curtains started to blow and when she looked at the window, there was all these black faces painted. Because that's part of the what's-his-name. The spirit is there. Every dot, every paint represents something on a blackfella. If he paints himself, he's not painting himself for nothing. Every dot, every stroke means something. And one voice was saying to the woman, talk to the spirits so that they will calm the waters so that the whales can come back in, so *kondoli* can come in.

Tom Trevorrow: We went down the Coorong with a group of schoolchildren, over the Forty-two Mile crossing and we were sitting on the beach talking to the children and sharing our culture and we looked out to the ocean and I saw a whale and a calf, diving in and out of the waves and heading down south. George: That was good. It was the first sighting since I was a little fella. The excitement at the return of the whales reminds me of the birth of the white buffalo calf called Miracle in Wisconsin, USA, and I tell the Trevorrow brothers about this rare event; it is understood as the fulfilment of the prophecy of White Buffalo Calf Woman, who brought the sacred pipe, the basis of Lakota religion, back to the people. Arvol Looking Horse (1994: 1), the nineteenth keeper of the sacred calf pipe, said that "a healing would soon begin" and along with it dreams and visions. The white calf holds the promise of renewal for Lakota and Cheyenne in particular and many others in a more general sense. When the buffaloes return to the Plains, all nations will be unified and live in peace. Early colonists slaughtered the sacred buffalo, just as the early whalers hunted *kondoli* to near extinction. Now the whales are returning and the sages of the society are finding meaning in the event. With the return comes forgiveness for the slaughter, the hope of redemption and new life. The voice of prophecy can inspire and confirm the wisdom of one's old ways and indicate new paths forward. The prophecy is one of a resurgence in traditional ways of regarding one's place in nature. The indigenous prophecy contrasts with the failed prophecy of progress based on technologies that control nature. Now, there is the sign, that the land will return, the whales will return, the buffaloes will return. When was the white calf born? asks George. I think it was the same time we saw the whale and its calf. "I'll look it up and fax you." The date was 20 August 1994.

And the whales are already come. They've had a whale come up, come in here and go right down to Salt Creek with a calf. And Tom and them, hunted the whale back, and this is where they used to come in, see, with high tide. And the blackfellas used to use the whales for transport and the whales talk, Maggie Jacobs said. Alerted to this belief, I paid attention to an item in the *Mail*, 19 August 1932, where Old "Sustie" Wilson (*c.*1830–1935) recalled Charlie Warner [Walker?], in the mid-nineteenth century, standing on a rock and calling the whales in or out. A beached whale was an occasion for feasting and one of the few times people could enter the territory of another without having to negotiate permission. It was also one of the few times one's *ngatji* would be eaten. Reuben Walker (1934: 186) says that people came from afar for "a feast of whale and a good smear of oil".

Kondoli was the original owner of fire, and there are various accounts, Ramindjeri and Yaraldi, of the theft of fire by scheming men who were later transformed into shark people.[5]

> *Kondoli*, a large, powerful man who lived in the east, possessed fire, which he guarded jealously. *Kuratje* and *Kanmari*, ancestors who later became fish, were sent to invite *Kondoli* to a feast so that they might acquire fire. However, when he hid his fire, *Rilbali*, the magpie lark man, threw a spear, and wounded *Kondoli* in the neck. *Kondoli* ran to the sea, dived in, and became a whale, which thenceforth blew water through the

wound. The steaming spout showed that there was fire (warm blood) inside. *Rilbali* placed his fire in a grass tree, where it remains today and may be brought out by rubbing. In another version, the shark gave the fire to the bird who, being unable to control it, set fire to the country, and today this country will burn readily. The wherewithal for making fire, iron pyrites (which makes sparks when struck with pieces of flint) was stolen by a man, *Ngarakkawi*, who to escape dived into the sea where he became a shark, whose sharp teeth are the flints.

Lindsay (1968: 18; Tindale and Long nd: 3) tells how Tindale learned of this Ngarrindjeri method of making fire. One day in the museum, Milerum picked up a piece of flint, struck it against his pocket knife and said, "My people made fire that way." Because this method was not recorded in the literature, Tindale initially thought he must have learned it from Europeans. However, Milerum persisted and explained that the flints were bartered from people to the south; the strikers came from a site in the Mount Lofty Ranges and when Tindale looked up the name of the site in his files, he found it meant "Place for Fire" (*ibid.*). Even Milerum, revered for his traditional knowledge had been doubted by Tindale. A place-name authenticated his knowledge. Unfortunately, there are many unrecorded place-names.

A number of women speak of the importance of the whale to women. No doubt the close kinship women expressed with the whale is a commentary on their recognition of a fellow warm-blooded mammal who bears live young, suckles them, and is extremely protective of them. When the whales are killed, when their young are slaughtered, human life is also imperilled. At another level, the locus of fire on land is in the grass trees, which are transformed rafts made by *Ngurunderi's* wives as they fled across Lake Albert. David Unaipon (1990: 20) states that the women were "bound" within the grass trees, to which I would add at the centre of the grass trees it is blood red, an evocation of the *narambi* state. Today women assert a link to *Kondoli*, the original owner of fire, and through the grass trees they are connected to the everyday source of fire. Imagine the spout of the whale, the steam rising from the fire, and how it replicates the shape of the grass tree. In pre-contact society, fire was life. It provided warmth during the chill winters, transformed the raw to the cooked, smoked the dead, was the symbol of unity in the ritual of "firestick marriage".[6] It was *Wururi*, a bad-tempered woman, who scattered the embers of fires. According to Penney (1842b) it was an old woman who stamped out the fires and thus brought forth the Murray River. So what do the women say about the connections?

Grace Sumner reports that her grandmother, whom she visited at her home at Port Elliot, knew a song about *kondoli*. This song was not recorded. The only women's songs we have are those of Pinkie Mack and they do not reach down to Encounter Bay where this song belongs. Perhaps Grace Sumner's grandmother sang the Ramindjeri song which tells of a mother and calf sporting in the white sand near the beach at Encounter Bay where they were in danger of being stranded. Some "evil minded" people hoped to be able to collect their oil for use in sorcery, but a man of the *kondoli* totem sings with "the wish" that the whale will go around the bay (Tindale 1931–4: 252-3). Was this a metaphor for Ngarrindjeri women raising children? What might Meyer, Tindale or the Berndts have learned about the whale had they asked women about the songs to protect and warn the mothers swimming with their calves? These questions remain just that: all the accounts are from male informants.

Signs from the Past and Present

Birds bring messages of death. Whales bring messages of life. In dreams, visions, and through contact with the spirits of the land, Ngarrindjeri weave a world of meaning, which is at once malignant and benign, filled with beauty and care but racked with anxieties, greed and malicious forces. In Lola Cameron Bonney's (1982) dream the old people appear as warriors of a previous era. While my grandfather was alive, I had a dream and all these tribal people were around. I could hear them talking in a low murmur and they were all standing around him and that must have been the spirit of all those warriors who died before. I was looking at all these people coming and they were just around his bed. But there was no one walking around the house and yet he was there and all around there were these naked, or semi-naked Aborigines from way back. It was about a month before he actually died, but I never really used to talk to people much about it, because they would say she's around the bend.

In Aunty Maggie's story, the old people who appeared wearing their ceremonial paint were from an earlier time. Their instructions created a link, a semblance of continuity with the past, when the whales were plentiful. Sometimes it is the recently dead who appear with a sign, usually for a bewildered, grieving close relative. Neville Gollan: My son used to live in the sleep-out part of the old home at Kalparin and I wanted to be there. One morning, not long after he died, I was awake early, six a.m. It was still dark and no-one was awake, so I went back to bed, and then I felt his weight come down on me. I could hear the breathing. I tried to move, but I couldn't. I tried to call out, but I couldn't. I was paralysed. I knew he had come back. I tried to throw off the weight. Then it lifted. There was no noise on the floor. I knew he had come back. It was not only me, but Jeffrey Upton also. Within a week, the same.

He told me too, confirms Victor Wilson as we read this section together. Neville Gollan's father gave him a sign, after which it was possible for his spirit to rest. Back in the early 1980s, with my mother, and my mother's younger brother, I wouldn't go into the house after Dad had died. My dad would clip me under the ear when he was alive. He'd say, "Listen and learn." [Neville demonstrates for me how he did this.] I was standing on the verandah with my back to the wall, so that nothing could come up behind me, and I got a clip. I took off. Next day I came back and I looked through the house. I looked around, but there were no loose floorboards. There was a vent on the wall, an air-hole, with mesh, and I pushed it away, and there were all his old dockets. After that, it went away. He clipped me to make me listen and learn. I was frightened to go into that house at night. I'd only go on the verandah. Once I found them, it all went away.

James Ngunaitpon told Taplin (6/1/1874) of his stepfather.

The old man had been in the reeds fishing and noosing ducks, when, as he came out, he seemed to hear some weapon thrown at him and whiz by his ear. He looked to see what it was, and immediately felt himself grasped by an invisible being, he supposed *Melape*. He grappled in turn and wrestled with his adversary and returned grapple for grapple. At first he seemed as nothing in the arms of his foe, but as he struggled on the invisible wrestler seemed to become less mighty as presently the old man saw the dim outline of a human figure struggling with him. As he did so, he felt the mysterious being burst away and he saw him no more.

(A slightly expanded version appears in Taplin 1873: 141-2.) The weight that immobilises and the ensuing struggle between the living and the paralysing force is a common theme in Ngarrindjeri stories of encounters with the recently dead.

To get to the old Needles homestead by car one drives along a sandy track. Four adult women and luggage in a compact car was probably not what Avis had in mind when I rented the vehicle, but it was a gorgeous summer afternoon, Genevieve was driving very slowly and I was taking notes. Veronica was talking about George Spender, her mother's grandfather, who was born at The Needles, and about her Aunts Vi, Lil, Pearl, and Nell (four of Alf Cameron's daughters). Nell was Veronica's special friend. The day she died I heard three knocks. I opened the door but there was nothing there. I thought, "I must go and see my brother," and he said, "There's a message from Meningie that Aunty Nell died." She always used to say to me, "Don't get asthma." [Veronica suffers greatly with her asthma and so did Nell.] Also, she'd say not to ask questions. The Needles is a place of which people would always ask, "How did you feel?" and follow with stories of visitations. Veronica: My mother came out here before she died, and was visited by the old ones. People talk about living close by to the dead so that they can talk to their relatives. Nonetheless, people say when they visit "The Needles"—near the burial ground which is located close by—that they get bad vibes.

Veronica Brodie at The Needles, 1996 (Diane Bell)

It is not only Ngarrindjeri people's spirits who roam, visit, and communicate. Several stories I heard involved outsiders. Taplin (1879: 135) denies this possibility but I heard a number of accounts of the power of Ngarrindjeri beliefs to encompass outsiders by their laws and thereby render them less fearful and foreign. Maggie Jacobs: Raukkan is a spooky old place, but the scariest story was, I was in Darwin. In 1942, when I was 21–22, they bombed Darwin and I was there with Nellie Sumner. We travelled around Australia, and we decided to go hitchhiking to Darwin. They were still picking up bodies when we got there. Nellie got married to a fellow from Jakarta, and went on a boat with them, and I stayed there until 1951 and the earth tremor, and then went to Cairns and back to Adelaide.

Well, in Darwin, Nellie and me, we used to play cards with this old Filipino–Portuguese fellow and he always had sick people in there, and he had his own medicine. One night, I was in an army hut, and that night we heard shuffling footsteps, like slippers. I said, "Come on, I know that's you." Grandpa Angeles we called him. He would come in looking for his daughter-in-law. I got up. I went to the door, but there was no one to be seen. It must have been him, his spirit. It happened two nights running. The third night I'd gone to see the women off after playing cards, and I saw this fellow, dressed all in white, and he walked through my house and next door. I saw the figure right over this street. It went between the next house and ours. When he got to the other side, he turned and looked at me. And he had no face or feet, but he had a hat on and he was all in white. "That's *muldarpi*," I said. Something was wrong.

We went to the hospital to see him that week. I remember the basketball was on, and we went to see him. He died the next day. In Filipino fashion, they lie them on the table, and then they all come up and smoke, drink tea and coffee and sing. We were sitting down at the window, and two little birds came in, and one sat on my shoulder. One of his daughters came and invited me to come over and sing. They used to gamble, and I used to too, but they asked me to put pennies on his eyes, and one on his forehead for luck. I said, "No, that's not my fashion." I didn't want to go in, but as soon as I saw the body, I knew that was the man who had walked through my house.

Sheila Goldsmith was ironing when we visited her at Raukkan. The view from her living room window across the lake is spectacular,

325

a wide-open vista of hazy blues. On this occasion I was asking her about signs. When my old dad passed away, we were living at Raukkan. The kids were playing inside. It was too cold to go outside, and they were frightened during the lightning. I covered the mirrors because they draw the lightning. I put aside the iron—it was a coal one—because it will attract the lightning. He was in hospital. When he passed away that day, a ball of lightning came through the kitchen window, and the kids screamed and when it came through, I knew he'd gone. That was a sign. I knew he'd passed away. I knew he was sick. He was away and I had no word, being the weekend no-one was around. I had thought he was OK. The Berndts (1993: 494) record that during storms, sorcery objects are hidden "because the storm smells the dead person's fat and red ochre with which they are smeared". People are reluctant to be out in storms and afraid of violent weather, with good reason. Tindale (1937: 110-11) says that storms were a good time for men to sneak about. *Ngurunderi*, it is said, had the power to still the storm (Tindale 1934–37: 93). Reading the signs, knowing the power of messengers and *muldarpi* is part and parcel of everyday Ngarrindjeri life and survival.

Powerful Presences

Glenys and Victor Wilson have a dining table that seems to expand to fit visitors, and the overflow is easily accommodated in their comfortable living room or on the shaded back porch. They are generous hosts: lots of hearty food and cups of tea that keep coming. We've had many happy and thoughtful exchanges around that table. But when Victor comes home and finds a group of women around the table, the focal point of the home, he does not linger, but slips quietly into another part of the house from where we can hear him strumming his guitar and softly singing. When he is called back, he sits on a low bench to the side of the table near the door. He is the visitor, a respectful man in the presence of female relatives.

On this occasion in December 1996, while Vicki Hartman, Judy Kropinyeri, Eunice Aston, Browning Gollan and I are waiting for Glenys Wilson to come home, we're talking about signs, about the Willie wagtail and the *mingka* bird: Vicki Hartman: I do remember my sister Eileen telling me about going to the bushes, and seeing that *mingka* bird had eyelashes. She was one of the main people who would tell us things. She'd round us up and yarn. It was mainly in the evening, and we'd be sitting in the bedroom, and she'd tell us stories. Mum and Dad would talk, too, but there'd be Aunty Pud, Uncle Mervin Carter there, too. We didn't always know what they were talking about, and I would never ask. We learned about the *ritjaruki* from the older people—Mum, Dad, and Eileen would say he was the messenger bird, and depending on how he was chattering, you could tell the message. When my sister died, two of them were talking away and banging into the screen. We knew someone must be dying. And then that night I heard that my sister Verna had died. Judy Kropinyeri continues: I moved into the house where she had died. I was lying there, just looking at the TV in the living room. I felt like there was someone there, and I tried to turn over, but I felt a presence. Vicki: She used to sleep in her bedroom, but the night she died she was in the living room, and I had her bed made up. Judy: I didn't know that. I must have been in her bed. Vicki: That's the only time I've ever experienced the "death smell", and she wasn't in the house, and I was getting everyone to scrub the bathroom, but I could still smell it, till she was buried. No one else could smell it. I've heard Aunty Pud talk about that before, and then it happened to me. It's not sweet, but it was different. Talking about these powerful presences is a serious matter and it is only older women who will name them and who may speak of the deadly sorcery practices. Even then, much is withheld.

Veronica Brodie: Some parts are confidential. It all depends how you tell it. I grew up, I guess you could say, in the world of knowing about *thumpamarldi*. My grandfather, Dan Wilson, was a *thumpamarldi*, like the *Kurdatja* man. He was out to get you, and lots of people have said to me, and in particular one of the Ngarrindjeri women, "Was your grandfather Killer Wilson?" And I said, "Yes, why? Why do you ask?" and I knew the answer, when I heard her ask me. She said because her grandfather told her that grandfather was a *thumpamarldi*. I said "Well, yes, he was," I said, "But why do you ask?" "Oh, he was after my grandmother and my grandfather, and they'd go out on walks and he'd tell them, 'Oh, look over there, look there's something over there, nothing there?' And if they turned their heads, well, bang, he'd hit them with a waddie; he'd do what he had to do and then leave. But they wouldn't look away, so he didn't have the chance to do what he wanted to."

327

I know from my father, I used to see little feather foot shoes,[7] outside my bedroom window, or outside the door, and I'd ask what they were. I was told, "Don't ask." I used to see *ngildjeri*, the bones, in a box, in a special box that he had. I'd see ochre in there, but I wouldn't touch; I'd just leave it alone and go away and play. And he used to be seen talking to other *thumpamarldis* up at Big Hill, so growing up with the knowledge of it used to scare me. I was frightened enough not to wander out at nights, or get tangled up in anything that involved *thumpamarldis*.

Eileen McHughes: Well, I always believed that the *muldarpi* was like a spirit creature, a ghost, that the parents would use to frighten the children so the children would behave, and the *thumpamarldi* is the one that would do the *millin*, and the *millin* is to bruise your body, or to get sung.[8] The bruise wouldn't show, but you could hear the person being caught, and the screaming. They'd look just fine and then they'd get sick and die. Veronica Brodie: My grandmother Glanville was telling us how Aunty Nan was caught by a fella from the North. She was *millined*, caught, like sung, by the *thumpamarldis* and they'd leave their victim and go away, and then, in time, she'd die a slow death. No doctors could understand what actually happened, how that sickness came to be. They had special skills and learnt the tricks of the trade and how to make the victim go on living a slow death.

Thumpamarldi will pull your tongue so you can't talk and they pull your ears, and that is part of the process of *millining*, and they fill your ears with sand. But they leave no trace where they've been, only the smell. When my aunt was caught, that was payback. It all depends what the situation is whether they leave a smell. Once we were down at Pelican Point and *thumpamarldi* must have been there. We could smell them. And Dad had to keep on washing down the tent. They put you to sleep and then they get you. They come from the west coast and from the north. They are not Ngarrindjeri. They come in for payback, or they come in if they're passing through. My grandfather Michael Gollan and my grandfather Roley Kropinyeri were telling me that Grandfather Mike said that when you got *millined*, just before you died, the person that *millined* you would come and see you and just before you died, you'd look up, you'd see that person and you'd lay back and you'd die. They'd have to do a payback, so someone would have to come and *millin* that person. Say it was Aunty Daisy here. Say if I *millined* her and Ellen knew about it, Ellen would have to come and *millin* one of my close relatives. Taplin (1873: 136) wrote of "acting upon the native principle if you cannot hurt your enemy, hurt his nearest relative."

Daisy Rankine: When the men or women done wrong to their tribe or their clan, they would be *millined* and put in their resting place sitting up, in their resting place [burial]. I know this is true, because my eldest uncle, he was *millined*, and that's where he was put to rest, sitting up in his resting place. That's all I can say. A range of infractions could provoke *millin*: especially breaking taboos, like the period of mourning for widows (Berndt *et al.* 1993: 391-2). All deaths were attributed to sorcery and thus one needed to know the signs of a sorcerer at work; how to take precautions; and when to seek remedies. The relatives did not rest until the culprit was found and the death avenged. Taplin (1873: 29) says that they "give themselves up to despair" and that women were particularly susceptible to sorcery. Tindale (1931–4: 163) mentions that the Ramindjeri have a special club with poisoned head used in the punishment of wayward women.

The key to understanding the importance that people place on relationships with each other, on certain places, and on the ramifications of careless speech, behaviour, or intent is the deeply ingrained fear of sorcery amongst Ngarrindjeri. The stories are vivid, chilling, and told authoritatively by people who were ensorcelled; who were brought back from an ensorcelled state; who have observed someone else in trouble; or who were sufficiently alert to pre-empt the ensorcelling, or distract the sorcerer. The knowledge being transmitted is first hand and concerns family members. While many of these accounts concern the older generation and will, I suspect, in time assume a mythic quality (especially the ones about being *millined*, of which I have heard a great number), many concern contemporary Ngarrindjeri and the accounts are accorded great explanatory value. Women know and talk about the necessary preventive measures: destroy food scraps, burn nail clippings and hair from a comb or brush, avoid eye contact with strangers, and don't wander about alone at night. Veronica Brodie, Eileen McHughes, Maggie Jacobs and Daisy Rankine have first-hand experience of the practice of *muldarpi* and *thumpamarldi*. These are topics they discuss with care. Although often dismissed as mere superstition, beliefs regarding sorcery continue to shape the Ngarrindjeri world, and, when one reaches back into the earlier sources, one finds that it was *Ngurunderi*'s teachings that provide the rationale. Milerum told Tindale: "*Ngurunderi* was the one who brought to us the doctor corroborees and sacred corroborees. At the ceremonies which were *narambi* or secret, only a few old women were allowed to be present, others being excluded (1934–7: 223). Ramsay Smith (1924: 267) considers the beliefs regarding care in disposing of body wastes and the bones of certain animals at some length, and writes: "If these things do not actually constitute religion, they are certainly the stuff that religion is made of, and the aboriginal's whole nature and actions must be restudied from this point of view."

Veronica Brodie: Grandfather Dan used to do a lot of this transcendental travelling.[9] He'd go into the wurley down by the lake, Lake Alexandrina. Down by the jetty there, they had a wurley, him and Grandmother Bessie. He'd tell her, "You sit outside my wurley; don't let nobody touch me for a couple of hours." They believed if you touched them while they was in this travelling, they could die. He'd say, "I'm going to see my people." Couple of hours later he'd come out and he'd tell her who he'd been to see, how they were, and so on. He'd come back into his body. He practised a lot of this sort of stuff and he said, "I learned it when I was a little boy on the Coorong and Kingston way." He was a man of many surprises and skills. Being brought up on the hummocks, he lived his life as a Coorong Ngarrindjeri man.

Tindale (1938–56: 73) relates a similar account of how a man, customarily placing himself in his own *ngatji*, can travel as a whirlwind.

A *mularpi* usually leaves the body flying on a *ngildi* or "flying spider web". When he returns he will break the *ngildi* so that no one may follow after him on it and do him harm. If a woman is watching over the body of a man whose *mularpi* is absent, she will know when he is about to return. She will see perhaps an owl on the branch of a tree nearby. Then the bird disappears over the hill and she will know that the spirit is returning and remark, "He will come soon." Then the man stirs; he breaks the *ngildi* and sitting up describes his journey and the events he witnessed."

In these accounts of out-of-body travel from Veronica Brodie and Milerum, we have good examples of how innovation may occur; of how practices from far away may be brought into the traditional repertoire; and a clear indication that women as well as men know how to read the signs.

Veronica Brodie: *Thumpamarldi* in my family, was a very frightening word and we knew that Dad was sort of mixed up in it a little bit, because often he'd take long walks by himself, up to the end of Big Hill. He'd lay around up there, or sit up there, and wait, and he'd be waiting and waiting, and one day my brother went up—he got worried—to look for him, and he growled at my brother. He said, "Don't ever follow me. What I do", he said, "is my business, man's business." So I mean, no one was allowed to follow. But we knew that he was sick and we thought he might have a heart attack or something, so my brother just, out of care, followed up there and got told off, got told to keep away.

Those sort of things, we knew they were there, but we respected his respect for those things that he was involved with. We wouldn't dare question any more and how deeply he was involved, we don't know, but we do know that it did happen in our family. And it frightened the lot of us. Some it didn't. Some tempted fate, and would go that one step further, you know, and sort of go into another tribe. Mainly it happened if you travelled north and carried on with one of the tribal women, well, one of their men would come down looking for you and follow you up, down to Raukkan, or Point Pearce, or wherever you lived. They tracked you down wherever.

It's not practised a lot these days, because I could say white man's law has come in now and it's taken a lot of our Ngarrindjeri law away from us. If our kids knew of it today, it'd be something they could look back on, and it would teach them discipline and respect, because for sure, one thing you never gave a *thumpamarldi* any cheek. You respected them the whole way. You know, you was too frightened to give them cheek, and discipline. If he told you to sit down, you sat down, and that was it, and you gave way to listening with a lot of common sense in your mind, and you thought, well, you know, I'm not going to upset him, because I don't want to be done in by him or hit by him, because we believe that, you know, one hit and they would kill you. This was how the old people used to bring us up to be, "*Thumpamarldi* get you tonight if you don't listen." Then we'd go to bed and we'd lie thinking that *thumpamarldi* going to come.

331

This fear continued. Veronica and her sister, Leila, were members of a group that Neville Gollan had taken to "The Needles". Veronica Brodie: It was a few years back. We went in the bus for the weekend from Adelaide about eight or nine years ago. We camped on the way to The Needles, at the camping spot, and we put up two tents, and we were sitting around yarning, and we heard footsteps going around the camp. Leila said, "Leave out cooked meat and food for it." So we did, and Leila and I got in the bus and we locked ourselves in. Next morning the food was all gone. They would have smelled our food cooking when they came by. They go looking, and it might have been the time of initiation, or they passed through looking for young men, and looking for a bit of food, and so we just left it there and they took it, they ate it all and went on their way. They didn't worry us.

Daisy Rankine: The meaning for *muldarpi* is with the sorcerer. They have their gear to point the bone at you, and amongst the gear that sorcerers work with, you know, is part of the hair, and the piece of bone, human bone, that's there and the bit of rag, or a pair of pants, and the human fat, off the dead [person], that's all mixed up and they put in for *ngathaguri*. My great-grandmother used to work with that, and her daughter and grandchildren wasn't allowed to go near her wurley. She had to sing out to her mother, and wait till her mother [Pinkie Mack] answered her, because she was doing her sorcery with her *maraldi* bones and those *maraldi* bones was handed down to her daughter.

In the desert regions of central Australia, the most feared individuals are the *kurdatja* men. These ritual avengers visit in the night, leave no footprints, and steal one's kidney fat, while leaving no traces of the incision. There is no cure. The victim sickens and dies. Transgressions that attract *kurdatja* visits are serious violations of the law: calling a prohibited name; looking at a prohibited object; visiting a restricted site. The identity of *kurdatja* is neither spoken, speculated about, nor revealed. Indeed, the *kurdatja* is not regarded as human. Mere mention of *kurdatja* evokes shudders of fear. This is not a matter for cross-examination. Similarly, for Ngarrindjeri, there are the *thumpamarldi*, who have the power to *millin*, ensorcel and bring havoc. There are *muldarpi* who roam after dark and sightings are taken extremely seriously. This is not about the memories of one's forebears, this is about now. Because,

Aunty Maggie said one night after telling a particularly chilling story, It is the living, not the dead that you have to watch out for.

Maggie Jacobs: *Muldarpi*'s a ghost. Yes, you can talk about it. There's *muldarpi* and then there's the *prupi*, that's the devil, see, and the *muldarpi* is a ghost, like now, you know. When Maggie Jacobs tells "ghost stories", the *muldarpi* at Graham's Castle is sure to be there. Legend has it that the ghost of Mrs Graham roams around at night. It was March 1996, and we were there preparing for the arrival of Judge Mathews and her party the next day. It was towards evening, we'd been inside, and the grannies had gone missing. The first thought was the swimming pool. Isobelle was in a panic, convinced that her granny had drowned, but we found them in the hall of the dormitory. They had built an elaborate cubby-house with the foam mattresses and were happily eating their way though a packet of sweet biscuits. The children were soundly ticked off and warned about the dangers of straying out of sight.

Maggie Jacobs: Well, last night, I don't know, I didn't hear a thing but Veronica did. Veronica heard a scream, see, and don't know whether that was Mrs Graham showing herself or what. But that's what I said to the kids this morning. She could have followed you, because, see, it was dark. We were always told if you don't do what you're told, you know, the *muldarpi* will be here, see. Like now, the kids last night, they were naughty, see, and then this morning I told them, but I didn't know that Veronica had heard this screaming at her window, see. I heard this sobbing and I walked up to Doreen Kartinyeri's room. She was awake. It wasn't her that made that noise. The scream was at my window and it frightened me more than the crying. It was crying. Whether it was just her [Mrs Graham] or not, I don't know, but this is what a *muldarpi* does. So I went into Veronica and I said to Veronica, "What did you hear?" and she said, "Aunty Maggie, there was a screaming at my window; somebody screamed and gave a yell at my window." Then I said this is the belief that we had when we was kids, you know. And of course I said to those kids, "Now you see what happens? When you were naughty," I said. "When you took those mattresses and you went and took those biscuits, now those biscuits would have belonged to somebody else who sits at the table." I said, "Now that's what you call stealing." See, we try to drum it into them, "That is stealing." You can't do that, because that's what I was taught when I was a kid. And I said, "Now through that," I said, "see, the *muldarpi* was here last night, at your window." Because we tell our kids, we tell them, you see. Veronica Brodie: I was lying there awake. Why should it come for me, I thought? I don't think it was the kids playing up. It only comes when there is a problem. Maybe she could sense there was trouble and it was the ghost of the castle, that old lady.

Over and over again, women told of the consequences of behaving improperly; of how one touched an item she shouldn't have and that's why she is the way she is; of how this one ate a such and such and that is why her family has suffered. One has to be constantly vigilant. Eileen McHughes: With your personal hygiene and things, we weren't allowed to do *karnjis* [urinate] outside unless you covered it up. We weren't allowed to leave our *tuwis* [hair] laying around. Any part of your body or clothing you weren't allowed to leave outside. You could easily get sung. And even today I believe that. Any of my fourteen grandchildren I'm teaching them. Any part of the person, nail clippings, body fluids and waste could be similarly used. Victor Wilson agrees he was taught the same thing: When we were kids on the Coorong we were always taught to cover up *karnji*, because someone could find it and *millin* you.

Taplin was delighted when the first young men at Raukkan agreed to have their hair cut, rather than allowing it to become matted and be torn out in tufts at initiation. Requiring that children have their hair cut before they could attend school was another strategy. Taplin waged war against the rituals that required hair string, but Raukkan residents continued to believe, and act on the belief, that hair could be used to ensorcel. Doreen Kartinyeri (1989: xiv) wrote that when her grandfather cut the children's hair, he'd say, "Come on boys; pick all your hair up off the ground and burn it in the fire," for fear that the hair would be used to "sing" them.[10] Maggie Jacobs: When you get a haircut, you know, I usually ask for my hair back, because when we comb our hair, we don't throw the hair around anywhere; we burn it, because *muldarpis* might get it or *thumpamarldi*, that's a sure thing for a *thumpamarldi*. And *thumpamarldi* can pick up your hair, and if he's got a fancy to you, he'll get you. That's the hair. And clothes, you never put your washing out on the line; you put it out in the daytime, and you take it, especially your gundies [underwear], you don't leave them on the line.

334

Especially when people are away from home, and are vulnerable to visits from strangers, they take great care with the washing.

These beliefs and practices are current today. I would see women bring in the washing before dusk and in the evening hear the accompanying lecture; or comb their hair, then gather up the hair caught in the teeth of the comb and carefully put it in their purse or handbag, sometimes in an envelope kept for that purpose. Stray hair was not discarded casually. A simple gesture may be part of a wider belief system, but it will be learnt as "That is what the older people said we should do", or "That is what my mother always did and I believed it was important and so I do it today." Something as mundane as combing one's hair may be indicative of deeply held beliefs about personal identity, relation to sacred stories, and fear of sorcery. Practical behaviours are tied into a larger world view, although not everyone can specify the linkages. What is critical and what is still believed is that one should exercise care in the disposal of things that are of one's flesh and that includes one's *ngatji*.

Eileen McHughes: I actually would like to tell you about my grand-daughter, the one that was being naughty. Four of my grandchildren live with their grandfather in Adelaide, and the little boy, he's really light, he'd pass for white, and he wants to be a tribal traditional Aboriginal, and that's his wish. The little girl was being naughty. She's six. They asked me to tell them about my grandparents and my history, so I told them about my great-grandmother, Lizzie Martinyeri. My grandchildren wanted to know about, like who they were related to and old Lizzie. So, I was telling the children about her because she was the one that made my grandmother Adeline sick because of the discipline that was handed down by Lizzie, and Adeline tried to interfere, and so she was made very sick. So I was telling my grandchildren this and the little girl was playing up, and I said: "Right, you've had it; I'm going to sing you", and she looked at me and she said, "You can't, Nanna." I said, "Yes, I can," I said, "Go on you boys, get some of her hair for me." So they got the hair and they put it in the envelope and she said, "You're not really going to do it, are you, Nanna?" and I said, "Yes, I'm going to; unless you listen and be good, I'm going to do it." Anyway, she wormed her way round me and she asked for her hair back so I gave her the hair back and I said, "Just remember though, I've got your photos in my bag. If I hear that you're naughty, I'm going to do it; I'll make you very sick." When we went back, she said, "Nanna, I was sick. I've been sick for about three days", and I said, "Well, next time you'd better listen, hey?" So she believes it now, that I can make her sick.

Three major modes of sorcery—*millin*, *ngagthari* and *nyeleri*—are fairly consistently noted from Taplin onwards. Taplin (1873: 29) records his experiences of the entrenched beliefs about sorcery in his ethnography, and in his journals we can read of his daily struggle with what he sees as blind superstition. Interestingly, in terms of the nature of change, his journal includes a reference to the introduction of *neilyeri* at Raukkan sixteen years earlier.[11] That *neilyeri* was an innovation is not mentioned in his published work (1879). By then he had formalised his knowledge and was interested in setting out the taxonomy of sorcery practices, against all of which he actively campaigned. As a snapshot of sorcery practice, his threefold schema works, but it masks the dynamism of Ngarrindjeri culture. Elders had begun to respond to the undermining of their authority which Taplin's assault on the marriage system, navel cord exchange, and mortuary rituals represented. They sought stronger and more fearful ways of impressing upon dissenters the dire consequences of setting aside these rituals and arrangements. Albert Karloan and Pinkie Mack both had the impression that sorcery was intensifying (Berndt *et al.* 1993: 290) and this is not unusual in situations of stress, dislocation and depopulation.

The Berndts (1993: 371) record that Albert Karloan's father was known as *ngaragi*, strict, a person adhering to the traditional mode of life, and that he would punish his son. From the stories of Ngarrindjeri women today, we can see that this value persists, as does knowledge and fear of sorcery. Beliefs in sorcery co-exist with Christian beliefs. I ask Veronica Brodie about Dan Wilson's relationship to the church. "Grandfather Dan was a Christian, and he knew that sorcery business." Leila Rankine had balanced her "culture" and Christianity also, and so did Aunty Koomi and Fofon. "It's nonsense to say you can't have both," says Veronica Brodie. On her kitchen bench Veronica has her favourite Psalm, 118: "This is the day the Lord has made, and we will rejoice and be glad in it." She reads and says, "We all have our days." We cannot speak to

Leila Rankine (1980) about her experiences, but we can read her poetry wherein she records some of her beliefs about "Spirits". The "Old Ones" warned her not to stray from the firelight at night.

> Our "old ones" spoke in whispers, of others long since passed.
> Who came at night to visit, and warn of things to come.
> The spirits of our people, are still with us today.
> They live beyond the fire-light, with the stars, and Milky Way.

And in "Pay-back" Leila Rankine (*ibid.*) writes:

> No-one, hears his movements
> but dead-bodies fat, is smelt.
> Quick, wash your face with water,
> or he'll put us, all to sleep.

Through the Wilson line, knowledge of the skills, habits, and meanings of the practice of sorcery have passed from generation to generation. The grand-daughters of Dan Wilson know a great deal, as do their brothers. Similarly skills, knowledge and objects have been handed down in Pinkie Mack's line. Their knowledge is not from books although, when we turn to the texts, the same information, albeit in more abstract and generalised terms, is there. What the oral accounts illuminate is that the practice of men and that of women is not identical. This is particularly plain in the practice of midwives from these lineages.

Putari Practice

Everyone feared Great-Nanna [Louisa Karpeny] because she was one of the sorcerers, with the *maraldi* bones, says Daisy Rankine. Eileen McHughes recalls: Old Lizzie was a *putari*, you know. I think there's different meanings to it, but I believed that it was because our Grandfather Mike told me she had a little bag of tricks, so I suppose that was what you used to sing people with, or like sorcery bag, I suppose, and then someone else says it's a doctor, so I'm not quite sure. I am inclined to believe my Grandfather Mike, because he knew her, I didn't. The practices of sorcerers intent on doing harm, native doctors intent on healing, and midwives intent on caring for mothers and their babies form a tangled web. There is little definitional or conceptual clarity in the written sources and, as Eileen McHughes illustrates, even those who are the descendants of experts in these fields are not quite sure where to draw the line. I think the confusion arises in part because those who had been through the doctor ceremonies instigated by *Ngurunderi* could use their power for good or evil. This appears to have applied to both men and women. Where there is a gender difference is in the situations where male and female doctors used their powers. There were specialist bodies of knowledge and it is apparent that women's expertise as midwives, known as *putari*, was not duplicated in men, although they might also be called *putari*. In some ways it is similar to the issue of both men and women being considered *narambi* at certain points of their lives. For both it meant "dangerous and separate" but it was experienced with reference to different situations in their respective life cycles.

So what were the male *putari* doing? As a youth, Milerum was present at a clan camping site just opposite Goat Island, when a gathering of *putari* set about curing those who had been the victims of *mankambuli*, "bone-magic" (Tindale 1934–7: 93-5). At this site, *Ngurunderi*, in his role of healer, had been asked to allay the fears and effects of *mankambuli*. Milerum recalled when the *putari* gathered, his father included. Acting for *Ngurunderi*, these *putari* treated people from as far away as Robe. Late in the day, as the people assembled, the women began to sing. They sang, not the loudly bawled songs used at ceremonies on other occasions but more gently for their chants were not ordinary ones about events which happened, but were ones with secret meanings. They were doctor songs asking the unseen *Ngurunderi* to intercede. Each doctor present sang his own song and the women audience would take up each refrain "gently" as they heard it from his lips. Then at dusk, men painted and feathered appeared from the west, dancing, approaching and reaching out to the sick, and diagnosing their condition. For those who had been boned, the *putari* performed a ritual with pressure, heat, smoked emu feathers, and, after a struggle, finally removed the bone, the point of which was then stuck into the bark of a tree. The exit wound was rubbed with emu oil and a pad of a spider web was put on it. The skills learned through these ceremonies come from

Ngurunderi, but the sorcery practices which gave rise to the need for healing pre-date *Ngurunderi*. There is not, however, a division between the destructive practices of the pre-*Ngurunderi* sorcerers and the nurturing ones of *putari*.

The stock-in-trade of the doctors varied, but it appears that *putari* could use their healing powers to undo the work of those who knew sorcery (Tindale 1937: 109-10; 1941: 223). Karloan's father used *tu:mi*, hair string, in his curing practices and could thereby see through his patient. Hair string wound around the head would give a doctor "X-ray vision" (Berndt *et al.* 1993: 261). *Tumi* can be used for good in the hands of *putari* and for evil.[12] Reuben Walker (1934: 207-9) writes of *putari*, who can heal, and witch-doctors, who can kill, as interchangeable: "They live in fear of the Putharee [*putari*]— would point finger and curse and person would die. The witch doctor was wiping out his own country." Moriarty (1879: 52), the police trooper at Goolwa, states that the *pooteri* uses various herbs, roots and she-oak to treat boils and sore eyes. Taplin (1879: 44-50) is far more interested in cataloguing diseases and calculating mortality rates than in native doctors, to which he devotes one paragraph. He identifies *kaldukkes*, *wiwirrar* and *puttheras*, who "profess" to treat the sick, with incantations, seaweed and hot steam baths. These "artful rogues" are, in his view, pretending to be doctors. When sorcery is blamed for a death, Taplin (4/9/1867) considers their work to be a masterpiece of the devil. Meyer (1843: 107) also has *wiwiri-malde* for a doctor "who drives away sickness". A "conjurer and trickster", says Reuben Walker (1934: 209) of Yami Rankine (of Hindmarsh Island) who, with his opossum bag, red handkerchief, a few pebbles and cord of human hair, treated a patient. Despite the confusion, it appears there were specialties and that the names were not entirely interchangeable. One of the earliest mentions of the practice of native doctors is by Meyer (1843: 90; see also Brough Smyth 1878 Vol. 2: 261-2) in his entry for *parraitjeorn*, a Ramindjeri term that literally means "a seaweed man". This "doctor . . . pretends to cure diseases by chewing a small piece of a red-coloured sea-weed which he gives to the patient, bidding him conceal it about his person. As the weed becomes dry, it is supposed the disease will evaporate with the moisture."

Taplin's journal entry of 2/5/1862 sets out the way in which men are made into *kaldukke* in a ritual, said to drive the men mad and endow them with the ability to ensorcel with *ngatji* remains (see also Taplin 1879: 134). Everything struck by a black spear used in the ceremony is *narambi*. While running around in their demented state, painted with white chalk, the *kaldukke* are said to be under the influence of *Melape*, the great master sorcerer. This is a rite of passage which draws upon the power of the ancestors, which by reference to the category *narambi* identifies this practice as part of religious practice. Informants for the Berndts and Tindale also detail the nature of doctor-making ceremonies, and introduce some new questions. Tindale (1938–56: 67-73), working with Albert Karloan, states that it was men who distinguished themselves in fighting, or who were feared for their sorcery powers, who were known as *ku:lkuki*. However, it appears that Albert's knowledge came to him through his patriline, rather than his prowess at hunting or sorcery. From the Berndts (1993: 489), we learn that Karloan's father's sister, with whom Albert sometimes worked, was a sorcerer and was brought before the *tendi* for use of her powers. Albert also credits his mother with saving his life when she guided him away from a track taken by a sorcerer (*ibid.*: 481). It appears that the whole family was skilled. Perhaps, within each family, certain knowledge was transmitted, but it was only when one's practice was recognised as worthy that one was known as a doctor.

In terms of ritual knowledge, we find that both older men and older women have skills and that some are particularly associated with older women. In a section on "Witch Doctor", Walker (1934: 207-8) writes of the feared power of old women to point and curse a person, who would eventually die. He recalls that, somewhere between the ages of nine and twelve, he saw scores of children poisoned. "The unfortunate children had to suffer for the Parents. It was sweet revenge for the old hags. She may have lost a relation that another tribes men had bruised to death. It was wo unto the children of that tribe. The old hags reaped quite a harvest." The *narthungarie*, made of hair or bone, and a "good soaking of dead man's fat", is left in place, and when the intended person shows a sign of having been affected, the danger is made explicit. "I have seen the native go to a shadow", writes Walker. "The old girls always kept a good supply" (see also Taplin 6/3/1861). Here we have women handling and owning the ritual and meting out justice on a grand scale.

During a visit to Goolwa, Tindale recorded Walker (1934: 208) as saying the old women had more voice than anything in camp. They were the ones who had voice about who killed a person and would talk a man down and they did as the old women wished. It appears the older women had quite a deal to say, not only in the use, but also in the barter of these feared ensorcelling items. They knew about and practised sorcery. With regard to diagnosing and treating the ills that arise from such practices, Walker describes a scene where the doctor, Old Yamie Walker, signalled to his wives who set up a chant which continued for some time. It would give a strong man the creeps, Walker (1934: 209) says of this melancholy sound.

So, older women knew and sang the songs associated with doctor business. There was a common core of knowledge, and a few exceptional women knew some of the senior men's practices.

What were the female doctors doing when they were with other women? We have no first-hand accounts from the nineteenth century, although we do have some clues. Tindale (1934–7: 158) defines the term from a male perspective: "*Putari*, a witch doctor; an older man claiming to have special, usually malevolent powers". Meyer (1843: 81) knew the practice to be gendered: *Mokani*: "a black stone, something like a hatchet, the head fastened between two sticks, which are bound together, and form a handle. There is a sharp edge, which is used to charm men, while the other end of the stone is blunt and rough, and is used to charm women. It is used for the same purpose in the same manner as the *plongge*." Berndt *et al.* (1993: 193) recognise the special expertise of female *putari* as concerning "midwifery and menstruation, as well as . . . contraceptive measures and so forth". Doreen Kartinyeri speaks with pride of how Aunty Rosie's midwifery skills were praised; how Aunty Laura had never lost one mother. But, as Eileen McHughes and others attest, female *putari* are doing more than dealing with reproductive matters.

Today, although most people are willing to allow the benefits of antibiotics and the like in treating certain aliments, their explanations of why certain people get sick at particular times, and why

341

some treatments are more efficacious than others, owe much to beliefs about sorcery, knowledge of bush medicines, their ability to read the signs, and their reliance on experts, such as *putari*. Eileen McHughes' knowledge of her environment harks back to her childhood and the families with whom they camped. My brother Kevin knocked a wart off, and it was really bleeding. My mother didn't like the sight of blood—she'd freak out when she saw a lot of blood—and I saw Aunty Laura gathering up all these cobwebs and I said, "What are you going to do with those?" and she said, "That stops the bleeding," so she wrapped them round my brother's finger and it stopped. Daisy Rankine concurs, Cobwebs were good for bleeding. Doreen also speaks of Aunty Rosie using cobwebs in her *putari* practice. I probably would have missed Tindale's (1934–7: 95) mention of a spiderweb pad had they not spoken of this practice.

Eileen McHughes learnt about bush medicine from her family, which included *putari* Lizzie Martinyeri. Then there was the old man's beard that they used to collect from down the Pines. They'd boil it up and it was used for chest complaints, like bronchitis. [I've also been told it is good for aches and pains of arthritis and rheumatism.] And with the she-oak apples, they'd boil the apples up and they used to drink that. Doreen Kartinyeri: You could eat the fruit, but for sickness they were boiled. They had the rock bowls and they used to build a fire around them. Eileen McHughes: There's a grey kind of plant—it's rather prickly—and we used to eat the roots of it that was in the ground. And the *thalgi*, thistle, you could eat it, have it for celery, or you could use the milk out of it for warts and things. For asthma, goanna fat, and when I'd say that I'd seen one, I was asked why didn't I catch it. Well, I can't catch goannas. I was never been taught how to. In my experience people never claim knowledge of skills or knowledge they don't have. It is dangerous and disrespectful to do so.

Muriel Van Der Byl calls the Hindmarsh Island "a medicine place" and there is widespread knowledge about herbal and folk remedies in the Ngarrindjeri community. There is also a strong belief in the efficacy of the treatments and a particular pride in stories of people healed. Tindale records that Joe Walker's daughter Emma, who was being treated for tuberculosis at Encounter Bay, was expected to die, but she recovered after her father took her back to his camp on the

Coorong and treated her with a native medicine, compounded from red mallee roots, ordinary eucalyptus roots and a native sarsaparilla plant (Tindale 1938–56: 262). Mr H. F. Dodds of Lalawa Station in the Lake Albert district, who related this tale to Tindale, said that in 1956 Emma was still alive, had married and had children.

Another reason for the thinness of, and confusion in, the ethnographic record is, I think, that these are not matters about which people talk openly. To mention certain words, to call certain names, is to evoke the presence and power of forces which may disturb, harm and bring sickness. In part, also, the conceptual framework of the recorders, which poses a radical opposition between magic and religion, as well as between superstition and true knowledge, serves to locate much information about the practice of medicine, the role of doctors, rituals to do with the body, as profane activities pursued by quacks and charlatans. The reporting has a decidedly ethnocentric tone about it. Would one say, of a priest, that he "pretends" with bread and wine at communion? Probably not. If the beliefs that underlie the practice were the subject of scholarly comment, it would be more likely to speak of the doctrine of transubstantiation.

So, if one were to extend respect to Ngarrindjeri practices, what are the relevant beliefs to be considered? Firstly one has to accept that all illness, premature death, and misfortune are the result of sorcery; that an adversary can use your likeness, your name, your *ngatji*, body fluids and wastes, or food scraps, as if they were you;[13] that the ceremonies by which doctors are made were instituted by *Ngurunderi*; and that the acquired skills and knowledge of a native doctor can be used to cure and to ensorcel. It would also be helpful to appreciate that, despite the masculine language of the sources, there were women *putari* and there are women today who have retained some of the knowledge and practice of their female forebears. People know who had the skills of a *putari* and who had the powers of a *thumparmaldi*. The lines of transmission are clear. Eileen McHughes learned from her grandfather, as did Veronica Brodie. Daisy Rankine is heir to the knowledge of Aunty Laura; Doreen Kartinyeri has stories from her Aunty Rosie. This oral knowledge complements the written sources and, as far as the women are concerned, it tells us more.

343

The *Mulyewongk*: A Story for All Ages

Muriel Van Der Byl: You'd be swimming in the late afternoon and they'd call, "Get out of the water. The *mulyewongk* will get you." We'd get out. Val has felt it and so have I. *Mulyewongk*. Great word. I can hear the creature bubbling up and bellowing from the depths of the lake. It's big and 'airy. Muriel Van Der Byl begins in explaining her vision of the long-haired monster that takes children who stray too close to the water's edge. This was the first story I was told by Ngarrindjeri women in January 1996. At that point I wasn't sure whether it was because the women assumed I'd know about the legendary bunyip, or if the story had further significance, but it certainly was at the forefront of their minds when I asked about childhood, and stories about sites where they'd lived, holidayed, or visited often. The Karpeny sisters spoke of the *mulyewongk* at Marrunggung; others spoke of the creature at Tailem Bend; some of the mechanical model in Murray Bridge. One story concerns the presence of a female *mulyewongk* in the waters around Hindmarsh Island (see Chapter 10). Commissioner Stevens (1995: 278) dismissed the Seven Sisters Dreaming as a Ngarrindjeri story on the basis of what she took to be a lack of written documentation. Similarly, in the absence of written texts, Jane Mathews (1996: 171ff.) was urged to dismiss the *mulyewongk* in Ngarrindjeri lands as a story of creative power and to understand it as "one of the many mythical creatures which inhabit the everyday world of the Ngarrindjeri". However, this division of the world of belief into "mythic creatures", which it would appear can be dismissed fairly easily, and "*Ngurunderi*-like" Dreamings, which should be respected, is problematic. The spirit beings might pre-date *Ngurunderi*, but they interact with him in his travels and thus become part of his story and creative sweep through the Lower Murray. They are not frozen in time. Also, because spirit beings are local in nature, theirs is often the story that belongs to a place and is known by a particular family. The way in which this local knowledge is then enmeshed in the larger accounts of the travels of the major Dreamings may not be as well known. This level might be thought of as the macro-design, and it would have been visible in large regional ceremonies. These are no longer performed. Fortunately, there are clues in the written sources where we can glimpse some of the interconnections between the localised spirit beings and the more mobile macro Dreamings.

On first hearing of the *mulyewongk*, I understood the story as a cautionary tale for children and an exhortation to mothers to be ever watchful of their children, but I know stories exist at different levels and that different people may know different details. It was told to me at a time when the issue of what women knew and believed about their bodies was being contested. So whenever the conversation turns to *mulyewongk*, I take note. One afternoon while we are sitting around the Wilson kitchen table in Murray Bridge, the conversation turns to the disciplining of children: Vicki Hartman (née Kropinyeri): Things like the *mulyewongk*, that's how we were disciplined, to never go alone. You were always with your brother or sister, and you always had to be home before dark. You would never come home after dark, especially south of Tailem Bend, where the cave was. We were not allowed to go out too far, and there was definitely no swimming until after the dandelions were out. Eunice Aston (née Sumner): I'm younger than Aunty Vicki, and I was brought up around the lake, and when we were brought to the river we were told about the *mulyewongk* at Tailem Bend, and how the hollow was the entrance, and therefore we had to be careful all along there. Judy Kropinyeri: My father would go under the water and come up and scare us. But that mechanical *mulyewongk*, it was nothing like ours. It is offensive. We've got a real one. Vicki Hartman: We used to say, "Poor whitefellas, is that all they've got?" [the mechanical version]. Eunice: We've said that a lot. Judy: It just upset us. But what could we do?

In conversations with women I routinely hear the *mulyewongk* being associated with the swimming season, dandelions, health and discipline. We were told that the fever—the yellow fever—would come while the dandelions were out, and that's why we weren't allowed in the water. I still use it with my kids. Vicki Hartman, Judy Kropinyeri, and Eunice Aston all agreed on this. Aunty Fofon's (Rankine 1969) story focused on the Seven Sisters, and did not mention the *mulyewongk*. Of course we don't know what she might have said if asked. Taplin (1873: 62) associated illness with the booming sound made by the creature. "The natives also dread a water spirit called Mulgewanke . . . they think it causes rheumatism to those who

345

hear it. He is represented as a curious being, half man, half fish, and instead of hair, a matted crop of reeds."

Isobelle Norvill has this to say about the *mulyewongk*: Pop Wilfie [Varcoe, the brother of Mumadie], he was a story-teller and if we were very good we were allowed to go down there and he'd tell us stories. He used to talk about the *mulyewongk*. Mum said that they [the creators of the mechanical *mulyewongk*] didn't even get that the *mulyewongk* was hairy. If something wasn't right, she'd just walk away. She treated it with disdain and said to the kids, "If you want to know about the *mulyewongk*, go talk to the old fellows." The "old fellows" have left some traces in the written record and there are still stories being told. *Mulyewongk* have been reported at various places in the Lower Murray and lakes. Some live in complex colonies, exhibit human-like emotions, recruit humans as new members and transform them through the exercise of their powers of sorcery; and *mulyewongk* are associated with certain rituals. On closer acquaintance I am finding the *mulyewongk* to be more and more fascinating, and I am becoming less and less satisfied with its classification as a quaint tale the sole purpose of which is to terrorise children. *Mulyewongk* are interwoven with other knowledge of the rhyme and rhythm of Ngarrindjeri lands, but which aspects are emphasised depends on the who, when, and where of the question. Berndt *et al.* (1993: 181) describe how the head and body of the young man just through his initiation is washed with a slimy swamp weed that grows along the river side and is associated with the *mulyewongk*. It is this weed that the *mulyewongk* also use in transforming their human captives.

Mulyewongk sites are most definitely off-limits to children, but they also carry a range of restrictions that take us into the domain of sacred taboos. The scope and nature of the restrictions that apply to *mulyewongk* are consistent with places and forces designated *narambi*. Tindale and Long (nd: 11) note that only old men may fish at the *mulyewongk* site at Murray Bridge. Further down river, men canoeing past Brinkleys Landing would make the children lie down for fear of the *mulyewongk* that left the water and went up the hill to its cave. None would pole past after dark (Tindale 1930–52: 269). Jacob Harris told Alison Harvey (1939) that, before his people would go past the place, they painted their faces with mud in a design that extended down the nose and across the forehead and cheeks. Fragments to be sure, but these snippets from the "old fellas" indicate that there is more than one story to be told of the *mulyewongk*. There are a number of *mulyewongk* sites known today, and a number are recorded in the literature, as Clarke's (1994: Fig. 3.9) map indicates. Taplin (1873: 62) writes of the booming sound of the *mulyewongk* in the lakes and numerous sightings, including one by his son. On a trip with Karloan down the Murray, Ronald Berndt (1940a: 166) recorded the site Mupulerwong (Mypolonga), which Karloan thought to be a "derivation of mulduwank". Berndt names its home as the "dark recesses of the many caves and shelters scattered along the banks of the Lower Murray", but thinks it probable that these "spirits" are owls. Tindale (1930–52: 269) identifies a cluster of sites: one in the cliffs at Pomanda, another at Kongarng (about two miles south-southwest of Alan McFarlane's Station and another taking in Jertang (Brinkleys Landing) and a cave at Masons Hill (Marrunggung). The Karpeny sisters detail this site for me. It is one of the better-documented *mulyewongk* places, which is not surprising, given that the Karpeny clan has maintained close oversight of the area. The stories associated with sites to which there has been restricted access are less well represented in the written record.

Steven Hemming (1985) has extracted the primary material from George Taplin, Ronald Berndt and H. K. Fry for the *mulyewongk* of the Lower Murray. Each author cites the story of the boy who was captured by a *mulyewongk* and subsequently saved by his father, but in each account there are variations. Mark Wilson (1868–1940) was the primary informant regarding *mulyewongk* in the 1930s although Tindale (1930–52: 269) says he also checked the story with David Unaipon. Fry provides the most detailed version of Mark Wilson's story (Hemming 1985: 14-15). After an eight-year-old boy was taken at the water's edge, the father "got his emu feathers that were wrapped around the kidney fat of a dead body called Ngrnooyee" and rubbed his own body with this anaesthetic in preparation for the rescue. Thus fortified and armed with waddies (clubs), the father dived in and found the passage to the *mulyewongk* home. "He crawled up and found them gathered about the little boy. They had a fire and were chanting a corroboree over him, to make him a *mulyewongk.*" Taking his emu feathers, the father enters, induces sleep in the captors, and returns to land with his son whose face and hair already showed signs of turning into a little *mulyewongk*. The tribe joyfully chants songs of the father's prowess and, after emu and goanna fat have been applied all over his body, the little boy recovers. Here the rescue is achieved through knowledge of sorcery which is more powerful than that of the *mulyewongk*. In Taplin's account (1873: 138; 16–17/9/1862) of this "legend", which is not attributed to any particular person, the father ties a line around his waist and, while his friends hold onto the line, performs certain incantations. He finds his son amongst the sleeping *mulyewongk*. Again the father relies on his powers, ones derived from *Ngurunderi's* law, to wrest his son from the dark forces and return him to the land of the living. The consequences of children being taken to the monster's lair, dramatised in these stories, told by adults to adults, take us deeper into the story.

Karloan told the Berndts (1993: 203-4, 422-4) that children were warned that washing their hands of grease after eating fish or duck on the bank of the river would attract the *mulyewongk*. In his account the captured child, whom Karloan had known as a young man, died after being rescued. As in Mark Wilson's version the father uses a cord, here identified as hair string, but when the child is brought to shore it is weed that is scraped from his body and there is no mention of his being anointed with oil. The child eventually dies for, as Karloan believes, a person either is taken and becomes one of them, or is rescued and dies because they have sung over him and made him one of them. The *mulyewongk*, he notes, "were no laughing matter" (*ibid.*: 207).

Berndt (1940a: 168) names Marrunggung as the place where the boy was taken and magically recovered by his father. Tindale (1930–52: 269-73) recorded the same story, but in his rendition the tribe begins to wail at the loss of the child as part of the mourning behaviour and, as noted above, the site is totally avoided after dark. Alison Harvey recorded the story from Pinkie Mack on 12 June 1939 with more precise details regarding the preparation of the anaesthetic, and in her account the boy is placed on an ant bed so that the weeds which cling to him may be eaten off. Henry Rankine

(1991: 121) learnt the story from his father, but in his version there are two boys playing at the water's edge and only one of them is taken. Each of these accounts tells the same basic story, albeit with significant differences in details and emphasis. We are fortunate in having a number of versions of this particular *mulyewongk* incident and the range of information available in each should alert us to the problems of relying on any one account as the authentic version. It is most probable that there are other accounts of the rescue that have not been written down. It is also possible that there are other versions of *mulyewongk* behaviour which have not been recorded anywhere. Where stories have an "inside" or "restricted" component, it is convenient to represent them as the story of a monster and to let the children's version be the one that is told widely. That way, more probing questions are not asked. But, there are several indications from the "old fellas" that *mulyewongk* were more than child's play. In two sources there are accounts of the *mulyewongk* interacting with *Ngurunderi*. Thus the *mulyewongk*, as a being, becomes part of the founding drama of the Ngarrindjeri world.

"It was while camped here [near Masons Hill at the entrance to Lake Alexandrina] that he was disturbed by a being called Muldjewangk which broke holes in his set nets so that he and his wives suffered, because they were unable to catch even lesser fish than their favourite Murray Cod," write Tindale and Pretty (1980: 50). Until Elymann's journals were translated,[14] this was the only reference which linked the *mulyewongk* to *Ngurunderi*. Elymann's journal entry of 18–19 June 1900 interweaves the *mulyewongk* with the presence of *Ngurunderi* and the configuration of the Southern Cross. From an old man in one of the tents on the beach, Elymann (Courto 1996: 287) learns that

> here their god Narrandurie made his presence known by means of the noise concerned during his trek from east to west. The same has been heard at times since the beginning of the world. A long time ago the Blacks saw him and it is reported that he has the figure of a big man. When he came here he instructed the Blacks to hold the magic-honour. Then corroborees were organised to honour him.

On 22 June Elymann writes further of his conversation with this old man regarding the relationship of *Ngurunderi* and the loud noise "It is always to be expected when 'the two little milk-white spots on the other

349

side of the Southern Cross' do not show themselves. Shortly before it occurs, one sees small rainbows before sunset" (*ibid*.: 247).

So how much is in the ethnographic literature on the subject of bunyips? A search on the World Wide Web reveals a vast literature out there on bunyips elsewhere in Australia. Professor John Mulvaney responds immediately to my request for a copy of his "Research Report" (1994) on the "Namoi bunyip". Derived from a word in the Wergaia dialect of the northwest of Victoria, "bunyips", Mulvaney reports, come in a range of guises: fur, feathers, fins, teeth, tusks, and hairy human-like beings. Barrett (1946: 9) adds that this amphibious animal inhabits shallow lakes and lagoons and deep shadowy holes in the rivers. When Aborigines draw bunyips, no two are the same. My bunyip bibliography grows. In Brough Smyth's (1878 Vol. 1: 435-44) review of the sources on bunyips for southeastern Australia, he mention its habitats as deep waterholes and the sea shore; its supernatural power over humans and ability to cause death, sickness and other misfortunes; and its elusive character. Lola Cameron Bonney (1980: 16-17) writes of "The Lake Monster" who inhabited a lake in Victoria and captured a swimmer who ignored the warnings of locals. By reaching back into the literature, we see that *mulyewongk* have a wider range of features than a waterlogged "boggey-man", though they certainly are known as that.

My daughter chuckles gleefully when I begin to tell her of the *mulyewongk*; she retrieves her children's books, *The Bunyip That Ate Canberra* (Salmon 1972) and *The Magic Pudding* (Lindsay 1930), from the basement of my Massachusetts home. She scours second-hand shops and finds Catherine Taplin's copy of *The Bunyip of Berkeley's Creek* (Wagner 1973) in Strathalbyn. This bunyip, she tells me, is having an existential crisis. He keeps asking "What am I?" and is told, "You're ugly." Only when he meets another bunyip is his beauty recognised. This bunyip is happy with his own kind. Bailey, Steven Hemming's daughter, tells me you get a rash on your bottom if you try to kill a *mulyewongk*.

While in Murray Bridge, we pick up a flyer with a message from "Bazza the Bunyip", prepared by the Department of Environment and Natural Resources. We see his image on ferry crossings. "Don't muck up the Murray," he growls. His rules include exercising due care with fire, water, litter, farmers' property and animals, local flora and fauna, firearms and historic sites, but nary a mention of Aboriginal sites and Heritage issues. At the Sturt Reserve, near where Albert Karloan camped and was interviewed by Ronald Berndt in 1939, we stop to photograph the mechanical bunyip. One afternoon Genevieve disappears, finds the designer, and on return regales me with stories of the history of the mechanical *mulyewongk*. The exhibit was opened in January 1972, and for twenty cents in the slot, one can peer

The BUNYIP will only work on 20c coins. The BUNYIP appears TWICE.

The mechanical *mulyewongk*, Murray Bridge, 1996 (Genevieve Bell)

351

through the mesh gate into a constructed cave and see the moulded fibreglass monster rise from its murky waters, bellow, and descend. An infant bunyip, added in the early 1980s, clings to its side. We photograph it, but really need a flash. Doreen Kartinyeri laughs when she sees the photograph and tells of how her grandson was terrorised when Papa Syd activated the beast before she could warn the child.

The *mulyewongk* has frightened children and puzzled scientists who have speculated over the possible bases of the stories and sightings. The material from the Lower Murray has been part of their deliberations. As early as July 1847 the Sydney Museum displayed a skull, supposedly of a bunyip which had been found in the Lower Murrumbidgee (Holland 1990: 520-1; Barrett 1946). In search of a scientific explanation, Clarke (1994: 132-5) reviews the various explanations. In his journal (20/6/1860), Taplin notes that the cannon-like sound is heard especially in winter and the natives say it is *mulyewongk* "breaking up gum trees which float down the Murray. . . . I heard it twelve times in 10 minutes." On 18/1/1870 Taplin reports a sighting of some strange animal spouting out on the lake more than six kilometres off. "We have heard Moolgewanke very much lately." Like later observers Taplin was curious regarding the origins of the noise. He is disinclined to believe it is a creature; he points out that each claim that one has been washed up is later explained, be it the carcass of a horse, or a platypus (29/11/1865). Berndt *et al.* (1993: 13) mention a large bone of some unidentified animal set within the cliff face, which is said to be the skeletal remains. In talking about the creature, Aunty Daisy volunteers "Dugong", and tells me that after the 1956 flood an unidentified mammal was seen. She mentions a boat tipped over at Murray Bridge near the willow. It takes a very powerful animal to do that. This is a living story. I hear of a site up-river from Swan Reach where boats used to dump rubbish in a *mulyewongk* hole. From Tindale and Long (nd: 11) we know there was a *mulyewongk* site at Murray Bridge that was a sacred site and that the bridge pylons were desecrated. The paddle-steamers may have churned up their homes, but the *mulyewongk* are still in the waters of the Lower Murray. Tom Trevorrow tells me that the *mulyewongk* site at Swan Reach was another breeding place. There are still things people do for the *mulyewongk,* he adds quietly. Could there have been *mulyewongk* increase rituals? Rites of propitiation?

There is agreement that *mulyewongk* live in dangerous aquatic environments: in places where branches and weed intertwine; where deep water presents a danger; where the waters are murky and swirl. Children should not stray to the water's edge in these places, no-one should dally near their caves. From there on, individuals and families offer a range of accounts of *mulyewongk* behaviour and significance. They interweave the *mulyewongk* with a range of beliefs about sorcery, illness, and survival. All contain a cautionary element regarding disturbance of their habitat. Given the history of disrespect for bunyip places, and lack of appreciation of sacred rites associated with these places, it is hardly surprising that some stories or parts of stories have been withheld. The children's version has been lapped up by whitefellas, most of whom are comfortable with the notion that Aborigines have "legends" and "just so" stories. It is some time before Val Power tells me of Harvey Karpeny, who is the keeper of the knowledge about its whereabouts. There are more stories known to the Karpeny clan, but they and others are not about to put this information in the public domain. Henry Rankine (1991) has spoken of the *mulyewongk* in public forum but does not consider the story to be open to any and all retellings. Eileen McHughes told me about the *mulyewongk* at Tailem Bend in January 1996, but it was another year before she talked about its home and even then she was uncomfortable in going into detail. As we shall see in Chapter Ten, the *mulyewongk* has significance for women on Hindmarsh Island.

Fear of Foreigners, Small People, the Dark

"They are in perpetual fear of malignant spirits, or bad men, who, they say, go abroad at night; and they seldom venture from the encampment after dusk, even to fetch water, without carrying a firestick in their hands, which they consider has the power of repelling these evil spirits," wrote Angas (1847: 88-9). Albert Karloan told Tindale (nd, f) of "little mythical night-people who had to be kept away by using lighted torches when attending fishing nets". Woods (1879: xxxiii) observes: "A corrobboree never takes place except on a bright moonlight night—for the natives have a great objection to moving about in the dark."

353

While I imagine stories about the ills that befall children who stray were always part of the Ngarrindjeri repertoire, I can't help wondering whether these stories did not assume greater importance after contact. There were now added dangers that might befall unattended children and many reasons to fear what lay beyond the comfort and security of one's family camp. Smallpox had wiped out whole families and the dead were buried where they fell, often without proper rituals. The whites came, stole women, interfered with sites, and massacred. On missions and reserves Ngarrindjeri found themselves living with strangers on strange territory. Children were removed and put in homes far away from their families. It was no longer possible to maintain marriage arrangements. One response to so many changes, and feelings of lack of control (apart from resorting to sorcery) could well have been to focus on those signs that offered an explanation, those rituals that offered comfort, and those stories that offered a sense of security. If one kept one's children close by; if one told a story of the dangers of wandering off alone, of being about after dark, perhaps the world would become a safer place. Jack Koolmatrie (Ely 1980: 29) noted, "Our teaching is sound." Children could get lost, kidnapped or murdered. Pragmatic and spiritually charged explanations co-exist with little apparent tension. A story which began as an account of an extraordinary event in time becomes a general explanation for certain categories of behaviours.

The story of the cannibalistic *prupi* at McGraths Flat may originally have been told to explain the meteorite which hit the area but, by the 1930s, it had become a cautionary tale for mothers to keep an ever-watchful eye on their children. Tindale (1938), on the basis of information from Milerum, provided the "legend" of Prupe (*prupi*) and Koromarange, two clan-sisters who lived near McGraths Flat. Tindale (*ibid.*: 18) takes this to be an example of that "stratum of stories" which deals with "individuals of unequivocally human origin" who, like everyday folk, have a *ngatji* but who never are translated into a *ngatji* form. There were *prupi* at other sites, and the word has the general meaning of bad. Harvey (1939) records a story of a *prupi* who leads men astray by calling them and misleading them like children. This is a good example of the way in which a story can function at different levels. Pinkie Mack identified *prupi* as a spirit woman who lived in a wombat hole at Kuyutung, northeast of Poltuwar (Poltallock) on Lake Alexandrina, in Piltindjeri clan territory (Berndt *et al.* 1993: 204). There may be other *prupi* locations, just as there are *mulyewongk* sites, of which we can know little from the literature and I would not presume to confine them to one area or to legislate their personal characteristics. One striking feature which is noted by Clarke (1994: 127ff.) is the localised nature of these "spirit beings".

Lola Cameron Bonney (1990: 12-13) tells of "The Yallamurrie, or the Cave of the Little Women" located between Naracoorte and Keith in South Australia, where women with pale, pink-coloured skin and long black hair dwelt. "According to the laws of the Aboriginals, they were forbidden to men", and any men they captured were used and "killed as soon as their stud duties were no longer required and all boy babies were treated in like manner". The story concludes with an account of what happened to two white men who did not respect this women's cave. Aunty Lola believed that the little women died out with the coming of closer settlement.

Lola Cameron Bonney (1982) told Roger Luebbers: There was a little man came out watching, trying to shoot a duck, he heard this sound in the *winggis*, sedges. He wasn't scared. He just couldn't move. He wasn't able to move a muscle. They are stark naked, fair-skinned, with black beards . . . And he was laying on his side, waiting for the ducks, and he could hear the wind through the *winggis* out on the lake and he said, "I couldn't even turn my neck, I couldn't turn back, I only lay there and looked at them. I was paralysed. They just looked at me. He walked up and pushed me and rolled me on my back and sat on me. He was looking at me and he had the coldest behind on my chest, and then he pulled my beard. And after a while he got off and stood there a while in the bushes just looking up." She then says, "I've seen this happen myself" and goes on to describe an incident in which she was involved.

There are numerous accounts of little people such as the *Taikuni*, who were said to be about a foot or two in height, but otherwise said to look just like human beings (Berndt *et al.* 1993: 207, 8). Tindale (1974: 93) mentions *Tharkun*. Karloan knew of a little island, Ru:puli, where mythical night people had to be kept away by using lighted torches when attending fishing nets (Tindale nd, c). Pinkie

Mack believed that little people had numerous camps along the shores of Lake Alexandrina, near Poltuwar in Piltindjeri territory (Berndt *et al.* 1993: 207). A tribe of little people, sometimes described as red-haired, lived in the Karnji Cliffs at McGraths Flat. Mark Wilson (Tindale and Long nd: 9) said that they make tormenting noises in the night. Harvey (1939) tells the story of the pygmy men who sometimes act as guides to lost men and sometimes led them astray.

Little people roamed about, especially at night. They pelted the unsuspecting with stones, and lured them away with their shining eyes. Vicki Hartman told me of the red eyes, and Eileen McHughes said not to look directly in the eye of strangers for fear of ensorcelment. I'm not sure whether any of these are about the same beings, but they are all cautionary tales and they augment references in the literature about the need to avoid eye contact with certain categories of person and the dangers of being out after nightfall.

We were told not to whistle in the dark, Jean Rankine and several other women had told me. Taplin (27/6/1861) noted:

> The children are, I find, very superstitious and the old people endeavour to make them more so. They were telling me last night of a being named Karungpe who lives in Wyirrewarre, who comes to the smouldering camp fire in the dead of night, scatters the embers and causes one person in the camp to die. They likewise say that the spirit of Tippoo's father goes about with a rope to catch people. They say it is dangerous to whistle in the dark lest Karungpe should catch them.

It is after dark that the spirits begin to move. Jean Rankine agrees: I still take orders from my elders. They told us not to come to the burial grounds after four o'clock. We can't come up here because that's when the spirits start to move, especially the soldier. He's the one. He sits in the left corner. He's been picked as the guardian of the burial grounds. It's not all Ngarrindjeri here. We've also got white people and Maori here and we're proud of it. The stories belong to particular places and as such belong to certain families.

Fascinating though it might be to contemplate, I am not going to attempt a taxonomy of this collectivity of beings, beliefs, and practices. There are rich pickings to be had in the ethnographic literature, but the topic of sorcery is not one people are prepared to discuss in great detail. It is too dangerous. I do not see this unwillingness to "go public" with the dangers of loose speech and behaviour, or to provide the details of particular case studies, as an indication of the lack of knowledge. I have been present when knowledgeable persons have been at a site where a close relative was *millined* and observed the gravity with which the matter is addressed. I have heard the tone in which threats of sorcery are uttered. I have seen the chagrin occasioned by the availability of sources that detail sorcery practices. I know that to simply say certain words can bring an otherwise friendly conversation to a shudderingly chill conclusion.

In my view, the importance of the narratives of beings such as the *mulyewongk*, *mingka* bird and *rijaruki* is the high level of interaction between the spirits and the living; their power to influence contemporary society and individual fates; their ability to communicate with the living; their explanatory value in analysis of why misfortune befalls some and not others. A host of shape-changers, malignant and benign, clever people, sorcerers, little people, people with red eyes, and spirits of the dead, routinely appear in this interactive drama. Localised and often highly personalised stories ground the activities of these beings in the rhythms of seasons, storms, tides, the particularities of the geography and history of the Lower Murray and lakes region of southeastern Australia. The creative period called "the Dreamtime" is not a remote and isolated moment in Ngarrindjeri history. The land remains alive with meaning and full of signs of significance. As W. E. H. Stanner (1979: 113) wrote in 1962: "Aborigines thought the world full of signs to men: they transformed the signs into assurances of mystical providence; and they conceived life's design as fixed by a founding drama." Sometimes only fragments of the stories of this drama are known, but the consequences of violation of the restrictions encoded in the tales are known and hence there is a reverence for these stories. This is the rationale for protecting places. Bad things will happen. From everyday behaviour—sitting in a certain way, walking in certain places, gathering foods in others—to specialist knowledge of sites and their significance, all have stories which blur the line between the pragmatics of daily behaviour and the power of the spirits to intrude, guide, teach and allow for change.

357

Part Two

The Politics of Knowledge

Previous page: The Murray Mouth, Slide 3. Published in Nick Harvey. (1983).
The Murray Mouth.
South Australia: South Ausralian Teachers Association
(Department of Lands, May 1966)

Respecting the Rules:
Oral and Written Cultures

Whose Knowledge? Whose Rules?

Jean Rankine: We learned a lot from Grandmother Lola Sumner, and that knowledge will never die while we are alive.

Thus far, Ngarrindjeri voices interwoven with various other sources have carried the text. It is now time to unpick some of my careful weaving and examine the fibres, the intent of the design, the qualifications and interests of the designers, weavers, and recorders of Ngarrindjeri stories. Who knows what? Who may acknowledge knowing what? Who are the authorities? What can we, do we, might we, should we know about Ngarrindjeri? What value are we to place on the sources, oral and written? How are we to read the silences? Although there is a considerable body of literature dealing with Ngarrindjeri, and I have been drawing on it in the preceding chapters, it is not true that there is nothing more to be learned of Ngarrindjeri history and culture. However, there are serious constraints on what might be known, by whom, under what circumstances, and what might be repeated under what conditions. In the next two chapters I am stepping back a little to pursue a number of questions regarding the politics of knowledge in a culture which privileges the spoken word (i.e. the Ngarrindjeri with whom I have been working) and the politics of knowledge in the broader Australian society which privileges written accounts. What happens when the two value systems become intertwined, as they have for the Ngarrindjeri? Today Ngarrindjeri read the historical record and find representations of their forebears that variously confirm and contradict what they know from their "old people". They read accounts which they believe should not be in the public domain. They read those Ngarrindjeri authors who have also left a record of their perceptions of their culture. Were it not for the current controversy over the status of restricted women's knowledge, questions about the relationship between written and oral texts might be ones about which to theorise. However, the value placed on the sources, oral and written, is no longer solely a matter of theorising. As has become evident through the Royal Commission and legal aftermath, the weight to be attached to various sources has serious consequences for Ngarrindjeri and researchers alike.

Questions regarding the who, when and where of it have become the stuff of cross-examinations, investigative journalism and letters to parliament. Anthropological assessments of the bases of authority of the elders, the rules of transmission of knowledge, and the assertions by Ngarrindjeri of sincerely held beliefs have not been sufficient to establish the bona fides of sacred places. In *Tickner v. Chapman* (1995) the Federal Court said that the Minister should have read the restricted women's submissions. In the negotiations concerning the release of confidential material to Judge Mathews (1996: 39-40), it was clear that in her view, without knowing the content of the stories, the Minister could not be satisfied that building a bridge would desecrate the site. The content of the story provided the rationale she sought, the link between the concepts of "significance" and "desecration". But content, without an understanding of cultural context and etiquette, does little to advance one's certainty regarding the "authenticity" of the cultural knowledge. In Part One I have been exploring context. Let me now turn to etiquette. By this I do not mean the social conventions of polite society, but rather "properties of conduct", as in the Webster dictionary definition. In an oral culture these "properties of conduct" assume a far more important role than in a print-oriented society, where there are many ways of conveying information other than in face-to-face situations. In an oral society these "properties" are the law, and the sanctions for violators are known. That is the power of the cautions contained in the stories. That is the power of the word.

Here are three field work moments that dramatised for me the extremely sensitive and difficult task I had embarked upon in writing about Ngarrindjeri ethnography and, more importantly, the nature of balancing of authorities and rights of access that Ngarrindjeri face in their daily lives. They concern my negotiations with Henry Rankine regarding sources which I wanted to use in this book. In early 1996 he had alerted me to a problem in dealing with written sources when I first sought access to the Tindale papers in the South Australian Museum. In Henry Rankine's view, there was information from his grandfather, Clarence Long, and other Ngarrindjeri with whom Tindale worked, that was not to be read by women, and the whole manuscript was to be treated respectfully. Even published texts that contain transcriptions of what had been said required permission. The word is still owned. On this occasion we had been out at Raukkan, but had missed Henry Rankine who was in hospital in Meningie. His wife Jean insisted that he was expecting us, so late that afternoon, with Henry in extremely good form and conversing with his grand-daughters in Ngarrindjeri, while working on my pronunciation, I sat down to ask him about three documents.

The first concerned a story, one with female protagonists, and I wondered if gender was important to the story. I asked if I could reproduce his account of the three sisters in the lake. In the version reproduced in Clarke's (1994: 135) thesis, the story is credited to "an Aboriginal source". Henry confirmed he was the source. Then, in customary Ngarrindjeri style, he dictated a contemporary account that grounded the story for the listeners. There are three sisters in the lake [Alexandrina] that we have always been told about. One will hit your boat (a flat-bottomed boat, a dinghy), one will tip over your boat, and one will drown you. You have to watch the weather, because the lake can be quite smooth, and in twenty minutes it can be quite rough. There are three waves close together. They come down all of a sudden. This story was passed down from the old people. Henry had learned it from his grandfather.

Then came the story that demonstrates the wisdom of the old people in reading the signs. My children, one day, it was a nice day, a beautiful day, and they wanted to go for a swim. I said, "Wait twenty minutes," because I could see what was coming. They were saying, "Can we go swimming in another five minutes?" And then I said, "In another ten minutes, wait another ten minutes." I was looking at the leaves, and

363

they were moving. I could see the storm coming. I said, "All right. Go swimming." The kids just got across the road, and the sand was flying, and the sand stung their legs. I said, "Now what if you'd been in the lake?" I've been on the lakes, I've lived in the lakes. When you're going out hunting for swan eggs, and when travelling around the lakes, it's important to know the weather. We have better forecasting than TV news. Our forecasting is outside there. The dangerously changeable nature of waters of the Coorong and lakes is evident in Taplin's journal, in Tindale's notes, and in contemporary story-telling.[1] The treacherous waters of Murray Mouth have claimed many lives, and one might say they have also protected many sites.

The second moment concerns a "find" I had made in a section of Tindale's papers. I asked Tom Trevorrow about *Ngurunderi*'s camp at Goolwa, a story I had heard both George and Tom tell, and I had wondered if *Ngurunderi* had interacted with any other beings while he was in the vicinity. From a sketch map in the Tindale papers, it appeared there were other active Dreamings at Goolwa. Who told it to Tindale? Tom asked. "Milerum, at Salt Creek, 1926," I said. This level of precision in the record is one of the joys of working with the Tindale material. In that case, Tom said, you had better ask Henry Rankine about using it. I had begun with Tom because the content of the story concerned an episode in the journey of *Ngurunderi* about which Tom and his brother George had given evidence to Judge Mathews, but Tom considered it to be Henry's prerogative regarding access. After Henry had read it, and we had agreed on conditions of use and access, including that it not be commercialised, I was then able to show it to the Trevorrows. "Can I use it?" I asked Henry. If it will help.

The third source I brought to Henry Rankine was a one-page transcription of his mother, Mrs Annie I. Rankine, MBE, recounting an aspect of the story of the Seven Sisters constellation. The Pleiades were once young girls and their story, like that of *Ngurunderi*, sets out an important aspect of the law for Ngarrindjeri and explains certain relationships between the land and sky, the living and the ancestors. The Rankine document is in the Australian Institute of Aboriginal and Torres Strait Islander Studies (AIATSIS) in Canberra and has no restrictions as far as access and citation go. Philip Clarke

(1994: 123) had quoted from it in his thesis. Yet Henry Rankine did not consider the transcription to be in the public domain. He had not been asked if it could be used, and further he did not want it quoted out of context. So I showed him my copy from the institute library. He read it, and asked why I wanted to use it. I explained I wanted to quote the whole section where his mother tells a story about the Seven Sisters, a Dreaming which the Royal Commission had found did not exist in Ngarrindjeri culture (Stevens 1995: 278). I told him I was interested in the way in which his mother told the story. It was a story which recalled her father, Clarence Long and shows him to be actively enforcing Ngarrindjeri law.

Annie Rankine (1969): My father used to tell us children of a special group of stars which is called the Seven Sisters, and before they were moving we weren't allowed to swim because the dandelions were in bloom then, and it was said that when the dandelions are out the water is still chill, and this is why our people are very strict and don't allow us to swim.

When the flowers all died off and the stars moved over a bit further, this is when we were allowed to swim because in that time the dandelion flower which would cause a fever to anyone would not be out to make us sick. So this is how we were taught the old people's way of living.

Many a time I tried to sneak past, go down to the lake and get away from my dad, but he would be waiting right on the dot for me, and then one whistle from him; we'd know that straightway we had to run, we knew we were wrong. All this will be in my memories and I'll never forget, because it remains so dear to me; taking notice of my father, being brought up that way; this will ever be in my memories.

And that's all I have got to say on the stars.

This is not a mythological account that is locked in a past era. It is a story that speaks to the living. Whenever I have heard other women tell this story about the dandelions, they chorus, And we don't swim while they're in bloom.

You can use it, said Henry of his mother's transcript, And you can use the material of my grandfather, if it will help, but remember, he'll be watching you. "Thank you, Henry." I would rather sign my name on the front sheet on documents in the AIATSIS or State Archives and thereby agree to be bound by their conditions of use and access. I would rather be subject to any number of codes of ethics, than have the spectre of Milerum, Henry's grandfather, Annie Rankine's father, Grandfather Clarrie to this generation of elders, Tindale's major source, the "last initiated man of the Coorong", looking over my shoulder.

A Two-Way Dialogue

I have only included those stories I have permission to repeat. I have respected—regretfully, I add—the wishes of those who did not want to be part of the project. There has been no covert research. People have known when I am taking notes or making tapes, and they have had the opportunity to read what I have written about them, to comment, correct and engage me regarding my analysis. This sort of dialogical research is always an interesting strategy. On the one hand, the feedback one gets from having one's "informants" read their own words is invaluable. Factual errors can be minimised, and the Ngarrindjeri who speak here have an interest in getting it right. They are also a reflective lot when it comes to what it is to be Ngarrindjeri. They have asked me questions which, for one thing, enriched my understanding of social change, and at times threw me into deep despair. How could I ever draw all the material together? How, in a written text, to do justice to the lilt and tenor of a story-telling tradition which relies on interaction with the audience? What to do when people, including me, clearly had different ideas about what something meant? On the other hand, dialogical research raises the question of censorship. Does having one's "informants" read a manuscript mean that what I have written must be "politically correct"? It could, but for a number of reasons I think not. In the past I have not shied away from publishing views, analyses and texts that were controversial, unwelcome in certain quarters, and I have been roundly and soundly set upon by colleagues, the media, Aboriginal organisations and lawyers. In short I have not toed a line in order to keep the peace, secure funding, or to please. I am neither an over-trained human tape recorder, nor a gun for hire. Throughout I am making plain the conditions under which people have spoken with me and the nature of the questions I asked.

During my visit from November 1996 to January 1997 visit, I was concerned to establish what could and could not be in the public domain and to ensure each individual consented to my use of parts of their stories. I needed clearances for the stories they had told me and stories they had told Judge Mathews. However, my Ngarrindjeri friends were not going to be contained by what had already been said. People continued telling me stories. I'd read a story back, ask about certain details and would find myself being told another story by way of illustrating the answer. Patterns emerged. I was getting a sense of their repertoire and the themes of their stories. At the same time I was working through archival material and getting a sense of the continuities and discontinuities in the written record. By May–June 1997, I had a draft that incorporated their voices with my analysis and the written sources. I had marked up the text by highlighting each person's name and I had a key to each chapter. Not only did I need individuals to read the sections in which they spoke and to see how I had organised the book but, as a safeguard for all concerned, I needed a method to indicate that each section had been read by the appropriate person. This was to be a labour-intensive exercise and I feared I would not make it through the many hundreds of individual references that needed to be read. "Get it signed," said the lawyers, "Tape the sessions." Given Ngarrindjeri attitudes to taping and that we were putting in ten- to twelve-hour days, this was not a practical strategy. Having people initial paragraph after paragraph of a 400-page manuscript was too like taking a deposition and bureaucratic exercises in which people place little faith. Instead, after the first few sessions, I found a simple tick (check) in the margin sufficed. It was visual and had the sense of "OK". I was impressed by how scrupulous people were. They would not read the words of others unless those words had been ticked off. The word was owned. Permission was needed.

As the manuscript filled up with page after page dotted with ticks, people began to talk with me about what others had said, to add their perspective, to provide more details, to confirm that I had indeed chosen to reproduce stories that spoke to core values and beliefs. Negotiations around the manuscript constituted an ongoing process and there was hardly a conversation when I was not being told something new. We'd be reading along and the story-teller would say: Now tell the story about so and so. "Turn the page," I was able to say on a number of occasions. It's there." Yes there is a sequencing to stories. We know that much? said one woman when she saw my weighty folder and all the ticks. That's what culture is? said another. We have plenty of that. At each of these sessions I would write directly onto the text. Read it back. More comments. Redraft. I wore out several of the eraser-tipped propelling pencils I was using. I wrote on the back of the page and keyed it into the text. By the end of the first week the manuscript had a life quite independent of me. More documents came out of back rooms; more stories. I had anticipated that people would be meticulous about reading their own prose, but I had not anticipated their preparedness to engage with me and my analysis and their interest in the structure of the book. They were taking the idea of feedback very seriously and there was an order to things. It was at this point that I knew I was no longer thought of by them as a consultant on an application under the Heritage Act. They were genuinely interested in what I thought, and how I had figured it out. If I was taking their ideas seriously, they would respect mine. I learned that not only were they gifted story-tellers and songsters, they were also interested in symbolic analysis. They could stand back and argue about the pragmatic and religious underpinnings of their beliefs. I recalled Tindale (1986b) writing in tribute to Milerum as a colleague, and as an anthropologist in his own right. The Ngarrindjeri with whom I have been working have also become colleagues. After four years of dealing with various experts, the media, legal system and anthropologists, they have developed sophisticated understandings of how they are represented by others and they have astute questions about how these images are constructed.

Despite my desire to make this project one in which we might all delight—and it has been a delight getting to know a number of Ngarrindjeri men and women—I have retained the right to final cut, so to speak. I have abided by the restrictions placed on certain categories of knowledge, as I am bound to do by a code of ethics that counsels "first do no harm", but it has been my decision as to what is included and how it is analysed. Of course, had I decided, on the basis of my research, that the society was bankrupt and had written in this vein, I would expect not to be welcome back. I would most certainly have exacerbated an already difficult research situation for anyone who might follow. But this is not my view of the society. I would not have chosen to pursue the writing of an ethnography had that been my position. I would probably have alluded to my work on the Ngarrindjeri Heritage Act application in an article and returned to the other research projects that I had put on hold in 1996. I began, as I pointed out in the Prologue, with a host of questions raised by the Ngarrindjeri application. I have continued to pursue these and have added others. I have done so not as a consultant but as one with a deep interest in social change, feminist ethnography and epistemologies, Indigenous peoples and Australian society. We all have reasons for undertaking research and writing. We all bring certain ideas to our projects. Thus, as well as making my methodological approach plain, I am also reflecting on how my interests, field experience, and training shape the weave of my analysis.

But I cannot leave it at that. As anthropologists, we become part of the ways in which access to knowledge is negotiated. Our field work dialogues generate ideas and histories. We find ourselves more at ease with some people rather than others. We make choices. We have resources, material resources, over which there may be some competition. At times we are trusted with privileged knowledge and such investments are not made lightly. We come to understand the underlying dynamics of the politics of knowledge in particular communities. Ian Keen (1994) walks a fine line in his analysis of Yolngu ceremony. How to talk about a system without breaching confidences and without undermining the authority of the key players by disclosing their strategies? "I cannot write in detail here about the actual content of esoteric knowledge, but the chapter will outline its structure," writes Ian Keen (*ibid.*: 227). This had also been my position in *Daughters of the Dreaming* in 1983. It was possible to understand the religious life of Aboriginal women without having to disclose the inner meanings of songs, symbols and stories. It is also my position on the Ngarrindjeri material. It is possible to know that certain stories exist and that they shape behaviour without being privy to the details. For instance, I do not need to know the details of the Easter story to know that the cross is an important Christian symbol.

In common with other oral cultures, the Ngarrindjeri place restrictions on access to certain places, knowledge and relationships. Thus believers must be prepared to abide by the rules and that includes not knowing, perhaps never knowing, the inner meanings and details of certain stories. Anthropologists may observe how these restrictions create hierarchies of knowledge, how certain individuals may then maintain authority and power over others; and they may come to appreciate why those others accept the "properties of conduct". One may believe in the power of a story, yet not know the details. For the anthropologist, questions such as to whom may I speak; who can see my notes; and what can I publish? are not mere pragmatics. They go the core of the politics of knowledge in Aboriginal societies, a politics which is conducted according to "properties" such as the relationships of the sacred to the profane, of men to women, of young to old, of family to family, and place to place. For nigh on two centuries these relationships have been shaped by factors beyond Aboriginal politics, but the contesting of the existence of women's knowledge in a number of public forums (the courts, the media, professional journals) has generated new concerns. How is dissent to be understood? What is the nature of belief? What constitutes knowledge and by whom is it legitimated?

Ngarrindjeri knowledge is no longer completely under the control of Ngarrindjeri. It has been recorded by a range of persons. Once written down, it is subject to new "rules" of access and to "foreign" protocols, such as laws concerning archives, Freedom of Information, and copyright. Once cultural knowledge is written down, it is endangered because then it can be read by inappropriate persons, who, on a "need to know" basis, may gain access to files. They do not need to demonstrate a right to know according to Ngarrindjeri conventions. They need only abide by Anglo law. This undermines the power of those who are responsible for the story, and their right to determine when a story is told and to whom. The value of the knowledge diminishes. This, in part, explains the antagonism of many Ngarrindjeri to research on their heritage in libraries and field research by anthropologists. They cannot do much about what has already been written down. Much of what is in existing sources is not material that they consider "open" and much of it they believe to be inaccurate, but they can do something about what is happening now. And they may well find that Australian law, in some respects, is beginning to recognise the relationship between knowers and the known. The addition of "moral rights" to the rights of a "creator" (i.e. writers and artists) in proposed moral rights legislation is one way of giving legal force to the relationship. Words and images are more than things to be protected as one would protect property. Not only must they be attributed, but the way in which they are used must honour the intent of the creator.

Side-bar Dialogues

The research and writing of this book entailed many different dialogues, some with Ngarrindjeri in person, some with lawyers, and others with colleagues. Each exchange had its own rules and conditions; each had its own sanctions. I have been as thorough as I can, but I do not claim to have worked with all Ngarrindjeri nor to have read every word written about Ngarrindjeri. There are people living further up the river I have not contacted, and there are people living in other states. There are the "dissidents" and the family who had been part of the Mathews application in 1996 to protect the proposed bridge site, but did not wish to be associated with this book. The bibliography indicates where I have been in the libraries and archives, but not all "gatekeepers" to collections dealing with the Lower Murray have been welcoming.[2] Further, I am all too aware of the divisions amongst Ngarrindjeri concerning social scientific research. These pre-date the Hindmarsh Island bridge proposal but are now indelibly stamped with its mark. There are those who believe that no good can come of committing their knowledge to writing; there are others who, increasingly, are of the opinion that the time has come for their knowledge to reach a wider audience than is possible within an oral culture. Also, there are some older people who are supportive of this project but who, for a number of reasons, including health and reluctance to expose themselves to ridicule in the media and courts such as they witnessed during the Royal Commission, are more comfortable communicating through their younger kin. Respect for one's elders, as I have pointed out, is a central value and it has many facets. As an elder, one does not need to be in the front-line if one chooses not to be. And, none of these positions is monolithic. Amongst those who favour more openness and work collaboratively with researchers, there are differences of opinion regarding the best way to proceed; and amongst the "dissidents", there are significant differences of opinion regarding the role of "traditional knowledge" or "Ngarrindjeri culture" in their lives.

As I mentioned in the Prologue, I had hoped to be able to spend some time with the "dissidents". This was not to be. I have had no direct dialogue with these women. Although initially well disposed, their lawyer, Nicolas Iles, after consultation with his clients, informed me they believed I had already made up my mind on the matter of "women's business" because I had been a consultant to the "proponent women". He stated that his clients had already been rigorously cross-examined during the Royal Commission and that I should consult the transcript of their evidence. In his view, his clients had been badly treated and did not wish to be questioned further. If I wanted to know what they thought, they were on the record for all to see.[3] My dialogue was to be restricted to written texts generated in a legal forum. I explained to Iles that I did not wish to discuss so-called "women's business" with them. Rather I wished to discuss life histories. I was writing ethnography, not a polemic about the Royal Commission. Of course anyone working in this area does so in the shadow of the bridge controversy, but I was no longer a consultant. I was pursuing questions I found interesting about contemporary Ngarrindjeri culture, not just the proposed bridge site and the "women's business". I was not engaged in a forensic exercise or a rehash of the Royal Commission. I gave his clients the option of reading what I had written about them before it went to the publishers. At his request I put this offer in writing.

At the time of our exchange I had not made up my mind regarding what his clients did or did not know. I still don't know, but I do know what is in the sources about "women's business". Were the "dissidents" aware of what Meyer (1846), Taplin (1859–79) and Tindale and Long (nd) had written about women's seclusion during menstruation and childbirth? I wondered. Did they know what the Berndts (1993) had written about girls' puberty rites? Had they seen the Angas drawing of the young girls on whose body the marks of these rites are visible? It simply is not true that there are no records of women's rituals that are under the control of women. That was not my invention. The existence of women's places and rituals has been noted from the earliest of observers down to the present. What this means for the particular issue of Hindmarsh Island is, of course, another thing. It requires context to understand. My mind was being made up on the basis of research not ideology. I was interested to talk with the "dissidents" about the same things that I had been discussing with others: weaving, songs, family and friends, favourite camping places, beliefs about burials, signs and sorcery, knowledge of bush medicine, *ngatji* and language. If they said they knew nothing of "women's business" or of Hindmarsh Island, then I would not have pursued them as experts on those topics, though I would have been interested to explore the significance of their beliefs with them.

After my exchanges with Iles in November 1996, I spoke in December with Dr Ron Brunton, an anthropologist who works at the Institute of Public Affairs and who has published a number of critiques of the anthropologists who have worked with Ngarrindjeri and on other contested sacred sites (Brunton 1995, 1996a, b). Brunton has undertaken no field work in Australia, but he was in regular contact with the "dissident women" and he volunteered that they had sought advice from him as to whether they should talk with me. Claiming not to know my politics, Brunton told me he had advised them against talking to me. He would, however, have encouraged them to speak with anthropologist Professor Jimmy Weiner of Adelaide University, whose politics he did know. That I am required to be of a particular political hue in order to gain an audience is surprising to say the least. In Brunton's view, Dorothy Wilson, Dulcie Wilson, Bertha Gollan, their relatives and friends showed courage and integrity without which the Royal Commission would not have been established: all they wanted to do was to tell the truth (Brunton (1996b: 8). Brunton (*ibid*.: 7) wrote of how he was the only anthropologist, apart from Jones and Clarke, who had "attempted to contact them and hear their stories".

"Why", Brunton asked me, "have you not spoken to the dissidents before?". Because, I explained, when I was under contract as a consultant, it would have constituted a conflict of interest. During the Mathews application I was not permitted to speak to a number of persons who had prepared submissions on behalf of the applicants in previous inquiries, nor could I speak with the anthropologists working for Mathews, or with the other parties. Many documents, even ones in the public domain, like Philip Clarke's doctoral thesis, were under an embargo. Speaking to the "dissidents", who were the clients of another party, was completely out of the question from January to June 1996. But it was now the end of 1996. I was no longer encumbered by that consideration. I hoped to meet with the "dissidents" in person, and to have them be the authors of their own lives. Perhaps, at that stage, I should have sought them out individually, but, if indeed they did not wish to speak to me, I thought that would constitute harassment. I am sure they could have contributed a great deal to my research and I had understood they were distressed that their opinion was not being sought. I had read elsewhere they had expressed some dissatisfaction with those who spoke only to the "proponents" and not to them. For instance, Dulcie Wilson (1996b) was distressed that the churches were supporting the proponents without hearing her side. In the *IPA Review* she repeated her concerns and added: "My own local television and radio station in Mt Gambier did not seek to have one interview with me, even though the dispute was making national headlines" (Wilson 1996a: 40-2). Journalist Chris Kenny (1996: 169ff.) complains that Doreen Kartinyeri would not be interviewed and cites (*ibid.*: 234-5) Bertha Gollan's criticism of the ABC and the churches: "They didn't consult us. Not one of us, did any member of any denomination come and speak to us." I can only say I tried.

Thus, in representing the dissidents' position(s), I am forced to rely on those documents which are in the public domain. This solution is less than perfect as the questions they have been asked and the contexts in which they have been asked are focused on Hindmarsh Island and "women's business". The situation is not conducive to developing a nuanced understanding of a culture as complex as contemporary Ngarrindjeri culture. The lawyer–client relationship consists of taking instructions and giving advice. Its aim is to construct a case. It contrasts with participant-observation field work, through which one establishes qualitatively different relationships. Unlike lawyers, anthropologists' communications are not covered by legal privilege and thus, potentially, our field notes can be subpoenaed. Establishing trust in the field relies on the personal relationships we forge rather than a legal relationship, and usually—although Hindmarsh Island threatens to be the exception —we are around for a lot longer than a lawyer on a case.

For well over a decade I have been arguing that as anthropologists we need to work towards promoting a more subtle understanding of anthropological practice amongst lawyers and the general public. At present, anthropologists who work in the applied field run the risk of having lawyers dictate their practice; of finding their "expert opinion" shaped by the rules of evidence and the demands of a particular case. Much of this was thrashed out in the 1970s in land rights hearings in the Northern Territory. Gender-restricted knowledge presented a problem, but various strategies were devised and where there was goodwill on all sides workable solutions were found (Bell 1984/5; Rose 1996; Keely 1996). The hearsay rule was relaxed. People gave evidence in groups, on site, and ritual performances became ways of demonstrating attachment to country, but disputed sacred site claims are contested in different ways. The very fact that they are in contention raises the volume.

I accept when I am working as a consultant that I am bound by certain legal constraints. If I find they violate my ethical code or would breach agreements into which I have entered in the field, I decline the work. This can have far-reaching consequences of which I am all too aware. But unless anthropologists can say no, I believe our professional status is compromised and in the long run that is to no-one's advantage. When I am funding my own research, as I am now, I do not expect to have to seek permission from lawyers who may have an interest in the outcome of my work. I see such a move as a dangerous fetter on free speech, and one that impinges on the whole society, not just those interested in Aboriginal affairs. I do not wish to be put in a position where I need to tailor my findings

375

or leave out compromising details. On the other hand I do not wish to be sued for millions of dollars, or find myself in breach of Section 35 of the South Australian Heritage Act. Prudence required that I have lawyers read the text and advise me regarding liabilities.

Respecting the Rules

Veronica Brodie: I wasn't going to tell anybody because it wasn't the right time . . . You have to earn the right to know the knowledge. Daisy Rankine explained to Jane Mathews why she could talk about some things but not others: We weren't allowed to speak out about what's under the waters or what's up in heaven and that something is holding me back now, the feeling I'm getting is very strong. There's a lot I can release, but I'm getting my sign. *Miwi* is what is holding us together with our knowledge and bringing it out. Albert Karloan, according to Tindale and Pretty (1980: 51), "gave his information freely and willingly to all who he felt would treat it with the respect it deserved". However, once on the printed page, this condition can not be honoured.

How cultural knowledge is generated, maintained, managed and transmitted; how responsibilities for and rights in knowledge are articulated; how access is structured; and how violations are punished—these lie at the heart of the survival of Aboriginal societies. Who knows what; who sees what; who hears what; what can be acknowledged as being known; with whom one might communicate; what is the significance of the restrictions; what is the nature of exceptions—these are all topics that anthropologists working with Aboriginal peoples in Australia have necessarily confronted. Knowledge is indeed power. It is a precious resource, jealously guarded. To understand the nature of the exercise of power in Aboriginal society, one needs to know something of the values, beliefs, and histories of groups and individuals. It is not a commodity to be traded in an open marketplace. Knowledge is embedded in social relations: those of gender, age, land affiliation, trade, ceremony, kinship and marriage. In this system access to knowledge is restricted and passed by word of mouth, and people move closer to the core of sacred knowledge as they demonstrate competence. Such a system needs clearly articulated rules for the transmission of knowledge (i.e., to whom, when, under what circumstances, with what consequences, and so on), and these rules must be accepted by participants in the system. This what I have called the etiquette of an oral culture.

"My word is my bond" is familiar enough as an expression. But pause for a moment and consider a world without written contracts, where history is carried by word of mouth; a society without libraries, dictionaries, encyclopedia and archives, not to mention computers and the Internet. In such a system, how can one know what is true? The human memory is fallible. Are such peoples without history? Clearly they value knowledge about the past, not just as flights of imagination or entertainment, but as potent signs for the living, as capable of influencing the future and as worth fighting over. Further, it is too simple to characterise an oral culture as hostage to individual human memory. There are objects, passed from generation to generation, that carry histories of the maker, resources and the land. Things as diverse as a century-old mat, a carved stick, a ritual basket, a canoe tree, a section of land that has been cleared, burnt out, hit by a meteorite or flooded, carry a history and cry out for interpretation. Does this mean that we have no check other than the word of the story-teller, or of the person who inscribes meaning on an event, thing, or relationship? I think not. Like good scholars everywhere, Ngarrindjeri cite their authorities and sources when they tell stories. When, they invoke the name of an elder as the author of a song, story, and design, they do so with respect. If the authority is no longer alive, the right to invoke that name falls to the descendants and, as we shall see, not just any member of the family. Place in family and connection to place are also important. This is not a world of oral anarchy. There are rules, and like rules elsewhere they are kept alive by being tested and confirmed, or contested and revised to accommodate "the conditions", as Isobelle Norvill said.

As we have seen, people are explicit about the respect due to their elders, the dead, and the land, but there are also other factors to be taken into account in understanding who knows what and who will own to knowing what. It is also important to know by whom one was told and when. Mostly these factors are not presented as "rules" in any formal or abstract sense, but if I asked why, I'd be given an explanation which entailed the balancing of structural factors, such

377

as closeness of blood relation, place in family, physical location, age, and gender, plus more individualistic reasons such as personal preferences, lifestyle and residential choices. The explanations arose quite naturally and others present would nod in agreement. Auntie Maggie was telling me how she had learned about certain aspects of Ngarrindjeri culture and why she could not talk about it in certain contexts. I just know what I was told by my grandmother. I was fifteen when she died in 1942. I sat around the campfire to get my knowledge and I kept it in my heart. Mummy Lola and Granny Koomi [Veronica's mother] were people who talked to me too. But I don't like to mention what I know in front of her grand-daughter, Janice Walker (née Rigney). Mummy Lola told Janice a lot of things and we leave it up to the families. I wouldn't be disrespectful and flaunt the knowledge. So stories may sometimes be told outside the family but the right to use the knowledge remains with the family. Invoking the authority of the elders must be done with respect, and those with whom their knowledge is being shared should be respectful also.

To speak of the business of others, one needs permission. Doreen Kartinyeri needed Eileen McHughes' permission to discuss her family lines; Jean Rankine needed the permission of Grace Sumner and Sheila Goldsmith to speak on behalf of the women at Raukkan. George Trevorrow agreed he knew Aunty Leila's *ngatji*, but added, One of her family can tell you that. That was her personal *ngatji*. That was hers. When I asked about using the photograph of George and his brother Tom scattering the ashes of Aunty Leila, I was told to ask her sister, not the person who took the photograph, not the persons in the shot. The person from whom one seeks permission depends on the nature of the question and the knowledge which remains embedded in the social relations of its production. In deciding whether she could speak on certain matters to Jane Mathews, Veronica Brodie asked Hilda Wilson (née Varcoe), the grand-daughter of Old Willy Rankine who was born on Hindmarsh Island. Old Willy Rankine (1866–1941) had married Clara (1865–1925), sister of Jacob Harris (Veronica Brodie's mother's father). Their daughters, Olive Rankine (1889–1966), Muriel (1890–1925), Ivy (1899–1966) and Beryl (1904–61) were the midwives. Hilda Varcoe,

Olive's daughter, married Robert Wilson (Veronica Brodie's father's father's mother's son's son). Veronica deduces that the knowledge of *putari* practice came through the Harris lineage: I think that's where Hilda Wilson's mother and aunty got the skills of the *putari*. It was from Clara when Aunty Ollie was growing up. However, the story which Veronica was seeking permission to use did not come from Aunty Hilda, but from Veronica's sister, Leila Rankine. "Why did you ask Aunty Hilda?" I ask Veronica. Having been entrusted with women's business, I have to respect what's there and I didn't know how much to tell. Hilda Wilson is what I regard as an elder, and before I did anything to upset her, I asked her. Veronica Brodie told me and she added that she sought permission of an elder with a blood line to the island. Hilda Wilson has chosen to speak through her younger women relatives, who have been protective and repeat only that which she has sanctioned may be shared. Even when she chose to sing "*Pata winema*", she did it through Major Sumner. Her family members were to be the beneficiaries of her knowledge.

One has to wait and show patience. Doreen Kartinyeri: I couldn't push my grandmother into telling me very much about things that she felt I shouldn't know. There were appropriate times at which certain knowledge was transmitted to young women. Judy Kropinyeri was told, Your aunty will tell you about women's business when you get older. And for middle age, as Sarah Milera explains: My mother died when I was fourteen. She was a powerful woman. Aunty Belle and Nanna Tinggie also taught me. I've had to suppress what I know. I can't say I know everything. Daisy Rankine, at sixty, is a young great-grandmother: My daughter has just turned forty-one years old and I haven't told her any of our tradition or lifestyle. She wasn't ready for the knowledge I had from my grandmother. *Pakanu* [Pinkie Mack] and George were raised as Karpeny and she told me a lot about her traditional lifestyle when I was just the age of fifteen. Ellen Trevorrow is willing to wait: A lot of things I wasn't taught, like Mum says, one day she's going to start talking about things with me. I actually missed out on a lot of sharing time at night, so I don't know what's going on, but I believe in my elders; I strongly believe in them. And I love them for what they're doing and I'm sorry that all of this has happened this way for my elders, because it's drained us all.

379

When I did ask, I was told I was a pig with big ears, so I was never allowed to ask, Jean Rankine tells me. But Gram—I say Gram, not grandmother, because I've got so much respect—she taught me to be the person I am today. She's given me strength. And my Gram told me there were things I would find out when I grew up, about certain places, and about women's things. But unfortunately I lost all my family so I never found out. So I know there is something there and I believe it, because she told me, as to finding out what it was, I don't know. Some admit to hanging around, staying quiet, and hoping that they would be allowed to stay. Doreen is recognised as being the one who did ask questions and found a way of doing so that was respectful. Grace Sumner: Doreen asked a lot more questions than I did. So I wonder if that's why she got taught more.

You need to know the personalities, says Vi Deuschle. Your grandparents wouldn't let you get away with being an "empty head". They were very strict. Albert Karloan, according to Catherine Berndt (1994b: 537), was eager to learn. Dreams and other clues singled him out as worthy of instruction. It was not sufficient to be told, or to be the member of an important lineage; other mundane and idiosyncratic factors intervened. Aptitude, attitude and availability are all considerations regarding who knows what.

Then there are things one can't acknowledge knowing until the older person has passed away. When the mother died the sister automatically took over, says Veronica Brodie, but she knows there are other factors. Back in 1969 Leila knew all this and I said, "Well, why didn't you tell me then?". She said, "Well, you know, we couldn't because of your lifestyle." It wasn't told to people who gossiped or women who gossiped; it was told to women who they knew would respect and hold the women's business at heart because of its sacredness—not because of the secrets of it, but because of the sacredness. And when I got up in the Royal Commission, I got up there to clear my mother's name. You can't talk about my mother like that. It's been a real heartache. This notion that one had to be a worthy recipient, to know how to keep one's word and to abide by the code of respect, is often cited as a reason some were not told about sacred matters. They were taught the cautions—that way they were protected—but the deeper significance and inner meanings were withheld.

380

Several of the "dissident" women mention that at Raukkan everyone knew everybody's business and that they were in and out of each other's houses all the time. So, they ask: "How could vital information about women's business have escaped our attention?". For instance, Rita Wilson, now in her late fifties and living in Millicent, looked back to the first twenty years of her life spent at Raukkan and asserted, "if it was 'women's business', all the women would know" (Stevens 1995: 268). Bertha Gollan, one of the leading "dissident" women, now in her late seventies, says that in the forty-five years she lived at Raukkan, she never heard anyone mention Hindmarsh Island and the waters around it as of "special or sacred significance to Ngarrindjeri people" (*ibid.*: 259). She ran errands for her mother, who did a lot of baking but, although she "would often stay and chat" with the older women, she "never heard any talk of 'women's business' and it was never suggested there might be any secret knowledge to be passed onto her" (*ibid.*: 258).

Bertha Gollan (née Wilson) was born 1920, the daughter of Charles Wilson and Mary Watson, whose father was Moandik from Kingston (Stevens 1995: 258); she has left few traces in the written record regarding her views on "traditional culture". We do not know what the old women with whom she chatted told her, only what they did not. There may be many reasons why she was not told, and without being able to talk with her it is difficult to know what constitutes "women's business" for her. One clue may lie in her endorsement of assimilationist ideals. Like her sister-in-law Dulcie Wilson, Bertha Gollan (Department of Education 1990: 163) in 1988 is quoted as saying, "I could honestly say I've never run up against prejudice and I've worked amongst white people and New Australians at the hospital and I was their equal." On leaving school Bertha Gollan worked as a domestic, and later she worked in the hospital at Point McLeay. I wonder whether she was paid the same rate as a white girl doing comparable work? Had she been a white girl growing up in South Australia she might have become a certificated nurse, or even a doctor. The Aboriginal Studies course guide (*ibid.*) suggests that some explain Bertha Gollan's experience "as due to the fact that she was fair-skinned and therefore met with less prejudice". Her perception of what constitutes "prejudice" can be queried; her experience cannot be generalised to other Ngarrindjeri, who most certainly have been subjected to prejudice. Like Dulcie Wilson, Bertha Gollan defines "equality" as "sameness".

Those people who grew up around large extended families off the mission appear to have heard a wider range of stories and to have learned the rules in concrete situations. Liz Tongerie: Our people who lived off the mission and were independent, they could speak freely of traditional things. For example I have been told a lot of things by Aunty Lola, I know other people have not been told. Growing up in fringe camps provided many opportunities to learn. George Trevorrow: We would hear our old people talking and get an understanding of the layout of our country. If there was a bit of a fire going and the old people were telling stories, sometimes they let us crawl up near their legs and lay down and listen to the stories, if they were meant for us. If they were not meant for us they would look at us like that and one look, you moved, you went away out of earshot from them because they were talking about business that you should not be hearing as a kid.

It is difficult for some stories to be told, and difficult for some to be heard. There are good reasons why some stories are not known by certain individuals and why, even if "known", are not repeated. Liz Tongerie said to me, Everyone does not have to know everything. A number of younger women say, with respect, and knowing they will be told when appropriate: We do not know what our elders know, but we believe them and support them. Or, Just because I don't know doesn't make it a lie. One does not claim to "know" until it is appropriate to do so; this moment, often ritualised in a formal handover, occurs when it becomes obvious that the senior person is near the end of her life. The persons on whom the knowledge is bestowed will already know much, but are not able to claim the status of knower until the appropriate time. Knowing the appropriate time may be a matter of reading the signs. When Aunty Maggie says, The ancestors are coming out and showing themselves, she implies, this is our sign to speak out. Aunty Daisy says her *miwi* is telling her to speak on some matters and observe silence on others.

The timing of the handover of restricted material, of knowledge that is dear to the elders, is contingent on a number of factors. In one ceremony I attended in central Australia, women who had rights in a particular dreaming "gave away" songs, dances, and ritual paraphernalia to another group of women resident some 320 kilometres away who had interests in the dreaming, but with reference to different sites. Through the handover ceremony, the "bestowers" made "public" (only senior women were present) the "gift". In fact the other women already knew a great deal about the songs, but they could not use them until given permission. The givers had been suffering "troubles", and through their actions hoped to restore peace in their community. Had one asked the newly enriched women before the handover what they knew, they would not have been forthcoming. In fact I had heard them deny they "knew" anything about that particular segment of the dreaming. "Knowing", and acknowledging that one "knows", are different things.

The Ngarrindjeri Aboriginal Studies course for secondary students, prepared with the assistance of elders such as Laura Kartinyeri and Leila Rankine (Department of Education 1990: 51), explains that one who obeys the laws gets knowledge and may achieve the status of elder; whereas one who disobeys will be punished and remain unimportant and ignorant. The "Teaching Guide" (*ibid.*: 12) cautions that some background will be needed before students begin questioning elders. "They will give information when they feel their audience are properly prepared to be told." I mention this publication because it is interesting that schoolchildren are being taught about the complexities of cross-cultural communications and the oral testimonies of elders, some now deceased; and because the material pre-dates the Hindmarsh Island debate regarding the transmission of knowledge in Ngarrindjeri society. Debates regarding the concept of "elder" run through the anthropological literature on Aboriginal society (Berndt 1965) and the Ngarrindjeri, with their *tendi*, being one of the few Aboriginal nations to have such a governmental structure, are of great interest. Despite the *tendi*, Ngarrindjeri elders, like authority figures across Australia, are persons of high standing in the religious domain. It is their knowledge and their meaning-making that marks them out as leaders.

383

If one wishes to learn, then one must be present, quiet and respectful. This is not an experimental system of learning. Children are socialised into respect for elders who are not to be second-guessed. Further, the consequences of undisciplined inquiry are known. It is dangerous to oneself and to loved ones. There are dangers in claiming to know when one doesn't, in lying, in speaking out of turn, in hearing things that are intended for others. It is not smart or clever to think one might be able to ease restricted information out of an elder. One may learn from one's nanna or aunt more often than from one's own parents, who have the daily responsibility for care. In my view the constant referencing of the authority of the elders and the ways in which their knowledge is held dear, respected, and protected against abuse, indicates continuity from one generation to the next. The "rules of respect" I saw in operation amongst the Ngarrindjeri are consistent with the ways in which the "old people" exercise religious authority in other parts of Australia where I have worked.

The ability to control access to knowledge is critical to maintaining authority and the integrity of the system. It is as critical as protecting the place about which the knowledge relates, because, in a sense, the place and the knowledge of the place fuse. Susan Woenne-Green (1987: 2), writing of Uluru and the necessity of ensuring that access to sacred areas is restricted, states that "it is not just physical access that must be restricted. Knowledge concerning such areas must also be preserved and protected from inappropriate use. It must, therefore, be restricted. . . . Information about a place is as much a part of it as the materials of which it is composed. The thing and its meaning cannot be separated". This insight has profound implications for the way we research, write about, and attempt to protect sacred places. Restricting knowledge has a purpose other than establishing who has authority within a particular community. Some people continue to "feel" the pull of their places; they are drawn to the sources of spiritual power, to the knowledge that is held dear. For them, this knowledge, hedged in with restrictive rules, is the knowledge that connects one to the land, to the ancestors, and to the key values of the society. Second-guessing what the sages know, cannot sustain the system. Rather, it is the belief that there is a core to the system, and the belief in that core of knowledge, that it is known to the sages of the society, that sustains.

Knowledge is currency, writes Eric Michaels (1985) of central Australian Aboriginal society; it circulates according to an economy of country, seniority, and gender (Rose 1994). And this is also true for Ngarrindjeri. The wealth of the society needs to be carefully managed, for if it were allowed to circulate freely, the society would be bankrupt. In the playing out of power with respect to access to resources, certain foods were made taboo, not because they were scarce, but to demonstrate that certain categories of persons could be disciplined and restrained. So, too, with knowledge. Everyone cannot know everything. If the authority of the elders is to be exercised, then restrictions, often seemingly arbitrary to an outsider, needed to be instituted. This system of restrictions and prohibitions is a way of teaching discipline and respect for the pronouncements of elders. The mystery of the restricted, of the sacred, may appear extremely trivial to outsiders, but from within the story it pushes one in a certain direction: for the Ngarrindjeri, it is in the direction of respect, and discipline, to follow rules without disputation; in other religious systems, it may be towards compassion, forgiveness, retribution, or transcendence.

With Respect to Gender

In listening to the the Catherine Ellis language tapes from the 1960s, I was struck by the differences in the styles of self-presentation of knowledge by the men and the women. The men will make statements of their authority while also stating they know little, whereas the women never make a statement about how much they know, but rather say they have forgotten, don't know, or offer a mumbled answer. James Brooks Kartinyeri, who died in Goolwa in 1963, says, I have given you the best I can. There is no other person around Point McLeay, or around the District or the Lakes who can give you what I've given. Ellen Brown, when asked if she knew any songs, said that she couldn't tell anything about songs; then some ten minutes later she sang the "*Pata winema*" song several times over. Ellis did not pursue Nanna Brown for her knowledge. Instead, there are many tapes of David Unaipon and James Brooks Kartinyeri. The form and style in which the men communicate their knowledge makes them easier and more satisfying "informants". It may be that the men have had greater contact with outsiders and therefore are more comfortable with the question-and-answer format, but it may also be that women's knowledge is better accessed through participating in their daily lives, through hearing stories told *in situ*, and through building relations of trust over time.

When it comes to knowledge that is "dear" to people, gender and age cross-cut in multiple and dynamic ways. Male elders and female elders know some things in common; some of it can be repeated, some not. In addition, there is knowledge that is gender-specific. Doreen Kartinyeri: Now, I've learned things about Ngarrindjeri men that I don't repeat, but I was told them for some purpose. I did say when they were doing the *Tjilbruki* Trail around the coast that's men's and then at Granite Island, they asked me to go in, but I said no. The Ngarrindjeri Committee was negotiating about that and then, not much long after, Hindmarsh Island came on the agenda for the government and so I felt, well, this time it is *mi:mini*'s [women's] so I've got to start speaking out. So I did. The disputes over development issues have forced people to articulate principles which hitherto had been implicit in behaviour. One mechanism for protecting gendered knowledge has been to maintain gendered spaces: that way, the question of what do you know of the knowledge of the opposite sex does not arise. The Royal Commission changed that situation.

George Trevorrow tried in every way possible to explain why he couldn't speak on the matter of "women's business" to the Royal Commission, but the rules by which he was abiding and those of the cross-examiner were not congruent. His knowledge of *ngatji* and what that meant for his understanding of the environment informed his concerns about protecting the waters around Hindmarsh Island: that was his "business". It complemented women's knowledge, but he respected the restricted nature of their "business". On 16 November 1995, David Smith, Counsel Assisting the Commissioner (G. Trevorrow 1995: 6423-6), sought clarification of what George Trevorrow knew and believed:

Q. But you didn't know anything about the content of the women's business.

A. No, I still don't know any of the content.

386

Q. It may be that a bridge to the island from the mainland would have no effect on—

A. It is still going through our waters.

Q. I beg your pardon.

A. It is still going through the waters.

Q. You don't say the waters is the women's business, do you?

A. I'm saying the importance of the waters.

Q. The importance of the waters is something to do with women's business, is it?

A. It very well could be, but it is important to the Ngarrindjeri culture because of the meeting of the waters. I didn't want to say this, but the place of the waters relates to what we call—the Ngarrindjeri people call Ngatji, which is each clan group's symbolic totem, so to speak. Those places like that is where these things breed, where they live, where they feed, all those things. You upset the totem area, you are upsetting everybody. But I don't expect you would understand that, the Ngarrindjeri Ngatji.

Q. Let me put a suggestion to you: what you are talking about is a disturbance to the environment. Is that right?

A. No, more than that. To what those Ngatji are to the people. They are not just animals and fish and snakes and things to us. They are real. They are more like people. Spiritual.

Q. So it is really nothing to do with women's business, is it?

A. It is combined with all those things. . . .

Q. You were saying that the island is significant because it is a place of women's business, and that a bridge linking the mainland to this place of women's business would be a desecration. That's what you're saying, is it?

A. Yes, there is no way—

Q. And you don't know, do you, by necessity, a jot about what the women's business is, do you?

A. (*Witness shakes head*)

Q. So you cannot tell us, can you, in what way a bridge would affect that spirituality of the island, which is women's business, can you?

A. No, I have no way in the world of trying to explain that to you. I never come here to talk about the women's business on that site.

Q. You are not in a position to talk to us about it, are you?

A. Because I can't, I'm a man.

387

Q. That's right. So your objection to the bridge really comes down to an environmental objection, isn't it?

A. No, a spiritual.

Rather than pursue the significance of *ngatji* as spiritually charged, and apparently ignorant of the enduring nature of the "friend, protector and countryman" translation, Smith returned to the theme of other cross-examinations: Aborigines had been co-opted by the environmentalists who were opposing the bridge. The ways in which interests of various parties may converge and diverge was outside the scope of the questioning. Any overlap became evidence of possible appropriation, manipulation, and fabrication. Smith (*ibid.*) continued:

Q. Is there some other spiritual aspect to the island which would be affected by a bridge, is there, not women's business?

A. I just finished talking to you about it, Ngatji related.

Q. I want to put a label on it so we can understand it. Is it the case that what you are talking about—that is, that a bridge cannot go to the island—is to do with some other spirituality of the island, not women's business?

A. I'm talking about my business.

Q. Can you tell us as much as you can about that.

A. I said it just now, N-G-A-T-J-I.

Q. Which is what you are talking about, is a question of protecting the environment from a lot of people coming to the island and ruining it. That's what it is, isn't it.

A. You interpret it as environment, I don't. We have different interpretations it seems. We cannot, as Aboriginal people, separate environment and culture. They go hand-in-hand.

Q. In this sense, that you are at one with the conservation movement, aren't you, who were interested in stopping the bridge to protect the birds, the wetlands, the natural habitat that's provided for bird life on the island.

A. I doubt very much whether they would know much about Ngarrindjeri Ngatjis. They wouldn't know nothing.

Q. That's much the same sort of argument though, isn't it?

A. No, nowhere near it.

Q. You want to protect the environment.

A. Nowhere near it.

Q. The Ngatjis, that is the bird symbols and totems for the clans and people, are in fact the wildlife, aren't they?

A. As you view them, yes.

Q. Why are they different from—

A. Because—no, I can't talk to you about that. It is plain to see you would never understand that anyway.

Q. I am suggesting to you that your objection to the bridge, in the end, boils down to really protecting the island from too many people coming onto it and the degradations that would lead to in terms of wildlife, plants and that sort of thing. That's what it is about, isn't it.

A. Well, that's what you are calling it.

Q. You say it is more than that, do you?

A. Yes.

That men and women may share an interest in protecting a place, but appeal to different stories, or aspects of a story, in explaining their concerns has been well documented in Northern Territory land claims. Important stories and sites often have a women's side and a men's side. There are ceremonies that have a women's side and men's side. That is the nature of complementarity. George Trevorrow would not speak of what Doreen Kartinyeri knows and she would not speak of what he knows. Yet each knows the other has their own business and it remains that. Jean Rankine explained how in her family this gendered knowledge is transmitted: Both Henry and myself feel that the old people have passed something on to us. My daughter, my children, will know everything, especially my daughters. When I leave this world, they'll know. I'm passing it onto them and Henry is passing things onto his sons and grandsons. I'm passing it onto my daughters and grand-daughters. The Berndts (1993: 363-4) record the role of the father to teach the son and the mother to teach the daughter. When there are violations, if the father doesn't punish the son, others will. This is still the case. In the case of a young unmarried woman who has a child, thereby demonstrating she has not heeded her mother's teaching, she is ridiculed. The young man, however, is flogged. The sanctions, like the teachings, are gendered.

389

Doreen Kartinyeri has also tried to explain the law which is specifically women's knowledge: Grandmother's lore is never tell a man and that's my teaching from a young girl. Maggie Jacobs: I mean I can't say those things to a man. Veronica Brodie: We're breaking a traditional law by telling it. It was never told to men. Doreen Kartinyeri continues: The "grandmother's lore" is the stories passed on from mother to daughter and it comes from the grandmother. I never heard Point Pearce women say that, only the Raukkan women. Aunty Rosie said, "Whenever I tell you, don't go *yanun* [talking] to the *kornis* [men], never do this. You must promise me you'll never do this." And, I have tried to fulfil that promise. It is important when we say "grandmother's lore" as that gives the connection between mother and daughter, but it's not always the actual mother. Pinkie Mack's family had daughters all the way and Louisa was old when she died and Pinkie too. If one woman had all sons, those sons would have wives. It would still come from the grandmother, go over to the in-law side and come back again. Mutha Bess [Rigney née Gollan; Matt Rigney's grandmother], she had all sons, no daughters. So the story would have been passed down through their wives. It has to go through a woman. And I could name all my uncles, their children would have learnt the stories from their mother that came down to the daughter-in-law, so it was still the grandmother's lore.

Eunice Aston (née Sumner) explains an even more complex set of considerations of kin, knowledge and respect. It involves a discussion amongst sisters Nell, Pearl and Mary regarding which of the grand-daughters might be told the Seven Sisters story. Nell and Pearl have no daughters, but Mary, the youngest, has three, and Eunice is the daughter of the youngest, Jessie Sumner. Eunice did not have seniority, but she was present and interested. I was starting to be told the story of the Seven Sisters by Aunty Pearl, but I was the grand-daughter of Mary, the youngest sister of Nell and Pearl. I got told a bit, the beginning of the story of the stars, but that was the end of the learning until I was a lot older. Aunty Pearl was telling the stars to me; and Aunty Nell was disputing her right to tell it. Aunty Pearl said I could be told because I was the only daughter who was home. She said, "They're not here, they're learning the white man's way." My mother had older sisters, Mary and Fran, and they had daughters. So they should have learnt before me. Thus the rule that knowledge passes through the eldest daughter

390

may have to be varied to accommodate circumstances, but this will not be done without contestation.

The lines of transmission of knowledge that Doreen Kartinyeri describes as the grandmother's lore also appear to underwrite the system of "royal titles" in use in the nineteenth century. Under this system important leaders were known by the title "King" or "Queen" and the handover to the next generation was formalised. It is not possible to say how much these titles are an adaptation of the system of governance known as the *tendi*, but it is clear that the individuals who bore the titles were knowledgeable and highly respected. Daisy Rankine's grandmother was known as Queen Louisa, and the title passed down the generations to Laura Kartinyeri. In 1987, on September 5, she was eighty-five, we had a big ceremony in Meningie, and the title "Queen" was bestowed on her. "What does the Queen have to do?" I ask Aunty Daisy. She has to keep the traditions alive, hold onto the sacred beliefs, genealogies, and she needs to know when to bring it out into the open. Aunty Daisy currently has permission, but she is not yet the holder of the title, which is with her aunt Wilhemena.

The transmission of these "royal titles" was noted in the *Register* of 11 May 1927, where Ethel Wympie Watson (maker of the 1939 sister basket) explains how she inherited the title from her aunt "Queen" Catherine Gibson and speaks of the accompanying ceremonies. My Aunt Catherine told that when she was made Queen, there was big doings. Days of dancing, and making feast, and all the wurlies full of people. Then she wore some native beads, and the chief one of the tribe made long talk, and there was much corroboree. So she became head of us all. But when I was made Queen, it was not so big a time. We went away back into the bush, and there were night fires and corroborees, and I wore the beads too. I have already heard of the beads from Shirley Peisley, who remembers them as a significant part of ceremonies.

The ceremony for "Queen" Ethel sounds very similar to Aunty Daisy's account. It appears that, as with her lineage, the title goes from mother to eldest daughter, through the sisters and then to oldest daughter of the oldest of that sibling set. I asked Doreen what she knew of these royal titles: I asked Aunty Rosie about Queen Louisa at Raukkan and King Tommy as Point Pearce. She said we never had any royalty, only elders, but some of the first ones who ever communicated with whitefellas were given the title and that's where the "Kings" and "Queens" come from. She told me, "You might come across some photographs of the old people with a plate, like the shape of a half moon, around their neck. You'll see it and know." It was quite a long time till I saw a photograph with it on. Queen Ethel got the title from Queen Catherine, she took over. Aunty Laura got the title "Queen of the Ngarrindjeri" in 1987. It is a big honour and you would have to know as much as possible about the women's side of stories and ceremonies and know all the women's stuff and respect towards other issues. Clearly the titles "King" and "Queen" are colonial artefacts, but the relationship that is being negotiated is not. As we saw, at the Sturt Re-enactment in 1951, Pinkie Mack exercised Karpeny authority in keeping the songs and story alive. New forms, especially ones that were pleasing to the colonial powers, were often grafted on to old ideas. These complex processes require dynamic models of social change.

Taking Time and Talking in Riddles

It could take three months, three years for them to tell you that one story complete, Neville Gollan explains. You'd be invited in and given a little bit of knowledge and depending on your behaviour, if they thought you were worthy, you'd be given the stories. Not all were given stories. When it was men's business, if they thought you were worthy, it would be, "Come here, we want to talk to you for a minute," and they'd tell you something. And they'd leave you at that and they'd pass the word. I don't know how they did it. They'd say, "Don't you remember what they spoke about down there?" and if you said, "No," there was no more said and you would know no more. Step by step, with the elders waiting to see if you comprehended before taking the next: it is an apt analogy, given the belief that one is being guided towards greater enlightenment, to decoding the riddles that a person such as Leila Rankine was said to employ. George Trevorrow: Like I said, I spent a lot of time with her up and down the Coorong living and camping and making educational things for, you know, and she was able to tell me a lot of things. She never spoke straight out and told me things. She was one of the elders that spoke almost in riddles. She would say something to you if she had any concern. You'd have to go away and think about that. Then the answer would come to you later, what she really meant.

I hadn't thought about it before, but that's what she was teaching me about. I had to wait to be older before I understood. I have heard women say that over and over. Veronica Brodie was visiting Encounter Bay: I'd never seen a whale in my life and there were three of them. Their big tails were going up in the air, and smashing down, and all of a sudden this came to me, you know, what Leila was talking to me about and I felt that something was finally coming back to the Ngarrindjeri women at last and the story has got to be told. We have to start telling it again because certain things are coming back. But I can't tell it while that male Minister is there, and it's a beautiful story, you know. Liz Tongerie's memory was jogged by the tapes: I was listening to the tapes of Aunty Lola and Uncle Ron being interviewed by Steven Hemming in the 1980s and I want to transcribe them. Some while back I went down there to Kingston and collected plants with them. We had labelled all the plants, but when we came back to the house, I just left them at the back door, and when I left, I forgot them. I kicked myself afterwards. I was so angry with myself. I wanted to photograph them before they lost their colour and now all I have of them is what is in my head. But now, when I hear the names of the tape, I can recall that picture in my head.

Eunice Aston found similarities between her knowledge and that of stories she was reading. I got half the story of the Seven Sisters from my aunty, and then I saw a book at school, and I thought, "This is what Aunty Pearl was telling me," and I told my father, and he was upset because he couldn't tell me. And then my grandmother died, so I couldn't learn from there. I was thinking, there's a lot more to this than is in the book; the book was only one page. It just said how the girls went off, and they then were rejoined and went to heaven. Knowledge acquired in fragments is sometimes recalled later when another event calls it to mind; when the significance of the story is grasped; or when the person has matured sufficiently to recognise the meaning of the story.

Story-telling is not a passive activity. All those present are part of the process of finding meaning. For example, when Henry Rankine retold the story of the three waves for me, he told it in the style of his mother: there was the account of the danger and its present-day relevance. Making explicit the significance of the story for those present is part of the responsibility of the story-teller and it is one that Ngarrindjeri story-tellers, I have heard, take seriously. At the end of a story, which concerns a past event, there is a lesson drawn for the living. It is the "same story", but it is told in a way that is sensitive to the needs and interests of the audience. I have now had the opportunity to hear a number of stories recounted by Ngarrindjeri elders, sometimes the same story by the same person, and some even concerning occasions on which I was present. I am struck by the way in which the stories are grounded in the specificities of person, place and time, while illuminating the moral universe. To strip off these details as editorialising is to miss the significance of the telling. Through story-telling, the oral culture can be reinvigorated, absorb new elements, and bring them within Ngarrindjeri control. A story which refers to a house, a motor car, store-bought food is not ipso facto "non-traditional". Rather, it illustrates the vitality and capacity of the culture to change, just as language absorbed new items in the nineteenth century.

Story-telling is not just about content. It is, David Unaipon points out, more like a dramatic performance and it contains the truths of his people. In the Preface to his 1924–5 manuscript, he writes of stories handed down orally for thousands of years: In fact, all tribal laws and customs are, first of all, told to the children of the tribe in the form of stories, just as the white Australian mother first instructs her children with nursery stories . . . I have used the simplest forms of expression, in order that neither the meaning nor the atmosphere may be lost . . . The Aboriginals are great story-tellers. The *Mun-cum-bulli* (the wise old man) telling the story puts in every detail. [Acts, gestures, dramatises, intonation] . . . He leads his hearers from point to point in the story. A little simple legend told to the tribe under primitive conditions would take all the evening to relate. The Aboriginals have a myth connected with nearly all the constellations, and bright stars in the heavens. No wonder the story-tellers of today find the written record to be lacking. It fails to engage the reader in this interactive process of finding meaning.

I am reminded of the homilies I have heard delivered by various speakers in the chapel at the college where I teach. I was not raised Catholic, but I attend the mass at the beginning of the school year and at graduation. It is an opportunity to be part of the community life of the college and the homily is instructive in many ways: the choice of text and homilist, the mode of exposition and the congregation response. Present are proud parents, expectant students, teachers (lay and religious), and watchful administrators. In the homily one hears "serious talk" about living together. It is not only the homilist who moulds the message: the listeners interpret what they hear according to their experience, needs, and knowledge. This is no less an authentic religious experience for the range of readings of a text by different homilists and the range of responses by those listening. Even with a religion that holds the written text to be the word of the divine, there is a place for reflection and shaping of the message by those present.

The Trouble with Books

Eileen McHughes: If it is printed by a white person, no offence, but if it is printed by a white person, then they believe it, but they won't believe us if it's oral. Veronica Brodie drew the distinction between written and oral traditions in a different way. Speaking of her mother, she said: She believed in their religion, but they loved their culture and they never let go. In Veronica's words: They're beautiful things and they make you wise and then you appreciate Ngarrindjeri culture.

For believers, the power of the stories is overwhelming. To be in the presence of such truth should, they reason, be sufficient. How can one hear the story of the Seven Sisters, or *Ngurunderi*, or *Nepelli* and not be awed? These are precious gifts of wisdom from the old people, heirlooms to be cherished. Henry Rankine, like many of his contemporaries, expresses a preference for knowledge handed down from generation to generation: I didn't get this from books, I got it from my mother. Whitefellas want to make everything transparent, but I was taught if you could see through someone, they're no good. Eileen McHughes points out she knows things that are not in the published sources: I learnt about *thumpamarldi* from my grandparents. My grandmother Connie, on the Varcoe side, had an uncle called Old Wongyu. Now, I reckon he must have come from over the west, because she said about this woman that was out after dark and got caught by mistake. Old Wongyu made this woman better. He got this glass or something from out of that woman's head. I believe that it was one of Aunty Gracie's relations. So that's not even in a book, is it, Aunty Grace, so how could I read about it? Maggie Jacobs agrees: I don't read much at all and I mean I did know about what Veronica said about the beginning of that story. That's her story.

Sarah Milera also knows she knows of matters that are not in books: My knowledge comes from the law of the *Rupelli*. Ronald and Catherine Berndt still didn't get it. The last *Rupelli* died in the 1970s, not in the nineteenth century. He was our protector and no-one would persecute him. He was always there for us kids. George Koolmatrie had it from the Manggurupa law. He was a law man. Serious matters are not in the Berndt book, but they are things that people know. I know, because every day I get a message. I wrote the story about the fish, the *pondi*, and *kondoli* and *thukapi*—it's a traditional story of the Ngarrindjeri. Most Ngarrindjeri have seen *A World That Was* (Berndt *et al.* 1993), but few own a copy. At $69.95 (when it was in print) it was beyond the reach of most Ngarrindjeri. Daisy Rankine: I was too poor to buy one, but my children bought me one, for my birthday, because my grandmother is in that book, but it was stolen out of my house and I can't afford another one. I was just glancing through it, but I'm not one to sit down and have a good study on books you know. Most say they haven't read the book. They gave up on the genealogies. They were turned off by the "sexy" stuff. Not that this generation are prudes, but that is not how they wish to be represented to the outside world. Jean Rankine reads Taplin and says she loves it. The descendants of David Unaipon have copies of his material and point to his accomplishments with pride. Most respect the Tindale materials, but also fear that some of his data should not be in the public domain; that the details are too close and too precise. When I was checking the transcript of what people had told Jane Mathews, and asking if I could use certain stories, a number of people expressed the view that they knew what they had said and stood by it. George and Tom Trevorrow read bits of theirs, and I read parts to them. Both said, "It's OK", and then added parts that addressed the topics we were discussing at the time. Tom said, "I'm not much for reading," but he remembered exactly what he had said.

When knowledge comes from a book, people say so, but more by way of having found something that supports or clarifies a story they have from their old people, than as a discovery of a new fact. Even

396

Doreen Kartinyeri, who is an experienced researcher, would take the word of a respected elder, over that of written sources. Many Ngarrindjeri point to examples of the inadequacy of the written record, and these inaccuracies challenge the right of the descendants of the "old people" to be the authors of their own lives. It is disrespectful to ask if an elder knows of what he or she spoke. When it comes to genealogies, the records of anthropologists may paint quite a different picture from that of a family member. Doreen Kartinyeri has shown that these records are fallible but, once written, the "fact" has a life of its own. It can be photocopied and broadcast widely. Ngarrindjeri can and do discriminate amongst the written sources. Doreen Kartinyeri, for instance, places greater trust in Tindale's material than in the Berndts'. She knows the conditions under which each was recorded and the manner in which it was written up. Neville Gollan gave me a good critique of the historical literature on the wreck of the Maria in 1840, but he preferred his father's version which drew on first-hand accounts. The bases of his opinion on the sources were scholarly. Many times I noticed that a Ngarrindjeri elder was asking me the same questions a rigorous historian would ask about documents. And, it was not just the who, where, and why of it. There were consequences for the living in terms of whose voice has been heard, heeded, repeated, and by whom.

There is a false security in going to the written record to settle disputes, yet such texts have to be seen in terms of the conditions under which they were produced. For instance, my father's birth certificate had the wrong date on it because his birth was registered by his father, who confused the day of the week on which he was born. It is not a mistake that most mothers are likely to make. In our family we always took grandma's word for it, over the document from the Register of Births, Deaths and Marriages. But then, when she died, we found she had mis-stated her birth year and was in fact five years older than we thought. Her reason for understating her age was not a matter of bad memory. Perhaps as a young married woman she had not wanted to be known as older than her husband. Perhaps in her middle years she had wanted to hold on to her youth. I never had the opportunity to ask her many sisters about the story of their much younger sister.

Staying Silent: Speaking Out

We leave pieces out to protect it, Neville Gollan says of visits to special places he has made with those he does not wish to incorporate within his world. George Trevorrow (Department of Education 1990: 25): We'll always hold back some, that way we got something, otherwise you drain it all out and it's all gone. Daisy Rankine says of her Nanna Laura: So when any of us would mention women, she would start hitting a tin washing dipper. She didn't want her voice recorded. I left it up to her what she was going to do. No-one else to speak but herself, you know. Veronica Brodie said of the story Betty Fisher recorded from Koomi, Veronica's mother: She would never tell a white woman anything she didn't need to. And I hear: Mummy Lola was very strict, even with language. She wouldn't have her photograph taken. Now there are different reasons for these various silences. Some have to do with restricted knowledge, some with the fear of ridicule; all have to do with maintaining control over how widely known certain things may be. Vicki Hartman and Eunice Sumner spelt it out for me. Vicki: So much has been taken away already. They'd say, "I'll tell you so much, no more." It was a way of being respectful and respecting knowledge. Eunice: It was a way of protecting us too. They were being careful so we would not be ridiculed.

Strategic silences and diverse reasons for maintaining them were noted by a number of early observers, and they resonate with those given in the late twentieth century. The Lutheran missionaries Teichelman and Schürmann (1840: v) complained that their 1840 studies with the Aboriginal people around Adelaide were hampered because of the "extreme reluctance, for a long time, to inform the inquirer". Taplin (11/12/1869) writes that there are activities that "They don't want me to see." His son Fred Taplin (30/3/1889) stated: "Dread of ridicule makes it almost impossible to obtain correct information from the semi-civilized black as to manners and customs of his forebears." Ramsay Smith (1924: 191) observed: "The Blackfellow waits until he is asked about things, or until he gets a concrete subject to form a text." That Ngarrindjeri elders keep their own counsel is not new, but were they simply withholding from whitefellas or also withholding from the next generation?

In 1988 Laura Kartinyeri (Department of Education 1990: 153) suggested it was both: The old people never used to teach the young people. They wanted to stop the white people learning. They wouldn't let us say anything. Referring to what the old people had told her she said, Never tell anything to grinkaris [whitefellas]. Secrets. Everything had to be secrets (Salgado 1994: 43). Annie Koolmatrie (Ely 1980: 32-4) remembers that information was withheld from her generation. When her parents sat down to talk with their friends in language, "we were never around. You were seen and not heard." She and her husband Jack speculate that the older ones didn't want to talk and even when they asked, they say "let it slide, see. We couldn't go back to our old laws again" (*ibid.*). Doreen Kartinyeri's Aunty Rosie was wary of whitefellas. In the late 1950s Doreen Kartinyeri recalls a visit by Fay Gale to Point Pearce. Doreen later worked with Fay at Adelaide University, but this first meeting was when Fay was doing her doctoral research. The women knew that Gladys Elphick, a respected Narrunga elder, was bringing a white woman to Point Pearce and they had organised a meeting. Doreen, ever eager to learn, decided to attend. On the way to the office she called into see Aunty Rosie, who did not wish to be part of the meeting and warned Doreen not to talk to white women. Out of respect for her elders, Doreen did not say anything and thankfully was not asked anything. She was young, after all, and they were talking about the history of the place. After the meeting, in all truthfulness, she was able to report to her aunt that she had not spoken to the white woman. On that occasion Aunty Rosie's knowledge was not recorded. Some seven years later, when interviewed by Cath Ellis (1966: LA 106), Aunty Rosie provided answers to a series of questions, but the tape does not capture the wealth of knowledge reported by her close family.

The mission forced a great deal of activity underground and the assimilationists rewarded those who espoused Western ideas. But there was resistance. There was subversion. The withholdings were strategic not wholesale. There were old people who invested in the generation of elders born in the 1920s and 1930s, i.e., the current generation of elders. The Berndts thought of Pinkie Mack as the "last generation" but it would appear her daughters knew many things that were not shared with outsiders. Cath Ellis (1963–5: 15) said that David Karpeny, forty years old in 1971, was a "typical Karpeny in his unwillingness to part with any information". She was aware he was withholding information from her. It appears that Laura Kartinyeri was of a similar disposition to David Karpeny and was being true to her family tradition when she was interviewed for the Education Department publication. Tonkinson (1993: xxi) likens the withholding of information to a "crisis of confidence" of the elders regarding the transmission of knowledge to the next generation. "It is clear", he writes, "from hints provided by the Berndts . . . that the elderly Yaraldi from whom they gathered data on the old traditions had not been disseminating this information among their fellows." In the absence of a ceremonial context which could vivify the meaning of certain stories, songs and symbols, the old people had limited ways of passing on certain knowledge to the next generation.

For instance, Pinkie Mack was a great singer and had learned *pekeri* songs from her father's father and father's sister, but was not allowed to sing them until she was a mature woman (Berndt *et al.* 1993: 215). By this time there were few left with whom she could communicate. So when she told the Berndts (*ibid.*: 154) that she didn't remember her initiation songs, what did this mean? It is hard to tell from their depiction of the exchanges. Was it that she didn't want to talk? It was an inappropriate context in which to talk? She didn't care to remember? With whom would she have sung those songs? With whom would she have spent long hours preparing for ceremonies and rehearsing the songs? It is in these contexts that meaning is accessible. According to Catherine Berndt (1994a: 639-40), Pinkie Mack said "she was lonely for the past" and "after Albert Karloan's death, the only remaining fluent Yaraldi speaker". She may have been observing a restriction of knowledge out of respect for the dead, or she may have felt, given the assimilation era and the operation of the Aborigines Act, that there was no point in remembering. She did express some ambivalence to the Berndts about the value of recording her memories (Tonkinson 1993: xxii). Tonkinson is careful to reiterate that the Berndts make no claims to comprehensivity; that they acknowledge and discuss the limitations on their study as "memory culture", not participant-observation; that a comparative work was not their intent; and that the memory of their several informants was fallible (*ibid.*: xix–xxiii). The upshot is that we don't know what Pinkie Mack knew of her initiation songs.

Nor can the Berndts tell us what Pinkie Mack told her daughter, and what her daughter could "know" from the context of her mother's and other elders' behaviour. She had the *maraldi* bones, which Aunty Daisy said were handed down from daughter to grand-daughter. The Berndts were not present at the times when stories were told, sites visited, and mats made. However, we know from Pinkie Mack's grand-daughter that a great deal of information has been passed down, and is being played out in the changing circumstances of the late 1990s. The knowledge was not buried with Pinkie Mack. Daisy Rankine has precise knowledge of clan boundaries; the power of *miwi*; the grandmothers' lore; the sacred knowledge associated with weaving; and is reflective about her complex of Christian and Ngarrindjeri stories.

There may have been a "crisis of confidence" in the 1940s—there may even have been a deliberate breaking of the circle—but knowledge did survive and today it is highly valued by many Ngarrindjeri. Further, for a number of reasons, some elders are moving to share and open up what they know and to make it available to the next generation. Daisy Rankine: We held onto our knowledge, but the time has come for us to speak out. To bring out what has been hidden for so long. Some of our people, the families, were afraid to speak out, but it is time that our voices should be heard. We are the descendants of our loved ones and it is time to speak out to help our younger generations and to have something for them for the future. The same as what I'm doing, as what was given to me. The knowledge that is handed down from generation to generation. There is, I think, a shift under way, and it owes much to the contesting of knowledge that has been transmitted orally and "investigated" by the Royal Commission. As a counterpoint to this move of certain elders to begin sharing their knowledge with their young people a little sooner, is a move to hold closer and place restrictions on certain knowledge being shared with white people.

It is not fear of ridicule that informs some of the current holding back, but the demonstrated inability of outsiders to observe the rules; to show respect for the old people, the land, and the dead; to maintain knowledge boundaries drawn by age, gender, family, place, and so on. The breaches of etiquette are not a light matter, and they are not matters for litigation. The breaches endanger the lives of others. In the face of grossly offensive behaviours, the elders simply withdraw. George Trevorrow gave up trying to explain his beliefs to the Royal Commission. Daisy Rankine was deeply distressed about the way in which the name of her aunt, Pinkie Mack's daughter, was being besmirched. My late aunt was calling for me and Sue Lawrie wouldn't have known that she was calling for me. And all that time it was so hurtful for me when I read in the Royal Commission that she needed me to be there. She always warned me there were too many strange people around her, coming into the community. She was still living in the fear with what she grew up with, holding back her knowledge, her sacred beliefs. We all hold that sacred knowledge of our parents, who we respect. Their names were never mentioned after they passed on, which is one of the spiritual sacred beliefs of our respect for our leaders, our late loved ones. We keep things quiet.

It is easier to keep track of who knows what in an oral culture than in a culture that relies on written texts. If all important knowledge is transmitted orally, it is possible to know who has been told what. One knows who is present and, should there be any careless talk, one will know that it was someone who was present who has spoken out of turn. This control over one's word plays out in different ways. I have seen people ask others to leave if it was considered inappropriate to talk in their presence. I have seen speakers simply glide onto another topic so gracefully that, unless you knew the body language and other clues, the move would be almost undetectable. I have seen women blanch or stiffen when asked a question that would require a breach of their code to answer. Usually the indication is polite: "I can't talk about that," or "Ask so and so". Signals that a topic should not be pursued are delivered with dignity, almost apologetically. I'd love to be able to tell the story, Veronica said one day. It is so beautiful, but I promised I wouldn't. The knowledge that they hold dear and sacred is believed to be so powerful that, if one were to be told, and was capable of listening, one would stand in awe and wonder of the beauty and majesty of the story. Unfortunately, over

402

the past four years in particular, not all who have heard have listened, and the disrespect for the old people has been painful to endure.

On several occasions when Aunty Maggie has been asked a question about women's practices that could open up an area into which she will not stray, she says, by way of alerting the questioner of the dangers, Well, I mean, I can say that, the women had one side, you might as well say women initiating, and the men had the other side see. Tom Trevorrow, when asked about women's knowledge, said, It's for them to say, if they're going to. George said, I can't go any further explaining. That's for women to talk about now. Both men and women react strongly to any suggestion that this line might have been crossed. George: If any of the men, or myself would have said anything in regards to personal things of our women, we would have been severely dealt with and forever more and we'd have been recognised as those sort of people. It is not only Doreen Kartinyeri who becomes angry when a man speaks out of turn; other men are also dismayed. One may apologise, but the harm cannot be undone.

Usually, if knowledge should not be shared, or if it is inappropriate to be present in a certain decision-making forum, people simply absent themselves. During the taking of the Aboriginal evidence in the Warumungu land claim, 1984, there was one site in which three groups expressed rights. The judge sought to solve the problem by convening a meeting with all three to settle it once and for all. Politely, but quite resolutely, certain people simply absented themselves and pleaded out-of-town business. The rights in the area were not going to be settled by a round-table negotiation convened by an outsider. Veronica Brodie is clear that there are questions she doesn't ask, shouldn't ask, and won't ask. I don't know what Doreen knows, and I'd swear that on my dead son's oath . . . I did tell them [the Royal Commission] I knew something, but I didn't volunteer the information.

One reading of the silences has been to equate "I don't know" or "She didn't say" with ignorance. But the silences of the Karpeny clan cannot be read as ignorance. Laura Kartinyeri was indicating that the "old people" rarely tolerated questions from youth. There are silences and there are lacunae. We need to exercise care in attributing significance. Radcliffe-Brown (1918: 240-1) cautions that, just because neither he nor Taplin was able to document an organised totemic ritual, "this must not be taken as evidence that such a ritual does not exist". Iris Stevens (1995: 274) reported that Vena Gollan did not know the word "Kumarangk" for Hindmarsh Island. That may be so, but there are middle-aged people alive today who learned the name from their elders and the name is in Berndt *et al.* (1993: 15) and in Tindale's place-name cards. Vena Gollan's lack of knowledge is not sound evidence that the name is of recent origin. Bertha Gollan could tell the Royal Commission nothing of the practice of *putari* although she had delivered many babies. Was there nothing to be known, or was information being withheld?

Doreen Kartinyeri: The women did the training for the girls. Mothers do the same for their daughters, about menstruation, hygiene, preparing for the first birth and the stories are passed down. My grandmother tried to tell me, but I said that I already knew. When I was put out to work for white people. When I went back to Raukkan my Nanna warned me about what I wasn't to do and I said I know. She used the Aboriginal word but I had the same information from both sides, that doesn't make me a fabricator. Bertha and them say they were told nothing. I can understand for Dulcie, her mother died when she was thirteen. I can't imagine Uncle Bruce, who she lived with, telling her, but you would have expected her aunty and grandmother to because they were close. Bertha in the Royal Commission said she was delivered by Granny Pinkie. Surely she would have learned more. According to Aunty Laura these midwives learned how to deal with complications and under hard and poor conditions. But Bertha said she'd learned how to deliver babies but nothing else. In 1966, when Bertha was in her mid-forties, Aunty Rosie outlined traditional childbirth practices to Cath Ellis (1966: LA 106), as did other Ngarrindjeri women such as Bessie Rigney (1965: LA 125a-126a). It is consistent with the little that Pinkie Mack told the Berndts (1993: 142). The knowledge was still with Ngarrindjeri *putari* and being passed down according to the grandmothers' law. Just because we do not have tapes of other midwives such as Nanna Laura, there is no reason to believe that their knowledge was any less rich. Bertha Gollan's ignorance cannot be explained by an absence of *putari* practice when she was growing up, or when she was a mature woman.

A Community of Belief and a Culture of Dissent

Neville Gollan: I have knowledge and I know what I'm speaking about. The younger ones know about what I've passed on and they put me there, as an elder. George and Tom, I nursed them and carried them when they were smaller, and they know what I've passed onto them. They know I know the country. I'm still doing that, passing onto others. One interesting aspect of Ngarrindjeri authority structures that has become visible during the various legal battles is the role of delegation, and the community support on which it relies. George Trevorrow explained to Judge Mathews: If you don't have community support, you can't speak on a topic. You need to have prior consultation and the community shares the weight. You have others present. They're our recorders, watching what we talk about. In central Australia, people use the word "witness", which has legal and religious referents. Lewis Rigney, Doug Milera, Neville Gollan, Bruce Carter and Victor Wilson provided the support for Tom when he spoke: We are only speaking because we've been "elected" to share our culture with you. So, it's not just me—Tom Trevorrow—or George Trevorrow or Neville Gollan. Delegated spokespersons, once endorsed, are expected to field all the questions of outsiders and thereby protect the old people. They are put in this position because they are trusted by members of the community of belief, and they remain in this position as long as they retain the trust of the community. The need for prior consultation in order to establish who will speak, and also often to determine how much should be said, slows down negotiations. When asked a question about sensitive matters, the first response is often, "I don't know", or "I can't say", and it might well be quite true. One doesn't know if one may speak until the correct persons have been consulted, a consensus achieved, and a spokesperson nominated. This process might be seen as an adaptation of the practices of the *tendi*, where there were notions of representative governance through the person of the *Rupelli* who could speak on behalf of his clan. Ngarrindjeri are certainly arch bureaucrats. They attend meetings, worry over who will chair it, who gets sitting fees, the voting procedures, the agenda, what is a binding decision and so on.

All members of a society do not need to know all things about that society to be considered a member or to function as members.

But they do need to know where they can turn for advice, and they need to have a degree of trust in their experts and their experts need to know that they are believed. Victor Wilson: Michael Gollan told me about it and he was eighty-two when he went. I believe Grandfather Mike. Within an oral culture, knowledge is restricted to certain persons; for the system to work, those who are not privy to the "inside knowledge" must accept the authority of those persons who are, and honour the wisdom of the restrictions. They must be willing to believe without "knowing". Feelings play an important part in keeping this system alive. A younger person will "feel" the pull of the place and this relationship will be further legitimated by an elder who may then choose to explain a little more. Younger women may well not know the content of particular stories but they trust their elders. A number of younger women affirmed this for Jane Mathews. Ellen Trevorrow: I know I'm not a liar, and I know my elders are not liars. Helen Jackson of Raukkan: When I was young growing up, I was taught to respect my elders and although I didn't know about women's business on Hindmarsh Island, I believe my elders are telling the truth. Cathy McHughes: I know my elders know. I know that I believe that there is women's business associated with Hindmarsh Island. Janice Rigney: We support our elders and we just believe in our *mi:minis*. Connie Love, Doreen's sister, simply says, You'd have to be mad to tell lies.

Doreen was chosen as the spokesperson for the women, but she was not alone. She was backed by those who believed in the stories and accepted the authority of their elders. Jean Rankine: Doreen is a person who is always special in our community and I am sure they would have known that and that is why they told her. I am glad that there are some women who can pass it on. I'm sorry that I wasn't told, but I think then, it just wasn't the right time to be told. So I'm glad for these other people but when, if, they want me to know, they'll come and tell me. In my grandmother's day, nothing of our culture was allowed to be in the open. It was all behind locked doors because they could walk into our homes. They were allowed to tell us what we could buy from the shop, which was so many pounds of sugar and even our meat was rationed. We were restricted. Grace Sumner: I believe Doreen and I also believe Mrs Daisy Rankine. She knows a lot. Since all this has blown up, I have been talking to the elders and I know a lot more now than I used to. I believe what they are telling me. . . . I believe in God and as a Christian I cannot condemn the dissident women. Others knew through the power of their *miwi*. Judith Kropinyeri: When I went to Hindmarsh Island I has this really strong feeling of belonging. I truly believe in the women's business. When an elder such as Aunty Maggie, Daisy or Doreen, "tells" younger women, or those who missed out on learning in their youth, details of certain stories, she licenses their "knowing". The women already have had feelings, already know fragments, and they believe that there are significant places, that the land is alive, and that the elders are the custodians. The teachings of their elders then become part of a process of confirmation and connect the feelings and fragments back to the stories of the old people.

Decisions once made are kept with a reverence I have rarely seen amongst my non-Ngarrindjeri friends and colleagues. Once one has given one's word, it is binding. It is not a game or a matter of honour such as "I'll tell you but you mustn't repeat it." This is a word given in an oral culture and it truly is one's bond. The community consultation affirms in a public way the authority of certain individuals and henceforth they are the spokespersons. The first conversation I had with Aunty Daisy in January 1996 was pleasant and she was very helpful on aspects of history. I was just getting to know people, and I tried talking with her about her grandmother of whom I had read a great deal. Whenever the conversation appeared to be heading towards the subject of women's knowledge, she would deftly change direction. Then her daughter, Ellen Trevorrow, arrived and I began talking with her also. Her mother protested: I can't talk about these things. Doreen Kartinyeri was elected our spokesperson and I gave my promise. After Ellen explained that I was employed to work with the women, she relaxed, but still was not prepared to talk openly. Doreen had been deputised and she was the one to ask. By deferring to the elected person, Aunty Daisy could get on with her life and not be bothered by questions. Her silence did not indicate ignorance: far from it.

Because of the respect due to one's elders, and to their knowledge, not only do younger people within this community of belief not know what the elders know, but one elder may well not know what another knows; but this does not shake their faith in the authority of

407

the old people. Veronica Brodie: Where did I learn it from? From my sister, that's the only one I've ever learned it from, no one else. I don't even know if Doreen knows the same as I know, you know, and I think that I'm the only one that holds that story at this moment in time, you know. Ellen Trevorrow: What I'm doing is not only for my elders, it is also for my children. Men who do not know the content of women's stories also believe in their elders. The faith they have in the word of older knowledgeable people, both women and men, is strong. Cyril Trevorrow: If the old people say it's true, I believe them. Paul Norvill: I don't know too much, but I believe my uncles and aunties. Alan Jackson: I totally support the women's business too. All that I learned from Aunty Dodo, one of my elders whom I respect and know that whatever she has learned when she was growing up is the truth and I have no reason to disbelieve anything she has said. Cyril Trevorrow: All my aunties here, all my other relatives, all the elders, I believe in what they say too. Kenny Sumner: "I believe that women's business does exist." Marshall Carter: I strongly support the women and believe in what they are doing. Edward Wilson: I knew about women's business from when I was a kid. Women and men, young and old, members of a number of families, are part of this community of belief.

The men's belief and support of the women is underwritten by their understanding of the complementary nature of gender relations in their society. Neville Gollan: I knew the men's business and I do believe that there is women's business. Well, as far as I am concerned, I have been told that you weren't told much about this, that you were told nothing about women's business, because it was strictly women's. And I do believe there was women's business. I believe very strongly to that. Tom Trevorrow: That women's business on Kumarangk—I believe in it, because I know very well that it's always been told to me that there's men's business and women's business. And women's business was to be respected, on both sides. And I believe when some of the elders telling me about that place, this . . . women's business I believe. I don't dispute it, because they got no reason to tell lies about anything like that. George Trevorrow adds, We're not liars. We have nothing to gain from this silly business. What is the motive? We don't have to lie. This is our country. It is our belief here. We don't have to lie about anything. We're disappointed that people are doing this to us. We're disappointed for the

408

children who have been through this. We're disappointed for the adults that have been through this. We're going to work very hard to make people aware our culture is living. They can say what they like. It's still going to be there at the end of the day. Frank Lampard: Yes, cobber, there is women's business, and there is men's business. Henry Rankine: I heard talk that there was [secret women's business], but I don't know nothing [about it]. But I'm sure it's there."

As an elder, one is owed respect, and one's authority is very rarely challenged. Certainly I have never heard an elder questioned within earshot. But an elder who has been nominated to speak for others is accountable to that community, and this responsibility is onerous, especially when the media is quick to sensationalise any appearance of disagreement. On the few occasions when I have heard the pronouncements of an elder queried, it has caused enormous pain for those present. I think one of the unhappiest moments I can remember during the last two years was when a woman was sufficiently disillusioned to say of another, "I am not going to call her 'Aunty' any more." The status of "elder" is not conferred lightly and I'm not sure it can be rescinded, although the past several years have sorely tried the system. It will take a while to see what the consequences will be, but, on the basis of what I have seen, especially in terms of who is being trained, consulted and heeded and who is being invested with knowledge, I think that the long-term effect will be to strengthen the authority of the elders and intensify the respect in which they are held. The elders who have not proved worthy of the title are not publicly denounced; rather, they are no longer consulted or cited. It seems to me that the system by which one becomes an elder is sufficiently rigorous to withstand challenge. It may even be strengthened in the process.

The challenge to the authority of elders such as Doreen Kartinyeri that is manifest in the testimony of the "dissident" women can be understood in several different ways. On the one hand, we may say that the dissidents don't wish to be part of the rules of respect and the community of belief around those elders who "know" and who have supported Doreen Kartinyeri. From their evidence to the Royal Commission, it is apparent they have developed their own critique of Ngarrindjeri traditions and it is at odds with that of those who

409

have endorsed Doreen. On the other hand, perhaps some still consider themselves bound by the rules but do not consider particular individuals to be worthy elders. There are, in fact, a number of different positions adopted by the dissident women. But because I am restricted to what is in the public domain via publications and the Royal Commission, I cannot explore a full range of opinions. Dorothy Wilson, who is the only one of the women to assert that there had been a deliberate fabrication, has said little outside the Royal Commission. To understand her position, one needs to know a great deal about Aboriginal family politics and the operation of the Nungas Club in Murray Bridge. She touched on several aspects in her testimony (1995: 686) but these are personal matters about which outsiders are loath to comment. I have not been able to talk with her so I shall not comment either. It is interesting to speculate why it is that since the Royal Commission, Dulcie Wilson has been the only one of the dissident women pursuing what it means to speak of "culture" and "tradition". Dulcie Wilson speaks out of a position defined by assimilationist politics. She has no need for elaborate consultation because that is not her frame of reference. She has challenged both the individuals who were claiming to be custodians of the culture and the process by which they were nominated (Stevens 1995: 267). Later, in the *IPA Review*, Dulcie Wilson (1996a: 38) wrote of manipulation and intimidation. "They were afraid to speak out for fear of reprisal" and "it saddened me to see young women being manipulated to believing whatever they were told about women's business" (*ibid.*: 40). The *South Eastern Times* (Anon 1996) reported that Dulcie Wilson told the Millicent Men's Probus Club that those opposing the bridge had pulled the wool over Minister Tickner's eyes. In her view they had neither authority nor knowledge because a "majority of these Aboriginal people were not born in the outback" (*ibid.*). But there is no suggestion from any of the Ngarrindjeri applicants that they were born in remote parts of the continent. They were born on or near their traditional lands and are proud of the ongoing attachment and the responsibility they exercise for the land.

Dulcie Wilson's depiction of the bases of authority and her open challenge to Ngarrindjeri spokespersons owe much to her Salvation

Army teachings. She becomes a Christian martyr who, strong in her faith of her righteousness, will stand against the majority. She will not be coerced. During her "quiet time of prayer", she was reading from the Book of Joshua (1: 7): "Have not I commanded thee? Be strong and of good courage. Be not afraid; neither thou be dismayed, for I the Lord thy God will be with you whither ever thou goest." When she read this, Dulcie Wilson (1996a: 38) writes, "I burst into tears. I knew that this was my mission no matter what the cost—and cost it did." Her mode of fulfilling her mission is informed by what she believes constitutes "traditional" Ngarrindjeri culture and its relevance to people today: "On my bookshelves at home I have a book about Aboriginal myths and legends. Some are beautiful stories, others depict acts of cruelty and sorcery. While these myths and legends were part of our early tradition. I certainly would not want them to be the basis of our day-to-day living. What I am really saying is this: if people are going to accept women's business on Hindmarsh Island, they must also accept all of the culture and tradition as well, and not just the convenient bits."

Dulcie Wilson's strong belief that "Australia needs a society in which Aboriginal and white people can work together in harmony" is one theme of her talk (Anon 1996). Thus Aboriginal people who make claims to a distinctive heritage which still informs their behaviour are standing in the way of the assimilation she so desires. Stories which concern sexual practices that are not part of mainstream society and could be construed as "primitive" must be rejected. The notion that the only "real Aborigines" were born in the outback and that people in the settled south no longer can be called "traditional" plays off a static modelling of what constitutes "tradition". It is to be equated with "tribal culture" like that of the Pitjantjatjara in the north of South Australia. Because the Ngarrindjeri no longer stage large ceremonies, hunt and gather their food, or communicate primarily in Ngarrindjeri, in her view, they cannot be considered "traditional". This a view shared by many commentators on matters Hindmarsh and with regards to claims made by Aboriginal people not living in so-called "remote communities". However, questioning the depth of traditional knowledge, is not the same as making accusations of fabrication. Some popular literature may well romanticise "traditional culture", but the elders of this generation who learnt the stories from their elders do not shy away from the cruel, malign and wilful behaviour of the creative ancestors. Dulcie Wilson's either/or approach, coupled with a static model of tradition, does not really address the matter of who knows what. Nor does it illuminate what is or was the status of Ngarrindjeri beliefs or practices.

Dulcie Wilson has access through books to a range of representations of religious stories, including ones dealing with Aboriginal culture, and she couples this with notions of the individual as embedded in Western democratic practice and the stress assimilationists placed on Aboriginal people aspiring to the values of the dominant society. This makes it possible for her to express scepticism regarding the word of certain elders. While, as we have seen, a story may often take many forms, these versions rarely come into direct conflict with each other. A person is not asked to decide between two accounts of the creation of the Murray—not, that is, until the recent contesting of women's knowledge. Of course, people have their own ideas about who is more knowledgeable than others, and they sometimes express doubts about the accuracy of an account. However, for Dulcie Wilson, a choice must be made. There is one truth, and her Christian teaching demands she tell it. Not only were young Ngarrindjeri being led astray, but sympathetic white supporters are also being misled "into believing that Ngarrindjeri are still living a tribal existence" (Wilson 1996a: 40). In 1995 there was an audience ready to listen to the story Dulcie Wilson (née Rigney) had to tell.

The existence of alternate forums (for example the courts and the media) wherein disputes may be pursued has significantly undermined the authority of the elders. Taplin was well aware of this and exploited his power to provide options to dissenting youths as a way of breaking the authority of the elders. They need not undergo initiation ceremonies. No longer would they be banished or ensorcelled if they disobeyed. They could live as Christians on the mission. Doug Wilson and I had just attended a meeting where everyone had had their say, as was considered proper, but where one person had refused to be bound by the group decision. Doug Wilson drew a comparison with times past, when the rules were strict. He

412

recalled some of the sorcery practices of which his sister had spoken, stories passed down in the Wilson family: They would have taken them away for the better of the tribe. A dispute would never have got to the stage that this one has over Hindmarsh Island. The laws were severe. Trouble-makers didn't survive. They had ways of killing that would look like person died of natural causes. There was bruising, and there was the taking of dead fat, and the smell was like being downwind of a fox, or you could use a sharp bone and pull the inside out and die a slow death. The choice of method depended on the seriousness of the crime. That's one reason for not roaming around after dark: you would go inside, or else there would be trouble. Such summary justice is no longer possible. Although we may debate the human rights implications of the traditional legal system, it is clear that today the elders do not have the sanctions to back their authority that they had before contact.

The role of dissent in maintaining this system of authority is complex and, I would point out, there have always been challenges, (although previous challenges were not face to face, and certainly were not fought out through the media, the courts and academic conferences, nor did they have a bottom line of many millions of dollars). The Berndts (1993: 211) note a long-standing dispute between Karloan and Milerum regarding the use of bullroarers in the Lower Murray. Other researchers have recorded how the knowledge of another may be disparaged. Archie Blackmore, who died in 1933, considered Milerum to be a "young man [who] . . . knows a lot about the Coorong; nothing about our country" (Tindale 1930–52: 57). Old Alf Cameron, remembered old people dancing and singing, but claimed not to know anything at all because it was too long ago, and he had been very ill; he told Ellis (1962–6: (3) 14) that he was sure his son Scottie didn't know anything. Ellis found otherwise. The knowledge of youth is routinely minimised by older people, and there have always been different opinions and perspectives; to a certain extent they have been honoured, disagreeable though that may have been. There were formal ways for resolving some disputes, and for others it was a matter of time.

Where clan boundaries were disputed, one had to wait to see how the matter would be resolved. The effect of the Royal Commission has been to interrupt and freeze an ongoing process. Because a

413

number of persons who are players did not appear in that forum and thus were not cross-examined, the perspective on the process is partial at best. I am reminded of land claims which are heard while rights of succession in a particular territory are being negotiated. It may be that there are no senior men at one generation level in one lineage but in another lineage, perhaps with the same great-grandfathers, there are. This claim may be challenged by a group with rights in the major Dreamings for the area but not the specific sites within the disputed area. There would then be a period of ambiguous ownership, and depending on whom one asked, one would record different data. Such matters cannot be resolved by a court, though a court may well become a resource that one group can exploit better than another. One may fit anthropological models of ownership better than another, or have more documentary evidence than the other and thus be appealing to the print-oriented reviewer. But ultimately, if the resolution of contested claims to power, resources and land is to be binding, it has to be credible to the participants.

Dulcie Wilson had placed herself outside consensus by claiming she had not been told by the old people and she didn't believe the accounts of this generation of elders about the existence of restricted knowledge. However, she had been present and even contributed during sessions when her husband Lindsay Wilson, and his contemporaries Marj Koolmatrie and Maggie Jacobs, were being interviewed by Steven Hemming. Dulcie stated that she remained interested in her culture and had never abandoned her Ngarrindjeri heritage (Stevens 1995: 266). This aspect of her self-presentation is something about which I would like to know more. What did she know about the *mingka* bird, the Willie wagtail, or the *mulyewongk*? What stories was she told about weaving? These are not matters which were pursued by Counsel Assisting. Of another of the "dissidents", Dorothy Wilson, just fifty, with links to the McHughes, Karpeny, and Gollan families, we do know she was told about such things when she was growing up (Stevens 1995: 270-1). She also was taught the cautions: Don't throw bones or hair clippings into the fire, don't sweep up and throw out into the dirt at night (*ibid.*). The danger she associated with the bones was the smell they made. Without talking to her, it is difficult to know how much more she was taught about these aspects of Ngarrindjeri culture, but she clearly was being given the instruction appropriate to a young person. The reasons for these cautions are not revealed lightly. As we saw with Veronica Brodie's account of sorcery practices in her family (see Chapter 6), and as I have witnessed on several occasions, people do not like to utter the names of the travelling spirits in the presence of adults, let alone children. From her testimony, it appears that Dorothy Wilson does not consider these items of cultural knowledge to be particularly significant, yet they are windows onto a larger world of traditional knowledge for those who are interested. As I have said, one can be Ngarrindjeri and not take a great interest in such matters in one's adult life.

What then can be said of the "dissident" women's position on the knowledge claims of elders who believe in the existence of restricted women's knowledge? Deane Fergie (1996: 13) points out that, of the twelve "dissident women" who gave evidence, "only one could be construed as a claim of fabrication". The others have more to do with what they believe on the basis of what they were not told about what they understand to be "women's business" and what they were not told of the importance of Hindmarsh Island. None asserts they were explicitly told by a respected elder that there was no women's business, or that Hindmarsh Island was not a site of special significance to women. All the women, except Dorothy Wilson, can be understood as saying there is a gap in their knowledge. It is the value they place on this lacuna that varies. In a footnote Fergie (*ibid.*) illustrates the five different positions adopted by the dissidents.

First: *Hindmarsh Island was never mentioned when I was growing up.* This was the position of Rocky Koolmatrie (1995: 859), daughter of Henry Koolmatrie and Isabel Trevorrow, a first cousin to Sarah Milera, who grew up at the One Mile out of Meningie (Stevens 1995: 272).

Second: *I never heard about women's business in relation to Hindmarsh Island, but do not assert that it does not exist.* This was the position of Phyllis Byrnes (1995: 977), whose mother's brother was married to Aunty Rosie (Stevens 1995: 272); of Jenny Grace (1995: 1308, 1309, 4230), the daughter of Margaret Lindsay, whose father was Nathaniel Kropinyeri and who, from an early age was raised by his wife, Aunty Rosie (Stevens 1995: 272); of Marguerita Wilson (1995: 3388); of Vena Gollan (1995: 870, 872, 887) daughter of Bertha Gollan; and of Audrey Dix (1995: 1308), another daughter of Bertha Gollan, who never heard any mention of "puberty or childbirth or other private matters" (Stevens 1995: 267).

Third: *I was never told* (implying that she doesn't believe). Margaret Lindsay (1995: 2227), Nathaniel Kropinyeri's daughter, adopted this position.

Fourth: *I was never told and I don't believe.* Beryl Kropinyeri (1995: 3410), the older sister of Dorothy Wilson and one who had spent time with Janet Smith (Stevens 1995: 270) and other Karpeny women; of Dulcie Wilson (1995: 3269, 3284, 3291, 3292), Bertha Gollan's sister-in-law; of Betty Tatt (1995: 1180, 1183) daughter of Garnet Wilson and Dulcie Rigney (Stevens 1995: 26); and of Bertha Gollan (1995: 953, 626, 925).

Finally there is *Dorothy Wilson's allegation of fabrication by men at the "mouth house" meeting.* Of this occasion there are competing narratives which were not fully explored by the Royal Commission (Mead 1995: 188). One account came from lawyer Tim Wooley, who as an officer of the court is held to a particularly high standard, and whose memory accords with the account provided by George Trevorrow.

Jane Mathews (1996: 121) writes of a once harmonious community which is now racked with in-fighting. From all the accounts we have of Ngarrindjeri society it appears there were disputes aplenty in the nineteenth century and there were mechanisms for resolving them. They occurred within families and between groups. They implicated successive generations. It is a romantic reconstruction of traditional society to cast it as without friction. It is also patently false to depict indigenous society as homogenous. There were scholars, philosophers, leaders, skilled artisans and gifted orators, just as there were individuals with bad tempers, faulty memories and few words. It may be true that that the "dissidents" and applicants are all inter-related and that all have been exposed to Christian religious teachings, but it does not follow that they all have the same level of access to knowledge, have exhibited the same attitude to learning, or have demonstrated the aptitude that would invite further investment of knowledge. There are dramatic differences within families which have to do with personalities, individual histories and so on.

Are these divisions set in stone? In the past there were groups who became enemies and remained so for generations. There was also reconciliation and rapprochement. Doreen Kartinyeri: All my life I've had disagreements with peoples or in-laws and I've always made it my business to make up. Even though the women who spoke out against me in the Royal Commission, I still sent them invites to the book launch for *Ngarrindjeri Anzacs*. I didn't feel I had a right to hold a grudge because of the significance of the book. The descendants of the soldiers had a right to be there and I sent them an invitation. I saw Betty and Shirley [Garney Wilson's daughters] outside the church and escorted them to their seats. I sent invites to Bertha and Dulcie but they didn't attend but some of their children did. Left alone, the deep wounds created by the Royal Commission and its aftermath might be healed by generosity such as this. The trouble with the printed word is that it gives a permanence to disputes and limits the possibilities for other stories to be told.

417

Sorting the Sources:
Writing about the Lower Murray

Who has Fabricated the Ngarrindjeri?
Throughout I have been locating the Ngarrindjeri who speak in this book as members of certain families, as of a certain age, as living in a particular place and interacting with me in specific situations. I have also been indicating the qualifications and interests of the authors of the written sources. What is the nature of these sources? What are their strengths and weaknesses? How does one access them? Under what conditions were they produced? What construction the written sources might or might not sustain has been at the core of much of the controversy surrounding sacred sites and women's restricted knowledge in the Goolwa, Hindmarsh Island, Murray Mouth region, and commentaries on the Royal Commission have significantly shaped the way in which such questions might be answered. The oral sources have been scrutinised in the media, courts and parliament. What might be learned from a similar scrutiny of the written sources and of the relationships between the observer and the observed? For those who did field work, there are significant differences in the amount of time spent with Ngarrindjeri: some are better qualified than others, some are better observers than others, some had language skills, some worked through interpreters, some used questionnaires to gather data, some lived amongst the people. Each had reasons for setting down his or her observations of Ngarrindjeri, each asked distinctive questions. Personality, age, gender, religious affiliation, training and so on all shaped the written record. At different periods we get different snapshots of Ngarrindjeri life.

In the past few decades the Ngarrindjeri have begun to speak of their own lives and have found that text books, protectors' reports, missionaries, government inquiries, and university-based researchers have already defined who they are and have considerable power to dictate who they might be. From the Royal Commission came the claim of a comprehensive and exhaustive record. "If the definition of ethnographic work was broadened to include any historical record of the beliefs and customs of Aboriginal people, then the Lower Murray would be one of the most recorded areas in southern Australia," opined Iris Stevens (1995: 41). Philip Clarke (1995a: 158) spoke of the over 500 references he had used in his thesis.[1] With such a wealth of documentation, how could the existence of a body of restricted women's practice have been overlooked? And what of the claims by Philip Clarke (1995a: 176) of a long history of women researchers, and by Philip Jones (1995: 4269) of the existence of a tradition of feminist anthropology in the Lower Murray? Steven Hemming (1996: 25) suggests it is Clarke and Jones who have been party to an "invention" of a Ngarrindjeri ethnography. What of Taplin's Narrinyeri: a doomed race? What of the Kukabrak of the Berndts: lives brought to us through the memories of two remarkable individuals? We might ask: Who has fabricated the Ngarrindjeri? Can we find any certainty in any of the sources? I think we can, but it is going to require a more nuanced approach: it is not enough to assert that if it is not in the written record, it does not exist.

Critiques of the ways in which Indigenous peoples have been represented in the written record have had a profound effect on the practice of anthropology. Greater attention is now paid to the nature of relationships established in the field. Anthropologists have begun to write reflexively, to bring the reader into the field with them: the cool, detached observer has become more of a participant. Greater attention is also being paid to how Indigenous peoples are located within larger socio-political networks and how these relationships shape their lives and their identity politics. How to write of the resurgence, revival, and re-emergence of "custom" in places such as the Pacific, Native America and now Australia, has been hotly debated by Indigenous scholars and anthropologists, amongst others.[2] Thoughtful commentators on these debates are careful to state that they are not passing judgement on the authenticity of a particular performance or practice—to do so would require a detailed, far-reaching analysis of historical, political, economic factors. Rather, they seek to clarify ways in which traditions emerge, adapt, absorb, accommodate, disappear and reappear. Ultimately, this is a naive wish. Once debates about "the invention of tradition" escape the conference circle, the analyses will be appropriated by those who have an interest in delegitimating certain practices. These critics will not be bothered by the need to know about context, or history, or comparative cases: in fact, they have an interest in isolating individuals and stripping them of such traces (Linnekin 1991: 447). Nor will they be interested in the reflexive turn in anthropology: instead the problematic nature of ethnographic authority becomes a way of challenging all anthropological expertise. Explorations of new spiritualities, of concepts of syncretism, of the ways in which Indigenous peoples are contributing to new theologies, will be appropriated by those who wish to argue that it is after all the environmentalists, feminists, or new agers whose ideas inform those fighting to stop a bridge being built to Hindmarsh Island.[3]

The postmodern turn in anthropology—which nurtures the "invention of tradition" debates, where discourse becomes a "free play of signifiers"—limits the ability of members of dominated communities to circulate their own signs, stories and meanings. They may do so only through another party and according to their rules of print, rules which carry their own taint of post-colonialism, sexism and racism. As Linnekin (1991: 462) and Briggs (1996) argue, the "invention of tradition" mode of framing cultural knowledge can lead to the denial of rights. It may allow destruction of sites. Bureaucrats and experts have access to archives which they use to enhance their authority as the representers of ethnographic truth. They have less access to oral histories, and their debates regarding authenticity reposition such histories. Oral knowledge becomes less authoritative. However, these critiques of the "invention of tradition" school do not lessen the authority of archives and those who guard them. The "invention of tradition" scholars do not set out to disenfranchise the natives—indeed, many have little to do with the natives of whom they write—but their postmodern critique is a two-edged sword. On the one hand it

421

encourages stylistic innovation and pays attention to difference but, having declared truth dead, it falls into a relativistic sink-hole. All voices are equal: none is to be preferred over another. Although it is unpopular in some quarters, I think that anthropologists can and should make explicit the basis on which one analysis is preferred to another, and I'm not talking about high theory. There are stories that capture the spirit of a place and its peoples more faithfully than do others. These are subtle truths. They do not sit well in a seven-second sound bite. They require context, getting to know a range of histories and politics. They require being there.

By way of bringing the reader into the world of the Ngarrindjeri with whom I have been working, I have introduced members of several families who have spoken of their old people. Those who were alive in the 1850s, are often termed "the first generation". They were the first to be given Christian names and to be organised into families that approximated to European standards, with descent being traced through the father's line. However, Ngarrindjeri reckoning is more complex than that. It has had to deal with the abduction of women, various liaisons with non-Ngarrindjeri, the offspring of such unions, children being taken away and institutionalised, and complex adoptions within the community. Being able to specify a blood relation with the first generation, in a sense, erases the pain of the intervening irregularities, indignities and insults. Thus to be able to say "I am the great-grandchild of Louisa Karpeny" as Daisy Rankine, Val Power and Muriel Van Der Byl can; or "the great-great-grandchild of Peter Pulami" as Sarah Milera and Maggie Jacobs can; or "the great-great-grandchild of Mulparini and Ben Sumner" as Doreen Kartinyeri and Edith Rigney can; or "the great-great-great-grandchild of this couple" as Isobelle and Victor Wilson can—such knowledge brings one back to the land, to the Murray, to the lakes and the Coorong. As we read this, Val reminds me that Pulami was Louisa Karpeny's first husband, so the lineages are even more intricately entwined. There are many ways of reckoning these family relationships, as Doreen demonstrated by reference to Eileen McHughes' genealogy. This tracing back to the land is expressed in several ways. As we have seen, stories belong to places and to people and both are owed respect.

The generation of elders who were the major informants for researchers in the 1930s and 1940s are often written about as "the last generation" of people with traditional knowledge, the last to go through initiation, to sing the songs, and to speak the language. It is their memories that to a large extent define Ngarrindjeri culture in the ethnographic literature. What Albert Karloan, Mark Wilson, Clarence Long, Reuben Walker and Pinkie Mack chose to tell Catherine and Ronald Berndt, Dorothy and Norman Tindale, or Alison Harvey of the ways of their forebears has become the standard against which the knowledge of the current generation of elders is assessed. Indeed, I have heard it said that contemporary Ngarrindjeri knowledge of traditional life is only possible because they have these records for reference. Sometimes we have recordings, or transcripts of conversations, and we have the musing of literate Ngarrindjeri, but the lives of the "informants" of the researchers of the 1930s and 1940s, for the most part, are glimpsed through the interests of the field worker. By way of contrast, the elders of the 1960s and 1970s—Rosie Kropinyeri, Laura Kartinyeri, Janet Karpeny, Leila Wilson, Rebecca "Koomi" Harris—come to us through their descendants as well as on tape recordings made by linguists, ethno-musicologists, oral and social historians.

The notion of last and first generations as establishing benchmarks obscures the depth of knowledge, the contexts within which knowledge has been acquired, and the fact that the current generation of elders grew up with the so-called "last generation". To be sure there were powerful interventions by church and state in their lives, but this generation of elders heard stories in context; they heard them over and over; they saw their relevance in their lives and came to understand the significance of what they were being told; and they jealously guarded what they knew. In the face of mission repression and state intrusion in their lives, the old people held onto the only thing that could not be taken away, the knowledge of their stories. During the assimilation era, fearing they would be mocked and not wanting their children to be ridiculed for their "primitive ways"—a situation, no doubt, that produced a degree of self-loathing—the old people, especially those on the mission, spoke to each other, withheld a good deal from their children, and feigned ignorance with inquisitive whitefellas. Their stories and the observations of interested descendants are now being passed on and woven back into the daily lives by this generation of elders. They are assisted by the records left by the last generation, artefacts in museums, photographs, letters, and in knowing how to read the land. They look to the written record not to find themselves but to show whitefellas that their old people were wise; kept their own counsel on some occasions and opened up on others.

Rod Lucas (1996: 40) has written of the privileging of anthropological knowledge which values "collection, appropriation and textual rendering" over that which employs "an epistemology based on social relationships and negotiated disclosure of sensitive cultural information". "Here", writes Lucas (*ibid.*) of the Royal Commission, "was a politics of knowledge laid bare." Here I am particularly interested in pursuing a critical reading of the sources on women, whether generated by women or men, or husband-and-wife teams. For convenience, and so that we may see to what degree representations of the peoples of the Lower Murray reflect different eras and possibilities, I am working through the texts chronologically but I am also paying attention to the individual recorders. Is there any value in sources which assume that Aboriginal religion is an oxymoron and that cast women as sexual but not social beings? If such sources are read critically, I suggest, we can glean a great deal. Even the silences tell us something. What of the claims to be comprehensive? The record is incomplete, as all the trained observers admit. What of the claims of a tradition of feminist ethnography in the Lower Murray? There have been women in the field, but their projects were not conceived as feminist. However, their data can contribute to feminist ethnography. How to understand the velocity of change in the Lower Murray? When is a tradition no longer a tradition? I suggest that change is a constant, that it was part of the system. The stories Ngarrindjeri tell of their land are grounded in the stories of their old people. So, what does it mean to speak of the "invention of tradition"? Who is doing the inventing? Again I ask, who has fabricated the Ngarrindjeri? Native or anthropologist? I suggest there is a difference between "invention" and the ways in which meaning is inscribed on the land through direct experience.

The anthropologist may well present an analysis that no one Ngarrindjeri would offer. In part, that is what distinguishes an ethnography from oral histories. However, I suggest it is possible to privilege gender in our analyses and still be able to present an account of the lives the peoples of the Lower Murray that is rigorous, resonates with the written record and incorporates Ngarrindjeri reflections.

The Royal Commission found fabrication; anthropologists write of social constructs; postmodernists play with the "invention of tradition". I type with a stack dictionaries at my feet—they're too heavy for the desk—I reach for the Macquarie, then the Webster, Funk and Wagnall, and Oxford. Not much disagreement:

- To fabricate: to construct, to assemble, to devise or invent.
- To construct: to form by putting together parts; devise; a complex image or idea resulting from a synthesis by the mind.
- To invent: To originate as a product of one's own contrivance.

How then to distinguish a construct from a fabrication? Both carry the idea of making something new, which is to invent. Commissioner Stevens wrote of a fabrication and implicated a number of people in its construction. However, the motive underlying the fabrication, and the means by which it was accomplished, remain vague. Rather, a number of hypotheses regarding the means by which the claim that there was "secret women's business" associated with Hindmarsh Island and which came to be part of the letter written to Mr Tickner by Doreen Kartinyeri in May 1994, were pursued in the media and by Stevens.[4] To my mind, there is a distinct difference between deliberate fabrication and the ongoing process of meaning-making in an oral culture. I have been tracing the shape of this through Ngarrindjeri concepts of *miwi*, *ngatji*, the importance of signs from the land, past and present, from the living and the deceased. How far can the written sources inform a search for answers?

First Sightings: Writing the Ngarrindjeri into existence

The Ngarrindjeri of the first written records rarely speak in their own voices. They are rendered passive, mere shadows in the landscape; they are stereotyped as the wild and violent men of the Coorong, or seen as people in need of education and medical assistance at Encounter Bay. A line here, a name there—reclaiming the Ngarrindjeri from the historical records is a painstaking task. Hoping to hear from just one Ngarrindjeri, I read all manner of histories of the settlement of the state of South Australia. I try to imagine what the view from the shore must have been; to locate myself on the other side of the frontier.[5] The earliest recorded intrusion into Ngarrindjeri territory was that of Captains Flinders and Baudin, who met in 1801 and named the bay after their encounter. They knew nothing of the people watching them from the shore or their names for these places. Both men missed the Murray Mouth, but they left traces on the land. Matthew Flinders' party slaughtered numerous kangaroos, and his log records that the island he named for this bounty was uninhabited. It was nearly thirty years before overland exploration and movement of stock would generate a written record, and not until the 1840s that any systematic observations were published. By then the Ramindjeri of Encounter Bay knew a great deal about the *kringkari*, as they called the whitefellas. These returning spirits kidnapped their women, killed their animals and desecrated sacred sites. And those who followed the ships did not simply sail on. Some made permanent camp on Kangaroo Island, where a rough and ready community of whalers, sealers and escaped convicts took hold long before the colony of South Australia was proclaimed in 1836.

When the first interactions between Ngarrindjeri and non-Indigenes occurred, we cannot be sure. The early unofficial settlers did not keep journals. What little we know of the interactions of these men with Ngarrindjeri comes from visitors to the island who, in letters, logs, diaries, dispatches and interviews, recorded what information they could glean (Bull 1884). However, in their songs, language and story-telling the Ngarrindjeri were making meaning of the newcomers and the catastrophic events in their lands. One story which has become emblematic of "first contact" was recorded by Taplin (15/2/1871). Some years ago, when white sailors stole three women from the coast near Rapid Bay, the women escaped and swam across the Backstairs Passage to return to their husbands. The two without children found a dinghy and made it safely home, but the woman with the child still strapped to her back was found dead on the shore. Had this story not been written down by Taplin, the episode might well have become the basis for another story of women who, like the wives of *Ngurunderi*, attempted to escape across the waters. The difference would be that these women were attempting to return home to their own *ruwe*. As a historical moment, the story is recorded in what might be taken as a gender-neutral voice, but the experiences it represents are gender-inflected. The European frontier was almost exclusively male, and it was a dangerous place for women. Little wonder that women ran away when the *kringkari* approached (Angas 1847: 58, 68).

The whaling stations were predominately male establishments around which local people camped and also found employment. The possibility of getting a "good smear of oil" and perhaps a feed of whale meat was no doubt enticing, but the mass slaughter of whales was dangerous in a number of ways. The availability of oil increased the opportunity for sorcery. The killing of *Kondoli*, an important *ngatji*, was tantamount to murder. In some oral accounts the killing of whales is cited as provoking the killing of *kringkari*. The whales would come into the shallow waters to calve and there they were easy prey. The songs that had the power to sing the mother and calf out to sea, away from the evil sorcerers, could well also have been used to curtail the activities of whitefellas. However, as the whale population decreased, it was obvious this was not working. Again, this is only surmise, but, given the intimate association of whales with women, and the celebration of the protective nature of whales with their calves, perhaps in yet another way women were being cautioned about their child-care responsibilities?

Other strange forces were at work in Ngarrindjeri lands. Small-pox had ravaged the population. Here was another danger for children, and yet another reason for the telling of stories concerning the care mothers should exercise. The Ngarrindjeri had named the condition *poke wallin* (marked by smallpox) and long incorporated the epidemic into their world of evil powers. *Poke wallin* had become associated with a *muldawali* who came out of the Southern Cross and led the spirits who had died to Kangaroo Island, the land of the dead (Tindale 1937: 112), also the first place where *kringkari* had settled. Evidence of the number of people who followed this *muldawali* was in the "many bones in the sandhills of the Coorong" of those who had been "beckoned" and followed (*ibid.*). The land stood as mute testimony to the tragedy. Captain Jack told Taplin (31/1/1860) that, at the time of great sickness, mounds measuring 1.2 to three metres were made to bury the dead: "They say that so many died that they could not perform the usual funereal rites for the dead, but were compelled to bury them at once out of the way" (Taplin 1873: 45, 81). At Pultowar, on the shores of Lake Alexandrina, one mound was opened and found to contain scores of human skeletons arranged in rows. Taplin supposes these were smallpox victims (*ibid.*: 45n). In the first decades of the nineteenth century, a period of many untimely deaths, sorcery accusations increased. Taplin (17–18/8/1859; 6–9/8/1860) wrote that sorcery was to blame for the population decline and the people up-river were to blame for an influenza epidemic. We have no contemporary eye-witness accounts of the smallpox epidemics, but we can be sure that its unprecedented character and its human toll had significantly changed the society that the "first white men" observed.

Captain Charles Sturt (1833), who in 1829–30 navigated the Murray River to the Southern Ocean, was the "first official contact" by land. His numerous sightings attest a curious population not entirely naive in the ways of whitefellas. As his party crossed Lake Alexandrina, they saw that the natives were lighting warning fires to signal the passage of the intruders (*ibid.*: 163). At the Murray Mouth they were well aware of the consternation their presence was causing (*ibid.*: 172). Ngarrindjeri stories also recall Sturt's journey. Jenny Ponggi hid in the rushes as Sturt sailed down the Murray into the lake (Tindale 1938–56: 260). Stirling (1911: 17) took down Louisa Karpeny's account of two soldiers and a man on horseback. He reasons that it could not have been before the 1836 proclamation of the colony. He gives her age as about ten or twelve in 1840, but others have reckoned her birth date as closer to 1821 than 1830. She could have been recalling Sturt, as her family now states. If so, she would have been about nine. Whatever the occasion, the information that these young women were frightened and hid is an important part of the meaning of the story, and is important in terms of our understanding of gender relations on the frontier.

428

In 1831, hard on the heels of explorer Sturt, came Captain Barker, sent by the Governor of New South Wales to look for another opening to the sea in the lakes region (Hastings 1944: 81ff.). He swam the Murray Mouth, compass strapped to his head, and, after being sighted on one of the sandhills on the opposite side, was never seen again. Perhaps the Ngarrindjeri on the south side killed him. Perhaps he drowned. Woods (1879: xvi) suggests he was "eaten by the natives". Whatever his fate, the Ngarrindjeri had little reason to trust whites. From the descriptions in both Sturt (1833) and Hastings (1944) of the fires that were lit and the massing of armed men, the Ngarrindjeri could well have believed the *kringkari* were in danger of trespassing on a sacred site. They had gathered to ensure they had the numbers necessary to overwhelm the intruders should they stray too close.

Then in 1840, when the colony of South Australia was only four years old, news of a massacre of the survivors of the *Maria*, wrecked near Kingston, reached Governor Grey in Adelaide.[6] The stories of warm welcoming natives of the Kaurna Plains were now contrasted with tales of treacherous murderers. It was a "return of the tribe to actions of extreme ferocity, and no doubt to cannibalism . . . the whole of those on board were slaughtered, not one being left to relate the horrid tale" (Bull 1884: 116). The *Gazette* of 13 August 1840, carried an account of the discovery of the bodies, wherein Dr Penney and Mr Pullen report finding "legs, arms, and portions of bodies visible, partially covered with sand" (*ibid.*: 117). The colonial response was quick. Major O'Halloran, dispatched by Governor Grey to bring in the offenders, "identified" the culprits; after a court martial that violated all known rules of evidence, he delivered summary justice. At Palgarang, the site of the massacre, in full view of their families, hands bound behind their backs, he hanged the two men. To his captive audience, he then delivered the following speech: "Black men, this is white man's punishment for murder. The next time white men are killed in this country, more punishment will be given. Let none of you take these bodies down; they must hang till they fall to pieces. We are now friends, and will remain so unless more white people are killed . . ." (Bull 1884: 121-4). Given the strict rules about the handling of the dead and the fears of sorcery associated with the dead, this colonial object lesson must have angered and terrified the Ngarrindjeri present, and those who later heard the story.

Tindale (Adelaide *Advertiser* 7/4/1934) recounts the story of the *Maria* as "it survives in the minds of the descendants of the people responsible for their fateful end". A party of twenty-six men, women and children survived the shipwreck. They were escorted and passed safely from clan to clan until they came to the northern boundary of the Karagari clan. There, in thick scrub country near Lambert Point, opposite Dodd's Landing, several of the sailors "interfered" with the local women. Pinkie Mack substantiated this point (Berndt *et al.* 1993: 292-3). From Milerum and Harry Lampard come stories of Pamputung, the place where the crew was murdered after crossing from Kondolindjerang (place of the whales) to the mainland side of the Coorong. This beach site was a Tuuri clan place for landing and drying *kundi* rafts (Tindale nd, d). According to "native tradition", a young white girl survived, and after some confusion regarding her human status, was cared for and wandered with the women for "two years" until discovered, when she was seized by a party of police and taken to Goolwa (Jenkin 1979: 57). Ngarrindjeri today offer several inter-related stories regarding this turning-point in their history of interactions with *kringkari*. One has to do with violation of sacred places; the other with the violation of women. Both stress that the newcomers did not behave according to the rules and were punished accordingly. The body of land and the bodies of women were to be respected.

The Ngarrindjeri, writes Taplin (1873: 6), never forgot the punishment. To be sure it was shocking, but this was also an area in which calamities abound. The general area of the *Maria* massacre was where the smallpox associated *muldawali* beckoned, the cannibalistic *prupi* lived, and a meteorite struck the ground. It was where George McGrath was murdered in 1844. The latter event is recalled in the name McGraths Flat, which, along with Barker's Knoll and Maria Creek, inscribed Ngarrindjeri violence on the land. That of the settlers is recorded in oral histories and occasionally in written records. Pinkie Mack told the Berndts (1993: 293) that, when it was discovered that some Aborigines had killed a sheep on Tatiara Station, "members of the local group were shot and their bodies burnt". There are other tales I have heard of strychnine poisonings. Stories of floggings are so routine as to be barely noteworthy, and are reported nonchalantly by local perpetrators (Becke 1899: 126-9).

By the 1840s, the people of the Lower Murray had been in contact with the *kringkari* for some two generations, English was spoken at Encounter Bay (Jenkin 1979: 44) and venereal disease was rife amongst the local women. What stories might Ngarrindjeri women have told of the *kringkari* who violated their lands and bodies and with whom some established long-term relationships? What of the children of these unions? By the time systematic records were kept, much was made of the "problem of half-caste children", but by then Ngarrindjeri had incorporated aspects of the whitefella's culture in their language and story-telling. In that sense they had exerted some control over the colonisers. However, like the "ants" of Alf Watson's metaphor, the whitefellas kept coming. By the 1840s the period of "pacification" was giving way to that of the missions and protectors. Now was the time to write of the language and beliefs.

A Dying Race: Recording Nineteenth Century Ngarrindjeri

1840s: Surgeon, missionary, artist

Documents concerning this period are in the public domain, but I am sure there is more to be found in various archives. The whaling industry at Encounter Bay created the conditions where learned men such as surgeon Dr Richard Penney and Pastor H. A. E. Meyer were able to learn local languages and record legends while caring for bodies and saving souls. Penney, who served as surgeon at Encounter Bay from 1840 until his death from consumption in 1844, understood well that Sturt's arrival heralded a new era. In the first part of his epic poem, "The Spirit of the Murray", Penney, writing under the pseudonym "Cuique", says: "Now scent destruction in the air/And watch around with ceaseless care./Alas! those harbingers of woe" (Foster 1991: 39). For the *Ngurunderi* story, as recounted in the poem, Penney (1843) relied on two young men:

> One of them belonged to the Currency Creek, and the other to the Wationg tribe. I asked one of them "how the Earth came to be?" He answered "that there was no Earth at first, only water." I then inquired,

"who made the land?" and, to a series of questions, received from one and the other the following particulars. The narratives were contained in little interlocutory tales, which the boys said their mothers and the old women were accustomed to tell them.

So Penney heard of women, if not from women. Penney (1842b) chided the many people who doubted "that the intellect of the Australian native is of sufficient calibre to construct sentences of poetry, or even originate poetical ideas". Through his correspondence with various officials, and contributions to the *Examiner*, we hear of Penney's concerns regarding the future of the Ngarrindjeri. For example, he wrote to A. M. Mundey, Private Secretary to the Governor, setting out his ideas for a comprehensive plan to civilise the natives, and offering advice on what might be expected of employers (Penny 1841). Penney (1842a) claimed to be "passionately attached to the district of the Murray and lakes". The records of this classicist, adventurer, and advocate for justice are a rich ethnographic mine. His time amongst the Ngarrindjeri may have been short and plagued by ill-health, but he did make several expeditions through the region; learned some language; wrote of *Ngurunderi* (Ooroondooil); and provided insights to local and social organisation (Clarke 1991; Foster 1991). Penney's is a varied record; his choice of medium, an epic poem, intriguing. What was it about this expressive form that he found so attractive? Was a straightforward description too dry and dull to convey the mystery and magic of what he had learned?

The primary interest of H. A. E. Meyer, a Lutheran missionary at Encounter Bay, 1840–6, as with other nineteenth-century missionaries who recorded language and legends, was to find ways to facilitate conversion to Christian religions. His attempt to describe and systematically analyse the language of the peoples "in the vicinity of Encounter Bay, and (with slight variations) by those extending along the coast to the eastward around Lake Alexandrina and for some distance up the River Murray" is the first we have in the written record. In the opinion of linguist Maryalyce McDonald (1977: 3), it is "brilliant and extensive". One thing Meyer established was that the Encounter Bay language was quite distinct from those of the Adelaide region, but Meyer (1843: iii) acknowledged that his account of the language is neither complete nor perfect. Although short, his *Manners and Customs of the Aborigines of the Encounter Bay Tribe* (1846) provides a straightforward catalogue of key Ramindjeri beliefs and practices which addresses the lives of women and men. In it I found the earliest observation of ceremonial separation of the sexes.

By far the best snapshot we get of mid-nineteenth-century Ngarrindjeri peoples is in the writing and drawings of naturalist George French Angas, who travelled through the area in 1844. Angas displays his sense of privilege, decidedly ethnocentric language, and a tendency to stylised representations. Nevertheless, his drawings and prose capture some of the majesty and mystery of Ngarrindjeri lands, the industry of its people, the seasonal round, ceremonial life, the sex division of labour, and individual personalities. In casting his keen eye over the various native encampments he came across in his journeying, Angas (1847) offers glimpses of daily life, and his depictions of hunting, gathering, and preparation of food reveal a people with skills well honed to the seasons and environment. Whether cooking in the embers at Wellington at George Mason's encampment, finding fresh-water mussels in the muddy flats, carrying the catch in a net bag slung over the shoulder, or using a mussel shell as a knife or another shell for spoon (*ibid.*: 53, 55, 61, 92), the Ngarrindjeri he meets are skilled workers and, for the most part, greet his party with generous offers of food and lodgings.

Women appear muted and in the background of most of the early colonial records. Penney, Angas and Meyer set down what they saw, and it is significant that they saw little of women. There were other people in the Lower Murray in this period who did not write of their experiences. George Mason was at Wellington (1840–1875/6) and Angas (1847: 52, 55, 76) observed the ways in which Mason has been assimilated into the lives of the local people. Indeed, the Berndts (1951: 205) believe Mason should be the subject of a separate study. I agree. However, I know of no publicly accessible sources, apart from his testimony to the 1860 Select Committee, that might illuminate Mason's perceptions of the Ngarrindjeri. From that record it is apparent that Mason's Ngarrindjeri lived a less constrained life than those at Point

McLeay. For one thing, they played cards.7 The Karpeny clan has stories of Mason, stories which may offend some moralists but which indicate how tight people were with information they wished to keep private. Mason was Pinkie Mack's father, but there is nothing of his relationship with Louisa Karpeny in the written record. Two years after Pinkie Mack was born, he gave evidence about the problems of "half-caste" children and the "bad" black girls who were running around. Could their lot be improved? Mason (1860: 81, 85) mentions Agnes, one of three "half-caste" girls, aged thirteen, whom his wife had taught to read and write. What stories did Ngarrindjeri women tell his wife? There were few white women around, and Mason (*ibid.*: 81) testified that the sex ratio was one woman to three men amongst the Ngarrindjeri. Women were in demand. How was this explained in story and song? What stories did the women tell each other of *kringkari* who fathered children, paid for sex and spread disease?

The 1850s–1870s: Records of a dying race

The research librarians in the Mortlock Library, Adelaide, are helpful. I sign onto the rules. No pens, only the stubby little pencils. These are precious records. One box at a time and give fair warning when you need the next. Soon I have the relevant boxes of papers labelled "Edith Gertrude Beaumont and other members of the Taplin and Blackwell families", which contain the journals of George Taplin (1859–79), clippings, photographs, booklets, notes on lectures, drawings and other memorabilia. Leafing through the material, I get a sense of the man, his deep attachment to his charges and his desire to have others understand his "Narrinyeri". George Taplin (1831–79) arrived in Adelaide in 1849 from England, studied for the Congregational ministry, and spent a few months at Currency Creek. From there he moved to Port Elliot, where he opened a school in 1854, before settling at Point McLeay in 1859. Taplin (1879: vii), who considered his studies would benefit both science and the subjects themselves, wrote: "No doubt people have often given them serious offence by unwittingly offending their prejudices." The journals, which cover the period of his ministry at Point McLeay, repay close reading. Unlike the more formal tone of

The Folklore, Manners and Customs of the South Australian Aborigines
(1879), *The Narrinyeri* (1873) and *Grammar of the Narrinyeri Tribe*
(1878), in the journals one meets the people with whom Taplin is
dealing on a daily basis. His chief source for language, James
Ngunaitponi, David Unapion's father, comes to life, along with
Taplin's convert Teenminnie (the wife of Pelican) and Captain Jack.
His days were busy: as well as his writing, he had buildings to plan
and construct, sick people who needed care and souls in dire need of
saving. Taplin was not a detached observer of tradition. As we have
seen, he was actively engaged in eradicating certain traditions and
often unaware of the ramifications of his interventions.

Taplin's translations of scriptures into the local language may be
the earliest texts we have in Ngarrindjeri. Still, he was probably half
a century behind the contact frontier and thus outside influences
had already operated on what he might learn. Taplin also testified
before the Select Committee on Aborigines of 1860 and wrote
numerous letters regarding the conditions at Point McLeay. From
these sources, well chronicled in Graham Jenkin's *Conquest of the
Ngarrindjeri* (1979), we can learn a great deal about Taplin the
man, as well as his Narrinyeri. However, the lively individuals of the
journals evaporate as Taplin distils what he knows of the people into
a sketch of the culture in *The Folklore* (1879). This book was based
on questionnaires distributed to "all keepers of aborigines depôts
throughout the colony".[8] These officials were on the spot, but had
no particular training. But, because of the consistency of the replies,
Taplin (1879: 33) was inclined to think he had tapped the truth
about the Narrinyeri. On a personal basis, Taplin grieved deeply
after the untimely death of his closest woman friend Teenminnie in
1869 and declared he found it "much more pleasant to deal with
the women than the men. They are so much more tractable and less
self-conceited" (27/12/1859). However, the forty-eight questions
which documented the fundamental features of his Narrinyeri
society largely ignore women (1879: 5-7).

In the absence of any systematic colonial effort to record the lives
of the Aborigines in South Australia, J. D. Woods (1879: vii) set out
"to preserve and to place before the public, in a collated form, some
of the few accounts" that existed. He included the 1878 expanded

version of Taplin's 1873 *The Narrinyeri*; Wyatt on the Adelaide Tribe; Meyer on Encounter Bay; and Schürmann on Port Lincoln. All except Wyatt, a Justice of the Peace and Protector of Aborigines (1837–39), were men of the cloth. These were the men who had the time and inclination to write of "Native Peoples". This slim edited volume has become the standard reference for the period. Woods (*ibid.*) is aware that the accounts are not "sufficiently complete to furnish the materials for a full history" and does not see any possibility of remedying this situation: the people are rapidly disappearing. Writing that Aborigines "have disappeared almost entirely except in the interior", Woods (*ibid.*: ix-xi) bemoaned the imprecision of what was known of the distribution of the surviving peoples throughout the state. When Woods (1879: xxxiv) turned to the subject of women, he noted the food taboos, harsh treatment, and the disproportionate number of males to females (2203 to 1750,) which he put down to infanticide (*ibid.*: xi). Taplin (1879: 43) also made special note of the few children in Goolwa and Port Elliot in the 1874 population statistics he collected. He credited the mission, where women outnumbered men and where there were more children, with saving lives. Woods (*ibid.*: xi) attributed the downward slide to "habits and practices, religious or otherwise, helped to cut the races short; and infanticide, as well as cannibalism". Taplin (1873: 119-20) reasoned that, given their inability to invent language, they must have "descended to their barbarism from a state more nearly approaching civilisation; and their language must be the remnant of what was then in use amongst them". Thus the passing of the peoples of the Lower Murray could be attributed to Manifest Destiny. They were to be "exterminated" by their own "barbarism" (*ibid.*: 122). Women were noteworthy because they were dying faster than men and not reproducing.

Dr Wyatt (1879: 159) who believed he was documenting the last days of a dying race, expressed concern about infanticide and prostitution, and he repeated some extraordinary opinions about the decreased fertility of women who have had sex with whitefellas. Driven by a sincere desire "to ameliorate the moral and physical condition of those degraded specimens of humanity", Wyatt (*ibid.*) also anticipates "complete annihilation": record-making is critical.

The Ngarrindjeri described in Woods are deeply scarred, literally and figuratively, by the tragedy of the *Maria*, the smallpox epidemics, and the death of Captain Barker. As such, they exist in time and place. Woods (1879: xxiv-xxv) writes of their distinct territories, with definable boundaries, and he appreciates their attachment to land: "Without the land the aboriginal native could not exist." He understands the impact the fencing of lands has had on their lives, and the implications for the future. Taplin (1879: 43) expands on this theme: "We have deprived the native of their country, sadly diminished their means of subsistence, and introduced a state of affairs more fatal to them than the barbarism in which they before lived." Given that Taplin's mission regime significantly shaped this "state of affairs", his reflections strike a bitter chord. The missionaries and protectors had the power to approve and disapprove, to provide a moral compass in a period of dramatic change, much of their making. The directions they provided mariginalised and constrained women.

Century's End: Learned Gentlemen and Armchair Anthropology
For the most part, as long as they are in English, these records are easy to access, even in US libraries. Between Taplin's death in 1879 and the anthropological researchers of Tindale and the Berndts in the 1930s and 1940s, a number of men visited and wrote of the Ngarrindjeri. Others drew on the existing sources and made the Ngarrindjeri a case study in works that brought together examples from different regions. Australia became a laboratory for testing social theory, and an opportunity to glimpse the last remnants of the hunter-gatherers living in their natural state. Some, like J. J. East (1889: 1), in a paper read before the Field Naturalists' Section of the Royal Society, 16 July 1889, made breathtaking generalisations: "But little difference is observable in the general appearance of the native throughout the whole continent of Australia. They are of the same colour, have no defined religious belief . . .". Their "many savage customs" likewise vary little across the land (*ibid.*). Others who, unlike Meyer, Taplin and Wyatt, had little or no contact with the Ngarrindjeri, drew on field-based accounts and questionnaires to produce comparative studies of the "natives". The two volumes of

437

Brough Smyth (1878) rely on extracts and summaries from Meyer and Taplin, as does Howitt (1904: 672-5). Save for Mrs Smith (1880) on the neighbouring Boandik in Victoria, no women took notes or produced comparative studies in the written record.

Then there were note-taking tourists with medical qualifications. Paul Erhard Andreas Elymann, a man with a deep disdain for women and a preference for company who shared his "gentlemanly" and scholarly interests, made three visits to Australia. His journal entries and account of his eight days at Point McLeay in 1899 help fill some of the gaps between Taplin and the accounts of Tindale and the Berndts. Vivienne Courto (1996) has translated these documents; she argues their attention to the who and where of his visits makes them a valuable adjunct to *Die Eingeborenen der Kolonie Südaustralien* (1908). In Elymann's journals we learn that Daniel Wilson was still making weapons and kept a "set" of throwing and striking weapons and a narrow shield in his room; that accounts of *Ngurunderi* travels, the *mulyewongk*, and fire, were still being told. A decade later, William Ramsay Smith (1924, 1930) travelled through Ngarrindjeri lands and, like Angas (1847), was captivated by the wild beauty of the landscape. In *Southern Seas*, Smith (1924: ix) severed the shackles of "scientific descriptions" and wrote to share "the joyous freedom" of his experience. Perhaps, like Penney, he sensed that mere prose would not convey his encounter with "other". Mostly Smith separated his theorising on the origins of Aborigines (1924: 209-26) from his observations of daily life, but when it came to dealing with the "problem of half-castes" (*ibid.*: 172-3), he drew on Mendel's theory of genetics.

Then there were those with an interest in local and social organisation. R. H. Mathews (1841–1918), a prolific writer, did some work by correspondence, and some by field observations; he broke new ground in his 1904 paper on the Aboriginal people of New South Wales and Victoria. Had he "discovered" a system hitherto unreported? His work as a land surveyor for the South Australian government and a Justice of the Peace afforded opportunities to carry out inquiries. From drawings by Angas in which the cicatrices are clearly visible (see p. 517), we know that Ngarrindjeri women practised this rite, but Mathews (1900) does not mention ritual body scarring in his survey of the southeast. Similarly, A. A. Radcliffe-Brown (1881–1955), the first professor of anthropology at the University of Sydney, synthesised and systematised much of the material on Ngarrindjeri social organisation and undertook field work in the Lower Murray, but he fails to explore how women's practices might alter his model of the patrilineal clan. Like the other learned gentlemen, Radcliffe-Brown (1918: 228) admitted that his work was incomplete.

Museums and Memory Culture: Tindale, Berndt *et al.*

On my November 1997 visit to the South Australian Museum on busy North Terrace, Adelaide, I asked the receptionist if I could speak to someone in the Anthropology Department. She froze. "Anthropology Department?" I knew there was one. I had been into the vaults the year before, but had thought it polite to be announced rather than wandering into the area of offices and store-rooms in the wing where the researchers work. She referred my question to a passing security guard. "Anthropology Department?" I explained who I was and what I was doing. We all laughed, but the story is indicative of the tensions in the museum. Since its creation in 1856, this museum has seen its share of controversies, many of which are shared by museums around the world: the repatriation of sacred objects and skeletal remains, the curation of sensitive material. "Who owns the past?" Indigenous peoples have asked. During the last decade or so, there has been a reorientation of museums. As Hemming (1995: 103) writes, "museum artefacts are re-entering the Aboriginal community" and with that move comes new relationships between Indigenous peoples and the museum. Museums have become interpretive centres rather than the keepers of the past. They have begun to incorporate native voices, ideas, and researchers. None of this has been uncontentious. The descendants of the original songsters, story-tellers and makers of objects have views on how their heritage should be lodged, accessed and interpreted. As I have pointed out, I needed to consult with Milerum's grandson before reading or citing the Tindale collection. The status of this collection and access to it have been matters of contention and rancour. The scars of those exchanges are still raw.

Over the years the South Australian Museum has provided an important locus for the study and preservation of the material culture of the Lower Murray, mapping, the recording of local family history, mythology and genealogies. Sir Edward Stirling's association with the museum extended from the 1860s to the 1920s, during which period he gathered material culture and recorded stories concerning "traditional culture" (Tindale and Pretty 1980: 50). We can thank him for speaking with Jenny Ponggi and Louisa Karpeny in 1911. Tindale was appointed ethnologist in 1928 and, as he puts it, "occupied himself for the next forty-five years in improving upon this record" (*ibid.*). More recently, anthropologists Deane Fergie, Rod Lucas and Peter Sutton, cultural geographer Philip Clarke, lawyer turned historian Philip Jones, oral historian Steven Hemming, and family history expert Doreen Kartinyeri have all worked at the museum and all, albeit in different capacities, have been caught up in matters concerning the nature of the written record and women's knowledge.

The Tindale Collection

I spent more time with the Tindale material than any other single source because the level of detail is unrivalled, his notes are grounded in the specificities of time, place and person, and the length and depth of his association with people in the Lower Murray is unparalleled. I could spend another year working only with this material and still not be done. In the thirteen folders known as "The World of Milerum", associated data folders, journals and card indexes, I have found material that yielded new insights and accounts. It was not easy, however.[9] Much of Tindale's material consists of unnumbered loose-leaf ring binders and shoe-boxes of vocabulary cards: citation is nightmarish. The material is not yet indexed, so my idea of its extent is imprecise. While I was working with the material, which was then housed in the director's office, I was under constant surveillance by museum staff and asked to explain myself more than once. I sat, in full view of all passing through, on the edge of the long couch in Chris Anderson's office, balancing the folders on my knee, and took notes in a book perched on the arm of the chair. The aching back was worth it. Being able to compare

Tindale's field-notes against later interpretations in published works is a rare privilege and, given the climate in Australia at present, likely to become more so. His handwriting is an acquired taste, but repays perseverance: the penned version is not always the same as the typed, and the published form is usually further edited. George Spender's song of the bridge across the Murray in Tindale (1937: 234) makes no mention of the desecration of a *mulyewongk* site caused by its construction. That information was available only in a handwritten field-note, as were other insights to which I have alluded.

Norman B. Tindale (1900–93) amassed a remarkable database. He records how things are done, not just assertions about the doing of them; he gives case histories that flesh out cultural principles; and he makes the ecological basis of land relations explicit. Here is one that concerns what he terms "typically women's work": the making of digging sticks variously used to control dogs, as a weapon in fights with other women, and in the getting of a living.

> [This] involved one of the few occasions they were ever allowed to have use of the male-treasured hafted stone axe. Various trees provided useful sticks. In the Tanganekald area, stout growths of mature whip-stick mallees were considered good choices. If a woman saw a potentially good stick, and had the leisure, she would sometimes not want to obtain an axe but could build a small fire to windward against the base of the coveted stick and over an hour or two char or burn it through. The heating of the wood hardened it and the part to windward would char more than the opposite side. When the stick was free, she could trim by scraping away the charred wood. In a further stage, either there or back in camp, she would partly bury the future digging end of the stick, selectively heaping hot coals over it to continue the shaping, removing it from time to time to scrape away further bared wood with stone or shell until she had a desirable tapered and fire-hardened digging end on her stick. This charring action appears to have hardened the wood when it had not advanced too far. Thus the digging point can actually be considered as "tempered". (Tindale and Long nd: 2)

There are no accounts of this richness and detail about what women are doing when they are engaged in women-only activities. Tindale wrote best of what he witnessed first-hand and heard from eyewitnesses. Unfortunately, most of the material is unpublished. Tindale is quite clear that certain places, practices and things were restricted, but ethical questions regarding who may repeat what Tindale was told are being negotiated in the 1990s, in the aftermath of the Royal Commission.

Although there are valid criticisms to be made of Tindale's generalisations about Australian Aboriginal territoriality, his work in the southeast was so detailed and has such a time depth, that one can reconstruct the who, where and what of it in his genealogies, site maps, and notes on mythological meanings. He kept detailed journals, in particular *Murray River Notes* (1930–52) and the three *Journals of Researches in the South East of South Australia* covering 1931–56. From these he extracted vocabulary items on cards and cross-references to his maps, on which he also made notations. This is material with which one can truly engage in re-analysis. Reading Tindale's (nd, b) "Informants File", where he lists the dates on which he spoke to each person, I get a sense of the intensity of the interactions with Milerum, Albert Karloan, Pinkie Mack, Reuben Walker, Mark Wilson, Granny and Creighton Unaipon, John "Sustie" Wilson, Alf Watson, Frank Blackmore, George Spender, Ethel Watson and others. Tindale's work with women is slight compared to his close relationship with Milerum, but he did talk to women about ceremonies, land and *ngatji* and, as noted above, his conversations with women contributed to his understanding of land tenure. He does credit Granny Unaipon, with whom he talked (11/2/1934) when she was near one hundred and still mentally clear, with causing him to revise his 1974 position on clan structure (Tindale nd, f). However, Tindale's major debt is to Milerum, who, as he grew older, became concerned at the loss of knowledge about his people. Milerum sang, told stories, made coiled baskets, and spoke in his own language, Tangani, and his mother's language, Potaruwutj. Tindale writes of Milerum as friend, intellectual and travelling companion on whose remarkable life are inscribed major changes of the past sixty-five years. In January 1996 when I first read the material generated through this remarkable collaboration, it was housed in the Old Barracks in the museum. It was there, in the shade of the grapevine during the summer months, that Milerum worked with Tindale. Unlike the question-and-answer method of other researchers, between Tindale and Mil erum things

442

would arise spontaneously, even serendipitously. This was how Tindale (Lindsay 1968) learned of such diverse matters as fire-making and the interdental "th" and, as we shall see, important things concerning birth rituals.

Today Milerum is remembered fondly by the older generation. Aunty Maggie recalls: Milerum was respected. If he told us a thing, we couldn't answer back. If Grandfather Clarence said so, that was it. Milerum was my neighbour and he was like a grandfather, he and Grandmother Polly. After school I'd come home, dragging my shoes, and he'd be there, and he'd say, "Well, my girl, come along." And he'd show us what we could eat and not eat. Milerum would have half a dozen following him. He had an old frying pan. He would buy boiled lollies, black drops, and everything, and he'd stand on the corner, just up from the church, and there was a horse trough there, and he'd stand on the corner and bang the pan, and he'd have a couple of this and that, and we'd line up, and old Fred Dodd, and Mummy Lola Sumner, and her brother. I knew old Grandfather Karloan, and old Grandfather David. David Unaipon was a very spiritual old fellow. Well, they all were. I remember Tindale, but not the Berndts.

The Berndt Book

Working primarily with Albert Karloan (1864–1940), Mark Wilson (1868/9–1940) and Pinkie Mack (1858–1954), Ronald and Catherine Berndt (1993: 281) were determined to provide an account of "a world that has now entirely disappeared" and it was to be one in which Ngarrindjeri today would read of their heritage (*ibid.*: 298-9). What was Kukabrak society really like (*ibid.*: 281)? In fulfilment of a promise made to Albert Karloan some fifty years earlier and with assistance from John Stanton, *A World That Was* appeared in 1993, three years after Ronald had died and a year before Catherine died. The couple wrote down and translated 188 pages of texts with interlinear translations, mostly from Albert Karloan; forty-one pages of genealogies (half by Karloan and half Mack); twenty-two pages on traditional foods, and nineteen on songs, mostly from Pinkie Mack: this forms an enduring contribution to the study of the peoples of the Lower Murray. And the Berndts understood that there was more to be learned. They write: "in no way did we exhaust their

443

extensive repertoire of Kukabrak knowledge", and "there are bound to be some inaccuracies" (*ibid.*: 282, 511).

The Berndts went on to become distinguished scholars. Ronald Murray Berndt (1916–90) became the professor of anthropology at the University of Western Australia, where he was simply known as "Prof". Catherine Helen Webb Berndt (1918–94) taught in the department, but she did not hold a full-time position.[10] They continued as a research team, publishing together and separately. The accomplishments enumerated in respective obituaries are many, but in the 1940s they were at the beginning of their careers. The initial work by Ronald Berndt with Karloan was undertaken before he had completed any anthropological studies. He was affiliated with at the South Australian Museum as an "Honorary Assistant in Ethnology", having been appointed in 1938 (Berndt 1982: 49). Indeed, it was Ronald Berndt's interactions with Karloan which he credits as propelling him into anthropology (Berndt *et al.* 1993: 3). Catherine Berndt had studied anthropology in Dunedin, New Zealand, but Ooldea was her first contact with Aboriginal peoples. They arrived there as newly-weds in June 1941 and left at the end of the year. They had completed their first piece of joint field work. Sometime in 1942 they headed off to Murray Bridge.

How long were the Berndts in this field? From sources available to me, it is not possible to reconstruct all the details, but what can be known is important. *A World That Was* (Berndt *et al.* 1993) draws on three field trips to the Lower Murray. During the first visit, from November 1939 to February 1940, Ronald Berndt, in the company of artist James Wigley whose sketches appear in the book, worked with Albert Karloan (*ibid.*: 3). In 1942 Ronald and Catherine Berndt camped at the Hume Pipe Company site, Murray Bridge for six months (*ibid.*: 3-4). There they worked intensely with Albert Karloan, but they acknowledge that they only recorded a fraction of what he knew (*ibid.*: 6) and that there was always unfinished business at the end of each session. They must have met Pinkie Mack during this period, though they make no mention of working with her. Mark Wilson had died earlier in 1942 and thus Catherine Berndt did not have the opportunity to work with him. The Berndts did not return to the Lower Murray until May 1943, for Ronald's third trip and Catherine's second. In February that year Albert Karloan had died, in circumstances that were obviously distressing for the Berndts and no doubt others who knew him and relied on his wisdom (Berndt *et al.* 1993: 7). It is not clear how long the 1943 trip lasted, but it certainly did not extend into 1944. During it the Berndts (*ibid.*: 7) visited Point McLeay, East Wellington and Meningie, but they do not mention how long they stayed in any of these places. In another article, Catherine Berndt (1989: 10) offers a clue. She says that in the early 1940s "we covered together" an area "including Point McLeay, Murray Bridge, Tailem Bend, Meningie and Wellington", and that "we camped for several months at Murray Bridge to be near Albert Karloan". After he died, "we were allowed to camp in the shearing shed at Brinkley Station, to be near Pinkie Mack and her family at the Brinkley Native Reserve" (*ibid.*: 12). From my reckoning, at the outside, Ronald spent sixteen months in the field, but it was probably closer to a year; and Catherine, a year, but probably closer to nine months. At a maximum Catherine could have spent several months at Brinkley near Pinkie Mack in 1943 but, given the other places they visited during that stay, it was probably a much shorter time. There is also evidence of some social visiting when Pinkie Mack came into Adelaide and attended singalongs at other people's houses (C. Berndt 1989: 13).

I have gone to some trouble to reconstruct these details of the Berndts' field work because, if I am to rely on their work as comprehensive, I need to know that it has a correspondingly comprehensive base. Time in the field is important, but so are field-work methods. Their "procedure in the field, as far as recording traditional material was concerned . . . was to suggest a topic on which one or the other could speak" (Berndt *et al.* 1993: 10). The result is the taking of oral histories, the recording and transcribing of songs, rather than participant-observation field work. There is little sense of the daily lives of the peoples with whom they were camped or of the dynamics of the various field locations. The tenor of life at the One Mile at Tailem Bend would have been quite different from that of the mission at Raukkan, or the community at Brinkley, but we get no sense of that texturing of Ngarrindjeri lives and no sense of the contexts within which the material was collected. In

445

another study (Berndt and Berndt 1951), which draws on the same field work, they provide quite vivid descriptions of each of the locations at which Ngarrindjeri live.

There is another window onto their 1940s field work which illuminates their approach; it demonstrates their engagement with an assimilationist model of Aboriginal society, treatment of women and their assumptions regarding the Lower Murray. Written in a different voice, *From Black to White in South Australia* (1951: 18) is an account of the "Aborigines' changing circumstances in one part of Australia". In the introduction to the book, Professor A. P. Elkin spells out his model of cultural adjustment, which includes the problem of making the transition from the stage of "official Protection" and "intelligent parasitism" to assimilated members of the wider society. The "mixed bloods"—his term—have "lost" their culture, and their only option is assimilation. *From Black to White* owes much to Elkin and to his understanding of the nature of Aboriginal society. The language is that of the 1950s. The Berndts write of the "remnants", and the rising population of "part-Aboriginal children". Most of the anecdotal material focuses on men and their concerns. Of the women they (*ibid.*: 214) say a "few act as domestics", but the majority are not employed. They note fights which come into court and the problem of drinking and prostitution (*ibid.*: 216, 217, 223); but the bulk of the material on women is in the section on sexual behaviour (*ibid.*: 220-6). Here Pinkie Mack, although not identified, is the subject of one of their expositions (*ibid.*: 221-3). On the "general adjustment" of people in the region, they write that there is "no more than a trace of the old aboriginal culture, and nothing of its essential structure and principles" (*ibid.*: 229).

In a number of subsequent publications Ronald Berndt (1974, 1982, 1989) revisited their field work in the Lower Murray and offered conflicting narratives about the title of the 1951 book.[11] It seems to me that his inconsistencies may indicate some uneasiness over the raw material and their 1950s assimilationist language. In 1989 he put forward a far more subtle modelling of change: one that allowed that attachment to place and family remained key values, but that saw the Ngarrindjeri choosing to participate in mainstream

Australia in their future. Ronald argues that he and Catherine adopted, perhaps more strongly than Elkin himself, the desire to right injustices and redress negative discrimination, and he claims that this may have been the "first 'applied anthropological' research of its kind carried out in Australia" (Berndt 1982: 51-2). Why were the Berndts working on "memory culture" with people they considered to be "remnants" in 1939, 1942 and 1943? Fay Gale (1990: 70) suggested that Ronald Berndt, "because of his German ancestry, was virtually held under house arrest". But Catherine Berndt told Gale that this was incorrect and he was not "under question for being of German descent". In security documents obtained by Geoff Gray,[12] there are letters concerning a complaint made by Berndt that his flat had been searched, a denial of same from the local police, and questions regarding Berndt's knowledge of people who had been interned during the war. These personal experiences may explain why it is so difficult to work out the Berndts' exact dates in the field in 1943. It does appear that they were anxious to head north: in 1944 they accepted appointments as anthropologist-welfare officers on Vestey's large pastoral holding in the Northern Territory. That work remained unpublished until 1987.

A World That Was, researched in the 1940s when exemption tickets were being issued to those who were considered "white", was published in the 1990s when these assimilationist moves had been discredited. It appeared in the year Native Title was recognised as part of the common law of the land and the peoples of the southeast had began to contemplate how they might register their rights in land. They care very much what is said about them but were not consulted directly regarding the publication of the book. Had it not been for the Hindmarsh Island Royal Commission, the book, expensive and quickly out of print, would have become part of the Berndt œuvre; the discipline would have taken up the issues it raised in conferences and through learned articles. Were the Ngarrindjeri really so different from all other Aboriginal societies? What weight can be attached to this research? In my view, from what can be reconstructed of the Berndts' field work, it is sound to rely on the book for a perspective on what a respected senior Yaraldi man wished to communicate in the 1939–40 and 1942 to a young male student of anthropology, and what a senior woman thought appropriate to transmit in 1943 to a young woman student. *A World That Was* is an invaluable contribution to our knowledge of the peoples of the Lower Murray, but it cannot answer all the questions one might ask.

Recording the Word: From passive to active voice

In the 1940s and 1950s and even into the 1960s, it was assumed that, with the passing of the last initiated men from whose memories traditional culture might be reconstructed, only fragments could be recorded in the settled south. Exhorted by assimilationist polices to attain the same style as other Australians, older Aboriginal people held onto their knowledge. The younger people were taught to be ashamed of the "old ways". To protect their children from ridicule and to protect their knowledge, the old people stayed silent. When they did speak, it was to trusted women and men, and it was not to be repeated to whitefellas. This is the climate in which Cath Ellis (1963–5) set out to establish what was known "within a 200-mile radius of Adelaide". In four notebooks, on a number of tapes, and in associated documentation, there are brief references to the parents of the current generation of "elders". Of Rosie Kropinyeri (née Rigney), who was in her seventies, Ellis (1962–6 (4): 4) says she "did know legends, but couldn't remember them"; but even when Aunty Rosie sings, and begins to volunteer information about *putari* practice, it is not pursued. Hughie McHughes (Ellis 1965: A124b), born in the 1890s, always referred to Ellen Brown as one who seemed to know a considerable amount, but her knowledge was not pursued with any rigour. Ellis (1962–6 (1)) comments:

> General impression is that people exist in a cultural vacuum and have no outlet at all. They seem quite unable to take any initiative . . . David [Unaipon] remembers much (which is useless), but Banks and Archie did dance in the corroborrees, but they had all died out before they learned the songs. They seem to know nothing at all.

In fact they knew a great deal, and at times it comes out despite the questions and underlying assumption of Ellis that she too was recording a world that was. Nonetheless, Ellis (1963–5: 54) is explicit that there is more work to be done reclaiming what she terms "remnants of tribal affiliations alongside information on cultural and social transition". Through the work of linguists Cath Ellis, Elaine Treagus (1966) and Maryalyce McDonald (1977) some of the continuity of stories in certain key families, such as the Karpeny and Wilson line, can be glimpsed, and I have been able to fill some of the gaps between the Berndts' work and my own. These women worked with women, but there is no evidence that identifying the existence of restricted women's knowledge was part of their projects. None spent long periods of time in the field. Again, that was not the purpose of their work.

With the shift to policies of self-determination and self-management, Aborigines moved into active voice and began to publish their own accounts of the past. *Survivors in Our Own Land* (1988) compiled by Christobel Mattingley and Ken Hampton reclaims a number of Nunga voices and weaves them into the historic record. *The Ngarrindjeri People* (1990), the Aboriginal studies book of the South Australian Department of Education, draws on the oral testimonies and asks new questions of the historical record. Here is a different sort of recording of the word. Annie Koolmatrie and her husband Jack recall the strictness of the old people and ceremonial life in *Murray/Murundi* compiled by Bonita Ely (1980). During the 1980s and 1990s oral historical projects have flourished in local communities and oral testimonies have become part of the written record. At the South Australian Museum, Steven Hemming worked with a number of old people and generated an invaluable tape archive. In his *Troddin Thru Raukkan*, we hear this generation of elders speaking at the 1994 Reunion. Again and again I heard that his patience and respect towards older women established him as a trustworthy recorder. Even so, there were topics he did not broach; there were topics that he was told were not for men and there were topics that were not even mentioned. Hemming (1996: 26) had known Doreen Kartinyeri since 1980, but she had carefully manoeuvred around gender-sensitive topics; she alerted him to issues only when it was absolutely necessary, as with the *Ngurunderi* exhibit (see p. 102). He had known Aunty Maggie for some eight years, but only recently has she begun to talk more openly.

It is not only historians and anthropologists who are tapping the oral sources and forging new understandings of the past. In the course of archaeological research, Roger Luebbers interviewed a number of Ngarrindjeri, including Lola Cameron Bonney (1982). From his reports (Luebbers 1981, 1982) of the Northern and Southern Coorong, it is evident that he involved the Ngarrindjeri Heritage Committee in his work. Input from contemporary people was a central part of his research design, and provided valuable insights into Ngarrindjeri cultural heritage and the existing links being maintained with their traditional past (Luebbers 1996). In 1979 his work took him to Hindmarsh Island, where he assessed some sites including two burial complexes. He ultimately abandoned plans for further work there when permission to work on private property was not forthcoming. Neale Draper, an anthropologist/archaeologist with the Department of State Aboriginal Affairs, who had worked on the matters concerning the bridge area since 1988, also recorded oral testimonies as part of his research. In the work of both Luebbers and Draper we hear directly from women about their knowledge of the land. Through Draper some of the Tindale material was introduced into the Royal Commission. Through Luebbers, some of Tindale's material, especially that concerning a restricted men's site, was introduced into the Mathews Report (see p. 273). Draper also made good use of local histories where, although the focus is on local white families, Ngarrindjeri stories are sometimes heard (Morison 1978; McLeay and Cato 1985; Padman 1987).

Potentially the most significant account of Ngarrindjeri produced in the 1990s is Philip Clarke's doctoral thesis. In this cultural geography of the Lower Murray he aims to "fill the gap" in the literature regarding the relationships of people "to land and places of significance within it" for a people whose landscape has been "modified by rural and urban development" and who are continuously reinventing culture (Clarke 1994: 1). He too incorporates the words of Ngarrindjeri, but for the most part the "informants" are not identified. Not only does this raise questions about whether or not people consented to be in the work, but it also makes it difficult to know whether one is getting a Ramindjeri,

Tangani or Yaraldi perspective—important if he is tracking land-based relationships. Hemming (1996: 31) writes that because Clarke "develops a model of alienation it restricts his understanding of social change". Further, Hemming notes, Clarke's focus is the people at Raukkan, and the relations to land he pursues are economic. Missing is the view from the fringe camps, town, cities, and homes. Then, when Clarke writes of "humanised landscape", he slides to the masculine, with no thought that it might be gendered (Hemming 1996: 38; Clarke 1996: 145). One of the significant limitations of the thesis is that it does not draw on the Berndts' (1993) book— "one or two minor things have cropped up" since he submitted his thesis, Clarke (1995a: 158) told the Royal Commission—or on the Tindale journals and maps, where relations to land can be traced in exquisite detail. Nonetheless, like the other sources, I have found it useful for re-analysis.

In his acknowledgements Clarke identifies a number of people on whose knowledge he has drawn, but many have reservations about his field-work methods and view his use of their stories as appropriation. Doreen Kartinyeri recalls: And I told him about the flowers, the feather flowers, very important, because in the olden days they used to use them as part of their corroborees and the ceremonies. So he did get information from me, he learnt things from me over the years, but not as an interview for his thesis; I didn't even know he was doing his thesis. So we're very, very hurt and disappointed in Philip Clarke's thesis because so much stuff that he's got in there that he said he got from these people and these people were never interviewed by him; they were interviewed by Steven Hemming.

In November 1996, Vi Deuschle asked me to sit a while at Tandanya and explain to whom fieldworkers are accountable. Who did he speak to? I asked my aunty, who talked with Steven Hemming and Philip Clarke was there, but Steven Hemming was talking. How was my aunty to know what he was doing? Vi has pursued her concerns at anthropology seminars at the University of Adelaide. I wanted other anthropologists to know how we feel about it. I went to raise it. When he said "this just came out in the nineties", now if he is attacking the report and the women, I want to know who has he talked to? Did they know what he was doing? Vi also had concerns about the Berndt book. It takes the word of young women as expert, and she [Catherine Berndt] spends a few days there and then she's an expert. And of the Royal Commission: We said "sacred" not "secret". I said to Steve Kenny, "Will we ever be able to redeem ourselves?" The people on the bench are pronouncing their own value judgements, and are really dependent on the lawyers to set them straight and the so-called "anthropologists" but they were not even experts.

On Silences, Assumptions and Censorship

In the foregoing survey of the sources I have highlighted the contexts within which data were recorded as a way of exploring the strengths and weaknesses of the written record. The record is partial: much is left unsaid, overlooked, or simply ignored. For the most part, the recorders admit there is more to be done. The questions asked and the assumptions underlying the questions reflect of deeply entrenched cultural attitudes about Aborigines and women. From first contact till the work of Tindale, the Ngarrindjeri come to us via explorers, doctors, artists, missionaries, protectors, police-troopers, colonial officials, all men of their times who addressed issues of political, social and scientific interest to themselves and their readership. They kept journals, wrote travelogues, compiled vocabularies, documented "manners and customs", and pronounced on the passing of a people. With the exception of Radcliffe-Brown, Mathews and Stirling none has any claim to anthropological credentials. From the 1930s onwards come more men, and a few women; more reclamation work, and some with an interest in contemporary lives; more short-term visits, and a few long-term relationships. What distinguishes these recorders is that they have some expertise in the field of Aboriginal studies, whether as linguists, historians, geographers, archaeologists. Anthropologists have not flocked to the Lower Murray—not until the Heritage applications for protection of the proposed bridge site that is. By then the field was so politicised it was difficult to undertake field work.

It is tempting to place the greatest weight on the earliest recordings as the most accurate, authentic accounts and free of the political taint of later work. Philip Clarke (1994: 64) argues that: "In spite of their biases . . . these records as accounts of pre-European Aboriginal culture are more reliable than most of the survey and reconstructive-type ethnographies compiled in later periods."[13] Sometimes this is true. Angas recorded body scarring on women, but Mathews missed it. Reviewing Mathews' work, Hartland (1906: 153) cautioned that, in the case of denials that a thing could exist just because it was not observed by another, "the wise student . . . does not necessarily refuse belief . . . he knows that the evidence of twenty witnesses who did not see an alleged event is often of little account beside the evidence of one who did see it". This applies both to those things Mathews "discovered" and to those things he fails to report. There are practices that the Berndts and Tindale document in the 1940s that are not mentioned in Taplin. Tindale (Tindale and Long nd: 9) suggests that when a new generation looks at the data compiled since Taplin, they will realise that, even though we know more, "we will always lack a full picture". The date of publication is not a sure sign of accuracy. There are other reasons for silences and omissions. Some are personal, some professional, some to do with the mode of collecting data.

Taplin (1873: 61, 143) omits those legends of Meyer which were "too indecent for general readers" and finds one exclamation "too obscene to be translatable". When women's behaviour strayed beyond the bounds of decency but was still of interest to scholarly gentlemen of his generation, Woods retreated into Latin footnotes, where one finds sexual matters considered too graphic to be described in English (Woods 1879: xii n; xiv n). Taplin preferred to stay silent. There are no words for female genitalia in Taplin's (1879: 125-41) English to Narrinyeri vocabulary. I assume that we should look to Taplin's missionary sensibilities to explain this silence, not to Ngarrindjeri anatomy. *Yuppun*, the word commonly used for "sex", is translated as "laying down" by Taplin (1873: 133). Taplin's silence on some terms, his mistranslations of others and his embarrassment regarding lewd women's songs should give us pause. Taplin's "Narrinyeri" were censored and self-censoring.

There certainly was sex to be reported. Protector George Mason, was the father of Pinkie Mack, but the Berndts say nothing of that, despite their purported closeness with Pinkie Mack and her lack of prudery (Berndt *et al.* 1993: 11). It may be a strategic silence but,

453

given their frankness and interest in sexual themes, it seems unlikely. Daisy Rankine, who is completely open about this aspect of her family history, smiled when I asked her why it was "unknown" in the 1940s: Her children knew. I was told when I was about fifteen. There was Frederick Taplin, who took over as superintendent at Point McLeay in 1879 and cut quite a different figure from George Taplin, his very proper father. Fred Taplin's regime was marked by repeated allegations of sexual misconduct, finally vindicated, according to Ngarrindjeri accounts, in a mysterious fire which killed him just as he was to answer to the Aborigines' Friends' Association for his behaviour (Jenkin 1979: 171ff.). Esther Butler claimed she had had sex with Fred Taplin but the investigators found no charge that could be proved (*ibid.*). What did older women say of those women who had had sex with Taplin? Another silence. In official inquiries, such as the Select Committee on Aborigines of 1860 and the Royal Commission of 1913, which established the "truth" about sexual relations on the frontier, women are spoken for and about.

Assumptions about Aboriginal peoples, their intellectual capacity, the nature of their beliefs, their place in the human race, and their ability to survive, all had a profound impact on the questions asked. Later observers were not as explicit as Woods (1879: xxxviii), who wrote: "Without a history, they have no past; without a religion, they have no hope; and without habits of forethought or providence, they can have no future." Nevertheless, these observers were sure that they were witness to the passing of a way of life. Manifest Destiny of the nineteenth century simply gave way to concepts of "culture loss" in the twentieth century, where the "last initiated man", the "last ceremony", the "last traditional songster" and the "last *Rupelli*" spoke of "memory culture". Of course, it is extremely convenient to be able to declare that one worked with the "last". As an "expert", one then has command of the field, so to speak. However, the descendants of the "last" initiated man and woman, and of others who were not canonised by either Berndt or Tindale, know quite a bit of value and what they know informs their daily lives.

Tindale and the Berndts, writing in the 1930s and 1940s, were working in an anthropological climate where the "real people" lived in the north and the "remnants" in the south. Milerum never learned to read or write which, for Tindale, makes him more "authentic". By way of contrast, Tindale (1930–52: 107) is less that flattering when it comes to Reuben Walker, whose information he says was at times contradictory and limited to "details of the days of the degeneration of his tribe". These "scraps" inform much of Tindale's work on the Ramindjeri and also offer some of the few descriptions of women's presence and power in doctor-making ceremonies. Milerum, Karloan, and Pinkie Mack were valued "informants" because they knew things others did not. This is why they were sought out. There are few who would question the authenticity of these voices. Did everyone know what Milerum and Albert Karloan knew? No. The value of their memories is that they are singular individuals. In the 1990s there are several key individuals who, supported by a community of belief, articulate cultural understandings of their relationships to land, but we hear the challenge that if no-one else knows the story, it is a dubious tradition (Mathews 1996: 174; Tonkinson 1997).

It makes a big difference how the records were generated: by first-hand contact or correspondence; by trained researchers or local pastoralists. Taplin's questionnaire in *The Folklore* (1879: 5-7) was dependent on the quality of the persons answering the questions, and the questions themselves significantly limited what might be learned. Taplin (1879: 5-7) asked: "What rites and ceremonies are used in the initiation of youths to the state of manhood?" There is no corresponding question for women, of whom it is assumed they are "given in marriage". The only question is "by whom?" Marriages were alliances between families; notions of women being "given" do not get one far in understanding the rituals of a traditional "firestick marriage". Police Trooper Moriarty (1879: 50-3), stationed at Goolwa, had some skills and his answers merit a separate entry. Of interest is that he notes that property of a man is divided between the widow and the children. Women, it would seem, had some rights. The sketch of the Narrinyeri which Taplin (1879: 34-42) derives from the answers has become a standard reference. The "facts" are repeated and recycled in other sources. Establishing a "fact" by repetition is not unusual in the early record. For example W. A. Cawthorne (1927: 74) repeats, without citation, the details of burials in the Encounter Bay area which appeared in quotation marks (also with no citation) in the 1843 Annual Report of M. Moorhouse, Protector of Aborigines, and which are detailed in Meyer (1846). The 1860 Select Committee established the "facts" about women in a similar way.

There were also nineteenth-century assumptions about womanhood based on the Victorian ideal. Women should not toil. "Amongst them the woman is an absolute slave," writes Woods (1879: xvii). The custom of women getting up and working directly after birth is part of their wretched condition (*ibid.*: xviii). Secure in the knowledge that "religion" is not part of the native experience, Woods (1879: xxx) does not pursue questions regarding what the women and men might have been doing. Taplin, a man of deep contradictions (Gale 1989: 126), makes mention of women: he wanted to ameliorate the lot of women, but he did not ask about their ceremonial life or Dreamtime stories. He was horrified by the practice of infanticide and the sexual licentiousness of *ringballin*. He thought the women's lamentations at the death of a husband to be "only convention" (14/11/1859), and in his view the custom of marrying outside the group led to fights and should therefore be curtailed (28/5/1859): "It makes the women furious inciters to vengeance, and deeply interested in the wars of the tribe, which are always about females stolen or else killed by their husbands." But then Taplin, who worried about women being beaten by their husbands, wrote: "Everything which raises the woman and makes her independent of the man, is to be encouraged" (9/12/1859). This did not include recognising the power women might derive through those marriages which Taplin found so disruptive.

Women were not asked about their interests in land. It was simply assumed that Aboriginal women on marriage, like women in the dominant society, ceded their rights to their husbands. One of the problems I have with the patrilineal patrilocal exogamous clan that appears in the writing of structural-functionalists like Radcliffe-Brown (1918) is that it is not clear where women are located within the system. They are born into the clan of their father. After marriage they take up residence in another country, that of their husband, where they must enjoy hunting and gathering rights in order to

456

survive. Women join and live with the horde of their husband, says Radcliffe-Brown (*ibid.*: 222, 237). From women themselves, it is clear they remain members of their natal clan; that is their family, that is how they reckon *ngatji* affiliation. The interests in their husband's clan and what will be the clan of their children are residential and use-based. The land-owning group (clan) cannot be the same as the residential group (horde), a distinction which subsequently came into focus (Elkin 1938). Had women been made visible as persons with interests in land, the inadequacies of the patrilineal clan model would have been apparent. Instead, it took many land claims and precise on-the-ground mapping of land-based relationship to demonstrate the lack of fit between the anthropological model and the lived reality (Bell 1993a: 237-8).

The silences can be instructive. Angas (1847: 58, 68, 87, 159) maps a gendered world when he notes women's fearful reaction to the presence of his all-male party. Meyer (1846) does not assume that men are the only ones with a ceremonial life but, with limited access to women's domain, he was at a disadvantage in providing details. The answers to Question 46 of Taplin's questionnaire (1879: 53) state that an initiate is "not allowed to speak to, or take, or use anything that has been handled by a female until his beard and whiskers are again plucked which completes the ceremony"; this is a window onto a world of gender restrictions. Silences may also indicate that insufficient time was spent in the field. The Berndts (1993) did not record Karloan's initiation site. Tindale (1930–52: 145, 199) did. Catherine Berndt (1994b) gives the date as 1884, and in the Berndts' joint work (1993: 172) it is 1882. Ronald Berndt (1940a) recorded the *Ngurunderi* story, but no songs about his travels. Luckily Tindale (1937, 1941) did. Silences may also indicate straight-out sexism. Elymann (Courto 1996: 59) accuses Aboriginal women of "superstition, mean-spiritedness, pettiness, belligerence, gossiping and scandal-mongering". Clearly he will not be asking about the "inner meanings" women attribute to certain behaviours. To be fair, he also found white women to be deficient. Somewhat ironically, several Ngarrindjeri who had told me of the existence of this manuscript held out the hope that it would contain something about women. Not all were as explicit as Elymann, but the result was much the same. We certainly do not hear from women, though we hear of them; and the information is usually about their bodies as sites of pleasure, reproduction and disease.

Lower Murray "experts" have a well-established tradition of disagreeing with each other which significantly predates the Royal Commission of 1995. There is no agreement in the sources as to who the Ngarrindjeri are. We have "Taplin's Narrinyeri", a term which Clarke (1991: 96) has suggested represents a "reinvention of tradition"; the Berndts (1993) use "Kukabrak", a term known to few in the Lower Murray today. Tindale (1974) terminates Ngarrindjeri country at Cape Jervis, while the Berndts (1993: 394) bring Ramindjeri country to just south of Adelaide. Tindale and the Berndts have harsh things to say about each other and about Taplin. Tindale (Tindale and Long nd: 9), complaining that Taplin never really understood the underlying structure of the Ngarrindjeri, describes *The Folklore* as a "monumental compilation" which "gathered together data of priceless interest", and regrets that Taplin "did not live to develop any comprehensive study". Regarding his additions to the second edition of *The Narrinyeri* in 1879, Tindale (*ibid.*) is of the opinion that "in later years the anthropological aspects of his work were being overshadowed by his humanitarian and missionary efforts". In a slightly drier tone, the Berndts (1993: 121) state: "We think that Taplin misunderstood a great deal of what was going on at Pt McLeay". The Berndts (*ibid.*: 2) describe Tindale as an "ethnologist at the Museum in the mid-1930s", with access to only a few elderly men and women, whose "material is limited no doubt because of his Museum commitments at that time". They note that a "major manuscript by Tindale is currently in preparation" (*ibid.*), but do not seem to countenance the possibility that it might add depth to their work, which was undertaken with fewer people and over a much shorter period of time than Tindale's was. Ronald Berndt (1982: 49-50) writes that he saw little of Tindale who, having been trained as an entomologist, might be considered an "amateur" anthropologist. Berndt went to Sydney to study with the "professionals".

Tindale (Tindale and Long nd: 5) says that, in his absence during the war years, Ronald Berndt had access to some of his notebooks and "in a few cases he has used my data unknowingly repeating in print some of my already published words so that in a few cases original ownership will not always be clear". On the other hand, Tindale (*ibid.* nd: 6) considers that it is "unfortunate that the Berndts neither read the early published data nor have had access to the data gathered from Ivartji and men such as Milerum". The Tindale material is an excellent antidote to a Yaraldi perspective of Taplin and the Berndts. However, most of it is unpublished. This skews our understanding of the society. We do not know what is happening along the Coorong and around Encounter Bay. The Berndts have little or no information on clans in those regions, including Hindmarsh Island. It is also unfortunate that the Berndts did not consult with this generation of elders.

Is there such a discordance of ethnographic voices that we have only personal snapshots of particular moments? If one makes plain the questions with which one begins, the interests that drive one's research, and one's methodology; if one is prepared to allow that the presence of a fieldworker is an element in the production of knowledge; if one can allow that all representations are partial, perspectival and situated in time and place, and do so without disappearing in a postmodern abyss of multiple subject positions or opting for absolute cultural relativism, then, yes, I think we can write ethnography that will be worth reading. It will be ethically grounded, it will be nuanced, and it will honour difference. It will be consciously located in time and place. This is ethnography from which we might be able to distil more enduring truths than one generated under coercive, sexist, racist, or homophobic conditions.[14]

On Women, Feminists and Ethnography

According to Commissioner Stevens (1995: 41): "A number of female anthropologists and ethnographers have worked in the Lower Murray area, including Dorothy Tindale, Alison Brookman (née Harvey), Catherine Berndt, Judy Inglis, Faye [*sic*] Gale, Jane Jacobs and Joy Wundersitz." Philip Clarke (1995a: 176) nominated Catherine Berndt as "one of the first feminist anthropologists in Australia working with Aboriginal culture". Philip Jones (1995: 4269) spoke of a tradition of feminist anthropology dating from the 1930s in the region and the "very strong commitment to investigate women's life, both in a practical sense and the spiritual dimension of that life". How then could such a significant cultural fact as the existence of an esoteric body of women's knowledge have escaped the attention of so many learned, skilled, and worthy women? Fay Gale (1989) had already urged a reconsideration of the early records and pointed to evidence in Edward John Eyre's journals of women's ceremonies. Steven Hemming (1996: 25) provides an alternate reading of the sources to demonstrate that the "long-term existence of secret women's business associated with Hindmarsh Island was entirely plausible". Philip Clarke (1996: 142) in revisiting his position that "it was very unlikely that the alleged secret sacred women's business as it related to Hindmarsh Island would have existed before early 1994", argues that there is a lack of fit for such a possibility with the ethnography of the Lower Murray, which "affords men's business and women's business an equal footing and, therefore, so much interconnection, that it can't really be separated out" (*ibid.*).

I have suggested that there is ample material in the existing sources to indicate that women were sacred at certain times and that on those occasions women were separated from women and in the care of senior women. These are necessary conditions for the generation of esoteric knowledge privileged to women. To know what is going on in these female-only domains requires a woman researcher, and not just any woman. She needs to be trusted, and stay around long enough to establish rapport; in most parts of Australia, it helps if one has children and even some grey hair. What one is told as a young woman is not what one is told as a grandmother. Each can collect valuable data, but it is the feminist attention to reflexivity that allows the reader to understand the ways in which the ethnography is embedded in particular relationships forged at particular times by particular persons. So, what of the women who worked in the Lower Murray?

Alison Brookman (née Harvey) is the joint author with Mountford (1942) of an article on women in the Flinders Ranges and another on a Yaraldi fishing legend (Harvey 1943). Tindale (nd, b) wrote of Alison Harvey in his "Informants File": "During the 1940s while staff shortage occurred in the Ethnology Department, she was an honorary assistant, and was able to gather very useful geographical and other details of Yaraldi legends . . . resulting in seven research papers on Australian native culture". In the course of the Royal Commission, Alison Brookman (1995: 4570-99) gave evidence regarding her notes of her 1939 visit with Pinkie Mack and painted a much less productive portrait of herself. Both Tindale and Mountford had wanted her to investigate if women had a "secret realm" which might parallel that of the men with whom they had worked in other parts of Australia (1995: 4574-5). She had already worked with Mountford in the Flinders Ranges for two weeks (1995: 4573), although she stated that she had only helped with the writing of the article on "Women of the Adnjamatana" (Mountford and Harvey 1942), not the research (1995: 4592). Of her Ngarrindjeri work, she supposed he had given her questions for Pinkie Mack with whom she spent time on 12 and 24 June 1939. Tindale had indicated that Pinkie Mack was the keeper of women's knowledge and thus this was the one person with whom she spoke (1995: 4587).

Harvey's field-note that birth was "secret" became the subject of extensive cross-examination. As she explained, it was "secret" in the sense that, for practical reasons, men and others not involved kept out of the way of a woman giving birth. It is hard to know how one would establish this as fact, but even if it were so, there could still be women's secret rituals performed at this moment in women's lives. At the time of her interviews with Pinkie Mack, Alison Harvey was twenty. Her BA was in classics and history. Her only experience of Aborigines was casual contacts on holidays and through her volunteer work in the museum. While it is laudable that Mountford and Tindale recognised the need for a woman to talk with the women, it was unrealistic, if not slightly contemptuous, to expect a young inexperienced classicist to be able to learn of restricted material in a couple of afternoons. Catherine Berndt (1989: 6) wrote of what an additional six months at Ooldea might have achieved in terms of gaining the necessary trust and fluency to learn of women's ceremonial life there.

Dorothy Tindale (1939), who accompanied her husband on the 1938–9 Harvard–Adelaide University Anthropological Expedition, kept "Notes on School Children and Menstruation". The front page of the exercise book reads: "These notes were made by Dorothy M. Tindale under direction of N. B. Tindale". In all, there are about thirty-six pages of handwritten notes, only a small part of which refers to Point McLeay women. There are, however, names and dates so one can know whence her information came. Like Alison Harvey, Dorothy Tindale was working under the direction of a man. Both women asked the questions deemed appropriate by these better-qualified and more experienced men. They asked about topics which were deemed suitable for female researchers: women's reproductive lives, their role as mothers and care-givers. Dorothy Tindale did elicit some helpful notes on birth practices to which I shall be turning in the next chapter, and Alison Harvey's extremely careful transcripts of language indicate the precision with which she recorded. Both Dorothy Tindale and Alison Harvey were engaged in the first step in a feminist ethnographic project—recording women—but neither expressed any interest in feminist theory nor demonstrated any engagement with feminist practice. Neither made any claims to be feminists.

Judy Inglis (1964: 115) an anthropologist who worked with the mission populations, acknowledged that they were often very knowledgeable about their kin, work history and moves, but she wrote: "Part-aborigines in this area no longer have a distinct culture. The reserves at Point Pearce and Point McLeay are simply rural slums." Through a careful study of genealogies and oral histories of the descendants of "six first-generation half-caste couples", Inglis mapped the ways in which the segregated populations of the missions scattered as their members moved out into "new forms of employment and new forms of interaction with members of the white society" (*ibid.*: 131). In her article "Aborigines in Adelaide" (Inglis 1961) she canvasses similar material. Inglis certainly includes women in her statistics and genealogies, but there is no particular focus on women.

Fay Gale and Joy Wundersitz, both geographers, writing of *Adelaide Aborigines* (1982) offer insights regarding the shifting demographies of the Point McLeay population on which I drew in Chapter 4. Gale's commitment to making women visible in her work is of long standing—*Women's Role in Aboriginal Society*, edited by Gale (1970) was the first of its kind in its engagement with feminist issues—and *We Are Bosses Ourselves*, also edited by Gale (1983) incorporates Ngarrindjeri voices.

Catherine Berndt's work, especially that which draws on her relationship with Pinkie Mack, is where we learn most directly of Ngarrindjeri women. Pinkie Mack's life, 1858–1954, spanned the century from the establishment of the mission to the height of assimilation era; she provided information to Tindale, the Berndts, and Alison Brookman. She was said to be the last woman to have gone through some women's initiation rituals. Her places were within Yaraldi territory and, through her marriage to John Mack, she had visited and knew others up-river. Without having some indication of her range of stories, it is hard to determine which country she knew in detail and which by implication, extension, and inference. Her songs of lament for the Piltindjeri and her retelling of the story of Crow (Berndt *et al.* 1993: 459-62) point to her continuing attachment to the clan territory of her "social" father. Tindale writes of meeting Pinkie Mack in March 1933 and of the topics they discussed, including the *ngia-ngiampe* relations, initiation, genealogies, *ngatji*, and a story of killing children at Jol:urum.[15]

How long did they spend with Pinkie Mack? The Berndts make no mention of working with her in 1942. Where did they meet with her in 1943? Of Brinkley (Berndt *et al.*: Plates 7, 27) and Raukkan (*ibid.*: Plates 8, 45) we can be sure, but how many other times were there? They had so many other commitments in that period and I wonder if Catherine did not spend part of her time at Murray Bridge while Ronald was working with Karloan, in preparing the Ooldea Fieldwork Report for *Oceania* (Berndt and Berndt 1942–5).[16] Did the Berndts ever travel with Pinkie Mack? It would appear not. Neither of the Berndts could drive. The material we have from Tindale of restricted places comes from his site visits with Milerum. The Berndts (*ibid.*: 10) are quite explicit that their sessions were conducted in or around the dwellings of Karloan at Murray Bridge and of Pinkie Mack at Brinkley. They are similarly explicit about the long days spent with Albert Karloan and his dedication to recording his culture (*ibid.*: 4). Pinkie Mack expressed some ambivalence. "However, she soon warmed to the task of teaching us what she thought we should know about Aboriginal people and Aboriginal life in that region. She was able and anxious to check over with us some of the material obtained from Karloan" (*ibid.*: 7). She checked data, but was she invited to initiate conversations? Was she asked about topics of importance to women in her own right?

There are many other unanswered questions. Was Catherine ever alone with Pinkie Mack? Her field-work style was "independence within a framework of interdependence", a pattern of "being together-but-separate" style, and it was also her view of the relationship between sexes in Aboriginal society (Kaldor 1988: 11; R. and M. Tonkinson 1994). Isobel White (1994) recalls several situations which demonstrated the extreme closeness of the Berndts as a couple and informs her view that "They certainly thought as one." Their teamwork resulted in many jointly authored pieces. The times they worked separately (while being together) are the basis of work that reveals the existence of knowledge and practices that are restricted to men or to women (C. Berndt 1950, 1965; R. Berndt 1952). In the Lower Murray, Ronald Berndt certainly spent time man-to-man with Karloan; but it is moot whether Catherine spent time woman-to-woman with Pinkie Mack. In her article reviewing her work in South Australia, Catherine is quite explicit about the benefits of having worked with the women by herself on other occasions, but makes no mention of it in the Lower Murray. Aunty Daisy does not recall any women-only sessions. Of course, she may have been absent or sent away.

How well did Catherine Berndt know Pinkie Mack? In an encyclopaedia entry, more concerned with Pinkie Mack's marital history, sexuality and nostalgia for the past than the breadth and depth of her knowledge, Berndt (1994a) describes her as "lovable and kind, dignified and passionate about what she saw as injustice, quietly courageous". Berndt approved of Pinkie Mack's use of feminine wiles, noting that she knew when to argue, cajole or persuade and was known as being able to get "anything out of that man [Chief Protector of Aborigines]". Without access to field-notes or reports such as the one from Ooldea, we cannot know what Catherine Berndt asked Pinkie Mack or when. If the 1951 book is any indication, it concerned sex, not the more esoteric readings of sexual symbolism that are available as one is brought deeper and deeper into the meanings of stories, songs and ceremonies. Even so, it appears Catherine did not know the identity of Pinkie Mack's father, a significant silence if we are to accept that women's secret knowledge would not have escaped her notice.

Was Catherine Berndt an equal partner in the production of *A World That Was*? In the jointly authored book which contains a chapter on the Lower Murray, there is a footnote to "R. M. Berndt, *Jaraldi Society*, unpublished manuscript" (Berndt and Berndt 1951: 84n). In 1961 in another jointly authored work there is another footnote to Ronald Berndt's two-volume manuscript "A Reconstruction of Yaralde Society (Berndt and Berndt 1961: 104 n 57). In 1974 Ronald is still referring to the unpublished material on the Narrinyeri as his alone (Berndt 1974: 27) and noting the need for reassessment of the material. According to John Stanton, curator of the Berndt Museum, who helped to complete the book, the first ten chapters of the manuscript were drafted by Ronald in the 1940s and the remainder was written in the 1980s jointly by Ronald and Catherine.[17] No wonder the section on birth has Pinkie Mack commenting on men's data rather than being the primary informant (Berndt *et al.* 1993: 142). From the appendices, it is clear that Pinkie Mack and Albert Karloan did not participate equally in the generation of material for the book. Karloan is the primary informant and the Berndts say as much. He worked from dawn to dusk and was committed to making this record of his culture (*ibid.*: 6, 282). Pinkie Mack, on the other hand, when they met up with her in 1943, was mourning the death of her grandson, Hurtle Sumner, and certain topics would have been set aside. Having Pinkie Mack check and supplement the record is not the same as hearing from her in her own right. Pinkie Mack's input does not completely lay to rest the matter of bias towards either sex in the reporting or conceptual framing of the book (Berndt *et al.* 1993: 11).

Catherine Berndt (Berndt and Berndt 1942–5: 220, 230) had written of "women's life" at Ooldea, of "their secret life, in which men have no share". Why did she not pursue the matter with the Ngarrindjeri, which was her next field-work site? While in the field at Ooldea, the Berndts were living in a community of several hundred

465

people, which swelled to four or five hundred during times of ceremonies and fell to around eighty when people dispersed after rain (*ibid.*: 8). They reported that each day there would be people "passing to and from the Soak, returning from hunting, obtaining water or collecting rations", and others who "assembled to gossip sitting round our fire" (*ibid.*: 7). "Very few of the women speak English", wrote Catherine (*ibid.*: 208). At least once a week in the evening, they could attend an *inma*, public performances which were open to the community (*ibid.*: 154), and were also able to report on secret women's rites and secret men's rites (*ibid.*: 154, 254). This is in stark contrast to their field situation in the Lower Murray, where there were no large ceremonial gatherings, no large seasonal population movements, and no abundance of fluent speakers from whom to record stories and learn language. At Ooldea there were good reasons to pursue questions regarding women's life, women's stories and women's business. It was there being played out. In a sense, it could not be avoided. As Catherine Berndt (*ibid.*: 1942–5: 3) acknowledges what she calls the "sex-dichotomy", it was not productive for a researcher to "overstep the allotted boundaries". This was a gendered field: women worked with women and men with men. But when the only woman with whom Catherine felt it was appropriate to talk about the old days was Pinkie Mack, there were less compelling reasons to ask about those aspects of women's lives that concerned all-female gatherings.

Could Catherine Berndt have overlooked secret women's business if it existed in the Lower Murray? I am suggesting it is possible. She was new to the field—in fact it was her husband's field-work site which she shared for some months in 1942 and 1943. She was a junior partner in this project, although she was more advanced than her husband in terms of her anthropological studies. She was young and childless, a woman who shared little of the life experience of Pinkie Mack, by then in her eighties and a great-grandmother. In 1942–3 Catherine Berndt had many calls on her time: the Ooldea manuscript, the acculturation study and so on. There is every possibility that Catherine did not spend time alone with Pinkie Mack, and if she did it was minimal and did not involve questions regarding a "secret life". It is my sense that Catherine was always a dedicated, meticulous and careful researcher, but that she saw no reason to work alone with women in the Lower Murray. Such things belonged in more traditional areas. Catherine would certainly have been aware of the work of Phyllis Kaberry (1939). I do not know when Catherine Berndt read Kaberry. Some of the language in her Ooldea material is reminiscent of Kaberry's, but Berndt does not cite her work there, only later. Questions of the sacred and profane were not ones which engaged Catherine in her work with Pinkie Mack. Her six-month stay at Ooldea certainly establishes her as fieldworker, and her field-work methods were rigorous, but Ooldea was not the Lower Murray. The Berndts asked different questions of these very different sites. They were integrated into the lives of the people in very different ways and established qualitatively different relation-ships.

What of the claim that Catherine Berndt is the foremost feminist ethnographer of the Lower Murray? Catherine was certainly a woman who worked with women and understood that field work was gendered, but she chose to distance herself from the label feminist. She was not engaged by feminist theory. Nonetheless her work is a contribution to feminist anthropology. Her MA thesis, "Women's Changing Ceremonies in Northern Australia" (1950) and 1965 article on "Women and the Secret Life'" are classics, but Catherine believed that "setting the record straight for women should not be at the expense of men" (Kaldor 1988: 10). According to Susan Kaldor (*ibid.*), Catherine was "brought up to believe in the basic overall equality of both sexes and also in the need for reform . . . a rather formidable figure, kind but used to having it her own way"; and she "did not come into anthropology as a militant feminist". As Catherine aged, she worked in more "traditional" communities and began to develop an appreciation of the depth of women's culture; she worked through various models of gender relations that might best explain her field-work experience. She wrote of complementarity, the two-sex model, independence and interdependence.[18] As feminists began to critique the male bias of much anthropology in Australia, she attempted to find an intellectual space that offered comfort with past work and a framework for future writing.

467

Looking back on her field work at Vestey's, Catherine Berndt claimed that she learned much of women's secret rituals, which women did not mind sharing as long it stayed within the region (Kaldor 1988: 11). Of course, this is impossible once one publishes material. Kaldor (*ibid.*) explains it by reference to there being "so much intrusion the situation is different now, and for reasons of privacy as well as secrecy, Berndt is considering not publishing such material except in the most general terms". Drawing on her experience from elsewhere, and with the benefit of hindsight, Berndt reasons that, given more time, she could have mapped the women's knowledge of land and myth. Much of her work is still unpublished, including a long-promised volume on women (Berndt and Berndt 1942–5: 260); her fieldnotes will not be available until 2024. We do not have Catherine Berndt's final word on the subject of women's lives in the Lower Murray.

A tradition of feminist anthropologists

I am having some difficulty endorsing the notion that there were a number of feminist anthropologists who paid attention to the practical and spiritual aspects of women's lives in the Lower Murray. The feminist tradition, if we want to call it that, is the grandmother's lore of which Doreen Kartinyeri spoke; it is the passing down of titles and knowledge of which Aunty Daisy spoke; it is the stories of strong women on the Coorong of which Liz Tongerie speaks; it is the importance of whales of Aunty Maggie's stories; the sacred waters of Sarah Milera's testimony; the Seven Sisters Dreaming of Veronica Brodie's; and the many women's stories of the dandelions and when it is safe to swim. The blood lines running through Pinkie Mack, Koomi Wilson, the Kropinyeris and Kartinyeris are well attested in the written record, but not the content of the stories. These are the authorities. Thus when Doreen Kartinyeri wrote to the Minister, Robert Tickner, on 12 May 1994, regarding the importance of the site to women, she cited her elders as sources. Her attempts to find support in the written record became part of the Royal Commission narrative of fabrication. The report of Deane Fergie (1994), which details the women's knowledge, makes plain the way in which the story was negotiated into print, the nomination of Doreen

Kartinyeri as the spokesperson for the group, and the difficulties that women face in bringing their stories forward.

The report has a history. In June 1994 Deane Fergie of the Department of Anthropology, University of Adelaide, was commissioned by the Aboriginal Legal Rights Movement (ALRM) to prepare "An anthropological assessment of the threat of injury and desecration to Aboriginal tradition by the proposed Hindmarsh Island Bridge Construction". Initially, Fergie's brief of 17 June 1984 was "to facilitate" a meeting between Professor Cheryl Saunders and Ngarrindjeri women. She had not conducted field work in the area and was careful to say so, but she had known Doreen since 1988 and they enjoyed a collegial friendship based on trust and mutual respect, enriched by each observing and talking with the other about their work practices. In the course of the ALRM consultancy, Fergie found herself invited to a women-only meeting at which she was not permitted to take notes, and she subsequently had various conversations with Doreen Kartinyeri and Sarah Milera. On 26 June, nine days after the initial brief, she was asked to prepare a report which would go to the Minister. She spoke to a number of other people and eight days later, on 4 July, submitted a 32-page report, to which was attached an envelope containing the restricted women's knowledge, marked "To be read by women only". Her documentation of the existence of "women's business" which was associated with Hindmarsh Island, the Goolwa Channel, Murray Mouth and Lake Alexandrina concerned an area "vital to the reproduction of human beings and the cosmos more generally". More specifically, within the corridor of the proposed bridge were sites which would be damaged if the bridge was built. The driving of pylons into the ground would be tantamount to driving a stake into their own bodies. The building of a bridge would create a permanent link between the land and the island and would cover the sacred waters. Fergie's report and her evidence to the Royal Commission have become centrepieces in the contesting of the ethnography of the Lower Murray.

How might a feminist ethnography of the Lower Murray be constructed?

"What are the women doing?" would be my starting point. Women are unevenly reported and under-reported as social actors; they are not relied on as sources; their practices were considered loathsome and licentious by missionaries; their contemporary claims have been trivialised and dismissed as fabrications. But there are traces. The longer I have with the sources, the more I find that supports statements that have been declared insupportable or impossible. It is a brave individual who makes categorical pronouncements regarding what is not, with reference to an oral culture that has been so imperfectly recorded.

The second and closely allied move is a strategic reading of the reclaimed and existing texts. For instance, when Pinkie Mack— according to the Berndts, the last initiated Ngarrindjeri woman— says she doesn't know her initiation songs, what did she mean? Here one must pay attention to context, be reflexive, heed the silences as well as the utterances. With respect to research with Ngarrindjeri women, I point out the prurient interest in women's bodies that the sources exhibit; an understanding of this is a critically important context for reading the sources "against the grain". Taplin's charges lived in repressive times and we hear from them through a filter. The informants of the Berndts and Tindale spoke in the age of assimilation, before feminist social scientists drew attention to the gendered nature of knowledge and the consequences the insights of feminist epistemology has for research in societies where there are gender-based domains. The Ngarrindjeri who write, speak, sing and know today seek the fulfilment of the promise of self-determination. More women are speaking and with more confidence. So how are we to understand what is being said?

The third set of questions concern methodologies and epistemologies. How would one design a research project that might provide insights into women's worlds? How does one adjudicate between competing accounts? If younger people say one thing and older people say another, if men offer one account and women another, does one have to read one account to the exclusion of the other? Does one negate the other? We need more nuanced models of societies, which acknowledge that information is not evenly distributed through any society; that knowledge is negotiated; that there may be more than one explanation for a particular phenomenon.

470

Of Courts, Consultants and Armchairs

The Royal Commission and various hearings have generated a formidable record of testimony, reports and articles dealing with the area of the proposed bridge, the politics of the proponents, the dissidents, anthropologists, and the courts. The Ngarrindjeri have become public property. Their genealogies, stories, conversations, and fights have made news. Most consultants' reports have involved minimal field work and have been conducted under less than perfect circumstances. A number of anthropologists, archaeologists and historians have worked on matters Hindmarsh, but not all reports have been published or made available within the hearings, let alone to a wider public. Robert Tonkinson gave advice to Commissioner Stevens but was not cross-examined on it. The reports of archaeologists Vanessa Edmunds, Neale Draper, anthropologists Rod Lucas and Deane Fergie, historian Steven Hemming, cultural geographer Philip Clarke and his fellow museum employee Philip Jones became part of the Royal Commission. They were unavailable to me until near the end of the Mathews Report process. The confidential appendices to Fergie's report were never made available. Most of the reports are still not public documents. I believe that copies can be found, but I have not tried. I have used only those documents which are in the public domain.

During the Mathews Report, Drs Peter Sutton, Nancy Williams, Myrna Tonkinson, and Roger Luebbers, Professors Francesca Merlan and Marcia Langton were approached by the Justice Mathews to serve as an expert panel. Marcia Langton (1996) stepped down and delivered a fine analysis of the case in Adelaide in March 1996. Roger Luebbers also did not serve, but he made his material available to the applicants in report form. A report of Peter Sutton's became public because it was quoted by Mathews in her report which was tabled in parliament, but no other documents were forthcoming. Nancy Williams certainly prepared materials for Judge Mathews, but it is not clear what the role was of the other members of the panel. Geoffrey Bagshaw and I worked with applicants, and Ken Maddock and Grayson Gerrard worked with the Chapmans. None of our reports, save what was quoted in Mathews, has been made public. This case has drawn in many senior people. What has been learned?

471

The first anthropological study of the Heritage issues associated with the area was prepared by Rod Lucas. "The Anthropology and Aboriginal History of Hindmarsh Island: A Report to Binalong Pty Ltd and Aboriginal Heritage Branch Adelaide (1990)" was based on fourteen days' work. It was written before the Tindale material was available and before the publication of the Berndt book, although Lucas had seen the latter in typescript in early 1989. In the existing sources, Lucas found no records of sites of mythological significance on Hindmarsh Island and recommended consultation with Aboriginal groups. His account of the alienation of land on the island draws on local histories and newspaper reports, indicating that the history of the area is yet to be written. We are still in the reclamation stage.

This has not stopped the armchair anthropologists, like the learned gentlemen of a century ago, from expressing their opinions. In the media, at conferences and in print, James Weiner (1995a, 1995b), professor of anthropology, University of Adelaide, has struggled with the notion of "secrets". Ron Brunton (1996a, b, 1991) has become one of the "authorities" on sacred sites in Australia, yet, to the best of my knowledge, he has not conducted any in-depth field work with Aboriginal people. Professor Robert Tonkinson, who followed Ronald Berndt in the chair in the Department of Anthropology at the University of Western Australia, has positioned himself as an expert commentator of the "Hindmarsh Island Bridge Affair". Tonkinson (1997: 6) explains his involvement as stemming from his writing the foreword to the Berndts' (1993) book:

> Although I had never worked in the area, I was a former student, colleague and friend of the Berndts. My brief was to comment on the Berndts' field work and its significance, and to situate their findings concerning Ngarrindjeri culture in the broader literature on Aboriginal Australia, with reference especially to issues such as leadership, politics and gender relations, which have been topics of debate in recent decades. Near the outset of the Royal Commission, which was held in Adelaide, I was asked by Counsel Assisting the Commissioner to advise them on matters pertaining to anthropological evidence.

Tonkinson was not called upon to give evidence, but he did meet with Counsel Assisting in Adelaide and also spoke briefly with the Commissioner.[19] In summary, he thought there was a "possibility"

of "secret women's business" but argued "on the basis of the anthropological evidence alone, serious questions arise as to how such a
hugely consequential body of knowledge could have remained so
restricted, and how its status as a secret-sacred category could have
failed to leave a visible imprint of any kind" (*ibid.*). But it had left
an imprint for those with the eyes to see.

Let me offer two examples from my own field work to illustrate
the importance of participant-observation field work. In 1976–8 in
central Australia, I spent a great deal of my time with the older
women in women-only camps, called *jilimi*. These camps were
located near the women's ceremonial area, which was very similar to
the description of the site for the young girls' puberty ceremonies
amongst the Ngarrindjeri. No-one could get to the area without
being seen approaching, and men avoided the area scrupulously. I
always travelled with women who were my classificatory sisters and
who shared the major kin avoidances that I should observe if I was
not to endanger those with whom I was travelling. I thought
nothing of the route I took. Then one day, in one community,
when I was being driven by a white community advisor who knew
the community well, we took a completely different route through
one area. I asked him why he'd gone that way, and he replied that
was where the Aboriginal men with whom he worked took him.
There was no reason why he would ever have seen or heard the
women on their ceremonial ground. He knew they had a camp but
he had been taught to avoid it, as I was taught to avoid the men's
areas. On another occasion, in a community further north, a group
of women had decided to stage a ceremony which marked the
transition to womanhood of one the girls in that community. The
men went off hunting that day and took the missionaries with
them. The women did not advertise what they were about to do,
but it was spectacular, and it required that they have full control
over the camps, the river, and all approaches. If it is possible to live
in a community and not visit women's places or be around during
their ceremonies, then it is possible not to "know".

Along with the return of the armchair anthropologists has come a
reassertion of an outmoded notion of the role of museums as the
guardians of knowledge. There is a deep unease with the new role of

museums as interpreters of the past, as incorporating diverse voices, as sorting through hitherto unrecorded meanings that are being attached to places, peoples and cultural practices. Of course, museums have always had a interpretive function, they have always dealt with meaning; but the focus on material culture masked this aspect of their practice. The active voices of Ngarrindjeri, a range of voices, voices which can not be filed away, are challenging this order, just as women who insist they know something the museum has never recorded threaten the masculine character of the written record.

Finding Meaning in a Changing World: A constant

It is convenient to believe that the ethnographic records of the mid-nineteenth to mid-twentieth century have captured "tradition" and to argue that, as Ngarrindjeri have become increasingly enmeshed in the cash economy, been missionised, and taught to read and write, they have "lost" their culture. Indeed, this is the language used by some Ngarrindjeri themselves. Where there are no written records to which one might turn to explore changes over the centuries, and where the religious ideology, underwritten by strict adherence to the law of the ancestors, is resistant to change, the image of a timeless native in a timeless land flourishes. Anthropologists arrive at a particular moment and establish an ethnographic baseline of "tradition" against which all other accounts and behaviours are read and, most often, found to be wanting. Of course, there are other ways in which we can tap into change than through written records and, although inherently conservative, Aboriginal religion did not stifle all imagination and creativity. But the image of the traditional Aborigine as "firmly fettered by rigid bonds of tradition" (Strehlow 1947: 5) is entrenched in popular imagination, and it is a comforting story for those who would dismiss contemporary interest in culture as politically motivated.

It might also be convenient to divide the contemporary worlds of Aborigines into modern people and traditional people (Cowlishaw 1988; Merlan 1991). Yet, as Francesca Merlan (1991: 350) points out for the Jawoyn and the Coronation Hill controversy, the juxtaposition of modernity with traditionalism unrealistically sets one group against another and ignores the nature of the conditions under which Aboriginal people have accommodated change. Few anthropologists have paid attention to urban populations, though the work of Basil Sansom with town campers in Darwin is a beginning. Work in the rural sector, such as that of Gillian Cowlishaw (1988) also identifies important questions for a study of Aboriginal populations who have long experience of living with non-Aboriginal populations. Ian Keen (1988), Jeremy Beckett (1994), Diane Barwick (1963), and Marie Reay (1949) have explored the distinctive Aboriginal cultures of the southeast. These are not "poor whites in black skins" but people who have fashioned lives within changing worlds,

In this dichotomy between the remote and the settled, Aborigines in the north still have "traditions", whereas those in the settled areas have remnants, memories, and museum projects. The latter are the stuff of reclamation, but not worthy of being considered "traditional"; their contemporary social practice is not the stuff of anthropological research. They can be left to the sociologists, oral historians and archaeologists. When it becomes apparent that there are still people who are concerned about their cultural heritage, and moreover are still imparting the knowledge of their forebears to their children and grandchildren, and are claiming that their daily social practice is resonant with the stories of their ancestors, such individuals are treated with suspicion. Where did they learn such things? Must be from books. If not from books, certainly from outsiders. It cannot be authentic knowledge if it does not tally with the early records and/or approximate the life of people in the remote areas. However, the modern/traditional, settled/remote, pristine/political dichotomies overlook the dynamic nature of Aboriginal societies in their pre-contact past, as well as their capacity to adapt, absorb, and survive today. Certainly Ngarrindjeri culture has changed with changing conditions, but change was also part of the structure of the culture. Today *ngatji* bring messages. The land is alive with signs of intent, foreboding, and significance. *Miwi* can still bring one home. Weavers use new materials and bind families in complex ways. Songs that initially addressed specific historical moments over time become associated with more general needs and anxieties. The songs which today capture the struggle of

475

knowledgeable Ngarrindjeri to protect their places will, in a generation or two, become songs of pride and determination. Language has always had the capacity to absorb new concepts, as have stories. In the nineteenth century we know of "traditions" learned from neighbours that were seamlessly woven into the local culture. An instance is *ngildjeri*, which Taplin noted was a recent form of sorcery; by the time Berndt *et al.* (1993: 261) wrote of these practices, *ngildjeri* had become part of the traditional repertoire. In an oral tradition, these changes would not be subject to outside scrutiny regarding their authenticity.

It might further be convenient to believe that, prior to the advent of Aboriginal land rights and issues of access to resources, which can pit one group against another, there were no divisions within Aboriginal communities. In this romantic vision of Indigenous peoples, there was caring, sharing and no conflict. Although clan territories were relatively well-defined, there was fission and fusion, and issues of contested leadership to be addressed. Tindale (nd, f) writes that clans were often of a "volatile, unstable character with disputes leading to breakaways to some members and their adjustment but changes of totem to emphasise their quasi-independence". Pressure on clans came from shifts in population, climate, flora and fauna, as well as disputes, leadership struggles, killings, jealousy and competition for spouses. Tindale (1941: 241-2) offers the example of a Kaurna woman at Rapid Bay, married to a Ramindjeri man who lived at Goolwa. When he died, there were moves to get her to remarry locally so that the rights she held, from her deceased husband, for permission to spear sharks would be retained within the community.

There were divisions within and between clan groups, and there were individual likes and dislikes. There were struggles for leadership. Clarence Long and Albert Karloan, who are the sources for most of what we know of the 1930s and 1940s, did not get along together and disagreed over basic issues such as the use of bullroarers in the Lower Murray (Berndt *et al.* 1993: 211). To depict small kin-based societies as harmonious is an act of romantic retrospection which denies full humanity to members of such societies. There may well be an idealised model which depicts a conflict-free society but,

476

like contemporary notions of "happy families", the reality is somewhat different, as the current statistics on domestic violence indicate. The power struggles, which are well documented in the songs of Milerum, were over land, resources, and marriage alliances. Ronald Berndt (1965: 178) alludes to strategies that the Manggurupa clan employed to gain ascendancy in the *tendi*. Looking back, all one sees is that a particular person was the *Rupelli*, sorcerer, or a ceremonial leader. One does not see the power plays. Yet from the songs and stories we know that there were such struggles.

To argue that Indigenous people were trapped in a world of tradition that tolerated no change is to confuse statements regarding the religious "dogma of immutability" with the reality of accommodation of changing circumstances: what I have called the "necessary and continuous process of reinvention" (Bell 1993a: 90-4). The former creates a stable and secure framework within which change can be negotiated. As Stanner (1966: 169) writes, "They attained stability but avoided inertia." The circumstances under which change occurs is not a free-for-all, but rather a delicately balanced system of checks and balances. Institutions like the *tendi* played an important adjudicatory function; individual dreamers and mystics were "given" knowledge; and expert story-tellers wove the threads into seamless garments in which a community of believers might wrap themselves.

In the desert regions, through song, dance, painting, ceremonies, hunting and gathering, at each generation level, within each family and community, the culture is made anew. With each new initiation, each new songster, the culture was reinvigorated. For the Ngarrindjeri, each case reviewed by the *tendi* brought into being new law; each marriage established new relationships; and every birth brought new possibilities of exchange. In the desert regions there are people who are prolific dreamers, to whom new songs, designs and stories are revealed. The past is constantly being "refound" and "reincorporated" into the present. It is up to the older people to help interpret the experiences within the lives of those present at the telling, singing, and dancing of the dreams. The Ngarrindjeri have their mystics and dreamers, persons to whom knowledge is revealed in dreams. They also have their experts to assist in interpretation, and a community of belief within which these are made known. One of the shaping forces of the past twenty years has been cultural revival in a political climate that has increasingly acknowledged the position of Aborigines in Aboriginal society and their contribution to Australian culture. This has played differently in the "remote communities" of the north of Australia, from the "settled south".

Within the timeless, romanticised world of "tradition", the landscape, the religion, system of land tenure, governance, kinship system, language, all are fixed. Although the broad brush paints a land created by key ancestors such as *Ngurunderi*, there are different versions of his exploits. There are even different explanations of the creation of the Murray Mouth. At the level of site location, there is also accommodation of change. For instance, with reference to the location of an important whale site, Kondilindjerung, the Berndts and Taplin agree, Tindale disagrees and Radcliffe-Brown found no clan associated with the site (Berndt *et al.* 1993: 310). This is neither surprising nor evidence that Ngarrindjeri are fabricating sites. Rather they are reading their landscape and ascribing meaning in a way that is consistent with key values of their society. Whales were (and still are in certain respects) important animals to the Ngarrindjeri in terms of their spiritual identity and as a physical resource. Whales might beach at different parts of the coast, the coast line is subject to change through storms and so on, and currents may shift; given these facts, it is hardly surprising that an important whale site might move, or that there might be more than one such site. The meaning of the same story or song may be given different emphases depending on the relationship of songster or story-teller to their audience. There are many ways of being "traditional" and it does not require that everyone believe the same thing, or know the same thing. It does, however, require respect for one's elders and their ability to find meaning in a rapidly changing world.

Fred Myers (1986: 64-8), writing of the Pintupi of Central Australia, describes the process of deductive reasoning by which landscape is assimilated to narrative structure, and the underlying impulse to find explanations within the framework of known stories for anomalous formations is satisfied. A younger man had "found something" and was not sure whether he had discovered a valuable mineral for which the traditional owners of the site might be grateful, or whether he had desecrated a site for which he might become the subject of sorcery. After careful inspection of the colour and texture of the reddish rock, the older men, knowing that in the Kangaroo Dreaming story a kangaroo had been killed some eight kilometres to the east, speculated that this formation was the sloppy contents of the gutted stomach. The site and its features were thus brought within the world of the pre-known. I have seen women reasoning in a similar fashion in central Australia, where a particular stand of plants is found at a location not previously visited. It is assumed to have been made by the same Dreaming who created other stands. As Myers (*ibid.*: 67) writes, the transformation of space into country and attaching of story to object "is part of the Pintupi habit of mind that looks behind the objects to events and sees in objects a sign of something else . . . The landscape itself offers clues about what might have happened." Ngarrindjeri also look to their elders to explain and their elders, guided by their *miwi*, do so within a framework of known stories and relationships between persons and places.

Ian Keen (1994: 296-7) writing of the Yolngu of Arnhem Land, a people whose stories and ceremonies have become standard references in the study of Aboriginal religion, points out, "Yolngu assimilated introduced ritual forms to their own mythology, and interpreted old forms in terms of mythologised newcomers." Mervyn Meggitt (1962: 119) writing of the Warlpiri of central Australia, the group who have come to be known as "the" desert people points out that the subsection system was less that 150 years old at the time of his field work. Although the Ngarrindjeri do not have the breadth of ceremonial life still enjoyed by the Yolngu, an elaborate system of social classification like the Warlpiri, or the control over their country the Pintupi enjoy, they too have demonstrated that change was part of their system and could be accommodated within their conceptual universe. They too look for meaning and significance in places for which they have strong feeling. They too read the signs.

479

Although it must remain speculation, it appears from the data of Tindale and the Berndts that Ngarrindjeri lands were also in flux at the time of first contact. Tonkinson (1993: xxvii) and the Berndts (1993: 29) note that the changes in clan membership occurred through segmentation and succession. "It would seem that even in times before white contact, conflict and adjustment had been a factor in continuing adjustment of tribal and clan boundaries," wrote Tindale (1938–56: 63). It appears "that even in times before white contact, conflict and adjustment had been a factor in continuing adjustment of tribal and clan boundaries" (*ibid.*). The Yaraldi had already moved into Tangani land. There were clashes at the Murray Mouth. The Tuuri clan split, with some members moving closer to the Yaraldi and learning to speak their language. A period of readjustment and even instability followed such moves. *Ngatji* affiliation of the newly formed groups needed to be settled; access to restricted places and rights in clan rituals likewise. One example entailed the breakaway group using the female form for the secondary *ngatji* instead of the male (Tindale 1934–7: 75).

Any records made of the land tenure system while any of these rearrangements of relations of people to land was in progress, might produce several different perspectives on who owned what tracts of land. "The whole of the Western Desert cultural area was, at the time of arrival of the Whites, in a state of transition, in which indigenous cultural institutions were undergoing transformations without having yet achieved any kind of balance," Annette Hamilton (1982: 103) concluded. This finding, based on a careful analysis of existing sources, has had profound implications for the ways in which Aboriginal relations to land are to be understood. Are we looking at discrete, descent-based clans? Are groups formed around economic or religious interests? Do several, internally contradictory principles apply? Certainly we know that Ngarrindjeri lands were in flux at the time of official settlement of the Lower Murray, but it was not a situation of whim or chaos: rules regarding succession can be specified (Tindale and Long nd: 12).

Tonkinson (1978: 113), writing of the religious life of the Mardudjara of the Western Desert, identifies "four related aspects of its internal dynamism". First he notes the diffusions of new rituals,

480

songlines and objects between groups within the desert. Ngarrindjeri ceremonies with people from up-river allowed such diffusion, and Pinkie Mack was one of the agents of transmission of such knowledge. Second is "ritual innovation at the local level". The innovation through individual dream-journeys, of which Tonkinson (*ibid.*) writes, is rather like that described by Tindale and Veronica Brodie. These "private revelations" must fit within the given religious schema but, as we have seen for Ngarrindjeri also, they are a way in which new ideas, forces, relationships and events may be brought within the pre-known world and thus be made amenable to the law. And, says Tonkinson (*ibid.*), although individuals are denied "an innovatory function in ritual creativity, they nevertheless have the vital task of translating piecemeal information into highly structured and integrated wholes." Rather like the weaving of family, the circle of language, the rhythm of the seasons, the world is and can be made whole. Third, Tonkinson notes the "discovery of sacred objects" left behind by the Dreamings which is consistent with Myers' experience and my own. Last, Tonkinson looks to the "the exploitation of myths inherent flexibility". As Keen argues, as I have pointed out for the Ngarrindjeri, there are many ways in which songs and stories may be interpreted. Max Charlesworth (1983: 386) summarises: "Within the framework or 'canon' provided by the foundation charter of the Dreaming there is a good deal of innovation and change and re-interpretation and adaptation."

Let us agree, then, that change and accommodation of change were part of the system. However, over the past century, the velocity of change has intensified. It has gone in new directions and at a speed over which local peoples had no control. There are good reasons why certain practices are no longer current, but this is not to say there is no distinctive Ngarrindjeri culture; that it cannot be described; or that Ngarrindjeri cannot articulate its distinctive features, its kinship system, language, privileging of feelings and interactions with the spirits of the land, governance structures and beliefs about land. As Ian Keen (1994: 297) writes: "The enterprise should be, therefore, not to record changes to a 'traditional' order (Cowlishaw 1987), but to trace trajectories of transformation in relations, powers, trends, events, and the forms into which people

481

try to shape their worlds." I have not attempted an exhaustive account of such trajectories, but rather indicated how contemporary beliefs and practices are a complex weave of knowledge from the old people, a continuing dialogue with the land through story, song, weaving, feather flowers, visiting places, burials, respect for the elders, a privileging of the spoken word and personal experience, accommodation of changing circumstances and a fierce determination to care for place they hold dear. The task of finding meaning in what Tonkinson calls "piecemeal information" and rendering it relevant today falls to the elders, not just old people, but those wise in the ways of the land and its people.

9

Women's Beliefs, Bodies and Practices

Gendered Work: Gendered Analyses

Women's Work: Raising children, tending the home fires, domestic, private, profane. *Men's Work*: earning a living, political, public, sacred. A woman Pope? Pope Joan notwithstanding, I doubt it. Women are potential polluters of the sacred. A man making school lunches every day? Possible, but rare. Male is to female as the sacred is to the profane as the public is to the private as the political is to the domestic. Stereotypes, to be sure, but these dichotomies are pervasive, persuasive and often unexamined. Critiquing this sex role stereotyping, feminists have pointed out that sex types are culturally constructed, not biological givens: not all societies expect men to be rugged individuals, not all societies expect women to be submissive, not all members of those societies who do have such expectations comply with the gender prescriptions. Those who defy, rebel, subvert, mock, and ignore pay a price and it is a gendered price. A woman who steps outside the expected role is anomalous, feared and ridiculed. A man who steps outside the masculine role can also expect to be the brunt of jokes, but the man who makes school lunches is unlikely to invoke the same intensity of anger as an ambitious woman who speaks her mind, heads a government or a church. The gender line he has crossed has taken him into the realm of the relatively powerless. Anyone if they have a mind can do women's work, but a man's work takes skill, that is why it is rewarded at a higher level, and taken more seriously. Isn't it?

Feminist ethnographers have explored gender relations in other societies and other periods and found a variety of ways in which a man can be a man and a woman a woman. Whether or not what it is to be man has always been considered more prestigious than what

483

it is to be a woman, in all cultures, throughout history, is by no means settled. There are those who would argue that sexual asymmetry is universal and those who would say it is historically constructed. That is a debate for another time. My interest here is first to establish what Ngarrindjeri women were actually doing. Was there work that was women's and work that was men's? Next, was woman's work solely concerned with physical survival or did she also labour spiritually? Was women's contribution to the reproduction of the Ngarrindjeri world more than the physical act of giving birth and raising children, of gathering food and making artefacts? Lastly, if women were co-producers with men of the spiritually charged world in which they lived, how were they initiated into the mysteries of this inner world? If women's work was complementary to that of the men, does that mean that there were no restricted gender-specific practices? Given that women were secluded from men and men from women at certain times, it is possible to argue for the existence of knowledge that was also gendered and kept apart? All of this questioning is to provide a context for answering another set of questions: What does a claim to the existence of "women's business" mean to the Ngarrindjeri of the written sources and the Ngarrindjeri caught up in the contesting of the sacredness of the Goolwa, Hindmarsh Island, Murray Mouth area? What is "women's business"?

Whose work? During Ngarrindjeri mortuary rituals, women keen; they do not build the burial platform, or tend the fires. Nor do they roam in the ti-tree groves. They are an integral part of the practices but have a specific role, as do the men. Ngarrindjeri fear the dark and take precautions to minimise the dangers of night travel. Milerum told Tindale of burning strips of gum tree bark which were waved in the air: One of the chores of women, on occasions when camps were to be made on the coastal side of the Coorong, was the gathering of supplies of such bark against need as illuminance on the treeless dunes. (Tindale and Long nd: 6). Milerum again: Shellfish gathering was a constant chore for Tangani women both in the Coorong, in the sheltered waters at recognized places, and generally along the whole length of the open ocean shore (*ibid.*: 3). Both men and women worked fibres. Women collected the rushes and made baskets while gathering flax into the two stranded string for fishing lines and nets, the treating and rolling was men's work (*ibid.*). Both men and women fished but Milerum adds, For men there was hunting, spearing, the use of the boomerang, fish traps, canoes and large nets for catching emus, for the women there was hunting small animals, lizards, opossum, and gather[ing] roots, grass seeds. They were responsible for the milling of food, the cleaning and cooking of vegetable foods for hulling and husking (*ibid.*: 11). This sex division of labour was part of the flow of daily life which Angas (1847: 54, 84) observed: "The men were out fishing in their canoes, and the women and girls being busily employed in gathering bulrush-root for supper, they did not arrive at their fires until after sunset." On Lake Alexandrina, Angas saw parties of eight to ten women venture several miles from shore on rafts propelled by a pole (*ibid.*: 90). These were probably the distinctive rectangular-shaped *kundi* which appear in Angas's drawings. In their appendix on "Traditional Foods", the Berndts (1993: 554-76) have a column headed "Division of labour and how caught". There are jobs for boys such as trapping small rodents; tasks undertaken by men with clubs, spears, traps and nets; women's catching of yabbies, tadpoles and sprat; and food like mussels, gathered by women, men and children. For the most part women are gathering and men are hunting.

These ethnographic notes on the sex division of labour in Ngarrindjeri society call to mind arrangements for other hunter-gathering peoples living in rich coastal zones (Hiatt 1970). There was men's work and women's work. From around the age of six or seven, boys were to be found with the men and girls with the women. Spending significant amounts of time in the same-sex groups, boys and girls experienced the getting of a living, a feeling for land, hearing the stories and learning the law in ways appropriate to their gender. Girls formed significant relations with their mothers, aunts and grandmothers as teachers, as did boys with their fathers, uncles and grandfathers. In addition to sex-specific activities, a number of tasks were undertaken jointly by men, women and children, and there were some that could be done by either men or women. Some tasks, like making bag wurlies, required the sex-specific skills of both men and women. From the literature and people's stories, it appears that, for the most part, men and women manufactured their own specialist tools, but there were exceptions that dramatised the nature of the restriction. In that wonderfully detailed description of how women tempered their digging sticks (yam sticks), Tindale comments that this was "one of the few occasions they were ever allowed to have use of the male treasured hafted stone axes" (see p. 441). Women, Tindale (1968) tells us, did not use sharp tools lest they hurt people in a fight— itself an interesting footnote in the role of women in conflict.

For the Ngarrindjeri, the division of labour is better understood in terms of a continuum rather than as a sharp either/or division. At either end there are activities which are known as men's and women's respectively, but in between is a subtle, shifting set of context-dependent activities, entailing co-operation, and indicating men's and women's interdependence. Taplin's journal entries indicate that new activities were incorporated into the existing notions of what was the proper work for men and women. When he set James Ngunaitponi to cook in the school, the women rebelled (Taplin 30/11/1864). On another occasion, the men were furious that girls had been offered refuge in the store where they could come into contact with the flour that was *narambi*. Women were also expected to do certain tasks by missionaries and employees. At Goolwa they were engaged on needlework (*ibid.*: 16/4/1862), and fine work it was too. Young girls also learned how to play gender stereotypes of the *kringkari* to their advantage. Reuben Walker (1934: 204) comments that the old people had lost control over young girls who, if threatened, would taunt, "You touch me. Tell policeman for you." Women also understood and subverted Taplin's view that "women's work" was less prestigious than men's. They "neglected" their unpaid housework in favour of other paid work, a perfectly rational preference, it seems to me.

In terms of understanding those activities which are sex-specific, we need to distinguish between accounts which are based on first-hand experience, and those that are second-hand, based on other accounts. For the most part this consideration has not been accorded great weight. Men recorded men's activities and, sometimes, when women were present, their activities were also noted, but not always. Taplin (1873: 4 n) observed: "It is common for natives to omit any mention of the women." Apparently for Taplin, women weren't "natives", just women. We have some accounts of what is going on in all male domains, such as when Angas (1847) met the *narambi* man (see p. 278), and some accounts of ceremonial life where men and women are working together, like Reuben Walker's (1934) account of doctor-making ceremonies, but we have no first-hand accounts of what was going on in women-only spaces. We know they exist: Angas (1847: 58, 87) saw women run away to them; boys are taught to avoid them (Berndt *et al.* 1993: 153), but we don't know what is happening in any detail. And no great premium was placed on learning about women-only activities. If nothing came to light in a afternoon or so, then it was probably because there was nothing to report. Men made better informants anyway and it was assumed they could speak for their women. When not, one could ask the missionary's wife. Thus Taplin's (1860) wife told him what she had been told about "half-caste children" and he told the 1860 *Report of the Select Committee of the Legislative Council upon Aborigines*. This fourth-hand datum then became the nineteenth-century record for the Ngarrindjeri: it was official, authentic, and in print.

It is not surprising that we know more of women's work in child-raising and food-getting than of their religious life. The male observer might see a woman collecting cockles, but would not be permitted to be present at a key moment in a woman's life like birth—that was definitely the business of women. To complicate the picture, many of the commentaries on women's rituals were written after the practices had been driven underground or ceased. Despite the reluctance of embarrassed observers who did not record the details, and despite the retreat into Latin, we do have some accounts of nineteenth-century ceremonial life in which women participated, and some oral histories from the twentieth. But, as I pointed out in Chapter 8 (see p. 456), assumptions about what is "natural" for men and women can pre-empt certain questions, and in Chapter 6 (see p. 337ff.), that women *putari* specialise in matters concerning women's reproductive lives. If we assume birth is physical labour alone, we will not pursue the *putari* as engaged in work that effects the life of the spirit. If weaving is studied solely as a fitting craft for a woman, then the symbolic and sacred dimensions will be obscured. Stories of birthing and stories of weaving implicate one's *miwi*, but there was no question I asked to elicit that. I was told little by little, and watched to see if I understood. I am well aware I still have much to learn.

Of course most of the nineteenth-century commentators dismissed the beliefs of men and women alike as mere superstition. By the twentieth century, with the publication of Freud's *Totem and Tabu* (1914) and Durkheim's *Elementary Forms of the Religious Life* (1912), Aboriginal beliefs and practices were worthy of research, but in their analyses women practised magic, not religion; women were profane, not sacred. Géza Rohéim (1933), for example, was the first to ask specifically of central Australian Aboriginal women what they were doing in their ceremonies. From within his psychoanalytic framework, he asked two questions: "What sort of person is she?" and "What are her work, her plays, her interests in everyday life, her passions, anxieties and pleasures?" Not surprisingly he found women had no religion or corporate ceremonial life, only personal magic. This was the period within which Tindale began his work with Ngarrindjeri, and from his notebooks it appears, with a couple of exceptions, he worked and travelled with men. Their stories become the standard against which to measure later versions. For example, we know the *prupi* story as published by Tindale (1938) but Brookman's account (Harvey 1939) is grounded in the lives of those known to the story-teller and suggests that the *prupi* leads men astray as if they were children. Mature men would not necessarily wish to share this perspective with a male anthropologist.

The pioneering work of Phyllis Kaberry (1939) notwithstanding, the gendered sacred/profane dichotomy, persisted well into the period of self-determination. In the 1970s Ken Maddock (1972: 155) characterised women's ceremonies as of interest to women, and men's as having consequences for the whole society, had wide currency. On the basis of research undertaken by women anthropologists, Maddock (1982: 138-40) revisited and revised his position somewhat, but the idea persists that women's religious life is of lesser reach than that of men's. As I argued in the previous chapter (see p. 456), we need to know what research questions were asked, by whom, of whom and under what conditions before we make global claims about what exists, what doesn't exist, and what it means. By and large, women researchers have demonstrated a greater propensity to reflexivity than have their male counterparts (Bell 1993b). On returning from field work amongst women, any woman who made authoritative statements regarding the nature of religious practice in a particular part of the country could expect to be challenged: "But you only worked with women. How can you know what the men were doing?" Yet men have been making authoritative statements on the basis of work with men and such challenges were rarely made, and even now are shrugged off (Bell 1993a: 276-300). The inability of Australian anthropology to grapple with the issues raised by Hindmarsh Island illustrates this all too well.

The particular texture of the division of labour in Ngarrindjeri culture is one where the interdependence of the sexes is marked, as the Berndts (1993) and Tonkinson (1993: xxix) point out. This has led some to conclude that there is no gender-restricted domain of knowledge or practice. As Philip Clarke (1996: 142) puts it, with "so much inter-connection, . . . it can't really be separated out". But I think it can and should be sorted out. What were the women doing? Reclamation is the first step in the feminist ethnography I set out in Chapter 8 (see pp. 469–70). What the sources, written and oral, tell us about the beliefs and practices of women in an empirical sense is a different question from what I, as an anthropologist, might charac-terise as the relations between the men and women. I might say that gender relations are egalitarian, complementary, matters of dominance and subordination, or dependence and interdependence. In the debates around Hindmarsh Island, the nature of gender relations and the existence of separate rituals for men and women have been conflated. Prying them apart is a fraught task because the sources on which I am relying already take a position, and often it is one that is highly ethnocentric, not based on field work, and sexist to boot.

The omission of women from cultural accounts and a willingness to theorise man as a universal is not an ethnographic quirk. In the wider society women are not key decision-makers, nor are they authoritative spokespersons in those domains where important societal resources are negotiated: in the economy, law, religion, and politics. Women are present, but for the most part have a long way to go before achieving parity with men. Thus, making women visible, whether with reference to Aboriginal society, or with reference to women in general in Australia, challenges understandings of social relations in a way that can be deeply disturbing. It calls attention to the ways in which our social worlds are constructed and it calls attention to agency by bringing women into active voice. It problematises what has hitherto been presented as a "natural" division of labour. At a deeper level, beyond the gendered binary oppositions of public/private and political/domestic, is a cluster of intriguing questions about how we might gain access to the worlds of those whose voices have not been recorded (e.g. women, minorities, indigenous peoples, the working class). These questions take me to the second and third parts of a feminist ethnography.

Sacred Moments: Sacred Relationships

Joined by **miwi** My *miwi* wisdom is telling, it's not the right time to speak. It's just spoken to women, says Daisy Rankine of a sacred belief. *Miwi* starts with the cord and when cut, the child is initiated. Karloan told the Berndts (1993: 245) that the old people "used to say that the miwi was a way to the true religion". Certainly *miwi* is a sacred word to be uttered with respect, and people with a strong *miwi* are respected. The feelings associated with one's *miwi* are relied upon in identifying sacred places and truth. But, in "Retrospect", the final chapter of *A World That Was*, the Berndts (*ibid*.: 288) qualify the centrality Karloan accords to *miwi*: "In all cases the miwi with its power was an essential attribute with more supernatural than religious associations." Here again we see the reluctance of the Berndts to locate key Ngarrindjeri beliefs within the religious domain. On what basis are we to distinguish between superstition and religion? What does this distinction mean in this context? It appears to be as arbitrary as was their distinction regarding the religious nature of Karloan's initiation (p. 175) and, as we shall see, their distinctions regarding birth and sacred rituals.

The Berndts (1993: 134) state that a person's *miwi* was made up of the *miwi* of each parent, but "as long as the physical attribute of being Aboriginal can be identified as such, the child will have that *miwi*". Thus children with a non-Aboriginal parent were still considered to be Ngarrindjeri and, where the non-Aboriginal parent

490

was the father (as it was in most mixed marriages), the mother's *miwi* was what shaped the child. As pointed out on p. 224, Yaraldi people stated that the *miwi* did not change throughout the centuries, so the *miwi* of a contemporary Aboriginal was believed to be the same as it had been at the beginning of time.

Because the *miwi* passes through the umbilical cord into the stomach at birth and the navel indicates the positioning of the *miwi*, the person with whom one has exchanged navel cords (*ngia-ngiampe*), also shares one's *miwi* (Berndt *et al.* 1993: 287). To greet one's *ngia-ngiampe* partner, one clasps the stomach and throws out one's hands, thus symbolising same stomach, same soul (*ibid.*: 245). Taplin (1873: 139) calls this gesture one of thanks. Tindale (1930–52: 111) describes another *miwi* sign given to a young fully initiated man, who is seated in the "place of honour". "One of the elders came, sat face to face with the initiate and grasped initiate's left hand with his left and the boy's navel (*pulangki*) with his right hand. He would flick (click) his fingers away. This was a sign that he belonged now among the men." Initiation, for young men, is a form of spiritual rebirth wherein they are transformed from boys into men. Here we have their very connection with the woman of whom they were born as the basis of the sign that confirms them as now within the world of men. Elymann (Courto 1996: 291) says that strangers may be welcomed with a hand gesture from the stomach. At other times greetings between men were by the left hand to draw each other close and the right arm to hug. Women, did not use this gesture but hugged each other close and rubbed their mouths over each other's faces (Tindale 1930–52: 113). Here is a case where both men and women have a particular characteristic, i.e. *miwi*, but its power and significance are marked in different ways. Was the women's greeting in some way related to women's understanding of their *miwi*, or to another set of relationships altogether? As we are reading this, Tom Trevorrow nods at his brother George. You see people today and they flick out their hand in greeting, from the stomach. Not all who use this gesture, Tom explains, necessarily understand the significance, but that does not lessen its sacred origins. It is learned by imitation and its meanings are revealed according to the rules.

491

Since Taplin (1873: 32-4) drew attention to the custom of the "navel cord exchange", it has been remarked upon by all serious scholars of Ngarrindjeri culture.[1] In his journal of 9 November 1859, Taplin wrote: "The boys and young men keep a bunch of feathers tied up together and in the middle of which is the preserved navel string (cut off at birth) of the individual to whom the bunch belongs. If any young man gives this bunch to another the other must never come into his presence thereafter." By 7 March 1861, Taplin, having noticed, over a period of time, that Agnes would not speak to Waukerri and his brother, nor go near them, discovered the reason. "It appears that Agnes' father gave the *kalduke* [bunch of feathers] in which was her navel string, to Waukerri's father." On 23 September 1869, a decade into his stay, Taplin wrote with some satisfaction regarding the power of Christianity to break down native customs, because "these men cast aside all thoughts of *ngia-ngiampe*, and under pressure of religious concern, sought counsel from the very man whom native law forbade them to speak to". In so doing, Taplin had significantly undermined an institution which was critical to good relations between groups as far away as the Darling River, and the other side of the Mount Lofty Ranges. By intruding on Ngarrindjeri birthing practices, he had also weakened the role of the *putari*, a task that western gynæcological and obstetric practices continued in the twentieth century with hospitalised births.

Working with Milerum, Reuben Walker, Albert Karloan, David Unaipon and Mark Wilson, Tindale provides a number of intriguing insights showing that this exchange and the associated rituals and relationships touch many aspects of Ngarrindjeri life. Under the heading "Navel String Relation", Tindale (1930–52: 113) elaborated on the practice known as *witjuti* by the Ramindjeri. As soon as the navel cord was severed from the child, it was carefully treated with ashes, dried, smoked, parcelled up and sent away to another tribe or clan. A navel string would be received in exchange. The relationship thus established endured for life, and *ngia-ngiampe* partners are said to be like the same flesh. They could never speak directly to each other, but were required to take the part of the other in disputes and provide safe haven in times of trouble. In fact, Tindale comments that "to hear some of the natives praising their *witjuti* one would think they never did anything but good" (*ibid.*). Gifts of food and weapons also accompanied the exchanges, but the main role of the partners was to act as intermediaries in trade relations between their respective groups. This ensured access to distant and sometimes hard-to-obtain items such as ochre, stone, special woods for weapons, and even seasonal foods not regionally available (Tindale and Long nd: 1).

The relationships established through the exchange implicated both families and continued through the generations. Exactly how this played out is not completely clear: we do not have sufficiently detailed case histories to work out the rules. From what is available, closeness and distance, both physical and genealogical, are important factors. According to Tindale (1931–4: 208), the Wanjakalde would not enter into the exchange relationship with the Tangane, or the Millicent natives, or the Ramindjeri, because "they were too friendly for this to be done". Marriage alliances with those groups facilitated access to these countries. Unaipon was a source for Tindale on this topic, and when asked how he had learned about the relationship, "he protested that he lived it" (*ibid.*: 92). One of Taplin's (7/1/1871) triumphs had been to convince David's father, James Ngunaitponi, to refuse to honour the relationship, so it would appear that David pursued his own course, despite his commitment to Christianity.

Midwives and **miwi** The descriptions of the Berndts (1993: 119-21), like those of Tindale, are short on information about women's role in the exchanges. The Berndts (*ibid.*) simply state that "when a woman gave birth, the midwife cut the navel cord". Was the midwife related to the mother's family? Midwives travelled in order to be with expectant mothers. Was there some logic other than availability to work? According to the Berndts (*ibid.*), the child's father gave the cord to the distant partner. Now Milerum and Pinkie Mack were *ngia-ngiampe*, and perhaps some further questioning might have established who actually cut the cord, who wrapped it, and who transported it. These were questions George Trevorrow had asked of his mother (Thora Lampard) with reference to his relationship with Aunty Beatty, a woman who continued to be a presence in his life. Muriel Van Der Byl told a story of being named after the midwife who delivered her (see Chapter 4, pp. 227-8). But all the Berndts (1993: 199) state is: "After the navel cord was removed, it was tied up in a bunch of feathers (*kalduki*). When the intermediaries arrived, the navel cord was handed over to them and became *narambi* (taboo) to the donor." This may be the ideology of the relationship, but Pinkie Mack admitted that on occasions she had spoken to Milerum. Of what? When? Why? We leave the old ways sometimes, she told Tindale (1930–52: 62) rather shamefacedly of this lapse.

The relationship, once established, implicates whole families and continues through generations. "The reaffirmation rite was similar, with the maintenance of the conventional obligations. The person who received the cord told his children about the special relationship and responsibilities associated with it" (Berndt *et al.* 1993: 119). And these were strictly enforced. For the Berndts, these were male-to-male negotiations. So, was there a relationship between Milerum's father and Pinkie Mack's family? Her father was a white man so was the exchange negotiated through her mother, or through an uncle, or through her social father? Tindale says the latter is how her clan affiliation was reckoned. Is there a continuing relationship with the children of Pinkie Mack and those of Milerum? Did the fact that Pinkie Mack and Milerum were not supposed to speak directly to each other have any effect on their respective relationships with the Berndts and Tindale? The Berndts (*ibid.*: 117) admit that, while the ritual exchange aspect may have fallen into disuse, certain obligations and responsibilities continued into the 1940s—from my field work, I'd say into the 1990s.

The Berndts, like Taplin, credit the child's father with handing over the cord, but Tindale (1938–56: 27), in conversation with David Unaipon and Mark Wilson, learned that it always goes to the mother's side of the family. On another occasion Unaipon said, "The cord is dried and given to a woman of a distant tribe who is not a blood relative" (Tindale 1931–4: 92). So do the Berndts mean that the father hands over the cord, but that he gives it to his wife's relatives, or have they collected a different "tradition"? Has "woman" been conflated with "mother's side"? Both Mark Wilson and Albert Karloan were Yaraldi, so it is unlikely it is a matter of regional variation. Did the role of the father change after contact

494

with whites? Frederick Taplin, writing in the *Adelaide Observer* (6 April 1889), cites an example of a temporary relation established to deal with the pragmatics of a particular situation. Were different options available? According to Reuben Walker (1934: 209) the exchange implicates both boys and girls in the initial generation, but only the sons of the succeeding generations. However, this is contradicted by Unaipon's evidence that Mrs Karpeny followed on from her father. Of course, individuals could have several networks of *ngia-ngiampe* partners through relationships established at different generation levels. Was there a point at which some relationships fell into disuse? Usually the Berndts are precise about the nature of the kin relationships involved in rituals, so are we to assume that in this case they don't know? Didn't ask? Thought it irrelevant? Or that people were not forthcoming on the topic? Taplin (1879: 41) admits that he could never find out the reason for the custom. "The natives could not tell me." From this silence it would be folly to assume there was no reason. Today people know about the relationship. Margaret Brusnahan, who was raised in an orphanage and not reunited with her mother (Henry Rankine's father's sister) until age sixteen, tells me, My Mum knew about it and she passed the knowledge down to me. My grandfather sent David Unaipon an umbilical cord as his spiritual brother.

The taboos associated with speaking to one's navel exchange partner, apparently also applied to the place associated with the origins of the custom. Tindale relates that Karloan had told him that, as a boy, when he "travelling past Tut:uar in Ngaralta territory in a canoe, he would hold his mouth closed with his hand because the country there belonged to his *witjuti* . . . In his secret guardian clan territory, he dared not speak or even mention the name of the place" (Tindale and Long nd: 1). In the Berndts' (1993: 352-3) account of what I take to be the same story, which they date at 1877, they relate how *Ngurunderi*, in his travels down the Murray past Bell's Landing, Mumerang, instigated the custom. At this site a granite rock stands as a visible sign of the navel cord. Karloan said the men painted their faces, averted their eyes and poled past the rock in silence. This rock was sacred (*narambi*) and as they passed it they thought of their *ngengampi*, the power of the relationship, and of their obligations; they thought this out of their *miwi*, the opening to which was the navel. Here, *miwi* relationships and restrictions indicate a sacred place and a sacred origin of the tradition.

Out of passive voice and into action The predominantly male-oriented descriptions raise questions for a researcher with an interest in women's lives. First, I would point to the lack of agency attributed to women and use of the passive voice. Who was cutting the cord and tying it in feathers? I want to ask Milerum, but he was not present at the cutting of the cord and maybe that explains the passive voice. Are the bunches of feathers in which the cord was transported of the same configuration as the feather flowers the women made and sold on the missions, or do they resemble those held by men in the *kokolaimi* "game" described by Tindale (1931–4: 78, 118, 233), and David Unaipon (1924–5)? There, two teams of men compete for a "ball of emu feathers" in what sounds like a wrestling match that ends in a weapons fight. Second, I would ask, if the relationship is like "same flesh", and the partnership established through the exchange has the same *miwi* as the cord giver, does this not mean that women are key actors in reproducing the Ngarrindjeri spiritual world? During labour and birth, the *putari* is in charge. The Berndts (1993: 199) acknowledge that the healing powers of a *putari* "involved not only the *ngatji* as such but the power to control it, and effecting a cure was dependent on the *putari* drawing upon the strength of his *miwi*. However, they are reluctant to take this insight further when it comes to female *putari*, the umbilical cord and *miwi* power. Women had a role to play in the establishment of the *ngia-ngiampe* relationship. They did not simply cut the cord and passively hand it over; rather, they had their own set of rituals which were conducted at birth, when no men were present.

Men knew about the existence of birth rituals and the associated symbols. David Unaipon claimed that the round stones with concentric circles found on old sandhill sites around the north shore of Lake Alexandrina were connected to the rituals associated with the cutting of the cord. Tindale (1938–56: 27) terms this the *ngia-ngiampe* "cult" and recorded Unaipon as saying that women would place the umbilical cord on such a stone before it was sent off. Mark

Wilson thought the stones, eight inches or more across, were made of slabs of Victor Harbor granite. "Neither felt that they had retained full knowledge of the 'inner meanings' of the custom" writes Tindale (*ibid.*). What might the women have known? We can't simply dismiss the stones and associated ritual, because no-one thought to pursue the matter with women, especially the *putari* who handled the cord.

Chapter 17 of David Unaipon's (1924–5: 188-92 and compare Smith 1930: 216-17) manuscript, which is devoted to the topic of *Nhung e umpe*, points to these meanings. His description of what he calls "a law itself" is punctuated on several occasions with references to Christianity, but the Ngarrindjeri ethnography and the editorialising of the preacher are easily separated, as I noted in Chapter 2 (p. 86ff.). In fact, it feels as if the references and allusions are there as a way of making the telling of the story "safe" for his audience and less threatening to those who see such "customs" as the work of the devil. Unaipon confirms that it was *Ngurunderi* who brought the ceremonies, and he outlines the wrapping of the cord in a roll of emu feathers. His assessment of the high status of midwives echoes what Ngarrindjeri say today:

> Now it is only the privilege of a certain female members of the tribe that is selected to give the gut, she must be a daughter of a mother who was selected for a navel gut. These mothers must come from a direct line of noble womanhood, good pure moral character and she submits the gut to a *Moo cum bulli* (that is the Philosopher of tribe) and it remains in his possession until he sees fit or thinks it proper to present it to a tribe.

If there is a break in the line of women, the next of kin on the mother's side takes up this "great and important position". According to Unaipon, it was a "coveted position, each girl when they are educated to become good women strive for this position". At this point Unaipon says that he "would like to call your attention to the Christian faith and he cites Luke 1, verse 42, "Blessed art thou Mary . . .". The virtues of which he writes may sound like those of Victorian womanhood, but they are also those of Ngarrindjeri schooled in the "grandmother's lore" and support what today's elders say of that wisdom and the lines of transmission through women, albeit in more pragmatic English.

Unaipon's account moves straight back into the ethnography:

Now the gut part of the intestine of the mother and child has great significance to us. We look upon it as coming from within a part of a woman where dwells all good wishes of pity and sympathy. There are two parts embodied in this gut. First that of the well trained moral of perfect womanhood which is recognized with a good deal of reverence. Secondly there is that portion of the childish innocence and purity which offers itself for a great development of life in itself as a challenge to its capability to develop itself to prove the inheritance a mother's quality. Thirdly the navel cord is symbolic of a story that binds the peculiarities of mother to child. As mother and child are linked to each other before birth so the *Nhung e umpie* must be so linked as mother and child. The navel cord is the physical reality so *Nhung e umpe* should be so true love, true fellowship, true pity. Let this symbol bind you. Now we look upon the navel cord with reverence.

Unaipon's account of the significance of the cord and *miwi* with his stress on morals could also be construed as an "invention", or a Christian innovation, but the underlying structure of the relationships he is describing are the same as in the other sources. The difference in Unaipon's account is that women are represented as physical and spiritual beings, and a moral force in their society. The idea that the bond between mother and child can be symbolically replicated in order to "make family" elsewhere is one that resonates with stories of women's weaving as binding in family.

Taplin (1873: 51) translates *ngiampe* as "back or loins"; Tindale (nd, e) gives *ngia-ngiampe* as "friend of my loins". Today people speak of the "life line" and say the power of one's *miwi* remains in the cord. Cutting the lifeline is a commitment and an honour. It's initiation into life, Tom Trevorrow told me. Men are not around when it is happening. They stay right out of it. There was more understanding about what life was about then. George Trevorrow explained the interconnections: Our *miwi* is a very, very strong spiritual thing, you know. We shouldn't be talking too much but it's where everything comes from, that's the lifeforce, that comes from the *kalduki*, from the *miwi*, the cord from the mother to the child. It's the lifeforce that gives things life in our spiritual beliefs. We are not going to understand this tradition by treating it in isolation. Neither George nor Tom has read Unaipon and neither, it seems, had the Berndts.

498

When women speak about *miwi* and the navel cord, they do so in hushed tones. The only conversations I have had about *miwi* and *ngia-ngiampe* in mixed company have been at Camp Coorong, but even then men have got up and left the group at certain times. When both men and women were present, the subject was treated respectfully, a little anxiously, and much was being left unsaid. In June 1997 I'm sitting at the conference table in the office at Camp Coorong, with Tom, George, Ellen and her mother: an unlikely place to be having this conversation. It is too cold to be outside, and I have the manuscript laid out in sections. Ellen Trevorrow listens intently as the men begin to talk about "traders", the navel cord and *miwi*. I was only seventeen, straight out of school, when my first son was born, and he was handed over to a close mate and she became like a godmother to him. Anything I needed she'd get me. I didn't know about the navel cord exchange. It was only with my older son. I didn't hand over my younger sons. I did it without knowing. Her mother nods: It was the power of *miwi*. "Handing over" is the language of the navel exchange, just as "given" is for songs and "finding" is for babies.

In the notes of Dorothy Tindale and Alison Brookman (née Harvey), we catch sight of what was transacted at the birth moment in the late 1930s. One Point McLeay woman told Dorothy Tindale (1939): You take a toadstool when it is dry and powdery and put the red powder on the navel. This is supposed to dry it up. A later method is to toast a rag and put it on the navel. The earlier method with the "red powder" is most likely a reference to red ochre. We know from the material on *narambi* that red ochre is a sign of danger, healing, and prohibition, and here are women handling it, in a women-only location. This is a sacred moment in Ngarrindjeri terms. Alison Brookman (Harvey 1939) noted *wi:tjuti* [navel cord relation] and *narambi* [sacred] on the same page. Pinkie Mack told Brookman that, after the cord was cut with a mussel shell, the ends were tied off with sinew. The Berndts (1993: 142), probably from the same source, state that the *putari* broke the cord with a twist of her hands. Pinkie Mack continues: The child is wrapped in a soft weed of fresh water growth. When the wrapping is taken off the cord, it is left covered with a floury substance like a cap. The child is not washed. When the covering is removed after one or two days, it is clean.

Then we have the words of someone who did speak to a *putari* and who was present at a birth. Eighteen at the time, Doreen Kartinyeri recalls: The only time I took part in helping was when I had to chop the wood and cart the water. The boys had been told to get lost and they went without first chopping the wood. And then Aunty Laura said, "You better get some more water, my girl." I done three trips with the kerosene tins on the yoke over my shoulder and filled up the copper and kept ladling the water out with a big dipper. I made a little bed in a box with a rug. That was December 1952 for the birth of Janice Rigney. When a baby is born, the cord is cut and tied near the mother. You leave a part for the baby, and a part between the knots. You wait for the palpitations to stop, and when it dries, it shrinks from four or five inches to about two. Aunty Laura said you have to let it fall away by itself. It's the lifeline, and when it drops off the child is ready to survive by itself. It has the lifeline. Once this happens, the *miwi* is within the child.

I was bathing the new baby, Janice Rigney, and Aunty Laura said not to get the cord wet, to keep the *pulanggi* dry. I made a dressing with cotton wool, and wrapped it in a stretchy singlet, put it on the navel, and then bound the body with strips of the singlet. Aunty Laura said when it falls off to bring it to her. She took it with reverence. I don't know what she did with it. Neither do I. No-one has volunteered the information, and the death of Laura Kartinyeri is much too recent to decently ask. Later, Doreen tells me: All the boys were calling her my little sister. I called her daughter and now she has the nickname "Daughter". She felt like my daughter too. Doreen's account suggests that the exchanges were still current in the 1950s for babies attended by *putari*. Sisters Val and Muriel say that certain midwives moved into Adelaide and thus women could still be attended by a *putari* into the late 1950s. Doreen has continued to reflect on the significance of Aunty Laura's instructions. When my first child was born, the cord dried and fell off after five days. I just got rid of it and he died at seven months. I have often wondered if I did the wrong thing.

Born of Woman

Doreen Kartinyeri and I have been working through this part of the book since 5.30 a.m. We left off late the night before, later than Doreen likes to be up, but she wanted to read it carefully. The thin

500

sun of that June morning was barely warming us, dogs were playing around the water tank, Point Pearce was waking up. Neighbours called over the fence as they walked past. We were still in our night clothes overlaid with sweaters and dressing gowns. The men give us a wide berth. They'll remember us talking together, Doreen jokes. "Can I tell these stories of midwives?" I ask. She agrees I can and that I should tell them along side those in the Berndts, Tindale and Taplin. The way you write it is not how I heard it, but it is the same story. I could hear my Aunty Rosie talking. She wouldn't have used those words, but that what she was saying. I haven't read *Maiyanu* David [Unaipon] but that is my teaching too.

On a tape made by Catherine Ellis (1966: LA106) we hear Aunty Rosie at Point Pearce January 1966 speaking: They used to tell us about when you got married . . . get one picked from another tribe, and never see them and marry them with firesticks and walk on out with these firesticks and they'd have to follow on . . . and that's all there was to it. "What about childbirth? Did you have anything special things the old folk taught you about childbirth?" asks Ellis. Well one old lady told me the way they used to sit down in the old times . . . now they are so particular about hygiene and all that. "It was a wonder they didn't get blood poisoning," she said. This was an elderly old lady, Mrs Close her name was. She told me they used to have the baby and they could travel next day. I couldn't get over it. I said, "What did they used do?" I said. After they had the child they'd sit over a big hole and have a little bit of a fire with a coals in it and pour water over it for the steam to rise. Do you think that would be very effective? [to Ellis] I think it would and then they'd just get up and shake themselves and it would all come away. Fellow linguist Luise Hercus, whose voice is audible on the tape, pursues the name of the wood which was burnt, but neither she nor Cath Ellis asks more about childbirth. In the background we can hear young children fussing and Aunty Rosie telling the boys to please not shake the table. This was not the environment in which more intimate matters would have been broached.

We'd first listened to this tape out at Point Pearce in December 1996, almost a year ago, and almost a year after Doreen had first told me of these practices. Doreen was delighted and filled in details as we listened again and again. The midwife to whom her aunt has

501

referred was Eva Close, born in the 1860s she tells me. A photograph of Eva Close sitting next to Granny Unaipon, also a *putari*, can be seen in the Wilson genealogy (Kartinyeri 1990: 37). They are stern-faced women, dressed in the formal attire of Victorian ladies, but they also knew the rituals of Ngarrindjeri birthing. I have listened to this tape with other women who, like Doreen, are delighted to hear it and comment that she's not telling everything. How could she? It is a fifteen-minute interview with children underfoot.

Doreen tells me of another *putari*. Now Aunty Laura always had a dinghy—a lovely little dinghy. So when Aunty Laura lived at the Three Mile at Tailem Bend, she would row down to Raukkan. When she lived at Marrunggung and Raukkan, she would row up to Three Mile camp out of Tailem Bend and she would stay with the women for a couple of weeks before the babies were born. And when children were sick a message would get to her and she would go down and sit with those children. And she said that out of all the confinements—and I said, "How many were there?" and Aunty said, "I don't know, lost count, there would be well over a hundred." And I said, "That's wonderful." She said, "There was only one baby that I ever lost"—and she was very sad.

Muriel Van Der Byl: Us girls looked for our closest relatives when we got ready to go to deliver. But in them days you would have the ones that were chosen to be midwives for that particular time of the year or whatever. Some of them would be going away and when they go you have to call them because a lot of the people went away for different times of the year—some seasonal picking—some of them didn't go to the picking but they used to prefer to go and work in the packing sheds after the fruit was all picked and dried out. You looked at the lifestyle, the social life of the Ngarrindjeri people from Raukkan, I can see the pattern of them.

Eileen McHughes: We weren't allowed to ask questions. However, we'd overhear because if you've got big ears you tend to hear more than you should, and I heard quite a lot from my ancestors down there. I remember my brother and I sitting on the cliff one day, waiting because my Aunty was about to give birth, and we were waiting to see this baby run out of the rushes, because that's where we thought it came from. Then we heard it crying behind us and Aunty Laura actually delivered that baby and that was my cousin, Trevor. Aunty Pud was very sick. She was haemorrhaging and Aunty Laura fixed her up. I saw her gathering up all

502

those cobwebs and she said, "That stops the bleeding." By the time they got the doctor down—and they had to go up in the horse and cart to get the doctor—and if it wasn't for what Aunty Laura done my aunty would have died. The *putari* were often the only assistance available to women living in fringe camps, and it is not surprising that those raised in these environments have knowledge of birthing practices. When they gave birth, Eileen explained, they used to dig a hole and line it with seaweed and they'd squat. It was always just the women and Aunty Laura said because this is our land. Giving birth on the land intensifies the attachment to the land. I have heard women, here and in central Australia, complain that hospital birth removes that intimate relationship. Giving birth on the land adds another layer to the significance of *ngatji/ngatjurul* as birthplace. In 1965 Mutha Bess (Bessie Rigney) was describing for Cath Ellis (1965: LA 126a) the deep trench, lined with green weed from the lake, that was prepared for the birthing mother, when a Ngarrindjeri woman, not identified asks in the background about her Ngarrindjeri name. Mutha Bess says she was born down the Coorong, on her country, and given a name for the place on the country. Once again children are playing in the background and she passes onto another conversation.

When I asked Isobelle Norvill about midwives, she thought for a bit and said, You know I think at Point Pearce the midwives were Ngarrindjeri, but I'll check it with one old lady because if you know something but are not quite sure since you've been separated for whatever reasons, then further down the track you go back and ask and check so you're not passing on false information. A couple of days later, she confirmed it. The three sisters, Ivy, Ollie and Belle, they were all Rankines and their father was born on Hindmarsh Island, near where the old cheese factory was. They got the name from those first Rankine on the island. The knowledge tracks from Hindmarsh island to Point Pearce to Raukkan and back. Ollie, Ivy and Belle were midwives and I was delivered by Ollie and Ivy, she married a Karpeny. I was one of eight and my Dad would say: "The babies are coming, Go and get Ollie and Ivy." And that was my job. I was the runner.

Doreen Kartinyeri: I remember the story that was told to me by Aunty Ivy Karpeny, before I went to Point Pearce in 1954. There was a woman that, the baby apparently died just before she was ready to

503

deliver. Aunty Ivy went and sat with this woman and she realised that the baby had died. So she sent to get the doctor down and Aunty Ivy said don't move her. The doctor stayed for a while and then he had to go back to the hospital to another patient from Maitland, and Aunty Ivy sat there through the night and the next day and kept giving her broth and rabbit soup and the baby started to deteriorate and Aunty Ivy had to stay with her five days and kept rubbing her in a circular way around the *pulanggi* and stomach part until the baby came away from her and until everything was safe. Aunty Ivy was a middle-aged woman then. So for her to use that skill. She was highly recommended. She was very respected for what she did. She stayed at that mother's side when the baby had died already—and the mother sort of drifted off into a coma so they couldn't move her as the shock would kill her. Taplin (1879: 48-9) also praised the skill, tact and presence of mind of midwives.

Pinkie Mack, Aunty Laura's mother, had acted as a midwife, and her account of the role of the *putari* repays close reading. Just before the last three labour pains, the *putari* would call to the child to come without delay and the mother would cry in pain. Today, Pinkie Mack said, the child does not hear its mother's cry . . . This is a sad thing, she added, because not having heard its mother's voice at delivery the child will not be good, for the voice of its mother makes them good" (Berndt *et al.* 1993: 142-3). In an oral culture, the spoken word is life. Until a child cries, it is not human. From Pinkie Mack's account, the first sound a child hears, the first sign of Ngarrindjeri culture it experiences, comes from the mother and the *putari* calling life forth and thereby ensuring a safe delivery. From the neighbouring Boandik people, Smith (1880: 506) reports that in her pain a mother "beats herself with her fist; the nurse tells her kindly to have patience, and to soothe her, will repeat all the names of her tribe. If the child is born (a girl), and the nurse says, 'Here is a wife for the last young man I named'." James Dawson (1881: 38), writing of the Western District of Victoria, says that if a child appears to be stillborn, "the nurse repeats the names of all her acquaintances in her own and neighbouring tribes" and should it recover the child takes the name and henceforth enjoys special attention from that person. Doreen listens and adds: The story I was told was that you've got to talk to the baby and the mother is encouraged to talk to the baby and not scream because that pushes the child back in. And it is hard not to scream when you're in labour. In each of these examples the midwife is connecting the child with her social world in a significant way.

The Berndts' information on birth was primarily from Karloan, who obtained it from his wife's mother Jean Perry, and from the sister of Peter Martin and Tommy Martin and from Old Dick Martin's daughter who was an excellent midwife. "The information was further supplemented by details given by Pinkie Mack" (Berndt *et al.* 1993: 142). We hear little of what women are thinking, doing, feeling. "The usual pattern of the birth was that, on feeling the onset of labour pains, a woman would sit down in her and her husband's camp while he left to sit on the opposite side of the main camping area or at least some little distance out of sight behind a windbreak" (*ibid.*). Brookman (Harvey 1939) says that young married women were allowed to be present at birth and are shown the correct way of handling cases. This would be an important stage in their education and one of which we know nothing. How many children did a midwife need to have before she could practise? I have heard women say one. Mountford and Harvey (1941), writing of the Adnjamatana, say it was three. Neither Catherine Berndt nor Alison Harvey had children when they undertook field work. Does it matter? In other regions there is ritual knowledge that can endanger women who are yet to bear children and women take great care not to place others in harm's way.

There is general agreement that women moved to women-only spaces for birth from the earliest records on (Meyer 1846). What of the men? "Some men, at such a time, would prefer to go out hunting or fishing to take the matter off their mind and be diverted from worrying," write the Berndts (1993: 142). They might also be avoiding a space where rituals that are privileged to women are taking place. Brookman (Harvey 1939) noted that in birthing camps women were fed by other women and "may not eat anything that is speared or caught in a net". Under "Jaralde Tribal Sex Life", Tindale (1930–52: 51) wrote: "When a baby was born the other children and the male parent were compelled to avoid the mother until the appearance of the new moon." It would appear there were rules associated with this seclusion. It was not just a matter of preference, as the Berndts imply, but a series of deliberate acts informed by the rules of Ngarrindjeri culture.[2]

In their comments on Aboriginal doctors, the Berndts (1993: 193) note, "there were also female *putari* but their special area of expertise concerned midwifery and menstruation, as well as contraceptive measures and so forth". Karloan said he had been told about this by Elizabeth Maratinyeri. "Granny Lizzie", as she was called by Aunty Rosie, was a Tangani woman who died during the 1920s. "She was a well-known *putari* and midwife who had served her apprenticeship with Yaraldi and Tangani female *putari*. This also brings up a further point: there was no embarrassment on the part of men and women discussing such intimate details" (*ibid.*: 141). It may be that the matters can be discussed to a certain extent, and that her skills were through training that men also undertake, but she was the person with the specialist knowledge and she was the person who was present at births. Midwives served an apprenticeship: they were skilled. In the written sources we have no details of what they actually did based on direct observations. They may have been verbally open, but in terms of content highly restricted. In the Berndts' (*ibid.*: 144) assessment: "There was no ritual at the birth of a child, except indirectly through the *ngengampi*. The natural act of giving birth was in itself a ritual manifestation which brought together the physical and spiritual attributes of a human being." It seems to me that the *ngengampi* practice, along with beliefs concerning *miwi*, were absolutely central to Ngarrindjeri culture, to the development of the individual and to the establishment of relationship with distant clans.

Was birth sacred? Tindale elicited an answer from David Unaipon by accident. He had asked whether he had ever seen any stone walls for fish traps in the Coorong area. Unaipon wanted to know whether I was confusing them with the "sacred *ngyangangyampe* stones" in his country, which were stone cairns built over the site where the afterbirth was buried and said to occur in the Lake Alexandrina area. (Tindale 1930–4: 92; see also 1974: 81). Thus, in Unaipon's view, the stones were not only to mark where afterbirth was buried: he considered them sacred and they bore the name of the relationship. The place, and the marker for the place, connect one to the spiritual world, to a custom instigated by *Ngurunderi*. The cutting of the cord and the preparation of it for sending to the *ngengampi* partner was literally in the hands of women. We have not heard the testimony of a midwife who had been present during a birth, cord cutting, and sending of the navel cord. Without this, we cannot say that women participated in a "natural" act and dismiss the possibility that cultural knowledge was being negotiated by women with women on these occasions, and that there were specific practices that took their form from the narratives of the ancestors. I do not know what it means to say there was "no ritual" but that birth was a "ritual manifestation". Such an assessment strips women of all agency. From other accounts of their roles in doctor ceremonies by Reuben Walker and their talents as sorcerers by Milerum, I find it hard to dismiss the possibility of rituals associated with birth. It is likely that women's powers, based on their access to the law, included songs, stories and ritual paraphernalia. There was no participant-observation field work with women *putari* undertaken, and those who knew were not telling *kringkari*. We do, however, have the stories of *putari* such as Aunty Rosie, Laura, Koomi, Ivy, Beatty, and Ollie that have been passed down to this generation. Not all told stories. Doreen: Aunty Myra was a midwife but she wouldn't tell me anything.

Rites of Passage: Coming of Age for Ngarrindjeri Girls

Birth, puberty, marriage, death: these and other crises in one's journey through life are marked by rituals. Arnold van Gennep in his classic *Les rites de passage* (1960, first published in 1908) provided a synthesis of the available ethnographic material. He concluded from his worldwide analysis of the ceremonies that accompany these "crises of life" that there were three distinct phases: separation, transition, and incorporation. The passage, or transition, that was being marked would determine which aspect was emphasised. Thus marriage ceremonies stress integration, while mortuary rituals process separation. For van Gennep, the rites of passage from one stage to the next facilitated the regeneration necessary for social life to continue. The rites renewed energy. This renewal can be seen in the seasonal round in Ngarrindjeri lands, the ceremonial cycle which followed the stars, the rebirth of spring.

507

While much of van Gennep's work is dated, his schema illuminates Ngarrindjeri practice. We know something of their elaborate mourning rituals which ease the passage from life to the land of the dead. There are ritual exchanges at birth which establish relationships that continue down the generations. At marriage, there was a firestick ceremony, during which the families of the couple symbolised the new union with a new hearth. At puberty, boys went through initiation ceremonies. They were captured from the women's camps, kept secluded in their *narambi* state; required to observe numerous taboos; taught the sacred stories; and finally, as newly born men, reintegrated into mixed company. But what of girls? The different stages in a woman's life are marked linguistically, and these categories provide clues regarding what were considered to be significant transitions within the culture. For instance, Reuben Walker (1934: 205) explained a complicated system of naming whereby spouses address each other differently after the birth of a girl and a boy.[3] Women are named according to their age, marital status and reproductive history; as we shall see, status was also marked ritually.[4] The puberty rites of the Ngarrindjeri females were graduated. They began at first menstruation and continued through cicatrisation to the next significant rite of passage for a woman, giving birth. I ask Eileen McHughes for the name for a young girl, and she says *yatiki* from her Granny Connie. In other sources I find *yatuka* (Berndt *et al.* 1993: 164), *yartuwe* (Taplin 1873: 131) and *yartooka* (Unaipon 1925–6).

The Yatuka First menstruation was the physical sign that a young girl was about to make the transition to womanhood. Interestingly, accounts in the ethnographic literature concerning menstruation provide far greater details of the rituals, taboos, practices and key relationships than are available for those associated with birth or the establishment of the *ngia-ngiampe* relationship. To me this indicates that many of the practices were current or within the memory of the older generation from whom they were recorded, and that the rituals had significant meaning for the participants. Missionaries may undermine marriage practices, ban large ceremonial gatherings, and even destroy ritual objects; state health authorities may confine women in hospital for birth and cut the cord with surgical scissors; but it is somewhat harder to intrude on private beliefs and behaviours concerned with menstruation. To be sure, traditional community-based rituals that had to do with marking the passage from girlhood to womanhood were curtailed, but women continued to learn about women's bodies from other women and that is something that neither state nor church has yet successfully controlled.

Val Power was told as she was getting into womanhood, they would say . . . go to your Aunty Janet. She will tell you. Liz Tongerie explains how her aunty taught her: Your mother never tells you anything about growing up, and then they bring in the "old aunties", and then *they* tell you about it. Aunty Lola (well, she was really my cousin), was brought in to tell me. After my mother had passed on, and my grandmother didn't tell me anything, Aunty Nell and Aunty Pearl were there, too. They were down at the Coorong at Boundary Bluff. That's part of our culture—it's not the immediate family who tell you. She was in Dimboola, and they brought her over here. I was twelve, and it was good to see her, and I wondered why she was coming. We were away from everyone else, and she was telling me. I presume it was my grandmother who invited her. They were talking about who told each one, and they were reminiscing about other cases of bringing someone in—my grandmother, who said I was a special girl.

The idea that birth and menstruation (in fact anything to do with women's blood) was the concern of women runs through the ethnographic literature. Writing in the 1840s Meyer (1846) details the way in which, at birth and menstruation, women camp separately, away from the general camp. Women call out to warn men. Should they come near, the men's hair will go grey and their strength will fail. Indeed, such was the young woman's power, that young men could not even see her footprints. On cold nights, the young woman wore fur slippers which kept her warm and also covered her tracks. "The matter of keeping warm at this time was regarded very seriously," say the Berndts (1993: 153). Here is a fine example of a behaviour which can be explained in several ways: the girls were being protected by being kept warm and the boys were being protected by being kept out of all contact. It was said that if a

509

young man saw a girl or woman in that condition they believed they would become prematurely grey-headed and sexually impotent (*ibid.*: 154). Thus there was a prohibition on being present and a consequence for violation. Women today know this story and a great deal more, but are not prepared to put the information in the public domain.

Pinkie Mack describes how, at the first pains, a girl was taken by her female kin, most likely in the company of a *putari*, to a special separate place some hundred metres from the main camp. A windbreak and a hut were built and she stayed there for several days (Berndt *et al.* 1993: 142). The Berndts tell us the girl was fed by her mother, sisters and female matri- and patri-parallel cousins (i.e. the women of her matriline and her potential sisters-in-law). During the day she sat over a fire, much the same as at birth; at dusk she moved to the women's camp where she stayed with older women. Pinkie Mack describes the criss-cross ritual designs, in her words "like a brooch", that were painted on a young girl at the time of the "changes" (Berndt *et al.* 1993: 154). She explains that "an older woman (probably a *putari*)", also using the "stem of the grasstree (*ngalaii*) dipped in the girl's blood, would tap the muscles below her shoulder blades and then her chest to make her healthy and strong". There were songs to accompany this rite, but Pinkie Mack told the Berndts she could no longer remember them. What symbolic associations may there be in the use of the grasstree—with its red centre, the locus of fire, memorialised as the raft of *Ngurunderi*'s wives—being used to paint the design? What ancestors' names were evoked in the exhortation to grow strong? What we can know, is that this was a women's ritual, with designs, songs and ritual paraphernalia, and under the control of women who knew the law and whose knowledge was respected.

Menstruation was a time of seclusion, a time when the young girl and others in the community had to abide by strict rules lest they fall ill. Tindale (1953: 143) recorded: "So dangerous was this that a husband or father or some near relative of a girl kept her apart— boy children must not know about women's blood." The Berndts (1993: 369-1) write that boys, on pain of death, are warned to keep away from menstruating girls, and that it is her family who exact revenge. It is dangerous for men to have sex with menstruating women (*ibid.*: 361-3). Taplin, although in somewhat ethnocentric language, also commented upon "the separation of the women on account of 'ceremonial uncleanness'. Women are obliged to reside in a hut apart during the whole time of their defilement" (scriptures nd). And in his journal, 14 June 1864, Taplin wrote:

> I find that during my absence Mr. Roberts and Mr. Stanley have disregarded the native customs with reference to the uncleanness of women. These I have always observed and respected, as I think they are decent in their mode of life. The natives have in consequence been much exasperated at Mr. Roberts and Mr. Stanley. They attribute some sickness to their conduct I believe.

Again, there are consequences to violating the rules. Taplin's imputation of notions of uncleanliness reflect his Christian upbringing. For the Ngarrindjeri, the blood, like red ochre, was dangerous, sacred and forbidden; but to make the leap to pollution one needed to import Judaeo-Christian beliefs where the sacred blood is that of sacrifice and the profane blood of women defiling. David Unaipon was alive to this distinction when he told Elaine Treagus (1996), who had asked for the word "blood" in Ngarrindjeri, "We don't use that word a lot. You have in Hymns and everywhere . . . washed in the blood but not us".

Taboos are common in rituals that mark the transition from one stage to another. Pinkie Mack said that all fish were taboo, but Karloan, relying on what his second wife's mother had told him, said that women usually ate fish (Berndt *et al.* 1993: 154). Tindale (1930–52: 5) notes "women are not allowed to eat fish caught with nets. They believed it would drive the fish away nor were they allowed to eat animals killed with a spear. They must live on vegetable foods and herbs." These are similar to the taboos associated with birth. Great care was taken to make sure no men, especially young men, ventured near the young girl (Harvey 1939). No men could observe what took place in her specially constructed hut, and none would come near the camp where she slept. However, men might catch sight of her at a distance. The warning signal was the sitting position adopted by women at this time. A man who saw a woman in that position knew to go no further. Old people kept a watchful eye on young boys and "if they inadvertently played nearby they would receive a flogging" (Berndt *et al.* 1993: 153).

It is difficult to read past the prejudice and preconceptions about menstruating women, because this topic is not part of public discourse in western society, any more than it is in Aboriginal society (if for different reasons). But if we can put preconceptions aside, we can see that this moment in a woman's life had repercussions for the whole society. At this time she was *narambi*. In particular, she could endanger young men, especially young initiates. The Berndts (1993: 154) state "the girl did not wash and was in fact debarred from going near any water that might be used for drinking". Brookman (Harvey 1939) also recorded the prohibition against entering the water. Tindale's observations about young men and young women locates the danger they represent to each other in a broader context by comparing the situation of menstrual blood and red ochre. "Girl children did not have to avoid menstrual blood [but] no girl dared touch anything belonging to a *narambi* lest she get red ochre on her" (Tindale 1930–52: 263). Men who were red-ochred were *narambi* and drank through a reed so as not to touch the water. Girls had to take great care not to come anywhere near the secluded men, not to cross their paths, eat their flour, or touch something they had touched, and to keep out of the water. As the reciprocal Tindale (1953: 143) records: "Women had to be very careful also lest menstrual blood should come near. Much bloodshed and fighting had its origins in neglect of these rules for nothing starts a fight quicker than fear that a boy may be hurt with menstrual blood." Here is a good example of complementarity in gender relations. Young men and women both had to observe taboos to do with food and water during their respective periods of initiation, but the content of the taboos was different. Young men in their *narambi* state had to drink water through a reed and the foods which they could not touch were extensive. They were, as people further north sometimes say, "all same but different".

What a man might know of the activities of women-only groups is clear in Reuben Walker's (1934: 214) notes on menstruation: The old girls were very particular about the young women, married or single. When a female was having their Monthleys, a spear would be stood up on top of the camp as a warning to the young men were not allowed to go into the camp where the spear stood as a warning. She was not allowed to intermingle . . . till her time was up. It was necessary to have a signal to warn men not to trespass, and the older women were the gatekeepers and teachers. What we don't and couldn't expect to get from Walker, is what the old women told the young girls for whom they were responsible. That is restricted to women. They were very "particular", and Tindale didn't pursue the matter. Had he, would knowledge of content of these beliefs and practices confirmed the existence of women's rituals? I think not. The structure, the precautions, and the teaching relationship between older and younger women have all been reported. We know that there was a time and place, respected and avoided by men, wherein women instructed women in the business of being a woman. The content may help us to understand the symbolism of Ngarrindjeri rituals, the relationship of blood to ochre, the nature of the taboos on water, but the sources are clear: women had ceremonies that were closed to men.

But I still ask: What had the girls been told? Cath Ellis (Ellis and Barwick 1989: 29), working with the Antikirinja and their knowledge of songs, comments that she was told that "in former times much knowledge had been passed from women to their grand-daughters during the period of isolation at menstruation. With the erosion of this practice of isolation, the whole process of transmission of traditional women's culture was placed in jeopardy." Once girls were in school and their comings and goings were monitored, it became increasingly difficult to observe the practices associated with menstruation. Tindale observes that teachers "can never keep a girl in school after the age of 12" (Tindale and Long nd: 4). Several women talked to me about how they had left school at this time. This is not something that one is likely to find documented in official statistics because their absence and silence avoid the need to explain to an outsider. It may not even have been made explicit to the young girl at the time, but the absences are full of meaning to a knowledgeable insider. As mentioned in Chapter 2, Doreen Kartinyeri had alerted the white males working on the *Ngurunderi* exhibit in 1988 that the sitting position of the woman was that of a menstruating woman. There are not too many old people who might have seen it and known, but I didn't want to take the risk.

From a wide range of sources—Taplin, Tindale, Walker, Harvey, Smith, Jenkins and the Berndts—we can discern clear patterns. We have a separation of the girl from the community and especially from men; behavioural clues in terms of how women sit; statements regarding her *narambi* state; several enumerations of who would be present; precautions that women should take; and there were consequences for non-observance. Pinkie Mack even mentions songs. What were they? Whom did they invoke? What did they ensure? Pinkie Mack and Albert Karloan disagreed over food taboos. Perhaps they also had different ideas about songs. The sources are consistent with what we know of Ngarrindjeri beliefs. Keeping warm, covering one's tracks, particular postures, food taboos, physical separation, avoidance of certain areas are all part of Ngarrindjeri women's lore. And Isobelle Norvill had not wanted her grand-daughter to miss out on some of the things that she felt hollow inside about missing out on. In some families young women are being instructed. Doreen Kartinyeri: We're still teaching that, training the young girls from birth on how hygiene, their own hygiene, how to look after their bodies, how to prepare their bodies for womanhood. My Aunty Rosie said menstruation was like the flowing waters, you shouldn't interrupt it. It's got to flow, like the waters.

Cicatrisation Women's bodies were marked by cutting and burning as part of their initiation.[5] On the first occasion the marks are burnt into the girl's arm, whereas on the second, the marks are cut into her back. These *manggi* (marking) ceremonies were the "official" Ngarrindjeri recognition of the physiological changes that the young woman was experiencing. As with other rituals where women's knowledge about women's bodies was transmitted, men were excluded. "A large group of women would accompany the girl into the scrub, where they prepared a cleared space and built fires" (Berndt *et al.* 1993: 154). Important ceremonies often alternate in mood: solemn, joking, quiet, raucous, light and dark, and it appears that during the marking ceremonies *all* women of the local camps would go out to make fun at this time (*ibid.*). This use of humour to divert attention and to break tension is a familiar pattern in

Aboriginal ceremonies; Reuben Walker (1934) comments on it in male initiation.

During the ceremony, write the Berndts (1993: 154), the "women would sit in a large circle with the novice in the middle and chant special songs referring to a girl's puberty. (Again, these songs were not remembered.)" The rituals were under the guidance of a *putari* who seared the designs with burnt twigs into the girl's flesh, which had been moistened by her spittle. Tindale (1931–4: 61) says the blood was caught and used in *ngildjeri* practice and that this was a time when women learned something of their *ngatji*. "Marks emblematic of the totem were cut by the Tangane on the outer part of the upper arm. An early photograph of a woman shows this and is readily recognisable as a lizard . . . Long cuts were made by men but only short ones by women." Thus the girl, like the boy, was introduced to part of her heritage and made part of the corporate life of her clan. "During this operation, the girl made no murmur. Any expression of discomfort or pain would have spoilt the ritual, which was an introduction to cicatrization" (Berndt *et al.* 1993: 154). Endurance of pain is a central component of male and female initiation also, and Unaipon (1924–5) sees it as central to learning discipline and respect. The young woman is clearly being honoured by all adult women, and although we have no record of the songs from Pinkie Mack or stories told, we can infer that important gender-specific knowledge was transmitted. We certainly can't say it wasn't. Women now in their sixties and older say this was the time they began to learn about the business of being a woman.

According to the Berndts (1993: 155), shortly after the marking of the arms, there is a second cicatrisation where, once again, the women gather at their "*narambi* place". There, while the women sang, the girl would hunch over,

> bending forwards while a *putari* or another influential elderly woman sat immediately behind her and prepared to cicatrize her. A piece of broken mussel shell or a *maki* (flint) knife was used to cut six rows of parallel broken lines on her back, each about half an inch long, arranged horizontally to extend over the back from shoulder to shoulder. The skin was cut slightly inwards and raised, and then red ochre was rubbed into it. After healing, this left heavily defined scars that remained throughout life.

515

It took some time for these cuts to heal; in the meantime the girl, in considerable pain, remained in the women's camp and under their care. The position adopted by the young girl is that of the woman giving birth. The pain of the cuts prepares the young girl for that life crisis. In the version of the Seven Sisters Dreaming provided by David Unaipon (1924–5), the young women who are seeking to prove their worth go through an ordeal similar to the one Pinkie Mack described to the Berndts. Again, the infliction of pain, the imprinting of designs, and the need for stoicism are familiar aspects of Aboriginal rites of passage.

Once the young woman had been through the marking of the arms and the legs, she was considered a woman and ready to assume the responsibilities of Ngarrindjeri women. As a sign that she was now a woman she wore a *kainingge* (pubic fringe), visible in the drawing by Angas (1847) of the "Girl of the Lower Murray Tribe near Lake Alexandrina". She wore this skirt until after the birth of her first child, at which point her husband would tell her to set it aside and pass it onto a younger woman, probably a younger sister or female matri-parallel cousin (Berndt *et al.* 1993: 155). Meyer (1846) adds the husband burns it if she is barren.

Girl of the Lower Murray Tribe
near Lake Alexandrina
South Australian Museum Anthropology
Archives (G. F. Angas 1845)

The symbolism of a girl's puberty rites and the actual practice of birthing are remarkably similar, and this is worth pursuing. To the Berndts (1993: 155), "The meaning of cicatrization is not clear." So, if the meaning is not clear, how can women be said to have no esoteric knowledge when the only informant says she doesn't "know"; hasn't been through the whole ceremony; and won't talk about the songs that were sung for what she did go through—even though she is known as a great singer? The meaning may have been quite clear to those present and to Pinkie Mack as well; it may have required further elucidation; context; most probably there was no one meaning. The fact that the designs were of the girl's clan country, and that she was kept separate from men, red-ochred, considered *narambi*, and was instructed by older women, indicates that this rite of passage was part of admitting a women into the inner meanings of Ngarrindjeri symbolic knowledge. She was in the presence of the sacred. Certainly Pinkie Mack emphasised that it was an outward sign indicating that a girl had passed from one stage in her life to the next. The setting aside of the pubic fringe and its transmission through the matriline is an articulation of the line of descent of knowledge about women and their fertility (*ibid.*: 155). This is not knowledge that passes through the patriline as *ngatji* affiliation should.

Depilation Although there are references to male rituals that entail the plucking of hair, there is none in the published ethnographic record regarding women. Are we then to assume it didn't happen? There are references in the *Ngurunderi* narrative that the young wives pluck their pubic hair and thereby indicate that they have not yet borne children, but there is nothing regarding the practice of Ngarrindjeri women. In Tindale and Long (nd: 3) there is a note headed "Initiation" with the symbol for woman beside it. This is the only description I have located for this practice although one can infer it from other references. In Tindale's account, depilation was one of the rites of female initiation practised by the Tangani. The women ceremonially seized the young woman, wrapped her tightly in a skin rug with her face covered, and then surrendered her to the men, who sang songs over her as she lay on the ground. She was expected to lie still while the hair was plucked, and henceforth "she was avoided by all men of her own clan and was expected thereafter to remove such hair as it appeared. After being given in marriage, she was supposed to continue the depilation herself until she had her first child after which she ceased to continue." It was at this point that she gave the pubic fringe to a younger sister. The name for the fringe, *kainingge*, echoes *kaingani*, the term for young male initiate. The young woman had to pluck her pubic hair until the birth of her first child and the young male initiate had his beard plucked. Here is another example of complementary rites for men and women which are "all the same but different".

Tindale's note not only shifts the ethnographic understanding of Ngarrindjeri rites of passage, but does so in a way that adds another dimension to the nature of gendered knowledge. Men are involved in one of the rituals that mark the passage to adult status for a woman, but all men must totally avoid all women during the previous segments of the initiation and after this one, her fellow clan members must totally avoid the young woman. Such exceptions serve to dramatise the later separation. Their closeness to the young virgin is highlighted by their subsequent distance from a clanswoman, one who is now marked with the designs, one on whose body the land is inscribed. The women's depilation rite was Tangani; this might explain why the Berndts heard nothing of it from Pinkie Mack, who was Yaraldi.

What Business? The "dissident women" made various claims concerning what they had been told about birth, menstruation and the changes in their bodies. Bertha Gollan, now in her late seventies, was born and educated on Raukkan, where nine of her eleven children were born. She was delivered by Pinkie Mack and also assisted an Aboriginal nursing sister, Faith Coulthard, in delivering babies. Still she heard nothing of secret "women's business". Iris Stevens (1995: 258-9) reports: "The young girls were not told how babies were born and they had to experience the changes in their bodies on their own." Dulcie Wilson claims that, although she knew many respected elders and had three births assisted by Ngarrindjeri midwives on the mission, "there was no discussion with her elders about fertility, menstruation, or childbirth. There was no instruction or discussion whatsoever because they never talked about such things" (*ibid.*: 266). So they ask: How come Doreen Kartinyeri was told? Doreen Kartinyeri contends that Dulcie Wilson had no communication with Aunty Rosie, who came to Point Pearce in 1931, the year Dulcie was born. I can't remember her visiting, so how could she have learned or not learned? Dulcie was twelve when her mother died and she was brought up by Uncle Bruce. Dulcie says she doesn't know where Hindmarsh Island is, so why is she an expert?

As a young woman, Phyllis Byrnes also lived in the same household as Aunty Rosie when she was living in Adelaide. She claimed that "they did not live in tribal ways", that Doreen Kartinyeri did not visit, and that Aunty Rosie had no special interest in Doreen (Stevens 1995: 264). These observations are challenged by a number of people who remember the closeness of Aunty Rosie and her niece, but they are flawed in other ways. Rosie Kartinyeri did know about "traditional birthing practices". Inadequate though the interview may be, she did tell Cath Ellis enough about what Ngarrindjeri mothers and midwives did to indicate that she had the knowledge. What the "dissident women" were or were not told cannot be the threshold test for the existence of a belief or a practice amongst other Ngarrindjeri.

It is not just what they were told, it is also how they understand the term "women's business". When her mother died, Margaret Lindsay, just seventy, the daughter of Nathaniel Kropinyeri, lived with Aunty Rosie at Point Pearce and called her "Mum". Margaret Lindsay stated she believes that "there is some women's business but not here, not down our way . . . up north where there's a lot of traditional women, I believe they've got women's business" (Stevens 1995: 263). She had only recently learned of the existence of such practices in the north. What is interesting in this and the assertions of other of the "dissident women" is that they have internalised a definition of "tradition" which excludes themselves and an understanding of Dreaming stories that excludes their stories. Other women, like Betty Tatt, in her early seventies, said she knew about stories like that of the *prupi* but: "There was never any talk of Dreaming stories. Her mother did not tell her anything about childbirth nor of the changes in her body" (*ibid.*: 260). Clara Rayner agreed that there was no talk on the mission of women's business, but said that when she was about sixteen and living in

Murray Bridge, "her mother said that there was women's business in a place which she named but it was not Hindmarsh Island" (*ibid.* 275). Further, her mother spoke of secret women's business. When she asked her mother specifically about Hindmarsh Island, her mother said: "It's best not to look back at things. It's best to look at the future" (Rayner 1995: 4673).

Cath Ellis (1963–5 (1) 22) notes that Jerry Mason, son of Rita Lindsay and Robert Mason, told her in February 1963 that "initiation rites were very severe" and that "women also had initiation ceremony". Ellis also "chatted" with Annie Mason (Koolmatrie) and Rita, who remembered a long corroboree and could think of the words. "Will return later to see if she can remember the whole song, if not will just record the words," writes Ellis. There does not appear to be any evidence this was accomplished. Lola Bonney Cameron told Liz Tongerie and Steven Hemming that in the Coorong there were initiated women. "That means they'd gone through rituals," said Liz. "And that means there were stories."

Women's Bodies: The Subject of Inquiry

On the one hand, there is a dearth of first-hand accounts that take us into the world of Ngarrindjeri women and explores women's cultural knowledge. On the other hand, there is a great deal in the literature about women's reproductive lives, their health, and their relations with white men. In fact, there were at least three state-sponsored inquiries into Aboriginal matters in South Australia—the Select Committee of the Legislative Council upon "The Aborigines" (1860); the Royal Commission on the Aborigines (1913); and the Hindmarsh Island Bridge Royal Commission (1995)—which sought information about women's bodies, their functions and the need to establish the truth about their behaviour.

Although birth was under the control of women, infanticide and abortion could be practised. Men might have objected, but there was little they could do. However, once women came under surveillance by the church and the state, their bodies were monitored. The 1860 Select Committee set out to inquire into the state of the mission under Taplin's management, and women's reproductive lives were an item of the agenda for the medical profession (Dr Wyatt), the church

520

(Rev. Taplin) and the state sponsoring the inquiry. Women's own views regarding conception and birth are not sought. They are heard through a filter. This sense of entitlement continues when it comes to inquiring into the intimate details of women's lives.

Dr Wyatt (1860) was examined and testified as follows:

656– Have you considered that one cause of the diminution of their numbers has been the disproportion of the sexes?—I have not considered that as having very much to do with it, as the same relative proportion existed probably before we arrived, and there was a tendency to female infanticide.

657– Were you aware of that crime being ever committed by the natives?—It is reported to be often committed; and one case where it was proposed fell under my own notice.

658– At what period did that occur?—During my holding the office of protector.

659– What was the nature of it?—A female child was about, according to custom, to be sacrificed, with the consent of the mother, in consequence of her having, when the child was born, a son four years of age, which she was still suckling. She suckled the son after the child was born, and that was the plea which the men set up for the destruction of the female infant.

Taplin says that he was ignorant "for some time that it existed to such an extent that it does". He also gave evidence to the 1860 inquiry and his journal of this period is full of grisly descriptions of infanticide (26/6/1861); of eating new borns (4/11/1861); of the fate of deformed babies and multiple births (20/9/1861). He moralises on the laziness of women, which was, in his words, "nothing but sheer, inexcusable laziness" (9/5/1861). "I find that infanticide prevails fearfully amongst these tribes. I know several women who have killed three or four children." Taplin may put infanticide down to laziness, but from accounts from many other societies we know that infanticide has been one method by which women were able to retain some control over the size of their families, and to ensure that the child that was still at the breast— and children were breastfed until three or four—would survive. Where infant mortality is high and a child has survived to be a toddler, has begun to speak, has become in that sense human, that child is a greater investment than the newborn, who will be a drain on the mother and the clan.

One concern of the Royal Commission was the fate of mixed-race children, and indeed the subject of prostitution had been raised by Penney (1841). Taplin reported that his wife, in conversation with an Aboriginal mother, had learned why the women were fond of having children of white fathers (12/9/1860):

> It appears that the men do not like the idea of allowing their wives to prostitute themselves to white men—they are ashamed of it. So no woman is allowed to speak of it, and indeed none like to, or to tell the names of the white men who are guilty of this sin, but a popular fiction is allowed to pass current among them that the cause of the children being white is the women eating plenty of flour when they are pregnant. But they like to have white children, both men and women, because they excite more compassion among the white women and can obtain larger gifts of food and clothes.

George Taplin (1860) testified:

1404– Is there any punishment for incontinency on the part of the lubras?—The men dislike the idea of incontinency on the part of the lubras, yet they wink at it; and the consequence that half the children are half-caste.

1405– Is there no punishment among themselves?—No; they cover it up amongst themselves, by pretending that the white children are produced by the lubra eating too much flour while pregnant; yet the lubras have told Mrs. Taplin that it is a mere rumour circulated as they preferred to have white children, as they were the least trouble, and the whites sympathised more with them.

The strongest first-hand testimony comes from Reuben Walker (1934: 187) who as a young boy in the 1860s was treated badly by whites and blacks and called names because of his mixed-race heritage. The *Advertiser* (25/2/1865) quoted from the report of the Protector of Aborigines: "I am sorry to say that the appearance of half-caste children is as frequent as ever . . . I should recommend that a reward be given to the mother to tell who is the father, and then the man be punished on that information." Some interesting records would have been generated had that suggestion been pursued. The proposed Aborigines Bill of 1899 aimed to curtail liaisons between white men and black women but was rejected by the parliament. The 1911 Aborigines Act established the Chief Protector and in 1923 the Aborigines Training of Children Act allowed children to be taken away without permission and put into homes.

The 1913 Royal Commission, unlike the 1860 Select Committee, took evidence from communities in other states, but as for its 1860 precursor the Ngarrindjeri were central to the considerations (Jenkin 1979: 259-70). The commissioners appeared to have learned little in the fifty-odd years. They were more concerned to protect the white population from venereal disease than to care for the people who had contracted the condition or the children who were dying at Raukkan. They worried about the "half-caste" problem and debated how soon such children should be taken from their mothers. "They should be taken away directly they are born" said James Grey, the secretary of the State Children's Council. "If they are in the wurlie a week it is bad for them, but it is fatal for them to remain there a year" (quoted in *ibid.*: 264). The women were not asked what they thought. Given that most of the Raukkan population was of mixed race, such wholesale removal would have constituted genocide. Nowhere is there any suggestion that the "half-caste" problem raised questions about the behaviour of early male colonists.

The Hindmarsh Island Royal Commission of 1995 was also fascinated with women's reproductive lives, in particular the abortion of mixed-race children. Few men wrote about their sprees. Edward Snell was an exception. On 12 December 1850 he wrote: "In the evening MacKay and I visited the Worleys [wurlies] and had a spree among the Lubras". Mixed race children were certainly conceived in the Goolwa area. It was traditionally a meeting place for a number of groups, and after white contact, it rapidly became a trading place for the settler population. There was a well-established fringe camp, and babies were born behind the site where the old police station now stands. Prostitution was one of the worries of Protectors in the area. There are also stories of particularly debauched travellers who had their way with the women and left them to fend for themselves. Veronica Brodie: Leila told me things of women's business to do with womanhood, the babies and we knew before that many of the Aboriginal women were raped and they had white foetuses so, you know, when they aborted them they buried them here, on Kumarangk.

The Harvard–Adelaide University Anthropological Expedition, 1938–1939 was also fascinated with women's bodies and their reproductive lives. The South Australian Museum holds Dorothy M. Tindale's notebooks on "Menstruation and School Data", recorded during this expedition. Folded into her notes is a form headed "Sex History of Australian Aborigines, Board of Anthropological Research: University of Adelaide". It contains personal questions regarding menstruation, sexual intercourse, conception, and pregnancy, with no mention of confidentiality. There is no attempt to elicit anything to do with the knowledge that young women are given at the time of puberty or the relationship of the women who assist. There is no attempt to learn about the knowledge that is imparted at birth. Instead, there is a prurient interest in women's blood and bodies and sexual habits. The only indication that this form might address women for whom life crises are ritualised is a question about the possibility of cleansing after menstruation and birth.

I am ambivalent about citing these documents as I feel they are like personal medical records that should be kept as part of a patient's medical history. No doubt these were not considerations when they were recorded, but they are now, and the existence of such material raises an ethical dilemma for researchers today. Just because something was once in the public domain does not mean it should be permitted to remain there and be accessible. Knowledge is not free. I propose to respect the privacy of the individuals whose lives are represented in the notebooks. With the consent of the elders amongst the applicant women, I simply offer a summary of Dorothy Tindale's observations. Doreen Kartinyeri tells me: I don't want their names in public and I've asked for that material to be restricted.

From Dorothy Tindale's (1939) notes, it is apparent that women were not satisfied with the white nurse and looked back to the days of the "native nurse". Particularly interesting here is the identification of problems with the cord as the reason for ill-health and death. Written on the individual records are notes concerning various women's attitudes to the delivery of health on the mission. There are a number of complaints about the tardiness of the nurse in taking them to hospital and subsequent deaths; much anecdotal material about babies who have bled to death as the result of the cord being cut wrongly; too short says another; that one child, who had trouble since birth with the navel, died at seven months, and a list of other children. No babies were lost before the sister came, she records. This is certainly what Ngarrindjeri women say today. Dorothy Tindale portrays the nurse as lacking in sympathy, declaring the homes dirty and the mothers a bad influence, whereas in Dorothy Tindale's opinion, this is not so.

The Berndts (1993: 138) note that abortion was rare and "frowned upon" because of the impact it could have on the mother. "Men were said to be absolutely opposed to such a procedure, in which a pregnant woman's upper abdomen would be pounded by a friend but not by a *putari*, who would refuse to be involved". On infanticide of mixed-race children, the Berndts (*ibid.*: 135) comment: "While the traditional norm appears to have been to cover up or ignore cases of illegitimacy, radical changes occurred with the breakdown of the old sanctions and the collapse of the indigenous council." Infanticide might also be practised if the child was born deformed, a consequence of the mother eating fat while pregnant. This is a good example of the way in which food taboos were enforced: women were prohibited from eating fatty foods lest their child suffer, and therefore this was the first question asked should a child be delivered deformed: Have you been eating fat?

There is little in the ethnographic record about theories of conception, contraception, or the practice of abortion. Different women were told different things. I recorded one story of how to tell the sex of the unborn child. According to Unaipon (Tindale 1930–52: 51): "The children were told by the parents that the baby had been found by the mother in some spot associated with totem. In a swan's nest in the case of the informant's younger sister whose totem was black swan". Where women "find" the spirit, they have a measure of power in terms of "finding" the spirit at a place which is favourable to their interests in land and their aspirations for their children. This language is certainly attributed to *putari* also, who

525

tell a child, "I found you." Mutha Bess said her mother found a lot (Ellis 1965: 126a). Alison Brookman (Harvey 1939) recorded that the "theory of conception to be told to children was that children are said to be little and flying about in the air and they are dropped out of bag and they could be caught." She also notes that "when a young girl is first pregnant, she consults her mother regarding her condition and her mother says, look at the flying child. You can catch that child." She also records a number of bush medicines and remedies which are consistent with what I recorded. And Tindale (1931–4: 91) records, "on the Coorong the lizard Tiliqua was a *ngaitye* or totem animal. If a native girl stepped across the track of one of these, she would become pregnant."

The Berndts (1993: 137) say the thistle called *talgi*, which grew prolifically along the water's edge, was a contraceptive. Tindale and Long (nd: 1) say the native thistle, *talgi*, which has a milky sap, when eaten can prevent pregnancy. I have asked a number of women about *thalgi*. Sarah Milera: I know we used to use the thistle, *thalgi*. I used to cook it for my aunty out on the Coorong. It was for strengthening the blood. If it was a contraceptive, how come there are so many children? We all ate it, like celery. Doreen Kartinyeri: They collected them all the time and we'd clean the *thalgi* and eat it just like celery. Everyone ate it so it can't be a contraceptive. We'd dip it in salt and munch it. When the leaves are nice and soft you roll it up and eat it like lettuce. Leila Rankine's poem "Our Table Was Spread" mentions "gathering thulgies [a kind of soft thistle] by the score". When Tom and Ellen Trevorrow visited Holy Cross College, they asked about the class I was teaching that day. "Women's Studies," I said. "We're talking about the environment and women's health." Tom was not keen on being in an all-women class but, after walking around the campus and meeting people, he volunteered to come to join us. He and Ellen spoke eloquently of central aspects of Ngarrindjeri culture, of *ngatji*, *miwi*, and weaving. Then Tom began talking about plants and, knowing it would be of interest to this class, mentioned the kangaroo apple that is used as a contraceptive.

The prurient interest of observers and outsiders in women's bodies, their functions, and their sexuality that is manifest from the Royal Commission Select Committee of 1860 onwards, plus the interventionist mode of delivery of health services to women, were hardly conducive to sharing knowledge about things a woman held dear. The message is that one can't trust knowledge, generated by women, about women's bodies. Those mysterious, life-giving sites of fear and repression are to be controlled, not celebrated. Given the boundaries of the sacred shift, it is not surprising that access to certain knowledge about "women's business" has become more and more restricted while other information may have become more public. Part of the problem of seeing women's rituals as significant lies with the way women's bodies are perceived, and it goes a long way to explaining why women draw an ever-tightening veil of secrecy around their business. Initially, the rituals associated with women's rites of passage were driven underground by the mission. According to Catherine Berndt, women's ceremonies were the first to "disappear" (1989: 11).

Women's reproductive lives have been researched as the physical means of reproducing the next generation, as sites of pleasure, danger and revulsion, but not as an integral part of the reproduction of the Ngarrindjeri world. If the organising device of the research is the physicality of women's bodily functions, of puberty, menstruation, conception and birth, then each may be studied as a separate phenomenon, documented, and fragmented. In these analyses women become just so many body parts or functions. A researcher could extract information about each function, but little attempt was made to locate these moments in a woman's life within the context of the reproduction of Ngarrindjeri culture. Yet there are multiple clues in the literature and in contemporary women's beliefs and practices, that birth was both hard physical work and part of the spiritual work through which enduring key aspects of Ngarrindjeri culture were observed and practised. Throughout this chapter I have been posing the same basic questions while documenting the existence of women-only spaces: what was being transacted in these women-only spaces? It is clear that there is a body of specialised knowledge and that women are secluded with other women at key moments in the ritual cycle. It is not just the natural processes of birth and bleeding, but the meanings attached to these life crises, the rituals that encode knowledge about these sacred moments, and the difficulty of accessing such knowledge.

527

"Women's Business": What Is It?

Muriel Van Der Byl: This was the day Graham Jenkins launched *Conquest of the Ngarrindjeri* at Point McLeay and Val and I were cooking Ngarrindjeri way in the ground. We'd finished the preparations and we'd gone to pick up my boys at the Wellington caravan park and to change. At the turn-off we had a blow out and then it was like everything was in slow motion. We flipped over twice, over the fence and I saw my life and my boys. I was scared but then I saw myself looking after my boys, so I knew I would live. Then I saw a tunnel and there were hands on my shoulder. Val Power: What I saw was a great big black tunnel cloud and I could see all these people looking over a balcony. Muriel: We didn't talk about it for a couple of days as we recuperated. We were lying in bed and talking and I told her the voices said, "It's not your time yet. You've got women's business to finish off." Well we laughed it off, but now we're fighting for our survival. Val: We had the accident where Louisa's boundary of the Ramindjeri country is at the Narrung turn-off. Maybe it was the old fellas as powerful as they are.

Much of the disputation of the past four years turns on the existence or otherwise of so called "women's business". I have spent some time attempting to establish the provenance of this term in the anthropological literature.[6] The earliest use I can find is in Charles Mountford and Alison Harvey (1941: 156) writing of the Adnjamatana of northern South Australia. There it glosses a range of beliefs and practices very similar to those that are documented in the written sources and known to certain senior Ngarrindjeri women today. Interestingly, Ngarrindjeri women report the existence of more items than are noted by Mountford and Harvey for the Adnjamatana. First, an elaborate theory of conception is given in detail, but the reports of several Ngarrindjeri conception beliefs have few details. However, I think we should consider the *miwi–ngatji–ngia-ngiampe* relationship the framework for such a theory. Second, pregnancy and birth practices are almost identical to Ngarrindjeri practices and both observe food taboos. Third, no infanticide is reported for the Adnjamatana, but for the Ngarrindjeri there are reports in Taplin and the Berndts, and there was resistance from the husbands and horror on the mission. Fourth, at an Adnjamatana birth no men were present, except sometimes a medicine man and then only during the early stages. The Ngarrindjeri report female doctors/midwives and have elaborate business associated with the umbilical cord. Fifth, menstruation practices and fear of blood are similar for both. Sixth, at puberty rites no men are present. This is similar, with one exception, for the Ngarrindjeri.

Of course, we need to do more than quantitative analyses but, given that Ngarrindjeri women have been put forward as an exception in the Australian anthropological literature, this comparison has some merit. Placing their discussion of "women's business" in a social context, Mountford and Harvey (1941: 160) note that, for young children, "moral upbringing is moulded by their environment and the telling of stories and legends". Since women have primary responsibility for young children, the women must know stories. Unfortunately we have only fragments of the Seven Sisters story, but what we have links Ngarrindjeri practice with Ngarrindjeri law. One story already mentioned that is being told has to do with the construction of the barrages and the earlier building of the jetty at Point McLeay (see p. 269). It provides context for the women's fears regarding the damage that a bridge will inflict on their bodies and reproductive lives.

In continuing my literature search for "women's business", I turned to the work of women anthropologists such as Catherine Berndt (1950, 1965), Jane Goodale (1971), Nancy Munn (1973), and Phyllis Kaberry (1939), all of whom have written first-hand accounts of Aboriginal women's religious lives. On revisiting their accounts, I found reference to women's ceremonies, secret women's ceremonies, secret sacred women's ceremonies and women's rituals (all terms that I also use), but scant reference to "women's business". Jane Goodale tells me that, even when writing of the *muringaleta*, a Tiwi girl's puberty ritual, she did not use the term. Catherine and Ronald Berndt (1942–5) in their report on their Ooldea field work, write of "men's business" and "women's business". In the section on "Women's Life", Catherine (*ibid.*: 230) writes: "Their secret life, in which men have no share, centres round the ancestral myths and songs told by the old women. Young girls, children and men may not listen to these; they are women's business." She does not dwell on the term, but the "secret life" that she documents, includes a woman's own "special duties . . . her own sacred and magical life in which man has no share. She has a part to play in some of men's ceremonies, as he has in some of hers (e.g. the initiation ritual of both sexes)" (*ibid.*: 259). The section concludes with "the bulk of the data [are] being reserved for later publication and discussion". As we have seen, such publications were not forthcoming.

I also asked a number of colleagues when they first heard the term and the answers are fairly consistent. They heard it in the field from Aboriginal people and they read it in my work. In papers I gave in 1976, I spoke about the range of activities in which women were engaged and the ways in which they were belittled by being called "love magic" (a hang-over from the sacred/profane dichotomy), rather than being understood as part of the religious life of a community and as an activity which invoked the power of the ancestors. I argued that categorising activities as "magic" rendered women's religious beliefs about land invisible. At that time I did not gloss women's rituals as "women's business". I heard the term used routinely by Aboriginal people (and used it myself) while I was in the field in 1976–8. At that time "men's business" and "women's business" were useful shorthand for the complex of gendered behaviours in desert society. As I began to publish, and to undertake consultancies, I continued to use the term and heard it used more often at conferences. I have unearthed a submission I made to the Alyawarra Kaititj Land Claim in 1978, where I used the term to gloss the women's *yawulyu*[7] which was performed for the Aboriginal Land Commissioner as evidence of women's relationship to land. That is the first use of the term which I have been able to locate in a publication of mine.

Looking back, I have a sense that, at the time, the term "women's business" fell upon fertile ground. The late 1970s and early 1980s were a time when women, Aboriginal and Anglo, were engaged in debates, direct action and conferences to address issues of sexism and racism. The women in the field have compiled a formidable record of scholarship, but their research was not informed by the feminist critiques of knowledge that developed from the late 1970s onwards (Bell 1993a). The term "women's business" now has a life of its own and has been appropriated by mainstream culture. I cannot speak for its usage in common parlance today, but I can specify what I meant by the term in the 1970s. I can also suggest why it might still be useful; why it might be open to abuse and misunderstandings; and why, in each situation, we need to specify, rather than assume, what it might encompass.

In "Women's Business Is Hard Work" (Bell: 1981), I spelt out what I meant by the term for central Australian Aboriginal women's practice.[8]

> Crucial to women's status is their relation to Aboriginal law. In seeking to make plain to whites the importance of their law, Aborigines draw upon an extended work metaphor. The law is termed "business" and is made up of "women's business" and "men's business". No pejorative overtones adhere to the qualification of business as women's. Ritual activity is glossed as "work" and participants as "workers" and "owners". The storehouse for ritual objects is known as the "office". Ritual is indeed work for Aborigines, for it is there that they locate the responsibility of maintaining their families and their land.

In central Australia, there is "business time", usually around the Christmas holidays when people can gather for the business of "making young men" through initiation ceremonies.

By exploring the dimensions of "women's business" and pointing out that women's ritual activity was not simply individual activities that had to do with women's physiology, but rather behaviours integral to beliefs about land, the ancestors, and women's rights and responsibilities, I had hoped to draw attention to the importance of "getting it right" in the first place. I was trying to avoid the "add women and stir" recipe for Aboriginal culture, while seeking to acknowledge that distinctive and gendered bodies of knowledge exist. I had seen what had happened in Alice Springs in the late 1970s over the proposals to build a dam; had worked on issues of site registration in the Northern Territory (Bell 1983) and issues of law reform, particularly recognition of traditional marriage (Bell 1988). My constant refrain at the time was that it is not sufficient to consult only with men. Women, for example, have distinctive interests in how marriages are contracted and sustained (Bell and Ditton 1980). Women have interests in land that should be recognised in their own right. I had worked on land claims where women were brought forward to talk about foraging, but were not relied upon as witnesses regarding their relationships to land (Bell 1984/5). At one level, the argument ran, it didn't matter in land claims that were strong because the claimants would win anyway and adjusting the hearing to accommodate women was inconvenient. But it does matter, as we continue to find out. The consultative structures stay predominantly male, as do the land councils, and women are at a disadvantage in being heard in these forums. Too often they enter when a situation is already in crisis. There they find a dearth of senior women lawyers and anthropologists who can work on their claims, few women judges, few women ministers of Aboriginal Affairs. The mass media are titillated by claims that concern women's bodies, doubt that women know anything of any consequence, and are convinced they are being "stirred up" by feminists (Bell 1993a).

As far as anthropology goes, it is, I think, reasonable to say that "women's business" is not a precise term of art; it can be used to gloss a range of traditions, observances, customs and beliefs, that are, in certain critical ways, the province of women, albeit different in different regions. It may include practices associated with women's reproductive lives and women's bodies, but that does not exhaust the possibilities of beliefs and practices that might be encompassed by the term, nor does it mean that the knowledge encompassed by the term does not also relate to land. *Ruwe*, we saw in Chapter 5 (p. 262), fuses land and body in one word, and it is a gendered body and a gendered landscape that are implicated. One needs to look to context to determine what "women's business" means. The term has a wide currency now, but it is my sense that this is from the mid-1980s onwards. It is also my sense that, for better or worse, I had a hand in popularising the term. The above is not intended as an exhaustive review: it merely indicates the lack of anthropological discussion of the term "women's business" and flags the questions of power differentials.

The definition of "women's business" in the Terms of Reference for the Royal Commission cobbles together two passages from Deane Fergie's report of 1994, which in no way could be read as conceptual or categorical definitions of "women's business". For the purposes of the Royal Commission, "women's business" became "the spiritual and cultural significance of Hindmarsh and Mundoo Islands, the waters of the Goolwa channel, Lake Alexandrina and the Murray Mouth within the tradition of Ngarrindjeri women which is crucial for the reproduction of the Ngarrindjeri people and of the cosmos which supports their existence" (Stevens 1995: 4). In Chapter 6 of her report, "Defining the Women's Business and its Place in the Literature", Stevens (*ibid.*: 229-85) does little to clarify what the term might mean to those who have used it. Instead, not having had access to the contents of the "secret envelopes" and, with one exception, not having heard from the proponent women, she offers a list of features she has inferred from a range of sources. The result is a curious combination of attempts to guess the contents, informed by a belief that there was a fabrication by Aboriginal activists, feminists, and fellow travellers. Deane Fergie (1996) has unpacked the "inferential tautology" on which the findings of the Royal Commission are based; she shows how the focus quickly shifted from "women's business" to "secret sacred women's business". Unfortunately the scholarship and time entailed in such an analysis does not make headlines.

In the definitional section of the applicants' representation to Justice Mathews (1996: ix), there was no mention of "women's business"; rather they relied on "women's knowledge" and "restricted women's knowledge". These are the categories with which the women were comfortable. Over and over I heard people saying, it was the media that made it secret, we said "sacred". They spoke of the knowledge of "privileged women", not just any woman. During the oral representations, the women did not often initiate use of the term. More often it came from counsel in a question. Indeed "women's business" was rejected outright by a number of senior women, who said "women's rituals" instead. The term as understood by the Royal Commission and as it came to be understood by the general public was a poor fit with the wealth of knowledge in the community. I have avoided the term and instead have written of ceremonies, rituals, beliefs, practices, traditions and knowledge as appropriate. There is a good deal that is the business of women.

Deborah Bird Rose (1996) writes of women's business as including the knowledge, songs, dance, designs, story and myths which belong to and are transacted by women. Birth, she points out, can be seen as "the window through which the existence of the sacred is glimpsed". In glimpsing the sacred here, I have returned to the topic of *miwi* and the navel cord relationship (*ngia-ngiampe*) and to reinterrogating the sources on women's rites of passage. Whether the configuring of gender values around these facts is one of equality is not the point. There are specialists; there is a differential access to knowledge; there are rules for transmission and sanctions for violations. There is a strong basis for the existence of "women's business" in the sources, flawed, hostile, ethno-centric as they are.

What Do We "Know" about Women and their Business?

Given that the sources support the existence of women-only spaces and the existence of knowledge restricted on the basis of gender, age, place in family and so on, perhaps we should recast the question about "women's business". It is not how could the existence of restricted women's ritual activities have escaped the notice of so many observers, but why, when observers learnt something of women's activities, were they so reluctant to name it as significant in the ritual life of women and the religious life of the Ngarrindjeri? Rarely is a work devoted solely to what women do, think, feel and know. When women do appear, it is to supplement what men say (as did Pinkie Mack on the topic of birth); in some cases it is to highlight the way in which men appropriate women's life-giving powers.[9] I have been focusing on what women are doing. What this means in terms of gender relations is another question. The dispossession of land, depopulation through disease, the male character of the frontier and the prurient interest shown in women's bodies have all shaped what is the business of women and, more particularly, the power of women to pursue their business. Are women equal partners or junior partners? Is it appropriate to describe their roles as complementary? If so, does this preclude the existence of separate ritual practices which draw on knowledge that is gender-specific? How ever we might answer such questions is largely irrelevant to establishing whether or not certain practices occurred.

Catherine Berndt (1989: 11) writes: "Gender-based differences, in the sense of inclusion-exclusion, in religious and other affairs, were minimal" and suggests this as one of the remarkable features of Yaraldi society. Tonkinson (1993: xxix) goes further: "Yaraldi ceremonial life was public, and there was apparently no secret-sacred men's religious domain, which is rare in Aboriginal societies."

Yet there is ample evidence of a men's domain and a women's domain that was sacred, hedged in with taboos, and off-limits to the opposite sex. Ceremonial life was not public in the sense that any person, of any age, male or female, initiated or uninitiated, local or foreign should be present and "know". Tonkinson's assessment of Yaraldi ceremonial life is not supported by the Berndts' own work, let alone the material from Norman Tindale, Alison Harvey, Dorothy Tindale, David Unaipon, Reuben Walker, Milerum, Albert Karloan, Pinkie Mack, and many others.

When the Berndts (1993: 210) characterise Ngarrindjeri society as open with no restricted information and no secret-sacred ritual, they qualified this description in a footnote: "While a certain element of the male initiation ritual was said to be secret-sacred, the ritual as a whole was not." However, as we have seen, there were rituals which they did not record, and there are other ways of understanding what they did record. The Berndts (*ibid.*: 287) stress complementarity. It is at this point that I think they have conflated the nature of gender relations in Ngarrindjeri society with the existence of gendered knowledge, places and restricted access to same. There were times when women gathered with other women under the leadership of a *putari*, when songs were sung, rituals were enacted, and men were excluded. A seclusion is a seclusion; a prohibition is a prohibition; a women-only space is a women-only space. To be *narambi* is to be sacred, dangerous, separate—the presence of red ochre is an indicator that one is in the presence of the sacred. The structure of the activities associated with aspects of women's reproductive lives may be known to men, but they do not participate, and thus have no knowledge based on direct experience. Just as women sometimes had access to the men's axes, and were present at some men's ceremonies, there were occasions when men might be present at certain women's rituals. Women "know" about male initiation—in fact, some older women may even see some of the most sacred of objects—but they would not claim to be knowledgeable about them, even though, as we have seen, women may be present, or within hearing distance, at the most sacred moments in men's ceremonies. Similarly men "know" that women are secluded at certain times for ritual activity, but they would not claim to know the songs. The ritual worlds balance each other, they

535

are made of the same threads, but they are woven according to the themes being celebrated by men or by women: they are different and separate.

The Ngarrindjeri applicants who asserted the existence of "women's business" believed that disruption to the proposed bridge site would be a violation of that business, but they were not prepared to place certain parts of their stories in the public domain. After working with them, I wondered how one might write of "women's business" without violating the rules of who might know what. From work with women in other parts of the country, I know that there are women's practices and restricted knowledge; I have not been shown the details, but I know they exist, not as a matter of blind faith, but a matter of anthropology. Turning to the Ngarrindjeri record, here are eight features of their "women's business" which were disclosed to the Reporter Jane Mathews and which establish that there were women's rituals without needing to probe content.

First, the structure of men's and women's worlds. There is knowledge that is the domain of women and that which is the domain of men (see also Hemming 1996b: 22-6). Men "know" of "women's business" and may even have a presence at some ceremonies, but there is a separation and neither seeks to probe the content of what the other knows. Rather, one believes in the existence of the other because one is aware of the restricted nature of one's own gender-specific knowledge. Thus "women's business" is both the domain of women and exists in relationship to "men's business".

Neville Gollan: I knew the men's business and I do believe that there is women's business.

Maggie Jacobs: I mean, I can't say those things to a man.

Doreen Kartinyeri: Grandmother's lore is never tell a man.

Sarah Milera: There's other areas women just sat, because they were tenders of this land while men were out on their lore business, and they were doing lore.

Veronica Brodie: We're breaking a traditional law by telling it . . . it was never told to the men.

Bruce Carter: I strongly believe that there has to be women's business as well as [men's] . . . because there is men's business.

536

Daisy Rankine: I know of parts of the man's side . . . Now, whatever that was, women never questioned it. I don't know what significance it had, but all I was told was that men had the story as well.

Kenny Sumner: I believe that women's business does exist.

George Trevorrow: I never come here to talk about the women's business on that site.

Second, rules which restrict access to "women's business". The question "Do you know something you are not telling me?" requires a person to admit that a body of knowledge, the existence of which cannot be acknowledged, does indeed exist. To do so is an admission of "knowing" about "restricted knowledge" and, in this context, a statement about its content. (Consider that matters of national security have been protected by denying the existence of certain information-gathering bodies.) The existence of restricted knowledge is signalled by the taboos.

Doreen Kartinyeri: I couldn't push my grandmother into telling me very much about things she felt I shouldn't know.

Daisy Rankine: So we all have our different families, we all got our different beliefs.

Jean Rankine: If they didn't give me permission, I wouldn't have been able to speak.

Veronica Brodie: It's restricted to privileged women . . . before I could discuss it with the younger ones, I had to discuss it with the older ones first.

Third, the authority of the elders. In an oral culture, knowledge is restricted to certain persons; for the system to work, those who are not privy to the "inside knowledge" must accept the authority of those persons who are privy, and the wisdom of the restrictions. They must be willing to believe without "knowing", but be prepared to participate in the system nonetheless. Applicants often referred to their "feelings" as one way they "knew" about the existence of "women's business" and sites on Hindmarsh Island. This way of knowing requires an understanding of what Daisy Rankine called her "*miwi* wisdom". One's elders can confirm that feelings are indeed exercises of the intellect by validating the "feelings" about the significance of places and events. In this way one's *miwi* wisdom is strengthened and developed.

Maggie Jacobs: I don't read much at all and I mean I did know, but what Veronica said about the beginning of that story is—that's the story.

Veronica Brodie: They're beautiful things and . . . they make you very wise and you appreciate the Ngarrindjeri culture.

Ellen Trevorrow: I felt it in my tummy. I believe strongly.

Grace Sumner: I believe these things.

Judith Kropinyeri: When I went to Hindmarsh Island I has this really strong feeling of belonging. I truly believe in the women's business.

Helen Jackson: We believe what our Elders say.

Janice Rigney: We support our Elders and we just believe in our *mi:minis*.

Daisy Rankine: I left it up to her what she was going to do, no-one else to speak but herself, you know.

Fourth, "women's business" is sacred. The women emphasised that they were speaking about knowledge that was sacred, not secret, and that it was the media that had played on the secrecy aspect. To this I would add, issues of contested secrecy come into play in a complex way when an outsider probes Aboriginal religious knowledge. If one is operating within a system of restricted knowledge and is bound by the "respect system", the issue of so-called "secrecy" takes on a different hue. It is linked to the authority of the elders and to the protection of what is sacred; it is far from the taunt of "I have a secret", which invites the curious to seek out the contents by fair means or foul. There is a difference between "knowledge" that is embedded in social relations and for which people are accountable, and "information" that is depersonalised and can be traded in the "marketplace of ideas". The women who hold women's knowledge for Dreamings in the area were clear that it was their spiritual beliefs, and restrictions on such knowledge they sought to protect. In this sense "women's business" is a subset of particular Dreamings, not a free-standing tradition in and of itself.

Daisy Rankine: That women's business is very sacred to us.

Veronica Brodie: It was told to women whom they knew would respect and hold the women's business at heart because of its sacredness— not because of the secrets of it, but because of its sacredness.

Fifth, rules governing the transmission of knowledge concerning "women's business". For a system wherein access to knowledge is restricted, passed by word of mouth, and wherein people move closer to the core of sacred knowledge as they demonstrate competence, there needs to be clearly articulated rules for the transmission of knowledge. As we saw in Chapter 7, the who, when, and where of it concerns both structural and idiosyncratic factors.

Maggie Jacobs: It was from my grandmother.

Daisy Rankine: The thing that I mentioned is the knowledge that was given to me through generation to generation.

Doreen Kartinyeri: You must keep it to yourself and one day by and by . . . you will know who to tell.

Jean Rankine: My grandmother taught me to be the person I am today. . . . She's given me strength, she's given me knowledge to go on, because every day I feel that we're being tested not by just people here but by other beings.

Isobelle Norvill: I've got a granddaughter now and I bring her down here as many times as I possibly can and with the help of her aunties I'm teaching her so that she doesn't miss out on some of the things that I feel hollow inside about missing out on.

Daisy Rankine: I can let my daughter, now she's forty-one years old, carry on our traditional family title.

Veronica Brodie: I wasn't going to tell anybody because it wasn't the right time. You have to earn the right to know the knowledge, or to know of the women's business.

Sixth, the known consequences to disclosure of "women's business". The pain, anguish and illness that resulted from earlier disclosures imperilled the well-being of the discloser and others in her social field. The women only disclosed details of the Seven Sisters story after grave consideration, and they withdrew the material when they realised it couldn't be protected under the rules of a Heritage application.

Veronica Brodie: I don't want to say something and it's wrong.

Eileen McHughes: Lizzie was a *putari* and I showed what that meant.

Sarah Milera: I don't like talking about those cliffs. I can't say it here.

539

I don't want to bring trauma to my Ngarrindjeri women.

Grace Sumner: My grandmother was telling me not to go there, but we went there and I nearly drowned through that, not listening.

Seventh, "women's business" is about the sacred business of being a woman. The Royal Commissioner and the Reporters under the Heritage Act have sought the details about this aspect of women's knowledge. In working at the intersections of two cultural systems—one that privileges the written text and the other that regards knowledge as embedded in social relations—we have a dilemma. To protect their law, they have to breach their law. Further, to require that the details of a ritual and/or belief must be specified and that, without such a disclosure, the significance of the belief/and or ritual cannot be known is to deny the importance of the details already disclosed. Much information concerning "women's business" addresses the role of *putari* and birth, knowledge of medicinal plants, knowledge of the seasons and the getting of food; preparation of girls for womanhood and modes of behaviour, demeanour, speech and so on. It does not arise in response to questions about "women's business".

Doreen Kartinyeri: So right up until I was a young girl they were still working by the seasons and the stars . . . the Seven Sisters are the beginning of a lot of things for the Ngarrindjeri women.

Val Power: Now, when I was getting into womanhood, they would say . . . go to your Aunty Janet.

Veronica Brodie: Ngarrindjeri women learned about certain ways to behave from this story.

Daisy Rankine: She just don't want to talk about it. You know, being a midwife, she was a midwife . . . she knew about women's business . . . the first time I heard about women's business was . . . that sacred business . . . I was 15 years old then, when I started to know about life too as well, you know, and sacred women's business . . . I was just a teenager going through life then.

Val Powers: Your aunty will tell you about women's business when you get older.

Doreen Kartinyeri: She told about all those things and how she used to cut the cord . . . we do it differently now.

Sarah Milera: Some plants I have to keep secret because they belong to women and only women know about them.

Doreen Kartinyeri: That was training the young girls from birth on how hygiene, their own hygiene, how to look after their bodies, how to prepare their bodies for womanhood.

Eighth, Hindmarsh Island is not just any island. In the next chapter, I will explore the sacredness of the island and its surrounding waters, especially for women and their business.

Isobelle Norvill: I believe and very much so in the spiritual and cultural aspects of Kumarangk.

Maggie Jacobs: My grandmother told me that this is where things happen with women.

Doreen Kartinyeri: This would be like a place where women would visit regular, daily, as this is the closeness, the family closeness, the relationship between each clan.

Isobelle Norvill: She just told me this was a very special place for women . . . that she would teach me more when I became a woman.

George Trevorrow: We know that this is very special ground over there. It's important to women. I believe this strongly.

Maggie Jacobs: See because that island down there, it was no secret it was sacred. The women's business was on one part of the island and the men on the other side . . . it is all connected with women's business down there.

Veronica Brodie: I want to bring my daughters down here one day, sit them down over there on the sand opposite the mouth and tell them about the women's business.

Val Power: Hindmarsh Island has a connection with the whole Ngarrindjeri nation. It is the hub of the Ngarrindjeri nation and in particular what it means to Ngarrindjeri *mi:minis* for their spiritual beliefs and for our other rituals and beliefs.

Daisy Rankine: Hindmarsh Island is a place of our ancestors' spirits . . . the meeting of the waters, the Goolwa waters are sacred to *mi:minis* and the island belonged to them . . . I knew there was business about Hindmarsh Island and the water and Goolwa but we wasn't allowed to speak out.

Connie Love: I hope there is nothing will happen to Hindmarsh Island because there's women's business down there.

Val Power: Aunty Janet used to shudder about those things, and she also said that a lot of things went on at Hindmarsh Island which they don't practise today.

Muriel Van Der Byl: The whole island . . . she'd say, it was like a medicine place, like a hospital, but that's as far as I can go about that.

Closing the Circle

Negotiating what might be included in this chapter has been complex and I wish I had several more years of "being there". Each time people read what I've written, more stories are told. On this occasion Doreen and I have finished working through the manuscript. We talk all the way as we drive back into Adelaide from Point Pearce, and Doreen decides dictating into my little tape recorder is a good way of making a record of what she wants to tell me of her Aunty Rosie. The visit to Point Pearce has been stimulating. I am about to board the plane for Boston that afternoon and before I do I need to drop off some materials at Stephen Kenny's office in Adelaide. Doreen stays in the car, reading. She's reading this last section on circles. I am stuffing books and papers into suitcases. She has told me: When I'm on the country I feel safe enough to tell it, especially when I'm sitting in a circle. The recurrent symbol of the circle, the circular mat, the weaving that radiates outwards, these things I am being told in oblique ways are connected to women's work, to women's lives, to women's rituals. Aunty Daisy has said: The weaving is about our history, all the Ngarrindjeri past. As we weave from the centre out, we weave the Ngarrindjeri world, like our *miwi*. It is not cut into little boxes. Ellen Trevorrow said: With the weaving it was sharing time. From where we actually start from, the centre part is creating, you're creating loops to weave into, then you move into the circle, you keep going round and round creating the loops and once the children do those stages they're talking, actually having a conversation, just like our old people lived, sharing time. And that's where a lot of stories were told.

The anthropologist who has listened to these stories, observed the interactions and at times participated is still pondering the significance of circles: the *ngia-ngiampe* stones with the concentric circles mentioned by Unaipon, the ceremonies where women danced in a circle, "like a whirlwind" (1993: 216, 218) and sat in a circle to paint circles on the breasts of a young girl to encourage growth (*ibid.*: 154-6; Saunders 1994), and the circle of language. Then there is the story of the wives of *Ngurunderi* whose swimming in circles formed a semi-circular sandbar. I read of Milerum telling Tindale that his "mother incised circular marks on the skin cloaks and rugs which were used and temporary marks were made on the claypans where they were pegged out" (Tindale and Long nd: 9). In other parts of Australia, the symbol of the circle is commonly associated with women (Munn 1973). Do the large circular Ngarrindjeri mats give physical form to a central Ngarrindjeri symbol? Is the coiled design a way of thinking about the cycles of life? Weaving is said to evoke a sacred feeling and strong weavers have cultivated their *miwi*. Can we connect *miwi*, the navel and women's work? Like the weaving, the *miwi* embodies circular designs. Milerum gave the name *pulatanguka* to the basket made from two circular mat-like pieces, the centre of each of which was regarded as resembling a navel, hence the name *pulanggi* (Tindale and Long: 1). *Nakal*, the sister basket, says one of Tindale's cards, and refers to "a scribbled note in a small memo book". I haven't found it yet. But this basket continues to intrigue me.

At Camp Coorong, several weeks after the Basket Weaving Conference in 1996, just before we set off down the Coorong, Ellen, still weaving, had greeted me at the door with, You caught me. This time it is a sister basket that is to be photographed in Sydney for a show in Taiwan. Part of me goes with this, says Ellen. It's being photographed in Sydney this weekend to go to the exhibit. "Don't your fingers get sore?" I ask as I watch her pulling the rushes deftly through. No. I love it, and she is radiant. Into the sister basket is woven knowledge of life and women's importance in the creation and maintenance of their world. The stories that are being told belong in the 1990s. The power of sisters, of the two halves that form the whole, and of the inside space they encompass, are ways of thinking about the struggles and strengths of these weaving women. Ellen has now made a set of seven sister baskets and it is the Seven Sisters Dreaming which sets out the rites of passage for Ngarrindjeri women.

But I have a plane to catch. Doreen is holding the manuscript up when I get back into the car. I didn't know you wanted to know that, she says. Why didn't you ask? "I wanted to hear it from you, when you were ready," I say. As Doreen tells this story of weaving, her hands move to make a circle. She is pulling through the rushes and threading in the fillers. When you keep adding with the filling, you're adding another member of your family and you don't put them all in together, they're at different stages, just like with the family. The family is all different ages, from the tall ones down. And when you finish you're on the last strand of the rush, that is the filling, and when we do it that way, you can't even see where it ends. And that is like the *miwi*, because there is no end to the *miwi*. It's joined on at either end to the placenta and the baby. It's the lifeline.

The beliefs and practices associated with the navel cord weave new people into an ever-widening circle of friends and relations, just as does the navel exchange. To see these links we need to think beyond the division of art/craft and the body as separate from religious beliefs and practices. Like the greeting of close friends where the hands are thrown out from the stomach, like the power of the *miwi* through the navel, weaving draws together feeling and thinking. There is a rhythm and ritual to it, as Ellen Trevorrow said. Shirley Peisley and Vi Deuschle have explained that Ngarrindjeri knowledge is not segmented and compartmentalised into individual disciplines. Rather, it is highly integrated, and constantly renewed through contact with kin and country, and it is anything but static. Tom and George Trevorrow were at pains to explain how the different parts of the Coorong were interconnected, and the problem of putting information about places in little boxes. Women's weaving draws together the threads of Ngarrindjeri lives into circular designs which, like cycles in the natural world, should not be broken. The Murray River was like a lifeline connecting the living body of land (Berndt *et al.* 1993: 13). The umbilical cord is a lifeline—Jean Rankine says it can bring you home—binding mother to child, said Unaipon, down through the generations, carrying Ngarrindjeri identity for those who listen to their *miwi*, their elders and the land.

Sacred Orders:
A weave of clans, stories and sanctions

Kumarangk: "Not just any island"

"*This island is not just any island,*" sang Dot Shaw. "*It belongs to the Ngarrindjeri mi:mini.*" And it is from Ngarrindjeri women that I first learned of the significance of this tiny island that nestles in the crook of the arm of the Goolwa Channel. On my first visit in 1996 I heard fragments of stories of the creative ancestors whose bodies reside in this landscape, whose deeds laid down the law for the living, and whose travels link the skyworld above to the earth and waters below. On that trip I recorded three names for the island—Ingulang, Kumarangk, and Tarpangk; later I found all these had left traces in the written sources, where I also found a fourth, Rumarang.[1] This multiplicity of naming is not unusual: there were a number of different groups who had an interest in the island and each had its own name. Today Hindmarsh Island is most commonly known as Kumarangk, a name said to mean the place of pregnancy.[2] This name resonates for the women who feel deeply connected to the place, who cried the first time they visited, who believe in the stories their elders tell of the creative heroes, the powerful presences associated with the area and the dangers associated with transgression of the laws.

On subsequent visits I hear stories of the "first generation" who camped and worked on the island, and of the visits made by this generation of elders to the island. Before the barrages were built, the women tell me, you could walk across to the island and it makes sense that the island would have been a safe place for certain restricted ceremonies. Remember Veronica Brodie's story of the women telling the missionaries they were going weaving (see pp. 86–7). I am shown burial sites of the old people, of babies and of aborted foetuses. I am told of the removal of bones from development sites. On subsequent visits people point out middens, speculate about unmarked graves, and anticipate that more bones will be disturbed in future developments. I learn of the burial places for visitors at Goolwa—sure evidence that this was a meeting place of some stability. Favourite camping places and fishing traps are pointed out. I see the *lauwari* massing on the salt marshes, collect pelican feathers, note medicinal plants, and listen to the breakers crashing on the hummocks. Shading my eyes against the bright light reflected off the ocean and sand dunes at the Murray Mouth, I trace the contours of the currents and wonder about the ways the wind, barrages and human presence shape this opening to the Southern Ocean. Celebrated in song and story, this is a wild, wonderful landscape where fresh water meets salt, where wildlife abounds, and where Ramindjeri, Tangani, Yaraldi and Warki clans once met for ceremonies, trade, dispute resolution and to arrange marriages.

There is little to indicate to the casual visitor to Goolwa, Hindmarsh Island and the Murray Mouth that this area is of enormous significance to the Ngarrindjeri. In the Signal Point Museum at Goolwa there are displays which include information about the Ngarrindjeri, but there are no story boards at Amelia Park to tell the visitor about the importance of this camping site or about the extensive midden that runs along the Goolwa foreshore. There is nothing at the old court house about the caves on which it was built. *Ngurunderi*'s campsite is not flagged. The Seven Sisters' story is not told to those who cross the Goolwa Channel on the Hindmarsh Island car ferry. In part, this "invisibility" of the Indigenous past is a conscious decision of the Ngarrindjeri. In the absence of respect for Aboriginal sites and beliefs, and in the absence of strong enforceable legislation, the best mode of protection is to keep quiet about the location of places unless they are in immediate danger. Given the recent experience where the South Australian Minister for Aboriginal Affairs allowed work to be undertaken on registered sites, and the cavalier way bones have been handled in the past, the Ngarrindjeri have good reason to fear that a sign indicating the presence of a sacred site would invite vandalism. When parts of their stories have become public, they have been treated with contempt.

546

Reconciliation has a hollow ring when the sign to the "Murray Mouth" is defaced with the words "Black Pussy" and there is no public outpouring of disgust and outrage at this racist, sexist slur, no editorials, letters to the editor, or calls for religious tolerance. Had the graffiti been a swastika on a synagogue, the nature of the insult and threat would have been immediately apparent, but beliefs about women's bodies, especially black women's bodies, are not understood as part of sacred traditions.

The *ruwi* on which Goolwa is built, and the *ruwi* on which the marina is planned are not understood as the *ruwar* of the ancestors, to be held as a sacred trust by the living. Rather, to the casual observer, Goolwa is a tidy town. Clear signs point to the presence of whitefellas and the leisure activities that may be enjoyed in the area. I pick up brochures at the Tourist Bureau. There are trips along the Coorong, fishing off Encounter Bay to be enjoyed and more messages from "Bazza the Bunyip". I wait for the car ferry and, along with several other cars, cross over to the island. There may well be "peak times" when one has to wait for this ferry, but in all the times I have been back and forth to the island, it has been a pleasant crossing with little or no delay.[3] The trip takes a few minutes and affords the opportunity to view Goolwa, the channel and the island. As we pull away from the shore I look back at the paddle steamers docked at Goolwa. One is called *Mundoo*. "Who said they could use that name?" demands one of my Ngarrindjeri passengers. Another is named *Moolgewangke*. Same question.

Once on the island, I visit the marina which is just off Randall Road, the main road running from west to east across the island. I am thinking about how to represent my field work and hope these "snaps" will work (see Field Work Area map, pp. 24–5). I photograph the large modern dwellings scattered across the stalled housing development to the east of the marina. These houses stand in marked contrast to the older, more rustic farmhouses, built on the estates carved out by the early settlers on the island, and the clusters of holiday shacks that dot the shoreline. I photograph the Goolwa barrage, located between the town and the Murray Mouth. It holds back the sea water. The waters lapping the land on which the marina and the town are built no longer surge with the tides, nor is the Goolwa Channel flushed by the salt

547

waters of the Southern Ocean, the place where the salt meets fresh water is silting up, the land is salting up.

The alienation of the lands of the Ramindjeri at Goolwa and the Tangani, Warki and Yaraldi on Hindmarsh Island began early in the history of the settlement of South Australia. Whalers and sealers from the Encounter Bay area had already made inland forays (Lewis 1917: 4). Then, in December 1837, in search of a navigable outlet to the sea, Messrs T. B. Strangways and Y. B. Hutchinson became the first official white visitors to the island. They named it Hindmarsh after the Governor. The local people watched, as they had watched Sturt seven years earlier. Six natives were observed "on the cliff on the other side, who called and waved at us: from two of them having shirts on no doubt they had been to the fishery" (Hutchinson 1838: 6). Several years later, for £10 per annum Dr John Rankine of Strathalbyn rented the island as a cattle run from the South Australian government (Hodge 1932: 69-70). The next settler, Charles Price, swam his cattle across after Rankine refused access to his ferry, at the time the only existing connection to the mainland. Price camped his first night with local people who were fishing (Conigrave 1938: 8; Anon. 1883: 9). As the settler population increased, Ngarrindjeri men and women were drawn into work as labourers and domestic help (Conigrave 1938: 9, 21-2); others made camp in Goolwa. They were staying close to their own *ruwi*.

It would be helpful to be able to plot the pattern of white settlement on the island, and several researchers have begun this task.[4] If it resembles in any way that of other parts of Australia, some of the earliest settlement sites of whites will be on exactly those sites prized by the local people; and much frontier violence was the result of clashes over access to such places. There is one report of "an inexhaustible supply of beautifully fresh sweet water" in native wells at the western end of the island, which became places where the whitefellas' stock could drink (Anon. 1883: 9). What of the native people who relied on these wells for their survival? The land was being transformed by the grazing cattle and sheep and by the planting of crops and land clearance. It was also being mismanaged.[5] Some settlers took precautions against what they saw as "marauding natives" by fortifying their homes.[6] However, despite the alienation of land, disease, the violence which erupted around alcohol, and the armed settlers, some Ngarrindjeri hung on.

Reuben Walker (1934: 191, 209) remembered Yami Rankine and his two wives, Betty and Louie, on the island in the late-nineteenth century, but says that the days of the Ramindjeri were few. In his census of 1876, Taplin (1873: 43) enumerated ninety-four people at Goolwa. Maurice Newell said some twenty to thirty people were camping near his house at Newell's Landing until 1910 "when they were moved to Point McLeay" (McCourt and Minchan 1987: 148). This was the period in which Aboriginal people, who were said to "infest" the city of Adelaide, were removed to Point McLeay by the Protector (Mattingley and Hampton 1988: 6). By the mid-1920s and into the 1930s the population at the ration depot at Goolwa ranged between four and ten persons: Reuben Walker received three dozen rat traps in August 1924.[7] He was still working at age sixty-five; still close to his *ruwi*. Who were the people who called the area of Hindmarsh Island, Goolwa and the Murray Mouth their home?

Hindmarsh Island: A Complex of Clans

There is agreement in the sources that the land around Encounter Bay was Ramindjeri, and their stories concern the rugged coastline, off-shore islands, back scrub country, and the various flora and fauna of this area. Likewise there is agreement that the Tangani lived along the Coorong, and their stories tell of these waterways, of the hummocks and rich bird and fish life. Around Raukkan were Yaraldi strongholds, and their stories are of the lake and its unique flora and fauna. Each group had a distinct ecological niche and each told stories that reflected their location. When we focus on the Murray Mouth area, we find a meeting of peoples, languages and clan groupings. Indeed, today some say this is where the creation of the various dialects of the Ngarrindjeri occurred, and the story of Wururi recorded by Meyer (1846) suggests that this was the area where the one language became many.

Tindale (1974) and the Berndts (1993) agree that Ramindjeri, Tangani, Warki and Yaraldi all had interests in the area. However, which clans, which *ngatji*, and which language groups had rights in which parts of this area is less clear. There is some agreement at the level of sites, but little at the level of clans. To be sure, this was an area in flux. Semi-permanent populations had grown up around Encounter Bay, and Goolwa had become a ration depot where local peoples gathered. As the Ramindjeri population declined, there was a westward push from those in the more isolated areas of the Coorong into Goolwa. The Murray Mouth moves. The stories had to accommodate such changes in the living landscape as well as demographic change. The stories overlapped and intertwined. The intermingling of peoples at Goolwa could be accommodated to a certain extent. This was where clans gathered, but the clan system was sorely stressed and, as clans fractured, stories fragmented also.

From Tindale's (1974: 212-19) descriptions and maps, it appears that Hindmarsh Island was Tangani, with the Warki occupying the eastern and the western extremities of the island, the Ramindjeri at Goolwa to the Murray Mouth and Tangani on the Younghusband Peninsula. However, when I delve deeper and deeper into his raw data, the pattern of occupation of and access to Hindmarsh Island becomes more complicated.[8] It appears that the Yaraldi held the west, with the Tangani on the east and the Warki north of the Goolwa Channel. The Berndts (1993: 304), who were often working with the same informants as Tindale, offer radically differently patterns of land ownership: Warki in the middle of the island, Yaraldi to the east, Tangani in the west, Goolwa as Tangani and the Murray Mouth as under the control of Yaraldi clans. It is significant that each has recorded a landscape that is named and attributed to specific groups. In part, the differences may be accounted for by the nature of the questions asked about local and social organisation; they may reflect different field-work styles and length of time spent on site visits; they may be what the "informant" wanted or thought was appropriate to communicate at any given time; they may be how the "informant" represented the nature of the changes underway in Ngarrindjeri lands. How ever we contextualise the information regarding land affiliation, it is evident that Tindale and Berndt have mapped significantly different relationships. All the evidence points to the Murray Mouth region as a shifting complex of clans, sites, resources, and stories. This is where the river, their lifeblood, enters the sea; where *ngatji* proliferate; where the tongue of the Coorong shoots off to the east. Who might reside upon and exploit the resources of Hindmarsh Island and environs was in flux. We cannot take the clan information of Tindale and the Berndts as establishing a static ethnographic base line.

These two maps of Kumarangk show that a number of interests in land intersected in the Hindmarsh Island, Goolwa, Murray Mouth area. In the site mapping of the Berndts and Tindale, there is some

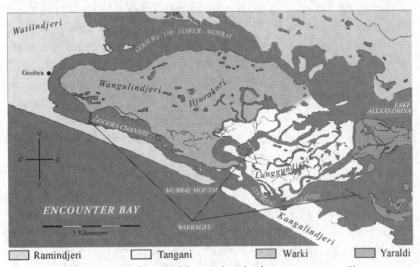

Ramindjeri   Tangani   Warki   Yaraldi

Kumarangk (after Tindale 1974 and other papers, see n 8)
(Map: Stephen Shaheen)

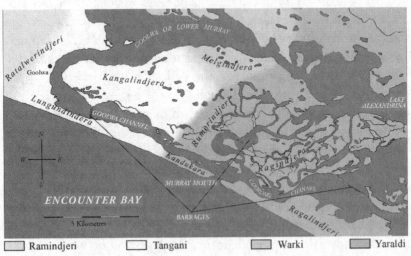

Ramindjeri   Tangani   Warki   Yaraldi

Kumarangk (after Berndt *et al.* 1993) (Map: Stephen Shaheen)

551

overlap of place names, although the Berndts (1993: 329, 309) do not mention a great number for the area. In brief, Tindale records that a Yaraldi clan, Iljorokori, occupied the southeastern half of the island facing the ocean mouth of the Murray River. Across Holmes Creek were the Tangani of the Lunggundjeri clan, who occupied Mundoo and Lucern Islands. In the northeastern part of Hindmarsh Island and in the northwest were the Wangulindjeri, a Yaraldi clan, who in earlier days, had held the whole of the island. Across the Goolwa Channel they were confronted by the Watiindjeri. They were a Ramindjeri clan who, in summer, also lived along the Murray shore of the Sir Richard Peninsula from Wateangk at the Murray Mouth west to Goolwa. In the autumn people hunted furred animals such as opossum, and in winter migrated to the wooded country north and northwest of Goolwa. Women gathered bracken fern rhizomes. The Melgenindjeri, a Warki clan, lived to the east of Finniss River, and the Meralda, another Warki clan, lived to the west of Currency Creek and Finniss River. The Kangalindjeri, a Tangani clan, took in Tauwitcheri Island, Long Island, the Mud Islands and the Younghusband Peninsula.

Let us now make this map dynamic. According to Tindale, the Iljorokori (Yaraldi) were an intruder clan of some three generations depth who had broken away from the Peltindjeri, living near Poltalloch on the southeast side of Lake Alexandrina. Tindale's note (nd, i) laments we know so little of the process by which this clan broke away and established itself because it would certainly flesh out our understanding of how change occurs. Their emergence as a new group was partly achieved by their having made a nominal change in their *ngatji* from *mangaraipuri*, the pelican of their parent clan, to *nori*, the pelican of the Rummerang clan. By the time Tindale was collecting data, they had come to regard themselves as a separate clan group. Albert Karloan said the break came at about the same time as the Manangki (his father's clan) split, that is, during the days of his great-grandfather. This territorial incursion we can date as just a little before white contact. In their early days, the Iljorokori had taken in one or two Tuuri clansmen of the Tangani tribe, and this would have further legitimated their move and possibly given access to local knowledge. It is evident that the Ngarrindjeri were adapting to and accommodating change, long before the 1840s. Reuben

Walker, who called the Iljorokori "Reumerunginja" (meaning of the Rummerang clan), offers an insider's view. When still a lad, Walker (1934: 187) married into the Lewarindjeri, another "tribe" of the Ruemerunginas. Of them he says Doctor Yami (Jimmy) Rankine, noted warrior and head of the tribe, and his wives Louie and Betty are the last members. When Walker includes the wives in the "tribe" he is not using the same notion of the land-holding group as Radcliffe-Brown, the Berndts and Tindale did. Unfortunately, the matter of women's affiliation to land was not pursued with Walker.

The Wangulindjeri (Yaraldi), who had their winter camps on the north of the island, took advantage of the firewood close by. In the summer they camped along the southern shore near Reedy Island, which was probably on or close to the border with the Iljorokori. The Wangulindjeri, according to Milerum, spoke a little like people to the west, and sometimes a little like the Bungandtitj people of the far southeast. From this, Tindale concludes that the clan was possibly an old one. They used bark canoes to meet the Watiindjeri (Ramindjeri) across the channel, and when Tangani visited they always camped west of Kultungath (Goolwa). Each group had separate camps. Lunggundjeri, a Tangani clan, lived on the north-eastern part of Hindmarsh Island, Lucerne and Mundoo; they exploited places as far west as Rat and Goat Island, and claimed the northern tip of the Younghusband Peninsula as their lookout. They had originally lived near Lake Albert in the area close to the Campbell House of today. According to Milerum, this clan spoke with a mixture of Yaraldi words and had "a funny way of talking". Their boundaries could not be clearly defined during Tindale's field work owing to the intrusion of the Iljorokori clan. This appears to be part of the westward push of Yaraldi and Tangani clans. By the turn of the century they had moved into Goolwa one focal site for surviving Ramindjeri.

In attempting to explicate the population movements in the area, Tindale states that, after the decline of the Ramindjeri in the late nineteenth century, the Lunggundjeri survivors shifted from Mundoo Island to Goolwa where, according to Reuben Walker, they spent their last days as a clan. There they clashed at the Murray Mouth as the Tangani spread west to Goolwa. Moriarty (Taplin

1879) the police trooper at Goolwa, in response to a question about legends, speaks of the Tanganarin. This was in the 1870s so the Tangani move into Ramindjeri country was well under way in the nineteenth century. The Berndts (1993: 329) locate their Lunggundjeri and Kanglindjeri further east than Tindale. This no doubt tracks the move into Goolwa and into Ramindjeri country, a move facilitated by the demise of the Ramindjeri and the attraction of services at Goolwa. This island, located at the intersection of a number of Ngarrindjeri interests, where the river, their lifeblood, enters the sea, home of whale, is not just any island. Entitlement to reside upon and exploit the resources of Hindmarsh Island and environs (not necessarily the same thing) was in flux.

In other parts of Australia, such a complex of clan interests in such a small space would indicate important resources to be exploited, as well as sites which may be recalled in the narratives of the formation of the region and ceremonial sites that needed to be kept under a watchful eye. The Berndts (1993: 15) write of the view from Raukkan, of looking across the lake to Point Sturt and of how "Hindmarsh (Kumarangk) and Mundoo (Multunganggun) and several other islands separated by numerous creeks and channels *protect the Murray Mouth*" (emphasis added). On Hindmarsh Island one is looking the other way, back into the lakes, to the inner reaches of the land "held by the sea", as Aunty Daisy told me. I look at the map with the river flowing through a network of channels to the sea and the way in which many clans and linguistic units converge on the area. Women knew the shape of the island as they rowed around it and the rhythm of the salt water and fresh waters, the flushing through the Murray Mouth. This knowledge is reflected in their beliefs about the area and encoded in the stories of the places and their relationship to each other. This is a fragile area, in need of protection, as the Berndts recognised.

Goolwa: A Complex of Activities

With the clans of at least three different languages on the island, and a fourth at Goolwa, reports of sweet water on Kumarangk and of beached whales at Kondilindjeri it is not surprising to find evidence of trade, ceremonies, and complex residential patterns in

554

the area. At intervals of several years, at large gatherings of people, called *mutjari*, disputes were settled, marriages arranged and initiations performed.[9] In 1850 Snell (Griffiths with Platt 1988: 187) left town to avoid the "great annual Fight" which was about to occur at Goolwa. As many as six marriages might be arranged at one meeting. One prompt for such gatherings for Tangani was seasonal abundance, such as when *munthari*, native apples, were ripe. More random, less predictable gatherings for feasting occurred when a "strong man" caused the beaching of a whale (Tindale 1974: 18). Then other groups would "invade" Tangani territory. It seems to me that where whales beach may well be affected by tides, storms and so on. Wherever the whales did beach became a place of feasting, sharing and the focus of much economic and ceremonial activity.[10]

In addition to the feasting at the Murray Mouth which brought different peoples together, there was the trade that focused on Goolwa. The Berndts (1993: 117) mention: "One other item of importance that found its way south was the native tobacco called *pitjuri* that came down from Queensland via the Dieri through Parachilna and was traded by the Ngadjuri to the Kaurna." The Ramindjeri clans traded "bundles of roots with the Yaraldi for hardwood spears, points and gum dampers (*ibid.*). As for the south-eastern trade route, they write:

> not a great deal was known about this at the time we worked with the local people. However, specially prepared potatoes, radishes and yams were traded, as well as smoke-dried freshwater fish, which was also distributed inland and south-east into Milipi country. Red ochre which Ramindjeri, Yaraldi and Tangani obtained during their visits to Mulgali was in turn traded through the Coorong to Mt Gambier. (*ibid.*: 118).

The highly valued quartzite flakes came from "Ramindjera hill people, as did flints used to make fire by percussion". *Kondoli*, the Berndts (1993: 235) say, danced so hard at the gathering at Kondilinar that sparks issued from his body. Here is the whale as the focus of feasting, fire and flint. Tindale (1974: 17) mentions Tauwitcheri Island, a small sheltered island which the Yaraldi residents called Tauadjeri, (Tawatjeri, Towodjeri), from *taua* for red ochre. This was a meeting place for the Ramindjeri and Yaraldi, who traded quartzite pebbles from Rapid Bay for axes and wooden weapons. Ceremonies took place there and a trade route went from Goolwa by the Murray Mouth, and across Hindmarsh Island (Tindale 1931–4: 46, 65-6). This is the route traffic would take across the proposed bridge and on to the island.

In Tindale and Long (nd: 6) I find one of Tindale's hand-drawn maps of trade connections. The arrows come down the peninsulas, down to Goolwa, tracing the trades in red ochre. By the time Milerum talked with Tindale, "the trade in red ochre was only a vague memory from the past, since they had other ways of obtaining it" (Tindale and Long nd: 10). What has been recorded illustrates the ways in which complex trades over a large area were facilitated by *ngia-ngiampe* trading partners (*ibid.*: 9, 10).

Goolwa's strategic location meant that traders could travel up the Murray, around the bay to Kaurna country, and across to Victoria (Berndt *et al.* 1993: 19-20). Of smoked fish, one of the trade items,

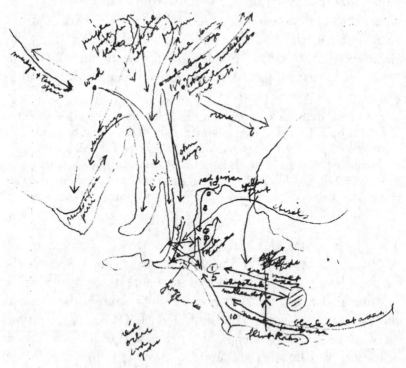

Red Ochre Trade in South Australia (Tindale and Long nd: 6)

various women tell me bits and pieces. Sarah Milera mentions these as a trade item at Goolwa. Edith Rankine recalls her Aunty Rosie making the little wooden frame over which she would smoke fish, and Doreen Kartinyeri tells me how she helped her Aunty Rosie to smoke and salt fish at Point Pearce. It was nothing to find a bag of salt in her cupboard, she says. At Amelia Park, Sarah Milera talks about the midden on which she stands and how its contents can reveal the changing times in Goolwa. This is where the approach to the bridge was first sited, through this history.

There were good reasons why the Ngarrindjeri have not been able to maintain a permanent presence on the island, but there are people who have stayed in contact with the area and their feelings for the sites are strong. Ironically, the bridge proposal has brought younger people into contact with the stories and places and has renewed an interest in the families who were associated with the island. The elders who are the custodians of the stories are ready to teach and guide the younger believers who are ready to learn. Visiting the island for the first time, in January 1996, I too knew this was not just any island. On subsequent occasions, sitting in the natural amphitheatre in the sand dunes on the beach facing the Murray Mouth, different groups of women continued to weave the strands of the stories they know. It is work-in-progress.

Different fragments have survived in different families and there are few occasions on which the whole might be celebrated. Indeed, there may be no neat, internally consistent whole. As we have seen, Ngarrindjeri stories, like those of other Indigenous people, tolerate a high degree of ambiguity. They may be read at a number of levels, and are contextualised by the story-teller to address the needs of the listeners, and this generation of listeners is focused on the sites at Goolwa, the Murray Mouth and Hindmarsh Island. But this is not to say that anything goes. I have been sketching the cultural framework within which stories are told, and as we listen to the stories of the island we can ask if they are consistent with that larger design; nor do they make a whole by themselves. The close scrutiny brought to bear on the fragmentary knowledge of those believers struggling to protect their places on the island and the surrounding waters, has created unrealistic expectations that pieces will fit and make sense.

We cannot know how the fragments might have been represented a century ago, but I have seen the earnest efforts of the weavers to read the signs, to believe that the circle will be completed, and to heed their *miwi* as they struggle with the ongoing process of finding meaning. Here are the bundles of rushes with which people are currently working. The stories are about the *Mantijinga* (Seven Sisters) and the *mulyewongk* in the Goolwa Channel, *Ngurunderi* and *Jekejeri* at Goolwa and *ngatji* at the Meeting of the Waters.

Mulyewongk: Cautionary Tales and Deeper Meanings

In Chapter 6, I set about reclaiming the fragments of stories we have about the *mulyewongk* and suggested that they concerned more than a frightening water creature: *mulyewongk* had a complex social organisation, interacted with *Ngurunderi*, and lived in places hedged in with taboos. None of the stories was from women. Then, in 1995 Daisy Rankine decided to open up part of what she had known for decades about the *mulyewongk*. She wrote "The Release of the Mulgewanki: A Summary of Oral History of a Meimeni" and in 1996 she shared it with Judge Mathews. To open up parts of the *mulyewongk* story, Daisy Rankine needed permission from her older sister Emily. We held onto it. We weren't allowed to let anyone know. It could have caused strife amongst our people and maybe they don't know anything about it and then there would be jealousy and the hatred for these things coming out. I feel free to talk about it now. I was going to bring it out on my sixtieth birthday, but my daughter Ellen began to show she was ready through her weaving and she took the initiative in locating her father, so I'm telling it now. There is more to come out, but not yet. I have seen Aunty Daisy decline to disclose knowledge that is of importance to her family. She is polite but resolute (see p. 447). Here is what she chose to make public.

I was told about the elbow at Goolwa as part of the woman gathering food. I was about fourteen or fifteen when I learned about the women's business of the island. It is the place of the *mi:mini*, and the story of the *mulyewongk* is about the survival of the land and what food to eat and all that. The stories are handed down from generation to generation to keep the descendants very careful about swimming in the water and for women to take care of their children. The story came through Pakunu Pinkie, to my mother, to me. We kept it quiet and didn't tell but the reason that I brought it out was that the water is sacred. The next thing they will do is that they will want to drain the river to see the *mulyewongk*. We had no voice, no right to complain, we had to keep quiet but the Goolwa River is sacred and the Murray River is sacred. And if they'd only believe our stories and accept our Ngarrindjeri culture, everything is so sacred to us.

The mother became a *mulyewongk* at the beginning of the story. It began at the elbow [Goolwa], where one Yaraldi clan was situated [towards the ferry from the marina on Hindmarsh island]. The women were finding food by the shoreline. At this time, the water was salty and the sharks would come in. There were no barrages then. While the woman was searching for cockles and watercress, the children were playing by themselves. The shark took the only child of the high chief, the Rupelli. The husband had done the wrong thing. He was lazy, and the wife, she had been looking for food and had not watched the child. The man went to look for his child, his only child. He went to another clan territory. He brought trouble on his own family and people by crossing a boundary on the women's island. The warriors from that clan territory were sent to *millin* him, even though he was a high chief, a Rupelli, because he had strayed onto their clan territory. But before the *thumarparldi* came to *millin* him, he and his wife decided to use their strong spiritual power to transform themselves. They could become anything they wanted and they became *mulyewongks* to protect themselves, otherwise they would have been dead. The husband went up the river, up the water in the channel [name withheld]. It's upstream through the lake to the lower river and under the cliff at Marrunggung. The husband and wife meet at Big Hill at Raukkan and that's why it's a spiritual place. *Prupi* used to hang around at Big Hill and that's why, this generation calls it an evil place. The Sumners were there. It was their family place. The *prupi* is there at Big Hill all the time. They [the husband and wife *mulyewongk*] meet at Big Hill and they will be fighting over who was to blame.

The woman *mulyewongk* drew from her mouth the water from the sea, she sucked the sea in and over the land, she opened the Murray to the sea and it mixed with fresh water so the salt water can preserve the sedges and can hold the land. This story is about before when *Ngurunderi* came down the Murray and carved out the river channel to the sea making it the river it is today. Before there were sand bars here and there, making stepping places to allow a walking trail through the three waters of the River, Lakes and Coorong, passing little islands around a main inland island of sacred significance to the tribal full blood inhabitants. This island is called Kumarangk even to the present day. The she-monster was always seen around the place where the child was taken. A cry would be heard like someone crying and it was an eerie or spooky cry which brought fear to the people, more fear to the children. Other families would call it *muldarpi*. From what we believed the *mulyewongk* was still living in the waters right down to the opening of the mouth of the Murray.

Like other accounts, Daisy Rankine's deals with the power of sorcery and the generation of *mulyewongk* by transformation. The manifestation of the *mulyewongk* at Goolwa, which Daisy Rankine tells us some families call *muldarpi*, has been sighted as a tangle of weeds floating past Goolwa and out to the Murray Mouth. Great quantities of seaweed were washed in through the Murray Mouth at Point Blenkinsop, a Lunggundjeri camping site on Mundoo Island, known as Mandumbari, which means "seaweed camp" (Tindale nd, h). These concentrations of weed are one possible source of the *mulyewongk* stories from this area. Large floating islands of weed are common through these waters. In December 1996 I saw one in the channel outside our camp in Clayton. Mark Wilson spoke of the "long trailing hair in the water that looked like water weed" (Clarke 1994: 132). The association of *mulyewongk* with *muldarpi* is also noted by Barrett (1946: 22) who says that the Encounter Bay tribe likened the evil water spirit to a gigantic starfish and called it *Mooldabbie*. Although there are no *mulyewongk* sites recorded in the

560

literature in this section of the Murray, Taplin (16–17/9/1862) reports a *mulyewongk* died and rotted at Rankine's Ferry (on Hindmarsh Island), a site very close to our Clayton camp. Taplin does not register any surprise at this location, which suggests to me that whoever told him the story believed the Goolwa Channel was a possible *mulyewongk* place.

Aunty Daisy's story of the two *mulyewongk* link her life at Brinkley to her life on the Coorong. The story also reminds us that there are two significant meetings of the waters: one where the Murray flows into Lake Alexandrina, and the other where it empties into the ocean at the Murray Mouth. Both, in her telling, concern Yaraldi territory, and both have *mulyewongk* sites. The two sites are connected through the marriage of the *mulyewongk*, and their relationship is made manifest by the sound of their fighting in the lake. Daisy Rankine's stories are grounded in her knowledge of local geography from her grandmother who taught her the stories of those places. She was a Yaraldi and that was what she taught me about. The island was shared by Tangani, Warki and Yaraldi. Like Doug Wilson, Daisy Rankine knows and respects clan boundaries. Like Leila Rankine, Daisy Rankine sometimes speaks in riddles. In her telling of the *mulyewongk* story she is spelling out knowledge boundaries and these are not mere lines on a map. They carry a highly emotional charge that can be observed. Recall Daisy Rankine's distress when standing on the clan boundary on Kumarangk Island (see pp. 220–1).

In the *Mulyewongk* story, as told by Aunty Daisy, we have a layering of deeds, actors and beings that vivify the landscape and give meaning to human institutions and human relationships with other beings. Her story concerns the nature of the world before *Ngurunderi* widened the Murray River. In this account a number of hitherto unrelated beings and practices are shown to be part of a larger design and their inter-relations are mapped. The institution of the Rupelli was already in place and it was through the misdeeds of one leader and his wives that the *mulyewongk* comes into being; that Kumarangk becomes a women's place; and that both good and bad elements are associated with the waters at Goolwa. The stories specify the consequences of transgression at a number of different levels. When the woman *mulyewongk* made the channel to let the sea water in to purify the land, it was a good thing; but the sharks followed, which was a bad thing. But this story is not in the past tense. Daisy Rankine also offers examples of recent sighting of *mulyewongk* in the area and of people hearing the cries of the woman near where the shark took her child. The *mulyewongk* is a living being which is still capable of damaging the living. Her story spells out one of the dangers those waters hold.

The Meeting of the Waters: Home for *Ngatji*

Leila used to come here, and she said when I go, you know where to take me, and we knew where. She used to come, and from here she could see all around the Coorong. She always talked about the place as spiritual, as the meeting of the waters. We had a discussion with the elders, and they thought to put her on the bayside, but we stood our ground and put her in the place where she'd be sheltered, said Tom Trevorrow. Leila Rankine's ashes were scattered at a site where she can over look the "spiritual waters", as I have heard the men and Sarah Milera term the wider area within which the salt and fresh waters mingle. And they said where the river meets the salt water, they said that's our spiritual place, Tom Trevorrow (1995: 6095) told the Royal Commission. On a trip down the Coorong with Tom Trevorrow, we stand at this lookout to survey these waters, the bay, the hummocks, and the barrages, the silt-laden murky lake waters and the crystal blue Coorong. On a clear day you would see the line where the lake water is pushing in the Coorong, says Tom.

At Ocean Bay, Tom tells me we are now within the *ngatji* breeding grounds. I photograph the display and a park notice regarding the waters of the Coorong. It explains that the fresh and salt waters of the area provide an important feeding ground for the water birds and migrating whales and that they also form part of a complex ecosystem which supports a wide range of aquatic plants and animals. There is nothing on the spiritual significance to the Ngarrindjeri. Tom points out where the mouth was in 1981. When the Coorong was tidal, it affected where the mouth was, and it was wide and deep, and you could take a boat up there. The seaweed would come in and up the channel, and go down as far as the Bonney Reserve. We'd pull out rolls of it, and the fish—mullet and *kongoli* (freshwater fish that can last in salt water for a long time)—would be there. They always travel in schools. We trek past the Murray Mouth through the barrage to Goolwa, and then back to Mark Point near where we have parked our cars. As we drive back through the Coorong National Park to Camp Coorong, Tom stops to show me the clear blue waters of the Coorong. The men are tracking the line of discoloured water. They're deeply worried about the health of the area. The meeting would have been back towards the barrage. George says, Near Long Point, just past Mark Point. You'd see a ripple, a colouration. Sometimes they're running into each other, when the water is rough, when there is wind, you can't see the channel where the lake water is coming in. The men are constantly monitoring the waters, the fish, the vegetation. I know I could spend years in these waterways and barely tap their knowledge.

George Trevorrow (1995: 6423-5) tried to explain the vitality of the region to the Royal Commission. He spoke of the *ngatji* related to the meeting of the waters, not of "women's business". He told the Commissioner, "I'm talking about my business" (see p. 388). He was not heard. During the Mathews hearing, he once again tried to explain. This time, he was able to tell the story the way he wanted and to stress his integrated world view: As we come through the mouth, you would've noticed all the different colour water. That's what we're talking about when we call it the meeting of the waters. Those waters, once they start mixing, that is the spiritual waters of this area, and of the Ngarrindjeri. This is where the major connections happen. This is the breeding place for all the *ngatji*, and everything that goes with the mixing of the water underneath the water, so it's very, very important to us spiritually, because those things, as I said, they are closer than a friend to you. They are nearly almost part of you. They speak to you, you speak to them, and this is the place where they all come to.

Years and years ago, they started draining the southeast and they've turned it into farm country. Because what we've been told from our old people is the country's on an angle, coming from the southeast. We've got underground waterways that run right through here where the water comes through. And we have the surface water that used to come through every year. We're not saying this was full, absolutely full of this precious water every year, all year round. But it certainly was for the better part of the year. It held good quality water and that water gave life. It gave life to what we describe as our *ngatjis*, that's like a spiritual connection between

563

us and the animals and the fish and the plants. We're linked into one thing. Our *ngatjis* live off those things. There's things that we don't see any more growing here, because the mixtures of the waters aren't here anymore. And that makes us sad.

This was not the first time George Trevorrow had spoken of the importance of the waters. In 1986, during the early consultations regarding the making of the video for the *Ngurunderi* exhibit in the South Australian Museum, he had spoken of the meeting of the waters as beginning near Pelican Point. At that time Steven Hemming (1986) recorded George Trevorrow telling part of his version of the *Ngurunderi* Dreaming to Winston Head, a South Australian Museum exhibition officer, and Vince Buckskin, the museum's Aboriginal liaison officer. It was, he told Winston, at Pelican Point that *Ngurunderi* sent a message to *Nepelli* to get "a crew together" in order to catch the giant *pondi*. By the time *Ngurunderi* arrived, they had circled *pondi* with their rafts and caught him.

> George Trevorrow: Yeah, at Pelican Point. That's where he cut up *pondi* in our versions of the story, that's where they pulled him to pieces and made different fishes.
>
> Winston Head: Did he make the fresh-water fish down there too?
>
> George Trevorrow: Yeah, because that's the meeting places of the two waters—the salt and fresh water. So as he broke him up he chucked pieces over into the salt-water and said you *mullowi*, he cut another piece up and said you *thukkeri* or whatever or *pilkari* and he made the different fishes for both waters.

A longer version appears in the Department of Education (1990: 51).

 From Raukkan Nepele saw Pondi at the place where the fresh and salt water meet. He pushed his canoe there and killed Pondi with his spear. Nepele put Pondi on a sandbar and waited for Ngurunderi. Ngurunderi met him there and the both cut Pondi up into many pieces. Ngurunderi threw each piece into the waters and told it to become a new fish.

"Nund Thukeri—you silver bream."

"Nund Pilarki—you callop."

"Nund Kunmuri—you mullet."

"Nund Mulawi—you mulloway."

Ngurunderi made all the fresh fish and salt water fish of the Ngarrindjeri. To the last piece, he said: "Nund Pondi—you keep being Murray cod."

On the *Ngurunderi* video, Henry Rankine recounts: "From Raukkan Nepelli saw *pondi* at the place where the fresh and salt waters meet." He killed *pondi* with his spear and then, when *Ngurunderi* arrived, together they cut up the giant fish and *Ngurunderi* named the fish species of fresh and salt waters. In accounts which reflect Yaraldi interests, such as that recorded by Ronald Berndt (1940a: 171), the newly created fish are thrown in the lake. In a later rendition, Berndt (1974: 25) says they were thrown into the river. In an account from Encounter Bay, the fish are thrown into the salt water (Meyer 1846). In the Spirit of the Murray, *Ngurunderi* (Ooroondooil) commands:

> Thou, Marma, to the sea descend,
> And from the parent stock,
> Fish of all kinds by Yilga send,
> With sea-shells from the rock!"
>
> (Penney in Foster 1991: 83)

Thus, *marma*, the generic for fish, is given the appropriate identity in different ecological niches, salt, fresh and at the mingling. In March 1996 Aunty Maggie Jacobs described for Jane Mathews her experience of some ten years ago at the site she called the "Meeting of the Waters", a site she indicated was between the barrage and the Murray Mouth: Well that's the place there, where I know of the meeting of the waters. That's where you can fish, one side for fresh water and the other side for salt water fish. I done that a few years back. You could sit in a dinghy and could throw one line over here for fresh water for *pilkari* and throw one line over here for salt water and catch both in one dinghy. That's what I learnt about the meeting of the waters and I've been there, seen the place. I've never seen so many birds in all my life as there, especially spoonbills. I knew there was a meeting of the waters but I didn't know until then, where. I don't know whether there are still meetings of the waters somewhere else, but I know that was the meeting of the waters and that was the time I was told that it was the meeting of the waters.

I had read in the Berndts (1993: 308-9) of one juxtaposition of *ngatji* that carried information about the actual meeting of the waters.

Kanmeri the saltwater jumping mullet, is the *ngatji* of the Kandukara clan at the Murray Mouth; *wankari*, the freshwater jumping mullet, is the *ngatji* of the Kangalindjeri on the southeast of Hindmarsh Island. The clans, positioned either side of the Goolwa Channel, one facing the ocean, the other within the tidal reach of the channel, thereby encode information about the respective habitats of mullet species. When I ask, Tom says that mullet jump in and out of the fresh water. The fresh water one is bigger that the salt one and some people say it is better but I like the salt one because I'm from the Coorong.

In their Appendix on "Traditional Foods", the Berndts (*ibid.*: 565) say that *wongkari* (*wankari*) is used for both fresh and salt. I ask Neville Gollan, who says that *kanmeri*, the Coorong mullet, is caught in the lakes but it likes the salt water. The Blue Mullet, also called the Sea Mullet and Jumping Mullet, will come into the Coorong, but is more at home in the ocean, around Victor Harbor, Neville suggests. We used to call it *krawi kanmeri*, the big *kanmeri*.[11] The mulloway and mullet can both live in fresh and salt water. They know the secret of that, but not the others. He adds, The fishes know the waters have changed. Now we are talking about fresh and salt water, Neville volunteers that the *lauwari*, the Cape Barren Goose, can convert salt water to fresh. That is his business.

There are ways in which several species and *ngatji* mediate between the fresh and salt waters. The relationship between these two ecological zones is addressed in a Yaraldi fishing legend recorded by Alison Harvey (1943). There the boundaries of the meeting of the waters are dramatised by the behaviour of the travelling red-billed gull ancestors who "avoid absolutely the salt water, first at Cold and Wet near the Coorong and subsequently in the islands near the Murray Mouth" (*ibid.*: 112). Jerry Schwab (1988: 94-5) was told that one reason for tensions between people at Point McLeay and Point Pearce was that one came from the fresh river water and the other from the salt water. Milerum told Tindale (nd, e) the fresh water of the Murray was *mungkuli*, fresh water, in contrast to Goolwa brackish and the salt water of the Coorong.

The relationship is also addressed in a note from an undated C. J. S. Harding manuscript, located in Tindale's (1930–52) papers. It reads as follows:

Narrinjeri—as a child he lived at Encounter Bay, knew many of the natives, talking their language, etc. He noticed that natives could never thread mullet on reeds for carrying and they expressed great concern at the thought of such a practice. They did not mind stringing them on any other form of support. Gurawa or Gulawa was the old name for Goolwa and meant, "place where fresh and salt water meet" or sometimes fresh, sometimes salt. The upper part of the lake was called by the name meaning, "Sweet Water" while the mouth was called, "Salt Water".[12]

Pinpointing a precise location for a site such as the "Meeting of the Waters" makes little sense. It has a shifting physical reality, and many factors which determine where it will be at any given moment: tides, barrage flow, seasonal floods. But it was a feature that has left traces in the written record.

The Ngarrindjeri called the Murray Mouth Wateangk on the northwest; opposite was a lookout point (Barker's Knoll) for the Lunggundjeri, a Tangani clan. These locations are relative to each other as the Murray Mouth has moved significantly over the years. Between 1949 and 1956 it moved northwest, between 1956 and 1960 southeast, between 1960 and 1965 back to the northwest, and between 1965 and 1967 back to the southeast (Harvey citing Thomson 1983: 4). My 1:250,000 map, with its 1987 date does not reflect the landscape through which I am moving, yet the existence of the Younghusband and Sir Richard Peninsulas is not disputed. In Ngarrindjeri, the names for the mouth, Tapawar, meaning opening, and Wateangk, meaning tail, are suggestive of the *ruwi/ruwa*, land/body relationship (see p. 262ff.), but there is no gender ascribed to the opening. Men and women had their own stories for this sacred space.

The insistence that the meeting of the waters is the breeding ground for *ngatji* is supported by the ethnography. In the Murray Mouth region, *ngatji* are plentiful, some clans having two or three. They include many birds such as blue crane, coot, cormorant, duck, eaglehawk, pelican, plover, red-beaked gull, a night bird, white-bellied sea-gull, pelican, spur-winged plover, little pied cormorant; several fish, including bony bream, mullet, shark; and various other creatures, whale, rabbit bandicoot, tortoise, snake, seal, spider, and water rat. In other parts of Australia, the power released when salt meets fresh water is encoded in religious beliefs and practices. Ian Keen (1990: 192-3) writes of how "images of the mixing of salt and freshwater, from rain-swollen estuaries into the sea, or from fresh water springs into the tidal flow in the mangroves, connote sexual connection and fertilisation and spiritual conception".[13] In Arnhem Land these stories underwrite ceremonial practice. Ngarrindjeri may not have performed their large-scale ceremonies for some time, and there is no written ethnographic record such as the one Keen has generated for the Yolngu; but the stories are still there and, like Yolngu stories, they concern conception, reproduction and fertility.

Doreen Kartinyeri: Those waters were meant to flow freely around the island with the tides coming in and going out. Eileen McHughes: So, for me, and it's really logical, if the salt water came up that far and the river coming down, all—everything would get flushed out into the ocean which kept all the environment balanced. It's like our bodies; if we don't drink enough water to flush out all the poisons, hey, we get sick. Daisy Rankine: We know the salt water preserved the land and is holding the land. She is preserving the land by drawing the sea in. If the mouth closes up, then the Coorong will be closed. it needs to be open to where the waters meet. Matt Rigney said that his grandmother, Mutha (Bessie Rigney née Gollan), told his family that when they put in the barrages in the late 1930s she was really upset, and she said it stopped the natural flow of life. It's like a blockage in an artery, and it stops the natural flow. If people don't drink water, people are getting sick, said Tom. Matt continues: And that's how I imagine it, when the women talk about being infertile. The fluids of the land, like those of the body need to be able to complete their cycles.

The men explained the situation to Jane Mathews. George Trevorrow: We know that our old people had a lot of problems in coming to terms with barrages being built on the water there, because it forced the water right back into this area, and actually sat it up on a lot of our important sites. Neville Gollan: A bridge would destroy some of our *ngatji*, like not coming along to let us know. This is what I could say, it's the best way that I could describe it. It'd destroy some of our beliefs or most of it because with that, if we're going back into there, this is why we're bringing you people down here to show you that those waters, the *ngatjis* down here, the *ngatjis* there, they all tie in together and they're all—they're a part of the Ngarrindjeri nation. The bridge would destroy the place by going in to the water. It is a real difficult thing to explain to you but this is the best way that I can do it. Building the bridge it would send *ngatjis* away from the area. They wouldn't be like they are now. As you saw yesterday when we went on that boat there were heaps of them flying around. That's the sort of impact we'll have on us. That's the best way that I can answer that.

Tom Trevorrow: I'd just like also to add a little bit to what Uncle Neville been talking about. Even from when I was grown up, *ngatjis* were taught to me and we were told by my elders to respect them and not to do anything to harm them because they are our friend. And when I got older and Uncle Neville told me, you know, that story of the *krowali* (see pp. 212–5), you know, that really enforced to me what my old people had been telling me about *ngatjis* and it really hit home with me and that's why I've got great respect for my *ngatjis* and for the other Ngarrindjeri clan groups *ngatjis*. I don't want to see them harmed any more, the same as the trees and everything that's all a part of it, I don't want to see that harmed any more. I'm frightened that if also, from a *ngatji*'s point of view, if a bridge goes ahead from Goolwa to Kumarangk—Hindmarsh Island— we see it that maybe the bridge might lead to further development which will lead to further destruction of our *ngatjis*, of that area, because that particular area is where all the *ngatjis* are. All the birdlife is. That's my great concern on that.

George Trevorrow: You see, Kumarangk, that area, is the central point for the Ngarrindjeri people and I don't want to go into it too much more but that's why all the *ngatjis* are there. That's the homeland. That's their area. All Aboriginal groups throughout Australia have got an area that is most significant to them, is very special, that is their centre point of their creation. That area is to us, that's our creation area and that's why so many of our stories, of our beliefs and our culture and heritage all revolves from that area outward upon the land of the Ngarrindjeri. It's a rich environment. It supports all the birdlife. You know, you could see that for yourself when you go there but to us as Ngarrindjeri people it's a spiritual environment. That's the most important thing to us about that area and we've sat back for many years and as I said, when the barrages were being built the old people didn't like that. Those old people are still around today. As I said before— yesterday I think I said—who didn't want them barrages being built but we had no say back then. We had no power, no control and the barrages they were built. But today we, as Ngarrindjeri Aboriginal people, have been given some power we think, some say, in protecting what's important to us for the survival of our future.

George Trevorrow did not invent the story of the meeting of the waters in 1995. He was on record in 1986 and there were witnesses to those story-telling sessions who were not sought out by the Royal Commission. The terms of reference were concerned with "women's business" and talk of *ngatji*, despite George Trevorrow's best endeavours, was dismissed as environmentalism. In the rush to address charges of fabrication of "women's business", the way in which "men's business" might support and complement the women's was passed over. The meeting of the waters concerns the spirituality and power of the meeting of the forces, and it concerns survival. This is where all the species proliferate. It is about the reproduction of the Ngarrindjeri world. It is about maintaining a balance of fresh to salt, of land to water, of life to spirit. However, it is not the only story which indicates the centrality of this area to certain Ngarrindjeri women and men. There are parts of the *Ngurunderi* story that are also critical to understanding the intensity of activities at Goolwa.

Ngurunderi and *Jekejere* at Goolwa

The *Ngurunderi* exhibit in the South Australian Museum has the towering figure striding along the peninsula, crossing over the Murray Mouth and continuing on, but *Ngurunderi* stopped at Goolwa and there drew in the waters that today form the Coorong. Tindale (1930–52: 102) writes: "This part may be apocryphal or truncated for The Pages are not visible from Granite Island and in other accounts it is Newlands Head or Rosetta Head which is his lookout." On sharing this insight with Reuben Walker, Tindale was told: "I know that *Ngurunderi* could see. He for instance looked from Goolwa and saw his two sons travelling down at the end of the Coorong. He wished them to come back, so he 'beckoned' to the water and it rushed right down; that is how the Coorong originated" (*ibid.*). So, *Ngurunderi*, the maker of the Murray River, the commander of the waters, who in drowning his wives created the waters Backstairs Passage, also created the Coorong.

According to oral traditions, *Ngurunderi* not only paused at Goolwa, he camped there, and the place he camped is right in the area of the proposed bridge: This place, Signal Point, I think most people know, is the central point for five of the major clan groups of the Ngarrindjeri people, and the five of them centres in on this point here just behind us [indicating the wharf area] where Signal Point and the cutting is. We believe there that's one of the last camps of *Ngurunderi* before he left this earth. It was a place where he sat in his *pulgi* [hut] and as the dead passed on, the spirits went to him, and he was the director of where they had to go, which home they were going to out of the major groupings. He pointed them in the right directions, George Trevorrow told Judge Mathews. Tom Trevorrow: The camp is where the railway crossing is, and in around the thing called Signal Point area there. That is all registered midden mounds there. They are recorded on file, I think, and you can see what's happened here. The cutting, you know, has been taken away, and all of our material has been pushed down into the edge of the water there. The beach has been filled in with the building of the dock. Once again, these activities belong to places threatened by the bridge proposal.

As far as the developers were concerned, the story of the way in which *Ngurunderi* at Goolwa was an example of the way in which new Dreamings "just keep bobbing up". Stephen Palyga (1996: 121-2), the solicitor representing the Chapmans, argued that the Seven Sisters was a new claim that "evolved" in the Mathews Inquiry, that "entirely new claims such as the Mulyewongk claim, came out of left field, and there was a claim that Ngurunderi had visited the bridge site". His concern was that new claims would just keep appearing unless the government passed legislation to prevent these vexatious women from using up the time of the courts and valuable public money. Such a richness of ancestral activity is just what one would expect of a place like Goolwa. And, as with other oral knowledge that has been dismissed and demeaned, there is support for the presence of *Ngurunderi* at Goolwa in the written sources. Meyer (1846) mentions *Ngurunderi*'s hut as a special place for the people of Goolwa who are guided to *Ngurunderi* by a line first used by his son. McLeay and Cato (1985: 16) mention that *Ngurunderi* would "take men to live with him forever if he came from the Goolwa or Encounter Bay people".[14]

It had always seemed improbable to me that there was not a *Ngurunderi* story associated with Goolwa: the elbow is so distinctive, the Murray Mouth such a significant confluence of waters. There are stories that relate to the area. One concerns *Kanmeri*, a male being: after his transformation into a fish rich in oil, along with his companion *Kuratje*, he met with *Kortowi* who lived near Goolwa (Tindale and Long nd: 7). But what of *Ngurunderi*? I was pushing on through the Tindale material in the South Australian Museum on Christmas Eve 1996, aware that I was about to be asked to leave because everyone else was in festive mode. I was trying to find all the references to *Jekejere*, a being, for which Tindale (nd, g) had a slip in his Vocabulary Cards of the Southeast of South Australia. All the entry for *Jekejere* said was ". . . about at Goolwa and there prepared a sandy beach before *Ngurunderi* appeared, *Ngurunderi* praised it and repaired it before travelling on to the west." In the Tanganekald Vocabulary Cards (Tindale nd, e) I found another reference to *Jekejere*, an ancestral male being who lived near Port Elliot, who made a sandy beach at Rawarangald, a great fishing place for schools of mullet. Again *Ngurunderi* praised the work of this ancestor. I found several ways into this story from the vocabulary slips. Tindale (1934–7: 30-2) recorded a conversation with Milerum at Salt Creek, 12 February 1934, headed "Additions to Ngurunderi Story", which locates this encounter between *Jekejere* and *Ngurunderi* as just before *Ngurunderi*'s wives strike out for Kangaroo Island.[15]

I check the place-names mentioned in the story. According to Tindale's Ramindjeri cards (Tindale nd, m), "Rawarangald" at Port Elliot is the place where the seaweed-covered rocks represent the remains of the pubic hair plucked by *Ngurunderi*'s wives. On the Tanganekald cards, "Rawarangald" is said to be "Frenchman Rock, Port Elliot; bay and point where shoals of mullet congregate—a great fishing place". It is likely that Rawarangald can refer to both the area and to a specific place within that area. It is also likely that the *rawa* of Rawarangald means "ancient", as in Rawakung (Raukkan) and Rawaldarang, the site at the western extremity of Hindmarsh Island. The chronology of the story is contained in the place-names. *Jekejere* was at these ancient places before *Ngurunderi*. He was making the beaches and preparing the land. He was also at a place associated with a ritual for young women who have not yet given birth. The only published reference to *Jekejere* I have found is in one of Milerum's songs recorded by Tindale (1937: 115-16), where the fine work of *Jekejere* is once again celebrated.

Then in the "World of Milerum" (Tindale and Long nd: 8) I found one of Tindale's hand-drawn sketch maps. The elbow at Goolwa is unmistakable. Tindale has drawn a line from Goolwa to a reference in one of his journals (Tindale 1934–7). By following up on this note I can determine that Milerum was his source. Milerum told Tindale that *Ngurunderi* was at Goolwa. To the best of my knowledge, none of the men has seen this; in fact, I don't think any of the people who have leafed through the papers has noticed it. I ask Tom and George Trevorrow about it (see p. 364) and was referred to Henry Rankine. I drive out to Raukkan and we spread the map out on his dining-room table. He and Jean examine it. He asks for my 1:100,000 map. Yes, it's the elbow all right. "Can I use it?" I ask. The answer is the same as ever: If it will help. When I show it and the notes to Tom and George Trevorrow, they ask: Will they believe us now? We always said *Ngurunderi* was at Goolwa. I ask about *Jekejere*. Yes. He was one of those fellows. I ask about the beach. It has been filled in now with the building of the dock. *Ngurunderi* was right at the site of the proposed bridge. Is this enough to reopen the Royal Commission? asks Tom. It shows we're not liars. True. None of the men could not have known about this material. This is the opposite of the so-called "late disclosures" about which the developers have been so exercised. The men have said all along that *Ngurunderi* was at Goolwa; now they have been vindicated in a sketch map and notes that Tindale intended to add to the *Ngurunderi* story, but never published.

The Pleiades: Stories of Sisters, the Seasons and Survival

They didn't have books to read to give them directions on how to dig for food or to do this or that for a child. Now you have books about how to bring up children and where to go to find certain places and things. Back in those days they only had nature, the sun, stars, and the moon to live and work by. We lived by the seasons. We were told not to swim in the springtime. If we asked why, we were told because we'd get sick. Veronica Brodie then drew a comparison with western practices. I know the pollens could give infections and there was rheumatic fever and children died who swam before the seasons were right. So the story gives directives about life, about preparing for womanhood, marriage and child-bearing. Ngarrindjeri women learned about certain ways to behave from this story.

Milerum's daughter, Annie Rankine (1969), was told not to swim until the dandelion flowers had died off and the Seven Sisters were moving (see p. 365). This practical advice which looked to the movement of heavenly bodies above and natural cycles on earth below was active knowledge in Annie Rankine's day and remains so in the 1990s. During November 1996, as the days warmed up, "Don't swim yet. The dandelions are still in bloom," was a constant refrain. And this practical wisdom, I learn, not only applies to the streams and rivers but for many it also takes in the local swimming pool. One hot November day I hear children pleading, "Can't we go swimming in the pool?" "No, the dandelions are still blooming," replies the prudent mother. "Well can't we just mow them down?" asks the child of the technological age. "Too smart for his own good," I'm told and the other women present nod in agreement. About the same time my daughter, Genevieve, was contemplating a swim, a treat for a visitor from the colder climes of the northern hemisphere, but she was told firmly by several of her "aunts" that it was not yet time to swim. Several weeks later when I asked about swimming, I was told, "Of course you can. The dandelions have gone." Milerum enforced the taboo with his daughter, Annie Long. Does this mean he also knew the women's story about the Seven Sisters? He knew it was dangerous, just as certain women-only spaces are dangerous. Neville Gollan says: Sometimes when it was a warm day in September, we'd want to swim but we'd get flogged and we were told we'd turn yellow, but he declines to say anything about the women's business associated with the Seven Sisters.

Dandelions are an introduced plant. Does this invalidate the tradition? I think not. As with the incorporation of swimming pools into the story, the use of an introduced plant is evidence of ways in which traditions can accommodate change. The practical aspect of the knowledge encoded in the story, the caution regarding the dangers of the waters has been rewoven into the changing landscape and has endured. The sacred core has been protected. We can only guess what other signals in the natural world were used before white contact. I remember the old ladies called Springtime "Billy Button time", when the lambs and everything was being born, young birds were coming out, you know, Doreen Kartinyeri muses, That was what they said. The flower-heads of Billy Buttons, which form a single yellow ball, not unlike the bright yellow flower of the dandelion, appear in spring and summer.[16] It may be that this native plant was the seasonal prompt that coincided with the rising of the Pleiades, but the introduced and now more prolific dandelion has taken its place. The details of the story which vivifies the prohibition on swimming have been mystified by the passage of time and would only have been known to a privileged few anyway, but the safety of children remains a concern for all. When full initiation cycles for men and women were practised, the connection between the waters, the plants and the Pleiades would have been made manifest in song, dance, and/or ritual design. Practical and esoteric knowledge would have been a mutually reinforcing weave. Today we hear the surviving fragments and can observe the respect for the cautions embedded in the story.

The story that most directly links the Pleiades to the waters around Hindmarsh Island and to women's rituals comes from Veronica Brodie. Where did I learn it? From my sister, that's the only one I've ever learned it from, no-one else. I don't even know what Doreen knows. I don't know if Doreen knows the same as I know, you know, and I think that I'm the only one that holds that story at this moment in time, you know. Other members of the Wilson family recall the Seven Sisters being a story that was told by Leila Rankine and her mother, Koomi, in its open form. Doug Wilson: My sister Leila would lie back and tell the legends of the Seven Sisters and stars. Margaret, Veronica's daughter, also remembers hearing the story from her grandmother, but she was too young at the time to appreciate what was being transmitted. I always knew a small story of the Seven Sisters. I believe that our Dreaming is real. It's not a myth. It comes from our rivers, our trees, our lands, unusual lands.

Throughout 1995, 1996 and 1997, Veronica Brodie held firm: I believe today and from what my sister has told me that what's there is very precious to us, in those waters. It's a part of the women's business in giving women directives and being one, I guess, who's been entrusted

575

with this story, I feel that I have to respect what's there, and I don't know just how much of it I can tell. It's a very big strain on me, in particular, because I know what Leila has passed on to me, what Mum gave her, that I want to tell it; I want to clear this air and I know that there's women like Ellen, Debbie, my daughters, and other young women out there, that we need to tell it to now, because like I say, we always say we'll tell it one day, but I may never be here tomorrow; I only live for one day at a time. I want to see everything go right and the stories that are hidden behind the Seven Sisters . . . There is just a little bit and I cannot tell it and I will not.

Veronica Brodie spoke of the Seven Sisters Dreaming to the Royal Commissioner in 1995 and to Justice Mathews in 1996. On both occasions she expressed frustration that she couldn't tell the entire story. After much agonising she did tell Mathews a little of the inside story. She did so in strictest confidence, believing that this piece of information would be sufficient to convince the judge of the importance of the area to women and the underlying rationale for not covering the waters with a bridge. In so doing, Veronica Brodie was walking the tightrope between the politics of knowledge in an oral culture and those of a text-oriented one. She had to balance the dangers of allowing information that should not be heard by men to be recorded, against the threat of injury and desecration of their Dreamings and land. There is a belief that the power of the story will be apparent to the listener, who will understand the investment of trust that sharing such knowledge represents. Veronica Brodie: They're beautiful things and they make you as you hear them, they make you very wise and you appreciate the Ngarrindjeri culture. Unfortunately this is not the basis on which Anglo law receives the stories. The stories contain "information", not wisdom being bestowed on one who is worthy. Indeed, a judge cannot be seen as being drawn into a reciprocal relationship with a witness, or as being under an obligation generated by now knowing the story. Once told, even in confidence to a judge, the story has a life of its own. It does not remain embedded in the relationships that allowed its telling.

The esoteric knowledge written down in 1994 found its way onto the desk of Ian McLachlan, MP. The transcript of the session when Veronica Brodie, Doreen Kartinyeri and Daisy Rankine divulged privileged knowledge to Judge Mathews was held in confidence, as

576

was the submission I had written regarding that evidence. However, in the great haste required to conclude the evidence and to distribute all materials to the relevant parties for comment, the confidential appendix containing my comments on the Seven Sisters Dreaming was distributed in error, by Jane Mathews' office, to other parties. It was this event that precipitated the withdrawal by the women of all confidential material generated between January and May 1996 for the application on which Jane Mathews was reporting.[17] If the breach of confidentiality had been an isolated incident it might not have been so traumatic, but this new breach was a re-run of the envelopes on McLachlan's desk (see pp. 24–5).

Veronica Brodie was a reluctant witness during the Royal Commission and only came forward to defend her mother's name when it had been placed in the public domain by the evidence of Betty Fisher. An amateur historian, with ties to the Narrunga of Yorke Peninsula, Betty Fisher had interviewed Koomi in the late 1960s. During the Royal Commission she had played a small section of tape on which Koomi's voice came through clear and true. She also had a page of notes of a story Koomi had told her of the Seven Sisters, and passages in her notebooks that related to Hindmarsh Island.[18] "There were seven sisters who were very beautiful. The mother could see around the earth, see everything. She was too big then. Said her daughters were too beautiful. Then she became too little. She needed to think about this. Her daughters were sent away into the sky so that they could stay beautiful for everyone. The mother looked for them and flowed out across the land seeking them. She grew tired and lay down. As she looked up at the sky she saw her daughters, she wept and the waters covered her searching places. She then gave the waters life and stayed at that place" (Fisher 1995: 6475). Throughout the Royal Commission and the Mathews Inquiry, Veronica Brodie insisted that the story as written down by Betty Fisher could be made public because her mother would never have told a white woman any more than she had to. But when asked if this is the story she also knew, she agreed and added, What Betty Fisher got was different from what Leila told me and what our mother knew. Stories, as I had pointed out with reference to the Ngurunderi story in Chapter 2, exist in different forms, and the Pleiades are no exception. They are indeterminate in number and are great travellers. Not surprisingly, there are a number of accounts of their adventures.

After the Mathews Report was done in June 1996, the months rolled by. It became apparent the findings of the Royal Commission, albeit flawed, would stand and that the legislation to facilitate the bridge would also stand. Veronica Brodie continued to reflect on her health and her responsibility to future generations. She decided that some of what her sister Leila had told her might be opened. Over Easter 1998, this is the part of the Seven Sisters story which she agreed should be placed in the public domain. In so doing she had the support of a group of Ngarrindjeri women.

 It begins with *Ngurunderi*'s cave which is situated under Signal Point [at Goolwa]. From the cave he looked across to the island. *Ngurunderi* felt it was his responsibility to look after the sky, the bird life, the waters, because he made the environment and the island. He was the god of the Ngarrindjeri.

His connection with the Seven Sisters was that he sent a young man, Orion, after the Seven Sisters to chase them and bring them back. They didn't want to be caught so they headed up to the sky, up and up and over the Milky Way and hid and there became the Seven Sisters.

When they want to come back to see their Mum, who is still in the waters—near where the ferry crosses, just a little over towards the mouth, to the south—there has to be a clear way, so they can return and they'll be returning shortly, when it gets cold, that's when they disappear from the sky. Then they come back down and go under the water to be with their mother. Their mother belonged to the Warrior Women of the Island.

The aspects of Aunty Leila's knowledge which Veronica chose to bestow on close Ngarrindjeri female kin and the subset of which she has now made public, tighten the weave encircling Kumarangk, the central characters of the founding drama and the law they established. Like *Ngurunderi*, the Seven Sisters have earthly manifestations and a sky presence; like *Ngurunderi* they allow communication between the earthworld and the skyworld. *Ngurunderi* was at Goolwa. The Seven Sisters are in the waters and the sky. Their unimpeded movement between the two worlds is necessary to allow the rhythm of life to be maintained, to allow for renewal. In the account from Koomi via Betty Fisher, there is a waxing and waning, perhaps the moon, which in Ramindjeri country is a woman. In the account via Leila, there is a cycling through the seasons. In both, a sacred order was celebrated, one that could be symbolised in ritual, song, story, dance, and body designs. In both, the mother remains in the waters which in Koomi's version the mother created.

Veronica Brodie spoke of the story giving directives about life, preparation for womanhood, marriage and child-bearing. In so doing, she distinguishes between the story of the Seven Sisters as a Ngarrindjeri Dreaming and the rituals established by the Seven Sisters, which she calls "directives" and "business". When full initiation, marriage and mortuary ceremonies were celebrated, the lore of the ancestors told in song, dance and story provided the charter for doing the business. The story of *Ngurunderi* tells of his travels in Ngarrindjeri lands and we learn *Ngurunderi* brought the doctor ceremonies, *Ngurunderi* performed the first platform burial. Similarly with the Seven Sisters, there are stories about their travels which link the waters with the stars that are reflected in the chill, still waters. There are also practices associated with the Seven Sisters which have to do with the rites of passage for young women as they mature.

The most elaborate written account of the Seven Sisters "business" is in David Unaipon's work (see p. 126ff.). In the story of the *Mungingee*, the Pleiades, he describes the ordeals that the young girls, *Yartooka* (*Yatuka*), willingly endure. Over a period of three years, they demonstrate they can control their appetites; endure the pain of tooth avulsion, cicatrices, and the perforation of the nasal septum; the discomfort of sleeping on a bed of ants; and finally that they can conquer fear. Unaipon (1925: 42-3), in the best story-telling tradition, then has his young women ground the story for their audience. The leader of the girls steps forward: "*Yartooka*, we have passed through the testings our Elders have prescribed and suffered much pain. Now it is the desire of the Great Spirit that you should go through the same testing . . . Will you not go and do as we have done?" The rites of passage are thereby established and the "*Yartooka* of the other tribes eagerly assented, so proud were they of the victory of their sisters" (*ibid.*). These rites of passage and the attendant knowledge are what Veronica Brodie called the "directives", and they are ones that mirror the seasonal round on earth. But just as Koomi would not have told a white woman anything that was restricted, similarly with David Unaipon. He knows the structure but has not directly observed the women's rites. In talking with Elaine Treagus (1966) about initiation, David Unaipon mentioned the *manjingki* (*mungingee*) and said "all our people can tell it". Not only has this story left traces in the written record, there is also the voice of David Unaipon testifying to the Seven Sisters as a Ngarrindjeri Dreaming.

The Dreaming story beings of the heavens gave them directives what they needed to live by or to do certain things by. It was like a Cosmic calendar, said Veronica Brodie. The Seven Sisters are the beginning of a lot of things for the Ngarrindjeri women, says Doreen Kartinyeri. Her account links important cycles in women's lives in terms of production of food (what is in season), with reproduction of the next generation, with the celestial order. The calendar is a very important piece of paper for every woman . . . So the Seven Sisters Dreaming to us is important because the stars, the moon, the sun controls the seasons. So right up until I was a young girl they were still working by the seasons and the stars. I would say that a diary and a calendar would be the two most important things that the Seven Sisters Dreaming would be able to tell Ngarrindjeri women over thousands of thousands of years. . . . they moved in certain circles. And in Spring when everything is being born that's when the sisters return, when swimming is restricted, when the waters are full of life, too dangerous for women to enter.

Unaipon's account of the rites of passage, I have suggested, need not be read as literal, but rather a setting forth of the values being communicated to young women. One of the trials of endurance not mentioned by Unaipon, but documented by Tindale, is that of depilation. Reuben Walker (Tindale and Long nd: 13) relates a segment of the *Ngurunderi* story that concerns when his wives were travelling west from Port Elliot. At the Chiton Rocks (*Jungeinju*), they sat down to pluck their pubic hair (*jungi*).

The rocks there formed a half circle and represent the hair cast aside by the two women [who] then travelled on towards the west. . . . At times the Wanindjeri camped on the eastern bank near the mouth of the Hindmarsh River. Rock, shellfish, crabs and crayfish were to be had among the rocks or where the weed covered rocks. This was likened to *jinggi* [*junggi*] or hair which in the tradition developed here because the two wives of the ancestral hero/explorer being *Ngurunderi* plucked hair from their bodies as a sign that they had not yet born children.

Here are the *yatuka* doing as the *Yartooka* of Unaipon's story did, as they were invited to do by the *Mungingee*. How is this rite connected to the Seven Sisters?

The answer is in Taplin (1873: 18), who wrote: "The Narrinyeri point out several stars, and say that they are deceased warriors who have gone to heaven (Wyirrewarre). They are Wyungare, and Nepelle, and the Manchingga, and several others." *Wyungare* is recognisably *Waiyungari* (the red-ochred man who becomes Mars) and *Nepelli* is *Ngurunderi*'s brother-in-law, but who are the *Manchingga* warriors? On hearing this term from Taplin, Milerum told Tindale it was "*Mantjingga*" (the Pleiades). Most probably this is the plural form of David Unaipon's *Mungingee*.[19] This continuity in naming is not surprising, given that Taplin probably got the name "*Manchingga*" from David Unaipon's father. But how is this related to the rite of depilation? I speculate that the *jingga/chingga/ingee* in these names of the Pleiades is a reference to *jinggi/junggi*, the word for pubic hair, as is the *Junge* of the place name *Jungeinju*.[20] What we don't know, because we know next to nothing of the wives of *Ngurunderi*, is their relationship to the *Yatuka*. Is there a story in which they are instructed by the *Yatuka* or did they arrive after this rite was established and, like all traditional Ngarrindjeri women following this rite, they plucked their pubic hair until the birth of their first child?

And what of the "warrior" status accorded these young women by Taplin, and also known to Lola Cameron Bonney and Liz Tongerie. Veronica Brodie (1995: 6234) had spoken of strong women in the Royal Commission. This, I think, is a further link with the Unaipon account. The *Yatuka* became strong women. They were warriors in the sense of their courage and endurance on behalf of all women. Ramsay Smith (1930: 331), no doubt drawing on Unaipon's story of the *Mungingee*, describes the heavenly tableau of that "bright and happy group Nepelle, Wyungara, and the Seven Sisters" who join *Ngurunderi* whence they watch over people below and bring "comfort and cheer" in the "Land of Heaven". This is the same configuration as in Taplin (1873: 18), but Smith translates Taplin's *Manchingga* as Seven sisters, a translation he must have got from Unaipon.

I think it is safe to say that the *Mungingee/Manchingga/Mantjingga* are young women warriors with a place in the Skyworld as the Pleiades. I also think one reason we hear little of this "warrior woman" tradition is because it was a Coorong perspective and one that extended into the southeast. Shirley Peisley's Gram told her how the Seven Sisters "travelled along the coast to very significant places". Like many major Dreamings, the Seven Sisters story has places where the deeds are recalled and where their bodies are known to have imprinted the land and waters, and accounts of how the Dreamings travelled from place to place.[21]

There is another common feature in the story of the wives and that of the sisters. Both are fleeing men, Orion in the case of the Pleiades and *Ngurunderi* in the case of his wives. This is a common feature of Pleiades stories across the continent and indeed in world mythology.[22] It is not surprising that there is a connection recorded between the Pleiades and Orion for the Ngarrindjeri also. The Berndts (1993: 164) name *Ngurunderi*, Crow, the Young Men and Girls, and *Waiyungari* as the four major Ngarrindjeri male initiation cycles. We know a great deal about the first, and last, but relatively little about the "young men and girls", or the Crow for that matter. Each cycle is associated with a Dreaming that has a manifestation in the skyworld; each is connected to a particular season. Thus ecological and ceremonial time run on the same cosmic calendar.

Mars emerges in spring, *riwuri*, and disappears in October–November, but because of his elopement with the wives of *Nepelli*, fishing is no good then. In summer, *luwadang*, from November to January, the Pleiades and Stingray appear and the fishing is excellent, especially for freshwater fish attracted to insects among the reed beds of the rivers and the lake. Those constellations disappear in autumn, February to April, the time of the Crow, and he lends his name, *Marangani*, to the season. The Berndts (*ibid.*: 366-7) credit Crow, who become a star, as responsible for the tides and propitious for fish. Crow disappears in October, the same time as Mars. Of *yutang*, winter, May to July, they simply say the "season coincided with the juxtaposition of certain stars" (*ibid.*: 76). But later they write:

We could say that *Ngurunderi* symbolized winter: this was conveyed in the search for his wives, in his setting of the scene and in his shaping of things to come. *Waiyungari*, on the other hand, was symbolic of spring: witness his hot-bloodedness, his personification as the red planet, his role as the contravener of law. [*ibid.*: 230]

What do Ngarrindjeri men today say about the Seven Sisters Dreaming? The caution about not swimming applied to both sexes, but it appears that gendered narratives also accompanied the taboo. Tom Trevorrow, like Veronica's daughter, had childhood memories of the elders talking about this Dreaming: Tom: I know very well because I learnt at a young age, I was I suppose about eight years old, when I first witnessed about the Seven Sisters Dreaming which relates to the Ngarrindjeri people and which relates to this area here. And it happened with me at the Old Three Mile Camp just out of Meningie. One of my elders was there and that's my wife's great-uncle—his name was Uncle Bigalong. He had a habit of pinching people and he pinched me and made me cry because when he pinched, he pinched hard. And when he pinched me, I started crying. He said, "No, no, no. Don't cry my boy. I'll do you the Seven Sisters." He was sitting around outside on the ground by the fire—my father was there, myself, Uncle Bigalong—and he started doing the Seven Sisters dance. And he danced around the fire for me and he was singing in Ngarrindjeri language and every time he'd stop, he'd point to the Seven Sisters. I'd stopped crying and I sat there and I watched him and he went on for about five minutes or more and he danced to the Seven Sisters. He said, "That's the Seven Sisters Dreaming." "Uncle Bigalong" is the Ngarrindjeri nickname for the late Hurtle Sumner, son of Pinkie Mack and brother of Laura Kartinyeri (see photograph p. 85).

Tom Trevorrow: And when I was about eight, that's when I first learned about the Seven Sisters and then I've learnt where it relates to and it relates here, to Hindmarsh Island, which we call Kumarangk. So that's something I know from a young age that I've learnt, from living in the camps, of the Seven Sisters Dreaming of the Ngarrindjeri people. I can't explain more to you. I just know that with Uncle Bigalong when he done the Seven Sisters Dreaming dance that he would not have done it if it was only related to women. So to my understanding of that it must be to the Ngarrindjeri men too, but there's more in depth to the women and we have not got access to the women's side of those Dreaming stories. On a lot of our creation stories, we have not got access to the women's side of those stories, but I saw Uncle Bigalow dance and I know that men had something too. This impromptu performance of the Seven Sisters dance would have taken place in or around 1962. At eight, Tom Trevorrow was at the age at which the Berndts say young men were being introduced to the stories of the stars. This part of the male practice was open.

Karloan (Berndt *et al.* 1993: 367) said of his initiation: "*Yatuka yarela p'rak manda yika p'rakunil inambul luwaldhaldham itji Waiyungari ngunumpulunil manda itji riwuri ngokunil ngunandja.* Girls when will rise because they are rising for summer time that one *Waiyungari* sinking because that one spring disappearing for us." The Seven Sisters Dreaming was associated with male practice at initiation. It was in the context of initiation that David Unaipon mentioned the Pleiades. Has any of the inside knowledge of men's account of the Seven Sisters survived? Neville Gollan shows me a photograph of James Ngunaitponi, David Unaipon's father, and points to the cicatrices on his body. That is the Seven Sisters Dreaming. At initiation men were marked with designs which indicated their rights and responsibilities in certain stories and places. It would appear the Unaipon lineage had an interest in the story of the Pleiades. The father bore the marks, the son told the story. Angas drew the little girl with the cicatrices. Pinkie Mack spoke of the rite of marking of the *Yatuka*. Men know of the existence of women's rituals, just as women know of men's. That is not what is restricted. It is being present at certain times and coming into contact with certain places, fluids, and persons that is taboo. So, why are men authoring accounts of women's rites of passage? There is no evidence that, up until the matter of the bridge, any women was ever asked about the Seven Sisters.[23]

Mantjingga: A Ngarrindjeri Dreaming

The Royal Commission found that the Seven Sisters story was not part of Ngarrindjeri tradition. However, there is evidence aplenty, in both the written and oral sources, to demonstrate that this is false (see Sutton 1996b). Many people speak of their general knowledge of the Seven Sisters. Maggie Jacobs: It's been, well, usual you know, the

Seven Sisters, like you'd sit outside on a moonlight night and they'd say, "They're the Seven Sisters." Lola Cameron Bonney is one who was said by her descendants to have talked about the Seven Sisters as central to the creation of the Ngarrindjeri world, but I have not been able to locate a tape or a written account of her own words on the subject. Clarke (1994: 123) writes of a "Lower Murray informant who told [him] that all Aboriginal people were believed to have originated from the Seven Sisters". Lola Cameron Bonney is almost certainly the source for this statement. On each visit to Trunceena I ask Peter and Meryl Mansfield, who have a number of tapes of Lola Cameron Bonney, if this story runs in the family. Lil [Lola's mother] used to talk all time, every time we met them, about the Seven Sisters. And they told us their people came from the eighth star in the seven sisters, which is the misty one, and they used to talk about that was in the Milky Way, and the black hole was called a goanna. Aunty Pearl was good on the stars. "She felt a connection with me," says Meryl. Peter agrees and Meryl continues, Aunty Pearl really knew the stars. We'd lie outside in summer, Uncle Ron, Peter, and I would sleep outside at Trunceena. Aunty Lola would say, "Don't think you'll see things in five minutes."

Indeed. This was knowledge that was taught through ceremonies, through practical experience and through taking a young person from one stage of enlightenment to the next as they proved themselves worthy and competent. If we could reach back in the memories of female sages of Milerum's age, we might be able to reconstruct something of the travels and exploits of these ancestral women. We might know who the eighth star was. Could it be related to the mother of the other accounts? Does it have something to do with the young boys who, the Berndts say, joined the young women?

The Pleiades are highly visible in the colder months in the northern hemisphere and in the warmer ones in the southern. Interestingly, in both hemispheres they are frequently represented as young women and indeed, at several hundred million years, one-tenth of the age of the solar system, the Pleiades are considered to be of adolescent age. The number of young women in this cluster is often given as seven and that is the number visible to the naked eye. With magnification, thousands can be discerned in this open (or galactic) cluster and thus it is not surprising to find that some stories

585

include an eighth star, or have explanations as to why some are brighter than the others. In Aboriginal stories, the closeness of the stars is explained by their being close kin: sisters should stay together for safety and through affection, shared rights in land, and shared responsibilities. Those who stray are endangered.

Milerum told Tindale: "There were seven or eight stars if you have a good look." The entry (Tindale and Long nd: 1) continues: "They were girls but one was a boy who went to them for fire because his fire had gone out; he did not return. There was another group of seven stars shaped like a stingray, the seven *ngawiri* or boys." The latter is probably the *Ngalwara*, six young men of the Berndts (1993: 164) and refers to Orion. Then in an entry, "Old notes from Karloan not dated but probably 1941" Tindale (nd, g) noted: "*Munaijeri*, one of the seven sisters stars who went away. *Maranjari* are stars." This may be a reference to the number which are clearly visible with the naked eye. The mention of fire in Tindale is inviting: the fire of initiation; of keeping the girls warm; the firing of the camp of the unfaithful wives (Clarke 1994: 113); fire and the whale; fire and the grasstree; and firestick marriages.

One mode of fabrication of "women's business" mooted by Commissioner Stevens was that the story of the Seven Sisters had been imported from Pitjantjatjara lands. It is true that the Pitjantjatjara have a Seven Sisters story but, like stories of the Pleiades, which are found across the continent and indeed throughout world history, it is embedded in a particular ecological niche and reflects and cultural concerns of the local peoples.[24] Here I emphasise that the women know the differences between their story and that of others, just as they know their weave and the men know their own carving. As Doreen Kartinyeri pointed out: I know it's different because of the landscapes. The stories were different, the areas were different, the reason they came down from the sky to the earth is different, the reason they went back is different. I didn't bring that story down here, because it's entirely different from what I learnt about here. The stars are part of their social world and the behaviour of the stars is intimately related to survival. Different societies observed the same stars, but the meaning they attributed to the movements and relative positions of the heavenly bodies reflected the earthly lives of the sages, scientists, mystics and meaning-makers below.

Across Australia there are many stories of the Pleiades wherein they are associated with seasonal change, fertility, new life and reproduction.[25] They are nearly always female, and most commonly are young women (see Sutton 1996b; Johnstone 1998). The major variations in stories of the Pleiades have to do with how they relate to the constellation Orion, which rises and sets just after the Pleiades; how they relate to the particular season in which they appear; which sites they create or imbue with significance; and the nature of the particular identities they adopt. Much depends on local geography, flora and fauna, but the Pleiades, in their various guises, do imprint the land before the travel to the skyworld. As Mountford (1976: 461) says of the early ethnographies: "These records, from Arnhem Land and the Flinders Ranges, coupled with those from Ridley and Langloh-Parker in New South Wales, suggest that this myth, in varying forms, covers a wide area." And they are travelling myths which traverse vast distances and interact with other Dreamings.

At times I have heard Ngarrindjeri women say that the Dreamings are "linking up" and "looking at each other". They do this once they are in the skyworld and their earthly manifestations also interacted. In her paintings, Muriel Van Der Byl has also explored the theme of the Sisters meeting up. This is a macro-view of ancestral activity, where members of the Seven Sisters group from one locale are in communication with those from another. Many of the stories of the Seven Sisters include sections where the sisters are separated, usually by a conniving man, and it is not uncommon across Australia to find Dreamings that communicate across wide territories (Tindale 1936, 1959; Barwick 1991). There are reports of large inter-tribal gatherings for the Ngarrindjeri in the nineteenth century, so there would have been occasions in which such communications could be modelled.

Sacred Orders: Everything in its Place

Doreen Kartinyeri: Aunty Rosie was telling me about the stars, not just the Seven Sisters, but everything in the sky. With the stars at certain times of the year, they knew to move. The stars, the moon, and the sun was like a compass, a calendar, and a clock. They never had watches. They'd move and know that the food could be plentiful when they come back next year after circling around. Tindale wrote of the stars marking the time of year and they did so in several ways. The sky drama encoded important information about the earth-bound reproductive cycles of various animals as well as the human species. Vega, the principal star in the constellation Lyra, appeared in the winter sky; it gave to the elders and doctor men the sign of the beginning of the mallee hen (*lauwari*) egg-laying season (Tindale and Long nd: 3). At this time the birds were not hunted and their eggs were forbidden to young men. In building her distinctive incubator mound, late in winter, the mallee hen scratches leaves and forest debris with her powerful claws and makes a harsh "scolding" sound. Its human manifestation, Vega, is a quarrelsome woman who continues her activities on earth. According to Tindale, Tangani men watched for the first appearance of *lawarikark* (literally, the mallee hen star) and delayed moving their camps across the Coorong waters in late spring so that they might gather the eggs, available from October through to early summer. In the early days of European settlement, access to the inland mounds, which entailed negotiating the Potaruwutj border to the east of Tangani territory, was still a matter of contention. "Old men knew when the eggs would begin to be laid, being guided by the star lawarikark seen at night near the end of winter". Other Aboriginal groups had similar ways of reading the stars. From western Victoria, Dawson (1881: 75) reports that, when Canopus is a little above the horizon in the east of the dawn sky, it is an indicator of the beginning of the egg-laying season of emus; and when the Pleiades are visible in the east an hour before sunrise, it is the time of visiting friends and neighbours.

Throughout the ages and across cultures men and women have looked skywards, found significance in the behaviours of heavenly bodies, and woven the astronomical knowledge derived from their observations into complex cosmologies. Agricultural societies co-ordinated their planting schedules and ritual calendars by the rising and setting of fundamental stars which provided a frame of reference for their activities (Ceci 1978). Their ceremonies and stories celebrated the changing seasons as mapped in the heavens. Seafaring societies negotiated the high seas without compass or chronometer.

Once the north star, Polaris, the pole star, was located, there was no doubt as to direction, no need to calibrate: north could be known with absolute certainty and one could sail safely home. In such societies the observable order of the skyworld provided a measure of security for those living out a more fragile, vulnerable existence on the earth below. As long as the heavenly bodies occupied their places, all was right with the world. While the rituals that address the "systematic cataloguing of relations and connections" may appear pointless to the outsider, in Levi-Strauss' (1966: 10) analysis of the "science of the concrete", formations such as the Pleiades become "sacred objects [which] contribute to the maintenance of order in the universe by occupying the spaces allocated to them". While the Pleiades can come and go with the seasons, the Ngarrindjeri will continue to live in a safe world.

The young age and high temperature of the Pleiades account for their brilliance and no doubt made them noteworthy, as did their tightly bunched formation. But their position in the heavens and coincidence with seasonal changes on earth made them a part of the maintenance of an order that had survival value in many cultures and over long periods of time. They are objects with a "sacred history" addressing both practical needs and deep religious wants (Eliade 1973: 5, 7-8; Ceci 1978: 31). Stories of such stars seamlessly weave knowledge for physical survival with religious beliefs and practices into a richly textured universe. The Seven Sisters are part of an enduring order of things for women. And, as we have seen, other stories entail a similar mapping of celestial order and earthly cycles. The boys were told about "various features of the environment: of the stars and phases of the moon," Berndt *et al.* (1993: 367) comment on Karloan's text about his pre-initiation training. And the girls?

Anyone who has camped out under southern skies knows the particular depth, density and brilliance of the stars. For millennia Aborigines have looked skywards, and in that vast vault of these southern skies they too have found significance. The rhythmic waxing and waning moon measured a monthly cycle. The constellations rose and fell with the seasons. This was an orderly world which gave rise to stories of routines of day and night, the cycles of life and death, and the phases of the moon. Surprise shooting stars, meteorites and comets punctuated the order and the idiosyncratic wandering planets traced their own time. Here Ngarrindjeri stories vividly illustrated the disasters that followed disruptions within the celestial order: the meteorite at McGraths Flat, smallpox and the Southern Cross, the aurora australis and eclipse of the moon engendered fear (Taplin 4–7/6/1859). The skyworld was a world in constant motion, full of significance and intent towards humankind. This was a drama that invited story-telling. Liz Tongerie recalls that her aunty always said: We come from the stars. Doug Wilson: In the night, after a meal, we had no radio or TV, we'd lie back and look at the sky and the stars. For each one, they had a story for how they got there, and they'd teach you all the sounds. The next day, they'd point out and say, "Why, he made that sound!" McLeay and Cato (1985: 18) wrote of the "golden path across to Goolwa" made by the equinoctial sun giving rise to the name "Nonpoonga", or "Place of sun on the water". It may well be that this story tells of the path to the camp of *Ngurunderi* at Goolwa, and that the line of the sun pointing to the elbow in September and March may be yet another piece of observed knowledge woven into Ngarrindjeri cosmology. What all these stories reveal is that Ngarrindjeri stories integrate the skyworld with that of daily life, and that there were stories that concern the Goolwa, Murray Mouth area.

Just as the land was gendered, so with the sky, and the important role of female sexuality is well documented. In the 1840s Meyer (1846) recorded stories of both sun and moon. The moon's sexual exploits rendered her so thin that she came to the attention of *Ngurunderi*, who ordered the waning woman-moon be driven away. "She flies, and is secreted for some time, but is employed all the time in seeking roots which are so nourishing that in a short time she appears again, and fills out and becomes rapidly fat." She is warned by other women not to eat too much lest she have trouble in giving birth (Berndt *et al.* 1993: 232). The Berndts (*ibid.*: 156) also refer to a long, but now forgotten, Ramindjeri moon myth that specifies the way in which the moon controls menstruation. The story of the moon's travels offers an explanation for the regular cycles of that body, provides advice on diet during pregnancy, and draws a metaphor with the cycles of human reproduction as manifest in changes in women's bodies from impregnation through pregnancy. On the one hand, the woman is shown as capable of surviving and flourishing through her own labours, but on the other, she is being warned by other women and *Ngurunderi* that she should exercise moderation in satisfying her appetite for food and sex.

Meyer (1846) specifies that the sun, also a woman, walks westward across the sky, and pauses overnight to rest with the spirits of the dead; the next day, glowing red from the warm skins given to her by her lover of the previous night, the sun continues on her journey. Of the moon and sun, the Berndts (1993: 233) write that they "mythologically speaking, provided two pillars within the structure of the co-joined worlds of the sky and the earth". The co-joining of the worlds, I point out, is achieved through the sexual activities and travels of these two women of the Dreamtime.

Weaving It Together

Daisy Rankine mourns the damage already done, but holding onto the enduring nature of the celestial order finds strength to continue: The landscape has changed with shifts in the sand but the spirits of our ancestors are still there. They are not gone from their homeland. They are in their resting places, but they are restless and still guiding us, their descendants, and they are still with us now. I recognise what they are telling us now. We must get our land back. We will not forget. We will not go away. We will not die. We will survive and live through our spirits in the stars. Our elders always said they would be with us in the Milky Way . . . The trees, the landscape might change, but the spiritual culture of the stars will last forever. Tom Trevorrow: The stories take you to creation, to God, and life. It's not the environment over there, it's our culture over there. The site down there, the Coorong, Granite Island, the Murray River, the lakes, they all link up together. Veronica Brodie: If that bridge goes ahead, other women will lose their Dreaming. It will break the cycle. Whites need to learn to leave sacred things alone.

The body of wisdom, often called "legends" and "myths" by outsiders, to Ngarrindjeri believers is a matter of fact. The wisdom connected with the Murray Mouth area is every bit as complex as the clan structure and every bit as difficult to confine within neat structures. The stories are of interest in themselves, but in getting to

591

know something of Ngarrindjeri lore, I have been intrigued by the inter-relationships between the stories, principal actors and special places, by the chronology of creation, and by the recurrent nature of certain symbols, metaphors, themes and motifs. Water, fire, the seasonal round. Stanner (1979) wrote of the founding drama, a creative era, known as the Dreamtime, when the land was given shape, form and meaning through the activities of the ancestors, most commonly called the Dreamings. In Ngarrindjeri lands the stories are of a complex, interacting world. There are a number of reasons why the written record is incomplete and the oral record fragmentary and jealously guarded. But we do know that the peoples of the Lower Murray, like Aborigines everywhere, looked to this creative period, and told stories of the coming into being of their world, and that today the veracity of these stories is known through their interactions with the land, their observations of the skies, their reading of signs of intent.

The return of certain species, like the whales, indicates that there is hope in revivifying the land. There is also forgiveness for the Ngarrindjeri from *ngatji*, such as whales, who were slaughtered by whites in the mid-nineteenth century. Sarah Milera elaborates: And birds, the pelicans which is important to us, have come back to lay eggs. Turtles have come back to lay eggs for the first time in a very long time, which is important to this because when we're doing something for our culture, the birds relate to it. They talk to us; they help us. We sit down and we talk as Ngarrindjeri people and we look at our people passed away and we look at the age that they gone at, thirty-five, forty years old. They're gone. I suppose I think myself I'm still lucky to be here today. You know, our life span has been cut in halves. You know, it's things that are affecting us is we've been forced to live another way that doesn't suit us. We've been forced away from our spiritual ties to the land and our spiritual ties to our *ngatjis* and everything that goes with it. We're worried as a people that anything more that go on we're going to be a dying race, we'll die out.

When I began this research I wanted to know how women's knowledge was constructed and transmitted. I wanted to know how their knowledge and men's knowledge was articulated. I wanted a context within which I might analyse the material that was broader than: do Ngarrindjeri women have "secret women's business"? A number of parties in the academy, media, parliament and legal system had inquired into and pronounced upon the who, where, when and why of Hindmarsh Island, but I did not begin with the question of "women's business" and in fact did not address it directly until the second-last chapter. I began with the weaving of women and the circular designs which radiate from the navel-like centre to take in family and stories. This was where women were telling stories of themselves, and their families. This was where women could author accounts of their own lives, in their own voices. In the past there had been a deliberate breaking of the circle, a sense of resignation and despair. Yet there were also key individuals who held close the knowledge that was dear to them. Fragments. Strands. In the 1990s Ngarrindjeri are working with the rushes they have to make meaning in radically changed and rapidly changing circumstances.

I have written of Ngarrindjeri culture as a thing made, like a finely woven mat. And yes, there are rents and tattered edges, but the tightly knotted core from which all weaving radiates has endured. Weaving was a most fortunate starting place. The weaving metaphor made intuitive sense to me but, as I began to tease out the fibres of Ngarrindjeri lives, I learned it was not just me. Weaving techniques and woven objects are a window onto Ngarrindjeri social life and cosmology, a way of thinking about family and a way of conceptualising the universe. It is no accident that the Ngarrindjeri lineages where weaving is a living tradition, are lineages where knowledge of land, lore and law is also alive. There is within the Ngarrindjeri community a high level of contestation of what it is that is being woven. This is indicative not only of the forces that have torn at the cultural fabric, but of the forces that actively work to make it whole again. I picture Aunty Rosie smoothing the rushes over the back of her knife; using the less than perfect rushes from Point Pearce for filler alongside the stronger, more pliable, enduring ones from Raukkan. She pulls the rush through and down to tighten the stitch. The mat grows and the design becomes clear as she coils outwards from the tight knot at the centre. I see Ellen doing the same today. I see other women "re-learning" what they knew as girls from women who learnt from their mothers. Each time I have explained the idea of a woven mat as a metaphor for Ngarrindjeri culture I have had

593

nods or recognition and approval. It allows that individual ideas are woven in strand by strand, pulled through, tightened, in a satisfying symmetry of design. The fragments are made whole again.

The weaving metaphor also acknowledges that strength resides in the interweaving of materials, that new items can be incorporated and interpreted within the stories told by the old people. Wire handles strengthen the baskets. Dandelions signal the departure of the Seven Sisters. New items are seamlessly woven into stories which still carry the colours, texture and scent of the land. And then there are things that the Ngarrindjeri with whom I have been working know to be a violation, a disruption, a threat to that order. When they explain the damage which will result from the proposed bridge, they look to the rules they have learned about their world, its structure and order; they know the dangers of violating their law. Here they have set out their stories. They need to be read in the context of their history, the land and their families. We can't block things off in little boxes. We've got to start and work our way through the body of the Coorong, said George Trevorrow, It's important to get that feeling . . . and how we feel about it.

Epilogue: Whither?

1998 was not the best of years and, as I write, it is yet to end. There had been some hope going into it. The High Court had agreed, 8 September 1997, to hear the Ngarrindjeri challenge to the *Hindmarsh Island Bridge Act* passed four months earlier on 12 May. The High Court, 20 October 1997, had ruled that in native title cases, Aboriginal men and women had the right to have gender-restricted evidence withheld from members of the opposite sex (AAP 1997). Perhaps, then the High Court would be prepared to grapple with the big questions embedded in the struggle of the Ngarrindjeri applicants to protect their sacred places. Their case has raised questions that go to the core of democratic values that many Australians hold dear. This is a country where the High Court in Mabo (1992) had set aside the flawed doctrine of *terra nullius* and found that native title was part of the common law of the land. This was a country where in 1967 nigh on ninety per cent of the population had endorsed a constitutional amendment to give the Commonwealth government concurrent rights with the states to legislate for Aborigines. Surely this was a country where fairness mattered.

It was an application under the Commonwealth Heritage Act which brought me into this field and the case continued to move through the Australian legal system as I began to write this book. In the Prologue I wrote of "being here and being there", of dislocations of time and space. In the chapters which follow I moved back and forth between the present and past tense, marking the immediate, tracing continuities and discontinuities, heeding the silences, scrutinising the sources. Let me now pick up the narrative of the case. It is very much of the here and now. In no sense is it a "world that was"

595

but it will make a big difference to the "world that will be". In late 1997, the Ngarrindjeri were asking that the High Court strike down a law which prevented the *Aboriginal and Torres Strait Islander Heritage Protection Act* 1984 from protecting their places. Places which would be desecrated should the bridge be built.[1] The law had had a rocky passage through the federal parliament and for some it had been easier to see the law go up to the court to be sorted out, than to use valuable political capital in debates regarding its constitutionality.

Those who care about Aboriginal rights are more inclined to address the proposed amendments to the Native Title Act occasioned by the 1996 Wik decision. There the High Court set out a framework within which pastoralists and Aborigines could co-exist, where settler and Indigene could share the country.[2] They found that Native Title was not extinguished by the granting of a pastoral lease, rather there would need to be negotiation, a word which invokes strong responses from conservative governments and development lobbies, for whom it is synonymous with chaos. The Prime Minister, John Howard, has done little to clarify and much to confound with his pronouncements regarding the need for balance and equality which he confuses with sameness.[3] When the Minister for Aboriginal Affairs, John Herron (1996), speaks on matters Hindmarsh, he talks about the need for closure, an end to this expensive long-running saga, a restoration in public confidence in government. He is yet to return the materials generated during the Mathews Report. The person who has been vocal on Aboriginal affairs is Queenslander Pauline Hanson, the ultra-conservative leader of the newly formed One Nation party, whose rise to prominence has been accompanied by hateful, racist rhetoric including claims that Aborigines were cannibals (Roberts 1997).

This is the background against which the High Court heard the Hindmarsh case in 1998. And the court that heard the Hindmarsh case is not the court that made the far-sighted decisions in the Mabo case of 1992. A series of resignations and appointments has significantly restructured the court (Lane 1997: 1). Cases involving the Heritage Act are rarely simple. It is legislation of last resort and of the ninety-nine applications brought under it, only two still stand (Evatt 1996: 9-11). Since the early 1980s there has been a concerted effort on behalf of development lobbies to delegitimate Aboriginal claims to sacred sites and in the nineties, Hindmarsh Island has become a target (see Brunton 1995, 1996a, b). It involves Aborigines from the settled south and it involves women: people who can be dismissed as having an agenda—be it environmentalism, feminism, or Aboriginal sovereignty. Further, there is dissension within the community. This is no neat, clear-cut case. But does that mean they should be disenfranchised? The issues raised by the Wik decision of 1996 concern who has rights in vast tracks of land and who has the right to negotiate rights to that land. These are the rights that are the stuff of politics and justice. There is little public understanding of what is being contested in the Hindmarsh case. Yet the quality of justice enjoyed by any society is only as good as that enjoyed by the most marginal, vulnerable, and disadvantaged. And the Ngarrindjeri who are bringing their case to the High Court are sorely in need of justice.

The Ngarrindjeri women and men who brought that first application under the Heritage Act in 1994 have not quit. For those who wish to see the bridge go ahead their continued litigation borders on the vexatious: What is to be gained by another inquiry? The expense is crippling and what more is to be learned? These are the points Minister John Herron (1997) raises when he introduces the "Bill for an Act to facilitate the construction of the Hindmarsh Island bridge, and for related purposes" into the House of Representatives in 1997. It is true the matter is tedious but it is also well to remember that persistent, committed litigants are part of the democratic process. Had there not been people who were prepared to challenge racist and sexist laws, women would not have the vote and Aborigines would still be subject to the repressive laws. The history of these Ngarrindjeri attempts to protect their sacred places may be discomforting and confusing—much of what has been written remains under embargo—but it is hard to sustain a charge of vexatious litigation.

These Ngarrindjeri are yet to have a determination in their favour. As I pointed out in the Prologue, in both of the section 10 applications brought under the Heritage Act, the reporter had been convinced the area of the proposed bridge was of significance to Aboriginal people and Aboriginal traditions (Saunders 1994; Mathews 1996: 183). The Tickner declaration of 1994 was quashed not because of anything the applicants did, but on legal technicalities. The Mathews Report (1996) was quashed because her appointment violated the separation of powers of the executive and the judiciary, not because of anything the applicants did. While these federal inquiries have failed to provide definitive reports that have survived at law, the South Australian Royal Commission (Stevens 1995), which found that the women had fabricated their beliefs in order to thwart the building of the bridge, remains intact. With one exception, the women being accused of fabrication, did not appear before the Royal Commission. They did not recognise the jurisdiction of the Commission that would investigate their religious beliefs. So their story was not told in that forum either. In fact, nowhere do we have an account of the women in their own words. All that is in the public arena is media interviews and conjecture as to what they know and believe. There is yet to be a properly constituted forum within which they might tell their stories and make their case with proper safeguards on confidentiality and with meaningful sanctions for those who breach confidentiality.

Increasingly, Heritage applications are being conducted along adversarial lines. There is little opportunity to hear about the webs of relationships within which sites and stories are located. And, as we have seen in the preceding chapters, there are many stories associated with Hindmarsh Island, Goolwa and the Murray Mouth area. To hear them we need context and we need to establish relationships based on trust and respect. Most commentaries on the Hindmarsh Island affair begin with the island nestled in the elbow of the Goolwa Channel. Legal inquiries have begun with the rectangle of land that takes in the approaches to the proposed bridge on the Goolwa and Hindmarsh Island sides and the waters between. Why is this piece of land so special? they ask. What makes the waters sacred? Show us your culture, they demand. Jane Mathews (1996: 200-6) sought a rationale for desecration, a rule that would explain the proposition that a bridge constitutes a desecration.[4]

I began with stories of Ngarrindjeri lives, relationships, places, beliefs, and struggles, as a context for this question. George Trevorrow (1995: 6365) had said: "If those old people were living today and seen what conditions we are in and what is happening with the culture,

598

they would have no hesitation about never speaking again." I imagine Leila Rankine, now keeping a watchful eye over the sacred waters from her resting place. What might she have said? I ponder her story-telling style, her propensity to talk in riddles, her Christian beliefs and her comfort in her culture. I ask her sister, Veronica and her sister-in-law Maggie Jacobs, "Would Aunty Leila tug at the fringe of the cleric's robe and demand a manifestation of his beliefs, insist that he explain the mystery of faith, the holy trinity, crucifixion and resurrection?"

At the core of the Ngarrindjeri world which I have come to know is the value placed on the maintenance of kinship ties and genealogies which bind Ngarrindjeri to land and to each other. I have written of Ngarrindjeri culture as a weave of people, places, distinctive beliefs and practices. Their stories tell of the stars and celestial lore, the power of the elements, and peculiarities of flora and fauna. They tell of pelicans, whales, Willie wagtails and *mingka* birds who carry messages regarding kin and country. They tell of the ills that befall individuals and communities when the rules are broken. Their stories resonate with the written sources. The responsibility of the living to care for country and to keep the stories alive has been severely challenged over the last century. In the face of colonisation of their lands, Ngarrindjeri were rendered relatively powerless, but not broken. The whales are returning to the Murray Mouth and with them hope and redemption. From the fragments of stories of the old people which have survived, the elders of today are weaving a world which incorporates the new, which provides meaning in a rapidly changing world, and which demonstrates respect for the things they value. And, it is a gendered world where men's and women's beliefs about their *ruwar* (bodies) are inscribed on their *ruwi* (land) in distinctive ways. For those who have the strength of *miwi* to know and to learn, the world-that-will-be is worth fighting for.

So, what does it mean for a secular state to provide legislative protection for the sacred places of Indigenous peoples? Can that protection be withheld or withdrawn from certain groups without eroding the religious freedoms of all? What is the quality of rights enjoyed by minorities? By women? It seemed to me in early 1998 that the High Court had a chance to say something meaningful about the Australian Constitution and the dramatic shifts in the relationship between the settler and Indigenous population of the last thirty years. And then there were questions which were not directly before the court but which will flow from a decision. Who determines what is sacred? What constitutes evidence of tradition? Can people in the settled south expect the same degree of protection of their places as people in the more remote communities in the north?

In February 1998 some twenty Ngarrindjeri made the journey to Canberra for the High Court hearing of their case. Hitherto this has been a place where Indigenous peoples have found a modicum of justice. How will the court understand this case? Using the last of my frequent flyer miles, I make a five-day trip to Australia from the USA for the High Court hearing. It's teaching time but my students are caught up in the case and drawing parallels with the rights of Native Americans and minorities in the USA. Some have heard the case reported on the BBC and read about it in the *New York Times*. It is difficult to explain to these young people who understand the

High Court, February 5, 1998
Left to right, back row Eunice Aston, Diane Bell, Doreen Kartinyeri,
Veronica Brodie, Hazel Wilson
Dorothy Shaw, Margaret Jacobs, Grace Sumner, Cherie Watkins
(Cherie Watkins' personal collection)

sixties as the Civil Rights era, why the Australian Constitution might have been changed in 1967 to allow laws that discriminate against Aborigines to be passed.

Before the case is heard there is another matter to be resolved. The most recent appointment to the bench, Ian Callinan, is known to have given a legal opinion on the validity of the Act at the request of John Herron in 1996 and, in 1995, at the request of Ian McLachlan, to have drafted terms of reference for a Royal Commission into the bridge affair (Campbell 1998: 3). The Ngarrindjeri Plaintiffs ask that he step down. There could be an apprehension of bias. He refuses. For two days we sit in the chill court and listen while bewigged learned gentlemen, and several gentlewomen, talk about the 1967 referendum and what it means. Where were they all in 1967? we ask each other. Don't they remember the groundswell for Aboriginal rights? Don't they remember there was no campaign for a "No" vote, that this was the moment when Australia acknowledged that Aboriginal people were to be counted in the national census? I remember voting. My daughter was only several months old and as I cast my vote I believed I was voting for a change that would remove discriminatory sections from the constitution. I may have grown up in a society that could pass repressive laws, but my daughter would not. At the end of the High Court hearings we leave Canberra confused. There have been some interesting questions debated such as: Are the Ngarrindjeri a race? What does the language of race mean in the late-twentieth century? I wonder. In anthropology it is an outdated and discredited concept, yet it is a powerful one in the hands of a Pauline Hanson.

25 February: Callinan, confronted with documents which demonstrate his poor memory and only five days before his fellow judges on the High Court will decide if he should step down, does step down (Kingston 1998: 1). The Hindmarsh decision came down on 1 April: five to one against the Ngarrindjeri. Justice Gaudron writes that the constitutional amendment of 1967 was poorly worded and was in effect a matter of "language and syntax".[5] According to this view, there was no shift in law that reflected the mood of the electorate; that gave force to the tenor of the campaigns for the "Yes" vote. In 1998, it now seems that the Commonwealth may pass laws "for" Aborigines

and that simply means "with respect to" Aborigines. It does not mean "for the benefit of" Aborigines. But what does this mean in real terms? What sort of laws might be passed? Well, not ones that constitute "manifest abuse", submitted the Commonwealth.[6] But how do we know when we have reached the point of manifest abuse? How far down the slippery slope do we need to be? Is the Hindmarsh Act a case of manifest abuse? At what point do we realise that abridging the rights of the vulnerable imperils the rights of all? Like the miner's canary which dies when the air turns foul, minorities, especially Indigenous peoples, act as an early warning. Beware, the litigants are telling us, the democratic air is turning foul.

Justices Brennan and McHughes write that the Hindmarsh Island Act was simply an exercise in partial repeal.[7] What the government giveth, the government taketh. But if there can be one amending/repealing act which restricts the ambit of the act, there can be others. Imagine, each time there is a contentious sacred site—and the ones that come to the attention of the Heritage Act nearly always are, that is the nature of the legislation—a "little law" could be passed to sort it out. Every time there is a group of "vexatious litigants" who wish to pursue their case, there could be another "little law" to resolve that. The case has considerably soured the climate in Australia around issues of Reconciliation, women's rights, Indigenous rights, and anthropological research. It has raised serious questions about the role of the media, courts and parliament in dealing with Indigenous people and women. Much mischief has been done. Justice Kirby, the one dissenting voice writes: "Each generation reads *The Constitution* in the light of accumulated experience. Each finds in the sparse words ideas and applications that earlier generations would not have imagined simply because circumstances, experience and common knowledge did not then require it."[8] How then might we imagine ourselves living as members of an international community? Who will hold the mirror in which we might see the reflections of a mature democratic nation?

The issues of justice raised by this case should concern all Australians but too many have tuned out. I understand why—the case is too messy, too complicated, too political and too dangerous to be involved in—but I am suggesting we tune out at our own peril. In writing this book, I have been thinking of ways in which to engage the reader, to provide a framework within which the Hindmarsh Island affair will be better understood. Over and above the legal-politico manoeuvres is a critical issue of the quality of justice dispensed through the courts and legislature. The questions this case raises could shape the agenda for a society with a civic commitment to justice for all, a society with a commitment that is reflective, that is not held hostage to competing interests, that sees through the anti-intellectualism of populist leaders, looks beyond the rhetoric of rights to the quality of justice enjoyed by minorities and women, and that refuses to allow the rights of the vulnerable to be sacrificed so that the status quo not be disturbed.

One of the great debates we need to be having in Australia concerns race relations, but we are having it obliquely. There was the refusal of the Prime Minister to apologise for the stolen generations and a grass-roots response of hundreds of thousands of Australians personally signing "Sorry" books. There was the rapid rise to prominence of Pauline Hanson of the One Nation party, the eleven seats her party won in the Queensland election of 27 June 1998, and the protest meetings and marches of ordinary citizens who were appalled by what she represented. The passage of the amendments on the *Native Title Act* on 8 July 1998 was achieved against a background of threats of an election on race, one that would divide the nation, and spurious arguments that equality meant all Australians should be treated the same. The damage done by a Hanson, Herron or Howard will not be eradicated with heavy-handed tactics. It will take courage, vision and leadership, qualities sadly lacking in the current parliament and court. It will take the enunciation of principles by which we might live together and honour core values of decency and fairness. It will take confronting the insecurities that feminism, Indigenous rights and religious diversity represent for those who are willing to believe that in the "good old days" things were better, before woman, native and other spoke in their own voices and insisted on being authors of their own lives.

Notes

Prologue

1. In Australia a Royal Commission is an inquiry directed to be carried out by the executive branch of government. The jurisdiction of the inquiry is defined by its terms of reference. It may simply ask for a report containing findings of fact and reasons for same or it may ask for a finding of fact and recommendations consequent upon the findings of fact. It may be conducted by a judge or a barrister or any other person. Judges are usually appointed to give such an inquiry a colour of judicial quality. It is possible to publicly dispute the findings of a Royal Commission but rather more difficult to convince a court to hear a challenge. See Thomas Edwin Trevorrow and the State of South Australia and Iris Eliza Stevens, in the South Australian Supreme Court, 1996. See also Mr Justice Kirby's reason for decision (dissenting) in the High Court ruling on the appointment of Justice Mathews as Reporter (Wilson and Ors v Minister, High Court 6 Sept 1996).

   The terms of reference for the South Australian Royal Commission into Hindmarsh Island of 16 June 1995 contained in Letters Patent from Dame Roma Flinders Mitchell, the Governor of South Australia, to Iris Eliza Stevens, a retired judge from the District Court of South Australia, required that she inquire and report on whether the "women's business", or any aspect of the "women's business", was a fabrication and if so "(a) the circumstances relating to such a fabrication; (b) the extent of such a fabrication; and (c) the purpose of such a fabrication" (Stevens 1995: 1-4, 311-5). Stevens was granted three extensions and reported on 19 December 1995. A Royal Commission is not a court of law but Stevens (*ibid*.: 5) conducted the Hindmarsh Island along the lines of a trial. The proponent women, with one exception, declined to give evidence and on the first day their legal representative read a statement setting out their reasons (Stevens 1995: 20-1).

2. The Hon. Elizabeth Evatt (1996) conducted a review of the *Aboriginal and Torres Strait Islander Heritage Protection Act* 1984 between 1 December 1995 and 22 August 1996. It was undertaken at the invitation of Robert Tickner,

Minister for Aboriginal and Torres Strait Islander Affairs, and submitted to John Herron who became the Minister after the March 1996 federal election. The Terms of Reference included (ii) matters of procedural justice in light of federal court judgments and appeals and, (vi) how secret/sacred information should be dealt with under the Act.

3. The Amelia Park site was registered pursuant to the *Aboriginal Heritage Act* (SA) 1988 and recorded at the Department of State Aboriginal Affairs Registry as an archaeological site.

4. See Muir (1996: 75) for an analysis of the media representations of the "proponent women" and the threat presented by their breaking of "feminine norms".

5. The Council for Aboriginal Reconciliation (1995), a bi-partisan group of Indigenous and non-indigenous persons, first met in 1992 and has as its agenda to "build bridges" for a better understanding between Aboriginal and Torres Strait Islanders and the wider community. It comprises twenty-five individuals (twelve of whom are Indigenous and eleven of whom are from the wider community). It is to work towards a better understanding between Aboriginal and Torres Strait Islanders and the broader Australian community. It identified eight issues as essential to the process of reconciliation. These include "understanding country" by recognising the importance of country and the nature of sacred relations to land; improving relationships by healing the ruptures caused through dislocation and dispossession of peoples, and valuing the diversity, strength and developing nature of indigenous cultures. Reconciliation meetings occur regularly in Adelaide and the concept is discussed by Ngarrindjeri, albeit in different ways. The applicants view the Royal Commission and much of the media reporting of their claims as hostile to the spirit of Reconciliation and any future possibilities of respectful partnerships.

6. *The Aboriginal Land Rights (Northern Territory) Act* 1976 and its complementary legislation of 1980, the *Aboriginal Sacred Sites Protection Act* has provided protection for sacred sites in the Northern Territory (Ritchie 1994; Howie 1981; Bell 1983). The Woodward Commission, which in 1974 had been asked to investigate how land rights might be recognised for the Aboriginal people of Australia had recommended a comprehensive plan for the entire country wherein there would be "needs based" claims for those who had been dispossessed and claims of "tradition" for those whose lands were not alienated. The first basis was dropped from the bill when the Labor Government lost the Federal election in 1975. When the new Liberal government legislated, it did so only for the Northern Territory. The issue of states' rights was certainly a consideration but by failing to pass national legislation, the Federal government left the matter of protection of sites with the individual states. Not until 1984 was there legislation enacted for the protection of sites across the country and this was the *Aboriginal and Torres*

Strait Islander Heritage Protection Act. This Act was premised on the concept of the Crown as owner and custodian of the cultural heritage of the nation. (The various Heritage Acts predate the Mabo decision of 1992 which recognised "native title" as part of the common law of Australia and gave rise to the *Native Title Act* 1993.) Thus in protecting Aboriginal heritage, the Crown is making special provisions rather than recognising a pre-existing right. At the time of writing, new Commonwealth legislation, which hands back much responsibility to the states, was working its way through the Parliament.

7. This matter was heard by O'Loughlin J. under the *Administrative Decisions (Judicial Review) Act* 1977. See Chapman v Tickner (1995) 37 ALD 1.

8. Tickner v Chapman (1995) 57 FCR.

9. Lawnham and Towers (1995); Attorney General Michael Lavarch (1995: 1691); Minister Robert Tickner (1995: 1795).

10. See Muir (1996: 74, 79) for an analysis of the media representations of the "dissident women" as defending the "good" name of Aborigines and identifying with the "suburban domestic interior, the feminine sphere".

11. See Fergie (1994: Title page). Doreen Kartinyeri recited these words at the Murray Mouth on 20 June 1994 and they became the title of the report Deane Fergie (*ibid.*) prepared for the Aboriginal Legal Rights Movement (ALRM), Adelaide, South Australia.

12. Throughout we were dealing with unrealistic practice directions and constantly moving deadlines which were the subject of complaints from a number of parties. Even solicitor Stephen Palyga (1996: 121), representing Tom and Wendy Chapman, complained about process. The Reporter's demand that everything, including her report, be complete by June became insistent after the March 1996 election which brought the Liberal Party, run by John Howard, into power.

13. Minister for Aboriginal and Torres Strait Islander Affairs v Western Australia. Full Federal Court, unreported, 28 May 1996. See, casenote, Hancock (1996: 12). The declaration made by Minister Robert Tickner, 6 April 1994, for protection of a site held sacred by members of the Yaruwu Aboriginal community was successfully challenged by the developers of the crocodile farm planned for that site. Carr J. on 7 February 1995, found that the decision making process had failed to comply with the requirements of procedural fairness. The matter was appealed by the Minister to the Full Bench of the Federal Court which agreed with Carr. However when the court wrote that the Minister must give parties "a proper opportunity to advance all legitimate arguments to avert a decision that might profoundly affect their interests" by disclosing relevant details, did that mean that all the details of secret men's business in this case, or secret women's business in the Hindmarsh case would have to be disclosed, or that it would be possible to summarise the beliefs without going into detail (see note 14). This case put the interests of those likely to be disadvantaged by a Ministerial declaration

on a collision course with the Aboriginal requirement that certain knowledge be restricted on the basis on gender. There are other bases (see Chapter 7).

14. In all, I prepared four confidential attachments: two accompanied the "Seven Sisters Report" (Bell and Bagshaw 1996) and two the "Desecration of Injury Report" (Bell 1996c). The women had already seen the lack of respect accorded to confidential material in the parliament, media and Stevens' (1995) publication of the genealogies (see Chapter 4). There were different sorts of confidentiality accorded to documents during the Mathews Report: (i) those confidential to the process; (ii) confidential on the basis of gender; (iii) to be read only by the Reporter and her advisors. The latter might be further restricted in combination with (ii). Mathews stated she would give less weight to representations that could not be read by other parties but she had no power to punish if these persons breached the confidentiality of the process. The disclosure that the so-called "secret envelopes" had been destroyed constituted a breach because that information was contained in a confidential representation to Mathews. Confidentiality types (ii) and (iii) were breached when my report on the women's confidential submissions to Mathews were circulated, in error, to other parties (see Chapter 10, note 17).

15. Dorothy Ann Wilson and Ors v Minister for Aboriginal Affairs, High Court of Australia, 6 September 1996, 189 CLR challenged the ability of a Chapter 111 judge to report to the federal minister under the *Aboriginal and Torres Strait Islander Heritage Protection Act* 1984.

16. Wilson v Tickner (1996), see note 15. It was not that the Court thought that Judge Mathews was not impartial but rather that there could be an appearance that the judge, as appointed by the Minister, would be acting as his agent. "Thus," wrote Gaudron J. (*ibid.*: 29) it is not a function that Parliament may confer on a judge of a court exercising judicial power of the Commonwealth." Kirby J. (*ibid.*: 30-60) rejected both the construction and constitutional arguments advanced for the plaintiffs and provided an analysis which repays careful reading.

17. Mathews, and most other commentators assumed that the Broome case meant all material had to be disclosed to interested parties in the interests of fairness (Tickner v Western Australia. WAG Nos 18 and 19, unreported judgment delivered 28 May 1996). The applicants withdrew their confidential material (ii) and (iii) and then, having examined the reasons for decision in the Broome case, sought to resubmit summaries of the material. Mathews rejected these attempts (see Chapter 10, note 17). Had the Mathews Report not been vanquished by the High Court ruling, her interpretation of the Broome case could have been challenged. There were procedural points which could have been raised, S. Kenny (1996) argued.

18. See Nicholls (1995/6, 1996). There are differing analyses of the way in which the media dealt with the claim of the dissidents and the proponent women. Chris Kenny (1996) argued that the ABC was partisan and virtually ignored

the dissident women. On the other hand Colin James writing in the Adelaide *Advertiser*, Christopher Pearson and Chris Kenny in the *Adelaide Review*, Frank Devine in the *Australian* and Geoff Easedown in the Melbourne *Herald*, have kept up a steady stream of criticism of the anthropologists and others who gave evidence in support of the "proponent women" and have cast the "dissident women" as brave souls who, along with Philip Clarke and Philip Jones of the South Australian Museum, have dared to tell the truth and have been punished (Brunton 1996a). For the most part the media were more concerned with following the Wik case and Native Title debates than Hindmarsh Island.

19. The judge had her own panel of experts on whom she could rely for advice. Drs Peter Sutton and Nancy Williams, senior, experienced anthropologists, visibly participated in the process. Her panel had originally included Professor Francesca Merlan, Dr Myrna Tonkinson (neither of whom appear to have been consulted) and Marcia Langton who resigned in March 1996 so that she might speak out on the topic at a conference in Adelaide. By empanelling this group Mathews had significantly depleted the pool of expertise available to other parties.

20. Maddox (in press) argues that there is tension between the value the Australian legal system places on freedom of religion and the requirement under the Heritage Act that there be evidence of the authenticity of the traditions on which a declaration might be based. She calls for "closer attention to be paid to technical issues of religious meaning and the nature of religious belief".

21. See Chapter 7 (pp. 372–3) for details of this exchange. One of the striking features of the position of the dissidents and the Chapmans was that the "proponent women" had not made themselves available and therefore were not to be believed. I had offered the dissident women the opportunity to read what I had written before publication. This was also my position with the applicants and, of course, raises critical questions about censorship, accountability and so on, which I discuss with reference to dialogical research also in Chapter 7. I note that Chris Kenny (1996: 243) is critical of the ABC "Media Report" for rejecting the chance to interview the dissidents, an opportunity I would have taken.

22. Section 35 (1) of the Act states: "It is an offence to divulge information about an Aboriginal site, object or remains, or about Aboriginal tradition, in contravention of Aboriginal tradition without authority. The Minister may give authority to divulge information" s. 35 (2). While I was writing my initial report for Justice Mathews, many of the reports to earlier inquiries, including all the anthropological, historical and archeological reports (Fergie 1994, Edmunds 1988, Lucas 1990, Luebbers 1981, 1982 as well as Philip Clarke's 1994 PhD thesis) were not available to me under penalty of section 35. This was a document I could access in a Public Library, but if I cited it, I could be prosecuted. The lack of access to this earlier anthropological and

historical research meant I had to duplicate research. Further, I was not permitted to speak to colleagues who had worked on the material during the Royal Commission, and did not meet with Deane Fergie until November 1996. While I was writing in an information vacuum, all the major parties to the Mathews Report had read the reports to the Royal Commission and thus I was at a distinct disadvantage. These are not good conditions under which to be offering an expert opinion. It is something akin to being required to diagnose a medical condition without a patient history.

23. Much of the Tindale material was brought back to Australia in 1995. I have been through the thirteen folders known as the "World of Milerum" which I cite as "Tindale and Long nd" and then give a number which indicates the number of the folder. The journals I cite by the dates covered in the notes. For the many other folders I have assigned a letter so the citation reads (Tindale nd, a). I have not been able to pursue all the cross references from Tindale cards to his journals, nor have I been able to check all the material in the "World of Milerum" against the journals. See also Chapter 8, note 9.

24. Appleton (1992: 284); Berndt (1940a: 167).

25. Berndt *et al.* (1993: 325); see also McDonald (1977: 12) *mnaeng-i*, Tindale (nd, e) *maneingai.*

26. See Hemming (1994a). Camp Coorong was established in 1987 by the Ngarrindjeri Lands and Progress Association. The focus of the cultural tourism program is education for school groups, special interest groups and tourists and this includes historical and contemporary accounts of Ngarrindjeri life. Their Cultural Heritage Centre opened 1988.

27. *Rawu* (old) plus *kung* (at). There are several place names which incorporate "*rawu*": Rawaldarang, a name on Hindmarsh Island and Rawarangald at Port Elliot. I would speculate that the name carries information about the chronology of the changing landscape of the Lower Murray (see p. 97).

28. There are many renditions and meanings offered for Goolwa. Gulawa or Gurawa (Morison 1978: 39) "the place where fresh and salt water meet"; Goolawarra (Wyatt 1879: 179); Kotungalt (Meyer 1843); Gutungald (Taplin 1873: 130) "place of cockles"; Kutunkald/Katunkald (Berndt *et al.* 1993: 222, 586); Kultungat/Kultungald/Ku:lawa was stated by the natives to have the meaning, "the elbow" from the word *ku:ke* but the actual derivation is more obscure (Tindale nd, j).

29. All population statistics are estimates and all can be challenged. I have erred on the conservative side. I have heard 4,000–5,000 offered as a reasonable figure. There are complicated issues of who is counted, by whom, when, and for what purpose. Clarke (1994: 57-63) provides a summary of the sources including Taplin's census-taking, Radcliffe-Brown's (1918) estimates and post-1967 census figures. Pre-European contact, estimates vary from 1,800 to 6,000; 1860s 1,000; declining to 511 in 1879; and in the 1990s increasing to 2,000–3,000.

30. See Chapters 3 and 10 for further discussion of the mappings of Ngarrindjeri lands by the Berndts (1993), Taplin (1873) and Tindale (1974). There is little agreement in their respective mapping of the clans of Hindmarsh Island/Goolwa/Murray Mouth area.
31. Tindale (1974: 133) for instance sees the Lofty Ranges as a geographic and ethnographic divide with circumcising and subincising peoples to the drier north and west and the Ngarrindjeri who feared their neighbours, to the east.
32. See Chapter 2 and the Chronology; see also Mattingley and Hampton (1988); Department of Education (1990); Jenkin (1979); Taplin (1879); Nile (1996); The Select Committee on Aborigines (1860); Royal Commission on Aborigines (1913); Wilson (1997).
33. See Bell (1993a, 1993b) for an extended argument on this matter and for my critique of the neglect of women, feminist theory, and the previous contributions of women scholars to the writing of ethnography.
34. See Chapter 2 on the tradition of literacy amongst the Ngarrindjeri. Lola Cameron Bonney, David Unaipon and Reuben Walker would each be worthy of a book and this generation of elders, if they so desired, could be recorded on audio and video tape for their descendants. Steven Hemming's sound archive, begun 1982, is one critically important resource and there are also many personal tapes made by Ngarrindjeri.
35. Thomas Lincoln Chapman, Wendy Jennifer Chapman v Luminis Pty Ltd ACN 008 027 085, Deane Fergie and Cheryl Ann Saunders, Federal Court of Australia, (SA), SG 33 of 1997. The application sought damages with interest and costs and claimed that, with respect to Deane Fergie, she had contravened s. 52 of the *Trade Practices Act*, or alternatively s. 56 of the *Fair Trading Act* in that her report was misleading or deceptive or likely to mislead or deceive.
36. See note 4. The Wilson Report (1997) was an opportunity for Reconciliation to be given some substance, but the current Prime Minister, John Howard (Woodford 1997) has consistently refused to apologise for the government role in separating Aboriginal children from their families and criticised the "black arm band view of history".

PART ONE
Chapter One

1. *Wukkin* (weaving) *mi:mini* (woman) is a phrase routinely used by Daisy Rankine and it also forms part of the name of the Ngarrindjeri Race Relations Basket Weaving (*Warkkin*) Association, Meningie. I have heard it from other women and had it explained as meaning "to wound" or to "pierce" as in the action of pushing in and pulling through the rushes, but also it has a vulgar meaning of "to poke". Meyer (1843: 106) has *wakk-in* as hurting; (Taplin

1879: 141) *wakkin* as wounding; Bonney (1990) *wuk-kin*, poke, jab. Meyer (1843: 74) has "*lagel*, making or weaving; spearing," and "*lakkin*, spearing; weaving". Taplin (1878: 17) also translates *lakkin*, as piercing to "make basket by piercing through and through as it is woven or sewn together". Thus there is some overlap in meaning but not sufficient to suppose that *lakkin* and *wakkin* is the same word. There may be a sound-symbolic connection where the "l" changes to "w" in certain meaning contexts or, the partial similarity in sound and meaning may be coincidental.

2. Within the Tindale collection there is a wealth of materials on various forms of baskets and fibres. I have begun the task of collating it and the file runs to some forty entries. Of interest to me are the distinct regional differences in materials and naming, the specialist items for men and women, and for particular tasks.

3. See Taplin (1873: 139-40, 141-2) *melapi*; (Berndt *et al.* 1993: 205) *mulapi*; Meyer (1843: 79) *melape*, devil, evil spirit, sorcery; Moriarty (1879: 51) *muldarpe*. The term *muldarpi* (*mularpi, mulapi*) is used differently by different peoples. I have heard it used interchangeably with *thumparmaldi* but the latter is a word that can endanger one's well being. Wyatt (1879: 167) says *dlarbe* could apply to the feared Adelaide natives.

4. Although missions dramatically altered the rules about not calling the names of the dead, I have noticed a number of Ngarrindjeri avoid using the names of the recently dead and simply use a kin term. See below note 17 and Chapter 4, note 10.

5. All references to the transcript of the Royal Commission (1995) are cited under the name of the person who is giving evidence or asking questions. I have also used this convention for the Select Committee on Aborigines (1860) and the Royal Commission on Aborigines (1913).

6. Chasing down these photographs, I am told that when the *Advertiser* took over the *News*, all the old records were destroyed. The quality of this copy is poor because it is an enhanced photocopy of the news clipping. I am grateful to Marian Thompson for tracking it down.

7. "Wurley" is a Kaurna word. The Ngarrindjeri word *ngawanthi* is still used by Margaret Jacobs; see Marj Koolmatrie and Lindsay Wilson in Hemming (1994a: 20).

8. Beckett (1993) explores the way in which one man, Walter Newton, negotiated the contradictions inherent in the colonial encounter and created a meaningful version of history from his knowledge of traditional stories, life experience and understanding of Christianity.

9. Giles and Everett (1992: 45-6) explain that a white missionary, Miss Gretta Matthews, who had learned the style from the Ngarrindjeri people, taught it to the Maung of Goulburn Island (N.T.) and from there the style migrated to Maningrida. See also Hamby (1995).

10. See Meyer (1843: 69) *kārute brŏke*, a basket made of two circular mats sewn

612

together; Tindale (nd, e) *pulatanguko*, a basket made from two circular mat-like pieces; *nakal*, sister basket (Tindale 1931-4: 85).

11. See Taplin (1879: 26). The Berndts (1993: 58ff.) call the *tendi "yanarum"*. This body took on a number of issues to do with sorcery and appeared to have the power of subpoena (*ibid.*). Tonkinson (1993: xxvii-xxviii) examines the claim that the Ngarrindjeri governance structure is unique in the context of Australia-wide debates regarding leadership, hierarchy and suggests we must allow for the impact of missions.

12. Under the *Aborigines Act Amendment Act* 1939, persons who were considered "white", because they had a non-Aboriginal parent, could be exempted from the operation of the Act. The exemption certificate stated that by reason of "character and standard of intelligence and development" they had "ceased to be an Aborigine for the purposes of the Act". Residents on missions were encouraged to gain exemptions, leave the mission and assimilate. Once exempted, people needed permission to visit relatives on the mission.

13. The Lower Murray Nungas Club was established in 1974 with funds made available by the Department of Education. It provided a centre for Aboriginal people in Murray Bridge and provided assistance with legal, health, welfare and education matters.

14. Further north in Antikirinja country, Ellis and Barwick (1989: 35) describe the regeneration of a song for young women and the respect shown by those present in not asking direct questions but waiting to be taught.

15. See Berndt *et al.* (1993: 314-5). This is the clan from which the head *Rupelli* of the inter-clan *tendi* was drawn. Sarah Milera is a descendant of Peter Pulami, often called the "last Rupelli" of the Manggurupa clan. Taplin (1879: 162) gives Pulami's clan as Rangulinyeri, but the Berndts insist this was a subsidiary of the Manggurupa clan which was "King Peter's clan" (Berndt *et al.* 1993: 513). In another place Ronald Berndt (1965: 178) suggests that this clan had not always been the dominant clan.

16. See Peter Sutton (1996a). I think the use of honorifics has been a way of incorporating outsiders, especially on missions where one was living with people one did not know and would not have known traditionally. It also is a way of dealing with the imposition of a system of naming which requires that each person has a unique name throughout their life and even after. Honorifics lessen the fear of sorcery with one's personal belongings, a name being one. It is my impression that kin terms are used on occasions where matters of tradition are being negotiated. In a similar vein, Marie Reay (1949: 44) remarks on the use of kin terms in rural New South Wales in times of crisis such as funerals.

17. Karloan describes the working of the fibre, including drying, twisting on the thigh and chewing (Berndt *et al.* 1993: 332).

18. With the introduction of the General Agreement on Tariffs and Trade (GATT) in 1993, the world's intellectual property rights (IPRs) regime

shifted from one in which different countries had different laws for protecting knowledge to the US patent system, which allows for patents on life forms. Indigenous knowledge (such as the medicinal properties of certain plants) can be "learnt" by researchers who can then isolate the active principle and patent it without any return to the people who have nurtured the knowledge over thousands of years. Transnational corporations may now "own" traditional knowledge. For a fuller treatment see Shiva (1997).

19. See Meyer (1843: 62, 74). *Warke laggel-in koyel*; the woman is making a basket. *Wark il lakk-in koye*; the woman is making (plaiting) a basket. From *warke* (woman), *laggel* (plaiting), *koyel* (basket). Taplin (1878: 17-18) chose *"lakkin"* as the paradigm of a native verb because it contained all the inflections of which he was aware.

20. Mason, then a corporal in the Police Force, was posted at Brinkley (Marrunggung) to keep the peace after the *Maria* incident of 1840. He was appointed sub-Protector in 1849 and, although he left the Police Force in 1856, he continued working with the people of the Lower Murray.

21. The dates are anything but sure. However, it is safe to say that there was one epidemic somewhere between 1814 and 1820 and another between 1829 and 1831 (Stirling 1911; Berndt, R. 1989: 64; Berndt *et al.* 1993: 292; Clarke 1994: 52-3). There was also a smallpox epidemic on the east coast which broke in 1789 out shortly after the establishment of the British penal colony at Sydney Cove.

22. On the four or so subsequent occasions when I have asked Daisy Rankine about this photograph, she has said she was ten. If the photograph was taken in 1943, she was seven. I have gone with seven, but I do wonder if perhaps the photograph was taken later.

23. The Berndts' papers, which were willed to the University of Western Australia are held under a thirty year embargo. In January 1997, under the provision of the Western Australian *Freedom of Information Act* 1992, eleven senior Ngarrindjeri sought access to materials which concerned their families and which they believed were contained within the collection. Their request was denied on the basis that everything was already in the book; that disclosure would be a breach of confidence and; that disclosure could reasonably prejudice future bequests to the Government or to an agency (Bapty 1997).

Chapter Two

1. See Hemming (1994b: 45-6). According to the catalogue (Hemming *et al.* 1989), the planning for the exhibit began in 1982 and entailed the active support of Ngarrindjeri communities and individuals, in particular Lola Sumner, Dick Koolmatrie, Henry and Jean Rankine, Doreen Kartinyeri, Marlene Stewart, George Trevorrow, Ronald Bonney, and Lola Cameron

Bonney. The account of *Ngurunderi's* travels, as narrated by Henry Rankine on the *Ngurunderi* video, was scripted by the South Australian Museum.

2. The Berndts offer different dates for Karloan's initiation. Catherine Berndt (1994b) says 1884 and in Berndt *et al.* (1993: 172) it is 1882. Tindale's (1930–52: 135-146) account of the initiation, recorded during a visit to Murray Bridge in 1938, gives details of the place, which is not Raukkan as the Berndts assume.

3. Under the *Aborigines Act* 1911, the Protector could allocate stock and land to his charges. Karloan applied in 1912 but got no response. His request for 150 pounds to purchase equipment so that he could travel with his son and present a show of songs and slides was dismissed as "ridiculous" by the Chief Protector (Berndt 1994b).

4. Clarke (1995b: 157) enumerates the different renditions of "*Ngurunderi*" in the literature: *Runderudie, Narrundi, Noorondourrie, Nar-oong-owie, Ooroondooil*. Accounts of this creative hero appear in Penney (1843); Meyer (1846); Moriarty (1879); Taplin (1859–79, 1873, 1879); Courto (1996); Laurie (1917); Smith (1930); Unaipon (1924-5, 1990); Tindale (1930–52, 1931-34, 1934–7); Tindale and Pretty (1980); Berndt (1940a); Berndt *et al.* (1993); Hemming (1994b).

5. See Foster's (1991) biographical sketch. Penney wrote under the pseudonym of Cuique in the local papers and the dates refer to the letters written under that name which accompanied each part of his epic five part poem, "Spirit of the Murray" published in the *South Australian Magazine*. In his letters Cuique writes that he discovered a bundle of papers including the manuscript near Port Malcolm in rubbish at an old settlement site. There is a certain irony in that the bundle was labelled "Secret Correspondence" (*ibid.*: 28).

6. Luebbers (1981) proposes a three-phase schema. The early settlement phase dates from around 6000 BP and relies on a single date of 5540 BP. The second, the intensive settlement phase, dating from 2350 BP to Colonial Contact, relies on his work at the Parnka site. During the third period, 1820 to the 1940s, some occupation of prehistoric sites continued and newer camp sites, reflecting new economic conditions, emerged.

7. Further entrenchment occurs when Dreamtime stories become part of the school curriculum. The South Australian Education Department (1990: 50-3) features the *Ngurunderi* story in its Aboriginal Studies course for year 8-12.

8. See also the cross-examination of Philip Clarke by Stephen Kenny (1995: 3744-8).

9. Laurie (1917: 660-2) casts *Ngurunderi* as a mighty hunter who was angered that all the animals had escaped. He caught the mammoth animals and tore them into pieces and now there are only small emu, kangaroo, turkey and so on.

10. This mission and the one in Adelaide run by fellow Lutherans C. W. Schürmann and C. G. Teichelmann were closed after failing to reach agreement with Governor Robe who insisted that all missions should work to convert

Aborigines to the Church of England (Jenkin 1979: 43-6, 81; Department of Education 1990: 120-22; Mattingley and Hampton 1988: 100, 175).

11. See Taplin (1864a, b) and his Journal entries of (23/4/1862, 29/10/67; 6/2/1865); Jenkin (1979: 106-8).

12. A driving force behind the Select Committee of 1860 was a complaint of local landowner, John Baker, who saw his territorial interests threatened by the mission (Jenkin 1979: 83ff.; Mattingley and Hampton 1988: 183).

13. These arguments are popular with certain organisations, politicians and individuals who promote the idea that to be treated equally one must treat everyone the same. However, it is necessary to distinguish between equality and equity. If people are unlike, then to treat them the same is unjust. A person in a wheelchair is not the same as an able-bodied person when it comes to accessing buildings with stairs. To treat them as the same would not be an exercise in equality. Native title is part of the common law of the land. The rights Indigenous peoples may enjoy will flow from that fact, are not matters of special consideration.

14. See Schwab (1986) whose interview with Veronica Brodie sparked some of the memories recorded in this section.

15. I am playing off the title of Elkin's (1977) book, *Aboriginal Men of High Degree*.

16. There is a considerable and growing body of literature about David Unaipon. See Beston (1979); Jones (1989, 1993). Stephen Muecke and Adam Shoemaker are collaborating with Harold "Kim Kropinyeri" to publish a collected works of David Unaipon writing.

17. Unaipon was reported to have said of the pile of typewritten documents on which he was working, "An idle man does not produce work such as that." (Jones 1989: 11).

18. Ellis (1962-6 (2): 27) provides details of a session with David Unaipon at Adelaide University on 20 June 1963 when Mr Strehlow did most of the interviewing. In assessing Unaipon's assertion that there are no others besides Clarence Long who know any songs, she notes it must be remembered that (a) he is not liked by the local Aborigines; (b) he does not even know that those are Aborigines at Kingston; (c) he was away from home for twenty-six years doing lay preaching in Victoria, New South Wales, and Tasmania. This may well be so. There are many instances of people distrusting those who have been to other communities and who have read the records of early observers in the Lower Murray region. Today his knowledge is respected and he is referred to as *Maiyanu* (grandfather) David. Tindale (1930–52: 317-8) writes of Unaipon paying five shillings for each story and being told "lies" by young men.

19. James Ngunaitponi was converted by the Rev. Reid and became an evangelist amongst his people along with William Kropinyeri, Peter Gollan, Allan Jomblyn and later John Sumner, George Koolmatrie, Peter Campbell and William McHughes (Unaipon 1953: 7).

616

20. In late 1995 Steven Hemming, at the South Australian Museum, researched and helped prepare the displays for the launching at Tandanya of the $50 note, which celebrates Unaipon's achievements. The display included a piece of Unaipon's perpetual motion machine on loan from the family, and panels, which included the genealogy now at Murray Bridge.

21. Milerum (Clarence Long) had introduced Tindale to Reuben Walker and, on the several occasions they worked together, Tindale found him extremely helpful. After a visit 21–22 April 1934, obviously stimulated by the meeting and questions, Reuben Walker (1934) wrote a forty-page manuscript and three-page vocabulary, which Mark Wilson typed up on a rather disabled typewriter from the pencilled draft, and forwarded it to Tindale through the Rev. J. C. Jennison.

22. Veronica Brodie (1995: 6283-4) read one of her sister's poems to the Royal Commission. It was put to her that Christobel Mattingley had written the poems. This she emphatically denied (*ibid.*: 6508).

23. Meyer (1843) recorded what is now usually known as Ramindjeri (from the place name Ramong and *indjeri*, belonging to). Taplin (1873) was the first to offer a group name, "Narrinyeri", for the people of the Lower Murray. He understood the word to be an abbreviation of *Kornarrinyeri* (from *kornar*, men, and *inyeri*, belonging to) and to the encompass the eighteen *lakalinyerar*. These he understood to be tribes/clans, the members of whom shared a *ngatji* (totem) and were blood family (*ibid.*). Others, Taplin (1879: 34) noted, regard the word Narrinyeri as derived from "*narr*" plain, intelligible (referring to language). Clarke (1991: 94) views Taplin's use of "Narrinyeri" as a "reinvention of tradition". Tindale and Long (nd: 6) state Narinjeri is not "a valid tribal term".

24. In her MA thesis McDonald (1977) draws together the data on the languages up the Murray River, across to Adelaide in the west and into Gippsland (Victoria) in the east. She finds a degree of relationship amongst those extending up river, a relationship supported by the *Ngurunderi* story of migration. Ngarrindjeri have some possibility of communication with Cape Jervis Kaurna but not the Adelaide Kaurna. Ngarrindjeri may be "considered originally to have been a language of the Upper Murray not the Murray Mouth and contact with languages of the Gippsland area might have occurred over a long period before migration" McDonald (*ibid.*: 10).

25. See Taplin (1879: 34-6); Berndt *et al.* (1993: 58ff.). See Chapter 1, note 13.

26. These "loaves" which Reuben Walker (1934) says were four inches by twelve to eighteen inches, were kneaded and hammered into a solid block.

27. I have heard "Nunga" used by people in and around Adelaide and in Ngarrindjeri lands when people wish to signal that they are Aboriginal, generally in contra-distinction to being a whitefella, but when being more specific about their identity, people will say "Ngarrindjeri", or "Kaurna" (see Clarke 1994: 89-92).

Notes

1. As a girl Margaret "Pinkie" Mack was known by the name Karpeny (from the husband of her mother Louisa) and although she married again, she kept the name Mack, which came from her first husband, John Mack, whose country was up river.

2. This photograph, published in the *Advertiser* (12/2/1951), was said to have been taken on Saturday at Goolwa (except that on Saturday the party was on Hindmarsh Island). It appears to be in the evening, so I think the location is correct and the day incorrect.

3. Locating the originals of the above photographs involved a great deal of time and effort from a number of people. It is not completely clear who took these photographs. Doreen Kartinyeri told me she thought she had taken them with her "little camera". Lola Sumner gave the photographs to Steven Hemming to copy and they were then filed in the South Australian Museum. I first became aware of them in a publication by Bonita Ely (1980), where they are dated 1930. I could see Big Bert Wilson is in the photograph so I knew they were from 1951 and that was quickly confirmed by Bert's siblings Veronica Brodie and Doug Wilson.

4. I thank Robert Foster for telling Deane Fergie who told me of a reference he had found to the ABC Report (1951) and I thank Renate Klein for locating the ABC Archive Director, John Spence, who also deserves thanks for the prompt and efficient way he located the tape and dispatched it to me. Technology has considerably extended the reach of our fieldwork.

5. See Angas (1847: 66) Milendura; Taplin (1879: 34n) Milmenru:ru, Milenjeriorn, Milmenroora; Tindale (nd, e) Milmenyeriarn.

6. I would be most grateful to learn of any such records or to hear from people who were present and might be able to identify those present. The ABC sound archives do not appear to contain any further recordings of the ceremony, but access is restricted to in-house research for programming. The Commonwealth Film Unit is mentioned in the Sturt Report of 10 February, so there may be footage in their archives. There may also be personal recordings that have survived.

7. Pitjantjatjara songs, Tunstill (1995: 59-67) demonstrates, may contain words from auxiliary languages, archaic forms and even English. One effect is to mask the lexical meanings and focus attention on the enjoyment of the music. This leaves the power to teach and the authority to interpret with the song experts, while not excluding participation of those present who may join in the exclamations of appreciation, beat the rhythm, and dance. Marie Reay (1949: 96) reports that in New South Wales, women may croon songs (which are remembered from young women's ceremonies) to their children who are not told the exact meaning of the words.

8. Ellis (1962–6 (2): 31) noted that Mike Gollan recognised one of Milerum's

618

songs and knew that it was a Tangankald death fear song but said that he didn't know anyone except Milerum who knew the song.

9. See Hemming (1997a). These meanings have been pieced together by Hemming from a number of conversations and tape recordings including those with Flora Kropinyeri (Hemming 1984) and Annie Koolmatrie (Hemming 1988). I am grateful to him for the many discussions we have had about his song and for his willingness to locate interview and song materials.

10. These tapes were transcribed with the assistance of Barry Alpher.

11. Harvey (1939); Taplin (1879: 12) translates "basket" as *koyi*; McDonald (1977: 122) *koy*; Berndt *et al.* (1993: 563-4) have *koia* as a basket for mussells and a *koia* for yabbies.

12. *Nurlu* is a genre of public dance from the Western Kimberleys. The texts are received in a dream where the dreamer is taken on a spirit journey accompanied by the spirit of deceased kin *balangan* and/or conception spirits know as *ray* (Keogh 1996: 39).

13. In December 1932, Tindale transcribed two Yaraldi and seventeen Tangani songs, sixteen of which were later recorded on an Edison wax cylinder in November 1937 and January 1938.

14. Tindale (1930–52: 55-6) described Pinkie Mack as "a half-caste woman about whom I have heard . . . she knows more songs than any other Jaralde."

15. See Meyer (1843: 98) *tartengk*; Taplin (1879: 126) *plangge* native drum of tightly rolled skins beaten by hand as it lies on the ground and *tartengk* sticks beaten together; Campbell (1934: 30-1) notes women singing and beating rolled-up possum skins and dancing in the shake-leg style; Berndt (1993: 334) mention women playing drums and singing.

16. The Berndts (1993: 214-7) recorded four Pekeri, or "dream" songs which differed in content from the two recorded by Tindale (1937); see Meyer (1843: 102) *tuñgari* song; Tindale (1937: 102) *tungari*.

17. In Chapter 14, "Ceremony and Song, the Berndts (1993: 210-222) reiterate that the categories and distinctions they are making are by no means hard and fast; see also Ellis (1967: 12).

18. Similarly, for the Adelaide region, Teichelmann and Schürmann (1840: 34) list *Nguyapalti*, as learnt from eastern tribes, the singing of which prevented or stopped the spread of smallpox.

19. The Berndts (1993: 216, 218, 582; 1951: 89) offer two translations of this lament. They identify Maggie Pool (née Karpeny) as the composer of the song which addressed the 1880s move off clan territory onto the mission and other places.

20. See Amery *et al.* (1990) for a sampling of songs being sung and composed around different themes, in different styles, in English, Ngarrindjeri and mixes thereof.

21. Donaldson (1995) sees the timing of the assaults on language and ceremonial life as explanation for the lack of an English corroboree. Had ceremony

survived the loss of language, then some may have been composed in English.

22. See Marj Koolmatrie (Hemming 1994a: 13) who says: "The visitors used to come across to the school to hear the children singing in the school and look at the Aboriginal work, but at that time in the 40s they thought we was monkeys—even in the 40s, and how we used to sing."

23. In this section I am drawing on interview material with Leila Rankine (Breen 1989) which has been read to her younger sister Veronica Brodie for permission to cite.

24. This version is from Ely (1980). See also Amery *et al.* (1990) where a chorus has been added in Ngarrindjeri and the song retitled "Kurangk *Tungari*".

25. It is sung by Jeanette Wormaldi. Dorothy Shaw, Belinda Stillisano, and Glenys Wilson sing the chorus in Ngarrindjeri.

26. Marett *et al.* (1997: 5, 6) write of Bobby Lane (1941–1993) of Cox Peninsula (Northern Territory.) who mentions songs as "given".

27. This event was promoted as "A Journey for Peace; A Journey for Protest; A Journey for Knowledge", beginning 25 November in Adelaide and ending at Goolwa, 30 November 1996.

Chapter Four

1. Betty Fisher, an amateur historian who had worked closely with Gladys Elphick, a highly respected Narunga woman, had also recorded Koomi. Fisher came forward with the tapes and her notes of conversations about Koomi's knowledge of Hindmarsh Island and the Seven Sisters Dreaming.

2. *Wururi* was *ngatji* for the Retjurindjeri clan (Berndt *et al.* 1993: 308), a Yaraldi clan whose territory was just east of Raukkan. It was also *ngatji* for Tatjarapa, meaning "hill that is now broke up" which according to the Berndts (*ibid.*: 309) is Tangani but according to Radcliffe-Brown (1918) is Yaraldi. Of course, it could be shared territory. Both agree it is located on the southeast of Lake Albert.

3. See Taplin (1873: 53); Berndt *et al.* (1993: 41). The term *ngatji* is the basis of the kin term for father and mother's father in a number of Aboriginal languages (Alpher pers. comm. 1998).

4. See Berndt *et al.* (1993: 521). Taplin's regime required that converts have only one wife and William Kropinyeri, who had two, "chose" to stay with the wife by whom he already had children. The younger wife was returned to her family who were offended and were required to exact retribution. The father of William Kropinyeri was "*millined*", i.e. killed by sorcery (Kartinyeri 1996: pers. comm.).

5. Tindale (nd, f) has an untitled chart where he has correlated the various sources (see also Radcliffe-Brown 1918; Clarke 1994: 79-80). The Berndts (1993: 306-312) provide details of clan, *ngatji* and site affiliations along with genealogies

and also refer back to the earlier sources.

6. Radcliffe-Brown (1918) provides the most formal account of local and social organisation in the early literature. For him "clan" was synonymous with "horde". The former included persons related in one line (*ibid.*: 232); the latter could include land owning, co-residential and patrilineal descent groups. Both Tindale (1974) and the Berndts (1993) acknowledge that there are a number of ways in which clans were inter-related. Tonkinson (1993: xxvi) suggests that the Ngarrindjeri material may be read as evidence of the patriclan or as evidence of more flexible organisation.

7. See Radcliffe-Brown (1918: 232); Berndt *et al.* (1993: 27-30). Men who went through initiation together and married into the same clan were called "*wiruki*" (*werekend*) and neighbours with no kinship ties were *tauwali* (Tindale 1934-7: 7, 15, 13, 23, 29, 154).

8. During the gold rushes of the 1850s, the Chinese landed at Port Adelaide to avoid paying a poll tax in Melbourne and travelled overland to the gold fields. This story was told at one of the many wells sunk to accommodate the travellers. These wells tended to be on or near Aboriginal camping places and were places where people gathered, worked and stayed in touch with their country.

9. See Amery *et al.* (1990), songs 22 and 26. "*Mrildun* is about a parent longing for a child who has been taken away.

10. See Berndt *et al.* (1993: 274); Wyatt (1879: 163, 165); Reuben Walker (1934: 214). Taplin (15/11/1859) understood that names were taboo lest grief should be awakened and they should cut themselves but Taplin (7/10/1865) considered dead names a "nuisance and I shall treat it as such". Clarke (1994: 24) says that the name becomes taboo immediately after the church service on the day of the funeral.

11. The Berndts (1993: 511) state the genealogies are in the book for the purposes of interrelations, that there are bound to be inaccuracies; that they are from Karloan's perspective; and have not been correlated with the Point McLeay records. These reservations have not stopped others from treating the material as a superior record to what can be learned from actual people. Doreen Kartinyeri's material was available but is not cited by the Berndts. Tindale's material could have been of great assistance, especially at the upper generation levels.

12. Elsewhere (Bell 1985) I have glossed these family groups "contextualised cognatic groups": "contextualised" because which level will be invoked and when depends on the situation; "cognatic" because descent may be traced through either the father, mother or more often mother's father, but sometimes mother's mother (for the Ngarrindjeri I would add father's father's mother and mother's mother's mother); and a "descent group" because blood lines are important.

Notes

Chapter Five

1. See Meyer (1843: 97) *ruwe* as "land, country, birthplace"; Wyatt (1879: 175) *reerwe* as earth; Taplin (1879: 132) land as *ruwe*; and Tindale (1931–4: 156) *kuruwi* as ground.

2. In explaining male initiation, Karloan uses *ruwar* for the "body" of the initiate (Berndt *et al.* 1993: 381); *ruwuran* as "body" in the context of a healing and a *ngatji* messenger (*ibid.*: 417); *ruwalan* as the nerves of the body *ruwa* (*ibid.*: 422).

3. Barry Alpher (pers. comm. 1998) writes: For purposes of consistency and brevity (especially in tables), I take the noun plural marker as -ar (often written "a"; the difference is not material to the arguments below), with the nature of the final r probably a light alveolar flap (which is difficult to hear, in Yir-Yoront, a language, of Cape York Peninsula intonation-finally), since (i) Meyer always transcribes it "ar"; (ii) "r" is (very) occasionally written in Berndt *et al.* (1993), usually when a vowel follows (I assume they were overcompensating a tendency to use a vowel letter plus "r" to indicate a long vowel, hence omitting postvocalic "r" at times when it should have been retained); (iii) The Berndts were taking transcription without the benefit of sound recording instruments, and hence many words would have been repeated to them out of context with final (falling) intonation; and (iv) within the word, as in "ruwuran" ruw-ar-an "[I feel] my body" (*ibid.*: Appendix 4: 82), Meyer (1843: 51). The Berndts always write "r" where it is expected. Of possible relevance to the arguments below is that there appears to be more to the marking of singular, dual, and plural than the sources make explicit. There appears, for one thing, to be a connection between singular (and sometimes nonsingular) marking and definiteness. These questions await more detailed investigation.

   (1) Land. In the meaning 'land', *ruw* takes the same morphology as other ordinary nouns, such as *ba:m* 'girl', *ko:n* 'man', *kur* 'river, neck, voice': 'girl' 'man' 'river' 'land': singular– *ba:m-i, ko:n-i, kur-i, ruw-i*. (Berndt *et al.* 1993: Appendix 4: 97, 4: 104); plural– *ba:m-a(r), ko:n-ar, kur-ar, uw-ar* (*ibid.*: 87); singular, 'to, on, at', *ko:nangk, kur-angk* (*ibid.*: 12,14), *ruw-angk* (*ibid.*: 20, 32): singular– 'onto, into, up to' *ko:nald* (*ibid.*: 2), *kur-ald, ruw-ald* (*ibid.*: 125) etc.

   (2) Body. In the meaning 'body', the form *ruwar* occurs at times with singular reference and at times with plural reference; it is in all occurrences identical in sound with the plural of 'land'. The singular form *ruwi* (also spelt *ruwe*) occurs only with the meaning 'land' (note that a cognate form *ruwe* 'land', with initial flapped "r", occurs in the Dardidardi language of the Murray–Lachlan junction area). There appears to be no phonological reason to reject a hypothesis that the root *ruw* is the basis of both 'land' and 'body'.

   (3) What is the association in meaning?

   (i) The Berndts (*ibid.*: 26) implicitly derive *ruwa* 'body' from *ruwi* 'land' on the strength of Karloan's (the narrator's) assertion that blood (the mother's) and semen combine to make the child. The apparent suggestion is that, since the two parents come from ('are', in other Aboriginal languages) two different countries, the child's body is a combination of both. So far, the suggestion seems plausible. It might be objected however that Ngarrindjeri nouns can be marked for dual number as well as singular and plural (*ruwengk* 'two countries') and that two would be the logical number to choose. Against this objection: (a) it could be held that the plurality of lands represents all the child's ancestry, including that at grandparental and higher levels; (b) although the (prototypical, generic) child spoken of in this text is singular (*poli*), it is not only the child's body but also its blood (*kruwua*) and flesh (*ngolda*, also written *ngalda*) that are spoken of in the plural (as well as, of course the bones, *patpata*). 'Blood' seems elsewhere in these texts to be spoken of in the plural only when discrete quantities are meant (as when a sorcerer removes it by mouthfuls); 'flesh' is almost everywhere plural (*ngolda*, which can also mean 'complete' [*ibid.*: 155]) regardless of sense, although there are some attestations in the singular (*ngoldi*, *ibid.*: 130) a few times. On the assumption that there is no problem with mixed-up transcriptions (*ngold*, *ngald*), the usage of *ngold* in the plural for 'flesh', together with its sense 'complete', lends weight to the *ruwar* 'body:land' connection.

(ii) It could also be argued that the land:body metaphor is appropriate because in many Aboriginal languages the land is spoken of in terms mapped from human body-part words: in Yir Yoront the land's 'belly' is a swamp, its 'throat' a creek, its 'shoulder' or 'chest' the surface, its 'ear' a site, and so on. Also, in Yir Yoront, the extensions of 'land, place' include things like 'time', 'day', and 'state of mind': general notions of things in human consciousness. Counter arguments to this are that (a) many concrete objects are so mapped, as with the 'belly' (inside), 'head' (roof), and 'eyes' (windows) of a house and the 'nose' and 'cheek' of a spearthrower, (b) the logic suggests that the land should be spoken of as 'bodies' and not the other way around, and (c) as widely extended as the 'place' word is in Yir Yoront semantics, 'body' is not one of its senses.

(4) *Rupelli*. The term *rupulli* (Taplin 1879: 35) is glossed 'chief' or 'landholder'. The gloss 'landholder' suggests a connection with *ruw* 'land'. However, although there is a phonological connection of p and w in Ngarrindjeri (as in many Aboriginal languages)—compare the two halves of the reduplicated form *thupathuw* (<*thupthuw* <*thupthup*) 'sky, cloud'—the lenition (softening) of p to w in Ngarrindjeri seems to occur only at the end of syllables after the first (unstressed syllables). There are, therefore, objections on phonological grounds to relating the *rup* of *rupulli* to the *ruw* of 'land; body'. *Rupeli* is a frightener of disobedient children in (Berndt *et al.* 1993; Appendix 4: 92). The same phonologically grounded objections apply, and there is in addition no apparent semantic resemblance.

4. In their book, *The Speaking Land* (1988: 17) published before *The World That Was* (1993) but most probably written after, the Berndts are even more literal

in their reading of the land as body: "Ngurunderi, who at the beginning, stretched out his body, spiritually, along the lower River Murray in South Australia, with one leg extending along the Coorong and the other along Encounter Bay".

5. Neighbouring, but unrelated languages have similar imprintings. For example in Kaurna, Mount Lofty is called by the word for ears (Black 1920: 82; Teichelmann and Schürmann 1840: 76; Wyatt 1879: 161).

6. One of the difficulties with the sources is that it is not possible to say with any certainly which of the three "r" sounds (a glide, a tap or a rolled one) is being represented by the symbol "r" in these early vocabularies. Meyer (1843: 73) translates *kuri* as river, neck, and voice. Tindale (1938–56: 24) writes: "From Milerum I know that [kurangk] was the name of the 'narrow place' at the northern end of the long Coorong lagoon".

7. For example, there are several suggested derivations for Jaraldikald (Yaraldi) in the literature: Tindale (1974: 212) "Jarawalangan?", Where shall we go?" and David Unaipon (Treagus 1996) from *yare* as meaning "back". However, Unaipon rolls his "r" in *yare*, so maybe they are two different words.

8. See Clarke (1994: 114-5, 1996: 145), Hemming (1996b: 32 n 28) and Jones (1995: 4419-4426) regarding exchanges in the Royal Commission over the nature of gendered landscapes. There are a number of versions of the *Ngurunderi* story and in some, women have a greater role than others. There are sites which are the result of female agency and sites where women's bodies are memorialised. There are places where *Ngurunderi's* body is visible in the landscape but it cannot be said that the entire land is "feminine" or "masculine".

9. I remember those wall maps and their vivid colours from my own days of teaching in Victorian Primary schools in the 1960s and I have spent some time trying to find one of South Australia in the Map section of the State Library, the Education Department of South Australia and through antique map dealers without success. Maybe someone reading this book has one.

10. Luebbers (1996) notes that the large network of Ngarrindjeri weirs constructed in the inland swamp for small fish was recorded by the Surveyor General G. W. Goyder in 1860. There were also burials which Lola and Ron Cameron discussed with Luebbers.

11. Tindale (1941: 6) glosses *narambe*, as set aside, or sacred; Taplin (1873: 15-18) describes the initiation rites of males in their "*narumbe*" state and emphasises the prohibitions and restrictions that apply; Walker (1934: 206) highlights the associated taboos; the Berndts (1993: 140) understand that women are also *narambi*.

12. See also Taplin (1879: 40); Berndt *et al.* (1993: 127, 156); Tindale and Long (nd: 4) write of the chestnut teal, which was totally prohibited to red-ochred youths. The bird was the *ngatji* of a man who lived alone on his clan territory on the south shore of Lake Albert, just five miles from an initiation place where Tangani and Yaraldi gathered.

13. Veronica Brodie (1995: 6268-9) related a story she had heard at a meeting of the Friends of Kumarangk concerning a taxi driver who had taken bones from the island and had joked in the pub about possibly raffling them.

14. Smith (1924: 198); Angas (1847: 60, 94); Luebbers (1981, 1982); Stirling (1911: 11); Taplin (1897: 42). Reuben Walker (1934) wrote of placing the head on an ant hill so that it might be cleaned up to make drinking dishes or vessels.

15. A long-time resident of Hindmarsh Island, Maurice Newell reported numerous human skeletons, mostly in a folded-up position (McCourt and Mincham 1987: 148). The quickness with which bones are said to be smallpox victims needs to be read with caution.

16. Meyer (1843: 57) provides notes on four modes of burial for the neighbourhood of Encounter Bay. "Old persons are buried. The middle-aged are placed in a tree, the hands and knees being brought nearly to the chin, all openings of the body—mouth, nose and ears, etc—being sewn up and the corpse covered with mats, pieces of net or old clothing. The corpse being placed in a tree, a fire is made underneath around which friends and relations of the deceased sit and make lamentation. In this situation the body remains unless removed by some hostile tribe, until the flesh is completely washed away, after which the skull is taken to the nearest relation for a drinking vessel. The third mode is to place the corpse in a sitting posture, without any covering, the face turned towards the east, until dried by the sun, after which it is placed in a tree. This plan is adopted with those to whom they wish to show their respect. The last mode is to burn the body, which is practiced only in the case of still-born children, or those which die shortly after birth."

Chapter Six

1. See Dawson (1881); Smyth (1878); Bell (1993a: 12-3); Amery *et al.* (1990). The Willie wagtail, *Rhipidura leucophrys* likes human company and makes incessant movements (Wade 1975: 22-3).

2. But note, Unaipon (1990: 28) *Rich er Rookitty*; Bonney (1990: 21) *Ritch-a-Rookery*; Tindale (nd, g) *teriteritj* for Meintangk,

3. See Chapter 1, note 3.

4. See Wade (1975: 108;) Whitelock (1985: 48-9); Nance and Spleight (1986: 70-1); Blakers (1984: 144); Reader's Digest (1986: 194).

5. Meyer's (1846) account of the coming into being of the whale is substantially the same as that of Elymann (Courto 1996: 290) and the Berndts (1993: 235-6). Tindale (1930–52: 272; 1931-3: 252-3; 1934-7: 181-4) recorded versions from Albert Karloan; Frank Blackmore, and Milerum (Tindale and Long nd: 3). As with the *Ngurunderi* story there are regional variations and different emphases which I have not explored here.

6. These were arranged, formal unions symbolised by the fire stick which was carried by the young woman to her husband's camp (Unaipon 1924–5; Berndt *et al.* 1993: 35-7; Walker 1934: 205).

7. Karaigatatami (Tindale 1931–4: 169, 250; nd, e) slippers were used in secret killings (like the "*kurdaitja* shoes" of central Australia).

8. There is an extensive literature on *millin* but not all the materials in these sources are "open" and indeed some of considered dangerous. They are however in the public domain and the reader may consult them. The structure of beliefs they set out is substantially that described by the women in the texts included in this chapter. See Meyer (1846); Taplin (1873: 26-9); Angas (1847: 96); Walker (1934: 201); Moriarty (1879: 51-2); Berndt *et al.* (1993).

9. See Berndt *et al.* (1993: 463-4). This form of travel was one way of visiting the dead, strengthening one's *miwi*, and learning new stories and songs.

10. Taplin (4/7/1869) noticed that children did not like having their faces washed or hair combed but he put these behaviours down to superstition and treated the matters as ones of personal hygiene.

11. It's not clear if this is sixteen years before the journal entry, i.e. 1857 and thus before Taplin's arrival or sixteen years before the publication of the book and thus 1863. The Berndts (1993: 263-4) mention that Pinkie Mack emphasised the fat removal was a practice more prevalent amongst the people up-river (i.e. her husband's people).

12. Taplin (15/11/1861) wrote of the belief that by wearing a plaited hair band around one's head, one's sense of smell and sight were improved, and one could thereby better avoid harm; see also Berndt *et al.* (1993: 253, 258).

13. See Taplin (17–18/8/1859; 2/4/1862); Berndt and Berndt (1993: 253-8).

14. Vivienne Courto (1996) provided me with a disc copy of her translations in November 1996.

PART TWO
Chapter Seven

1. Taplin's journals contain a number of stories regarding the need for caution. The Rev. James Reid, for example, ignored his counsel and drowned (Taplin 24/7/1863).

2. Often I am dealing with material which is hard to check and if I have made mistakes or missed a reference, I'd be grateful to know. There are some papers I have not been able to access. I asked Philip Clarke for copies of several unpublished papers of his which I had seen mentioned in Jane Simpson's (1996) bibliography. He declined to share his papers with me although they had been made available to other colleagues.

3. There are sections of the transcript of the Royal Commission which are permanently suppressed and which concern testimony central to questions

regarding "women's business". So it is not entirely true that by reading what is in the public domain I can follow how the women were questioned and hear all the women had to say.

Chapter Eight

1. In her footnotes Stevens (1995: 47) cites Exhibits Numbers 3 and 4 but nowhere in her report in there a listing of the exhibits. Thus without access to other sources, one cannot know who is the source of this information. The arguments of several commentators like Brunton (1996a: 9) and Tonkinson (1997) rely on there being an extensive written record.
2. In a particularly helpful review of the debates concerning the "invention of tradition", Charles Briggs (1996) identifies key players, their interests, and their economic and political power. One area that requires further analysis is the perceived danger certain postmodern critiques, including the "invention of tradition", represent for Indigenous peoples.
3. A number of scholars are engaged in rethinking contemporary religious practice and beliefs across Australia and moving beyond the models of the "old" and the "new" to more nuanced understandings: see Swain and Rose (1988); Pattel-Gray and Trompf (1993); Maddox (1997, 1998).
4. An interesting exercise is to compare the narrative in Mead (1995) with that of Stevens (1995) and Chris Kenny (1996).
5. In the *Other Side of the Frontier*, Reynolds (1981) explored the meaning of contact for Aborigines and demonstrated that, contrary to the received wisdom of mainstream history, it was not too late to do so. There were still oral histories to be tapped and in the records of anthropologists, administrators, missionaries and local settlers, the voices of Aborigines are sometimes heard. However, Reynolds pays no particular attention to the frontier as gendered. In "An accidental Australian tourist" (Bell 1994a), I set out what a gendered analysis might look like for the period 1600–1800.
6. There are many accounts of the incident: see Hastings (1944); Taplin (1873); Jenkin (1979); Tindale (1937-41: 31); Angas (1847: 66); Woods (1879: xxii).
7. Unlike Mason (1860: 2276) at Wellington, who thought it an "innocent amusement", Taplin was much opposed to this practice and the Select Committee of 1860 feared this conflict in values might undermine the authority of Europeans.
8. See Taplin (1879: 1-3) for the questions: numbers 1–12 concern kinship, marriage and social structure; questions 13–15 governance and property; 16–17, 19.24, 28, 44–48 beliefs and practices; 25–6 material culture; 29–43 language.
9. The materials with which I was working had only recently been returned to Australia. When Tindale settled in the USA, he took much of his primary

research material with him and some copies remained locked in the museum. Amongst other things he was working on the "World of Milerum" (Tindale and Long nd). After Tindale died Philip Jones went to California in order to organise the return of the collection to Adelaide. Part was shipped by air and part by sea. The papers are currently housed in the Anthropology Archives of the South Australian Museum where they await the attention of a qualified curator.

It took the Museum from October 1997 to February 1998 and numerous reminders from me to obtain answers to my question regarding when the materials arrived and when they were available to researchers. Philip Jones tells me that the airmail component arrived in February and the materials were available as soon as they were unpacked, a few weeks later (pers. comm. 27/2/1998). The sea-freight component arrived during June 1994. This shipment contained the "World of Milerum" which, because it was considered to contain material already available in the journals sent by airmail, was not opened until questions were raised regarding its potential value during the Royal Commission (see Clarke 1996; Hemming 1997b). It was then unpacked, Jones supposes, in September/October 1995. The "World of Milerum" does comprise cullings from Tindale's journals, and map notations and so on, but I also found that there was information in the folders which went beyond the journal entries which Tindale had cross-referenced and that there were new syntheses and interpretations being put forward.

10. Kaldor (1988) represents this as a joint decision which allowed Catherine Berndt to pursue her research. The Tonkinsons (1994) say "like many of her female contemporaries Catherine never held a tenured full-time position." The fact that at the University of Western Australia, married couples could not work in the same department is to me a significant factor. Her part-time position may have been a matter of "choice" but it was a constrained one.

11. The Berndts (1982: 51) wrote: "We eventually revised and shortened [the manuscript] and gave it a more publicly acceptable title, *From Black to White*, but in another place he states the book was originally entitled "This Way to Freedom" but the publishers preferred the other title (R. Berndt 1989: 67). In their obituary for Catherine Berndt, Bob and Myrna Tonkinson (1994) write that it was a title that she "could never abide".

12. Australian Archives (Series No C123, Item number 16553). Box 89 of the Security Service Dossier concerning Ronald Berndt.

13. In response to Steven Hemming's (1996: 35) critique of his elevation of missionaries such as Taplin and Meyer to the status of ethnographers, and unbiased ones at that, Clarke (1996: 143) refers to his evidence (Clarke 1995a: 323) and thesis (1994: 64) where he asserts he stated that the early data "today is quite useful for reanalysis". Footnotes to the Royal Commission (1995) are often difficult to get to check because Stevens (1995) provides inadequate information. However, this exchange between Hemming (1996b, 1997b) and

Clarke (1996) can be cross-checked with Clarke's (1994: 64) thesis and he does not mention the usefulness of the sources "for reanalysis". Those words are in the transcript.

14. See Bell (1993b) where I outline feminist standpoint theory as a basis for feminist ethnography which takes women's lives as it starting point.

15. Tindale's (nd, b) file sheet on Pinkie Mack runs to one page whereas that on Milerum has five handwritten pages of references and notes. Tindale gives Pinkie Mack's clan as Peltindjeri, and her *ngatji* catfish from her sociological father and says that she is *ngiampe* to Milerum.

16. The fieldwork for *From Black to White*, which took the Berndts (1951) to the Musgrave and Everard Ranges in the northwest of the state, the mission at Ernabella, the town of Oodnadatta, the Lower Murray region and to Adelaide "was carried out chiefly between 1941–1944" (*ibid.*: 20). In this period they also managed to conduct an essay survey in Port Augusta, Quorn, Marie and Goolwa (*ibid.*: 226), spend June–December of 1941 at Ooldea and write "A Preliminary Report of Fieldwork in the Ooldea Region, Western South Australia" (1942–5). The latter is 341 pages long and contains extensive interlinear translations. Given all the other activities by which they were engaged, when was the Preliminary Report written? The first seventy pages at least must have been written before or during their 1942 Lower Murray trip; the section concerning "Women's Life" before or during their 1943 stint.

17. In an email to Deane Fergie, John Stanton (8/2/1996) states that "the original draft Ms, in two volumes, was written by Prof . . . the remainder of the book was written in the late 1980s from original field notes jointly by both Prof and Catherine and incorporated her material, particularly Pinkie Mack's side of things, including her songs of which she was a specialist."

18. See Berndt (1950; 1963; 1965; 1970; 1973; 1979; 1981; 1983; 1989). Tracing the way in which Catherine Berndt positioned herself as woman, but as one who had little time for feminist theory, would be an interesting project. Later.

19. Tom Trevorrow's attempt to have the findings of the Royal Commission set aside failed in Federal Court in July 1996 as did his appeal to the High Court in April 1997. Trevorrow argued he was denied natural justice because he was not permitted to know the substance of comments by, nor conduct a cross examination of, anthropologist Robert Tonkinson, who advised Justice Stevens in the Royal Commission inquiry. While the courts have required that the applicants disclose their restricted material in order to enjoy the protection that the law might afford their sacred places, the legal system has not furnished the applicants with all that they seek.

Notes

Chapter Nine

1. See for example Tindale (1974: 80-1; 1938–56: 27); Berndt (1993: 116-121).
2. Like Taplin, Mrs Smith's (1880: 5) language needs to be read in the context of the times in which she was writing, but unlike Taplin, she had first hand knowledge of women's practices for the Boandick of neighbouring Victoria. "The custom of the women is to retire to some pleasant part of the country to be confined, accompanied by a 'moitmum' (nurse). Her superstitious lord will not receive his spouse until her days of purification are over."
3. After the birth of a girl, the mother calls her husband *ngoka:wunpam:i* and after a boy *ngoka:wunngawari* but he never again mentions his wife's name. The father of a girl is addressed as *ereka:wunparmi* and of a girl *ereka:wunngowari* and the wife never mentions the husband's name.
4. For example: A young woman was *weiatuki* (Tindale 1931–4: 151), *bami* (Taplin 1879: 131); big girl *yartuwe* (Taplin: *ibid.*); *meeminnie* woman, female kangaroo (Wyatt 1879: 172); unmarried woman, *yingkitye* (Meyer 1843: 66), *wirrate*, woman whose child is dead (*ibid.*: 107); widow *maimuri* (Tindale 1931–4: 237), *yortangge* (Meyer 1843: 66); *kaluwandjeri* widow of several years standing (Tindale 1931–4: 168); old woman *wulu meiminin* (*ibid.*: 152); barren woman *plotye* (Meyer 1843: 93), having children, *plo-watyeri* (*ibid.*: 93).
5. See Berndt *et al.* (1993: 154ff.); *murumuru* (Tindale 1931–4: 61); *mangar, meramangye* (Meyer 1843: 77, 79); tattooing, marks of munggar, tattooing, *mungaiyuwun* Taplin (1879: 139).
6. Peter Sutton located an earlier reference in Daisy Bates (1933) "Moolyadabbin's father has been away beyond Goomalung (the place of the grey possum) on Bibbulmun "business"." However, is not clear what kind of "business " this is.
7. These land-based ceremonies have open segments and others from which all men and young children are excluded (see Bell 1993a). In this particular ceremony the women's excluded all men during the restricted segments, including the judge and his party.
8. This is the published form of a paper I delivered at the Wenner-Gren Foundation-sponsored conference, on "Women, Development and the Sex Division of Labor" in Austria, 1980 (Bell 1981). There I was addressing issues that were on the agenda of feminism and anthropology at that time: i.e. was sexual asymmetry a universal or were there more egalitarian societies and how might we know given the male bias in the literature? The feminist debates have grown more sophisticated and diversified somewhat since then. My interests now lie in the fields of feminist epistemologies and the possibilities of writing and doing feminist ethnography (Bell 1993a, 1993b).
9. In *A World That Was* (Berndt *et al.* 1993) "women's business" is covered in Chapter Eight entitled "Socialization", whereas "men's business", in Chapter Ten, is called "Male Initiation Cycle." Both chapters would be in the section of the manuscript cited as the work Ronald Berndt until 1974 and thus it is

probable that the inclusion of Pinkie Mack's information was an addition to an already-drafted chapter.

Chapter Ten

1. Yallop (1975: 81) has Ingulang for Hindmarsh Island and on the map in Berndt *et al.* (1993: 329) Angalang Creek is on Mundoo Island. It is possible that Ingulang was the Yaraldi name for the eastern portion of the island complex and that it took its name from the water way. Tarpangk, a Ramindjeri place name recorded by Meyer (1843: 50) may have been a name the people at Goolwa used for the island. I heard it at Goolwa. A fourth name, Rumarang from the place name Rumerang is recorded by the Berndts (1993: 329). This name I did not hear but then I didn't ask directly. I waited for the names to emerge in conversation at the island.

2. Kumarangk, appears in Tindale (nd, k) on the card for Rawaldarang as the "not localised" name for the island. Berndt *et al.* (1993: 15, 22-3, 319-20) also give Kumarangk as the name for the island. It may have applied to the Yaraldi or Tangani territory, or may have described a particular feature, a river, or the points (Taplin 1873: 130). It may, as the contemporary etymology suggests, be *kummari*, from pregnant (Meyer 1843: 73) and "angk", meaning "at" (Meyer 1843: 14, 54-5). Alison Harvey (1939) also recorded *kumari* as pregnant. However, which of the three "r" is being represented is not possible to determine. See Chapter 4, note 7.

3. One of the reasons the developers say they need a bridge is that the ferry cannot accommodate the number of visitors who would be attracted to a marina. Bridge proponents claim that the present car ferry is inadequate for the current usage and that one can experience long delays in getting across to the island. No comprehensive studies of which I am aware have been undertaken of the current usage so it is not possible to comment on the accuracy of this view. There is a priority lane for residents of the island. The ferry system of the lower Murray which crosses the river and lakes at various points is free and most visitors find the experience to be a charming interlude.

4. See Chronology which follows this chapter. I have not been able to spend the time in archives necessary to write a competent history of the island. There are local histories which make mention of the area (Conigrave 1838; Morison 1978; McLeay and Cato 1985), records of the Protector of Aborigines, articles in newspapers, the research undertaken by Rod Lucas (1990) and more to be done on oral histories with settler families.

5. According to the Agricultural Editor of the *Observer* (Anon 1883: 9) land had been "terribly mismanaged".

6. Norman Grundy told the Sturt Report (ABC: 1951) that this was the purpose of the musket holes at shoulder height in the old station at Riverside which his

grandfather had established in the 1860s.

7. See Depot Stores Ledger (1912–32). In these ledgers it is possible to trace some individuals and to get a sense of diet, clothing and work patterns.

8. In this section I am drawing together material from Tindale's (nd, c, h, i, j; Tindale and Long nd; Tindale 1931–4, 1934–7, 1938–56, 1953, 1974), his site maps, journals, place name cards, and loose-leaf folders on social organisation.

9. When people gather for ceremonies they also settle disputes, and establish alliances through marriage. Tindale (1937: 116) mentions a song Milerum sang about a widow who attempted to entice a young man into marriage as "illustrating how the Ramindjeri people controlled the actions of their fellow clans people". Tindale records a song "to make a widow not marry too soon sung about Goolwa, a song that shames and restrains the woman, the old women sing and are 'indignant.' They sing in derision as a way of expressing their censure of such behaviour" (Tindale 1931–4: 245).

10. See Tindale (1974: 24); Walker (1934: 186). Tindale (1937: 107, 122; 1974: 80) writes of the *kondoli tungari* (song) at the Murray Mouth and of the powers of men of the *kondoli ngatji* to cause and prevent the stranding of a whale. He gives the song as Ramindjeri. The Berndts (1993: 326) locate Kondilindjerung in Tangani country on the Younghusband Peninsula, as "the home of the whales" (*ibid.*: 15) within the clan territory Kondilindjera and having the ngatji *whale*, i.e. *kondoli*. Thus where whales beached themselves and was in the territory of the people with whale as *ngatji*. Taplin has the Kondarlindjeri as the Murray Mouth (West). In Radcliffe-Brown's (1918) view there was no such clan (see Berndt *et al.* 1993: 310). Today a number of people say that *kondoli* is the *ngatji* for the Murray Mouth.

11. The sources are anything but clear on the matter of mullet and that may well reflect the ability of mullet to live in different environments. Tindale (nd, e) has the following Tangani terms: *kanmeri*, mullet, yellow eye, *Aldrichetta forsteri*, a *ngatji* of the Kanmere clan; *jatarumi*, mullet, yellow eye, *Mugil forsteri* (Tom Trevorrow told me that I wouldn't see this one past Raukkan); *poronti*, sea mullet, *Mugil cephalus*, *ngatji* of the Marntandi clan, a very oily fish, taboo to young men, also known as *poronti* (Tom Trevorrow said he used to catch them when he was thirteen but they are very rare now); *ra:tji*, sand mullet, *Myxus elongalus*; *wankari*, jumping mullet, *Liza argentea*. The Berndts (1993: 309) have *wangkari*, jumping mullet or fresh water mullet; *wongkari*, jumping mullet of which there are fresh- and salt-water kinds (*ibid.*: 565); *wongkari*, freshwater mullet or jumping mullet (*ibid.*: 563). Then in the *Fisherman's Handbook* (Starling 1992), sand mullet, *Myxus elongatus*, "a streamlined attractive mullet with a more pointed head than most of its relations" (*ibid.*: 128-9); sea mullet, *Mugil cephalus*, also called bully mullet, hardgut mullet and the river mullet, "the giant of the mullet clan" which changes colour when it goes from salt- to fresh-water (*ibid.*: 130-1) and in Scott (1962: 133) I find that *Liza argentea*, the

jumping or flat tail mullet was previously *Mugil argentea*. I thank Susan Woenne-Green who helped unravel this fishy nomenclature.

12. This is the Charles Harding to whom Elva Morison (1978: 39) refers in her history of the Harding Family 1853–1978. She cited an article written for "Days that Speak" (16/3/1918) which when checked is under the byline of "Arcadian" (1918: 10), who is most probably Harding. The article mentions "Mooncarie" as fresh water which is probably Milerum's *Mungkuli* but does not appear in Tindale's (1930–52) note which is what started me on this search and I thank Marion Thompson for her perseverance in getting to the original source.

13. Keen (1994: 211) has further explicated these meanings. "The fish dances and songs were images of spiritual conception. In the related Cloudy Water songs, sung during the evenings in the Madayin ceremony as well as at circumcision and mortuary rites, the images of the Djang'kawu catching fish with their conical mats, collecting shellfish and putting them in their dilly-bags, were associated with the mixing of salt and fresh water, and connoted the processes of conception and reproduction, for the conical mat and dilly-bag were often interpreted as symbols of the vagina and uterus. But the symbols were multivalent; Warner's instructors saw fish as images of spirits of the dead (Warner 1937: 446). The ancestral action of catching fish could also connote the reincorporation of the dead into the ancestral domain and at least an implication of reincarnation."

14. When I spoke with Nancy Cato (pers. comm. 5/1996) regarding the research and writing of McLeay and Cato (1985) book, she said that Leslie McLeay's source was old people in Goolwa and that she had also talked with Tindale.

15. Milerum, at Salt Creek, February 12, 1934 provided what Tindale (1934–7: 30ff.) recorded as "Additions to Ngurunderi Story": "Ngurunderi was the first man to tie hooks on spears. After that everyone did the same. Nepele and Ngurunderi talked by thungari, a secret talk at a distance, [an episode where he is speared and kills his attacker]. Ngurunderi sent message back to Nepele saying send my women to Tularang. Boys went ahead while Ngurunderi stayed at Ngururak-ngul (see map). Women had a pine pole to spear fish with. Left them by the bay. Pines still there. Mowantjang before you get to Tauadjeri no other clump this way on [?] used today.

Fixed up Sandy beach at Goolwa. Was next step after Mowantja. This beach was made by Jek:ejere before Ngurunderi came. You did well said Ngurunderi.

At Rawarangal make place for mullet schools to come in; great fishing place today. Ngurunderi said, "I must go on. My two women bother to me. You go straight on to Tankular" he said to women (Tunkalilla Beach). When Ngurunderi got there no sign of them saw them almost over to Kangaroo Island floated about, sulky not come back turned them into Ranjureng. Two sisters = the Pages. He went across to Kangaroo Island followed cliffs along found good place there and disappeared."

My only alterations to this field note of Tindale were to fill in his abbreviations (e.g. a tailed N for *Ngurunderi*, and "ng" for all other tailed "n"s. The note allows us to see where in the *Ngurunderi* narrative, this episode might have been located had it been available when the South Australian museum was researching the Ngurunderi exhibit (see map Chapter 2, "Pioneers of the Lower Murray"). See also Ronald Berndt (1940a: 178 n. 35) who refers back to Tindale's (1941: 115-6) mention of *jekejere* at Port Elliot.

16. Billy Buttons, also known as Bachelors Buttons, *Craspedia canens*, formerly known as *C. glauca* is a perennial herb. The tiny yellow flowers stand on an erect stem up to sixty-five cm high (Prescott 1988: 92-3, 54; Wrigley and Fagg 1996).

17. See Mathews (1996: 41-3). At a hearing 12/4/1996, Mathews provided the opportunity for the applicants to address the matter of satisfying the Minister regarding the issue of Desecration. "Mere assertions of inconsistencies or adverse effect could not suffice" to satisfy the minister that the building of a bridge would desecrate a site if "he did not know the content of the tradition," she asserted. On 30/4/96 Mathews reconvened the taking of oral submissions so that the women could reveal further details of the Seven Sisters story. The women did provide further details on the understanding that only women of Mathews' team, their own female advisors and the Minister would see it. The confidential appendix of mine which concerned this evidence was appended to a report lodged 14/5/96 (Bell and Bagshaw 1996) and circulated, in error, several days later. The applicants organised a meeting to discuss this breach of confidence and other related matters. Because people had to come from a number of different locations and had to engage in extensive consultation within their own families and communities (see Chapter 7), this could not be scheduled until 30/5/96. The Federal Court (Hancock 1996) decision in the Western Australian Crocodile Farm case came down on 28/5/96, two days before the day of their meeting and only served to confirm their decision not to allow the materials to go forward to the Minister. The lawyers for the Chapmans immediately requested that confidential material be forwarded to them and when the material was formally withdrawn by the applicants, the Chapmans commenced proceedings in Federal Court to prevent the withdrawal. They did not succeed and the material was withdrawn (see Mathews 1996: 44-5). Reporter Jane Mathews does not mention the breach of confidentiality in her report.

The decision in the Crocodile Farm case spoke of the necessity for "disclosure by the reporter in some appropriate way" (Hancock 1996). In close consultation with the women, I prepared an amended account of the confidential material which did not violate their law and which indicated in general terms the nature of the relationship between the story and the nature of the desecration that a bridge would constitute. Mathews (1996: 45) took the view "that the resubmitted portions did not advance the applicants' case in any material way". She also rejected other attempts to find ways to comply with the WA decision (*ibid.*: 46). Had Mathews' appointment not been quashed, her interpretation of the adequacy of the resubmitted material and the other proposals could also have been challenged. The resubmitted materials may have been found to be "appropriate" in terms of the WA decision and would most certainly have found favour in the Evatt (1996: 47pp.) Report recommendations concerning restricted material. An aspect of the way this case developed which concerns me as an anthropologist, but does not appear to engage lawyers in any immediate way, is the assumption that a minister, reporter, or legal counsel could, should, or would be able to pronounce on the adequacy of the content of an Aboriginal tradition. This comes perilously close to the law determining what is and what is not a "valid" or "authentic" belief or tradition (see Maddox in press).

18. One of Betty Fisher's pencilled notes was admitted in evidence at the Royal Commission but a second set of notes was refused (Brodie 1995: 6514-7). Mathews (1996: 49) had the paper subjected to forensic tests which generally supported Betty Fisher's account. (The paper was of the period in which the note had been generated but the pencil could not be dated. Pen ink could have been).

19. The singular marker is "i" or, as it often appears "e", or even "ee". Unaipon uses "u" as in "cut" to represent the short "a" and is inconsistent in his use of "g" as in "get" and "g" as in "gel". Thus I am reading the *Mungi* of Unaipon as the *Manji* and *Manchi* of Tindale and Taplin. I cannot be absolutely certain that I am reading the orthographies of Taplin, Tindale and Unaipon accurately. There are inconsistencies within each of the systems. With Unaipon I have the benefit of being able to listen to his tapes and compare these with his transcriptions (Treagus 1966).

20. The initial "y" sound, as in "you", of the word for pubic hair is represented by a "j" in these orthographies, in the same way as the Berndts (1993) use a "j" in Jaralde (which I have been rendering Yaraldi). That does not explain the "ch" in the Taplin rendition which is the "j" sound of "jet". It could be that reference to pubic hair is in the *ingga/ingee* ending and the *Manchi/Manji/Mungi* refer to the stars. In another place Tindale gives Munyaijeri for the Seven Sisters. The *Munya* may be the same word, but Tindale usually has "j" for the English "y" as well as "nj" (not "ny" for the "ny" sound in "onion". I have heard the word for pubic hair (sometimes extended to all body hair) pronounced with the "ny" sound and with the "y".

21. The *Kunkarungkara* women, for example, traverse vast tracts of the Great Western Desert and shape the landscape before becoming the Pleiades (Barwick 1991; Mountford 1938; Tindale 1936a, 1959).

22. See Dawson (1881: 100); Parker (1905); Sutton (1996b). The exceptions are certain Arnhem Land stories which depict the Pleiades and Orion as married (see Johnstone 1998: 55).

23. Where women have been asked by women researchers with an interest in women, separate women's stories have been recorded (Barwick 1991; Berndt and Berndt 1942–5; White 1975).
24. Stories from Arnhem Land and the Lower Murray contain references to the meeting of fresh and salt waters; those from colder climes concern "ice-maidens" (Parker 1905); and from the desert regions a search for water (Tindale 1936a: 176).
25. In the desert regions, for example, the Pleiades signal the dingo whelping season which is important for survival and ceremonies (Tindale 1959: 305).

Epilogue

1. *Doreen Kartinyeri and Neville Gollan v. The Commonwealth of Australia.* (1998) High Court of Australia 22, Canberra.
2. *The Wik Peoples v. Queensland and Ors.* (1996) 141 ALR 129; (1997) 2 (1) ALR 35.
3. In the Mabo decision of 1992, the High Court recognised that native title was not extinguished by the fact of British settlement. The Indigenous peoples of Australia have continuing rights in land not lawfully alienated by the Crown. Thus to argue that they are being granted or are asking for "special consideration" is false.
4. Maddox (in press) argues that Mathews' search for a "rule" is "a peculiarly Western and Protestant view of the nature and structure of religious belief systems". The expectation of a doctrinal elaboration is one generated by the theological, cultural and intellectual history of the legislating group rather than anything which might be found in the group the legislation is supposed to protect.
5. *Kartinyeri and Anor v. The Commonwealth.* (1997: para 29).
6. *ibid.*: (para 117: 3).
7. *ibid.*: (para 9).
8. *ibid.*: (para 132: 2).

A Ngarrindjeri Time-line

80 000 BP	Current earliest estimate of human occupation in Australia.
31 000 BP	Charcoal, possibly associated with human occupation, in Koonalda Cave, SA.
21 000 BP	Human occupation, Seton Cave, Kangaroo Island, SA.
20 000 BP	Extinction of most mega-fauna in Australia
16 000 BP	SA's oldest dated burial site, Roonka, Murray River.
15 000 BP	Peak of last ice-age—sea level over 100 metres below present level.
12 000 BP	Human occupation, Flinders Ranges, SA.
10 000 BP	Kangaroo Island cut off from the mainland by rising seas.
6 000 BP	Sea level rises to near present level.

Colonial Period

1789	Epidemic (smallpox, perhaps also chicken-pox) kills many Aborigines.
1800	Sealers and whalers active around Kangaroo Island and Victor Harbor.
1801	Explorers Matthew Flinders (English) and Thomas Baudin (French) reach Encounter Bay, SA.
1829–31	Second smallpox epidemic kills many Aborigines.
1830	Charles Sturt travels down the Murray River to the sea.
1836	South Australia proclaimed a colony; no treaty was made with Aboriginal people; English settler population: 941.
1837	Aborigines made British subjects.
	Dr W. Wyatt appointed Protector of Aborigines.
	European population increases to 2,500.
	Continued presence of sealers and whalers.
	Ongoing exploration and establishment of an overland trail along the Murray River—expeditions led by Hawdon, Bonney, Eyre and Sturt.

Murray River Aboriginal migration into Adelaide commences.

Dresden Mission Aid Society send Christian G. Teichelmann (German) and C. W. Schürmann (German) to SA.

1839   Venereal disease creates health problems for Aboriginal people at Encounter Bay. Settler population: 14,000.

1840   The ship, *Maria,* sinks off the Coorong and Aborigines kill all survivors, except one girl.

H. A. E. Meyer established Lutheran mission at Encounter Bay.

Overland stock route along the Coorong through Ngarrindjeri lands. Settler population: 17,300.

1841   A punitive expedition led by Protector Moorhouse and Sub-Inspector Shaw results in the shooting deaths of forty or more Aboriginal men, women, and children at Rufus River.

E. J. Eyre appointed a Protector of the Aborigines at Moorundie, on the Murray River, to "maintain the peace".

1842   *Waste Lands Act* (SA) sets aside land for public use including for benefit of Aboriginal people.

Colonial government regulates Aboriginal behaviour—any Aborigine annoying shopkeepers or found naked could be locked up for 24 hours.

1843   H. A. E. Meyer book on the Encounter Bay language published.

1844   *Aboriginal Orphans Ordinance* (SA) passed; Chief Protector of Aborigines becomes legal guardian of "every half-caste and other unprotected Aboriginal child whose parents are dead or unknown".

1846   Mission at Encounter Bay closed.

1853   Riverboats bring more travellers to the Murray River Region.

European settlement continues to expand into interior regions of SA.

Environmental degradation disrupts traditional subsistence patterns.

1857   South Australia gains self-government—Aborigines no longer protected by the Colonial Office in London.

Aborigines' Friends' Association founded in SA.

Office of Protector of Aborigines abolished and responsibility transferred to the Minister for Crown Lands.

1859   George Taplin established a mission at Raukkan on the shores of Lake Alexandrina.

1860   Select Committee of Enquiry into conditions of Aborigines in SA. Aboriginal population continues to decline. Fourteen ration depots operated by SA government.

1868   Commissioner of Crown Lands takes over role of Protector.

1869   *Waste Lands Amendment Act* (SA) makes it easier for European settlers to gain land; more Aboriginal people are forced off their own lands.

1876	*The Criminal Law Consolidation Act* (SA) established that an "Aboriginal native" could publicly be executed at the place of the crime, (repealed in 1952).
1879	George Taplin dies.
1892	Minister of Agriculture and Education assumes responsibility for Aboriginal Affairs.

After Federation

1901	Australian states federate; legislative responsibility for Aborigines remains with the states; Aboriginal people explicitly excluded from national census and national legislation.
1911	*Aborigines Act* (SA) makes Chief Protector legal guardian of every Aboriginal and "half-caste" child; also confers the power to confine Aborigines to reserves. Chief Protector of Aborigines declared "curator" of all Aboriginal property.
1913	Royal Commission of Enquiry on Aborigines (1913–1916). Aboriginal men from Point McLeay and Point Pearce testify.
1916	SA state government takes over Point McLeay mission from the Aborigines' Friends' Association.
1923	Passage of *Aborigines (Training for Children) Act* (SA) empowers the Protector to commit Aboriginal children to educational or vocational institutions for their "care, control and training".
1925–26	Anthropologist Norman Tindale begins fieldwork in SA. After 1931, Milerum (Tangani) assists Tindale.
1930	Re-enactment of Sturt's voyage for the 100 year anniversary of his exploration of the Murray River region. Aborigines at Raukkan participate in re-enactment celebrations.
1934	Chief Protector given considerable powers over all aspects of Aboriginal life.
1935	Construction of barrages commences on Murray River: Tauwitchere, Ewe Island, Boundary Creek, Mundoo and Goolwa Channel barrages completed by 1940.
1936	*Police Act* (SA) makes it illegal for non-Aboriginal people to live or travel with Aborigines.
1938–39	Norman Tindale leads a major data-gathering expedition to almost every Aboriginal settlement in eastern, southern and south-western Australia. Jointly funded by the University of Adelaide and Harvard University.
1939	*Aborigines Act Amendment Act* (SA) abolishes the Office of Chief Protector and the Advisory Council and establishes the Aborigines Protection Board.
	Aboriginal people enlist and fight in World War II.

Anthropologist R. M. Berndt begins fieldwork in the Murray River region, joined by his wife, Catherine, in 1942.

1940   Aboriginal population divided by SA state government's use of Exemption Certificates which prohibit mixed-race Aborigines from "consorting" with other Aboriginal people.

1941   Clarence Long – Milerum – (Tangani) dies, aged 72.

1942   Karloan (Yaraldi) dies in Murray Bridge, aged 79.

1951   Assimilation Policy Conference between State and Commonwealth authorities involved in Aboriginal welfare held in Canberra.

Second Sturt re-enactment along the Murray River region; three Ngarrindjeri ceremonial performances staged.

Publication of *From Black to White* by Catherine and Ronald Berndt.

1954   Margaret "Pinkie" Mack (Yaraldi) dies, aged 96.

1962   *Aboriginal Affairs Act* (SA), one of the most liberal in Australia, repeals the Aborigines' Protection Board guardianship of all Aboriginal children, but life on reserves continues to be restrictive.

Welfare Act (SA) proclaimed, establishing a new board of control known as the Aboriginal Affairs Board.

1965   *Aborigines and Historic Relics Preservation Act* (SA) provides limited protection of sacred sites, burial sites and other significant locations.

1966   Vinnie Branson (Kaurna) and Gladys Elphick (Kaurna) found the Council of Aboriginal Women.

Prohibition of Discrimination Act (SA).

Land Trust Bill (SA) moves toward granting Aboriginal title to land.

1967   David Unaipon (Ngarrindjeri) dies, aged 95.

National Referendum on Australian Constitution. Aborigines to be counted in a national census and the Commonwealth to have concurrent rights with the states to legislate for Aborigines.

Aboriginal Affairs Amendment Act (SA) gives reserve councils limited power to control who could visit their lands.

1972   Tent Embassy set up opposite Parliament House in Canberra; first time the Aboriginal flag was officially flown.

The Lower Murray Nungas Club established.

1974   Control of land at Point McLeay and other small pockets along the Coorong and Murray River transferred to the Aboriginal Land Trust. The Point McLeay Community Council assumed control over their own lands.

Land Rights Era

1976   *Aboriginal Land Rights (NT) Act*—first Commonwealth land rights legislation; applies only to the Northern Territory.

Racial Discrimination Act (RDA) brings Australia into compliance with United Nations Human Rights resolutions and charter.

1977   Binalong Pty Ltd, owned by the Chapman family, purchases land on Hindmarsh Island.

Equal Opportunity Act (SA) makes discrimination in employment, education and the provision of goods and services illegal.

1981   *Pitjantjatjara Lands Rights Act* (SA) in far northwest grants title to 102,630 square kilometres of land to Aboriginal people.

Rosetta Rigney (Aunty Rosie) dies, aged 87.

1984   *Maralinga Tjarutja Land Rights Act* (SA) in far west of SA grants freehold title over an additional 76,420 square kilometres to the Pitjantjatjara.

Aboriginal and Torres Strait Islander Heritage Protection Act (ATSIHPA), to protect and preserves places, areas and objects of significance to Aborigines.

1985   First Aboriginal Women's Art Festival held in Adelaide.

1988   Development of self-government in lands trust areas.

Cultural Heritage centre established at Camp Coorong.

Aboriginal Heritage Act (SA).

Edmonds' archaeological survey of Hindmarsh Island for SA Aboriginal Heritage Branch identifies eleven sites.

1989   ATSIC (Aboriginal and Torres Strait Islander Commission) established.

Ngurunderi Exhibit opens at the South Australian Museum.

Oct—SA government approves bridge construction, financed and constructed by Binalong.

1990   Nov—Lucas Report on anthropological and archaeological issues relating to Hindmarsh Island: substantial burial sites; no extant mythology which specifies mythological sites; recommends any potential developer consult directly with relevant Aboriginal representative body.

Native Title Era

1992   Mabo decision: High Court ruled that native title has not been extinguished by British colonisation.

Publication of *A World That Was*, R. M. Berndt and C. H. Berndt with J. E. Stanton.

1993   Passage of *Native Title Act*; establishes mechanisms for validating land titles called into question by the Mabo decision.

Mar—SA government signs a deed with developers and local government council binding bridge construction.

Apr—Final construction of bridge approved.

Oct—Lower Murray Aboriginal Heritage Committee requests protection of the bridge site area under *Aboriginal Heritage Act* (SA).

Nov—Horace Chapman and Co. Pty Ltd goes into liquidation.

Dec—Aboriginal Heritage Committee applies for federal intervention; protests underway, continuing through May 1994.

Dec 11—Liberal Government wins State election.

1994   Feb 3—S. J. Jacobs QC submits report "Enquiry into the Building of the Hindmarsh Island Bridge"; report yet to be made public.

Feb 15—SA Transport Minister, Diana Laidlaw, announces State Government intention to go forward with the bridge.

Apr—Receivers appointed for the Chapman companies.

Apr 20—Aboriginal Legal Rights Movement (ALRM) writes to Commonwealth Minister disclosing that the area is of mythological and cosmological significance and seeking protection.

May 3—State Minister for Aboriginal Affairs, Michael Armitage, grants authorisation under Section 23 of *Aboriginal Heritage Act* (SA) for destruction of Aboriginal sites in order for bridge to be built.

May 4—Ngarrindjeri meeting held to plan opposition to bridge.

May 12—National Minister for Aboriginal Affairs, Robert Tickner (Labor), issues temporary emergency declaration under Section 9 of ATSIHPA, stopping work for 30 days to allow further investigation.

May 26—Cheryl Saunders appointed to prepare a report under Section 10 of ATSIHPA, public notice issued make no mention of specific areas, nor of "women's business."

Jul 4—Anthropologist Deane Fergie provides ALRM with an assessment of the threat of injury and desecration to Aboriginal tradition posed by bridge construction

Jul 9—Cheryl Saunders reports to the federal minister of Aboriginal Affairs.

Jul 10—Robert Tickner issues a 25-year ban on development.

Aug 8—Binalong Pty Ltd goes into liquidation and Westpac Bank becomes receiver of Hindmarsh Island marina development.

1995   Jan 6—Package of materials relevant to to Saunders' report (including "secret envelope") mistakenly sent to federal Shadow Minister for Aboriginal Affairs, Ian McLachlan (Liberal SA) and copied by his staff.

Feb 7—Federal Court quashes Tickner's ban.

Feb 15—Tickner challenges Federal Court Justice O'Loughlin's decision to quash the writ of protection issued under ATSIHPA.

Mar 6—Ian McLachlan brandishes the "secret envelope" in federal parliament.

Mar 10—Ian McLachlan resigns from Opposition front bench for misleading the public.

Mar 13—Attorney-General Lavarch calls for Howard to return the documents.

Mar 26—Letter signed by Nanna Laura Kartinyeri (Ngarrindjeri) alleging the women's business was fabricated is introduced and tabled in SA Parliament. Premier Dean Brown calls for a Federal Inquiry.

May 19—Media reports that Hindmarsh Island significance was "fabricated by men". Several Ngarrindjeri women come forward to support media position—statements of Dorothy Wilson (Ngarrindjeri) and Dulcie Wilson (Ngarrindjeri) are backed by three other Ngarrindjeri women.

May 29—Doreen Kartinyeri awarded Honorary Doctorate, University of South Australia.

Jun 6—Chris Kenny's Channel 10 media report: Doug Milera (Ngarrindjeri) made up the "women's business" story.

Jun 8—SA Premier, Dean Brown, announces that Iris Stevens will head up a Royal Commission to determine whether there has been any fabrication. Tickner announces a new federal inquiry, which will be led by Federal Court Judge Jane Mathews, beginning after the Commonwealth appeal in Federal Court.

Jul 17—Doreen Kartinyeri (Ngarrindjeri) says she saw map of Hindmarsh Island in 1954, and was able to understand the significance of the island to her female kin.

July 19—First Hearing date of the Royal Commission in Adelaide.

Jul 27—Doug Milera (Ngarrindjeri) retracts his earlier statement, saying that he was drunk, spoke in anger and said things he does not, and did not, believe.

Aug 8—Betty Fisher, amateur historian, tells commission that elder Rebecca "Koomi" Wilson (Ngarrindjeri) told her Hindmarsh Island was "extremely secret and important" to Aboriginal women in a 1967 interview.

Aug 11—Bertha Gollan (Ngarrindjeri) testifies that she knew of no secret sacred significance preventing the bridge, and that she, and another elder who just died, had been threatened not to disagree with claims for religious significance.

Aug 25—Full bench of the Supreme Court in Adelaide decides that Armitage had not adequately consulted with "interested parties" before giving the Royal Commission the authority to allow information on Aboriginal culture and tradition to be disclosed.

Oct 20—Tickner appoints Justice Elizabeth Evatt to undertake a "comprehensive independent review" of ATSIHPA, noting that

"Submissions may be subject to release under the Freedom of Information Act 1982".

Dec 7—Tickner's appeal of decision to overturn the 25-year bridge ban dismissed in Federal Court: Tickner should have read the appendices himself.

Tickner announces Justice Jane Mathews will head the new federal inquiry.

Royal Commissioner Iris Stevens granted a third extension, to report on December 19.

Dec 19—Report of Royal Commission finds that women's business was fabricated; opposition calls for Tickner's resignation; Ngarrindjeri lodge a new ATSIHPA application.

1996   Jan 16—Senator Rosemary Crowley (acting on behalf of the Minister for Aboriginal and Torres Strait Islander Affairs) appoints Jane Mathews as reporter on the new application under ATSIHPA.

Jan 19—Mathews issues notice under Section 10 (3) of ATSIHPA.

Feb—Anthropologist Robert Tonkinson, delivers paper in Hawai'i, states he met with Counsel Assisting twice and Commissioner Stevens once; conceded possibility of secret women's traditions but on basis of anthropological evidence considered the likelihood of the existence of women's business remaining so restricted (as to have left no imprint in the record) was slim.

Feb 19—Chapmans lodge a writ in Federal Court alleging negligence by Tickner and Cheryl Saunders; claim $12,115,317.36 (including $786,000 in legal fees) in damages.

Feb 26—Wendy Chapman and son Andrew ordered by Magistrate David Gurry in Adelaide Magistrates Court to stand trial on Australian Securities Commission charges of failing to deliver records to the liquidators of two family companies.

Mar 2—Liberal party wins Federal election; John Howard becomes Prime Minister.

May 28—In the Crocodile Farm case Federal Court rules that confidential material must be made available to all parties in an appropriate form.

May 29—Mathews tells applicants they will have to withdraw confidentiality claims or withdraw segregated material.

May 30—Lawyers for Chapmans demand full disclosure of Aboriginal claims from Mathews; Ngarrindjeri applicants withdraw all confidential material.

June 20—Tom Trevorrow (Ngarrindjeri) lodges a case before the Full Bench of the Supreme Court (SA) seeking a declaration of denial of natural justice during the Royal Commission.

Jul 3—Justice Williams of the SA Supreme Court denies Trevorrow's right of appeal.

Sep 6—High Court rules six to one that Mathews' role as reporter is invalid in that it violates the separation of powers.

Sep 17—Mathews' report tabled; federal Minister for Aboriginal and Torres Strait Islander Affairs, John Herron (Liberal), announces special legislation to resolve bridge impasse.

Sep 26—Herron tables Elizabeth Evatt's report on ATSIHPA.

Oct 2—Trevorrow's claim rejected by Full Bench of the Supreme Court (SA) without comment.

Nov 7—Wendy Chapman and son Andrew convicted and fined $1,000 by the District Court of SA for breaching company law.

Nov 18–25—Indigenous Arts Festival, Weavers' Conference at Camp Coorong.

Nov 20—"The Untold Story"—Adelaide public meeting discusses the Hindmarsh Island case and implications.

Nov 25–30—Ngarrindjeri and supporters make a "Long Walk" from Adelaide to Goolwa as peaceful protest.

Dec 23—Wik Decision, High Court rules that the granting of a pastoral lease does not extinguish native title.

1997   Feb 10—ALP and minority parties (Greens, Independents and Democrats) combine to defeat special legislation which would have allowed bridge construction to proceed. Senator Harradine, (Independent Tasmania), casts a deciding vote.

Feb 14—Open letter to the Prime Minister from Ngarrindjeri women calling for both John Howard and John Herron to resign.

Mar 5—Wendy Chapman applies for a hearing in Federal Court seeking to force Herron to appoint a new reporter to hear the Ngarrindjeri ATSIHPA Application.

Apr 1—Thomas Trevorrow (Ngarrindjeri) submits High Court application for special leave to appeal Justice Williams' decision of 1996.

Apr—*Pauline Hanson: The Truth* published, sets out the philosophy of One Nation, a new ultra-conservative political party, led by Pauline Hanson (MP, Queensland).

May 1—Howard announces his "10 Point Plan" to amend the *Native Title Act* in light of the Wik decision.

May 12—Australian Labor Party retracts its opposition to the Hindmarsh Bill and withdraws its amendment requiring RDA compliance. *Hindmarsh Island Bridge Act* passes both Houses of Parliament, precludes the Ngarrindjeri from any protection under ATSIHPA.

May 21—Human Rights and Equal Opportunity Commission releases *Bringing Them Home*, its Report on the "Stolen Generations" finding that as many as 40,000 Aboriginal children were taken from their parents between 1910–1970.

May 29—The Chapman family files federal court proceedings against Deane Fergie and Cheryl Saunders, asking $69.62 million in losses accumulated through the halting of bridge construction.

May—Ngarrindjeri announce intention to challenge HIBA on the basis that it violates Section 51 (xxvi) of the Constitution, and/or RDA.

Jun—International Indigenous People's Tribunal in the United States hears from Ngarrindjeri people; renders decision which *inter-alia* calls upon the Government of Australia to "honour the spiritual and sacred traditions of the Ngarrindjeri People, treat them with the utmost respect, and ensure that they are taken into consideration; and provide for the presence of an international human right observer".

Sep 8—High Court rules that it will hear the Ngarrindjeri challenge to HIBA in February.

Oct 20—High Court rules that Aborigines have the right to have evidence of secret men's and women's business in native title cases withheld from members of the opposite sex.

Oct—Tom and Wendy Chapman regain control of the Hindmarsh Island marina.

Dec 5—Senate amends Howard's 10-point Wik bill; Senator Harradine instrumental in amendments; Prime Minister Howard rejects Senate's amendments to Wik bill; double dissolution of Parliament is threatened.

1998   Feb 5–6—High Court hears challenge to HIBA. Justice Ian Callinan, newest appointment to the High Court, refuses to step aside despite having previously given legal advice to the Minister for Aboriginal Affairs, John Herron, and to former Shadow Minister, Ian McLachlan, on the subject of Hindmarsh Island.

Feb 25—Justice Callinan stands down.

Apr 1—High Court rules 5 to 1 that HIBA is constitutional.

Jun 13—One Nation, led by Pauline Hanson, wins 11 seats in Queensland elections.

Jul 8—Senate passes the "Ten Point Plan" amendments to *Native Title Act* averting a double-dissolution of parliament. The amendments substantially modify and restrict indigenous rights. Senator Harradine (Independent, Tasmania) casts a deciding vote.

July 28—Page proofs of *Ngarrindjeri Wurruwarrin* to printers; Federal election pending; race likely to be an issue.

July—The Murray Mouth continues to silt up.

Bibliography

AAP. (1997). Secret business privacy backed by High Court. *Advertiser*, October 21.

ABC. (1951). The Sturt Report, Nos. 33-36. Radio Archives, Sydney: Australian Broadcasting Corporation.

Allen, Paula Gunn. (1984). Grandmother. In Rayna Green (Ed.), *That's What She Said* (p. 14). Bloomington: Indiana University Press.

Amery, Rob. (1995). It's ours to keep and call our own: Reclamation of the Nunga languages in the Adelaide region, South Australia. *International Journal of Society and Language*, 113, 63-82.

Amery, Rob, Kathryn Gale, Josie Aguis, and Chester Shultz. (1990). *Narrunga, Kaurna and Ngarrindjeri Songs*. Elizabeth, South Australia: Kaurna Plains School.

Angas, George French. (1844). *Original Sketches for South Australia*. Illustrated. London: T. McLean.

Angas, George French. (1847). *Savage Life and Scenes in Australia and New Zealand*. Vol. 1. London: Smith, Elder and Co.

Angus and Robertson. (1932). Angus and Robertson Correspondence Files, 1884–1932. Sydney: Mitchell Library (ML MSS 314/76).

Anon. (1883). Hindmarsh Island and Mr. Price's hereford herd. *Observer*, 24 November, pp. 9-10.

Anon. (1994). Dulcie Wilson speaker at Rotary Intercity meeting. *Southern Argus*, 24 November, p. 11.

Anon. (1996). Dulcie Wilson talks to Probus. *South Eastern Times*, April 29, p. 15.

Appleton, Richard and Barbara Appleton. (1992). *The Cambridge Dictionary of Australian Places*. Cambridge: Cambridge University Press.

Arcadian. (1918). Days that speak. *Saturday Journal LIII* (14,572), March 16, 10.

Australian Archives. (1940). Ronald Murray Berndt [Security service dossier]. C 123, item 16553.

Ayers, F. G. (1913). Minutes of Evidence. *Royal Commission on Aborigines*. Adelaide: South Australian Government Printer.

Bapty, Christine. (1997). Notice of Decision, Freedom of Information Application. Office of the Registrar, University of Western Australia, March 12.

Bibliography

Barrett, Charles Leslie. (1946). *The Bunyip and Other Mythical Monsters and Legends.* Melbourne: Reed and Harris.

Barwick, Diane. (1963). A little more than kin—regional affiliation and group identity among Aboriginal migrants in Melbourne. Unpublished PhD thesis, Anthropology, Australian National University, Canberra.

Barwick, Linda. (1991). Secondary documentation of the group project on Antikirinya (Andaratinja) Women, northern South Australia, 1966–8 expeditions. Unpublished restricted document deposited in the Library and Electronic Data Archive, Australian Institute of Aboriginal and Torres Strait Islander Studies.

Barwick, Linda, Allan Marett and Guy Tunstill. (Eds.), (1995). *The Essence of Singing and the Substance of Song.* Oceania Monograph No. 46. Sydney.

Bates, Daisy. (1933). Father and son—an incident in Bibbulmun history. *West Australian*, November 18.

Becke, Louis (Ed.), (1899). *Old Convict Days.* New York: New Amsterdam Publication Company.

Beckett, Jeremy. (1993). Walter Newton's history of the world—or Australia. *American Ethnologist*, 20 (4), 675-695.

Beckett, Jeremy (Ed.), (1994). *Aboriginal History: Aboriginal Myth. Oceania*, 65 (2).

Bell, Diane. (1978). Statement to the Alyawarra and Kaititja Land Claim Hearing. Exhibit 45. Alice Springs: Central Land Council.

Bell, Diane. (1981). Women's business is hard work. *Signs*, 7 (2), 314-337.

Bell, Diane. (1983). Sacred sites: The politics of protection. In Nicolas Peterson and Marcia Langton (Eds.), *Aborigines and Land Rights* (pp. 278-293). Canberra: Australian Institute of Aboriginal Studies.

Bell, Diane. (1984–5). Aboriginal women and land: Learning from the Northern Territory experience. *Anthropological Forum*, 5 (3), 353-363.

Bell, Diane. (1985). Report on the Warumungu Land Claim, July 15, maps, diagrams, bibliography, Exhibit 280. Alice Springs: Central Land Council.

Bell, Diane. (1988). Aboriginal women and the recognition of customary law in Australia. In Bradford W. Morse and Gordon R. Woodman (Eds.), *Indigenous Law and the State* (pp. 297-314). Dordretch, Holland: Foris Publication.

Bell, Diane. (1993a). *Daughters of the Dreaming.* (Second edition: new preface and added epilogue, pp. 274-324). Minneapolis: University of Minnesota Press.

Bell, Diane. (1993b). Introduction: The context. Yes Virginia, there is a feminist ethnography. In Diane Bell, Pat Caplan and Wazir Karim (Eds.), *Gendered Fields: Women, Men and Ethnography* (pp. 1-18). London: Routledge.

Bell, Diane. (1994). An accidental Australian tourist: A feminist anthropologist at sea and on land. In Stuart Schwartz (Ed.), *Implicit Ethnographies: In the wake of Columbus* (pp. 502-555). Cambridge: Cambridge University Press.

Bell, Diane. (1996a). A world that is, was, and will be: Ngarrindjeri women's traditions, observances, customs and beliefs. Appendix 7 to Report for the Applicants to the Commonwealth Hindmarsh Island Report, March.

Bell, Diane. (1996b). Ngarrindjeri oral submissions thus far: An interim Supplementary Report for the Applicants to the Commonwealth Hindmarsh Island Report, April 14.

Bell, Diane. (1996c). Injury and desecration: An anthropological assessment of the submission. Supplementary Report for the Applicants to the Commonwealth Hindmarsh Island Report, May 14.

Bell, Diane. (1998). Cross-cultural confusions: Indigenous traditions, legal confusions, and ethnographic uncertainties. Paper presented at "Tolerance, cultural diversity and pluralism: Reconciliation and human rights." Fulbright Symposium, University of Adelaide, April 14–16.

Bell, Diane and Pam Ditton. (1980). *Law: The old and the new: Aboriginal women in Central Australia speak out.* Aboriginal History for the Central Australian Aboriginal Legal Aid Service, Canberra. Revised edition, 1984. Canberra: Aboriginal History.

Bell, Diane and Geoffrey Bagshaw. (1996). Seven sisters dreaming: The Ngarrindjeri in perspective. A Supplementary Report for the Applicants to the Commonwealth Hindmarsh Island Report, April 30.

Berlo, Janet Catherine. (1991). Beyond bricolage: Women and aesthetic strategies in Latin American textiles. In Margot Blum Schevill, Janet Catherine Berlo, and Edward B. Dwyer (Eds.), *Textile Traditions of Mesoamerica and the Andes: An anthology* (pp. 437-479). Austin: University of Texas Press.

Berndt, Catherine H. (1950). Women's changing ceremonies in Northern Australia. *L'Homme, 1*, 1-87.

Berndt, Catherine H. (1963). The social position of women, commentary. In Helen Shiels (Ed.), *Australian Aboriginal Studies* (pp. 335-42). Melbourne: Oxford University Press.

Berndt, Catherine H. (1965). Women and the "secret life". In Ronald M. and Catherine H. Berndt (Eds.), *Aboriginal Man in Australia* (pp. 238-82). Sydney: Angus and Robertson.

Berndt, Catherine H. (1970). Digging sticks and spears, or, the two-sex model. In Fay Gale (Ed.), *Women's Role in Aboriginal Society* (pp. 39-48). Canberra: Australian Institute of Aboriginal Studies.

Berndt, Catherine H. (1973). Women as outsiders: a partial parallel. *Aboriginal News, 1* (4), 7-8, 21.

Berndt, Catherine H. (1979). Aboriginal women and the notion of the "marginal man". In Ronald M. Berndt and Catherine H. Berndt (Eds.), *Aborigines of the West: Their past and their present* (pp. 28-38). Nedlands: University of Western Australia Press for the Education Committee of the 150th Anniversary Celebrations.

Berndt, Catherine H. (1981). Interpretations and "facts" in Aboriginal Australia. In Frances Dahlberg (Ed.), *Woman the Gatherer* (pp. 153-203). New Haven: Yale University Press.

Berndt, Catherine H. (1983). Mythical women, past and present. In Fay Gale (Ed.), *We are Bosses Ourselves* (pp. 13-21). Canberra: Australian Institute of Aboriginal Studies.

Berndt, Catherine H. (1989). Retrospect, and prospect: Looking back after 50 years. In Peggy Brock (Ed.), *Women, Rites and Sites.* (pp. 1-20). Sydney: Allen and Unwin.

Berndt, Catherine H. (1994a). Pinkie Mack. In David Horton (Ed.), *The Encyclopaedia of Aboriginal Australia: Aboriginal and Torres Strait Islander History, Society and Culture* (pp. 639-640). Canberra: Aboriginal Studies Press.

Berndt, Catherine H. (1994b). Albert Karloan. In David Horton (Ed.), *The Encyclopaedia of Aboriginal Australia: Aboriginal and Torres Strait Islander History, Society and Culture* (pp. 536-537). Canberra: Aboriginal Studies Press.

Berndt, Ronald M. (1940a). Some aspects of Jaraldi culture, South Australia. *Oceania, 11* (2), 164-185.

Berndt, Ronald M. (1940b). A curlew and owl legend from the Narunga tribe, South Australia, *Oceania, 10* (4), 456-462.

Berndt, Ronald M. (1952). *Djanggawul. An Aboriginal Religious Cult of Northeast Arnhem Land.* Melbourne: Cheshire.

Berndt, Ronald M. (1965). Law and order in Aboriginal Australia. In Ronald M. Berndt and Catherine H. Berndt (Eds.), *Aboriginal Man in Australia: Essays in honour of Emeritus Professor A. P. Elkin* (pp. 167-206). Sydney: Angus and Robertson.

Berndt, Ronald M. (1970). *Australian Aboriginal Anthropology: Modern Studies in the Social Anthropology of the Australian Aborigines.* Nedlands: Published for the Australian Institute of Aboriginal Studies by the University of Western Australia.

Berndt, Ronald M. (1974). *Australian Aboriginal Religion.* (Four fascicles I-IV). Leiden: Brill.

Berndt, Ronald M. (1979). A profile of good and bad in Australian Aboriginal religion. Charles Strong Memorial Trust Lecture. Republished (1998). In Max Charlesworth (Ed.), *Religious Business: Essays on Australian Aboriginal Spirituality* (pp. 24-45). Melbourne: Cambridge University Press.

Berndt, Ronald M. (1982). The changing face of Aboriginal studies: Some personal glimpses. In Grant McCall (Ed.), *Anthropology and Australia: Essays to honour fifty years of Mankind* (pp. 49-66). Sydney: Anthropological Society of NSW.

Berndt, Ronald M. (1989). Aboriginal fieldwork in South Australia in the 1940s and implications for the present. *Records of the South Australian Museum, 23* (1), 59-68.

Berndt, Ronald M. and Catherine H. Berndt. (1942-5). A preliminary report of field work in the Ooldea region, Western South Australia. *Oceania,* 1942, *12* (4), *13* (1) (2); 1943, *13* (4), *14* (1) (2); 1944 *14* (3) (4); 1945 *15* (1) (2) (3)

Berndt, Ronald M. and Catherine H. Berndt. (1951). *From Black to White.* Melbourne: F. W. Cheshire.

Berndt, Ronald M. and Catherine H. Berndt. (1964). *The World of the First Australians: An Introduction to the Traditional Life of the Australian Aborigines.* Sydney: Ure Smith.

Berndt, Ronald M. and Catherine H. Berndt. (1987). *End of an Era.* Canberra: Australian Institute of Aboriginal Studies.

Berndt, Ronald M. and Catherine H. Berndt. (1988). *The Speaking Land. Myth and story in Aboriginal Australia.* Ringwood: Penguin.

Berndt, Ronald M. and Catherine H. Berndt with John E. Stanton. (1993). *A World That Was: The Yaruldi of the Murray River and the Lakes, South Australia.* Melbourne: Melbourne University Press at the Miegunyah Press.

Beston, John B. (1979). David Unaipon: The first Aboriginal writer (1873–1967) *Southerly,* September 334-351.

Black, J. M. (1917). Vocabularies of three South Australian languages, Wirrunga, Narrinyeri, Wongaidya. *Transactions and Proceedings of the Royal Society of South Australia, XLI,* 1-8.

Black, J. M. (1920). Vocabularies of four South Australian languages—Adelaide, Narruga, Kukata, and Narrinyeri—with special reference to their speech sounds. *Transactions of the Royal Society of South Australia, XLIV,* 76-93.

Blakers, Margaret. (1984). *The Atlas of Australian Birds.* Melbourne: Melbourne University Press.

Bonney, Lola Cameron. (1982). Taped interview with Roger Luebbers 11/5/1982.

Bonney, Lola Cameron. (1990). *Out of the Dreaming.* Kingston: SE Kingston Leader.

Breen, Marcus (Ed.), (1989). *Our Place, Our Music.* Canberra: Aboriginal Studies Press.

Briggs, Charles L. (1996). The politics of discursive authority on the invention of tradition. *Cultural Anthropology, 11* (4), 435-469.

Brock, Peggy (Ed.), (1989). *Women's Rites and Sites.* Sydney: Allen and Unwin.

Brookman, Alison (née: Harvey). (1995). Evidence. Transcript of the Hindmarsh Island Bridge Royal Commission. Adelaide: South Australian Government Printer.

Brodie, Veronica. (1995). Evidence. Transcript of the Hindmarsh Island Bridge Royal Commission. Adelaide: South Australian Government Printer.

Brunton, Ronald. (1991). Controversy in the "Sickness Country": The battle of Coronation Hill. *Quadrant,* Sept, 16-20.

Brunton, Ronald. (1995). Blocking business: An anthropological assessment of the Hindmarsh Island dispute. Tasman Institute. Occasional paper B31, August.

Brunton, Ronald. (1996a). The false culture syndrome: The Howard government and the Commonwealth Hindmarsh Island inquiry. *IPA Backgrounder, 8* (2).

Brunton, Ronald. (1996b). The Hindmarsh Island bridge and the credibility of Australian anthropology. *Anthropology Today, 12* (4), 2-7.

Brusnahan, Margaret. (1992). *Raukkan and other Poems.* Broome: Magabala Books.

Bull, John Wrathall. (1884). *Early Experiences of Life in South Australia and extended colonial history*. Adelaide: E. S. Wigg and Son.

Bulmer, John. (1994). Victorian Aborigines: John Bulmer's recollections 1855–1908. *Museum of Victoria, 1*.

Byrnes, Phyllis. (1995). Evidence. Transcript of the Hindmarsh Island Bridge Royal Commission. Adelaide: South Australian Government Printer.

Cameron, Alfred. (1913). Minutes of Evidence. *Royal Commission on Aborigines*. Adelaide: South Australian Government Printer.

Campbell, Roderick. (1998). Blacks ask judge to step aside. *Canberra Times*, 2 February, p. 3.

Campbell, T. D. (1934). Notes on the Aborigines of the South East of South Australia. Part 1. *Transactions and Proceedings of the Royal Society of South Australia, 58*, 22-23.

Campbell, T. D. (1939). Notes on the Aborigines of the South East of South Australia. Part 2. *Transactions and Proceedings of the Royal Society of South Australia, 63*, 27-35.

Campbell, T. D., J. B. Cleland and P. S. Hossfeld. (1946). Aborigines of the lower south east of South Australia. *Record of the South Australian Museum, 8*, 445-502.

Cawthorne, W. A. (1927). Rough Notes on the Manners and Customs of the Natives. (First published in 1844.) *Proceedings of the Royal Geographical Society of Australia, South Australia Branch*. Session XXVII, 47-77.

Ceci, Lynn. (1978). Watchers of the Pleiades: Ethnoastronomy among Native cultivators in northeastern North America. *Ethnohistory, 25* (4), 301-317.

Charlesworth, Hilary. (1997). "Little boxes": A review of the Commonwealth Hindmarsh Island Report by Justice Jane Mathews. *Aboriginal Law Bulletin, 13*, (90), 19-21.

Charlesworth, Max. (1983). Introduction: Change in Aboriginal Australia. In Max Charlesworth *et al.* (Eds.), *Religion in Aboriginal Australia*, (pp. 383-387). St Lucia: University of Queensland Press.

Clarke, Philip A. (1991). Penney as ethnographer. *Journal of the Anthropological Society of South Australia, 29* (1), 88-107.

Clarke, Philip A. (1994). Contact, conflict and regeneration: Aboriginal cultural geography of the Lower Murray, South Australia. Unpublished PhD thesis, Department of Geography and Anthropology, University of South Australia, Adelaide.

Clarke, Philip A. (1995a). Evidence. Transcript of the Hindmarsh Island Bridge Royal Commission. Adelaide: South Australian Government Printer.

Clarke, Philip A. (1995b). Myth as history? The Ngurunderi dreaming of the Lower Murray, South Australia. *Records of the South Australian Museum, 28* (2), 143-156.

Clarke, Philip A. (1996). Response to "Secret Women's Business: The Hindmarsh Island affair". *Journal of Australian Studies, 50/51*, 141-149.

Clarke, Philip A. (1997). The Aboriginal cosmic landscape of southern South Australia. *Records of the South Australian Museum*, 29 (2), 125-145.

Clifford, James. (1988). *The Predicament of Culture*. Cambridge: Harvard University Press.

Conigrave, Sarah. (1938). *My Reminiscences of the Early Days: Personal incidents on a sheep and cattle run in South Australia*. (Second edition) Perth: Brokensha and Shaw.

Council for Aboriginal Reconciliation. (1995). *Going Forward: Social justice for the first Australians*. Canberra: Australian Government Printers.

Courto, Vivienne. (1996). Translation of the Journals and Notes of Paul Erhard Andreas Elymann 1896–1912. Unpublished ms.

Cowlishaw, Gillian. (1987). Colour, culture and Aboriginalists. *Man*, 2 (2), 221-237.

Cowlishaw, Gillian. (1988). Australian Aboriginal studies: The anthropologists' accounts. In Marie de Lepervanche and Gillian Bottomley (Eds.), *The Cultural Construction of Race* (pp. 60-79). Studies in Society and Culture. Sydney: George Allen and Unwin.

Curr, Edward. M. (1886). *The Australian Race, Its origin, languages, customs, place of landing in Australia and the roots by which it spread itself out over that continent*. Vol. 2. Melbourne: Victorian Government Printer.

Dawson, James. (1881). *Australian Aborigines: The languages and customs of several tribes of Aborigines in the Western District of Victoria, Australia*. Melbourne: George Robertson.

Department of Education. (1990). *The Ngarrindjeri People: Aboriginal people of the River Murray, Lakes and Coorong. Aboriginal Studies 8-12*. Adelaide: Department of Education, South Australia.

Depot Stores Ledger. (1912–32). Accounts kept by issuer of stores at Depots. 2 vols. GRC 52/56.

Deuschle, Vi. (1983). Historical factors which have affected Aboriginal lifestyles since colonisation. In Fay Gale (Ed.), *We Are Bosses Ourselves* (pp. 86-88). Canberra: Australian Institute of Aboriginal Studies.

Deuschle, Vi. (1988). Foreword. In Christobel Mattingley and Ken Hampton (Eds.), *Survival in Our Own Land: Aboriginal experiences in South Australia since 1836, told by Nungas and others* (p. ix). Adelaide: Wakefield Press.

Dix, Audrey. (1995). Evidence. Transcript of the Hindmarsh Island Bridge Royal Commission. Adelaide: South Australian Government Printer.

Donaldson, Tamsin. (1995). Mixes of English and ancestral language words in Southeastern Australian Aboriginal songs of traditional and introduced origin. In Linda Barwick, Allan Marett and Guy Tunstill (Eds.), *The Essence of Singing and the Substance of Song* (pp. 143-158). Oceania Monograph, No. 46, University of Sydney.

Draper, Neale. (1996). *Kumarangk* (Hindmarsh Island, South Australia): Aboriginal Heritage Assessment. Prepared for the South Australian Department of State Aboriginal Affairs, and the *Ngarrindjeri* traditional owners of the Lower Murray Region.

Durkheim, Emile. (1912). *Elementary Forms of the Religious Life.* New York: Free Press.

Eades, Diana. (1981). That's our way of talking: Aborigines in south-east Queensland. *Social Alternatives, 2* (2), 11-14.

East, J. J. (1889). The Aborigines of South and Central Australia. Paper read before the Field Naturalists' Section of the Royal Society, South Australia, July 16, pp. 1-11. (Pamphlet, Mortlock Library of South Australia.)

Edmonds, Vanessa. (1988). An Archaeological Survey of Hindmarsh Island. Aboriginal Heritage Branch, Adelaide.

Eliade, Mircea (1973). *Australian Religions. An introduction.* Ithaca, New York and London: Cornell University Press.

Elkin, A. P. (1938). *The Australian Aborigines.* Sydney: Angus and Robertson (Second edition 1974).

Elkin, A. P. (1939). Introduction. In Phyllis M. Kaberry *Aboriginal Woman: Sacred and profane* (pp. xvii-xxxi). London: Routledge.

Elkin, A. P. (1951). Introduction. In Ronald M. and Catherine H. Berndt (Eds.), *From Black to White in South Australia* (pp. 11-17). Melbourne: F. W. Cheshire.

Elkin, A. P. (1977). *Aboriginal Men of High Degree.* St Lucia: University of Queensland Press. (Second edition).

Ellis, Catherine. (1962–6). Note Books 1-4, MS 2242. Canberra: Australian Institute of Aboriginal and Torres Strait Islander Studies.

Ellis, Catherine. (1963–5). Report on fieldwork within a radius of 200 miles from Adelaide 1963–65 assisted by A. M. Ellis. Unpublished manuscript held at Barr Smith Library, University of Adelaide.

Ellis, Catherine. (1964). Archive Tape LA 120a. Canberra: Australian Institute of Aboriginal and Torres Strait Islander Studies.

Ellis, Catherine. (1965). Archive Tapes LA 124a, LA 124b, LA 125a, LA 125b, LA 126a. Canberra: Australian Institute of Aboriginal and Torres Strait Islander Studies.

Ellis, Catherine. (1966a). Archive Tape, LA 106. Canberra: Australian Institute of Aboriginal and Torres Strait Islander Studies.

Ellis, Catherine. (1966b). Aboriginal songs of South Australia. *Miscellanea Musicologica 1,* 137-190.

Ellis, Catherine. (1967). Folk song migration in Aboriginal South Australia. *The Journal of the International Folk Music Council, 19,* 11-16.

Ellis, Catherine. (1984). Time consciousness of Aboriginal performers. In J. C. Kassler and J. Stubington (Eds.), *Problems and Solutions: Occasional essays in musicology presented to Alice M. Moyle* (pp. 149-85). Sydney: Hale and Iremonger.

Ellis, Catherine. (1985). *Aboriginal Music. Education for living. Cross-cultural experiences from South Australia.* St Lucia: University of Queensland Press.

Ellis, Catherine. (1994). Powerful Songs: Their placement in Aboriginal thought. *The World of Music, 36* (1), 3-19.

Ellis, Catherine, M. Brunton and Linda Barwick. (1988). From dreaming rock to reggae rock. In A. McCredie (Ed.), *From Colonel Light into the Footlights: The performing arts in South Australia from 1836 to the present* (pp. 151-172). Adelaide: Pagel Books.

Ellis, Catherine J. and Linda Barwick. (1989). Antikirinja women's song knowledge. In Peggy Brock (Ed.), *Women, Rites and Sites* (pp. 21-40). Sydney: Allen and Unwin.

Elmslie, Ronald G. and Susan Nance. (1988). William Ramsay Smith. In Geoffrey Serle (Ed.), *Australian Dictionary of Biography, II*, 1891–1939 (pp. 674–5). Melbourne: Melbourne University Press.

Ely, Bonita. (1980). *Murray–Murundi.* Adelaide: Experimental Art Foundation.

Elymann, Paul Erhard Andreas. (1908). *Die Eingeborenen der Kolonie Südaustralien.* Berlin: Dietrich Reimer (Ernst Vohsen).

ESA. (1927). A dusky ruler: Queen of the Aborigines. Chat with Ethel Wympie Watson. *Register,* May 11.

Evatt, Elizabeth. (1996). Review of the *Aboriginal and Torres Strait Islander Heritage Protection Act,* 1984. Canberra: Australian Government Printer.

Fergie, Deane. (1994). To all the mothers that were, to all the mothers that are, to all the mothers that will be: An anthropological assessment of the threat of injury and desecration to Aboriginal tradition by the proposed Hindmarsh Island bridge construction. A Report to the Aboriginal Legal Rights Movement Inc in relation to Section 10 (1) of the *Aboriginal and Torres Strait Islander Heritage Protection Act,* 1984.

Fergie, Deane. (1996). Secret envelopes and inferential tautologies. *Journal of Australian Studies, 48*, 13-24.

Fisher, Betty. (1995). Evidence. Transcript of the Hindmarsh Island Bridge Royal Commission. Adelaide: South Australian Government Printer.

Flood, Josephine. (1983). *Archaeology of the Dreamtime.* Sydney: Collins.

Foster, Robert. (1991). The spirit of Penney, a biographical sketch of Richard Penney. *Journal of the Anthropological Society of South Australia, 29* (1), 1-87.

Francis, Patrick Wilfred. (1913). Minutes of Evidence. *Royal Commission on Aborigines.* Adelaide: South Australian Government Printer.

Frazer, James George. (1959). *The Golden Bough.* New York: Criterion Books.

Freud, Sigmund. (1914). *Totem and Tabu: Some points of agreement between the mental lives of the savages and the neurotics.* Leipzig: H. Heller.

Gale, Fay. (1964). *A Study of Assimilation: Part-Aborigines in South Australia.* Adelaide: Libraries Board of South Australia.

Gale, Fay (Ed.), (1970). *Women's Role in Aboriginal Society.* Canberra: Australian Institute of Aboriginal Studies.

Gale, Fay. (1972). *Urban Aborigines.* Canberra: Australian National University Press.

655

Gale, Fay (Ed.), (1983). *We are Bosses Ourselves.* Canberra: Australian Institute of Aboriginal Studies.

Gale, Fay. (1989). Roles revisited: The women of South Australia. In Peggy Brock (Ed.), *Women's Rites and Sites* (pp. 120-135). Sydney: Allen and Unwin.

Gale, Fay. (1990). Obituary: Ronald Murray Berndt, 1916–1990. In Academy of the Social Sciences, Australia *Annual Report for the Year 1990* (pp. 76-78). Canberra: Academy of Social Sciences.

Gale, Fay and Joy Wundersitz. (1982). *Adelaide Aborigines. A case study of urban life 1966–1981.* The Aboriginal Component in the Australian Economy, 4. Canberra: Australian National University.

Geertz, Clifford. (1983). *Local Knowledge.* New York: Basic Books.

Giles, Kerry with Phillip (Piri) Everett. (1992). Two countries, one weave? *Artlink,* Winter, *12* (2), 44-46.

Giles, Kerry and John Kean. (1992). *Nyoongah Nunga Yura Koorie 1992 Adelaide Festival.* Adelaide: National Aboriginal Cultural Institute.

Gollan, Bertha. (1995). Evidence. Transcript of the Hindmarsh Island Bridge Royal Commission. Adelaide: South Australian Government Printer.

Gollan, Vena. (1995). Evidence. Transcript of the Hindmarsh Island Bridge Royal Commission. Adelaide: South Australian Government Printer.

Goodale, Jane. (1971). *Tiwi Wives: A study of women on Melville Island, Australia.* Seattle: University of Washington Press.

Grace, Jenny. (1990). Murray River Women. In Adele Pring (Ed.), *Women of the Centre* (pp. 158-172). Apollo Bay: Pascoe Publishing.

Grace, Jenny. (1995). Evidence. Transcript of the Hindmarsh Island Bridge Royal Commission. Adelaide: South Australian Government Printer.

Griffiths, Tom. (Edited with assistance from A. Platt) (1988). *The Life and Adventures of Edward Snell: The illustrated diary of an artist, engineer, and adventurer in the Australian colonies, 1849–1859.* Sydney: Angus and Robertson.

Gummow, Margaret. (1995). Songs and sites/moving mountains: A study of one song from northern NSW. In Linda Barwick, Allan Marettand Guy Tunstill (Eds.), *The Essence of Singing and the Substance of Song* (pp. 121-132). Oceania Monograph, No. 46, University of Sydney.

Guss, David M. (1989). *To Weave and Sing: Art, symbol, and narrative in the South American rainforest.* Berkeley: University of California Press.

Hamby, Louise. (1995). New ideas from Galiwing:ku. *Craft Arts International,* 33, 97-99.

Hamilton, Annette. (1982). Descended from father, belonging to country: Rights to land in the Australian Western Desert. In E. Leacock and R. Lee (Eds.), *Politics and History in Band Societies* (pp. 85-108). Cambridge: Cambridge University Press.

Hancock, Nathan. (1996). Case note. *Aboriginal Law Bulletin, 3* (82), 12-13.

Harjo, Joy and Gloria Bird. (1997). *Reinventing the Enemy's Language: Contemporary Native women's writings in North America.* New York: W. W. Norton.

Harris, Jacob. (1913). Minutes of Evidence. *Royal Commission on Aborigines.* Adelaide: South Australian Government Printer.

Hart, C. W. and Arnold R. Pilling. (1970). *The Tiwi of Northern Australia.* New York: Holt.

Hartland, E. Sydney. (1906). Review of Ethnological Notes on the Aboriginal Tribes of New South Wales and Victoria, by R. H. Mathews, 1905. *Man., 98* (9), 153-155.

Harvey, Alison. (1939). Field Notebook. AA 105 H. K. Fry Collection. Adelaide: South Australian Museum Anthropology Archives.

Harvey, Alison. (1943). A fishing legend of the Jaralde tribe of Lake Alexandrina, South Australia. *Mankind, 3* (4), 108-112.

Harvey, Nick. (1983). *The Murray Mouth.* South Australia: South Australian Teacher's Association.

Hastings, J. G. (1944, reprinted 1987). Tragedies of the Coorong. In Tom McCourt and Hans Mincham (Eds.), *The Coorong and lakes of the Lower Murray* (pp. 79-105). Beachport: Beachport Branch of the National Trust.

Hemming, Steven J. (1984). Taped interview with Flora Smith and Paul Smith at Murray Bridge, February. (In Hemming's possession.)

Hemming, Steven. (1985). The Mulgewongk. *Journal of Anthropology Society of South Australia, 23* (1), 11-16.

Hemming, Steven J. (1986). Taped interview with George Trevorrow, Winston Head and Vince Buckskin at SA Museum, June 7. (In Hemming's possession.)

Hemming, Steven J. (1987). October long weekend excursion. *Journal of Anthropological Society of South Australia, 25* (8), 1-8.

Hemming, Steven J. (1988). Interview recorded with Annie Koolmatrie, August 11. (In Hemming's possession.)

Hemming, Steven J. (1991). Lower Murray shields: an historical perspective. *Records of the South Australian Museum, 24* (2), 125-138.

Hemming, Steven J. (1993). Re-naming the "country": Aboriginal oral histories and site recording. Read at the Oral History Association of Australia Conference, Sydney.

Hemming, Steven J. (Ed.), (1994a). *Troddin thru Raukkan: Our Home: Raukkan reunion.* Raukkan: Raukkan Council and the South Australian Museum.

Hemming, Steven J. (1994b). In the tracks of Ngurunderi: the South Australian Museum's Ngurunderi exhibition and cultural tourism. *Australian Aboriginal Studies, 2,* 38-46.

Hemming, Steven J. (1995). River Murray histories: Oral history, archaeology and museum collections. In E. Greenwood, K. Neumann and A. Sartori (Eds.), *Work in Flux* (pp. 102-110). Melbourne: Melbourne University History Conference Series, 1.

Hemming, Steven J. (1996). Inventing anthropology. *Journal of Australian Studies, 48,* 25-39.

Hemming, Steven J. (1997a). Oral history, native title and Hindmarsh Island. Paper presented at the Oral History Conference, Alice Springs 3–7/9/1997.

Hemming, Steven J. (1997b). Not the slightest shred of evidence: A reply to Philip Clarke's response to "Secret Women's Business." *Journal of Australian Studies*, 5 (3), 130-145.

Hemming, Steven J. and Philip G. Jones, with Philip A. Clarke. (1989). *Ngurunderi: An Aboriginal dreaming*. Adelaide: South Australian Museum.

Herron, John. (1996). Evidence. Legal and Constitutional Committee of the Senate hearing on the Hindmarsh Island Bridge Bill, November 29.

Hiatt, Betty. (1970). Woman the gatherer. In Fay Gale (Ed.), *Women's Role in Aboriginal Soceity* (pp. 2-7). Canberra: Australian Institute of Aboriginal Studies (2nd ed. 1974).

Hodge, Charles R. (1932). *Encounter Bay: The miniature Naples of Australia, a short history of the romantic south coast of South Australia*. Hampstead Gardens, South Australia: Austraprint (facsimile reprint).

Hogan, Linda. (1987). *Mean Spirit*. New York: Ivy Books.

Holland, Julian. (1990). On the trail of the Bunyip. *Australian Natural History*, 23 (7), 520-521.

Howie, Ross. (1981). Northern Territory. In Nicolas Peterson (Ed.), *Aboriginal Land Rights: A handbook* (pp. 28-52). Canberra: Australian Institute of Aboriginal Studies.

Howie-Willis, Ian. (1994). Unaipon, J. In David Horton (Ed.), *The Australian Encyclopaedia of Aboriginal Australia* (p. 1117). Canberra: Australian Institute of Aboriginal and Torres Strait Islander Studies.

Howitt, A. W. (1904). *The Native Tribes of South-East Australia*. London: Macmillan.

Hunter, Elizabeth, Jane. (1913). Minutes of Evidence. *Royal Commission on Aborigines*. Adelaide: South Australian Government Printer.

Hutchinson, Y. B. (1838). A hasty account (written by the late Y. B. Hutchinson, January 1838, and copied by P. O. Hutchinson, a son, July 1889) of an expedition to Encounter Bay and Lake Alexandrina at the latter part of 1837. PRO RN831.

Inglis, Judy. (1961). Aborigines in Adelaide. *Polynesian Society Journal, 70* (2), 200-218.

Inglis, Judy. (1964). Dispersal of Aboriginal Families in South Australia. In Marie Reay (Ed.), *Aborigines Now: New perspectives in the study of Aboriginal communities* (pp. 115-132). Melbourne: Angus and Robertson.

Jacobs, S. J. (1994). Report on Goolwa-Hindmarsh Island Bridge Proposal and Associated Development on Hindmarsh Island to the Enquiry into the Hindmarsh Island Bridge to Crown Solicitor, Adelaide, February 3.

Jackson, Pompey. (1913). Minutes of Evidence. *Royal Commission on Aborigines*. Adelaide: South Australian Government Printer.

Jenkin, Graham. (1979). *Conquest of the Ngarrindjeri: The story of the lower Lakes Tribes*. Adelaide: Rigby.

Johnstone, Dianne. (1998). *Night Skies of Aboriginal Australia: A noctuary*. Oceania Monographs 47. Sydney: University of Sydney.

Jones, Philip. (1989). "A curve is a line and a line is a curve": Some of the truth about David Unaipon. *Adelaide Review*, July. *65*, 10-11.

Jones, Philip. (1993). David Unaipon. In John Ritchie (Ed.), *Australian Dictionary of Biography*, (pp. 303-305). Melbourne: Melbourne University Press.

Jones, Philip. (1995). Evidence. Transcript of the Hindmarsh Island Bridge Royal Commission. Adelaide: South Australian Government Printer.

Kaberry, Phyllis M. (1939). *Aboriginal Woman: Sacred and profane.* London: Routledge.

Kaldor, Susan. (1988). Catherine Helen Webb Berndt. In Ute Gacs, Aisah Khan, Jerrie McIntyre and Ruth Weinberg (Eds.), *Women Anthropologists: A biographical dictionary* (pp. 8-16). New York: Greenwood Press.

Karloan, Albert. (1989). "*Pata winema*" song. CD of soundtrack of the Ngurunderi Exhibit. Adelaide: South Australian Museum.

Kartinyeri, Doreen. (1983a). Recording Our History (As told to Milton Gale). In Fay Gale (Ed.), *We Are Bosses Ourselves.* (pp. 136-157). Canberra: Australian Institute of Aboriginal Studies.

Kartinyeri, Doreen. (1983b). *The Rigney Family Genealogy.* Adelaide: Aboriginal Research Centre, University of Adelaide.

Kartinyeri, Doreen. (1985). *The Wanganeen Family Genealogy.* Adelaide: Aboriginal Research Centre, University of Adelaide.

Kartinyeri, Doreen. (1989). *The Kartinyeri Family Genealogy.* Vols. 1-2. Adelaide: South Australian Museum.

Kartinyeri, Doreen. (1990). *The Wilson Family Genealogies.* Vols. 1-3. Adelaide: South Australian Museum.

Kartinyeri, Doreen. (1996). *Ngarrindjeri Anzacs.* Raukkan: South Australian Museum and Raukkan Council.

Keely, Annie. (1996). Women and land: The problems Aboriginal women face in providing gender restricted evidence. Paper read at "Land Rights—past, present and future—Conference", Canberra 17/8/1996.

Keen, Ian. (1978). One ceremony, one song: An economy of religious knowledge among the Yolngu of north-east Arnhem Land. Unpublished PhD thesis, Anthropology, Australian National University.

Keen, Ian. (Ed.), (1988). *Being Black: Aboriginal cultures in "Settled Australia".* Canberra: Aboriginal Studies Press.

Keen, Ian. (1990). Images of reproduction in the Yolngu Madayin ceremony. *TAJA, 1* (2-3), 193-207.

Keen, Ian. (1993). Aboriginal beliefs vs Mining at Coronation Hill: The containing force of traditionalism. *Human Organization, 52* (4), 344-355.

Keen, Ian. (1994). *Knowledge and Secrecy in an Aboriginal Religion.* Oxford: Clarendon Press.

Kendon, Adam. (1988). *Sign Languages of Aboriginal Australia. Cultural, semiotic and communicative perspectives.* Cambridge: Cambridge University Press.

Bibliography

Kenny, Chris. (1996). *Women's Business.* Potts Point, NSW: Duffy and Snellgrove.

Kenny, Stephen. (1995). Transcript of the Hindmarsh Island Bridge Royal Commission. Adelaide: South Australian Government Printer.

Kenny, Stephen. (1996). Evidence. Legal and Constitutional Committee of the Senate hearing on the Hindmarsh Island Bridge Bill, November 29.

Keogh, Ray. (1996). The native interpretation of Aboriginal song texts: The case of *nurlu.* In William McGregor (Ed.), *Studies in Kimberley Languages in Honour of Howard Coate* (pp. 255-264). Munich: Lincom Europa.

Kingston, Margot. (1998). Judge steps aside in Hindmarsh case. *Sydney Morning Herald.* February 26, 1.

Kluske, J. (1991). *Coorong Park Notes: Coorong National Park.* Netley, SA: National Parks and Wildlife Service, Department of Environment and National Resources.

Kropinyeri, Beryl. (1995). Evidence. Transcript of the Hindmarsh Island Bridge Royal Commission. Adelaide: South Australian Government Printer.

Kropinyeri, Mathew. (1913). Minutes of Evidence. *Royal Commission on Aborigines.* Adelaide: South Australian Government Printer.

Lampard, Henry. (1913). Minutes of Evidence. *Royal Commission on Aborigines.* Adelaide: South Australian Government Printer.

Lane, Bernard. (1997). Conservative tilts bench. *Australian,* December 19, 1.

Langton, Marcia. (1996). The Hindmarsh Island affair: How Aboriginal religion has become an administerable affair. *Australian Feminist Studies, 11* (24), 211-217.

Laurie, D. F. (1917). Native legend of the origin of Orion's belt. *Transactions and Proceedings of the Royal Society, 41,* 660-662.

Lavarch, Michael. (1995). Motion of Censure, House of Representatives, *Hansard,* March 7. p. 16.

Lawnham, Patrick and Katherine Towers. (1995). Secret sell-out. *Australian,* 10/3/1995.

Lendon, A. A. (1940). Dr Richard Penney (1840–1844). *Proceedings of Royal Geographical Society, Australia, South Australia Branch, 31,* 20-32.

Levi-Strauss, Claude. (1966). *The Savage Mind.* University of Chicago Press.

Lewis, John. (1917). Some notes on the early navigation of the River Murray: An address to the Royal Geographical Society of Australasia, South Australian Branch. Adelaide: The Society.

Lindsay, Norman. (1930). *The Magic Pudding: Being the adventures of Bunyip Bluegum and his friends Bill Barnacle and Sam Sawnoff.* Sydney: Angus and Robertson.

Lindsay, H. A. (1968). Art and artefacts. *Aboriginal Quarterly, April–June,* 19.

Lindsay, Margaret. (1995). Evidence. Transcript of the Hindmarsh Island Bridge Royal Commission. Adelaide: South Australian Government Printer.

Linn, Rob. (1988). *A Diverse Land: A history of the Lower Murray, Lakes and Coorong.* Meningie: Meningie Historical Society.

Linnekin, Jocelyn. (1991). Cultural invention and the dilemma of authenticity. *American Anthropologist, 93,* 446-449.

Lobban, Will. (1969). Interview recorded with Annie Koolmatrie, Harry Hunter and Evelyn Hunter. Tape Archive 1729A. Canberra: Australian Institute of Aboriginal and Torres Strait Islander Studies.

Looking Horse, Arvol. (AP/ICCC) (1994). White buffalo calf named "Miracle". *News From Indian Country, 8,* (18).

Lucas, Rod. (1990). The anthropology and Aboriginal history of Hindmarsh Island. A report to Binalong Pty Ltd and Aboriginal Heritage Branch, Dept of Environment and Planning, Adelaide.

Lucas, Rod. (1996). The failure of anthropology. *Journal of Australian Studies, 48,* 40-51.

Luebbers, Roger A. (1981). The Coorong Report: An archaeological investigation of the Southern Coorong. Unpublished report of the Department of Environment and Planning of South Australia.

Luebbers, Roger A. (1982). The Coorong Report: An archaeological investigation of the Northern Coorong. Unpublished report of the Department of Environment and Planning of South Australia.

Luebbers, Roger A. (1996). A Report prepared on behalf of the Applicants to the Commonwealth Hindmarsh Island Report. Adelaide: South Australian Government Printer.

McCourt, Tom and Hans Mincham. (1987). *The Coorong and lakes of the Lower Murray.* Beachport: Beachport Branch of the National Trust.

McDonald, Maryalyce. (1977). A study of the phonetics and phonology of Yaraldi and associated dialects. Unpublished MA thesis, Australian National University.

McGarry, Andrew and Georgina Windsor. (1997). Aborigines take bridge battle to High Court. *Australian,* May 15, 5.

McKeown, Keith Z. (1936). *Australian Spiders.* Sydney: Angus and Robertson.

McLeay, Leslie and Nancy Cato. (1985). *The Story of Goolwa and the Murray Mouth.* Adelaide: Wakefield Press.

Maddock, Kenneth. (1972). *The Australian Aborigines: A portrait of their society.* Ringwood: Penguin.

Maddock, Kenneth. (1982). *The Australian Aborigines: A portrait of their society.* Ringwood: Penguin. Revised second edition.

Maddock, Kenneth. (1988). God, Caesar and Mammon at Coronation Hill. *Oceania, 58,* 305-310.

Maddox, Marion. (1997). How late night theology sparked a Royal Commission. *Sophia, 36* (2).

Maddox, Marion. (1998). What is a fabrication? The political status of religious belief. *Australian Religion Studies REVIEW, 11* (1), 5-16.

Maddox, Marion. (In press) Religious Belief and the Hindmarsh Island Controversy. In George Couvalis and Cheryl Simpson (Eds.), *Cultural Heritage: Values and Rights* (pp. 67-79). Adelaide: Flinders University Press.

Marett, Allan, Linda Barwick, and Lysbeth Ford. (1997). Liner Notes. Rak Badjalarr: Wangga songs for North Peron Island (NW Australia) by Bobby Lane. Unpublished ms.

Mason, George E. (1860). Evidence to the select committee of the legislative council upon "the Aborigines". Adelaide: South Australia Government Printer.

Mathews, Jane. (1996). Commonwealth Hindmarsh Island report pursuant to Section 10(4) of the *Aboriginal and Torres Strait Islander Act* (1984). Canberra: Australian Government Printer.

Mathews, Robert Hamilton. (1900). Phallic rites and initiation ceremonies of South Australia. *Proceedings of American Philosophical Society, 32*, 622-638.

Mathews, Robert Hamilton. (1904). Ethnological notes on the Aboriginal tribes of New South Wales and Victoria. *Journal of the Royal Society of New South Wales, 38*, 203-381.

Mattingley, Christobel and Ken Hampton (Eds.), (1988). *Survival in Our Own Land: Aboriginal experiences in South Australia since 1836, told by Nungas and others.* Adelaide: Wakefield Press.

Mead, Greg. (1995). *A Royal Omission.* South Australia: The Author.

Meggitt, Mervyn J. (1962). *Desert People: A study of Walbiri of Central Australia.* Sydney: Angus and Robertson.

Merlan, Francesca. (1987). Catfish and alligator: Totemic songs of the western Roper River, Northern Territory. In Margaret Clunies Ross *et al.* (Eds.), *Songs of Aboriginal Australia* (pp. 142-168). Sydney: University of Sydney.

Merlan, Francesca. (1991). The limits of cultural construction: The case of Coronation Hill. *Oceania, 61*, 341-352.

Merlan, Francesca. (1998). *Caging the Rainbow: Places, politics, and Aborigines in a North Australian town.* Honolulu: University of Hawai'i Press.

Meyer, Heinrich August Edward. (1843). *Vocabulary of the Language Spoken by the Aborigines of South Australia.* Adelaide: James Allen.

Meyer, Heinrich August Edward. (1846). *Manners and Customs of the Aborigines of the Encounter Bay Tribe, South Australia.* Adelaide: South Australia Government Printer. (Republished 1963, South Australian Facsimile Editions No. 20. Adelaide: Libraries Board of South Australia.)

Michaels, Eric. (1985). Constraints on knowledge in an economy of oral information. *Current Anthropology, 26* (4), 505-510.

Momaday, Scott N. (1976). *The Names.* Tucson: Sun Tracks, University of Arizona Press.

Moorehouse, Matthew. (1860). Evidence to the select committee of the legislative council upon "the Aborigines". Adelaide: South Australia Government Printer.

Moorehouse, Matthew. (1990). Annual report of the Aborigines Department for the year ending 30th September, 1943. *Journal of the Anthropological Society of South Australia, 28* (1), 54-63.

Morgan, Marlo. (1993). *Mutant Message: Down under.* San Francisco: Harper Collins.

Moriarty, T. (1879). The Goolwa clan of the Narrinyeri tribe. In Taplin, G. (Ed.), *The Folklore, Manners, Customs and Languages of the South Australian Aborigines* (50-53). Adelaide: South Australian Government Printer.

Morison, Elva. (1978). *Recollections of the South Coast Area of South Australia 1853–1978. A History of the Harding family beginning in England in the mid 1700s.* Adelaide: Lutheran Publishing House.

Mountford, Charles P. (1938). Aboriginal Crayon Drawings III, The Legend of Wati-Jula and the Kunkarunkara Women. *Transaction of Royal Society of South Australia, 62* (2), 241-254.

Mountford, Charles P. and Alison Harvey. (1941). Women of the Adnjamatana of the northern Flinders Ranges, South Australia. *Oceania, 12* (2), 155-162.

Muir, Kathie. (1996). Media representations of Ngarrindjeri women. *Journal of Australian Studies, 48,* 73-82.

Mulvaney, John. (1994). The Namoi Bunyip. *Australian Aboriginal Studies, 1,* 36-38.

Munn, Nancy D. (1973). *Walbiri Iconography.* Chicago: University of Chicago Press.

Murphy, Jacqueline Shea. (1997). Review of "Reinventing the Enemy's Language". (Harjo and Bird 1997). *Women's Review of Books,* Oct. pp. 10-11.

Myers, Fred. (1986). *Pintupi Country, Pintupi Self: Sentiment, place, and politics among Western Desert Aborigines.* Smithsonian Institute Press, Washington, DC.

Nance, C. and D. L. Spleight (Eds.), (1986). *A Land Transformed.* Melbourne: Longman.

Nicholls, Christine. (1995–6). Misrepresenting Hindmarsh. *Arena Magazine,* Dec-Jan, 24-26.

Nicholls, Christine. (1996). Literacy and gender. *Journal of Australian Studies, 48,* 59-72.

Nile, Richard (Ed.), (1996). *Journal of Australian Studies.* Brisbane: University of Queensland.

Noye, John (Ed.), (1974). *The Coorong.* Adelaide: University of Adelaide Press.

O'Brien, May L. and Sue Wyatt. (1990). *The Legend of the Seven Sisters. A traditional Aboriginal story from Western Australia.* Canberra: Aboriginal Studies Press.

Ong, Walter J. (1988). *Orality and Literacy: Technologizing of the word.* New York: Methuen. (First published in 1982.)

Padman, E. L. (1987). *The Story of Narrung: The place of the large she-oaks.* Adelaide: Lutheran Publishing House.

Palyga, Stephen. (1996). Evidence. Legal and Constitutional Committee of the Senate hearing on the Hindmarsh Island Bridge Bill, November 29.

Parker, Catherine Langloh. (1905). *The Euhlayi tribe: A study of Aboriginal life in Australia.* London: A. Constable and Co.

Pattel-Gray, Anne and Garry W. Trompf. (1993). Styles of Australian Aboriginal and Melanesian theology. *International Review of Mission, 82* (326), 167-188.

Penney, Richard. (1841). Letter to A. M. Mundey, Esq., Private Secretary Acting. July 1.

Penney, Richard (aka: "Cuique"). (1842a). Letter to Editor, South Australian Magazine June 1842. (Reprinted in the *Journal of Anthropological Society of South Australia*, *29* (1), 41-3).

Penney, Richard (aka: "Cuique"). (1842b). Letter to Editor, South Australian Magazine 20/7/1842. (Reprinted in the *Journal of Anthropological Society of South Australia*, *29* (1), 54-6).

Penney, Richard. (1843). Letter to Editor, South Australian Magazine 6/11/1843, (Reprinted in the *Journal of Anthropological Society of South Australia*, *29* (1) 78-80).

Peterson, Nicolas. (1976). *Tribes and Boundaries*. Canberra: Australian Institute of Aboriginal Studies.

Prescott, Ann. (1988). *It's Blue with Five Petals: Wildflowers of the Adelaide region*. South Australia: Self published.

Radcliffe-Brown, A. R. (1918). Notes on social organization of Australian tribes. *Journal of The Royal Anthropological Institute*, *48*, 222-252.

Rankine, Annie. (1969). *Old Ways and New*. Ms No. 1439, recorder unknown, 11/3/1969. Canberra: Australian Institute of Aboriginal and Torres Strait Islander Studies.

Rankine, Daisy. (1995). The release of the Mulgewanki. (A summary of oral history by a meimeni). Typescript in author's possession.

Rankine, Henry J. (1991). A talk by Henry Rankine. *Journal of Anthropological Society of South Australia*, *29* (2), 108-127.

Rankine, Jimmy. (1994). *Rough Image*. (CD). Self-distributed.

Rankine, Leila. (1974a). What the Coorong means to me. In John Noye (Ed.), *The Coorong*. Adelaide: Department of Adult Education, University of Adelaide.

Rankine, Leila. (1974b). The actual present. Lecture given at the Goolwa Cinema, University of Adelaide, January 10.

Rankine, Leila. (*c.*1980). *Poems*. (Self-published).

Rayner, Clara. (1995). Evidence. Transcript of the Hindmarsh Island Bridge Royal Commission. Adelaide: South Australian Government Printer.

Reader's Digest. (1976). *Complete Book of Australian Birds*. Sydney: Reader's Digest.

Reay, Marie. (1949). Native thought in rural New South Wales. *Oceania*, *XX* (2), 89-118.

Reynolds, Henry. (1981). *The Other Side of the Frontier*. Ringwood: Penguin.

Ritchie, David. (1994). Principles and practice of site protection laws in Australia. In David Carmichael *et al.* (Eds.), *Sacred Sites, Sacred Places* (pp. 227-244). London: Routledge.

Roberts, Greg. (1997). Aborigines were cannibals. *Sydney Morning Herald*, April 22, 1, 4.

Róheim, Géza. (1933). Women and their life in Central Australia. *Royal Anthropological Institute Journal*, *63*, 207-265.

664

Rose, Deborah Bird. (1992). *Dingo Makes us Human*. Cambridge: Cambridge University Press.

Rose, Deborah Bird. (1994). Whose confidentiality, whose intellectual property? In M. Edmunds (Ed.), *Claims to Knowledge, Claims to Country: Native title claims and the role of the anthropologist* (pp. 1-11). Summary of Proceedings of the conference Session on Native Title, AAS conference, University of Sydney, September 1994. Produced by the Native Titles Unit, Australian Institute of Aboriginal and Torres Strait Islander Studies, Canberra.

Rose, Deborah Bird. (1996). Slouching towards obliteration: Reflections on the ambiguity of silence and speech. Unpublished paper.

Ross, Jacquelyn. (1997). In the arms of the Coorong: A weaving of hearts and cultures in Australia. *News from Native California, 10* (3), 25-27.

Royal Commission. (1913). *Report of Royal Commission on Aborigines*. Adelaide: South Australian Government Printer.

Royal Commission. (1995). *Report of the Hindmarsh Island Bridge Royal Commission*. Adelaide: South Australian Government Printer. (see Stevens).

Ryan, Lyndall. (1996). Origins of a Royal Commission. *Journal of Australian Studies, 48*, 1-12.

Salgado, Barbara (1994). *Murrundi Voices: Ngarrindjeri people's stories from the Lower Murray*. Illustrated by Nellie Rankine. Rural City of Murray Bridge.

Salmon, Michael. (1972). *The Monster That Ate Canberra*. Canberra: Summit Press Pty Ltd.

Saunders, Cheryl. (1994). Report to the Minister for Aboriginal and Torres Strait Islander Affairs on the significant Aboriginal area in the vicinity of Goolwa and Hindmarsh (Kumarangk) Island. Adelaide: South Australian Government Printer.

Schwab, Jerry. (1986). Interview with Veronica Brodie, 26 February. Transcription of Jerry Schwab's field tapes. Tape 7. Canberra: Australian Institute of Aboriginal and Torres Strait Islander Studies.

Schwab, Jerry. (1988). Ambiguity, style and kinship in Adelaide Aboriginal identity. In Ian Keen (Ed.), *Being Black: Aboriginal cultures in "Settled' Australia"* (pp. 77-96). Canberra: Aboriginal Studies Press.

Scott, Trevor D. (1962). *The Marine and Fresh Water Fishes of South Australia*. South Australian Government Printer.

Select Committee. (1860). *Report of the Select Committee of the Legislative Council on the Aborigines of South Australia*. Adelaide: South Australian Government Printer.

Shiva, Vandana. (1997). *Biopiracy: The plunder of nature and knowledge*. Boston: South End Press.

Shoemaker, Adam. (1989). *Black Words, White Page. Aboriginal literature, 1929–1988*. St Lucia: University of Queensland Press.

Simpson, Jane. (1996). Early language contact varieties in South Australia. *Australian Journal of Linguistics, 16*, 169-207.

Simpson, Andrea. (1995). Transcript of the Hindmarsh Island Bridge Royal Commission. Adelaide: South Australian Government Printer.

Smith, Christina, Mrs James. (1880). *The Boandik Tribe of South Australian Aborigines: A sketch of their habits, customs, legends and language; also an account of the efforts made by Mr. and Mrs. James Smith to Christianise and civilise them.* Adelaide: South Australia Government Printer.

Smith, William Ramsay. (1924). *In Southern Seas.* London: Murray.

Smith, William Ramsay. (1930). *Myths and Legends of the Australian Aboriginals.* London: Harrap.

Smyth, Brough R. (1878). *The Aborigines of Victoria; with notes relating to the habits of the natives of other parts of Australia and Tasmania; compiled from various sources from the government of Victoria.* Melbourne: John Currey O'Neil.

Spencer, Baldwin. (1914). *Native Tribes of the Northern Territory of Australia.* London: Macmillan and Co.

Stanner, W. E. H. (1966) *On Aboriginal Religion.* Oceania Monographs, No. 11, Sydney: University of Sydney.

Stanner, W .E. H. (1979). Religion, totems and symbolism. *White Man Got No Dreaming* (pp. 106-143). Canberra: Australian National University Press.

Starling, Steve. (1992). *Fisherman's Handbook: How to find, identify and catch the Australian angling fish.* NSW: Sandpiper Press.

Stevens, Iris. (1995). *Report of the Hindmarsh Island Bridge Royal Commission.* Adelaide: South Australian Government Printer

Stirling, E. C. (1911). Preliminary Report on the discovery of Native Remains at Swan Port, River Murray with an enquiry into the alleged occurrence of a pandemic among the Australian Aborigines, *Transactions of the Royal Society of South Australia, 35,* 4-46.

Strehlow, T. G. H. (1970). Geography and the totemic landscape in Central Australia. In R. M. Berndt (Ed.), *Australian Aboriginal Anthropology* (pp. 92-140). Nedlands: University of Western Australia Press.

Strehlow, T. G. H. (1971). *Songs of Central Australia.* Sydney: Angus and Robertson.

Sturt, Charles. (1833). *Two expeditions into the interior of Southern Australia.* 2 vols. London: Smith, Elder and Co.

Sumner, Major. (1988). Video of Hilda Wilson. Adelaide: In Sumner's possession.

Sutton, Peter. (1987). Mystery and change. In Margaret Clunies Ross *et al.* (Eds.), *Songs of Aboriginal Australia* (pp. 77-96). Sydney: University of Sydney Press.

Sutton, Peter. (1996a). Post-classical Aboriginal society and native title. Discussion paper published by the National Native Title Tribunal. Perth: Commonwealth Law Courts.

Sutton, Peter. (1996b). The seven sisters, women's fertility, and the Hindmarsh Island area. Report to Judge Mathews, 3 May.

Swain, Tony and Deborah Bird Rose. (Eds.), (1988). *Aboriginal Australians and Christian Missions*. Bedford Park: Australian Association for the Study of Religions.

Symons, Michael and Marion Maddox. (1997). Low card from the race deck. Melbourne: *Age*, 15 February.

Taplin, Frederick W. (1889). An Australian native fifty years ago. *Observer*. 31 March, 6 April.

Taplin, George. (nd). Illustrations of Scripture found amongst the native Aborigines. Adelaide: Mortlock Library.

Taplin, George. (1859–1879). Journal: Five volumes as typed from the original by Mrs Beaumont. Adelaide: Mortlock Library. (In the text citations are by date of entry in the journal.)

Taplin, George. (1860). Evidence to The Select Committee of the Legislative Council upon "The Aborigines". Adelaide: South Australian Government Printer.

Taplin, George. (1864a). *Lessons, Hymns and Prayers for the Native Schools at Point McLeay*. Adelaide: Aborigines' Friends' Association.

Taplin, George. (1864b). *Tungarar Jehovald. Yarildewallin. Extracts from the Holy Scriptures*. Adelaide: South Australian Auxiliary of the British and Foreign Bible Society.

Taplin, George, (1873). The Narrinyeri. Reprinted in J. D. Woods (Ed.), *The Native Tribes of South Australia* (pp. 1-156). Adelaide: E. S. Wigg and Son.

Taplin, George. (1878). *Grammar of the Language "Narrinyeri" tribe*. Adelaide: South Australian Government Printer.

Taplin, George. (1879). *Folklore, Manners and Customs of the South Australian Aborigines: Gathered from inquiries made by authority of the South Australian Government*. Adelaide: E. Spiller, Acting Government Printer, Adelaide.

Tatt, Betty. (1995). Evidence. Transcript of the Hindmarsh Island Bridge Royal Commission. Adelaide: South Australian Government Printer.

Teichelmann, Christian G. and C. W. Schürmann. (1840). *Outlines of a Grammar, Vocabulary, and Phraseology of the Aboriginal Language of South Australia, Spoken by the Natives in and for Some Distance around Adelaide*. Adelaide.

Thomas, W. J. (nd *c.*1960). *Some Myths and Legends of the Australian Aborigines*. Melbourne: Whitcombe and Tombs.

Tickner, Robert. (1995). Debate, House of Representatives, *Hansard*, 8 March, p. 1795.

Tindale, Dorothy. (1939). Notes on School Children and Menstruation. Note Book. Adelaide: Anthropology Archives South Australian Museum.

Tindale, Norman B. (nd, a). Folder: Jobs needing further attention before typing. Adelaide: Anthropology Archive, South Australian Museum.

Tindale, Norman B. (nd, b). Folder: Informants file. Adelaide: Anthropology Archive, South Australian Museum.

Tindale, Norman B. (nd, c). Folder: Tanganekald Data Folder. Adelaide: Anthropology Archive, South Australian Museum.

Tindale, Norman B. (nd, d). Folder: Tangane Place Names. Adelaide: Anthropology Archive, South Australian Museum.

Tindale, Norman B. (nd, e). Box: Tangane Vocabulary: Adelaide: Anthropology Archive, South Australian Museum.

Tindale, Norman B. (nd, f). Folder: Tanganekald Social Organisation. Adelaide: Anthropology Archive, South Australian Museum.

Tindale, Norman B. (nd, g). Box: Vocabulary of the South East. Adelaide: Anthropology Archive, South Australian Museum.

Tindale, Norman B. (nd, h) Folder: Tangane Clans. Adelaide: Anthropology Archive, South Australian Museum.

Tindale, Norman B. (nd, i). Folder: Jaralde Clans. Adelaide: Anthropology Archive, South Australian Museum.

Tindale, Norman B. (nd, j). Folder: Clan Data 2 – Potaruwutj. Adelaide: Anthropology Archive, South Australian Museum.

Tindale, Norman B. (nd, k). Box: Australian Place Card File. Adelaide: Anthropology Archive, South Australian Museum.

Tindale, Norman B. (nd, l). Box: Potaruwutj Vocabulary Cards. Adelaide: Anthropology Archive, South Australian Museum.

Tindale, Norman B. (nd, m). Box: Ramindjeri Cards. Adelaide: Anthropology Archive, South Australian Museum.

Tindale, Norman B. (1930–52). Murray River Notes. Adelaide: Anthropology Archive, South Australian Museum.

Tindale, Norman B. (1931–4). Journal of Researches in the South East of South Australia, Vol. 1. Adelaide: Anthropology Archive, South Australian Museum.

Tindale, Norman B. (1934–7). Journal of Researches in the South East of South Australia, Vol. 2. Adelaide: Anthropology Archive, South Australian Museum.

Tindale, Norman B. (1935). The legend of Waijungari, Jaralde Tribe, Lake Alexandrina, South Australia, and the phonetic system employed in its transcription. Records of the South Australian Museum 5, 261-274.

Tindale, Norman B. (1936a). Legend of the Wati Kutjara, Warburton Range, Western Australia. *Oceania*, 7, 169-185.

Tindale, Norman B. (1936b). Notes on the natives of the southern portion of Yorke Peninsula, South Australia. *Transactions and Proceedings of Royal Society of South Australia*, 60, 55-70.

Tindale, Norman B. (1937). Native Songs of South-East Australia. *Transactions of the Royal Society of South Australia*, 61, 107-120.

Tindale, Norman B. (1938). Prupe and Koromarange: A legend of the Tanganekald, Coorong, South Australia. *Transactions of the Royal Society of South Australia*, 62, 18-23.

Tindale, Norman B. (1938–56). Journal of Researches in the South East of South Australia, Vol. 3. Adelaide: Anthropology Archive, South Australian Museum.

Tindale, Norman B. (1941). Native Songs of South-East Australia. *Transactions of the Royal Society of South Australia, Part II, 65* (2), 233-243.

Tindale, Norman B. (1953). Murray River Journal. Adelaide: Anthropology Archive, South Australian Museum.

Tindale, Norman B. (1959A). Totemic beliefs in the Western Desert of Australia, Part I: Women who became the Pleiades. *Records of the South Australian Museum, 13,* 305-332.

Tindale, Norman B. (1968). Nomenclature of archaeological cultures and associated implements in Australia. *Records of South Australian Museum, 15* (4), 615-640.

Tindale, Norman B. (1974). *Aboriginal Tribes of Australia: Their terrain, environmental controls, distribution, limits, and proper names.* Canberra: Australian National University Press.

Tindale, Norman B. (1986a). Folder: Work in Progress. Adelaide: Anthropology Archive, South Australian Museum.

Tindale, Norman B. (1986b). Milerum. In Bede Nairn and Geoffrey Serle (Eds.), *Australian Dictionary of Biography, 11,* 1891–1939. (pp. 498-499). Melbourne: Melbourne University Press.

Tindale, Norman and Clarence Long. (nd). The World of Milerum, Stage A, Vol. 1-10. Adelaide: Anthropology Archive, South Australian Museum.

Tindale, Norman B. and G. L. Pretty. (1980). The surviving record: The old tribes of the Lower Murray Valley—Nanguruku, Ngaralta, Yarildekald, Portaulun, Ramindjeri, Tanganekald. A guide to their cultural landscape. In R. Edwards and J. Stewart (Eds.), *Preserving Indigenous Cultures: A new role for museums* (pp. 43-52). Canberra: Australian Government Printer.

Tonkinson, Robert. (1978). *The Mardudjara Aborigines.* New York: Holt Rinehart and Winston.

Tonkinson, Robert. (1993). Introduction. In Berndt *et al., A World That Was: The Yaraldi of the Murray River and the Lakes, South Australia* (pp. xvii-xxxi). Melbourne: Melbourne University Press.

Tonkinson, Robert. (1997). Anthropology and Aboriginal tradition: The Hindmarsh Island bridge affair and the politics of interpretation. *Oceania, 68* (1), 1-26.

Tonkinson, Robert and Myrna Tonkinson. (1994). Obituary: Catherine Helen Berndt. *Australian,* May 25.

Treagus, Elaine. (1966). Archive Tapes, LA 3462A, Australian Institute of Aboriginal and Torres Strait Islander Studies, Canberra.

Trevorrow, George. (1995). Evidence. Transcript of the Hindmarsh Island Bridge Royal Commission. Adelaide: South Australian Government Printer.

Trevorrow, Tom. (1995). Evidence. Transcript of the Hindmarsh Island Bridge Royal Commission. Adelaide: South Australian Government Printer.

Tunstill, Guy. (1995). Learning Pitjantjatjara Songs. In Linda Barwick, Allan Marett and Guy Tunstill (Eds.), *The Essence of Singing and the Substance of Song* (pp. 59-73). Oceania Monograph No. 46. Sydney.

Bibliography

Unaipon, David. (1913). Minutes of Evidence. *Royal Commission on Aborigines.* Adelaide: South Australian Government Printer.

Unaipon, David. (1918). In defence of the Aborigines. Adelaide: *Register,* 27 July.

Unaipon, David. (1924). Aboriginals: Their traditions and customs. Sydney: *Daily Telegraph,* 2 August.

Unaipon, David. (1924–5). Legendary Tales of the Australian Aborigines. Ms copy (MLA 1929 Cyreel 1134). Sydney: Mitchell Library.

Unaipon, David. (1925). The story of the Mungingee. *The Home,* Feb. pp. 42-43. (Reprinted in Beston 1979: 347-350.)

Unaipon, David. (1926). *Aboriginal Legends.* Adelaide.

Unaipon, David. (1929). *Aboriginal Legends.* Number 1, (Kinnie Ger: the Native Cat). Adelaide: Hunkin, Ellis and King.

Unaipon, David. (1930). *Native Legends.* Adelaide: Hunkin, Ellis and King.

Unaipon, David. (1951). *My Life Story.* Adelaide: Hunkin, Ellis and King Ltd. (Reprint of Annual Report of Aborigines' Friends' Association, from speech at Annual Meeting, March 1951).

Unaipon, David. (1953). Leaves of memory. *Aborigines' Friends' Association Annual Review, 95,* 6-9

Unaipon, David. (1954a). How the tortoise got his shell. *Dawn, 3* (11), 9.

Unaipon, David. (1959a). The voice of the great spirit. *Dawn, 8* (8), 19.

Unaipon, David. (1959b). Why frogs jump into the water: An Australian Aboriginal legend. *Dawn, 8* (7), 17.

Unaipon, David. (1990). Narroondarie's wives. In Jack Davis *et al.* (Eds.), *Paperback* (pp. 19-32). St Lucia: University of Queensland Press.

Van Gennep, Arnold. (1960). *The Rites of Passage.* Introduction by Solon T. Kimball, translated by Monika B. Vizedon and Gabrielle L. Caffee. Chicago: University of Chicago Press

Vietch, John. (1951). Goolwa packed for arrival of Sturt party. Adelaide: *Advertiser,* 2 February.

von Sturmer, John. (1987). Aboriginal singing and notions of power. In Margaret Clunies Ross *et al.* (Eds.), *Songs of Aboriginal Australia.* Sydney: University of Sydney, pp. 63-76.

Wade, Peter (Ed.), (1975). *Every Australian Bird Illustrated.* Rigby Ltd, Adelaide.

Walker, Reuben. (1934). The Reuben Walker Manuscript. In Norman Tindale, Journal of Researches in the South East of South Australia, Vol. 2. (pp. 185-214). Adelaide: Anthropology Archive, South Australian Museum.

Wagner, Jenny. (1973). *The Bunyip of Berkeleys Creek.* Ringwood: Penguin.

Warner, W. Lloyd. (1937). *A Black Civilization. A social study of an Australian tribe.* New York: Harper and Brothers.

Weiner, Annette B. (1976). *Women of Value, Men of Renown: New perspectives in Trobriand exchange.* Austin: University of Texas Press.

Weiner, James. (1995a). Anthropologists, historians and the secret of social knowledge. *Anthropology Today, 11* (5), 3-7.

Weiner, James. (1995b). The Secret of the Ngarrindjeri: The fabrication of social knowledge, *Arena*, 5, 17-32.

White, Isobel. (1975). Sexual conquest and submission in the myths of central Australia. In L. R. Hiatt (Ed.), *Australian Aboriginal Mythology*, (pp. 123-142). Canberra: Australian Institute of Aboriginal Studies.

White, Isobel. (1994). Obituary: Catherine Helen Berndt. *Oceania*, 65 (1), 1-3.

Wild, Stephen. (1987). Recreating the jukurrpa: Adaptation and innovation of songs and ceremonies in Warlpiri society. In Margaret Clunies Ross *et al.* (Eds.), *Songs of Aboriginal Australia* (pp. 97-120). Sydney: University of Sydney.

Williams, Nancy M. (1986). *The Yolngu and Their Land*. Australian Institute of Aboriginal Studies, Canberra.

Wilson, Dan. (1913). Minutes of Evidence. *Royal Commission on Aborigines*. Adelaide: South Australian Government Printer.

Wilson, Dulcie. (1995). Evidence. Transcript of the Hindmarsh Island Bridge Royal Commission. Adelaide: South Australian Government Printer.

Wilson, Dulcie. (1996a). Telling the Truth: A dissident Aboriginal voice. *IPA Review*, 49 (1), 37-43.

Wilson, Dulcie. (1996b). Appalled by the churches' stance. *Adelaide Review*, January 1996, p. 2. (Letter to the Editor).

Wilson, John snr. (1913). Minutes of Evidence. *Royal Commission on Aborigines*. Adelaide: South Australian Government Printer.

Wilson, Mark. (1985). The Moolgewauk (Bunyip). In the papers of H. K. Fry (held in the South Australian Museum), quoted in "The Mulgewongk" by Steven Hemming. *Journal of Anthropological Society of South Australia*, 23 (1), 11-16.

Wilson, Marguerita. (1995). Evidence. Transcript of the Hindmarsh Island Bridge Royal Commission. Adelaide: South Australian Government Printer.

Wilson, Ronald Sir. (1997). *Bringing them Home: Report of the national inquiry into the separation of Aboriginal and Torres Strait Islander children from their families*. Sydney: Sterling Press.

Woenne-Green, Susan. (1987). Public and private knowledge. Section 17, Uluru (Ayers Rock–Mt Olga) National Park Notes. Alice Springs: ANPWS.

Woodford, James. (1997). Push to recognize victim's trauma. *Sydney Morning Herald*, May 21.

Woods, J. D. (Ed.), (1879). The Aborigines of South Australia. *Transactions and Proceedings and Report of the Philosophical Society of Adelaide, South Australia for 1878–1879*. pp. 81-88.

Wrigley, John W. and Murray Fagg. (1996). *Australian Native Plants: Propagation, cultivation and use in landscaping*. China: Reed.

Wyatt, William. (1860). Evidence. *Report of the Select Committee of the Legislative Council on the Aborigines of South Australia*. Adelaide: South Australian Government Printer.

Wyatt, William. (1879). *Some Account of the Manners and Superstitions of the Adelaide and Encounter Bay Aboriginal Tribes*. Adelaide: E. S. Wigg and Son.

Bibliography

Yallop, Collin and Grimwade, G. (1975). *Narinjari: An outline of the language studied by George Taplin, with Taplin's notes and comparative table.* Oceania Monograph No. 17, Sydney.

Cases Cited

ALRM v. South Australia and Anor. (No. 1) (1995) 64 SASR 551.

ALRM v. South Australia and Anor. (No 2) (1995) 64 SASR 558.

Chapman and Ors v. Tickner and Ors. (1995) 55 FCR 316.

Chapman and Anor v. Luminis, Fergie and Saunders. Federal Court of Australia, (1997) (SA, SG 33).

Kartinyeri and Anor v. The Commonwealth. (1988) 152 ALR 540.

Mabo and Ors v. Queensland. (No. 2) (1992) 175 CLR 1.

Norvill and Milera v. Chapman and Ors. (1996) 1(2) AILR 238.

Tickner and Ors v. Chapman and Ors. (1995) 57 FCR 451.

Tickner v. Western Australia. (1996) WAG Nos 18 and 19, unreported judgment delivered May 28.

Trevorrow v. The State of South Australia and Iris Eliza Stevens. (1996) High Court (A 50).

The Wik Peoples v. Queensland and Ors. (1996) 141 ALR 129, (1996) 186 CLR 71.

Wilson and Ors v. Minister for Aboriginal and Torres Strait Islander Affairs and Anor. (1996) 189 CLR 1.

Permissions

Photographs

Permissions

149   Ngarrindjeri men painted and dancing at Raukkan, 1951. Reproduced with permission of SAM Anthropology Archives.

Ngarrindjeri men seated. Reproduced with permission of SAM Anthropology Archives.

359   The Murray Mouth. Slide 3 from: Harvey, Nick (1983). *The Murray Mouth.* Geography Teachers' Association of South Australia. Photograph: Department of Lands, 1966.

517   Drawing by G. F. Angas. Angas collection. Reproduced with permission of SAM Anthropology Archives.

All other photographs are from the personal collection of individuals named in the text or credited with the photograph. The publisher acknowledges kind permission to reproduce these photographs. Copyright on all photographs remains with the copyright owner.

Archives

I had permission from the Director of the South Australian Museum to read those materials of Tindale known as the "World of Milerum" (Tindale and Long nd), The Murray River Notes Journals, The Journals of Researches in the South East of South Australia, the various vocabulary boxes, folders and maps of the Lower Murray, the Note Book of Dorothy Tindale and that of Alison Harvey. I also spoke and wrote to Henry Rankine, of the Ngarrindjeri Heritage Committee, regarding my access to the materials of his grandfather, Clarence Long.

Permission also granted by Department of Education, South Australia for the use of their chronology in *The Ngarrindjeri People* (1990).

Audio

Permission was also granted to use audio materials from ABC Radio Archives for tapes of the Sturt Report, and tapes held in the sound archives of the Australian Institute of Aboriginal and Torres Strait Islander Studies.

Index

Index

as injury and desecration 16–17, 18, 21, 469,
536, 591, 638
impact on *ngatjis* 568–9
Hindmarsh Island Bridge Act 1997   32
Callinan steps down 640–1
challenge rejected 641–2
High Court challenge 31, 635, 636–7, 639–41
Hindmarsh Island Bridge Bill 31
Hindmarsh Island Royal Commission *see* Royal
Commission (Hindmarsh Island)
Hobba, Leigh 189
Hogan, Linda 14
Holland, Julian 352
Holmes, Tommy 132
Howard, John 636
Howie-Willis, Ian 105
Howitt, A. W. 174, 438
humour 142–3, 515
Hunter, Dora 187
Hunter, Elizabeth Jane 108
Hutchins, Allen 295
Hutchinson, Y. B. 548

Iles, Nicolas 22, 36, 372
Indigenous peoples, social justice 20, 642–3
Indigenous Peoples' Basket Conference 71, 543
infanticide 521–2, 525, 528
Inglis, Judy 105, 459, 462
initiation
men *see* men's initiation
Isobelle *see* Norville, Isobelle

Jackson, Helen 406
Jackson, Pompey 107
Jacobs, Jane 459
Jacobs, Margaret 28, 45, 46, 50, 55, 62, 63, 69,
110, 116, 143, 148, 200, 201, 256, 323, 414,
584, 600
barrages 258, 259
burial grounds 289–90
feelings 221, 223
knowledge 54–5, 218
"Meeting of the Waters" 565
muldarpi 333–4
respecting the rules 378, 382, 403, 449
signs 309
singing 182, 184, 187
whales 318, 319
Janet, Aunty *see* Smith, Janet
Jaralde 29, 505
Jaraldekald 29
see also Yaraldi
Jean, Mona 50
Jekejere 176
and *Ngurunderi* at Goolwa 570–3
Jenkin, Graham 104, 105, 106, 430, 435, 454,
523, 528
Jervis, Cape 29
jilimi 473
Jones, Philip 48, 128, 420, 440, 459, 471
Jones, Wood 130

Kaberry, Phyllis M. 467, 488, 529
Kaldor, Susan 464, 467, 468
kalduki 339, 340, 492, 494, 496, 498
Kalparin Farm 26
Kangaroo Island 92, 95, 266, 426, 427

Kanglindjeri 554
Kanmeri 320, 572
Karloan, Albert 49, 51, 58, 81, 132, 168, 206,
207, 209, 217, 336, 376, 443, 444, 445, 494–5
and Berndts 463, 465
burials 288
doctor-making ceremonies 340
initiation 279–80, 281, 457, 584, 589
Ngurunderi account 93–4
"*Pata winema*" 155, 159, 160, 162, 163
respecting the rules 380
Karpeni 232
Karpeny, Beatrice 227
Karpeny, David 400
Karpeny, George 52, 147
Karpeny, Louisa 43, 44, 51, 79, 80, 81, 84, 147,
177, 204, 337, 391, 428, 434, 440
Karpeny, Muriel *see* Van Der Byl, Muriel
Karpeny, Rosalyn 56
Karpeny, Val *see* Power, Val
Kartinyeri, Albert 205
Kartinyeri, Alma 73
Kartinyeri, Archibald 205
Kartinyeri, Doreen 11, 20, 28, 31, 45, 46, 48–50,
59–61, 63, 74, 102, 112, 120, 124, 126, 142,
185, 194, 221, 222, 230, 259, 334, 417, 425,
451, 468, 469, 513, 542, 568, 640
basket weaving 65–8, 543–4
burials 298, 306, 307
bush medicine 342
childbirth 504, 519
family affiliations 204, 205
feather flowers 74, 75, 76
gendered knowledge 386, 389, 390, 391, 403,
404, 449
gendered lands 269–72, 275–6
genealogies 232–4, 238, 239, 241–3, 244
lands 249, 254
navel cord exchange 500
religion 110–11
research scholar 136
respecting the rules 378, 379–80
restriction on transmission of knowledge 112–13
rites of passage 518–19
seasonal food 69
stories of Kumarangk 190–2
Sturt reenactment 146, 148, 152, 154
Kartinyeri, Dorrie 70
Kartinyeri, Dot 168
Kartinyeri, Edith *see* Rigney, Edith
Kartinyeri, James Brooks 73, 156–8, 159, 161,
162, 163, 164, 180, 193, 228, 231, 385
Kartinyeri, Laura 44, 63, 66, 84, 85, 117, 234,
392, 403, 500
gendered knowledge 383, 391
on telling whitefellas anything 399, 400
Kartinyeri, Noreen 56
Kartinyeri, Oscar 149, 180
Kartinyeri, Sally 229
Kartinyeri, Theo 276
Kaurna 29, 132, 137, 203, 210
Keely, Annie 375
Keen, Ian 88, 95, 165, 275, 369, 475, 479, 481, 568
Kenny, Chris 8, 23, 48, 272, 374
Kenny, Stephen 21, 22, 452, 542
Keogh, Ray 165, 166
Kestle, Girly 228

679

Index

Index

Index

Index